Facing History and Ourselves
Holocaust and Human Behavior

Dedicated to Dr. Henry Zabierek

Facing History and Ourselves
Holocaust and Human Behavior

Margot Stern Strom
William S. Parsons

Intentional Educations, Inc.   Watertown, Massachusetts

Cover design: Laura Tarrish

Cover objects: Prisioner's jacket from a concentration camp; Nazi armband; Star patch which Jews were required to wear; War relief button; Medal commemorating the Armenian Genocide; Carte d'identite courtesy of Regine Winder Barshak: The cartes d'identite were issued to residents of France by the French Police Department. If a resident was Jewish the card was stamped with *Juif* or *Juive* in red ink. A person was required to carry the card at all times; Letter written from a concentration camp.

Copyright (c) 1982 by Margot Stern Strom and William S. Parsons

Published by Intentional Educations, Inc.

Library of Congress Catalog Card Number: 82-80292

All rights reserved. No portion of this book may be reproduced in any form, or by any means, mechanical or electronic, or by any information storage and retrieval system or other method, for any use, without the written permission of the publisher.

Printed in the United States of America.

Contents

Overview 1

Rationale 13

Methodology 14

The Facing History and Ourselves Project 18

1 An Introduction 21

2 Society and the Individual 29

3 Antisemitism: A Case Study of Prejudice and Discrimination 45

4 German History: World War I to II 67

5 Nazi Philosophy and Policy 99

6 Preparing for Obedience 145

7 Victims of Tyranny 189

8 The Holocaust 227

9 Who Knew? Individuals, Groups, and Nations 267

10 Judgment 295

11 The Armenians
Part I A Case of Forgotten Genocide 319
Part II Do We Learn From Past Experiences? 346

12 Facing Today and the Future 383

Credits 405

Overview:
Confronting 20th-Century Genocide

The obstacles to learning about genocide, as it was first practiced in the 20th century upon the Ottoman Armenians and in its ultimate expression in the Holocaust, are great. It is not yet considered a serious subject for social scientists, nor is it covered by teachers or included in textbooks.

Although these two events are from distinctly different times and places, with particular victims and unique outcomes, with unique precedents and antecedents, practiced by different nations and their citizens, with different intensity, they have shared a common fate. Both of these events have been ignored, avoided, or denied and, if treated, revised beyond recognition by their survivors. Since most events of the 20th century have elicited intense scholarly investigation and reportage, this silence is particularly disturbing. We believe that when students are denied access to information about these events so that reflection on the meaning of these events is impossible, prevention is never given a real chance.

However, despite the paucity of materials and the lack of support for such a confrontation with history, there are a significant number of parents, community leaders, and educators committed to the belief that education must reflect the complex social and political realities of their world and that reflection on the history of genocide is a necessary part of preparation for adulthood and active citizenship.

These adults, like the students of the Facing History classes, warn that it is far too dangerous to foster a distorted view of history by teaching an idealized concept of government where things are presented as they ought to be, instead of as they are or were. To deny students the opportunity to think about effective ways to prevent abuse or to bring about change in their own institutions and lives creates an unnecessary and unfair handicap. Young adults may discover the discrepancy between fact and fiction too late to respond to events that demand of them courage and risk-taking.

Textbooks and teachers who fail to prepare students for the complexities of the social and political world produce disillusioned and cynical young adults who are vulnerable to unexamined prejudices, and who will acquiesce in simple governmental solutions to complex problems. This project attempts to give students access to history which is difficult and controversial. Because most students are given information about their world from the traditional textbook, and because they learn to make a difference in their world from the models that their teachers offer, we have chosen to present this history through the most widely used educational tool, the textbook. The *Facing History and Ourselves: Holocaust and Human Behavior* curriculum combines ignored history with a pedagogy which shapes the powerful material so that students can make use of developmentally appropriate activities and lessons.

Efforts to incorporate history about the genocide of the Armenian people and the Holocaust have evoked similar responses from the traditional textbook publishers. The following excerpt from a memo about a proposed Holocaust curriculum indicates the power of avoidance among American publishers:

The topic probably is regional in localities where there is a strong Jewish community; I suspect that there are a number of things already available for free from various Jewish groups. . . . Doubt many would give up that much time to the topic . . . to me, much of this is ghoulish. . . . I am sure a program can be effectively introduced, but not with average students and average teachers. . . . Much of what they're talking about can be handled effectively in college, but runs into lots of operational problems at the school level. . . . They're expressing a very high risk situation, with students sharing experiences and attitudes . . .[1]

A look at some of the other barriers to learning about these events illuminates the conventional taboos and motivations which have contributed to the suppression and avoidance of this history. No matter what the arguments are, they all contribute to the silence about 20th-century genocide.

Although the efforts to teach about the Holocaust are documented here, many of the same reasons for avoiding education in the classroom about the genocide of the Armenian people are given by teachers and administrators.* Many report the subjects are too controversial, too emotional, or too ethnic and that, since they were victim to the silence on these events in their own education, they cannot adequately teach about them now. So they perpetuate the silence. In the following letter by a German citizen writing to his wife about the recent German terrorism, one reads an indictment of all teaching:

For indeed, I am as German as the members of the Baader-Meinhof gang. I belong to their age. We were ashamed of our country. We were told what happened—the marching—the books—the Sieg Heils and the beatings, the loud brutal and vulgar crowds—the people we loved being driven out—Albert Einstein, Thomas Mann, Brecht—their books, paintings and music scores burned. Other people we had never heard of—those nameless millions who so silently went to the camps where their voices were gassed forever silent. This was no country to be proud of. We were also pained, lonesome kids amid adults who could not, must not, ever be trusted. How could I trust my parents who, balancing me on their knees, sang "Deutschland, Deutschland, Uber alles" with me? Who would make me call after a man in the street, a man I didn't even know, "Jew! Jew!" Who with my father—once a high-ranking officer—would tell me they'd never heard of any camps. And who, when I asked him about the 6 million Jews that had been put to death, insisted that it was 4.5 million—the figure I had quoted, he said, had been made up by the notoriously deceitful Jewish media—4.5 while my heart was counting— one and one and one . . .[2]

After reading this indictment, one questions how teachers of any curriculum about justice, law, civic responsibility, human behavior, and history could fail to consider how genocide, the taking of lives, became the policy of state decision-makers.

*Later in this overview there is a brief discussion about the universal vs. particular nature of the events of genocide as they relate to avoidance in education. For further information on this issue, readers might refer to the following authors: Yehuda Bauer, Henry L. Feingold, Henry Freidlander, Vahakn N. Dadrian, Dr. Irene Shur, and Lucy Dawidowicz.

Some teachers continue to report that it is blasphemy to draw lessons from the Holocaust or that "bad history" is best forgotten. Others fear that these histories are too easily mistaught even by competent teachers who have made careful plans and who are sensitive to the importance of the issues and to student reactions. For example, some teachers of the Holocaust have found that they risk encouraging glorification of power and identification with adventure, or increasing antisemitism and stereotyping. It is possible to present materials that are not appropriate so that students tune out or become paralyzed by the content. And in the face of such potential for abuse, many teachers and administrators refuse to attempt education about the Holocaust.

For those teachers trained to expect the historical method to yield a simple analysis for all events in history, these unprecedented events, at the same time repugnant and fascinating, defy simple formulas and conventional categories. Instead, the events demand a new and different system of scrutiny which honors the struggle and discomfort one feels at facing such history. The struggle is compounded by the inability of the traditional vocabulary used by most writers of history and literature to help make meaning of what is learned about the nature of human behavior. And so, instead of confrontation, which demands a leap in the imagination, there is only coping. As Arthur Miller wrote in the transcript for a TV play about Auschwitz, "We have learned something new about the human race, and the news is not good."

Outrage is the initial response to evidence of mass bestiality. Extended exposure then gradually bludgeons the mind until it becomes limp in stunned silence. After the helplessness of shock, follows a long period of painful reflection; and slowly, acceptance of the fact that one must come to terms with reality. The fragile trappings of civilized behavior are far more vulnerable to violent and evil forces than we are usually able to imagine. Yet, we must so imagine, in the hope that the likelihood of recurrence can be reduced.[3]

The problems involved in confronting information about contemporary nuclear issues and the potential for nuclear disaster are remarkably similar to those described in discussion about confrontation with the Holocaust. The unique challenge here is to recognize the similarities while remaining faithful to the uniqueness of each event.

Robert Jay Lifton has written about the impact of extreme historical circumstances on human behavior. He has interviewed Nazi doctors and survivors of Hiroshima and Nagasaki and lectures about a need to confront the history of the Holocaust and the danger of another nuclear horror far beyond the imaginations of even the survivors of the Holocaust and Nagasaki.

One must be open to discomfort or anxiety in order to perceive and to resist holocaust. . . . We may do better to speak of a struggle against numbing and turn towards awareness . . . .[4]

He urges us further:

Our present circumstances demand that we extend imaginative access to death to include massive death, collective death, holocaust with the possibility of total annihilation. That is asking a great deal of the human imagination.[5]

The impulse is to universalize all the events related to 20th-century genocide in order to better cope with the information. This denial of the particular victim and uniqueness of each event is particularly disturbing because such reactions contribute to avoidance. In the case of Holocaust study, the reasons for this denial are particularly complex. Henry Feingold writes: "The creative mind seems naturally prone to seek universal truths which somehow require a muting and even denial of the Holocaust's specific Jewish dimension."[6] In the classroom, if these events are mentioned, denial takes the form of subsuming these events under a generalized category of man's inhumanity to man. Some teachers say they are teaching about the Holocaust, yet they never mention the word "Jew," or explore the concept of the "war within a war" and its particular victims.

Yet, there are many teachers who are willing to be challenged by the universal and unique aspects of these events. Initially, they define the problem in the form of a question: Why is the Holocaust different from the experiences of the slaves in America? What about the native American experience? What is the distinction between genocide and the Holocaust? How is genocide of the Armenian people different from the Holocaust? Assuming they are inquiring with colleagues of good faith, the dialogue can begin here. As Hannah Arendt suggests, it is then we begin to think:

Thinking is the urgent work of a species that bears responsibility for its own survival... to do philosophy by criticism or agreement, to carry on thinking, the authority by which we survive in human form.[7]

Milton Meltzer answers the question, why single out the extermination of the Jews from the other innumerable crimes committed by the Nazis, this way:

... What is historically significant is its uniqueness. There is no precedent for it in Jewish history. Nor in the history of any other people. Civilians in the past have been massacred for what man called "reasonable" goals, utilitarian goals — to extend power, to acquire wealth, to increase territory, to stamp out opposition, to force conversion. What some power conceived to be in its self-interest was the reason behind the persecution.

But Hitler and the Nazis wanted to murder all Jews because they were Jews. Not because of their faith, not despite their faith. But because of what Hitler called their "race." He did not believe this "inferior" people had any right to share the earth with their "superiors," the Germans. So Jews — religious and unreligious — were exterminated. They were killed even when their deaths proved harmful militarily or economically, to the Nazis. It was a crime against all humanity, committed upon a body of the Jewish people. . . .[8]

The content of the struggle to understand the unique and particular aspect of the Holocaust revolves about the following fact. The Nazis attempted to annihilate European Jewry with the cooperation of the military, bureaucracy, and citizenry, no matter what the consequences to their nation.

A Jew was not doomed because of any set of activities undertaken voluntarily, not for adherence to orthodoxy, not for active political opposition to the Nazis, nor for membership in a proscribed political party. A Jew was doomed whether he was an assimilated or unassimilated Jew, a conservative or liberal in politics. Thus, the terrible perversity of the Nazi condemnation of Jews lies in the fact that this condemnation was rooted in the basis of one's being, not in what one had done or indeed could have done.[9]

This was not true in the case of the genocide of the Armenian people, for example, or the gypsies in World War II. In the case of the Armenians, there were some opportunities to survive by conversion and escape.

Gypsies appear to have been murdered as "asocials" (as were numbers of Germans — by a process of "Vernichtung durch arbeit"); and certain categories exempted as being valuable Aryan stock. . . . And, as in the case of the American Indians, there was a "brutal fight" for land and livelihood which ended when the land had been taken away from them; what was left of the Indian nations was then allowed to vegetate and, if they managed, to survive.[10]

But the history of the 20th century has taught that there is "no franchise on suffering" and, according to Henry Feingold, the Jewish people "are not in a contest to measure pain or degrees of victimization." He suggests:

[What is being measured] is the importance of the event in history, and that clearly the Holocaust is an entirely different event in the terms of its historical weight. Understood correctly, the claim of the Holocaust's uniqueness and particularity rests not on the fact that Jews experienced more pain and greater suffering than others, or that the evil they were compelled to confront was crueler. It is based on comparative historical development of modern Europe.[11]

According to Feingold, the Holocaust created a sharp break in the flow of history by annihilating Jews who had dispersed across Europe, an intellectual leadership which Feingold labels as part of a modernizing elite, a people committed to universalism and internationalism, who pressured for protection as they sensed a need for change in order to see a better future.

[This] universalizing elite, in the realm of ideas, and science and technology, was on the road to creating the basis of a society beyond the legal nation state.[12]

These thinkers and actors equipped with the ideas of the enlightenment and with a new belief in science, hoped for a modern world free from the yoke of hate and myth perpetuated in the traditional world by separate groups, religions, and old tribes. But instead of the protection of a world community for all, the power of some of Europe's nation states grew at the expense of certain people and groups and history changed drastically when the inventions of the modern world were used in the mass deaths instead of world peace. And so Feingold reminds us of the unusual weight of the Holocaust as an historical event; he writes, "History is not democratic; it does not assign equal import to like events."[13]

Those teachers who engage in a careful analysis of genocide will recognize the universal connections of these events to one another, and also remain faithful to the uniqueness of each event. One Armenian scholar reminds us that, "Amidst the welter of infinite details keynoting the unique characteristics of each episode, one may be able to discern and substantiate some outstanding common features. . . ."[14]

By acknowledging the tension between the universal and the particular characteristics of these two events, teachers can answer those who fear that a study of the Holocaust and the genocide of the Armenian people together will denigrate or cheapen the significance of each event. Consequently, they will fully honor and recognize the potential of their students to make meaning of history. They can be faithful to the uniqueness of each historical event, and make universal connections where appropriate.

We can attain universality only through particularity; there are no shortcuts. The more we come to know about the Holocaust, how it came about, how it was carried out, etc., the greater the possibility that we will become sensitized to inhumanity and suffering whenever they occur. If we take shortcuts we are in danger of losing all distinctions of what Yosef Yerushalmi calls the "debasement of our vocabulary." We may then have simply one more word which for a short time was a new and powerful symbol, but which quickly became emptied of all meaning.[15]

Opposition to teaching about genocide comes in many other guises. Some writers, because of certain personal loyalties or prejudices, deny that the events occurred and argue that any attempt to teach such history is false. For some teachers, for example, the publicity about the Holocaust by those who call Holocaust studies a conspiracy among the Jews to glorify the events, is enough to fuel their fears that they are introducing missionary education or support their fears of confronting long held unexamined prejudices. And so they, too, prefer to remain silent.

In the light of the literature of denial from those who claim there was no Holocaust or genocide of the Armenian people, and as others deny the uniqueness of each event, it seems especially critical to confront the power that revisionism, universalism, and denial have for educators and their students.

In the case of the Ottoman Armenians, one can begin to recognize how easily certain history is forgotten. It is obvious from the label "the forgotten genocide" that the impulse to cope with the history of the genocide of the Armenian people by ignoring, denying, or revising has almost been successful.

The fact remains that a nation guilty of genocide did indeed succeed in burying the story "in the pit of history." In part it succeeded because the Armenians are few, dispersed, and without a public platform to plead their case—from which astute and dangerous men can draw the conclusion that the world cares little for the fate of those who are politically impotent.[16]

Even though the French government during World War I originated the phrase "crimes against humanity" to describe Turkish acts against the Armenians, ". . . the world proved itself eager to forgive Turkey its crimes."[17] After the genocide, for example, Halide Hanum, an avowedly passionate Turkish nationalist, wrote about the horror of the human suffering among the Armenians. She said, "I know—never mind what I know, it was better to forget." She writes, "Of the massacres and violence it is best not to speak much—the sooner they are forgotten, the better."[18]

This plea to forgive Turkey was echoed just recently in a *New York Times* editorial:

... On the eve of the Fiftieth Anniversary of the genocide, the New York Times *suggested editorially that it was high time for the Armenians to forgive the Turks. Few Armenian readers of the* Times *missed the grim irony of the fact that this editorial appeared only a few weeks after the same newspaper had been decrying Germany's proposed statute of limitations on Nazi murders. But then it is common practice to refuse to recognize the meaning of the Armenian fate. In* Eichmann in Jerusalem, *Hannah Arendt dismissed their case as a "pogrom", and this February, as the Fiftieth Anniversary year drew to a close, Karl Jaspers was quoted in the pages of* Commentary *as denying any pre-Hitler precedent for genocide.*[19]

Rev. Vartan Hartunian, who translated his father's memoirs into a book, *Neither to Laugh Nor to Weep: A Memoir of the Armenian Genocide,* gives his response to those who forget:

Any crime that is forgotten or forgiven is a crime that has been sanctioned and blessed. The surviving victims must proclaim the truth, must insist on due punishment and must do all in their power to prevent the powerful in their advance toward corruption.[20]

Because the documentation is not extensive and the number of American scholars who read and speak Turkish and Armenian and who have access to the documents still held by Turkey is limited, revisionism is a serious problem.

Richard Hovannisian describes his experience as a writer and researcher in Armenian history as challenging "... for by its very nature the topic is extremely controversial, the facts often disguised, misrepresented, or undiscovered. Seeking history in a past shrouded in myth and distortion is a difficult, sometimes thankless pursuit."[21]

Even when there is significant documentation of the exterminations, the revisionists make the educator's task more complicated. For example, even some of the American Protestant missionaries changed their stories during the time that America was realigning itself with the new Turkish Republic, and Arnold Toynbee, who edited the primary source on the genocide, *Lord Bryce's Blue Book,* later changed his story. In 1917, Toynbee wrote:

Turks will say (after the war), we were at war.... The Armenians were traitors at large in a war zone. But such excuses are entirely contradicted by facts.

And after completing his editorship of *The Treatment of the Armenians,* he published a summary of its contents, *The Murderous Tyranny of the Turks,* in which he inserted a plea that the world remember these "unprecedented crimes" after the war, and insure against their recurrence.*

"Historians are always engaged in reinterpreting the past," writes Lucy Dawidowicz:

---

*He reversed his previous views on Turkish responsibility, according to Marjorie Housepian, "after he viewed the Turkish side in the Greco-Turkish War." But he later reversed himself again.

They do so sometimes on the basis of newly found documentary sources, sometimes by reconsidering the known data from a different political position, or by taking into account a different time span, or by employing a new methodology. Every historical subject has undergone revision as each new generation rewrites the history of the past in the light of its own perspective and values. But the term "revisionism" has applied specifically to dissident positions which are at variance with mainstream history on several subjects from the Civil War on . . . .[22]

But when contemporary revisionists argue that historical events never took place, as in the case of those who call the Holocaust a hoax or deny a genocide upon the Ottoman Armenians, then revisionism is a direct threat to education. "Most shocking of all," writes Dawidowicz, "these gross and malicious falsifications, far from being attacked and repudiated, have gained a respectful hearing in academic historical institutions in the United States."

As the following story illustrates, the effort to deny the Holocaust its historic reality often happens in ignorance.

Recently, Dawidowicz, scholar and author of *War Against the Jews 1933-1945,* was approached by a man associated with the Larry King radio show, a national network program, to appear with Robert Faurision, an associate professor from the University of Lyon, who calls the gas chamber and the genocide "one and the same lie . . . ." When she refused to appear, the journalist asked if she was against discussing "controversial" matters on the radio. His question implied that the historical fact that European Jews were murdered was a "controversial issue." It seems in his effort to see everything as an "issue," he has fallen into a serious trap, one that this curriculum tries to avoid. Her refusal to share the platform with those who avoid accepted historical scholarship and who appear under the guise of historian in an attempt to deny history, was, we think, an important statement to make. The documentation of the Holocaust is substantial; the impulse to change the past by ignoring the history, by denying the history, or by "revising" the history, even if by only a few, is disturbing.

Recently President Ronald Reagan made the following remarks about denial:

I'm horrified today when I know that . . . there are actually people now trying to say that the Holocaust was invented, that it never happened, that there weren't six million people whose lives were taken cruelly and needlessly in that event, that all of this is propaganda. Well, [there's] the old cliché that a picture is worth a thousand words. . . . Not only do we have the survivors today to tell us first-hand, but in World War II, I was in the military and assigned to a post where every week, we obtained from every branch of the service all over the world the combat film that was taken by every branch. And we edited this into a secret report for the general staff. We had access to and saw that secret report. And I remember April '45. I remember seeing the first film that came in when the war was still on, when our troops had come upon the first camps and had entered those camps. And you saw, unretouched — and no way that it could ever have been rehearsed — what they saw — the horror they saw.[23]

But unlike the case of the Nazi Holocaust, the documentation of the destruction in Ottoman Turkey was not so carefully kept to be later used at international war trials and as information to refute and counteract the deniers. This lack of documentation is a major reason for excluding education about the genocide of the Armenian people, and for the ongoing hostility of many Armenians to the present government of Turkey.

As for examining the official Turkish records, it is pretentious to expect that, if documents still exist, they would be made accessible to an American, or, for that matter, any researcher. The issue has been one of extreme sensitivity for every Turkish cabinet since the end of World War I. And even if there were no official Turkish records relating to the subject, what cannot be dismissed is the evidence of the thousands of eyewitness reports — made by individuals whose governments were allied with Turkey, in the detailed accounts of the survivors and in the extensive diplomatic correspondence. It is inconceivable that a scholar who has investigated the subject could remain unaware that the Armenian was eliminated not just in a few border districts, but in all the Armenian plateau and Anatolia.[24]

The debate over motivations and numbers continues to provide the major content for those writers who argue by omission or because of certain loyalties, that the Armenian genocide never happened.

Professor Richard Hovannisian cites the recent *History of the Ottoman Empire and Modern Turkey* by Stanford and Ezel Jural Shaw as one text that by omission and selection, attempts to deny that a policy of genocide of the Ottoman Armenians was carried out by the Young Turks. They argue, says Hovannisian, that the Armenians suffered terribly during the last two decades of the Ottoman Empire, but in the context of Ottoman history "... the Armenian experience was not unique to the Armenians...." There was no "conscious effort at extermination," they argue, but instead the world witnessed "the final breakup of a multi-national society as a result of a whole series of national revolts, terroristic attacks, massacres and counter-massacres, and famine and disease, compounded by destructive and brutal foreign invasions, in which all the people of the empire, Muslim and non-Muslim alike, had their victims and criminals, and against which the Ottoman government found itself powerless to act despite numerous efforts to do so."

Like Dawidowicz, Hovannisian sees the belaboring of the Shaws' revisionism as ludicrous. "Such uncritical acceptance and reiteration of Turkish denials, rationalizations, and subterfuge turns revisionism into falsification," says Hovannisian.

And today, the suppression of history continues, warns Terrence des Pres. In his recent review of Walter Laquer's new book, *The Terrible Secret*, which documents who knew what and when about the Holocaust, Des Pres wrote:

The activity of the American government to suppress the information on the Holocaust as it was learned from Europe is not so disassociated from the suppression of this history today — for whatever reasons: guilt, fear, or disbelief... it strikes me that the "terrible secret" is still in force, exactly as he described it, the combination of fear and shame, of psychological repression and political suppression, characterizes our own predicament today. We saw it in our response to Vietnam and Cambodia, we see it currently in relation to events in Latin America, and we may see it as we draw closer to nuclear war than we ever have been before.[25]

Ironically, though, there are many students and adults who witness the telling of these events of 20th-century genocide and massacres through the sophisticated technology of our visual media. Often they begin to believe what they see on television, but they have no way of understanding what they see. Today's classroom teacher has yet to find adequate ways to help students process the incredible amount of information and misinformation that they bring to class from television.

Does this openness to behavior . . .asks George Steiner, make us any better prepared, any more willing to act? Or has it on the contrary, made even thicker skin of our indifference? And all are accomplice to that which leaves them indifferent.[26]

The relationship of action to thought is also the subject of this reflection by Albert Camus:

I know that the great tragedies of history often fascinate men with approaching horror. Paralyzed, they cannot make up their minds to do anything but wait. So they wait, and one day the Gorgon devours them. But I should like to convince you that the spell can be broken, that there is only illusion of impotence, that strength of heart, intelligence and courage are enough to stop fate and sometimes reverse it.[27]

We must take very seriously the challenge we educators have to more adequately prepare our students for the complexities of their 21st century and heed their simple logic. Students argue, if certain events in history are omitted from their texts, their class discussion, how are they expected to recognize the abuses and power and humanity when they come again?

They recognize what Hitler meant about the lessons of history when he spoke to his troops before invading Poland in 1939:

Our strength is in our quickness and brutality. Ghengis Khan had millions of women and children killed by his own will and with a gay heart. History sees only in him a great state builder. What weak western European civilization thinks about me does not matter. . . . I have sent to the East only my "Death Head Units," with the order to kill without mercy all men, women, and children of Polish race or language. Only in such a way will we win the vital space we need. Who still talks nowadays of the extermination of the Armenians?[28]

". . . When the observation was made in 1939," wrote Feingold, "voices concerning the actions of the Turks had fallen silent."[29]

Students and teachers in this project have confronted the powerful barriers to their knowing about genocide and the Holocaust, and they have learned to be challenged by the dualities as part of their learning process. These historical events which defy our most traditional education methodology—when we listen, we cannot hear; when we watch, we do not really see; and when we read, we do not know—make us different.

This is a demanding academic experience. But it is also the sort of dialectical exercise that encourages a student to arrive by his own route at the threshold of insight or personal wisdom. Here is a curriculum that honors duality: process and product, head and heart, history and autobiography.[30]

Finally, then, this curriculum preserves, as only education can, the terrible events of 20th-century genocide, to serve as a living reminder of the power of the individual to make decisions which affect not only the protection of his or her neighbor, but the survival of the world.

After returning from the physical shock of Nagasaki, Jacob Bronowski wrote that all decisions about disarmament and other issues which weigh the fate of nations ". . . should be made within the forbidding context of Nagasaki; only then could statesmen make realistic judgments of the problems which they handle on our behalf."

He tried to convince his colleagues in government and in the United Nations of his idea. However, they pointed out to him that "delegates would be uncomfortable in Nagasaki."

We recognize that confronting this history will be uncomfortable. But by denying students access to this history, we fail to honor their potential to confront, to cope, and to plan to make a difference, today and in their futures.

Truly our students have begun to wonder, which for Plato is the beginning of philosophy. Applying that wonder to the everyday and matter-of-course, as Heidegger says, "accepting wondering as one's abode," they have begun to think.

One student wrote:

. . . Maybe in the future, this great chance of learning this history could affect how I reason, act, and maybe eventually what I might become, or do.

Or, in the words of another student:

Once a person has been subjected to the materials of the course, they can never again feel the same way about their own humanity or that of others.

Citations

Overview

[1] Unpublished memo from textbook publisher to a staff member about Holocaust curriculum, 1980.

[2] *New York Times,* Letters to the Editor.

[3] Bohdan Wytwycky, *The Other Holocaust* (The Novak Report, 918 F Street, N.W., Washington, D.C. 20004, 1980) p. 82.

[4] Robert J. Lifton, "Nuclear Awareness: In a Dark Time the Eye Begins to See," *The Broken Connection* (New York: Simon and Schuster, 1979).

[5] Ibid.

[6] Henry Feingold, "Determining the Uniqueness of the Holocaust: The Factor of Historical Valence," copyrighted by *Shoah: A Journal of Resources on the Holocaust* published by the National Jewish Resources Center, 250 West 57 St., New York, New York 10107. Spring 1981, p. 3. Reprinted by permission.

[7] Hannah Arendt, *The Life of the Mind: Thinking* (New York: Harcourt Brace Jovanovich, 1977).

[8] "Why Remember?"—introduction from *Never to Forget: The Jews of the Holocaust* by Milton Meltzer. Copyright © 1976 by Milton Meltzer. Reprinted by permission of Harper & Row, Publishers, Inc., pp. xv, xvi.

[9] Wytwycky, *The Other Holocaust,* pp. 39, 40.

[10] Yehuda Bauer, "Unique and Universal: Some General Problems Arising out of Holocaust Research," (speech).

[11] Feingold, *Shoah,* p. 10, 11.

[12] Ibid.

[13] Ibid.

[14] Vahakn N. Dadrian, "The Methodological Components of the Study of Genocide as a Sociological Problem: The Armenian Case," *Recent Studies in Modern Armenian History* (NAASR) 1972, pp. 83-103.

[15] Eva Fleischner, ed., *Auschwitz: Beginning of a New Era? Reflections on the Holocaust,* Reprinted by permission of the Cathedral of St. John the Divine, New York City and KTAV Publishing Company, New York City, 1977.

[16] Marjorie Housepian, "The Unremembered Genocide," in *A Commentary Report* (The American Jewish Committee, New York).

[17] Ibid.

[18] Ibid.

[19] Ibid.

[20] Vartan Hartunian, Talk to Facing History Teacher Workshop, July 3, 1981.

[21] Richard G. Hovannisian, "Rewriting History," *Ararat,* (Armenian General Benevolent Union of America, Summer 1978) p. 2.

[22] Lucy Dawidowicz, "Lies About the Holocaust," *Commentary,* December 1980, pp. 31-37.

[23] Ronald Reagan, address at Holocaust Memorial Rememberance Service, East Room, White House, 1981.

[24] Hovannisian, "Rewriting History."

[25] Terrence Des Pres, "Review of Lacquer's *The Terrible Secret*" *New Republic,* January 1981.

[26] Anthony Lewis, "After Auschwitz," *New York Times,* October 1, 1981.

[27] Albert Camus, *Notebooks* (New York: Knopf).

[28] Feingold, *Shoah,* p. 3.

[29] Ibid., p. 3.

[30] Lisa Colt, and Fanny Connelly, "Excerpts from Student Journals," Facing History and Ourselves Project, 1980.

Rationale

The *Facing History and Ourselves: Holocaust and Human Behavior* curriculum is specifically designed for adolescents, and their school and home community, to promote awareness of the history of the Holocaust and the genocide of the Armenian people, an appreciation for justice, a concern for interpersonal understanding, and a memory for the victims of those events.

Since the universal questions of morality and the lessons to be learned from a history of totalitarianism, racism, and dehumanization are not unique to the Holocaust, comparisons and parallels are made to past and contemporary issues, events, and choices when appropriate.

For example, when students think about why they study this history, they ask, "Can we learn from the past?" In this context, the "forgotten genocide" of the Armenian people, which happened just 25 years before the Holocaust, takes on new meaning. Students argue, if their teachers keep silent about the Holocaust and the Armenian genocide, they deny them the chance to prevent such an event from happening again.

This study recognizes ". . . that there were differences in degree, circumstances, and intent on the suffering imposed upon Jews, Gypsies and Slavs" and that the effects of Nazi brutality have left an indelible mark on the collective memory of them all. This study recognizes that what is unique about the Holocaust is that the Nazis used the tools of modern technology and the bureaucracy of a modern nation to carry out a policy of extermination of every Jewish person in Europe with the cooperation of citizens, army, and industry. The Nazis' thorough documentation of the event has left us with the details of human behavior in extreme situations that make this major historical event critical to any study in morality, law, and citizenship.

In this curriculum, students investigate the use and abuse of power, obedience, loyalty, decision-making, and survival as they further develop their notions of justice. They identify the role and responsibilities of the individual within a given society in times of choice. Materials and activities are designed to encourage students to struggle with issues and dilemmas that defy simple solutions. And when students confront the Holocaust, the war within a war, these materials help students make a leap in their imagination to think about the choiceless choices of the history. They study this history to learn that this event was not inevitable.

Students are stimulated to reason and think about the implications for a society that abuses civil liberties and censors freedom to think. They grapple with the role of the victim, the victimizer, and the bystander as they explore a wide range of human responses. Later then, they are compelled to think about judgment, in moral as well as legal terms.

Teachers and students report that the experiences they share while studying this curriculum encourage the sense of community and the impulse to be more socially active in times that demand personal courage and risk-taking.

Hannah Arendt asks, "Could the activity of thinking, as such,...be among the conditions that make men abstain from evil-doing or even actually condition them against it?" If we are to meet our present problems in human and creative ways, it is most urgent that we face history and ourselves.

Methodology

There is a danger that when a curriculum on the Holocaust and the genocide of the Armenian people is not taught appropriately students will feel overwhelmed or, in some cases, become detached so that they tune out. The *Facing History and Ourselves* curriculum is designed to provide to adolescents information and activities which engage and challenge their most advanced thinking and speak to their concerns in a setting which provides for group interaction and individual reflection.

Since the lives of early adolescents are centered in peer groups and mutual relationships, students are likely to be struggling with issues of loyalty, trust, and responsibility as individuals within groups. This curriculum must support and challenge students who are beginning to see themselves as unique individuals, but with a yearning to belong. The curriculum must help students whose newly discovered notions of subjectivity raise the problem of differing perspectives, competing truths, the need to understand motives and to consider the intentions and abilities of themselves and others. Adolescence is a time of major developmental transitions. Students need to think about thinking, to become aware of their own development.

One thing this course has done, it has made me more aware—not only of what happened in the past, but also of what is happening today, now, in the world and in me.
—from a student journal

This curriculum seeks to foster cognitive growth and historical understanding by using content and methodology that induce conflict and continually complicate students' simple answers to complex problems. Methodology has been developed to encourage students to understand more than one perspective in a dilemma, to place themselves in the position of another person, and to be willing to express ideas in class without fear of ridicule. Lessons are designed to encourage students to think about history and its relationship to their lives and to consider the consequences of decisions and actions as they explore the roles and responses of individuals and groups confronting difficult moral issues and dilemmas. They are challenged to complicate their thinking by not accepting simple solutions to complex questions of human behavior and history. Readings and films have been chosen which are about thinking. "Who had time to think, . . . It was hard to think," remembers one German citizen as he tried to understand what went wrong in Germany during the Nazi period. Other activities and materials are chosen to illustrate those aspects of a society or of human behavior which affect the decisions we make or which keep us from thinking. The lessons on the power of propaganda, and the activities and films on obedience give new meaning to the statement by philosopher Hannah Arendt:

Thinking, an activity without space or time, paradoxically requires space and time. Of all the forms of political organization that do not permit freedom, only totalitarianism consciously seeks to crowd out the ability to think. Man cannot be silenced, he can only be crowded into not speaking.

The initial chapters in the curriculum are designed to engage students in thinking about decision-making and the vocabulary of morality in their own lives as they think about the choices people have within a given society. The connecting chapters which present history on antisemitism, from World War I to World War II in Europe, and on preparing for obedience, provide critical content and lessons for thinking about the choices people had for making a difference. Students grapple with the actual range of human responses made during the decades of choice before the Holocaust began. Certain strongly held myths which students hope will give simple explanation to this history are dispelled when they realize how many years the citizens of Germany had to vote on policy, read Nazi handouts, decide on taking an oath, risk speaking out for the dismissed faculty colleague or for the Jews in their classes or in their neighborhoods. In these initial lessons students develop a vocabulary of decision-making and justice as an aid to reasoning.

When students learn about totalitarianism, racism, and the policy of living space, they make critical connections to the study of human rights. Questions about the protection of the law and the power of a demagogue make this history of dehumanization relevant to individual choice today. It is in these chapters that students begin to wonder, "What would I have done?" The lesson plans for many of the Nazi youth are described and, as they read the stories of the participants in the history, students think about the type of education which could support courage and risk-taking in the name of justice for all citizens.

Later, as students learn about the actual war within a war, and the systematic plans for carrying out the final destruction, students give up another strongly held myth which blames the Holocaust on a single madman, Adolf Hitler. As they begin to read about the involvement of citizens, the military, and the bureaucracy in carrying out the extermination, they are often shocked. Once again, the simple explanations for complex history fail them.

In the next chapters, the vocabulary of reason and choice which students explored in the initial chapters fails to help them confront the facts of the Holocaust. Thinking about extermination, its victims, its victimizers, and its bystanders, demands a leap in the imagination and a new "vocabulary of annihilation." The "choice-less choices" of this history of human behavior in extremity do not reflect the options between right and wrong but between one form of abnormal response and another. Now students learn that a confrontation with this history demands more than coping with the information.

Students investigate the range of human responses to the Holocaust when they read about individuals, groups, and nations who had a chance to make a difference. Some chose to act and some did not. Some students and teachers emphasize the acts of courage, which rekindle hope in humanity at the expense of the reality of the mass murder, human experimentation, and extermination of children, men, and women. It is easier to dwell, for example, on Denmark as a nation which saved its Jewish citizens than it is to learn about the roles of the Catholic church, the American president, and the collaboration in many occupied nations. To study heroes and heroines and to talk of human dignity is to distort and distract from the painful reality of the history.

As students think about judgment in moral and legal terms, the chapter "Judgment" provides them with an opportunity to learn about the international war-crimes trials, to read the testimony of the victimizers and victims, and to think about the consequences, punishment, revenge, and retribution for individuals and nations. When they consider that one of the twelve men sentenced to death at the Nuremberg trials was convicted of "turning neighbor against neighbor," and "breaking the moral backbone of a citizenry," the power of words takes on a new meaning.

Later, as students think about prevention, they study the genocide of the Armenian people, and in that history, they recognize familiar themes. How does a nation move from protecting its minorities to defining them as the enemy, eliminating them from the rights of human dignity, and finally taking their lives? How does the minority get cast as the enemy, the traitor? What steps toward genocide are common to the history of this 20th-century genocide and the Holocaust? Students are outraged at the attempt to keep such history from their studies. And they remind their teachers of the potential for education to make a difference in the lives of individuals, groups, and nations. We truly study the past in order to think about our future.

The final chapter of the curriculum is designed to help students practice thinking about how they can make a difference in their lives. How can they erase the graffiti, stand up for a friend in trouble, understand the headlines? If they can model how to take a stand without getting caught in dogma, if they can learn to listen to the reasoning of those taking another stand, if they can participate in dialogue, then perhaps they will not indict their teachers in the future as this German adult did:

Trust my teachers?... who taught me nine years of Latin, six years of Greek, two years of English, philosophy, science and fine arts, and yet were so clumsy at the fine art of teaching history.

Establishing closure for this curriculum can be as difficult as searching for a way to begin the study of the Holocaust and human behavior. On a practical pedagogical level, the organized classroom lessons must come to an end, and we offer some concluding activities. On the other hand, the questions and issues raised in this study are ongoing concerns. As one student put it, "This isn't the end, is it? I mean, how do you just stop studying it?"

For many of those who have become involved in this study, the challenge to learn has been genuine—to learn not merely by acquiring knowledge, but by applying that knowledge to their own lives, to reexamine themselves and their relationships with those around them in the light of what they have learned. To cite only two examples: one student struggled with the issue of prejudice because her mother really believed that Jews were evil; and a teacher commented that his involvement with this curriculum had really made him think, not only about himself, but about his teaching.

Throughout the course, students related the issues raised in the curriculum to their daily lives—contemporary events, other academic studies, television programs, and even the dispute on the ball field. There are many issues raised in this curriculum that students and teachers can see reflected in their own lives, and each may feel the impact at a different point. There is one point, however, at which it is virtually impossible to avoid confronting issues very close to home: any discussion of racism in the context of this study almost invariably draws parallels to racism within our own society and particularly within our own schools and neighborhoods.

In all probability, racial slurs, graffiti, and fights within the school setting will continue, but our experience and documentation indicate an expanded level of awareness of justice issues, for students and teachers. It is the challenge of a curriculum like this one, and the teacher training that accompanies it, to demonstrate that public education can involve students and faculty with the origins, growth, and consequences of racism, and can take at least one small step toward helping students become human. One of the most silently powerful tributes to the value of this curriculum was the student who, while studying the Holocaust, quietly erased the swastika from his notebook.

Responses to this curriculum were noted by parents and other teachers as well as by the students themselves. Parents reported that dinner-time conversations had changed; their children were asking questions, repeating stories, and probing — sometimes for opinions and sometimes simply for help in understanding. The English teacher reported that the content of the papers reflected the class discussions; a math teacher shared his experiences from World War II, and an art teacher came to ask what the students are learning.

The following responses reflect some of the spill-over of this material:

Can we arrange to have more time in the schedule to study this — it's good.

I don't think there will be another Holocaust if we keep on teaching about the Holocaust and the Constitution; all men are created equal.

You know, some people believe that if the people of your country did something bad before you were born, that you were guilty also and should feel bad. But it wasn't your fault. Really, all humanity should feel guilty in the same way we have a right to feel good about what the Danes did because we're all members of the human race..

Everyone in the class learned a lot about the Holocaust, but did they learn a lot about human behavior, because after all, that's why we learned about the Holocaust, isn't it?

Facing History and Ourselves

Facing History and Ourselves is designed to offer educators from a variety of classroom settings appropriate materials and techniques for bringing the history of 20th century genocide, the Holocaust and the Armenian Genocide, to their students. The text provides background information, resources for additional research, a summary of scholarly approaches to the issues concerning the recording, interpretation, and teaching of the events, and options for developing the concepts and themes of these histories. Activities can be used to enhance existing curricula in history, law, art, English, sociology, and psychology classes, adapted for electives at the high school or college level, or incorporated as a unit in junior high social studies or English courses.

Although the materials have been classroom-tested with a variety of age groups, they depend, finally, on the individual teacher to mold them to each classroom setting. One art teacher, for example, might co-teach *Facing History and Ourselves: Holocaust and Human Behavior* for seventeen weeks while others in junior high settings might offer an eight- to ten-week unit in English or social studies. There are many other models for adopting the lessons of this text. This curriculum presentation has the potential to interest and involve more than just the individual staff member who uses the text in class; it can become a multi-disciplinary, community participation program. When teachers, parents, and other adults in the community attend classes or adult education courses, and workshops are designed to invite participation, then this learning experience takes on a special vitality. As one student reported, "I knew this history was important because so many of my other teachers came to learn too!"

The Facing History and Ourselves teacher training and dissemination project was originally funded by ESEA Title IV. It provides resources and staff for those who seek information and support for bringing this program to their communities. Awareness workshops and individual planning sessions are offered at the Facing History and Ourselves Resource Center at 25 Kennard Road, Brookline, MA 02146, 617-734-1111 (ext. 335/355), or at a site convenient for those implementing the program. The project is recognized by the National Diffusion Network as an "exemplary model program worthy to be replicated across the nation." There are NDN facilitators in each state whose role is to advise and support those educators interested in adopting the project. Already many teachers, representing a variety of ages and ethnic, social, and economic backgrounds have participated in the development and dissemination stages of the teacher training project. Many of these teachers have provided valuable information to our staff as we designed ways to make this project work for others.

We wish to give special recognition to some of the people who dedicated their time and expertise, their lessons and suggestions, and especially their friendship to our staff since 1976. Information about their products is available at the Resource Center.

• Margaret Drew researched and prepared the Facing History and Ourselves annotated bibliography. She has recently updated the filmography, prepared originally by Sharon Rivo. Peg's dedication to this

project and her friendship to this staff have been invaluable. The revised bibliography/filmography is available at the Resource Center.
- Barbara Traietti Hearne, an art teacher, sat with social studies students as they learned this history. Later she prepared the lessons on propaganda posters, monuments, and visual thinking used in this text.
- Henry Zabierek and Ken Schwartz provided valuable research and support in the development of Chapters 4, 9, and 12.
- Lisa Colt and Fanny Connelly prepared the *Journal Book* which documents their experiences as they taught the original Facing History and Ourselves materials in their private school classrooms. The excerpts from their student journals provide a unique insight into how 8th and 12th grade students make meaning of the course.
- Joe Reilly, a kindergarten teacher, volunteered his talent as a collector of antique posters, newspapers, and magazines, and shared his documents with teachers and students.
- Father Robert Bullock, Elizabeth Dopazo, Professor Lawrence Langer, E. Spencer Parsons, Professor Erich Goldhagen, Sonia Weitz, Jacob Birnbaum, and Rose Murra, have spoken to students, teachers, and parents in classrooms and workshops. Videotapes of their talks are available at the Resource Center.
- Manoog Young, Professor Martin H. Halabian from the National Association of Armenian Studies and Research, Inc., Susan Carlin and Ross Vartian at the Armenian Assembly of America, Reverend Vartan Hartunian of the First Armenian Church of Belmont, Mass. and Professor Richard Hovannisian of U.C.L.A. have been especially helpful in the preparation of the Armenian material. At present Alvin Bedrosian and Ara Jundanian are preparing videotape accounts of Armenian survivors under a grant from Permanent Charities to the National Center for Genocide Studies.
- Professor Lisa Kuhmerker, a long-time friend of this project, edited the *Moral Education Forum* special edition on this project.
- Ina Friedman produced a slide tape with Lynn Simon's class in Cambridge, Mass. which documents the use of the curriculum there; and David Whittier has produced a videotape which is a montage of the project's efforts in the awareness workshops.
- Professor Marcus Lieberman of the Harvard Graduate School of Education designed various tests to measure the impact of the curriculum on students. Betty Bardige, a doctoral candidate, has analyzed student journals and provided our staff with a better understanding of the cognitive-developmental approach to moral development and the complexity of evaluating growth.
- Warren Green in St. Louis, Alex Grobman in Los Angeles, Rabbi Yitz Greenberg in New York, Franklin Littel in Philadelphia, and Hillel Levine of the President's Commission on the Holocaust are all engaged actively in supporting education on the Holocaust. Martin Goldman of the Boston Anti-Defamation League and Eleanor Blumenberg of Los Angeles have been especially helpful.
- Dr. Henry Zabierek and Dr. Robert Sperber formerly of the Brookline Public Schools have shown unusual courage in their support of this project. In fact, the administrators, school committee, students, parents, and civil service staff have provided a model for encouraging, developing, implementing and disseminating innovative teacher education.

- Father Robert Bullock and Dr. Max Laufer, energized by friends of the project such as Maxwell Burstein, Arnold Soloway, Robert O'Shea, Zezette Larsen, Sigmund Strochlitz, Jack Mendelsohn, and Alan Kay, have spent hours trying to find financial support to augment our federal funds, and to find permanent funding when the federal commitment was cut-back because its priorities changed.
- Lia Coulouris, who coordinates our fundraising activities, has given us hope in otherwise dark financial times.

We wish to acknowledge the commitment and dedication of Cathy McCarney, who assists the Facing History and Ourselves staff in every aspect of our work. She represents the attempt of this staff to try even when all seems impossible.

We welcome your inquiries, and compliment teachers for their dedication to education at a time when support is hard to find.

Margot Stern Strom
William S. Parsons

1 An Introduction

This thing would be so much easier to learn if it weren't true.
— 8th grade student

Overview

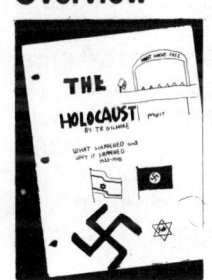

The Facing History and Ourselves Project seeks to give students access to events, both historical and current, which are usually avoided in classrooms and in textbooks.

In the initial meetings teachers and students discuss their expectations for the unit. One teacher decided to examine personal risk-taking as her goal for the unit. She wrote, "It takes courage to formulate opinions and to voice them publicly. It takes courage to listen long and hard to other points of view." One teacher found in her first class discussions with students their potential to reveal an ability that scientist Jacob Bronowski described as "...uniquely human: to draw conclusions from what we see to what we do not see...and to recognize ourselves in the past, on the steps to the present."[1]

Certainly this quotation by Anatoli Kutznetsov in his book *Babi Yar* connects the past to the present.

> ...Books are always being burnt. The library at Alexandria went up in flames, the Inquisition had their bonfires...books were burnt under Stalin, there have been bonfires in the squares under Hitler, and there will be more and more of them burnt. There are always more people to burn books than to wrote them . . . this is the first sign of trouble—if books are burned, that means things are going wrong. It means that you are surrounded by force, fear and ignorance, that power is in the hands of the barbarians.[2]

The following account of a parent who did not like what his son was reading for school is informative. The father, a selectman of a town in western Massachusetts, asked the school superintendent to remove the novel, *One Day in the Life of Ivan Denisovich*, from his son's senior-high literature course. The father objected to and was "disgusted" by the details of the life of a prisoner in a Soviet concentration camp. The description of a dialogue between two prisoners contained what he called "vulgarities." The father said he wanted "selectivity" not censorship. It is useful to begin to identify the question about censorship early in this unit since the issue of censorship plays a key role in this curriculum.

In 1978, the United States District Court for Massachusetts found that school committee members had been motivated by personal feelings about the theme and language of a poem in an anthology when they decided to remove the book from the school library. Therefore their criteria for judgment were unconstitutional and impermissable. The book went back on the shelves.

In New Hampshire, a board of education ordered all issues of *Ms* magazine removed from a high school library because some of the ads were "offensive" and some of the content politically objectionable. In 1979, the District Court of New Hampshire ordered the board to replace the magazines.

Students might consider whether their state's laws allow local school boards to remove books and periodicals from the school library. Joseph Cooper, a lecturer on law and journalism, suggests that would-be banners should ask themselves these questions:

1. What would you do if a teacher discussed the banished book or periodical in class? If reviews and excerpts were published in the student newspaper?

2. Are you being motivated by personal preferences, beliefs, abhorences? Have your political and religious dispositions influenced your assessment of the material? How about your particular notions of morality, decency, and taste?

3. Can you cite legitimate and substantial government interests that would be served by the proposed ban? Would you be willing to undertake, or pay for, an evaluation of every book and periodical in your school system's libraries in order to subject them to the same criteria?

4. Would you feel comfortable having to elaborate on why you find the material objectionable? Having to explain your motives? What are you prepared to do, go through, and spend to explain and defend your actions?

5. Do you like publicity? Notoriety?

6. Do you like lawyers? Courtrooms?[3]

Teachers report that discussions about developing a classroom atmosphere in which controversial issues and opposing ideas can be shared are critical to their preparation for teaching this history. Many define an agreement, or contract, with their students at the beginning of the unit which recognizes how difficult it is for adults and students to confront a history of racism and horror, and which seeks to help us face history and ourselves. Often the goals, expectations, and anxieties of the students are the same as those of the teachers. Also, many teachers are learning about this history for the first time. One teacher describes her attempt to reach an understanding with her students this way:

I told the students that the curriculum touched on a great many things that could hurt us all if we were not sensitive to one another's feelings. I stated that I was uncomfortable teaching the unit unless we could maintain an atmosphere of mutual respect. The contract included that each person could express his or her feelings without being put down by others.

And students responded to the initial class discussion this way:

I find that I'm not afraid to talk in front of the class anymore. I think some of the things that helped me not to be afraid were class discussions. You've taught us to respect what other people say, even if you don't agree with them. I used to be really afraid that the more popular people would laugh at what I said, but then I started talking and didn't really care if a person laughed.
—8th grade student

When the course first started it seemed like any other course, but it got better. We took notes and worked with books like a normal class but we mostly discussed this work. It doesn't seem like we're a class, but more like a group.
  —*a high school student*

This course has a lot to offer me, my classmates, and even the teacher. All I have to do is be sincere about it and get interested.
  —*a high school student*

Reading 1

Why Should Young People Study the Holocaust?
One student wrote:

What is going to make the course special for me is the connection it makes between past and present. As someone said in class today, the past should not be a refuge for us but rather a reflection on what is to come.

For years and years, parents did their best to shield their children from a subject they considered too depressing. Why burden them with the complexities and traumas of the Holocaust? One can understand their point of view; one can almost share their misgivings. For it is indeed too cruel a subject. What good is it to tell children of man's endless capacity to do evil? To describe to them atrocities that challenge reason as much as faith? They will grow up; they will find out. That was the prevalent attitude of parents.[4]

Using Reading 1

An Opening Day Discussion
Discuss why the study of genocide is avoided in classrooms and textbooks. Share the results of surveys of high school and college texts which reveal that information on the Holocaust and genocide of the Armenian people is avoided, ignored, or inadequately taught. Students might conduct their own survey.

When students are asked why so many people feel uncomfortable about learning this history, they respond:

• Maybe because there is violence in this unit, and people think that it will rub off on some of the kids.
• Maybe the parents don't want us to watch the violence in the movies, or maybe there is too much sex or nudity in the films.
• Maybe kids get nightmares from learning this unit.
• Maybe there are swears in the readings.
• Maybe the parents object to it because they think the teachers are teaching it wrong.
• Maybe adults object because it's just another experiment in school.
• Maybe the unit talks about something horrible which happened to one of the children's relatives and so their parents don't want the child to hear about it.
• Maybe we might not be able to understand parts of it so it might get boring for us.

Students remember this first lesson:

Then we began to study the Holocaust and Human Behavior, the unit which I was most interested in. At first we began to get into it slowly. I remember when you had us sit on the floor in a big circle to discuss why we were learning about the Holocaust. What do we think our parents think about us studying this certain unit, and why has it been kept such a big secret all of these years?

I'd also like to know how the others in the class feel. Are we drawn to this sort of thing the way we can't resist peeking at a gruesome car crash, or are we trying to examine serious questions in human behavior?

An Opening Lesson

The following discussion took place after a class read "Why Should Young People Study the Holocaust?":

Q: How would you respond to parents who want to shield their children from the Holocaust?
A: "The more people know, the less likely it is to happen again."
A: "Better that kids find out in school because if kids find out elsewhere, then they'll turn on their parents."
A: "We should study the Holocaust because we know more about human behavior today."
Q: What concerns should I as a teacher have in this unit?
A: "You must be careful of something being said that offends others in the class."
A: "The teacher must be careful not to force opinions on students."

Next, the teacher read the title of the curriculum, *Facing History and Ourselves.*

Q: What does "Facing History and Ourselves" mean?
A: "Seeing how history affects us."
A: "How we fit into the picture."
A: "How it affects us today."
Q: What do you think the unit is going to be about?
A: "What power can do to someone."
A: "What caused the Holocaust."
A: "Studying behaviors of people."
A: "A study of government and history."
A: "The attitudes of non-Jews in the world."
A: "How people in and out of Germany responded."

Later in this lesson, the teacher defined ground rules for this unit:

Trust
• We must respect each idea that anyone presents in class.
• I will not allow ridicule or put-downs.
• An attitude of trust is essential, and I will insist upon it.

Journals
• All of you are to keep all of your work in journals. Do not mark the curriculum booklet. Homework, notes, comments — all of these will be a part of your journal.

For homework, the teacher assigned the following questions for students' journals:

1. What do you think this unit will be about?
2. Why do you think we are studying it?

Reading 2

Keeping a Journal*

Many teachers and students keep a journal as they study this unit. In some classes the journals become part of the required assignments; in others they are voluntary. For example, in one class only one student kept a journal. In it she and her teacher carried on a running dialogue. But in another class, the journal provided the setting for a "silent dialogue with the self" while the classroom became the setting for group interactions. The journal can be a written record or a visual record; it can be a place for clippings or poems, private reflections and argument.

Author Joan Didion wrote,"I write entirely to find out what I'm thinking, what I'm looking at, what I see and what it means."

A journal, unlike a finished poem, story, or essay, remains alive, open, and incomplete, similar to the process of history itself, awaiting further entries.
—*a teacher*

Using Reading 2

Journals are a valuable supplementary activity to the *Facing History and Ourselves* curriculum. Daily autobiographical writings can chart for each student the process and progress of the course, illuminate his or her responses to it, and even function as a student advocate and support system.

Within the framework of this course, the journal becomes a means for each student and teacher to record, graphically and spontaneously, ongoing encounters with the moral issues that emerge from the course material. As students make their way into the *Facing History and Ourselves* curriculum they will in effect be bearing witness to their own living history, responding to their own growth and change during the course.

Every individual perceives the world through his or her own experience and understanding. A student's insights, questions, and memories have an internal reality that is both unique and valuable. If the student can record these perceptions with honesty he or she will have taken an important step toward self-understanding. What the students choose to confront in their journals can tell them much about who they are.

Much is required of the students who prepare to "face history and themselves." The curriculum goals include such formidable behavioral objects as "to foster growth and understanding by continually complicating students' simple answers to complex questions. To increase affective learning by providing opportunities for psychological insight, empathy, and moral commitment." The journal remains a constant throughout these pursuits and culminates in a tangible account of the delicate and painful process that can lead first to insight and eventually to understanding. "Give sorrow words" said Shakespeare. Or, as one senior student was moved to write:

This history is grim and it can build up inside and make you feel ugly and hopeless. At times I did. My journal was a confidant that no person could have been because it was always there. My journal was a daily reminder

---

*A complete lesson plan for using the journal with your class is available at the Facing History Resource Center and a complete record of the journal of two teachers and their students is available in book form at the Resource Center.

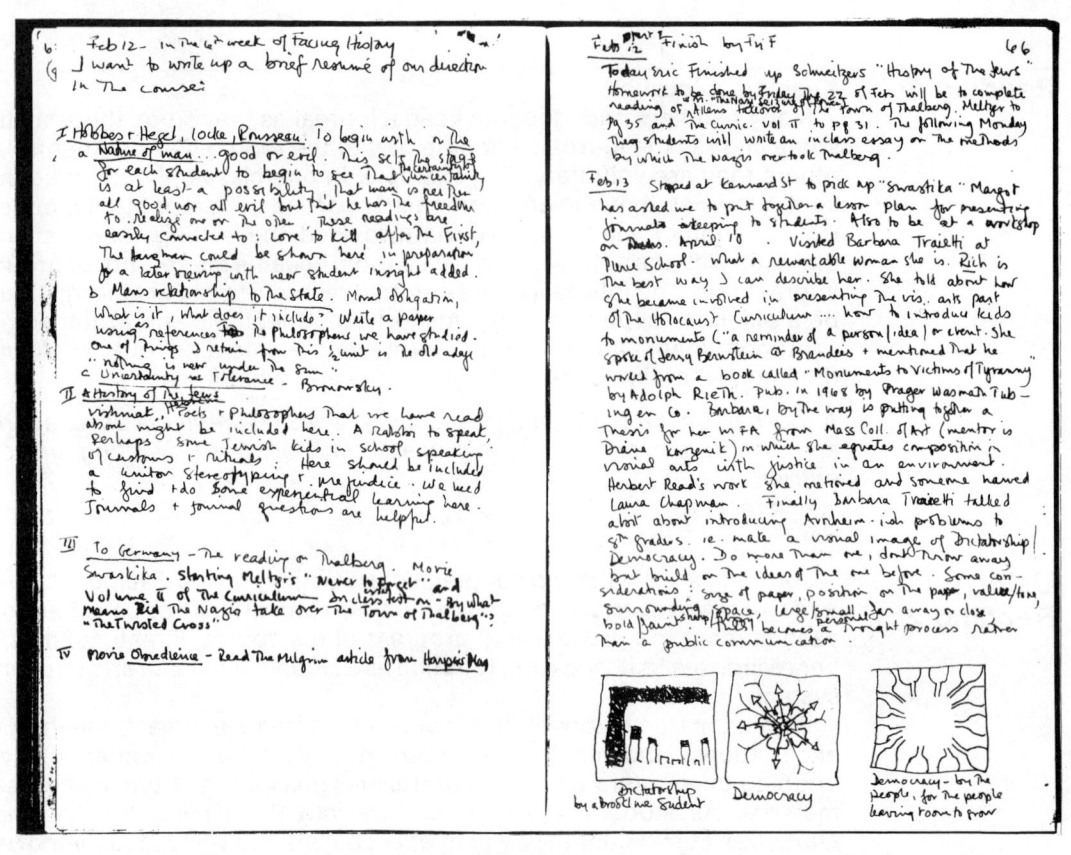

Two pages from a teacher's journal

so that when class didn't meet or there wasn't time to discuss something we wanted to, we held our own class with our journals.[5]

The following are sample journal responses of 8th grade students to their first class:

I hope that the students will take this course seriously. I also hope that people will use this course for their benefit. The course will be very moving and powerful, and I fear that people will make fun of people if they show emotion. I expect the course to help me figure out who I really am and what I truly believe.

I've always wanted to learn more about the Holocaust. I like studying humans and how they treat others. I think I will have to work at sharing my feelings with the rest of the class. However, everybody else is in the same boat.

I expect to learn more about the reasons people hurt each other. I also want to learn why prejudice exists in our society. I think it's the most incredibly stupid thing a person could feel.

I don't have any expectations, fears, or anxieties. What I am a little bit afraid of, though, is that I will find fault with myself.

These students anticipated the critical themes of the *Facing History and Ourselves* curriculum.

The following journal responses from high school students describe why they are taking the course:

It seemed a good device in which to explore myself more deeply. I have found through my summers of working with retarded people that it is hard for others to accept and understand those who are different.

I'm taking this course because I'm interested in the Holocaust itself but more importantly I am fascinated with the thoughts, beliefs, actions of the people of the time. Such a strange part of history. It is people who committed the Holocaust and I am a person.

Unfortunately I must admit that my initial interest in the Holocaust has been merely the grim fascination that it has held for me. What makes me think that in 1937 in Germany I wouldn't have felt like a superior Aryan if now I feel like a superior preppie. I'm not sure that I do feel like a superior preppie, but I am definitely going to take a hard look at myself and try to determine whether I am one or not. If I am, I have a lot of deprogramming to do.[6]

Reading 3

Building Vocabulary

Throughout this study there are words which we easily recognize, even know how to spell and associate with a meaning or an idea, but which we do not usually use in our daily conversation. If we were asked to give a definition, we might find it difficult. Often we know what a word means but we can't explain it. Instead of relying only on the dictionary definition, we can build *working definitions* for new words, and make these words an integral part of our vocabulary. Words, such as *conscience, consequences, motivation, bureaucracy, prejudice, rumor,* and *scapegoating,* take on new meaning as the curriculum moves from the opening chapters on the individual, society, and decision-making, through the actual history of the Holocaust. As information increases, our initial definitions become more complex. The following are two examples of working definitions that build to encompass more information:

Bureaucracy:
• is like a tree or an organization
• is like a work structure for business or society
• is like the system or structure which was set up to make the factory work in the story "The Bear That Wasn't" (foreman—general manager—3rd vice-president—2nd vice-president—1st vice-president)

Rumor:
• is information which may be true, but until you get it proved it is still a rumor
• is like when people blamed one group for the Black Death

Using Reading 3

When students become familiar with the idea of *working definitions*, they become actively engaged in vocabulary building. A working definition requires that a student continually expand the meaning of his or her vocabulary words. Students construct a definition according to their individual level of understanding. Basic definitions can be introduced as a class activity, and at different points in the curriculum students can redefine words as a result of discussion. Students select words to be defined, discussed, and shared. The following responses by two students indicate the value of identifying the use of vocabulary as a curriculum goal.

One thing did change—my vocabulary has broadened greatly. Now goals, genocide, and other words I never understood before, but had heard, I now use in my language a great deal.

Power—This word probably was the most powerful word we talked about this year. We learned about getting power, using power, and abusing power, and how this fit into much of the world's history.

Students may prefer to express abstract concepts by means of a configuration of lines and shapes in space. They draw their notions of democracy and dictatorship, for example, without using any representational forms such as people or things. Often these drawings portray many more ideas about a complex concept than would a verbal definition.

Students can be instructed to use different lines and shapes: heavy, light, curvy, zigzag, straight, sharp, or twisted, in different spatial relations to express their understandings or descriptions. Later, individual conceptions are shared in class and as the descriptions develop, they take on new meaning. For further information on visual thinking, refer to Rudolf Arnheim's *Visual Thinking*, University of California, Berkeley, 1969.

Reading 4

Materials List

Students maintain and refer to a materials list in which they record written materials, media, and activities used as the unit progresses. On this list students practice recording the names of guest speakers with the proper abbreviations, list and underline book titles, and record assignments. These lists provide a summary of the class activities and are especially helpful later in evaluation exercises.

Citations

Chapter 1

[1] From *The Ascent of Man* by J. Bronowski, ©1973 by J. Bronowski. Reprinted by permission of Little, Brown and Company.

[2] Anatoli Kutznetsov, *Babi Yar: A Document in the Form of a Novel* (New York: Farrar, Strauss & Giroux, 1970).

[3] Joseph Cooper, "If You Ban a Book," *New York Times*, Sept. 27, 1981.

[4] Elie Wiesel, "The Telling of the War," *New York Times Book Review*, November 5, 1972. Reprinted with permission.

[5] Lisa Colt, "Student Journals as an Adjunct to the Facing History and Ourselves Curriculum," Facing History and Ourselves Project, 1978.

[6] Lisa Colt and Fanny Connelly, *Facing History and Ourselves: Excerpts From Student Journals*, Facing History and Ourselves Project, 1980. (Hereafter referred to as Colt, Connelly, *Excerpts*.)

2 Society and the Individual

All that is necessary for the forces of evil to win in the world is for enough good men to do nothing.*
—Edmund Burke

Overview

In this chapter students are introduced to the concept of the role of the individual in society. Students develop working definitions for the terms *society* and *individual*, and brainstorm those aspects of society such as family, religion, political groups, school, grade, friends, race, town, city, state, nation, and values which contribute to the individual's identity. These intitial chapters present information about themes and concepts which will take on additional meaning as actual historical events are presented in later chapters. These chapters serve as an important foundation for the class, although it is not unusual to hear, "Where is the Holocaust? Why are we studying this first?"

Reading 1

Construct a Diagram: Various Aspects of Society Affect the Identity of an Individual

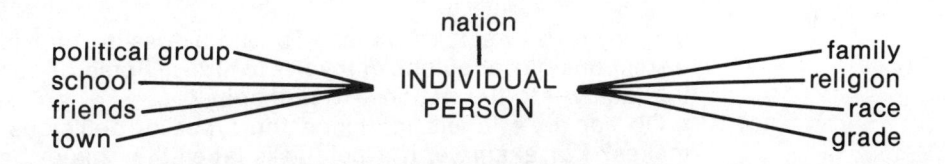

```
                              nation
                                |
    political group  ╲                            ╱  family
    school            ╲      INDIVIDUAL         ╱    religion
    friends           ╱        PERSON           ╲    race
    town             ╱                            ╲  grade
```

Using Reading 1

Students fill in the diagram with *labels* which society often gives to an individual, such as *follower, leader, believer, complainer, pacifist, conformist, nonconformist, coward, patriot, traitor* or *aggressor*. One class was asked to apply these ideas to themselves and construct personal diagrams. When the teacher shared his personal diagram with the class, his students were amazed that he, too, had so many identities. This lesson was the first of many in widening perspectives.

Questions about the role of an individual as a decision-maker in society are important to the curriculum. In class discussion or as a homework assignment explore the types of decisions an individual makes in order to maintain his or her identity in a society. For example, does the individual recognize a decision-making situation? Does the individual avoid or attempt to solve conflicts? Does he or she obey or

---

*Many of the historical quotations include the terms *man* or *men* used to refer to people. This usage reflects the period in which they were written.

29

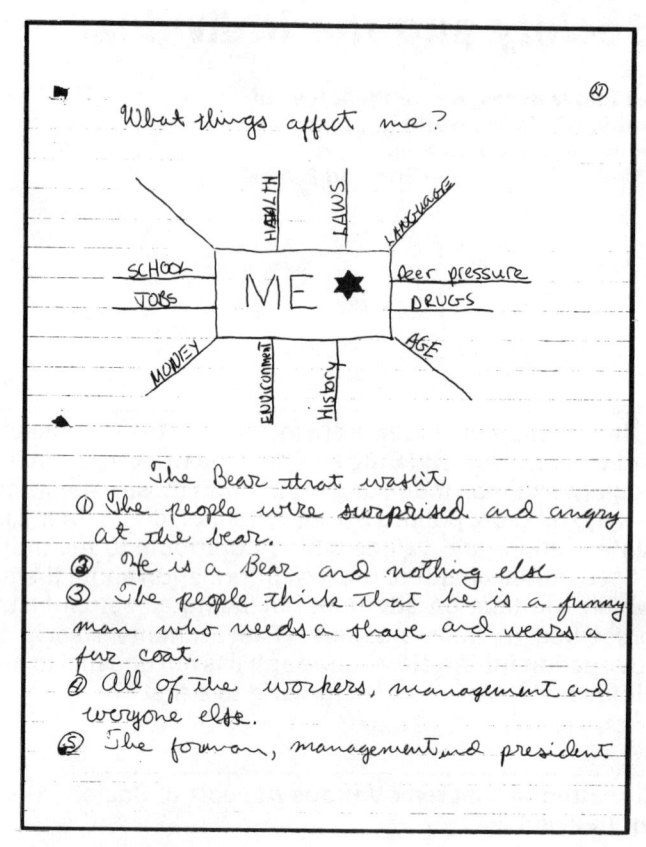

> *What things affect me?*
>
> HEALTH · LAWS · LANGUAGE · peer pressure · DRUGS · AGE · History · ENVIRONMENT · MONEY · JOBS · SCHOOL — ME ✡
>
> The Bear that wasn't
> ① The people were surprised and angry at the bear.
> ② He is a Bear and nothing else
> ③ The people think that he is a funny man who needs a shave and wears a fur coat.
> ④ All of the workers, management and everyone else.
> ⑤ The foreman, management and president

Page from a student journal

disobey laws or sets of values? To whom does the individual choose to be responsible, obedient, or loyal—to him-or herself—to the group—to the family—to the nation—to humanity?

Do society's labels influence the types of decisions an individual makes? For example, if a person is labeled by his or her friends as a bully, does the person choose to disobey rules and live up to that label as an aggressor? Why or why not?

Reading 2   *The Bear That Wasn't,* by Frank Tashlin*

Using Reading 2

Multiple copies of this book should be available so that students may enjoy the pictures, which enhance the mood and theme of the story. The story demonstrates the struggle between the bear's perception of his identity and the identity with which society labels him. Social studies concepts such as peer pressure, symbols of power (size of desk, name plates), bureaucracy, fear, brainwashing, indoctrination, isolation, and security are clearly developed in class discussions about this book.

*Multiple copies of *The Bear That Wasn't* by Frank Tashlin (Dover Publications) can be borrowed from the Facing History and Ourselves Resource Center at 25 Kennard Road, Brookline, MA. 02164. For further information, refer to the annotated *Facing History and Ourselves Bibliography Filmography* by Margaret Drew, available at the Resource Center.

When I first entered your room at the beginning of the year I was very uncomfortable because you showed me a lot of power I could not handle. Then when I read the book about "The Bear" I thought back when I first came to this school. How I was intimidated by the kids and how I used to laugh at the different people. I didn't understand why you were teaching us about prejudice, power, government, complex, idea. Then I realized you were building us up for the Holocaust.
 —8th grade student

The book you read about the bear, "just a plain old bear," hit deeply to what I have often felt intensely. I've often had nightmares that those who are close to me lose faith in me, stop caring, forget who I am. I run around trying to jar memories, and nobody seems to remember. It causes total isolation, aloneness. I forget about believing in myself, who I am, what I stand for, the point of living. What is life good for if we do not have an identity?
 —a high school student

Reading 3 "Harrison Bergeron," by Kurt Vonnegut*

The year was 2081, and everyone was finally equal. They weren't only equal before God and the law. They were equal every which way. Nobody was smarter than anybody else. Nobody was better looking than anybody else. Nobody was stronger or quicker than anybody else. All this equality was due to the 211th, 212th, and the 213th Amendments to the Constitution, and to the unceasing vigilance of agents of the United States Handicapper General.

Some things about living still weren't quite right, though. April, for instance, still drove people crazy by not being spring-time. And it was in that clammy month that the H-G men took George and Hazel Bergeron's fourteen-year-old son, Harrison, away.

It was tragic, all right, but George and Hazel couldn't think about it very hard. Hazel had a perfectly average intelligence, which meant she couldn't think about anything except in short bursts. And George, while his intelligence was way above normal, had a little mental handicap radio in his ear. He was required by law to wear it at all times. It was tuned to a government transmitter. Every twenty seconds or so, the transmitter would send out some sharp noise to keep people like George from taking unfair advantage of their brains.

George and Hazel were watching television. There were tears on Hazel's cheeks, but she'd forgotten for the moment what they were about.

On the television screen were ballerinas.

A buzzer sounded in George's head. His thoughts fled in panic, like bandits from a burglar alarm.

"That was a real pretty dance, that dance they just did," said Hazel.

"Huh?" said George.

"That dance—it was nice," said Hazel.

"Yup," said George. He tried to think a little about the ballerinas. They weren't really very good—no better than anybody else would have been,

---

*The author, Kurt Vonnegut, endured the fire-bombing of Dresden in World War II to write a science fiction story about a society in the future where ". . . everybody was finally equal." A transcript for TV based on this story is available at the Resource Center.

anyway. They were burdened with sash-weights and bags of birdshot, and their faces were masked, so that no one, seeing a free and graceful gesture or a pretty face, would feel like something the cat drug in. George was toying with the vague notion that maybe dancers shouldn't be handicapped. But he didn't get very far before another noise in his ear radio scattered his thoughts.

George winced. So did two out of the eight ballerinas.

Hazel saw him wince. Having no mental handicap herself, she had to ask George what the latest sound had been.

"Sounded like somebody hitting a milk bottle with a ball peen hammer," said George.

"I'd think it would be real interesting, hearing all the different sounds," said Hazel, a little envious. "All the things they think up."

"Um," said George.

"Only, if I was Handicapper General, you know what I would do?" asked Hazel. Hazel, as a matter of fact, bore a strong resemblance to the Handicapper General, a woman named Diana Moon Glampers. "If I was Diana Moon Glampers," said Hazel, "I'd have chimes on Sunday—just chimes. Kind of in honor of religion."

"I could think, if it was just chimes," said George.

"Well—maybe make 'em real loud," said Hazel. "I think I'd make a good Handicapper General."

"Good as anybody else," said George.

"Who knows better'n I do what normal is?" said Hazel.

"Right," said George. He began to think glimmeringly about his abnormal son who was now in jail, about Harrison, but a twenty-one-gun salute in his head stopped that.

"Boy!" said Hazel, "that was a doozy, wasn't it?"

It was such a doozy that George was white and trembling, and tears stood on the rims of his red eyes. Two of the eight ballerinas had collapsed to the studio floor, and were holding their temples.

"All of a sudden you look so tired," said Hazel. "Why don't you stretch out on the sofa, so's you can rest your handicap bag on the pillows, honeybunch." She was referring to the forty-seven pounds of birdshot in a canvas bag, which was padlocked around George's neck. "Go on and rest the bag for awhile," she said. "I don't care if you're not equal to me for awhile."

George weighed the bag with his hands. "I don't mind it," he said. "I don't notice it any more. It's just part of me."

"You've been so tired lately—kind of wore out," said Hazel. "If there was just some way we could make a little hole in the bottom of the bag, and just take out a few of them lead balls. Just a few."

"Two years in prison and two thousand dollars fine for every ball I took out," said George. "I don't call that a bargain."

"If you could just take a few out when you come home from work," said Hazel. "I mean—you don't compete with anybody around here. You just set around."

"If I tried to get away with it," said George, "then other people'd get away with it—and pretty soon we'd be right back to the dark ages again, with everybody competing against everybody else. You wouldn't like that, would you?"

"I'd hate it," said Hazel.

"There you are," said George. "The minute people start cheating on laws, what do you think happens to society?"

If Hazel hadn't been able to come up with an answer to this question, George couldn't have supplied one. A siren was going off in his head.

"Reckon it'd fall apart," said Hazel.

"What would?" said George blankly.

"Society," said Hazel uncertainly. "Wasn't that what you just said?"

"Who knows?" said George.

The television program was suddenly interrupted for a news bulletin. It wasn't clear at first as to what the bulletin was about, since the announcer, like all announcers, had a serious speech impediment. For about half a minute, and in a state of high excitement, the announcer tried to say, "Ladies and gentlemen—"

He finally gave up, handed the bulletin to a ballerina to read.

"That's all right—" Hazel said of the announcer, "he tried. That's the big thing. He tried to do the best he could with what God gave him. He should get a nice raise for trying so hard."

"Ladies and gentlemen—" said the ballerina, reading the bulletin. She must have been extraordinarily beautiful, because the mask she wore was hideous. And it was easy to see that she was the strongest and most graceful of all the dancers, for her handicap bags were as big as those worn by two-hundred-pound men.

And she had to apologize at once for her voice, which was a very unfair voice for a woman to use. Her voice was a warm, luminous, timeless melody. "Excuse me—" she said, and she began again, making her voice absolutely uncompetitive.

"Harrison Bergeron, age fourteen," she said in a grackle squawk, "has just escaped from jail, where he was held on suspicion of plotting to overthrow the government. He is a genius and an athlete, is underhandicapped, and should be regarded as extremely dangerous."

A police photograph of Harrison Bergeron was flashed on the screen—upside down, then sideways, then upside down again, then right side up. The picture showed the full length of Harrison against a background calibrated in feet and inches. He was exactly seven feet tall.

The rest of Harrison's appearance was Halloween and hardware. Nobody had ever born heavier handicaps. He had outgrown hindrances faster than the H-G men could think them up. Instead of a little ear radio for a mental handicap, he wore a tremendous pair of earphones, and spectacles with thick wavy lenses. The spectacles were intended to make him not only half blind, but to give him whanging headaches besides.

Scrap metal was hung all over him. Ordinarily, there was a certain symmetry, a military neatness to the handicaps issued to strong people, but Harrison looked like a walking junkyard. In the race of life, Harrison carried three hundred pounds.

And to offset his good looks, the H-G men required that he wear at all times a red rubber ball for a nose, keep his eyebrows shaved off, and cover his even white teeth with black caps at snaggle-tooth random.

"If you see this boy," said the ballerina, "do not—I repeat, do not—try to reason with him."

There was the shriek of a door being torn from its hinges.

Screams and barking cries of consternation came from the television set. The photograph of Harrison Bergeron on the screen jumped again and again, as though dancing to the tune of an earthquake.

George Bergeron correctly identified the earthquake, and well he might have—for many was the time his own home had danced to the same crashing tune. "My God—" said George, "that must be Harrison!"

The realization was blasted from his mind instantly by the sound of an automobile collision in his head.

When George could open his eyes again, the photograph of Harrison was gone. A living, breathing Harrison filled the screen.

Clanking, clownish, and huge, Harrison stood in the center of the studio. The knob of the uprooted studio door was still in his hand. Ballerinas, technicians, musicians, and announcers cowered on their knees before him, expecting to die.

"I am the Emperor!" cried Harrison. "Do you hear? I am the Emperor! Everybody must do what I say at once!" He stamped his foot and the studio shook.

"Even as I stand here—" he bellowed, "crippled, hobbled, sickened—I am a greater ruler than any man who ever lived! Now watch me become what I can become!"

Harrison tore the straps of his handicap harness like wet tissue paper, tore straps guaranteed to support five thousand pounds.

Harrison's scrap-iron handicaps crashed to the floor.

Harrison thrust his thumbs under the bar of the padlock that secured his head harness. The bar snapped like celery. Harrison smashed his headphones and spectacles against the wall.

He flung away his rubber-ball nose, revealed a man that would have awed Thor, the god of thunder.

"I shall now select my Empress!" he said, looking down on the cowering people. "Let the first woman who dares rise to her feet claim her mate and her throne!"

A moment passed, and then a ballerina arose, swaying like a willow.

Harrison plucked the mental handicap from her ear, snapped off her physical handicaps with marvelous delicacy. Last of all, he removed her mask.

She was blindingly beautiful.

"Now—" said Harrison, taking her hand, "shall we show the people the meaning of the word dance? Music!" he commanded.

The musicians scrambled back into their chairs, and Harrison stripped them of their handicaps, too. "Play your best," he told them, "and I'll make you barons and dukes and earls."

The music began. It was normal at first—cheap, silly, false. But Harrison snatched two musicians from their chairs, waved them like batons as he sang the music as he wanted it played. He slammed them back into their chairs.

The music began again and was much improved.

Harrison and his Empress merely listened to the music for a while—listened gravely, as though synchronizing their heart-beats with it.

They shifted their weights to their toes.

Harrison placed his big hands on the girl's tiny waist, letting her sense the weightlessness that would soon be hers.

And then, in an explosion of joy and grace, into the air they sprang!

Not only were the laws of the land abandoned, but the law of gravity and the laws of motion as well.

They reeled, whirled, swiveled, bounced, capered, gamboled, and spun.

They leaped like deer on the moon.

The studio ceiling was thirty feet high, but each leap brought the dancers nearer to it.

It became their obvious intention to kiss the ceiling.
They kissed it.
And then, neutralizing gravity with love and pure will, they remained suspended in air inches below the ceiling, and they kissed each other for a long, long time.

It was then that Diana Moon Glampers, the Handicapper General, came into the studio with a double-barreled ten-gauge shotgun. She fired twice, and the Emperor and the Empress were dead before they hit the floor.

Diana Moon Glampers loaded the gun again. She aimed it at the musicians and told them they had ten seconds to get their handicaps back on.

It was then that the Bergerons' television tube burned out.

Hazel turned to comment about the blackout to George. But George had gone into the kitchen for a can of beer.

George came back in with the beer, paused while a handicap signal shook him up. And then he sat down again. "You have been crying?" he said to Hazel.

"Yup," she said.

"What about?" he said.

"I forget," she said. "Something real sad on television."

"What was it?" he said.

"It's all kind of mixed up in my mind," said Hazel.

"Forget sad things," said George.

"I always do," said Hazel.

"That's my girl," said George. He winced. There was the sound of a riveting gun in his head.

"Gee—I could tell that one was a doozy," said Hazel.

"You can say that again," said George.

"Gee—" said Hazel, "I could tell that one was a doozy."[1]

Using Reading 3

Use the diagram presented at the beginning of this chapter as a model for diagraming Harrison Bergeron. Place Harrison Bergeron in the middle of the diagram and identify those aspects of his society which contribute to his identity. Discuss what the author means by the "dark ages of society." Why was Harrison described as "under-handicapped?"

Students are intrigued by the notion of a society that forces everyone to be equal. Students consider the positive aspects as well as the inherent abuses of forced equality.

The following quotations are from class discussions of Harrison Bergeron:[2]

I don't think everybody should be physically, mentally, or intellectually equal. Social and political equality is important. If everybody is to be equal in every aspect, the world would seem pretty grim—even more confusing than now.
  —a high school student

I hate to confess that I am one of the crowd. I dress like everyone else at school. I hate to say that I am not strong enough to be different, but maybe this will change after the course. I would like to learn not to be a bystander.
  —a high school student

Activity 4

*Love to Kill**

This film is an excerpt from the feature movie *Bless the Beasts and Children* in which a group of young campers are confronted with a difficult decision-making situation. Buffalo are being slaughtered for sport and the boys decide to break the law and attempt to free them.

Using Activity 4

Because the content of this film offers so many possible avenues of discussion, it is important to structure the lesson. Choose questions from the reading and discussion on "Harrison Bergeron" to focus the material. Should an individual go against society? When? Under what circumstances? What will the consequences be to the individual? To the society? As students view the film, have them list their own questions about the behavior of the main characters. The following is a list generated in one class:

• Should the campers have taken the law into their own hands? Do you think they had considered the consequences of their actions? Would you have decided to join the campers? If you believe your cause is right, is it all right to break the law? Who did the campers think they were helping—the buffalo—their own conscience—society? The leader of the camp wore an army helmet and spoke the language of war as he was saving the buffalo. Is there any significance in this metaphor?

• What do you think about the counselor? How else might he have handled the situation? What about the comparison he makes between the buffalo and the campers as "dings"? What type of kid would not be labeled a "ding"? What clues are there as to how the counselor felt in the end after the shooting?

• What do you think about the shooters' opinion that the killing of the buffalo is a "sport"? Are these shooters correcting an imbalance in nature? Is it right to kill animals that are considered useless? What about the way in which the shooters are killing the buffalo?

Since the film is shown early in the unit, and because it raises a highly engaging dilemma for the students, this discussion serves as an introduction to skills which will be needed for discussions of the sophisticated and complex moral issues raised later in this unit. The lesson should encourage students to initiate questions, clarify the issues of a conflict situation, define the dilemma, struggle with the vocabulary of conflict (motivation and consequences), draw analogies to past lessons in everyday situations, and struggle with the reasoning of their peers. In addition to defining the content of a conflict situation, students are introduced to a process for decision-making.

The following list, "What I Saw Happening," is one teacher's list of the skills that students were practicing during a class discussion:
• referring to notes and recording new information
• recalling yesterday's lesson and referring to other lessons
• restating a focused part of a summary
• asking other students for aid in recalling information, defining words

---

*Brief descriptions of films used in this curriculum are offered for those teachers who cannot obtain the films. Information about purchasing or renting these films is included in the bibliography/filmography available through the Resource Center. Many of the films in these initial lessons may already be a part of a school media collection.

- receiving additional information from other students
- redefining a statement or question
- recognizing and defining words
- writing their own questions
- posing lessons in the form of a question
- listening to one another
- using memorized work in the proper place
- struggling with concepts
- giving spontaneous thoughts and questions
- relating classroom issues to home and school life
- involving themselves in a process—time to think and struggle
- volunteering for tasks
- including other adults
- identifying major questions by assigning priority

Teachers, in workshops, have shared concerns about the appropriate methodology for introducing controversial materials. The following are teacher responses to a video tape of a class using the film *Love to Kill*.

I want to see more of the tapes on how to lead discussions. The little I saw was so enlightening. I find it difficult sometimes to get kids to really struggle with ideas; they are so prone to trying to come up with a facile answer and tune out.

As I watched the video tape, I thought a great deal about teaching group leadership—lots of choice and decision-making (who decides to answer which part of the question), modeling fairness in calling on students to speak using student material (their questions), and then comparing to teacher's questions—a good way to see teacher as involved, a partner in the process, vocabulary introduced at the right time and then applied, not just memorized. It is teaching methodology for thinking process.

After viewing the tape, I am more confident about finding conflict issues and developing discussion and I see the importance of modeling and of students learning the skill of quoting each other in discussions.

The following excerpts are from 8th grade students' end-of-the-year evaluations, which relate to these materials and methodology:

Another thing that I'm grateful for is having questions that don't really have conceivable answers. Because this helped me see what it was like for the people who don't raise their hand too often. I think I have become more understanding in this respect.

This year helped me very much to deal with decisions, dilemmas, and difficult situations. I've learned what it means to be a person in a society and what other people in a society do, to make a community.

I have grown a lot as a person because I can see how other people think. I also learned a lot of themes that I will see and encounter in my life. I have now faced the shocking realization that I'm not always right.

Most important of all though, is the fact that one of the biggest impressions social studies has made on me is that now, I can honestly say, I can take both sides of a dilemma and judge them accordingly. This has helped me in both social studies and in other things also.

Activity 5

After the First
This film is about a 12-year-old boy's first hunting trip and the reaction of his family to the event. This film serves as a parable with lessons about violence, agression, growing up, social conditioning, and family values.

The following questions are excerpted from the film guide:[3]

1. What does the scene in the kitchen reveal about the personalities of Steve's parents? Does it reveal anything about Steve himself?

2. What is Steve's mood as the film begins? As it ends? At what point does his attitude begin to change, and why? How would you describe Steve as a person?

3. The relationship of father and son is essential to this film. Examine that relationship as it is revealed:
- in the truck on the way to the woods
- when the father teaches Steve to use the rifle
- when Steve shoots the rabbit
- at the end of the film

4. The father's attitude toward hunting is typical of a certain set of values. What were some of the father's statements, and what do they reveal about his attitude?

5. Identify and describe the visual significance of the images, for example:
- the train
- the frozen surface of the lake
- the stream running free
- the close-up of Steve's eye, followed by the close-up of the rabbit's eye
- the flight of the birds
- blood on the grass
- the gun

6. How would you describe Steve's feelings as he:
- walks with his father at the start
- walks in the woods
- fires the gun for the first time
- watches the flight of the birds or swings on the vine
- sees his father kill the rabbit

Discuss violence as it is portrayed in the film. How does the father's attitude toward hunting apply to violence on a larger scale? (To war, for example.) Are there kinds of violence which are not physical?

Using Activity 5

The following questions and responses from a class discussion provide helpful guides for your own class discussion or for follow-up assignments in the journal.

Do human beings have a natural instinct to kill, or is it learned behavior?

Why does the boy shoot the rabbit? Is he trying to show his love for his father? Is he afraid to stand up for his own beliefs about what is right and wrong?

After the First *was a film that really opened my eyes to the ideas of human behavior and why people think, feel, and act the way they do. Is it taught or is it just adapted? Human behavior is also tied into the rest of the unit we've studied this year. The other film that got me thinking about this was* Love to Kill.
—8th grade student

A scene from the film, *After the First*

The more I learn, the more questions which are important to answer I come up with. Questions such as is there something that every person is born with which tells them that killing another person is wrong. If so, we are capable of being untrained from this instinct. I know for sure that we are capable of being trained to consider one person, or one group of people, as beasts or worms with no feelings.
—8th grade student

I guess it does get easier after the first time you do anything, good or bad. We talked today about how if you stick up for someone it, too, is easier each succeeding time. But the other side is that if you don't support someone you know or something you believe in, the reticence continues as a habit. Often when I hear people putting someone down, I play the easy role and don't get involved. When confronted with someone who is ardently against another person I usually say nothing. (Grunt, I do that alot.)
—a high school student

I couldn't believe how callous the father was to the son's feelings, yet I thought about this and came up with the conclusion that he probably went through the same thing himself. . . . He probably knew his son would grow out of fear and revulsion.
—a high school student

Reading 6

Quotations

"You are not born human; you have to be taught to be human."[4]

"The existence of this tendency to aggression . . . is the factor that disturbs our relations with our neighbors and makes it necessary for culture to institute its high demands. Civilized society is perpetually menaced with disintegration through this primary hostility of men toward one another . . . The fateful question of the human species seems to me to be whether and to what extent the cultural process developed in it will succeed in mastering the derangements of communal life caused by the human instinct of aggression and self-destruction."[5]

Using Reading 6

Discussion of these quotations will help to summarize the activities about human behavior and decision-making. Students described their reactions to the activities:

I really started to get into social studies when we started The Bear That Wasn't.

We then started doing discussions on Love to Kill, After the First *and* Facing History and Ourselves. *We always talked about why some people made the decisions they did, why people sort of went along with things and what people's reasonings were.*

"Harrison Bergeron" was a very good story. One of the best ones we read. We had very intellectual and complex discussions about why Harrison didn't want to wear handicaps and his parents really didn't seem to care, but they did, but because of their society it was hard for them to think the way they wanted to.

Everything in social studies was so systematic. Right when we talked about societies and why people do what they do, we stayed on the subject until we got everything out of it, until everyone could understand and/or at least have some knowledge of it.

We then, after learning the main concept of a society, went into the Holocaust, not exactly right into it, but we were carefully being taught how to handle, when the time came, to hear and see the hard facts about the Holocaust.

One thing I liked about our class was the discussions we had, only if they weren't boring (most of them weren't).

Reading 7

Raising a Crucial Question

What if there are certain individuals who insist their plan for how life should be lived was the one plan that would take precedence over everyone else's plan?

Using Reading 7

Students begin to wonder how it would feel if someone, wanted to have his or her plan made mandatory for all and ones own plan would be drastically reduced, or even eliminated? Their questions anticipate the critical question which is phrased later and differently as the history unfolds: How could this history have happened?

Students should be ready to engage in an inquiry exercise which focuses on how one person, in the hypothetical, might go about having his/her plan become the grand plan over all other plans.

Elicit such questions as: What steps would one take, and in what order to begin to move such a plan into completion? What groups would have to be affected and why? What aspects of the society would have to be changed? Would allegiances have to be altered and how? How would resistance be countered? Would education be involved—if so, how? If the society were complex, would the machinery and technology of government and economy be changed? Would individual choices for action be made which might counter the group's decisions or actions? When? Why? Under what conditions?

Reading 8

The Ascent of Man

Jacob Bronowski, a scientist, wrote about the choices people have for their existence. The concept of choice plays a significant role in this history.

Man is the only creature not locked into his environment. His imagination, his reason, his emotional subtlety and toughness make it possible for him not to accept the environment, but to change it. And that series of inventions by which man from age to age has remade his environment is a different kind of evolution—not biological, but cultural evolution.[6]

Using Reading 8

The Ascent of Man by Jacob Bronowski gives the reader a sense of time and a perspective on what Bronowski describes as "cultural evolution," which is applicable to these lessons. Students and teachers can construct a continuum together which identifies some of the major events in cultural history. The construction of a continuum reinforces the skill of categorizing the abstract and its completion allows students to see the evolution of specific cultures in relation to many of the terms listed below. They see that not all cultures have developed along the same lines; the Incas, for example, never developed the wheel or the skill of writing.

The following list might appear on a class continuum:
1. Ice Age
2. Fire
3. Survival
4. Nomads
5. Categories of culture
6. Agricultural Revolution
7. Wheat
8. Lever-plow (principle of physics)
9. Settlements
10. Villages
11. Domestication of animals
12. Wheel
13. Surplus
14. Government
15. Leisure time
16. Inventions
17. Communication
18. Conflict
19. War
20. Cities
21. Time (B.C. - A.D.)

The continuum provides students with one perspective on time. The continuum reintroduces important social studies terms, and prepares students for the gradual introduction to those persons and groups who have affected the cultural evolution of humans in both negative and positive ways. Teachers and students might speculate on the question whether the continuum shows progress. Examples of hunting-gathering people, typical of the nomads in early cultural history, exist throughout the continuum. One aspect of what makes our place on the continuum unique today is that there exist societies very different from our own which we can explore and from which we can gain perspective on our own society. Within today's world there exist people who live as did people in the beginning of the cultural continuum. Some of these people may be unaffected by technology; they are non-modern, traditional peoples. Consider how modern technology affects their lifestyles and their existence. Where will these people be represented on continuums in the near future? What happened to the Incas, Native American people, and the Bushmen, for example?

All persons make choices for their existence and sometimes for the existence of their families and friends; these plans we will call the grand plans; they exist for individuals, families, and groups. If we assume that individuals have their own grand plans, no matter how simple or complex, what might some be like? A father or mother might have a plan for the survival of the family; it might include plans for education and survival specific to their environment.

In this activity students and teachers begin to construct the critical questions which relate to later class discussions about the Grand Planners of history. Selected questions should be posted in the classroom for the duration of the unit. These questions could serve later in a final student evaluation for the unit. The following list of questions came from one class:

1. What is an idea?
2. How can one judge whether an idea is good or bad?
3. Why are bad ideas more powerful than good ideas?
4. How can we help our culture survive?
5. Who said people are ascending? Progressing?
6. Why would anyone want to conquer the world?
7. How do people who abuse power get power?
8. Is power always a negative thing?

Some teachers use a film called *Search for Knowledge and Certainty* from the PBS TV series *The Ascent of Man.* It is used in teacher education workshops to stimulate discussion about the use and abuse of ideas.

This film explores the themes of tolerance and dogmatism. Some high school teachers have insisted on using this film with their students. One high school teacher wrote the following about the film:

It is a demanding film that can be viewed in two class periods. The first reel is highly academic and difficult even for some seniors to fully comprehend. But by the end of reel 2 shape and meaning emerge and relate with triumphant clarity to both the Holocaust and human behavior. Bronowski's linkage of uncertainty with tolerance invites us to see human possibility in the midst of ambiguity.

A high school student responded to the film:

I think I understand now. There is no certainty. Bronowski shows that it is impossible to ever locate an electron's position exactly — any energy needed to view or locate the electron will move it — thus illustrating we can't be sure about anything.

One 8th grade teacher* assigned the following guide questions for his students who saw only reel 1 of this film. Included, also, are sample student responses:

Teacher's question: What is the difference between the ways an artist and a scientist would study a human face?

Student Response: An artist would probably see . . . the shape and contour, the different shades of color and different . . . textures in the face. She would look and see expression: happiness or sadness.

A scientist would look at the face and would see what heritage the person was from; she would look at the bone structure and discover what type or category it was from. She would try to find out if there was past illness in the face, and if so, what kind. A scientist would look at a face and would see scientific data more than the artistic beauty.

Jacob Bronowski discusses tolerance as a scientific necessity. Students made the following meaning out of his explanation on tolerance after their teacher asked them to examine how much tolerance they had as an individual in a specific situation.

When it comes to family members, my brother in particular, I am hardly tolerant. Example (one I'm sure you've heard before): When I have a friend over, usually my brother's home, too. Sometimes he just has to participate in what we're doing. Even if we don't want him to, he persists. It's not until he gets physically thrown out (and even that doesn't always work) or if it's time for his television programs will he leave.

With other people/members of family, I'm usually more tolerant. If someone else makes a mistake, I sometimes don't say anything, or if I do it's usually in fun. I'm not "out to get them," like I am my brother.

The oddest thing is, my family . . . seems to take all of my "intolerant" behavior in, along with my better moods. It could be that their fondness for me helps to cover up any misbehavior on my part. Or, maybe they have just developed a very high tolerance for me.

Tolerance is a very big part of friendship, because if you can't tolerate, you cannot live peacefully with your friends (or any other people for that matter). The word tolerance *is all about simply accepting other people and their differences.*

The teacher then asked: What do you think Mr. Bronowski was trying to say in the last moments of Search for Knowledge and Certainty, Part 2?

I think that the main point in this film is that people shouldn't try to be so powerful.

---

*Lesson plans like this one by Rob Levin are available at the Resource Center in Brookline, Massachusetts.

I liked the way the man said, technology does not kill people, ignorance does. . . . It proved that people can do crazy things because of their lack of knowledge.

This film said that no matter what materials we have, our most dangerous weapon is ourselves, and that all of the wisdom that we have can turn upon us if we become too sure of ourselves. This film accomplished a lot.

The teacher tried to help students relate the notion of what knowledge is to a previous social studies lesson. He quoted a comment about the five million American citizens who were Ku Klux Klan members in the 1930s, "[They] were not bad or vicious people. They were, for the most part, honest, hardworking, and God-fearing. They had been educated." Then he asked his students: Do you believe the above statement? What is there in that statement that you can or can't believe?

Citations

Chapter 2

[1] Kurt Vonnegut, Jr., "Harrison Bergeron," *Welcome to the Monkey House* (New York: Delacorte Press/Seymour Lawrence). Copyright© 1961 by Kurt Vonnegut, Jr. Originally published in *Fantasy and Science Fiction*. Reprinted by permission.

[2] Colt, Connelly, *Excerpts*.

[3] Joanne McPortland, *Presentation Guide: After the First* (Los Angeles:Franciscan Communications Center, 1973.)

[4] *Denmark '43*, (New York: Learning Corporation of America).

[5] Sigmund Freud, *Civilization and Its Discontents*, (Reprinted in *Center Magazine*, March/April 1981).

[6] *Ascent of Man* (New Jersey: Time-Life Multimedia).

3 Antisemitism: A Case Study of Prejudice and Discrimination

Nothing is so infectious as hate. . . .[1]

Overview

In this chapter we present antisemitism as a case study in discrimination. Initially, we investigate the phenomenon of antisemitism as it relates to all kinds of hatred, especially those familiar to our students, anti-black, anti-white, anti-Irish, and anti-other. In the initial chapters of this curriculum we explored ways an individual maintains his or her identity. And in this chapter we learn that groups, too, try to maintain their identities. One way a group or society develops its identity is to distinguish itself from other groups, through the characteristics that distinguish it from other groups, or through the ideas and ideals it advocates. If a group or society likes what it stands for, then what it stands for is "good," and what it is *not* can be construed as "bad." This way of thinking inevitably leads to prejudice, whether it is adopted by an individual or a society.

We examine the long tradition of antisemitism in order to think about how and why it was perpetuated. And to think about ways we can make a difference in stopping such hate.

As the history of anti-Semitism has shown, hatred of Jews invariably reflects larger crises in society which directly affect the lives of all. The resurgence of anti-Semitism points to a resurgence of other forms of intolerance and hatred. And that poses a profound threat to all democratic life and institutions.[2]

Before students can examine how prejudice and discrimination toward the Jewish people were transformed into a policy of antisemitism and racism in Europe in the 1920s and 1930s, they must examine how such hate is manifest today in their own lives toward the particular Jew, the Jews of a community, or the Jews of a nation. When students discover that antisemitism, like other prejudice, is a hate that for some people becomes a weapon in thought and also in deed, they understand more fully the complexities of human behavior as it was manifest in words, in action and non-action, by individuals and groups toward Jews before the Holocaust.

There are many factors which need to be considered when trying to explain why antisemitism emerges and intensifies in a particular period of history.

In his four-volume history of anti-Semitism, Leon Poliakov says that anti-Semitism has three main expressions: it appears in the context of social and political distinctions; it has theological characteristics; and it necessitates some racial distinction. In various historical periods one of these expressions becomes dominant. So, Poliakov characterizes the anti-Semitism of late antiquity as social or political; the anti-Semitism of the Middle Ages as theological; and the anti-Semitism of the modern world as racial. The dominance of one form does not mean that the others are not present, but only that they serve a subsidiary function to the dominant expression. Other scholars suggest additional forms.[3]

The anti-Jewish policy of Germany's Third Reich established social barriers, deprived Jews of their civil rights, excluded them from the economy, and ultimately resulted in the "final solution," the culmination within a European setting of centuries of antisemitism.

In the chapters that follow students study how antisemitism became transformed by racial theories and doctrines of the 19th century and led to policies of genocide.

Later in the chapters on the "final solution," the leap from the political policies of discrimination and expulsion to the carrying out of extermination of all Jewish people is documented.

Reading 1 About Hatred

Hatred begins in the heart and not in the head. In so many instances we do not hate people because of a particular deed, but rather do we find that deed ugly because we hate them. . . .[4]

Using Reading 1

In discussion about this quotation and its meaning students will anticipate the content of this chapter.

Have students add the terms *prejudice* and *discrimination* to their vocabulary list. As the units progress these working definitions will take on more meaning.

One student remembered her confrontation with personal prejudice this way:

I see prejudice now, in other people and in me; I'm afraid of old people, I get angry at shy people, I label (hippie, preppy, etc.). Prejudice grew, it was fed, watered, given sun, transplanted. Here choices are involved too. I made a choice to recognize my prejudices, to try to conquer them.
—*a high school student*

Reading 2 A Lesson on Prejudice and Discrimination

Prejudice comes from the word *prejudge*. We prejudge when we have an opinion about a person because we feel a certain way about the group to which that person belongs.[5]

Discrimination occurs when prejudicial attitudes are translated into overt actions against a particular group or a member of that group. Example: A person who says that all Mexicans are lazy is guilty of prejudice; one who refuses to sell a house to a Mexican is guilty of discrimination.

When prejudice and discrimination are applied to Jewish people we refer to this as *antisemitism*. We will not discuss the "errors involved in designating the Jews as a race; we need only note that they are a very mixed group, by no means purely Semitic, that there are many Semites who are not Jews and many Jews who are not Semites, that Semites are simply a branch of the Caucasian race, and that even were the Jews a distinct race the fact would create no consequences of importance for human behavior."[6]

In his book entitled *Anti-Semite and Jew*, Sartre attempts to describe what a person has chosen to become when he or she claims to hate all Jews. According to Sartre, an antisemite does not want to try to be rational or open to new truths that may challenge his or her opinions. The antisemite is like a stone that is "massive and impenetrable." This type of person is fearful of changing his or her opinions and therefore searches for simple answers in order to "distinguish between good and evil." An antisemite does not want to think, instead he or she wants only to find a simple explanation. The question, "What is evil?" is simple for the antisemite. "Jews are evil, therefore let us eliminate them. To eliminate an evil is to perform a good."

Furthermore, to be an antisemite means to lose one's individuality. As Sartre suggests, "Through hatred, the anti-Semite seeks out the protective community of men of bad faith, who reinforce each other through a collective uniformity of behavior.... The phrase 'I hate the Jews' is one that is uttered in chorus; in pronouncing it one attaches himself to a tradition and to a community—the tradition and community of the mediocre."[7]

Using Reading 2

One of the most difficult aspects of the inservice education part of this program has been the attempt to help teachers recognize and confront the unique and complex history and power of antisemitism. Many teachers would feel most comfortable if they never needed to mention the word "Jew"; if they could deal with the whole history of the Holocaust as just one more example of "man's inhumanity to man," with the Nazi Holocaust as very much like other historically documented massacres and mass murders.

If truth be told, some teachers are so uncomfortable at the thought of dealing with antisemitism and prejudice that this is a major reason they prefer not to teach about the Holocaust. Our experience has been that those teachers who found ways to deal with their own feelings, and strategies for introducing the topic of antisemitism into their discussions, found that the level of communication and student growth in their classes increased enormously.

As students think about how a group defines itself by what it is not, it is intriguing to think about how we distinguish between self and other. At what point does the use of such distinctions become abusive? A similar explanation of the "we vs. they" phenomenon that Sartre uses to describe the antisemite appears in the chapter on the genocide of the Armenian people (Chapter 11). This chapter explores how separate ethnic groupings of the Ottoman Empire kept the "we vs. they" distinctions alive and used them for political purposes.

Within the context of Jacob Bronowski's tracing of the development of culture in his *Ascent of Man*, the following historical explanation for the distinction between self and other and how these separations between us and them have taken on an antisemitic cast is intriguing.

This distinction emerges in prehistory in hunting cultures, where competition for limited numbers of food sources requires a clear demarca-

tion between your group and the other group, and this is transferred to agricultural communities in the development of history. Historically, this distinction becomes a comparative category in which one judges how like us, or unlike us, is the other, thus enabling people symbolically to organize or divide up their worlds and to structure reality. In the history of the West and within the relationships among Judaism, Christianity, and Islam, all too often [this distinction] has taken the cast of anti-Semitism.[8]

Reading 3

The Boy of Old Prague* by Sulamith Ish-Kishor

The story of Tomas illustrates how a young boy in the 1500s can learn to view the world through a lens distorted by hate, superstition, and rumor. Tomas grows up accepting without question all he hears about the people of the ghetto of Prague until his confrontation with the Jews of the ghetto challenges his beliefs.

Using Reading 3

This activity provides an opportunity for the teacher to read a story aloud to the class (about 3 class periods). Many teachers are intially timid about reading out loud to older students, but they find the experience worthy of the risk. Often teachers sanction only certain methods for presenting materials as permissible for older students and certain others as appropriate for young children when actually such choices are unnecessarily limiting. Exploring new ways to present materials by students can become another way to model how to be tolerant of new ideas. Helping students delay the initial rush of judgment to new and different approaches by encouraging them to learn in a variety of modes gives practice in widening perspective and respecting the "other."

After reading *The Boy of Old Prague*, students can relate the lessons on discrimination and prejudice to their own experiences in labeling and bias. And because the setting is another time and place in history it creates a distance that enables the student to speak more openly about the rumors, suspicions, and fears that they may have about Jewish people today. Often, though, class discussions are about other group hatreds. In many classes discussion about stereotyping of races different than their own begins here.

This activity reminds the teacher and students that sometimes a lesson does not come to a neat conclusion. It takes *time* to sort out one's own impression of a reading or a speaker. After a talk on antisemitism one student wrote:

The conversation was confusing, hard, I could feel that it was something very important. . . . If you were brought up to "hate" Jews and living in a community where this stands for everyone, how are you going to think? How are you going to act? Mostly you will hate Jews too. It is not necessarily your fault at all. Because you were brought up that way, and you respected your parents, and friends, and when you are a kid they are the ones you are going to follow. I liked the discussion a lot even though I didn't understand much.

*Published by Pantheon, 1962.

Reading 4

What Is a Pogrom?

Pogrom is a Russian term used throughout *The Boy of Old Prague*. Technically the word means riot or destruction but it has come "to stand for violence against Jews. . . ."[9]

One hundred years ago the peasantry in the town of Elizanetgrad in the Ukraine started a pogrom. They were encouraged by the aristocracy of St. Petersburg, who called for the "people's wrath" to "be vented on the Jews." A Russian writer of the time described the killings, rape, and pillage that spread from town to town as unending torture against that religious and ethnic minority.

But the Minister of the Interior told the Czar that pogroms were caused by the victims themselves. Later, a radical populist Russian writer, Marodnaya Valya, praised the pogroms against the "kikes" who "rob" and "cheat" the peasant and who "drink his blood."[10]

Often in the retelling of history, the listener questions the victim of violence instead of asking the critical question about why the victimizer created the situation. It is important to remember to refocus the questions of why to the victimizer. The victim never creates the situation of horror; the victimizer does.

Using Reading 4

This definition and brief history of the first pogrom will help students to understand the term as it is used in *The Boy of Old Prague* and later in the chapter on the victims of tyranny.

The fact that the history of the pogrom in Russia has been the subject of recent revisionism is important to note here because later, in the study of the Nazi race policies and of the Armenian victims, the notion that the victims are the cause of their own problems is repeated. And in historical interpretations, written to support certain national loyalties, the pogrom can be ignored, revised, or changed. For example, in 1979, the Soviet author Lydia Modzhorian refers to the pogroms as "so-called outbursts of anti-Semitism" that were "artificially exaggerated and widely used by Jewish entrepreneurs and rabbis. . . ." In her view, the "excesses" against Jews were not based upon religious or ethnic considerations, but rather were a "reaction to the exploitation to which the broad masses were subjected to capitalist enterprises."[11] This official explanation for a pogrom was created to diffuse the reality of the events. In this reading, students begin to recognize how the rumors and traditions of hate found in *The Boy of Old Prague* were active among certain people and groups in the late 19th century.

Reading 5

A Speaker Comes to Class

Scholars, theologians, or historians may be invited to speak to classes about the history of antisemitism. In many New England communities Father Robert Bullock of the Archdiocese of Boston talks to students about the distinctions between individual anger and group hatred. In this context, the discussions often focus on where the word *antisemitism* comes from and what role anti-Jewish laws and decrees have played in the history of the European nations and in the dominant religious institutions. Father Bullock asks students to consider the difference between *antisemitism* written with and without a hyphen. A person could be anti-Catholic, anti-Protestant, anti-Jewish, anti-black, because these refer to group labels. But since there is no such group as *semites* there should be no hyphen. *Anti-semitism* with a hyphen was a word coined by Wilhelm Marr in Germany in 1879, which meant "hatred of Jewish blood." This curriculum will use the word *antisemitism* to refer to those attitudes of hatred of Jews perpetuated through history.*

Using Reading 5

It is important to plan for a speaker by discussing objectives with the speaker and by preparing the class to listen, to hear, and to use the information. Often the message of the speaker can become an integral part of the students' learning experience and can enhance or be elaborated on in follow-up lessons. It has been our experience that teachers who invite other teachers and prepare them for the speaker encourage support for students' learning and enable their colleagues to deal with any spill over into their classrooms.

In one school after Father Bullock spoke to a group of 8th grade students, the teacher prepared for a discussion about "critical listening." This activity is particularly helpful for those times when some students may claim they didn't understand the speaker or that the speaker didn't represent their beliefs. After such a lesson, students are amazed at how much they really hear. The following questions guided the follow-up discussion:

1. What happens to you when you hear something new? Something different?

2. What happens when you hear information that conflicts with what you know? How do you react? What possible reactions are there? (Anger, defensiveness, listening, easy explanations, debating . . .)

3. In an attempt to think about what Father Bullock said, list five things you heard him say. Compare your list with other lists by students. Compare your list with the teacher's list.
   • What do the comparisons tell us?
   • Think about why each person selects certain things to hear, to remember.
   • What are some of the things in the list that you believe in?
   • What factors help affect what you believe in? Return to the identity chart in Chapter 2. Does your identity affect what you hear?

Reading 6

An Excerpt from *O Jerusalem* by Lapierre and Collins

The notion of "we vs. they" takes on meaning in this summary of historical anti-Judaism in Europe.

The early fathers of the Christian Church strove to emphasize the differences between their religion and its theological predecessor by forcing upon the Jews a kind of spiritual apartheid. The emperor Theodosius II gave those aspirations legal force in his code, condemning Judaism and, for the first time, legally branding the Jews a people apart.

Dagobert, King of the Franks, drove them from Gaul; Spain's Visigoths seized their children as converts; the Byzantine Emperor Heraclius

---

*Talks on antisemitism by Father Robert Bullock and Reverend E. Spencer Parsons are available on video tape at the Facing History Resource Center.

forbade Jewish worship. With the Crusades, spiritual apartheid (separation) became systematic slaughter. Shrieking their cry "Dues vult! God wills it!" the Crusades fell on every hapless Jewish community on their route to Jerusalem.

Most countries barred Jews from owning land. The religiously organized medieval craft and commerce guilds were closed to them. The Church forbade Jews to employ Christians and Christians to live among Jews. Most loathsome of all was the decision of the Fourth Lateran Council in 1215 to stamp the Jews as a race apart by forcing them to wear a distinguishing badge. In England it was a replica of the tablets on which Moses received the Ten Commandments. In France and Germany it was a yellow O, forerunner of the yellow stars with which the Third Reich would one day mark the victims of its gas chambers.

Edward I of England and later Philip the Fair of France expelled the Jews from their nations, seizing their property before evicting them. Even the Black Death was blamed on the Jews, accused of poisoning Christian wells with a powder made of spiders, frogs' legs, Christian entrails and consecrated hosts. Over two hundred Jewish communities were exterminated in the slaughters stirred by that wild fantasy.

During those dark centuries, the only example of normal Jewish existence in the West was in the Spain of the Caliphate, where, under Arab rule, the Jewish people flourished as they never would again in the Diaspora (outside of what is now Israel). The Christian Reconquista ended that. In 1492 Ferdinand and Isabella expelled the Jews from Spain.

In Germany, Jews were forbidden to ride in carriages and were made to pay a special toll as they entered a city. The republic of Venice enriched the vocabulary of the world with the word ghetto from the quarter, Ghetto Nuovo—New Foundry—to which the republic restricted its Jews. In Poland the Cossack Revolt, with a ferocity and devotion to torture unparalleled in Jewish experience, wiped out over 100,000 Jews in less than a decade. When the czars pushed their frontier westward across Poland, an era of darkness set in for almost half the world's Jewish population. Fenced into history's greatest ghetto, the Pale of Settlement, Jews were conscripted at the age of twelve for twenty-five years of military service and forced to pay special taxes on kosher meat and Sabbath candles. Jewish women were not allowed to live in the big city university centers without the yellow ticket of a prostitute. In 1880, after the assassination of Alexander II, the mobs, aided by the Czar's soldiers, burned and butchered their way through one Jewish community after another, leaving a new word in their wake: *pogrom.*[12]

Using Reading 6

In this chapter students may raise personal, theological, and historical questions that teachers feel ill-equipped to handle. However, questions concerning rumors, stereotyping, and scapegoating, which often played a part in relations between Christians and Jews, sometimes need to be discussed in order to study antisemitism.

Since the project staff has had the opportunity to travel across the United States, we have been reminded that the intensity of historical or contemporary antisemitism and anti-Jewish feelings or actions is tempered by the cultural, social, geographic, and ethnic history of a community, and that often ignorance, misinformation, and hate are directed against other minorities.

Some teachers report that their students raise questions about the deicide charge or the blood libel while others raise questions about the origins of religions. Students report that the adult world takes for granted that children have been taught basic comparative religious information but they also report that their simplest questions about one another's religions have not been answered and for some, until now, not even asked. One student wondered how he could have studied English history and early American history without a better understanding of the religious forces at play.

One way students traditionally explore more fully the questions raised by their school work is to talk with the adults in their own homes, to seek out the leadership of their own religious institutions, and to research for further explanation from the scholarship available on the subject. Often the process for gathering adequate information on the complex role religions have played in the history of the world is frustrating for the novice.

The following information is included for the teacher who may wish to help explore the power of certain rumors. Father Robert Bullock, in a letter to another Catholic priest, describes what he speaks about with children who are interested in the history of antisemitism.

My central purpose in the hour I teach is to talk about the nature and causes of antisemitism since there can be little understanding of the Holocaust without a clear and detailed awareness of this unique form of prejudice. I am careful to note that there are many roots of antisemistism and I am only dealing with one of them. I tell the students that it is a very painful task for us who are Christian to acknowledge that one of the roots of antisemitism is the way the New Testament presents Jews. This is not to say that the Gospels are antisemitic or that St. Paul was an antisemite in the way we understand today. But it is to say that the Gospels, Acts, and some of the letters can be used by antisemites to support their cause. This point is made in the text and footnotes of Nostra Aetate *and in the 1975* Vatican Guidelines for the Implementation of Nostra Aetate. *It is contained in numerous volumes by reputable Catholic and Jewish scholars. I often tell the students about Jules Isaac, author of* The Teaching of Contempt, *a book on this subject, who presented a copy to Pope John XXIII and helped inaugurate, some think, the process that led to the declaration in Vatican II.* The Anguish of the Jews *by Edward Flannery, former Executive Secretary of the Bishop's committee on Catholics and Jews, USCC, goes far beyond what I tell the students. The library on this issue is quite extensive.*

On the question of the deicide charge, I do teach that there is no such thing as collective guilt, a guilt that can be extended beyond those who were directly involved in the proceedings, then or now.

Individuals and institutions have kept alive certain myths and distortions to serve their needs. An explanation of the "blood libel"* challenges and defuses the power of such myths, and can be presented in the belief that information can combat myth. However, some information inadequately understood can reinforce negative stereotypes.

---

*Richard Hecht and Leon Poliakov provide additional information on the history of the blood libel.

Ellis Rivkin believes that the question, "Who crucified Jesus?" should be replaced with the question, "What crucified Jesus?" He gives the following explanation for the Roman death of Jesus:

What crucified Jesus was the destruction of human rights, Roman imperialism, selfish collaboration. What crucified Jesus was a type of regime which, throughout history, is forever crucifying those who would bring human freedom, insight, or a new way of looking at man's relationship to man. Domination, tyranny, dictatorship, power and disregard for the life of others were what crucified Jesus. If there were among them Jews who abetted such a regime, then they too shared the responsibility.

The mass of Jews, however, who were so bitterly suffering under Roman domination that they were to revolt in but a few years against its tyranny, can hardly be said to have crucified Jesus. In the crucifixion, their own plight of helplessness, humiliation and subjection was clearly written on the cross itself. By nailing to the cross one who claimed to be the messiah to free human beings, Rome and its collaborators indicated their attitude towards human freedom.[13]

"Generations of Christians," writes Dagobert Runes, "have been raised in hate and emotionally prepared for active antisemitism ... by the Christ-killer charge." He writes:

... Crucifixion in the manner described in the Gospels was the obligatory penalty for sorcery and high treason in the Roman Empire. Rebellious slaves as well as blasphemous rebels against the state religion were put to the cross in the Roman Empire time and time again.... There is no record of a single case in the whole rich and well-known history of the ancient Jewish people where crucifixion was ever used or urged upon an occupying military force.[14]

Language affects the steps toward dehumanization. We find that the use of language affects the level of tolerance groups have for one another. Words such as *parasite* and *vermin* have transformed the identity of individuals in the "other" group and made them seem less than human and therefore more easily threatening. These terms have fed modern antisemitism and Alex Bein suggests that, in our attempt to understand the phenomenon of antisemitism, we must look at the semantics of Jew-hatred. When the term *parasite* was originally applied to Jews in the Middle Ages, it was in a context of discussions of usury and interest. But thanks to the physiocrats and psuedoscientific theories of racial differences, the word *parasite* took on a physical reality. Bein states that:

... The fact that the Jews were seen in actual physical reality ... by way of images that were half comparisons, ultimately made possible the destruction wrought by the Nazis, using methods hitherto reserved for the extermination of bacilli, insects, and vermin. Similarly, the terms host people *and* guest people—*used by non-Jews and Jews alike—would also have to be examined."*[15]

Reading 7 Investigating Christian Roots of Antisemitism

In his article on modern antisemitism Richard Hecht states, "The challenge is how to convince young people from quite different racial, ethnic, and economic backgrounds that the quality of life is dependent on the quality of others' lives."[16]

Using Reading 7

Although historians of the Holocaust recognize the power of an environment of antisemitic teachings of hate, they caution us from making the leap from identifying the roots of historical Christian antisemitism to the creation of the Nazi policy of racism and genocide. However, it is instructive to consider how anti-Judaism was perpetuated and later condemned by the leading Christian churches.

As one explores the historical roots of antisemitism, it is important to recognize that what some historians, scholars, and people of faith consider historical documents, others consider to be indisputable words of God and therefore not open to analysis and interpretation. Most textbooks avoid bringing up these delicate subjects because it is so easy to offend one faith or another. Our attempt is to expose intolerance when it is directed at others. If certain documents and writings of innocent intent have been abused and used to hurt others, then there is merit in thinking about how this happened.

Some historians look to the early history of Judaism and Christianity and think about how groups maintained their identities during the troubled times of the Roman Empire. In this context it is interesting to see how the scattered groups of Jews maintained their religion and historical identity by refusing to become assimilated into the Roman Empire.

The followers of Jesus, viewed by the Romans as just another troublesome challenge to authority, began to form their new identity as Christians. Distinctions between Jews and Christians were defined during Roman times as new "groups" became different from "others." As new groups looked for converts, certain laws and traditions came under re-interpretation and became known as "old" in contrast to the "new" (old testament, new testament), and in time some negative connotations were institutionalized. For those who were interested in identifying a particular group of people as the enemy, there are writings of critical figures in Christian history that can be seen as "energizing factors which contribute to the pumping up of modern antisemitism." Some scholars look to the writings of Matthew and John, for example, as telling the story of the crucifixion of Jesus in different times to different audiences.

According to many scholars, Matthew wrote his version about 60 years after the death of Jesus, and John wrote about 80 years after the crucifixion, at a time when both Jews and Christians were being persecuted. Most believe that John was trying to persuade Greeks and Romans to convert to Christianity. A careful reading of these two writers will reveal one who identifies a particular group as responsible for the death of Jesus. Compare the Book of John (Chapter 18: verses 12 and 33; Chapter 19: verses 7 and 38) with the book of Matthew (Chapter 26: verse 47; Chapter 27: verses 11, 20 and 57).

In decrees and statements from the Ecumenical Council Vatican II, the Roman Catholic Church has responded to those who desire to blame Jews for the crucifixion of Jesus. The now famous *Nostra Aetate* of October 1965 contains the following guidelines and suggestions for Jewish-Christian relations:

• The Church condemns "all forms of antisemitism and discrimination."

- "Liturgical passages that show the Jewish people in such an unfavorable light" will be carefully interpreted by the Church to avoid prejudice.*

Later in history when Martin Luther led the Protestant movement in separation from the Catholic Church in Germany (1483-1546), he initially criticized the Church for its historic maltreatment of Jewish people. In 1523 he wrote a pamphlet entitled "Jesus Christ Was Born a Jew," in which he wrote that "... we ought to treat the Jews in a brotherly manner in order that we might convert them...."[17] But as the years passed his attitudes toward Jewish people changed from tolerance to intolerance. In 1542 he wrote *Schem Hamephoras* in which he stated, "Perhaps some merciful and holy soul among us Christians will be of the opinion that I am too rough with these poor and pitiable Jews, mocking and deriding them...."[18] And by 1543 Luther outlined his plan for the Jewish people:

They do not allow us to convert them.... I shall offer my faithful suggestion: first, that we burn their synagogues with fire; and what cannot be burnt shall be buried with earth, so that no man shall ever more be able to see any stone or remnant of it... secondly it is necessary to uproot and destroy their houses in the same way, since there we find they do the same as in their synagogues, and house them under some roof or other or in a cowshed like gypsies, in order that they may know that they are not lords in our land as they claim, but in exile and captivity... thirdly it is necessary that all their prayer books and their books of the Talmud shall be taken from them... fourthly, that their Rabbis shall be forbidden on pain of bodily punishment and death to teach henceforward... fifth, that the Jews shall be absolutely forbidden to move on the roads... sixth, that they shall be forbidden their usurious transactions and all their ready money and precious belongings of silver and gold shall be taken from them and placed under deposit... seventh, that the young and healthy Jews and Jewesses shall be given mallets, hoes and spindles and shall be required to earn their bread by the sweat of their brow....There is room for apprehension, to be sure, that they are liable to harm us... if they should serve us or work for us....Let us therefore use the simple wisdom of other peoples like those of France, Spain, and Bohemia... and expel them from the land forever.[19]

Among many Christian theologians today, anti-Jewish teaching is frequently referred to as the "teaching of contempt." As one contemporary Christian theologian wrote, "Most of the Nazi measures taken against the Jews—legislation excluding Jews from professions and forbidding intermarriage, the wearing of the yellow star, the ghetto—can be found in medieval Christendom. Only genocide was missing...."[20]

According to Father Edward H. Flannery, the Catholic historian of antisemitism, the new brand of antisemitism of the Nazis went beyond the scapegoating of the Jew or the suggestion that Jews were of an inferior race to the blaming of Jews for every problem, for destroying Aryan blood, for being the epitome of evil.

The missionaries of Christianity had said in effect: You have no right to live among us as Jews. The secular rulers who followed had proclaimed:

---

*Full text available at the Facing History Resource Center.

You have no right to live among us. The German Nazis at last decreed: You have no right to live.[21]

Activity 8

The Life That Disappeared

The Life That Disappeared, by Roman Vishniac, concerns life in the Jewish ghettos of Eastern Europe during the 1930s. The effects of anti-semitism are transformed from abstract generalities to personal life experiences.

Using Activity 8

Point out to the class that these are pictures of some Eastern European Jewish peasants and that their appearance and ghetto conditions are not representative of the living conditions of all Jewish people in Europe. Many lived in the urban centers of Germany and in other Western European countries. Simple stereotypes must be avoided. When students view *The Camera of My Family* later in the curriculum they are introduced to a cosmopolitan Western European Jewish family.

Dr. Roman Vishniac took his photographs just prior to the Nazi invasion of Poland; he realized that most of his subjects would probably soon vanish. His photographs "constitute the last pictorial record of a unique world that vanished only one year later." Some students will be familiar with a term used to describe the small village existence of Jews in the centuries before the Holocaust, the *shtetl*. The following reading gives vital background information about the Jewish community in Eastern Europe.

Reading 9

Who Were the Jews of Eastern Europe?

The following is an excerpt from *Never to Forget* by Milton Meltzer.

Who were the Jews of Eastern Europe? There were seven million of them living in that huge territory bounded by Germany on the west, the Dnieper River on the east, the Baltic Sea on the north, and the Black Sea on the south. Their settlement in Eastern Europe had started in the thirteenth century, with people from Bohemia and Germany. The Jews, expelled from the West during the next centuries, headed in many directions, but large numbers of them settled in the East. They were welcomed by the Polish rulers for the help they could give in the crucial task of building the country's economy. By 1500, the center of the Jewish world had moved to the Rhine. Their lot in the Middle Ages, contrasted with the horror of Western Europe, was not unbearable.

But the good life did not last long. Soon the epidemic of religious hatred and violence reached into the East, too, and the effect was catastrophic. Living conditions became as intolerable for Jews in Poland, Lithuania, the Ukraine and Galicia as they were in the other Christian countries. Church laws forced Jews into ghettos and branded them with the yellow badge. In the seventeenth century, a Ukranian uprising wiped out hundreds of Jewish communities, and hundreds of thousands — a third of the Jewish population — died by the sword, famine, and pestilence. Repeated pogroms left deep wounds in the conciousness of East European Jews, wounds which succeeding generations never healed.

The Jewish couple in this drawing lived in a small stetl in Eastern Europe. The drawing is based on an actual photograph.

When Poland was swallowed up by Russia, Prussia, and Austria after the defeat of Napoleon, a huge mass of Jews came under czarist rule. To keep the Jews out of the interior, the Czar mapped out a region all Jews were forced to live in — the Pale of Settlement. The Jews were allowed their traditional right of self-government in religious affairs, but the state restricted every aspect of life. Hundreds of anti-Jewish laws and regulations were applied mercilessly. No matter what czar sat on the throne, the persecution of the Jews continued. Anti-semitism was like an official faith, observed and respected everywhere in the Russian Empire.

In the 1870s, pogroms engineered by the government began to break out. Within a decade, new anti-Jewish restrictions and disabilities were piled upon the old. Under these crushing blows, one and one-third million Jews fled the Empire between 1881 and 1918. Most settled in the United States, but many went to Western Europe and elsewhere. More would have escaped if they had the means. But the majority of East European Jews were desperately poor. Most were factory workers, artisans, and petty tradespeople who worked fifteen and more hours a day, and lived on a diet of potatoes and herring.

They lived largely in the shtetls of Eastern Europe, the thousands of small towns scattered throughout the Pale of Settlement. The shtetls were essentially marketplaces for trading goods and services. The little towns were islands in a sea of poor, illiterate peasants. The Jews lived a separate life as a minority within the culture of the majority. During World War I, the Jews fell victim to both sides as the fighting moved back and forth. They were arrested, tortured, deported, massacred. Out of the war came the birth of Poland as an independent state. But it did not bring the Jews a better life. Not even to the small number of assimilationist Jews who came from the wealthy families. These "Poles of Mosaic Faith," as they called themselves, stressed their deep bonds with the Polish nation and their distinctness from the Orthodox Jews. In their own eyes, they were really Poles, not Jews... but the Poles didn't believe the Jews were Poles. Poland, like Nazi Germany, defined the Jews as a race. The Poles thought of the Jews as a strange people, a foreign people, a hostile people. . . .

[Even the assimilationist Jews who were esecially prominent among the leading scientists, artists, and writers were highly suspect to the Poles, although they did not join either the Zionists or the Bundists, two groups which fought for the right of Jews to live as a distinct people. The Zionists, who represented about 40% of the Polish Jews, were sympathetic to the goal of a national homeland in Palestine, and the Bundists, a socialist organization of Jewish workers, worked for a Poland where Jews would be given freedom and national equality.]

The great majority of Jews supported Polish freedom, hoping for recognition as a national minority and for equal rights. But most Polish political parties opposed these demands. Pogroms broke out the very day Polish independence was proclaimed. And, from this time on, robberies, beatings, and murders of Jews were everyday events. . . .The ancient antisemitism continued, fueled now by the rise of new fascist parties and anti-Jewish groups.

In the depression of the 1930s, antisemitic violence raged through the universities and the provincial towns. A new slogan appeared everywhere: "There is no place for Jews in Poland." The government-supported press was peppered with articles treating the Jews as an inevitable evil. In despair, the Jewish press forecast "a catastrophe for Polish Jewry." In 1935 a new Polish constitution abolished parliamentary democracy and replaced it with a fascist system. Nazi racial theories and practices were adopted. Plans were made to force mass emigration.

But most countries discriminated against Jewish immigrants. Only 117,000 Jews were able to leave Poland in the years between 1931 and 1938. Anti-Jewish riots broke out in many cities and towns. Jewish people were attacked, stores looted, tradespeople barred from markets and fairs. When a delegation of Polish Jews called on the head of the government's Nationalities Department to ask that steps be taken against antisemitic propaganda, he replied, "Nowadays everybody in Poland is antisemitic. We cannot assign police to protect every single Jew. We do not intend, moreover, to hang young people just for being antisemitic."[22]

Using Reading 9

This summary of how the Jewish people lived in Eastern Europe, particularly in Poland when it became independent, gives students certain historical facts within which to picture Jewish life before Hitler's defeat and occupation of Poland, and before the "final solution," which resulted in the Holocaust.

Students who have studied the development of the Constitution of the United States will be able to recognize and discuss how a democracy defends itself against dictatorship, and how it amends its constitution in order to give fuller protection to its minorities. Later, when students learn about the genocide of the Armenian people in Ottoman Turkey, they will learn about the discriminatory laws against the Christian-Armenian minority within a Moslem Turkish majority, and they will recognize the critical role the emergence of nation-states and Russian involvement played in that history as well.

Fiddler on the Roof, a Broadway play and film, and *Image Before My Eyes,* a recent documentary film, depict aspects of the shtetl life and modern life in Eastern Europe before the Holocaust.

Reading 10 Who Were the Jews of Germany?
The following is an excerpt from *They Chose Life* by Yehuda Bauer.

Jews first came to Germany from the Mediterranean world with the Roman armies, some 2,000 years ago, and have lived there ever since. In the so-called Dark Ages, they seem to have enjoyed reasonable security and public acceptance. But later, in the era of the Crusades (beginning in 1096 A.D.), conditions in Germany, indeed all over Central Europe, grew ominous for them. One reason was the mounting religious fanaticism and superstition of Christians; another was that Jews were in effect forced by Christians into the unpopular but necessary money-lending business, because the Church in those days forbade Christians to charge interest.

From the time of the Crusades, Jews were forced to live separately in ghettos. Popular hostility often erupted in violence. Forced conversion, pillage, expulsion and even massacre became common, sometimes inspired as much by a desire to get rid of inconvenient creditors as by religious zealotry. Persecution grew still worse with the Black Death, a vast plague epidemic in 1348-51, which popular superstition blamed on the Jews. Eventually, a large part of German Jewry fled eastward to what is now Poland, Lithuania, Czechoslovakia, Hungary, Rumania and Russia, and founded great new Jewish communities there.

After several centuries, things very slowly began to improve for those Jews who had stayed in Germany. In the early 1800s, they were let out of the ghetto; in the decades that followed, they were gradually admitted to most spheres of the larger society; and by the 1870s they were full and equal citizens under the law in every part of the country. Now feeling themselves part of the German nation, different from other Germans only in religion, they moved up rapidly with impressive achievements in commerce and industry, public service, scholarship and the arts.

Yet a large part of the German people never completely accepted the Jews as fellow citizens, and rejected their claim to being Germans while maintaining a religion and cultural tradition of their own. In Germany, as elsewhere in Europe, the old hostilities—religious, economic, political—were deeply rooted in Christian theology and its modern interpretations, and the more the Jews strove to be accepted, the more prejudice against them grew. Demagogues found them a convenient whipping boy for whatever ailed the society: wars, poverty, unemployment, "subversion," corruption. And despite the equality assured them by law, Jews remained virtually excluded from judgeships, full professorships, the higher ranks of government, and the armed forces, and a number of other positions of power and influence.[23]

Using Reading 10

The Camera of My Family, used in Chapter 7, portrays and documents the history of a centuries-old German family. Use parts of the filmstrip or the book *The Camera of My Family* appropriate for this reading.

Reading 11

One Student's View of the "Other"

The following reading illustrates a student's view of his contemporary school world:

Being a Jew at this school I often feel uncomfortable because of my different heritage. It is sometimes difficult for me to handle the greater extent to which a majority of the student body (people from old New England families) are established in society.

A large number of students here descend from the forefathers of this nation. Therefore they have stronger roots in society than members of my family (and many other Jewish families) that have been in America for no more than three generations. It was the great, great, grandparents of these students who founded institutions like this school and Harvard; started country clubs and established traditional social events like the Eliots and the Cotillion Balls.

Often I feel alienated from a majority of the student body, because, as a virtual newcomer in this society, I am not able to participate in many of the social events or to belong to many of the clubs that my fellow students frequent. (Though most of these institutions are open to Jews by law, we are not encouraged to join.) These restrictions inflicted upon me because of my religion affect my life at school. There are some students here who I will never know beyond a certain level because they have a life outside of school which I cannot share with them.[24]

Using Reading 11

In one school, the teacher felt the need to add information on the history of the Jewish people. She chose chapters from *A History of the Jews Since the First Century A.D.* by Frederick Schmeitzer.

The following journal responses indicate the range of ideas which these lessons provoked:

We're slowly but surely making our way through The History of the Jews. *It seems to me that their history and their religion are inseparable. One thing that never ceases to amaze me is that so many people died. I take such figures as 100,000 so lightly. Those people living and suffering in the Middle Ages most likely had the same wishes and desires as I do today. It's hard to comprehend that even today in our "advanced" society people are still dying.*

I think the only way to end racial prejudice is to realize that it is there, inside all of us. It's also important to expose kids to different ethnic groups and different social backgrounds.

Everyone tends to hide their prejudices at this school. Our prejudices surface as nervous jokes such as "All those Russian Commies should be shot." I heard that while sitting in the student commons today. Our biases are particularly acute because the majority of us are from the same ethnic group. There are so few minority members here.

Although I'm certain that prejudices do exist in this school, I can't say as I clearly see them.

It's a sad thing that American Jews today don't have a better understanding of their own heritage. But then I have very little perception as to what it means to be a Protestant.

One thing I find interesting is that it is because of the Jewish religion that the Jews were persecuted, but it is also because of the Jewish religion that they survived.[25]

Reading 12 **A Christian Response to Contemporary Antisemitism in Christianity**
The following is an excerpt from an article by Tom F. Driver* that appeared in *Christianity and Crisis* magazine.

We all noticed with alarm what was said at the "National Affairs Briefing" in Dallas last August by the Rev. Dr. Bailey Smith, who is president of the Southern Baptist Convention. Here are his words as quoted in the *United Methodist Reporter* (Oct. 3): "It is interesting at great political rallies how you have a Protestant to pray, a Catholic to pray, and then you have a Jew to pray. With all due respect to those dear people, my friends, God Almighty does not hear the prayer of a Jew.

"For how in the world can God hear the prayer of a Jew, or how in the world can God hear the prayer of a man who says that Jesus Christ is not the true Messiah? That is blasphemy."

Quite a number of Christians, including some officials of the Southern Baptist Convention, made public objection to what Dr. Smith said. I'm glad they did. But the fact remains that he said it. And when asked about it, he repeated it.

I recently sat in a body of liberal Christian educators who were asked to make a public, collective repudiation of Bailey Smith's declaration that "God does not hear the prayer of a Jew." The body refused to go on record as a collective body.[26]

Using Reading 12
The following letters to the editor appeared recently in *Time* magazine. Since Smith's statement, there has been a heightened interest in such statements made by representatives of the church in regard to the Jewish people.[27]

The Rev. Mr. Smith gives just another reason why global brotherhood will never be attained. It is unbelievable that anyone, especially in a leadership role, could deny the accessibility of God to any people.
—Mark Naigles, Providence

If God cannot hear a Jew's prayers, how could he hear those of Jesus, a Jew?
—Richard Nile, Hackensack, N.J.

---

* Tom F. Driver, Paul F. Tillich Professor of Theology and Culture at Union Theological Seminary (NYC), will shortly publish a book on Christology and ethics. This article is adapted from remarks delivered at a teach-in on anti-Semitism held at Columbia University in October 1980.

Violent acts against Jews have not disappeared as these newspaper headlines of 1938, 1980, and 1980 document.

Reading 13 "Now Swastikas in French"

In the following excerpt from an article by Flora Lewis, she argues that there is a "moral responsibility for opinions which incite to murder."

Italian, French, Spanish, British, German and other extreme rightists have held joint conferences, without open incitement to violence but with undertones of nostalgia for fascism.

In the last three months, there have been 40 attacks in France by groups whom the police consider neo-Nazis. They follow a mounting campaign of graffiti with swastikas and anti-Jewish slogans, anti-Semitic tracts, and threatening letters sent to Jews. Although there has long been official insistence, shared by a number of leading Jews in France, that anti-Zionism cannot be equated with anti-Semitism, the extreme right's old habit of focusing grievances on Jews generally is being reasserted.

The standard explanations are also flowing freely. Rightists blame it all on Soviet K.G.B. plots. The left blames dark forces within the establishment and the police. Sociologists mumble about frustrations caused by recession and unemployment.

Nobody really knows why, after left-wing terrorism seemed to be receding, the extreme right is now bent on murder. But the toll is mounting and the targets are more frequently Jewish.

Many who oppose violence nonetheless say things which give it intellectual justification. Alain de Benoist, a leading ideologist of

France's "New Right," wrote that "an intelligent racism, which has a sense of ethnicity, is less harmful than an intemperate leveling, assimilating anti-racism," and the phrase became a slogan of violence-prone extremists.

They are still few in Europe, the human beings who practice terrorism to intimidate societies in the direction of their sick dreams, just as the renascent Ku Klux Klan in the United States comprises few. And there is a dilemma for democracies which guarantee free speech and recognize only crimes of deed, not of thought.

But there is a moral responsibility for opinions which incite to murder. There is the proof of more than 20 million dead, the victims of the Nazi holocaust and of World War II, that a civilization which tolerates first a little evil talk, then shrugs off a few evil deeds, is launching itself toward a tragedy that spares no one. There is a strange, historic role of Jews as the bellweather victims of impending doom.

This is not just a matter for the police, just a matter for governments, just a matter for Europeans. It is the obligation of all who profess any love for life and freedom to reject with utmost resolution both the deeds and the thoughts which lead them, wherever they appear. It is an obligation, not only of decency, but of survival itself.[28]

Using Reading 13

What actions do students think would be appropriate responses to those responsible for "crimes of thought?" How does the first amendment of the Bill of Rights affect the decision? What is the dilemma for democracies according to Ms. Lewis?

Earlier in this chapter we discussed how anger is addressed toward individuals and how usually a confrontation between individuals who are angry at each other can bring some dialogue and possibly some resolution to the anger. But hatred toward a group is hard to resolve—how can a person confront a group?

George Haddad, Professor Emeritus of History at the University of California points out the complexities around the problem of understanding modern antisemitism in these approaches to the question, What is antisemitism? "Is it intolerance of the Jew as a practitioner of the specific religion of Judaism? Is it intolerance of a group of people? Or is it intolerance and dissatisfaction with the state of Israel?"[29] What are the dimensions of equating antisemitism with anti-Zionism and anti-Israel, he asks?

Later, while discussing the creation of the modern state of Israel, he says, ". . . Now, this whole business of anti-Semitism has become political. It is political anti-Semitism, because of the creation of Israel. Before 1948, before 1917, before the Balfour Declaration, anti-Semitism was connected with social community, religious practices, social practices."[30]

Lewis refers to the "old habit" of focusing all grievances against the Jews in general, the habit of "equating anti-Zionism with anti-Judaism. The anti-Semitism once directed at individual Jews and the Jewish people as a whole is now turned against the Jewish State. In the words of Irving Louis Horowitz,"the transformation is from pariah people to pariah nation."[31] This problem is particularly important today as explanation for the rise of extremist hate groups throughout the Soviet Union, Europe, and the United States.

Scholars argue that for years the long tradition of antisemitism in Soviet Russia has been revivified in the guise of anti-Zionism. In Soviet publications, "Every Jew, especially in the United States, is presented as a Zionist . . . the White House is a tool in the hands of the Zionists. Zionism is something the Jewish capitalists invented for their profit; the Zionists were partners of the Nazis; historically the Jews volunteered to live in the ghettos, so as to rule their host nations more effectively."[32]

In the view of one scholar, ". . . the individual Jew is not the primary target of this new anti-Semitism. The primary target is the Jewish national entity, the State of Israel. The particular form of anti-Semitism in America, where a canon of civility circumscribes behavior toward individual Jews, has now been transferred to the European community or to the world community."[33]*

Antisemitism in Islamic or Arab societies is a topic of investigation for some students interested in how historical antisemitism is transformed in the modern world. A careful study would demand that distinctions among European, Arab, Christian, and Islamic themes of anti-Jewish feelings and actions be recognized. Another factor worthy of study would be the history of the United Nations Resolution 3379, finally adopted by the General Assembly on November 10, 1975, which linked Zionism with colonialism, neo-colonialism, foreign occupation, apartheid, and racial discrimination.

The study of the association of Judaism, Zionism, antisemitism, and relevant nationalisms will reveal the complexities awaiting those of us in the world community who try to understand the present state of international politics in regard to the Middle East.

Activity 14   The Youth Klan and California Reich

- *The Youth Klan*, produced by CBS, Carousel Films, New York, 30 minutes. A documentary about the recruitment tactics of the Klan in the United States in the 1980s. It documents how contemporary antisemitism serves as a rallying point for the Klan.
- *California Reich*. This film documents the training of young children as they follow their families into the American Nazi Party today. The use of propaganda, indoctrination, hate slogans, and symbols are all a part of the "education of these American youth."

Using Activity 14

The growth of anti-Semitism is evidenced in the proliferation of neo-Nazi and fascist groups in England and on the Continent. The National Front in Britain now counts ten thousand members. The West German Interior Ministry in 1979 listed twenty-three explicitly neo-Nazi groups, six more than in 1977, with a membership of up to 14,000. In France, the outlawed Federation d'action nationale et Europenne (FANE) claimed 260 members.

The United States is not immune to the resurgence of explicitly anti-Semitic movements. Indeed, the Ku Klux Klan in the past few years has grown more politically active, open, and audacious in a drive to procure greater social acceptance. The Klan's drive is paralleled by the

---

*Harold Quinley and Charles Glock, in their book *Anti-Semitism in America*, suggest that the canon of American civility has confined antisemitism here to stereotypic expressions [e.g., the Jew as monied, or the Jew as pushy and intrusive]. This does not mean that these are not actualized in behavior at specific points in time or in specific contexts.

American Nazi Party, a number of white Supremacist groups, and renewed interest in and vigor of the old states rights movements...

There is also the intellectual right which expresses its anti-Semitism culturally rather than politically. The Groupement de Recherches et d'etudes pour la civilzation Europenne (GRECE) has an estimated ten thousand members and argues in a formally scientific way for the "natural inequality" of individuals and races.[34]

- Students could discuss what appeal these groups have for some youth.
- Students could comment on the following quotation, delivered by the Director of Jewish Affairs in London at a symposium on "Anti-Semitism in the Nineteen-Eighties."

I know it will be said that Hitler did not start with more than a handful of followers. This is true. But it is equally true that not every group of fifty crazy fanatics grows into a big political party. All of these groups are led by complete nonentities, and this is of paramount importance.

Citations

Chapter 3

[1] Dagobert D. Runes, *The Jew and the Cross* (New York: Citadel Press, 1966). Published by arrangement with Citadel Press.

[2] Richard Hecht, "The Face of Modern Anti-Semitism, *The Center Magazine*, March-April 1981, p. 27.

[3] Ibid., p. 19.

[4] Runes, *The Jew and the Cross*, p. 49.

[5] Irene Gersten and Betsy Bliss, *Ecidujerp Prejudice: Either Way It Doesn't Make Sense* (Franklin Watts, Inc., 1974) p. 8.

[6] Milton J. Yinger, *Anti-Semitism: A Case Study in Prejudice and Discrimination* (Freedom Books, 1964) pp. 5-6.

[7] Eva Fleischner, ed., *Auschwitz: Beginning of a New Era? Reflections on the Holocaust* Reprinted by permission of the Cathedral of St. John the Divine, New York City and KTAV Publishing Company, New York City, 1977, pp. 367-368.

[8] Hecht, "The Face of Modern Anti-Semitism," p. 19.

[9] William Korey, "The Way the Soviets Look Back on the Pogrom," *The Wall Street Journal*.

[10] Ibid.

[11] Ibid.

[12] *O Jerusalem*, Copyright © 1972 by Larry Collins and Dominique Lapierre. Reprinted by permission of Simon and Schuster, a Division of Gulf and Western Corporation.

[13] Fleischer, *Auschwitz: Beginning of a New Era?*, p. 165.

[14] Runes, *The Jew and the Cross*, pp. 30-31.

[15] Hecht, *The Face of Modern Anti-Semitism*, p. 21.

[16] Ibid.

[17] Edward H. Flannery, *The Anguish of the Jews* (Macmillan, 1965) p. 152.

[18] Leon Poliakov, *The History of Antisemitism* (Schocken Books, 1974) Vol. I, p. 219.

[19] H.H. Ben-Sasson, ed., *A History of the Jewish People* (Harvard University Press, 1976) p. 650.

[20] Eva Fleischner, "A Christian Theologian Looks at the Holocaust," (original article).

[21] From *Never to Forget: The Jews of the Holcaust* by Milton Meltzer. Copyright © 1976 by Milton Meltzer. Reprinted by permission of Harper & Row, Publishers, Inc., p. 15.

[22] Ibid., pp. 60-63.

[23] Yehuda Bauer, *They Chose Life* (The American Jewish Committee, 1973).

[24] Colt, Connelly, *Excerpts*.

[25] Ibid.

[26] Tom F. Driver, "Hating the Jews for Jesus' Sake," *Christianity and Crisis*, New York, Nov. 24, 1980.

[27] From Letters to the Editor: "Does God Hear Jews?" *Time Magazine*, Oct. 20, 1980, p. 5.

[28] Flora Lewis, "Now Swastikas in French," *New York Times*, Oct. 6, 1981, p. A-19. © 1981 by The New York Times Company. Reprinted by permission.

[29] Hecht, *The Face of Modern Anti-Semitism*, p. 28.

[30] Ibid., p. 33.

[31] Ibid., p. 27.

[32] Ibid., p. 27.

[33] Ibid., p. 27.

[34] Ibid., p. 18.

4

German History: World War I to II

What is the Third Reich in reality, a new order in the making or a holocaust, a national rebirth...
—H. Rauschning, 1939

Overview This chapter introduces students to the broadest outlines of German history before the Holocaust and explores the unlikelihood of a Nazi success in uniting Germany as it had never been united before.

One way to approach this chapter and the next one on Nazi philosophy and policy is to use the readings, charts, maps, and films to focus on the following questions:

1. What *events* or *ideas* did the Nazis take advantage of in order to gain support as they consolidated power?
2. What *techniques* did the Nazis use to consolidate their power once they had seized it?

The steps by which the Nazis consolidated their power and identified their enemies are similar to those taken by the Young Turks government to gain power and define the Armenian people as a threat to their security (Chapter 11).

Reading 1 **An American Remembers September 1930**

Milton Meltzer was fifteen years old when he first noticed the words *Nazi* and *Hitler* in the Worcester, Massachusetts, newspaper in September 1930. He remembers:

> ... I was starting my junior year in high school. I used to read the papers, but not very thoroughly — sports, the funnies, stories about local people, rarely any foreign news.
> But on this day something caught my eye in a report datelined from Germany. A hundred-odd members of Adolf Hitler's Nazi party had just been elected to the German legislature — the Reichstag they called it — and they had shown up for the first session wearing brown uniforms and shouting "Deutchland erwache! Jude verrecke!"
> The paper obligingly explained what those foreign words meant: Germany awake! Jew perish!
> Who was Hitler? What was a Nazi? Did the Germans take that slogan seriously? — "Jew perish!"
> It was those words that leaped out at me from the small print. I wasn't looking for them; I didn't know they would be there....
> Then why did my skin prickle when I saw those words in the newspaper?... Somewhere I had seen the word "pogrom" in print, knew it meant bloody riots against Jews, and linked it to the immigrants who, like my mother and father, had fled Eastern Europe. On the street I had

heard Jewish boys called "Kike" and seen them fling themselves upon their tormentors.

But for politicians to stand up now in public and shout that the Jews must die?

I shuddered. "That could never happen here, could it, Pa?" He looked up, then smiled to reassure me. "Don't worry about it," he said. "Hitler and those Nazis of his—they won't last long."

They didn't. Not in the long perspective of time. They took power in 1933; they lost power in 1945. Twelve years. It's the length of time most of us spend in grade school and high school. That's only about a sixth of the average life span.

But how do you measure the cost of those dozen years of Nazi rule over Germany and most of Europe? By the time Hitler's power was smashed, 29 million were dead. They were from many different countries, including Hitler's Germany and our United States.[1]

Using Reading 1

This reading raises the questions that most students come to this course asking: Who was Hitler? Who were the Nazis? Why did it happen? This chapter begins to give students information about the history of the person and his party. What students often forget to ask initially is: Who were the citizens, the followers, the neighbors, the teachers, the doctors, the farmers who decided to follow, to resist, or to watch?

Activity 2 **Map of Europe**

Using Activity 2

Begin by using a map of Europe. What is unique about Germany's location? What are the possible advantages and disadvantages of its location? What are the implications of Germany's location? What would it take to unify such a country?

Reading 3 **What Was Germany?**

Germany has never been a typically European nation. Both the geography and history of Germany are unlike other European countries. There is no such thing as a German "race." The "Germanies" have been so different and the divisions within Germany have been so great that there was no political unit called "Germany" until 1871.

Germany, located in the heartland of Central Europe, has never known well-defined national boundaries. Great Britain has an island, Italy has a peninsula, and France has its seacoasts and mountains. On the other hand, German boundaries have been artificial, impermanent frontiers.

Other geographical factors have served to impede German unity. Germany is divided more than any other European country by natural regions such as mountain ranges, valleys, plateaus, lakes, and the rivers Rhine, Elbe, Oder, and Vistula.

The lack of uniformity or "oneness" in Germany is further illustrated by its religious differences. Christianity and paganism have opposed one another throughout all German history. While most nations chose one religion, such as Catholic France or Protestant England, the Germanies remained permanently divided between Lutheran Germany and Catholic Germany. Religious wars took place all over Europe, but nowhere did they last as long or leave such deep scars as in Germany.

The German people had more differences among themselves than any other peoples of Europe. Their ethnic origins were of greater variety than any country in Europe. Goths, Vandals, Franks, Anglo-Saxons, and Slavs all combined to form the population of modern Germany. The country that was to make racial principle an official part of its policy had the widest variety of ethnic origins!

At no time in German history was there one strong central government able to control all the diverse tendencies in Germany. Other countries developed strong national states, but Germany did not. Around 1800 the map of Germany showed 314 states, 1475 estates, and 1789 independent rulers. Attempts to unify Germany were virtually impossible in the face of geographic, cultural, religious, and ethnic differences.

Germany, so long delayed in its unification, finally achieved it in 1871. The leader in that movement was the state of Prussia, which had emerged as a very important state in the 17th century. Frederick the Great (1740 - 1786), more than any other German ruler, set the example of military force for Germany to follow. "Negotiations without weapons are like music without instruments," he said. Otto von Bismarck (1815-1898), the Prussian chancellor who led the successful struggle for unification in 1871, championed the use of "blood and iron." Successful wars against both Austria and France culminated in the creation of the German state in January 1871.

The "Germany" that emerged in 1871 was in reality an enlarged Prussia. The king of Prussia became the emperor of Germany. The chancellor of Prussia became the chancellor of Germany. The various divisions within Germany were temporarily set aside. All these tensions were held in check as long as the Prussian soldier-state provided protection and security for all classes and all states. When this was no longer the case, such as in the German defeat in World War I, then all of the differences within Germany would again emerge.

What was Germany? Who were the Germans? How could the land of Beethoven become the land of Hitler? How could the greatest unity that Germany had ever known occur under Adolf Hitler? The dilemma that was Germany is illustrated in this quote by the British historian A.J.P. Taylor:

The history of Germany is a history of extremes. . . . "Germany" has meant at one moment a being so sentimental, so trusting, so pious, as to be too good for this world; and at another time a being so brutal, so unprincipled, so degraded, as to be not fit to live. Both descriptions are true; both types of Germans have existed not only at the same epoch, but in the same person.[2]

Using Reading 3

Develop working definitions of key vocabulary words. Ask students to make a list of the ways in which Germany differed from other countries. How unified was Germany after 1871?

Homework gives students practice in summarizing what they are learning. Often what students are learning is at variance with what the teacher thinks the students are learning. Teachers should not become so immersed in history that they forget skills work or the developmental level of students. They should check that the curriculum goals are being accurately translated.

For the first time in my history curriculum, the questions and answers about "why" it happened have been discussed. Not only "where," "what," "when," and "how."
—a high school student

Reading 4

World War I: The Unexpected War

After 1871, it was in the interest of the newly created German nation to preserve peace. In the next thirty years Germany was transformed from a predominantly agricultural country to a predominantly industrial state, and material progress became the outstanding feature of German life. In thirty years Germany achieved what it had taken England one hundred years to accomplish. By 1914, Germany was the outstanding competitor of Britain and the United States in world trade, in banking, in insurance, and in shipping. Germany seemed to be in a glorious age of economic prosperity and comfort. War seemed out of the question. No country seemed to want war and no one expected it.

Why, then, did war break out? On June 28, 1914, the heir to the throne of Austria, Franz Ferdinand, was assassinated by Serbian youths in Sarajevo, the capital of Bosnia (present-day Yugoslavia). Although this was a sensational event, no one expected war to result. Yet one month later Austria declared war on Serbia and by August 2, Germany, France, England, and Russia had all declared war.

World War I was unexpected and unwanted, yet it was quite logical in the sense that it symbolized the failure to resolve problems and tensions between countries. Chief among the underlying causes of the war were these:

Entangling, secret alliances—After 1871 no European country felt strong enough to rely solely on its own resources. Bismarck of Germany established the Triple Alliance with Italy and Austria. Eventually a rival alliance system, the Triple Entente, was formed among France, England, and Russia. The purpose of these alliances was to prevent war.

The alliances in practice often served to make war possible. Smaller countries within each alliance tended to be more aggressive. Countries supported one another blindly, regardless of their self-interest. The alliance system made it certain that any war would be of major proportions. The German ambassador Zimmerman explained the coming of war this way: "It all came from this damned system of alliances, the curse of modern times."

Nationalism—National pride and inflated patriotism became a new religion after 1871. Nationalism emphasized the uniqueness of each country: one people, one culture, one government, one identity, one purpose. History books were rewritten to glorify each country's achievements and gloss over its shortcomings. National self-glorification became the theme of writers who exalted their own cultures and ridiculed and detested others. To demonstrate their greatness, European countries acquired colonies in Africa and Asia, took pride in the defeat of enemies, and refused to believe that their nations could ever be wrong.

Militarism—After 1871 nations increased their armaments so that other countries would not attack. An armaments race began and the faster it went, the higher tensions mounted. Europe became an armed camp in the latter part of the 19th century, and only England did not have a military draft.

The growth of armies and scientific equipment made war a science. Thousands of trained specialists were needed. Plans had to be made for or against invasion. All of this gave rise to a powerful class of professional soldiers or militarists. With the concept of militarism, the army assumed controlling interest over the civilian government and the military way of life was considered to be the highest form of life.

Militarism and the huge supply of weapons inevitably led some to justify war on the basis that war brings out the noblest and most unselfish virtues in people and that war was an instrument for weeding out weak nations. War was justifiable to achieve what a nation wanted when peaceful methods failed.

Imperialism—The period from 1871 to 1914 witnessed a struggle for the establishment of colonies and control of Africa and Asia. European businesses urged their governments to acquire territory both as a market for the increased industrial productivity and as a source for raw materials. Nationalists urged the acquiring of territory for purposes of increased national prestige. This frantic scrambling for territory brought many nations to the brink of war and produced war in some cases: England fought in the Boer War in South Africa in 1899, Japan defeated Russia in 1904 - 1905, and three wars were fought in the Balkans in the period 1911-1913. All countries recognized no authority higher than their own and obeyed rules of international law only if they did not conflict with national interests.

Given these underlying causes, the coming of war seems logical. Yet few people expected it, and it came to all countries as a complete shock. There had been no major war since 1814.

The war itself was more shocking still. Sixty-five million persons were involved in the war and about 50 percent of them were either killed or wounded. There were 1,500,000 casualties in the first six months. Although the military leaders of each country promised a short war and Kaiser Wilhelm II of Germany promised that "the troops will be home by Christmas," the war was largely one of stalemate; it lasted four years. And the defeat of Germany meant a return to the tensions and differences prior to 1871.

Using Reading 4

This lesson attempts to illustrate the curriculum objective that history provides complex explanations for the past rather than precise predictions on the future. This section deals with the causes and results of the war and does not attempt to recite the details.

Each of the underlying causes will require explanation. Make use of the map of Europe to illustrate concepts such as "entangling alliances." If the war seems so logical, why was it so unexpected?

Activity 5

Good-bye Billy
This is a documentary film that surveys the history of the United States during World War I at home and at the battlefront.

Using Activity 5

Some students may wish to read further on particular phases of World War I. Others may wish to search out answers to questions left unanswered in class. The details of World War I are not commensurate with curriculum objectives.

Although this unit does not present materials about war, or treat questions about who decides to have wars, who fights them, and what purposes they have served, class discussions and student interest will certainly be aroused by the films of war. Hopefully, other units will present students with appropriate materials for considering war. Contemporary considerations of draft issues, for example, are critical for high school students who are immediately affected and who are almost at the voting age.

In the following reading about World War I, Philip Gibbs remembers the humor: "The more revolting it was," he says, "the more ... [people] shouted with laughter:"

It was ... the laughter of mortals at the trick which had been played on them by ironical fate. They had been taught to believe that the whole object of life was to reach out to beauty and love, and that mankind, in its progress to perfection, had killed the beast instinct, cruelty, blood-lust, the primitive, savage law of survival by tooth and claw and club and ax. All poetry, all art, all religion had preached this gospel and this promise.

Now that ideal was broken like a china vase dashed to the ground. The contrast between that and this was devastating. . . . The war-time humor of the soul roared with mirth at the sight of all the dignity and elegance despoiled.[3]

Reading 6

Germany from War to Peace

Peace came to Germany in November 1918 at the request of the Supreme High Command of the German Army. As early as September 1918, the Supreme Command demanded that the government request an armistice immediately. The news of the request for an armistice astounded soldiers at the front and produced mixed reactions.

Chaplain Raymund Dreeling wrote that when the government decided to ask for peace "it was as if a nightmare were over."

... What the average fighting man wanted and demanded was that an end should be put to the war and then peace and nothing but peace. ... No power in the world could have induced the average soldier at the front to take part in fighting that was to last still longer.[4]

But Ernst Junger viewed the end of hostilities differently. He wrote:

War, father of all things, is also our father. It has hammered us, chiseled us, and hardened us into what we are ... it has reared us for battle and we shall remain fighters as long as we live. ... That is the new man, the pioneer of the storm, the choice product of Central Europe. ... This war is not the end.[5]

The Germans had no choice but to sign the Armistice agreement. Failure to accept the terms of the Armistice would have resulted in the Allied invasion of Germany. Since the government of the German emperor Wilhelm II had collapsed on November 9 and the emperor had sought exile in Holland, the Armistice was signed by representatives of the newly created republic. The signing took place on November 11, 1918, at 5 a.m. in a railroad car in Compiegn forest in France. The fighting officially stopped at 11 a.m.

Germany's loss in World War I was particularly crushing. When Germany entered the war on August 1, 1914, the country was united as never before with "the spirit of 1914." Germany's carefully planned strategy to defeat France in forty days failed, and the war became a war of trenches. The stalemate was broken after the United States entered the war in 1917.

The victorious powers gathered at Versailles in France in January 1919 to draft a treaty of peace. Twenty-seven countries were represented and some countries sent as many as seventy delegates. One British delegate later described the conference as "having that sense of order of a riot in a parrot house."

The year 1919 was a high water mark for democracy in world history. The Allies (England, France, and the United States were the principal countries) had won the war and democracy seemed to be the wave of the future. President Wilson of the United States had taken his country into war "to make the world safe for democracy."

The Versailles Conference was dominated by President Woodrow Wilson of the United States, Prime Minister Lloyd George of England, and Premier Georges Clemenceau of France. Wilson had drafted a "Fourteen Points" statement in which he suggested that fairness and justice would remove any further incentive for war. England felt that a Germany that was weakened economically would be disastrous for all Europe, yet Lloyd George had to show some results that would justify England's large casualty toll. Clearly, any treaty would have to be a compromise settlement.

The treaty negotiations were further influenced by the fact that all countries had expected a short war and all had expected to win it. Countries had not raised taxes sufficiently to pay for the war, expecting that the losers would pay. Four years of bloodshed left the victors even more determined to punish the enemy who had made them suffer. Germany was not allowed to participate in the deliberations of the conference and only came to sign the agreement.

The treaty was signed on June 28, 1919, in the Hall of Mirrors at Versailles. The site was the same one used to proclaim the creation of the German Empire in 1871.

The right-wing German newspaper, *Deutsche Zeitung*, published the following statement on its front page on June 28:

Vengeance! German nation! Today in the Hall of Mirrors of Versailles the disgraceful treaty is being signed. Do not forget it! In the place where, in the glorious year of 1871, the German empire in all its glory had its origin, today German honor is being carried to its grave. Do not forget it! The German people will, with unceasing labor, press forward to reconquer the place among the nations to which it is entitled. Then will come vengeance for the shame of 1919.[6]

The Versailles Treaty has been called the most controversial treaty of all time. Since World War II some critics have labeled the treaty differently. Some have seen it as a just peace, others have considered it a harsh peace, and some others have viewed it as a just peace under the circumstances.

Using Reading 6

Any explanation of the rise of Hitler to power in Germany must include a study of the crushing loss of Germany in World War I, the Armistice, and the Versailles Treaty.

The teacher should introduce the word *armistice*. A working definition might be "the stopping of hostilities until a peace treaty is signed."

Discuss the term *treaty* and determine the criteria for what a peace treaty should accomplish. Raise some of the following questions: What is the ultimate objective of a peace treaty? What is a good treaty? Is it to stop all future wars? Is it to punish? Is it to be fair to all? Can a treaty prevent war and at the same time make all sides satisfied? Who should make the treaty? Have students make a list of the criteria for a good treaty. Ask students to list some of the difficulties and problems that surrounded the making of the Versailles Treaty.

Is it right to establish a treaty to prevent war if it is unfair to some countries? When students analyze the treaty in comparison to their criteria for a good treaty, their reactions are sharp. Be prepared for cries of "unfair" or "stupid" or "one-sided." Most students view the treaty as glaringly unjust. Refer students to their list of problems that surrounded the making of the treaty. On the basis of all the evidence was this (1) a just peace (2) a harsh peace (3) a just peace under the circumstances?

Reading 7

Synopsis of American President Woodrow Wilson's Fourteen Points for World Peace (January 1918)[7]

1. There should be no secret treaties.
2. There should be freedom of the seas for all.
3. Trade between nations should flow more freely.
4. Armaments should be reduced.
5. The boundaries between nations should be drawn according to the wishes of the people (self-determination).
6. The rights of the peoples not living in their own lands should be respected.
7. Foreign troops should be taken out of places where they were not wanted.
8. A League of Nations must be formed to keep peace among nations.

Using Reading 7

The Fourteen Points were written almost one year before the war ended! Students should analyze this document in the light of the criteria they have established for a good peace treaty. Is this a good model for a peace treaty? If you were a German leader, what kind of a peace treaty would you expect?

Reading 8

Excerpts from the Treaty of Versailles (June 28, 1919)[8]

Article
80. Germany will respect the independence of Austria.
81. Germany recognizes the complete independence of Czechoslovakia.
87. Germany recognizes the complete independence of Poland.
119. Germany surrenders all her rights and titles over her overseas countries.
159. The German military forces shall be demobilized and reduced not to exceed 100,000 men.
181. The German navy must not exceed 6 battleships, 6 light cruisers, 12 destroyers, and 12 torpedo boats. No submarines are to be included.

198. The Armed Forces of Germany must not include any military or naval air forces.
231. Germany and her Allies accept the responsibility for causing all the loss and damage to the Allied Powers.
233. Germany will pay for all damages done to the civilian population and property of the Allied Governments (The figure was later set at $33,000,000,000.)
428. To guarantee the execution of the Treaty, the German territory situated to the west of the Rhine River will be occupied by Allied troops for 15 years.
431. The occupation forces will be withdrawn as soon as Germany complies with the Treaty.

Using Reading 8

The Treaty of Versailles was the treaty that officially ended World War I. Refer to maps of Europe before World War I and Europe after World War I to illustrate some of the articles of the Treaty of Versailles, such as article 81 on Czechoslovakia.

Again ask students to apply the criteria they have established for a good peace treaty to the Treaty of Versailles. Is this treaty fair? Will the treaty stop future wars? What's good about this treaty? What's bad about it?

Reading 9

Weimar Republic 1919 - 1923

In 1919, after having been defeated in World War I, Germany established a republic. This democratic government was created so that the Germans might get a more lenient peace treaty from the Allies: England, France, and the United States. Although it was not inevitable that this government would fail, the wonder is that it lasted so long.

The Republic was created amidst the general exhaustion and shock of having been defeated in World War I. The military government had kept news of German defeats from the public and had created the impression that victory was imminent. No enemy soldier had ever set foot on German soil. The Allies had insisted that the Germans rid themselves of their military and civilian leaders before an armistice could be signed. Thus, the military lost the war but the new government was blamed for it. Later many Germans would insist that the government stabbed them in the back and the Nazis would brand these officials as "the criminals of November."

Germany was not prepared for a democratic government after World War I. Germany had always known strong leadership and it had been ruled by an emperor since 1871. Most Germans viewed the Republic as only an emergency solution, and others talked of "a Republic without Republicans."

The Weimar Republic was harassed on all sides. The Communists, having taken over in Russia in 1917, were eager to capitalize on the chaos and confusion in post-war Germany. A Communist manifesto of December 1918 proclaimed: "The rule of the working class is to be realized only through the path of an armed worker's revolution. The Communists are its vanguard...."[9]

Those who wanted a monarchy or strong leadership often resorted to violence to ruin the Republic. Anyone who supported the government was their enemy. Young people were told that it was for the good of

Germany to rid the country of "traitors." From 1918 to 1923 there were several hundred murders. In 1920 a General Kapp attempted to take over the government in Berlin, and Adolf Hitler was also unsuccessful in the state of Bavaria in 1923.

The inexperience with democratic government resulted in the creation of a variety of political parties in Germany, each with its own flag, salute, and newspaper. Since no one party could gain a majority of seats in the German parliament (Reichstag), the government changed hands frequently.

In 1923 Germany was beset with economic chaos. The political uncertainty and the money that had to be paid to the victorious countries of World War I made the German mark almost valueless. People carried shopping bags filled with marks. In 1923, the cost of a streetcar ticket in Berlin was 16,000,000,000 marks. The following table illustrates the fantastic inflation:

1914: 1 dollar equals 4 marks
January 1922: 1 dollar equals 191 marks
January 1923: 1 dollar equals 17,792 marks
November 1923: 1 dollar equals 4,200,000,000 marks[10]

The Weimar Republic miraculously survived the calamities of 1923. However, the savings of the lower and middle classes were wiped out, and many of these people became paupers. Since someone had to be blamed, the Republic was the scapegoat. Future governments would be more authoritarian and the ultimate benefactor would be the Nazi party.

Using Reading 9

Refer to maps of Europe before and after World War I. Germany, after a painful and unexpected loss in World War I, without a history in democracy and self-government, and in the midst of political, economic, and social chaos, created a republic that was vulnerable and susceptible to criticism and overthrow.

Introduce the term *republic*; a working definition at this point might be "a government that is subject to the votes of the people." After this reading students should be able to identify at least three factors that made it difficult for the Republic to survive. With all these difficulties, why did Germany create a republic? Introduce the term *inflation* and create a working definition. Discuss the effects of such inflation on an average German family.

The following are categories from a student worksheet:
• Creation of Weimar Republic
• Problems of the Republic
• Economic chaos

Reading 10

Description of the Announcement of the Republic

On the morning of November 9, 1918, Philip Scheidemann was at the Reichstag where he heard that Wilhelm Liebknecht intended to proclaim a Soviet Republic for Germany to the masses of people outside. Schiedermann was not about to let this happen. He addressed the people outside the Reichstag, proclaiming the German Republic. With his declaration, he ended the Bolshevik (Communist) threat by promising that the foes of Germany who promoted annexation and refused to reform the constitution were gone for good. Scheidemann proclaimed:

Workmen and soldiers realize the historic importance of today. Miracles have happened. . . . Everything for the people; everything by the people! Stand united and loyal, and be conscious of your duty. The old and the rotten—the monarchy—has broken down. Long live the new! Long live the German Republic![11]

Using Reading 10

Identify *Reichstag* (the German parliament), *Wilhelm Liebknecht* (a Communist leader), *Bolshevist* or *Bolshevik* (the branch of the Communist Party that took over Russia in 1917). Speculate on the role of the German citizens in the creation of the new government and discuss how this might affect their commitment to the Republic in the future.

Reading 11

Germany, 1924-1929

The period from 1924 through 1929 was one of comparative prosperity and calm for Germany. It was a breathing spell for the Republic, both economically and politically. Germany and the world calmed down and there was an upward trend in the economy.

The economic recovery of Germany has been called "one of the most spectacular recoveries in the world's entire economic history." Germany borrowed a great deal of money, particularly from the United States. In addition, the Germans copied many successful American business practices, such as standardization of parts, improved business organization, and the concentration of industries for purposes of efficiency. American influence was strongest from companies such as Ford, Chrysler, General Motors, and Eastman Kodak.

Germany became the most powerful industrial country in Europe and the most modern country on the continent. The German automobile industry became the largest in Europe. Germany was very productive in such industries as coal, steel, chemicals, and electrical supplies.

The Weimar Republic was given further credibility when Paul von Hindenburg, Chief of Staff of the German army in World War I, became president in 1925. Since the civilian government and not the military leaders signed both the Armistice and the Treaty of Versailles, Hindenburg was still seen as a war hero. Hindenburg was eighty, a believer in monarchy, and an outspoken opponent of the Weimar Republic. He did, however, operate within the limits of the constitution. He was a national institution, the image of a strong figure for the Republic.

However, the key figure in the period 1924-1929 was Gustav Stresemann, the German foreign minister. Like Hindenburg, he was a monarchist. In spite of this, Stresemann took a common sense approach toward Germany's problems. Stresemann wanted to build good will with other countries, despite the fact that this meant cooperating with those who had defeated Germany in World War I. Stresemann's chief goals were to lower the reparations payments that Germany was forced to pay to the Allies (33,000,000,000 dollars) and to gain German entrance into the League of Nations. The League was an association of countries that was a forerunner to the United Nations.

In 1925 Germany began a period of improved relations with France by signing the Locarno Pact. In this treaty, France, Belgium, and Germany agreed to respect each other's boundaries. The countries further agreed "in no case to go to war against each other."

In 1926 Germany was admitted to the League of Nations. The League was the brain child of President Wilson of the United States, who saw the agency as a means of preventing future wars. Stresemann viewed German entrance as providing an opportunity for Germany to state its case to the world and to work for changes in the Treaty of Versailles.

For his work in promoting international good will, Stresemann was awarded the Nobel Peace Prize in 1927. In 1929 Germany signed the Kellogg-Briand Peace Pact, which "outlawed war as an instrument of national policy" and limited its use to defensive purposes only. Many leaders had the feeling that the world was in for a long period of peace.

Stresemann also made progress for Germany in the matter of reparations payments to the Allies. In 1924 the Dawes Plan scaled down the amount of money Germany had to pay annually. In 1929 the Young Plan reduced the total amount of the reparations bill to 28,000,000,000 dollars and spread the payments out over 59 years.

Stresemann had accomplished much by attempting what was possible. Many problems still confronted Germany: the country was borrowing large sums of money, all Germans hated the Treaty of Versailles, and Germany was very much dependent on what happened economically and politically in the rest of the world. Nonetheless, this period of calm and prosperity serves to remind us that what happened in Germany later was not inevitable.

Using Reading 11

This reading demonstrates that the Nazi takeover of power was not inevitable; Germany during the years 1924-1929 experienced comparative peace and prosperity.

Have students research the political parties in Germany from January 1919 to March 1933. What percentage of the vote did each party receive in the elections during those years? Have students graph their answers. When were the low and high points for each party? Define *liberal, conservative, left,* and *right.* Introduce the terms *economic, social,* and *political* as vocabulary words useful in hypothesizing about why people voted as they did.[12] Which parties were in favor of the Weimar Republic and which were against it?

Introduce the term *reparations*; a working definition might be "payment to the victors for war damages." What words best describe Germany during this period?

Reading 12

Adolf Hitler and the Nazi Party, 1919-1929

What of Adolf Hitler and the Nazi party? Who was he and who were they? How could a "funny little man" with an eighth-grade education carry his party from its small beginnings in a Munich beer cellar to its dominant position in world politics in fourteen years? Was Hitler peculiar, or was it his success that was unusual?

Adolf Hitler was born in Austria on April 20, 1889. He was the fourth of six children. The first three children died in a diphtheria epidemic in 1888. A fifth child died of measles at age six. Only Adolf and Paula, born in 1896, survived. Hitler's stepfather, a custom's official, died when Adolf was fourteen. Hitler's first years in school were very successful and he got all *A's,* but at age eleven he entered a technical school where his grades became so poor that he left school at sixteen.

Hitler received unusual attention from his mother, perhaps to compensate for the loss of the first three children. She always encouraged him, even spoiled him. Hitler's mother died of cancer in 1907. Hitler disagreed with Dr. Block, the Jewish doctor, over the treatment for his mother, and blamed the doctor for his mother's death.

Hitler lived in Vienna from 1907 to 1913. In 1909 he applied for admission to the Academy of Art in Vienna and was rejected twice for lack of talent. He made a living by selling small paintings. Although he was eligible for military service in Austria, he managed to avoid it for four years.

In 1913 Hitler moved to Munich, Germany. Now twenty-four, he joined the German army and took part in heavy fighting in France in World War I. In October 1916, he was wounded in the leg and sent back to Germany. After returning to the front lines in March 1917, he was the victim of a gas attack by the British in October 1918. Temporarily blinded, he was recovering in the hospital when news reached him of the Armistice.

Hitler had entered military service as a quiet, reserved soldier. His commanding officer felt that Hitler had no capacity for leadership. He never rose above the rank of lance-corporal, although there were heavy losses in his units. Nonetheless, Hitler had demonstrated bravery and was decorated with the Iron Cross, which was most unusual for someone of such low rank.

The war had been the greatest experience in Hitler's life. He loved the comradeship, discipline, and excitement of army life. From these experiences emerged the central ideas he was to pursue later: his belief in the inequality of races and individuals, the heroic virtues of war, and the insistence that the German army was never defeated in World War I.

In 1919 Adolf Hitler was thirty years old. He was out of work; actually, he had never really worked. He returned to chaotic Munich, where he found many ex-servicemen's associations set up in oppositon to those who "lost the war": profiteers, politicians, and Jews who were blamed as those who "stabbed the army in the back." Hitler took a course in political instruction, which was given to soldiers, and became an instruction officer himself. The quiet soldier of the recent war who felt speechless in a small group was changing character.

In September 1919, Hitler was asked by the army to investigate the German Workers Party. The party had been organized in March 1918 and had tried to join workers and nationalists. Hitler met with a few party members in a Munich beer cellar, the Sterneckenbrau. Invited back, he joined the group as party member 7. Apparently Hitler believed that the only chance he had to play a leading role in German politics was with a party, starting at the bottom.

In 1920 Hitler transformed the party to the National Socialist German Workers' Party (National Sozialistische Deutsche Arbeiter-Partei— SNDAP). The Twenty-five Point Program of the party was announced on February 25, 1920. It seemed an obscure event, but future events proved it to be very significant.

By 1922 Hitler had become a well-known figure around Munich and in the state of Bavaria. He often hired a dozen beer halls and dashed from one to another to deliver his speeches. He always hammered away at his basic themes: hatred of Jews and Communists, the injustice of the Treaty of Versailles, and the fact that the German army had been sold out by pacifists and Jews.

One of his bitterest critics, Otto Strasser, wrote:

Hitler responds to the vibration of the human heart with the delicacy of a seismograph. . . .Adolf Hitler enters a hall. He sniffs the air. For a minute he gropes, feels his way, senses the atmosphere. Suddenly he bursts forth. His words go like an arrow to their target, he touches each private wound on the raw, liberating the mass unconscious, expressing the innermost aspiration, telling it what it most wants to hear.[13]

On November 8, 1923, Hitler and his followers attempted a Putsch (takeover of the government) in Munich. In the two-day struggle sixteen Nazis were killed. Hitler fled, but was captured on November 11. The Nazi movement was apparently over.

After a trial of twenty-four days, Hitler was given the minimum sentence of five years in jail. He was sent to Landsberg Prison near Munich. Prison life for Hitler was hardly a sobering experience. He grew fat, entertained many visitors, and dictated a book, *Mein Kampf (My Battle)*. Published in 1925, the book sold 9,473 copies that year.

Freed from prison in December 1924, Hitler found his party in shambles. The unsuccessful Putsch had taught him that the Nazis must come to power legally. All of Hitler's oratorical prowess was needed to rebuild the party and to recruit new membership.

Given the relative peace and prosperity of Germany during this time, who would join the Nazi Party? At this time Nazism united the disillusioned of every class: the army officer who couldn't find his role in civilian life, the ruined capitalist, the unemployed worker, the unemployed clerk, the university student who had flunked his examination, and the incompetent lawyer or blundering doctor. All of these people could exchange their shabby clothes for the smart uniforms of the Nazis and seek new hope in Hitler's promises.

Hitler and the Nazis proclaimed war as a normal state of life. Hitler felt that people could fight only if they had one common and permanent enemy. Historians disagree on the source of Hitler's antisemitism. He always claimed it came from his days in Vienna.

The Nazis proclaimed that the salvation of the world depended on the German race; it was the symbol of all creative genius. The counter-race was the Jews. The Nazi duty was to destroy the counter-race. Hitler had explained it clearly in a Munich speech on July 28, 1932:

The Jew has never founded any civilization, though he has destroyed hundreds. He possesses nothing of his own creation to which he can point. Everything he has is stolen. Foreign people, foreign workmen build him his temples; it is foreigners who shed their blood for him. He has no art of his own; bit by bit he has stolen it all from other peoples. He does not even know how to preserve the precious things others have created.[14]

The Nazis operated as a state within a state. Hitler's storm troopers (Sturm Abteilungen—SA) policed Nazi meetings and often broke up opposition party meetings. The Nazis did everything possible to attract attention; they used slogans, posters, and rallies. Party membership rose from 17,000 members in 1926 to upward of 60,000 members in 1928.

Despite the activity and dynamism of the party, the political stability of 1924-1929 hurt the Nazis. Nazi representation in the German parliament, the Reichstag, gradually declined. From 1924 to 1928 their membership dropped from 32 to 12. The party seemed on the way to permanent obscurity. Only a major calamity for the Weimar Republic could ever make the Nazis a factor in the German political scene.

Using Reading 12

In the previous section students learned about the Weimar Republic from 1919 to 1929. This section further supports the theme of the unlikelihood of Nazi success.

Students could develop a time line that includes the major events of Hitler's life from this reading or graph the rise and fall of Hitler's fortunes during this period. In either case, it should be clear that, despite the frenzied activity of Hitler and the Nazi party, the Nazi party by 1929 was relatively insignificant.

These lessons seek to demonstrate that the Nazi takeover was not simply a direct result of World War I, nor was it inevitable. Again, students see that there are no simple explanations to complex problems.

I can easily see how Hitler obtained his power, and all I can say for Hitler is he must be some psychological genius. I mean I can understand one person's callousness toward murder, but how could a whole population feel the same way no matter how badly off they were.
—an 8th grade student

Reading 13 Two Descriptions of Hitler

Ericka Mann was living in Germany at this time. She described Hitler as uneducated, unskilled in sport, weak, and uncourageous. She wrote:

... His shoulders are narrow and his hips broad; he will never be able to distinguish himself physically. As a boy he was nervous. His mother described him as "moonstruck," and in Mein Kampf, *he admits that he was difficult to handle. He had pneumonia at the age of thirteen, and during the War he suffered from temporary blindness, probably of hysterical origin. He was only slightly wounded; a more important injury was suffered in 1923, during his Putsch, when he dashed his shoulder against the pavement near the Feldherrnhalle. He threw himself to the ground the minute he heard bullets; and later, although he had sworn to kill himself if the Putsch failed, he escaped quietly. Mussolini drives, pilots his own plane, and is an exceptionally fine rider; Hitler is not even able to sit on his horse long enough to review a parade. It is eminently logical that he should desire "his" youth to be adroit and courageous, even though he himself is neither. He is giving them the "advantages" he missed, and they are to conquer the world.*[15]

The following letter, written in October 1923 by a woman named Anna, gives a very different description of Hitler. She describes the enthusiasm and deep conviction of his followers. They consider him as the man they can trust unconditionally, because he never promised too much or predicted anything that was not true.

I have never heard any other speaker (and I have, after all, heard many) who was so able to penetrate into the soul of the individual, who spoke with such a sense of righteousness about those confused German racial comrades who even today know no fatherland. To show them is the principal, and at the same time, the most difficult task. In my opinion, there is no man on German soil that can do more to awaken in all of us this love of our homeland and loyalty to our fatherland.... Unmatched rejoicing breaks out when he enters the hall, and he has to wait a long time until the shouting dies down. ... [At the Rossbach Rally in

Hitler at a Nazi rally in 1934

September] the hall was very nicely decorated with the old [Imperial] black-white-red flag, the swastika, and the Navy flag. The band played various marches, then came the individual units of the Fighting Union, threading their way through the audience and the rows of chairs like a gray-green snake. . . . The high point of the evening was not reached until Hitler stepped up to the podium. His appearance was greeted with an endless series of "Heils," and, in a few words, he spoke from his heart into the hearts of all.

You cannot imagine how silent it becomes as soon as this man speaks; it is as if all of the thousand listeners are no longer able to breathe. When he angrily condemns the deeds of those who have ruled our people since the revolution and those who now prevent him and his followers from settling accounts with those November big-wigs, cheers ring through the hall for minutes on end. There is no silence until he waves his hands repeatedly to indicate that he wants to continue speaking. . . . Adolf Hitler is so firmly convinced of the correctness of his nationalistic views that he automatically communicates this conviction to his listeners. God grant that, as trailbreaker to better times, he will be able to gather many more racial comrades under the Swastika. After all, every class is represented. Workers and lower-ranking civil servants, officers and storm troopers, students and old pensioners — all sit together, and all are in agreement with the great concept embodied in the person of Adolf Hitler. It is often said that where eleven Germans come together, ten political parties are represented. Here, however, I have never heard anyone say that Hitler should do this, or that he should have done that. Sometimes it almost seems to me as if Hitler used a magic charm in order to win the unconditional confidence of old and young alike. When one considers, however, that the common man, suffering from the spiritual malaise that goes hand in hand with economic misery, seeks stability and finds it in the one man who will not disappoint him, then one understands the jubilation that is evoked by his very appearance.[16]

Using Reading 13

Compare the two descriptions of Hitler. What do they say about the man? About each author?

Unlike Mann's account, the Anna letter is not from the writings of a public figure, nor even a semipublic figure, but from the pen of an obscure person who left no noticeable imprint on the course of history. We have here a letter written by an early convert to National Socialism, known to us only as "Anna"—describing her reaction to Hitler's oratory and personality as she experienced it shortly before the abortive Munich "Beer Hall Putsch" of November 1923.

Discuss the drama of the night marches, the role of goose-stepping, the theater of the mass rallies, and of Hitler's appeal and charisma.

Reading 14

Hitler as Leader

Hitler learned from the failure of the 1923 uprising that an open physical attack was foolish. "Democracy," he said, "must be defeated with the weapons of democracy." His revolution would have to wait until after he came to power legally.

Several recent studies of Nazi history conclude that Hitler had no blueprint for a totalitarian state. He improvised hastily to meet each crisis, both in his rise to power and in his exercise of that power once he attained it.

While never letting up on his rabid antisemitism, Hitler offered something for everybody except, of course, the Jews. To workers he promised jobs; to employers, fatter profits and freedom from union restraints; to the lower-middle class, status and self-respect; to the generals, a glorious army; to Germany, world supremacy; to the nations abroad, peace. He was the master demagogue; he understood crowd psychology; he knew how to manipulate issues, to mobilize the disaffected. Initially the mass of his followers came from the poor, the youth, the small tradesmen, and the handicraftsmen.

Hitler himself, not the program, was the sole unifying force. Despair with things as they were united his followers with their mystical leader. No one stopped to discuss what would be done once power was attained.[17]

Using Reading 14

In his analysis of *Mein Kampf*, George Sabine states that the leader according to Hitler is "neither a scholar nor a theorist but a practical psychologist and an organizer." As psychologist and organizer, the leader "manipulates the people as an artist molds clay.... No trick was overlooked: the advantage of oratory over written argument; the effects of lighting, atmosphere, symbols, and the crowd; the advantage of meetings held at night when the power to resist suggestion is low. Leadership works by skillful use of suggestion, collective hypnosis, of subconscious motivation."[18]

According to William Shirer, Hitler wanted to use the red, white, and black colors of Imperial Russia for his Third Reich. The swastika was designated as the new symbol, and as Hitler writes in *Mein Kampf*, "In *red* we see the social idea of the movement, in *white* the nationalist idea, in the *swastika* the vision of the struggle for the victory of the Aryan man."[19]

Reading 15

Ten Major Points of the Twenty-five Point Nazi Program, February 25, 1920

We demand:

1. A union of all Germans to form a great Germany on the basis of self-determination of peoples.
2. Abolition of the Treaty of Versailles.
3. Land and territory (colonies) for our surplus population.
4. German blood as a requirement for German citizenship. No Jew can be a member of the nation.
5. Non-citizens live in Germany as foreigners only, subject to the law of aliens.
6. Only citizens can vote or hold public office.
7. The state insures that every citizen live decently and earn his livelihood. If it is impossible to provide food for the whole population, then aliens must be expelled.
8. No further immigration of non-Germans. Any non-German who arrived after August 2, 1914, shall leave immediately.
9. A thorough reconstruction of our national system of education. The science of citizenship shall be taught from the beginning.
10. All newspapers must be published in the German language by German citizens and owners.

Using Reading 15

The partial list of 10 points can be used to challenge students to struggle with the questions: "How could people have supported the Nazi Program?" and "Could I support the Nazi Program?"

- Read the program aloud as students follow along in their textbooks.
- Ask if anyone has a response.
- Students should be given time to ask about words such as *abolition, surplus,* and *self-determination,* which need definition.
- Ask students if there is any statement on the list that they could support with more clarity. (Number 9 has proved to be a good beginning to the discussion. When asked if they or their parents felt the school system could be improved, many students had a great deal to say on this issue and eventually claimed that they and their parents could support point 9.)
- When students examine the list, some begin supporting various points and disagreement occurs. At first students ask, "Do you mean if I were a German living in 1920, would I support this program?" The teacher can push students to clarify what they think about the program themselves. What do they think about the idea of a treaty (point 2) that makes one country take full responsibility for a war?

One teacher remembers this lesson:

With the end of the period near, I left the class with a statement and a question: "Many historians claim that the Nazis were elected because millions of people could support most of the Nazi Program and close their eyes to those points which preached hatred toward a particular group. When do we close our eyes to things we believe are wrong or unfair? What things do we go along with or who do we follow regardless of what they say or do?

One boy approached me after class and asked, "Could we elect the Nazis in this country today?"

To give students a sense of the conditions under which the average German might have been introduced to the Twenty-five Point Program, ask them to read this document quickly, as if they had been handed the flyer as they walked along the street. As quickly as students have finished, ask them to turn the document over and write down as many ideas as they can remember. Sample student recollections and write them on the board. Then turn the document over and ask individual students to compare their lists with the number of points in the document. How much did students remember? How much would the average German have remembered? What do the results of this exercise mean? Can this explain why Hitler and the Nazis were not taken seriously, or does it explain why some Germans joined the Nazi Party?

Of the 25 points, 7 points dealt with Jews. "The program called for the denial of citizenship and public office to Jews, the expulsion of Jews who had immigrated, and the exclusion of Jews from the press. All German Jews were categorized as 'foreigners' and 'guests' of the nation."[20]

Reading 16 Political Party Programs

Two important political party platforms were those of the pro-Weimar Republic party, made up of Social Democrats and Centrists, and the Communist party.

Pro-Weimar Platforms

This party wishes to maintain the Republic and to allow Germany to take its place among the free governments of Europe.

1. We support the present German Republic so that freedom, democracy, and justice will live in the hearts of our German countrymen.

2. We will honor all of Germany's obligations, political and financial, in order that Germany's honor and respect will not be decreased in the eyes of the world.

3. We plan to create more jobs by undertaking an extensive program of public works.

4. We will establish unemployment compensation up to a six-month period.

5. We will cut government expenditures to lower taxes.

6. We believe in the right of those who disagree with the party to speak and write on those issues without interference.

Communist Party Platform

We are committed to the overthrow of the presently existing, oppressive Republic and all of its economic and social institutions. The party favors:

1. The abolition of private property.

2. The establishment of land reform programs, in which the government will take over the land and distribute it for the common good of all.

3. The ownership of all industrial productive forces by the government, so that they can be operated for the benefit of all the people rather than the capitalists.

4. A foreign policy that will build friendly relations between Germany and the Soviet Union, since both are allies against capitalism.

To the German people: The cause of your misery is the fact that French, British, and American capitalists are exploiting German workers to get rich themselves. Germans, unite to get rid of this terrible burden.

The following case studies are of German citizens who made decisions during this period.

Hermann Struts

Hermann Struts, a lieutenant in the German army, has been a lieutenant since World War I, when he fought bravely on the western front. Coming from a long line of military officers and having graduated from the German military academy, Hermann is proud of Germany's military tradition. His pride is personal, because Germany had always boasted a fine army that had secured the nation's well-being and leadership.

Yet Hermann has not been promoted for more than ten years. Because the German army has been so drastically reduced by the Treaty of Versailles, there have been relatively few promotions. In the old army, Hermann would have been at least a captain by now, because he is a resourceful officer. In all probability, he would have been a major. Hermann resents the Versailles Treaty, which forced Germany to give up its military tradition. He believes this has done irreparable harm to Germany's honor, and to his honor as a soldier. He feels that if the present government had vetoed the treaty and allowed the German army to resist it, neither Germany nor he would be in their present position.

Otto Hauptmann

Otto Hauptmann works in an electric motor factory in Berlin. Although his trade union has actively worked for better conditions and higher wages, it has not made many gains, primarily because the 1923 inflation and the present depression have sapped the entire economy. Otto believes, however, that the union would succeed if the economy were stable. As it is, the union has kept him employed. When many of his friends had been laid off, Otto's union had persuaded his company managers to keep the senior men. Factories where unions are weak had kept only the younger men, because the managers say they are more productive.

Otto has been worried by the ideas many of his fellow workers have expressed recently. . . . When the owners are forced to cut back production, they take it out on the workers. So the only way to end the depression is to let the workers control the factories and the government. Otto still believes that the workers get fair treatment as long as there are strong unions. Moreover, he thinks that managing the factories and government should be left to men who understand these complicated jobs.

Eric von Ronheim

Eric von Ronheim, chief executive of a Frankfurt textile factory, is extremely concerned about the present economic depression. Reduced production means lower profits for his company. If only Germany had not been treated so ruthlessly at Versailles, the nation would have sufficient resources to produce goods for consumption, and conditions would be far better. But the government has had to impose burdensome taxes in order to pay the reparations the Allies had demanded. Indeed, much of his own profits are going into these taxes. Moreover, the overtaxed Germans have little money to spend on German goods, and so demand is dangerously low. Since other countries are also suffering from depressions, there is almost no foreign market for German goods. Even if Germany were to come out of the depression, Eric knows taxes would be increased to finish paying the reparations.

Eric is also worried about the menacing number of communists in Germany who wish to organize the same kind of government as the Soviet Union has. If the communists succeed, the capitalists would receive no mercy from the workers. And Germany would become subservient to its old enemy, the Soviet Union.

Karl Schmidt

Karl Schmidt is a steelworker in the rich steel-producing Ruhr Valley. Like so many men in the Ruhr, however, he is out of work. The depression has forced many steel mills to shut down until there is a market for their goods. On the day Karl's mill closed, the owners announced that shrinking profits made it impossible to keep the workers on their jobs. Such might be the case, Karl reasons, yet the owners still live in big houses and drive expensive automobiles. Why are the owners protected from the economic slump while the workers suffer? The government is helping the workers somewhat with unemployment compensation, but the payments are hardly enough to support Karl, his wife, and their two children. Moreover, the government has declared that it has little money left, and it cannot continue the payments much longer.

As far as Karl understands, if the government would stop paying the reparations, perhaps it could help Germany recover. But Karl also knows that if the government stops its payment, the French might again occupy the Ruhr Valley, as they had in 1923. What is needed, Karl believes, is a government that is responsive to the workers—perhaps even one that is run by the workers, as some of his friends argue. And he feels Germany needs a government that can deny France and the other nations the reparation payments.

Wilhelm Schultz

Wilhelm Schultz is a peasant who works with his father on their farm in East Prussia. His uncle lives just a few miles away, in the area of East Prussia that the Versailles Treaty had sectioned off as the Polish Corridor. Wilhelm's uncle sends reports describing how the Poles mistreat the Germans in their country. Wilhelm's grandfather lives nearby in Danzig, but his relatives never visit him. Going to Danzig means crossing into Poland and contending with numerous travel restrictions. Wilhelm's schooling had taught him great love for the German heroes like Siegfried, and he was dismayed that his government had signed a treaty that subjected many Germans, like his uncle, to Polish rule. Then again, he watches people who violate basic Prussian values rise to respected positions in the government. He sees in them a distasteful lack of moral discipline, for they are often drunk and rowdy. This is not the way Prussians should behave, Wilhelm thinks.

Wilhelm and his father are finding times hard. The thriving port of Danzig had once been the market for his father's goods. Now it is difficult to ship goods there because they have to cross the Polish Corridor. Besides, the Poles have opened a rival port to take business away from Danzig. Moreover, the depression does not make things easier. Finally, the communists nearby in the Soviet Union are a constant threat to Wilhelm and his father, because they advocate the end of private property. Wilhelm and his father are proud to call their land their own, for this gives them added dignity. The communists want to take this land and this dignity from them—the last rewards the world seems to offer.

Wolfgang von Kohler

Wolfgang von Kohler, a prominent attorney who attended the University of Bonn, has a strong sense of the German cultural, literary, and historical traditions. He believes that the great gifts his people have contributed to Western civilization have been ignored. Wolfgang dreams of the newly created Republic uniting all of the German democratic traditions and leading the way to a totally democratic Europe. He is upset by the unfortunate methods the Weimar Republic often uses to repress the parties of the extreme left more cruelly than those of the extreme right.

However, Wolfgang's sense of justice is more outraged by the demeaning attitude with which the Allies, particularly the French, view the German Republic. He, and others like him, who believe in Germany and human dignity, would like to prove to these countries that the Germans are a great race.

Heinrich Munchen

Heinrich Munchen is the owner of a small Munich grocery store started by his father. For years his father had saved to send him to the university. But Heinrich chose not to go to the university, and the money stayed in the bank. In 1923 Heinrich had had a good use for it. His two sons were both brilliant; one wanted to be a doctor, and the other hoped to be an engineer. The money in the bank would have paid for their education. But that same year inflation had hit Germany because the government had printed so much money to pay the reparations. Since the money was not backed by anything economically solid, it had become nearly worthless. Two weeks before his older son was to leave for the university, the bank had called him to say that his savings were worth only enough to buy three postage stamps. This was certainly a blow to Heinrich, but it was more of a blow to his sons, whose futures hung in the balance. They asked him what kind of faith they could put in a system that ruined hard-working men.

Now in 1930, there seems little to be done to regain the losses. People are not making any money and, therefore, cannot buy as many groceries as they had before. And the competition from the big department and chain stores makes it difficult for Heinrich to compete. Again Heinrich's economic plight is no fault of his own. His sons once more question the system that has brought these hardships to their father and to them.[21]

Using Reading 16

These are actual case studies of German citizens and they are designed to give the history meaning in terms of an average German citizen as decision-maker.

One approach to this assignment is to divide the class into seven groups and assign a case study to each group. Ask each group to review the ten points of the Nazi plan and the two party platforms and then determine which of the parties the person in each case study would choose. Be sure each group has reasons to support its choice.

Another approach is to assign two groups to work on the same case. One group might decide that its citizen would support Hitler, while other students would disagree. The teacher should encourage each group to clarify its reasoning, identify the grievances, and discuss the weight and appeal of issues in terms of a final decision. What might finally make a citizen decide to support Hitler—fear? national pride? political stability? disgust with the Republic? We suggest that the teacher explain that four of the seven persons would definitely support the Nazi party

(Struts, von Ronheim, Schultz, and Munchen). Given the background of those citizens who supported the Nazis, what hypothesis might students make as to who supported the Nazis?

After the depression hit Germany in 1929, the Nazi party vote went from about 1 million to 6 million in the 1930 election. They were now the second-largest party. The people believed Hitler would do what he promised. By 1932 there were 6 million jobless in Germany and that year the vote for the Nazi party was 14 million.

Reading 17

The Twilight of the Weimar Republic, 1929-1933

The Weimar Republic faced two major problems in the fall of 1929: Gustav Stresemann died on October 3, 1929. Despite the fact that all Germans detested the Versailles Treaty and its war guilt clause, Stresemann had emerged to symbolize confidence and success. His successors were to symbolize more negative traits.

The United States' stock market crash of October 1929 would take its greatest toll on Germany. Stresemann observed:

I must ask you always to remember that during the past year we have been living on borrowed money. If a crisis were to arise and the Americans were to call in their short-term loans, we should be faced with bankruptcy.[22]

American financiers immediately demanded payment on their loans. The depression led to massive unemployment in Germany: 1,368,000 in 1929; 5,668,000 in 1931; 6,014,000 by 1933. Wages were cut and the jobless wandered the streets with cries of "give us bread."

These double setbacks revealed the weaknesses and mistakes of the Weimar Republic. The Republic had been like a candle burning at both ends, with the Communists on one end calling for a dictatorship of the working class and the Nazis on the other end calling for a dictatorship of the few. The Republic had been kind to most of its enemies. The German army had not been destroyed in World War I and the Republic used it to put down uprisings. Hitler had served only one year in prison for political treason. Only the Communists were punished ruthlessly.

The Nazis would gain the most from the Republic's troubles. While Hitler's rise to power might now be possible, it was not clearly inevitable. Many complicated explanations are available, but no simple solution exists.

The political scene from 1930 to 1933 resembled a corrupt political chess game with all participants invoking article 48 of the Weimar Constitution, which stated that the chancellor could rule by decree in emergency situations.

Herman Bruning, chancellor from March 1930 to March 1932, was the most humane of the group. Bruning was an intelligent economist (he later taught at Harvard), but he was a dull speaker and always sounded as if he were delivering a treasurer's report. In September 1939 the Nazis were able to get more members elected to the Reichstag; an increase from 12 to 107. Chancellor Bruning found it increasingly difficult to deal with this growing Nazi party; coping with the Nazis was now a major problem.

After becoming a German citizen in February 1932, Hitler challenged Hindenburg for the presidency. He conducted a whirlwind campaign and often flew from speech to speech, but Hindenburg still outpolled

Hitler 18,000,000 (49.6%) to 11,000,000 (30.1%). Since no candidate received a majority of the votes, a run-off election was required. In April, Hindenburg received his majority with 19,000,000 (53%), while Hitler polled 13,000,000 (36.8%). Hitler was a loser, but 13,000,000 Germans had voted for him in a free, democratic election.

Following the election, Hindenburg appointed Franz von Papen as chancellor. Von Papen sought ways of bringing the Nazis into a coalition government so that they might be under control. In the July elections of 1932, the Nazis had emerged as the strongest single party; they increased their Reichstag representation from 107 to 230. The Nazi representatives showed up at the Reichstag in uniform. Herman Goering, the second most important Nazi, was now appointed president of the Reichstag. Chancellor von Papen was not allowed to speak in the Reichstag because Goering would not recognize him. The wily von Papen, who later served the Nazis, proved to be a disaster; he would be replaced in December 1932.

Meanwhile, Hindenburg arranged to meet with Hitler in August 1932. Hitler was awed by the 87-year-old president, and performed badly. Hindenburg offered him the job of vice-chancellor, but Hitler refused. The Nazis suffered defeats in the November elections; their membership in the Reichstag declined from 230 to 196. Some Nazis despaired that Hitler might not get another chance to become chancellor.

On December 2, 1932, General Kurt von Schleicher became the last chancellor before Hitler. He convinced the senile Hindenburg that the Nazis could be controlled. One way to do this was to convince the Nazi leaders below Hitler to join the government. Von Schleicher hoped to convince these Nazis that if they remained with Hitler, they would never get a chance to gain power at all. Von Schleicher failed to bring them into the government and, as a result, he resigned on January 28, 1933.

Hindenburg now had little choice. He still regarded Hitler as a "bohemian corporal." He didn't want to appoint him, but Hitler was in charge of the largest party. Hitler had held out for the "best deal" and now he got it when Hindenburg asked him to form a "nonpartisan" government. At 11 a.m. on January 30, 1933, Hitler became chancellor.

Some people argue that Hitler's rise to power was a natural outcome of German history. Some see his rise to power as sheer luck. Others say it was nothing unusual, since dictatorships were established in over a dozen European countries by the 1930s. Still others point out that the German leaders underestimated Hitler and felt they could control him. The most important issue may lie in these words by the provocative British historian, A.J.P. Taylor:

The real problem in German history is why so few of the educated, civilized classes recognized Hitler as the embodiment of evil. University professors; army officers; businessmen and bankers—these had a background of culture, and even of respect for law. Yet virtually none of them exclaimed: "This is anti-Christ." Later, they were to make out that Hitler had deceived them and that the bestial nature of National-Socialism could not have been foreseen. This is not true. The real character of National-Socialism was exposed by many foreigners, and even by some German observers long before Hitler came to power.[23]

Using Reading 17

This reading documents the shattering of the relative peace and prosperity of the German nation, exposes the weaknesses of the Republic, and details how the German political leadership manipulated

Hitler into power in order to control him. This allowed Hitler to come to power legally. The complexity of the events reiterates the course objective that there are no simple answers to the complex question of how Nazi dictatorship came to Germany.

Before reading this, ask students to speculate on the meaning of *twilight*. Will this reading be about the end of the Weimar Republic? The beginning of the end? The "dark days" of the Republic?

Have students add to their vocabulary list such words as *decree*, *coalition*, and *nonpartisan*.

This reading seems ideal for the use of the political, economic, and social chart suggested earlier. It is an excellent source for gathering evidence. Who or what was responsible for Hitler's rise to power— politicians, the German people, luck, the depression? What was the "twilight" of the Republic?

Another approach is to discuss with students how the reading relates to the following quotation by John Snell. "Any system can stand in fair weather: it is tested when the wind blows." Discuss with students how the quotation relates to the Weimar Republic: In what ways was it tested? What winds were blowing? Why did it stand? (Keep in mind that Hitler was now chancellor of the Weimar Republic.)

Reading 18

Hitler: From Chancellor to Dictator

Adolf Hitler had come to power legally, but not as the result of an election victory or any wave of popular enthusiasm. The Nazis had suffered a loss of two million votes in the most recent elections of 1932, and they had never won over 37 percent of the popular vote. Conservative leaders in Germany convinced President Hindenburg to appoint Hitler so that he and the Nazis could be controlled.

Nazis were given only three of the eleven cabinet positions in the government, and all of those were minor posts. Outnumbered eight to three, Hitler was supposed to carry out the wishes of others. Hitler could not even report to President Hindenburg unless the vice-chancellor, Franz von Papen, was present.

Once in office, Hitler proved to be uncontrollable. He astounded and overwhelmed those who felt they had trapped him. Hitler made legal what others considered to be illegal.

What did Hitler do? How did he do it? How did he get away with it?

The following headlines describe the events through which Hitler became dictator of Germany. The list of definitions will explain key words.

HEADLINES

February 27, 1933	Nazis Burn Reichstag Building
	Berlin SA Involved
	Dutch Communists Blamed
February 28, 1933	Nazis Suspend All Civil Liberties
	Hindenburg Signs Hitler's Decree
	Hitler Warns of Communist Acts of Violence
March 5, 1933	Nazis Receive 43.9% of Election Votes
	Total Is 5,500,000 Greater Than Last Election
	Nazis Form Coalition with Nationalist Party
March 9, 1933	Nazis Overthrow Government in Bavaria
	Nazis Take Over Key Government Posts

March 23, 1933	Reichstag Passes Enabling Law, 441-94 Huge Crowd Roars Approval Outside Hitler Free to Make Laws for Four Years
May 2, 1933	Trade Union Powers Transferred to Nazi Labor Front Strikes and Collective Bargaining Outlawed Trade Union Leaders Sent to Concentration Camps
January 30, 1934	Hitler Decrees Law for Reconstruction of Reich German State Governments Abolished Powers of German States Surrendered to Nazi Party
May 20, 1934	Nazis Move Against Social Democratic Party Occupy Party Buildings and Newspaper Offices Nazis Confiscate Social Democratic Funds
May 26, 1934	Nazis Take Over Property and Money of Communist Party Communist Party Outlawed Communists Barred from Holding Public Office
June 19, 1934	Nazis Abolish Social Democratic Party Brand Social Democrats as Enemies of the People Social Democrats Barred from Holding Public Office
June 21, 1934	Nazis Turn Against Nationalist Party Invade Party Offices All Over Germany Abolition of Party Inevitable
June 30, 1934	Hitler Refuses to Incorporate SA into Army Charges SA Planned to Overthrow Government 400 of Hitler's Former SA Colleagues Killed
July 14, 1934	German Government Bans Formation of Parties Nazi Party Declared Only Party in Germany Severe Prison Terms for Any Violators
August 2, 1934	President Hindenburg Dies Hitler Takes Over as President and Chancellor Army Takes Oath of Allegiance to Hitler
August 19, 1934	Germans Vote to Support Hitler's Takeover of Presidency Vote is 90% Favorable—38,395,479 to 4,300,429 Voter Turnout is 95.7%
September 7, 1934	Hitler Addresses Nazi Party Rally at Nuremberg Declares Nazi Revolution at an End Vows No New Revolution in Germany for 1,000 Years

LIST OF DEFINITIONS

Bavaria: Second largest of the 17 states in Germany. Hitler had lived here in Munich, had joined the Nazi party here, and had tried to overthrow the Munich government in 1923.

Civil Liberties: Freedom of speech, right to assembly, freedom from illegal search, right to protection of property, etc.

Coalition: A group of parties that combine for common interest. In 1933 the Nazis (43% of the vote) joined with the Nationalists (8%) to form a majority.

Communist Party: International party calling for dictatorship of the working class. Had taken over government in Russia in 1917. Always committed to overthrowing the Weimar Republic.

Decree: A law dictated by the government leader without the vote of the law-making branch of the government. Article 48 of the Weimar Consitution permitted presidential decrees in emergency situations.

Hindenburg: German general in World War I, elected President of Weimar Republic in 1925 and 1932. Detested Hitler, but appointed him because he was leader of the largest party.

Nationalist Party: Party of upper-class who wanted a monarchy. Major opposition party to Weimar Republic. Joined with Nazis to form majority government in 1933.

Nazi Labor Front: Organized to bring the independent trade unions under control. Hitler needed control of trade unions to organize Germany under Nazi rule.

Reich: German government. Hitler called his government the Third Reich. The First Reich had been established in the 9th century, the Second Reich in 1871.

Reichstag: The law-making body of Germany under the Weimar Republic. It was elected by the people.

SA: Sturm Abteilungen, Hitler's storm troopers. Acted as police and army for Nazis. Demanded a larger role in German government after Hitler became chancellor.

Social Democrats: Played the largest role in establishing the Weimar Republic. Lost much support after the Great Depression of 1929.

Trade Unions: Organization of workers, a very large and powerful group in Germany. No previous government had interferred with them. Unions tried not to provoke Nazis, in order to preserve their organization.

Using Reading 18

This assignment will provide data of a different kind to sharpen students' data skills. It asks students to read a series of headlines and to synthesize the data to make a series of generalizations.

These headlines detail how Hitler moved from the role of chancellor where there were checks on him, to the role of absolute dictator where there were *no* checks on his power. It further demonstrates that the Nazi takeover of power was not inevitable; it had to be achieved.

Hitler had said that democracy was rule by "crazy brains." How does his rise to power in the German Republic give meaning to his statement?

Because the other political parties of Germany did not unite against Hitler, he became chancellor with less than a majority vote. Later the Nazis manipulated the two-thirds vote necessary to make Hitler the legal dictator. In 1934, after Hindenburg died, Hitler proclaimed himself Supreme Head of State and Commander-in-Chief of the Armed Forces, after uniting the offices of president and chancellor. Finally he asked for a plebiscite where he received a 90% Yes-vote.

Activity 19

Anatomy of a Dictatorship
This film is made up of film clips that document Hitler's rise to power. Key figures in this history are identified.

Using Activity 19

Ask students to evaluate the film. Raise such questions as: What does the film tell you that you already have learned? What does it tell you that you have not learned? What in the film disagrees with what you've learned? Is it a good film? Caution: without careful viewing, the students will assume Hitler's rise to power was inevitable.

Reading 20

How the West Was Lost, 1933-1939

Once in power, Adolf Hitler proved that *Mein Kampf* was not an idle document. Within six years Hitler violated the Treaty of Versailles repeatedly by moving troops into the Rhineland, fighting in the Spanish Civil War, annexing Austria and Czechoslovakia, and invading Poland. Not until 1939 did the Allies take a stand.

Why was the Treaty of Versailles not enforced? The truth is that it had never been enforced. Articles 168 and 169 of the treaty, which called for "elimination of the industrial capacity to make war," were never carried out. The German army had not been destroyed and the rebuilding started the day following the signing of the peace. Count Brockdorff at Versailles in 1919 said:

Since we Germans were summoned to Versailles and the Allies did not come to Berlin, we can easily play down at home the extent of our military defeat. We should be grateful to the Allies for this oversight. Thanks to it, we'll be able one day to resume and conclude this war. I'll make it my business to see that we shall then be in a position to make up once and for all our present fortunes. In the final battle, we shall be the victors.[24]

The Germans justified their rearmament by maintaining that they needed their industry to pay off their debts to the Allies. A civilian air force was begun, one that could easily be converted to military use. Military weapons were manufactured in Germany and in German factories in Switzerland, Denmark, Sweden, and Holland. By 1935 the Germans could openly announce that they had an army of thirty-five divisions (350,000 men) and an air force as large as that of England.

The mood after World War I in the Allied countries was one of pacifism and the active pursuit of peace. World War I was seen as a mistake and some people felt that the Germans had been blamed erroneously for the war. In this atmosphere German acquisition of territory could be viewed as just compensation for past injustices.

The United States had not signed the Versailles Treaty, had not joined the League of Nations, and now refused to lend money or sell arms to any warring country, be it aggressor or victim. The English mood was best exemplified by the Oxford Oath of 1933, a statement endorsed by university students in all parts of the British Empire, which pledged that no student in any part of the British Empire would fight under any circumstances. France, which had lost half of its men between the ages of twenty and thirty-two in World War I, built the Maginot Line, an elaborate defensive wall along the German border, in the hope that this would discourage war.

In this atmosphere Hitler took great risks, always against the advice of his own military advisors. In 1936 Hitler marched his troops into the Rhineland in open violation of the Versailles Treaty and the Locarno Pact. In the event they met any resistance, his generals were ordered to withdraw. Hitler could have been stopped, even defeated here. Instead, the Allies did nothing and reminded themselves that Hitler was only occupying German soil.

The Spanish Civil War of 1936 - 1939 provided further examples of

Neville Chamberlain's National Broadcast, September 21, 1938

How horrible, fantastic, incredible it is that we should be digging trenches and trying on gas masks here because of a quarrel in a far-away country between people of whom we know nothing. It seems still more impossible that a quarrel which has already been settled in principle should be the subject of war.

Do not be alarmed if you hear of men being called up to man the anti-aircraft defences or ships. These are only precautionary measures such as a Government must take in times like this. But they do not necessarily mean that we have determined for war or that war is imminent.

However much we may sympathize with a small nation confronted by a big and powerful neighbor, we cannot in all circumstances undertake to involve the whole British Empire in war simply on her account. If we have to fight it must be on larger issues than that.

I am myself a man of peace to the depths of my soul. Armed conflict between nations is a nightmare to me; but if I were convinced that any nation had made up its mind to dominate the world by fear of its force, I should feel that it must be resisted. Under such a domination life for people who believe in liberty would not be worth living; but war is a fearful thing, and we must be very clear, before we embark on it, that it is really the great issues that are at stake, and that the call to risk everything in their defence, when all the consequences are weighed, is irresistible.[25]

Poem

Dear Czechoslovakyer
I don't think he's going to attack yer
But even if he does
I'm not going to back yer.[26]

Hitler's action and Allied inaction. Hitler sent planes and tanks to help General Francisco Franco overthrow the elected Spanish government. The British response was typical of Allied behavior: England would not send help to any belligerents.

In March 1938 Hitler annexed Austria. The Versailles Treaty had forbidden any such *Anschluss* (union of Germany and Austria). Although the Russians were eager to oppose, the British refused. Six million Germans lived in Austria.

Hitler next demanded the Sudetenland of Czechoslovakia, an area where 3,000,000 Germans lived. France was bound by treaty to support Czechoslovakia and wanted to do so. Neville Chamberlain, the British prime minister, preferred a policy of appeasement, making concessions in order to preserve peace. Chamberlain flew to meet with Hitler twice and left assured that Hitler would make no more territorial demands after the Sudetenland. In September 1938, Germany, Italy, France, and England signed the Munich Pact, giving the Sudetenland of Czechoslovakia to Hitler. The bankruptcy of the appeasement policy

Wonder If Anyone Laughs At Me Any More?

was demonstrated when Hitler took the remainder of Czechoslovakia in March 1939.

Only now did the Allies realize that they had misunderstood and underestimated Hitler. Appeasement was based on the idea that dislike of war was common to all persons. Either the idea was defective, or Hitler's behavior was not that of a human being. On March 31, 1939, England pledged to oppose any further aggression by Hitler. Unwilling to fight for democratic Czechoslovakia, England now would fight over semi-fascist Poland. Hitler's invasion of Poland on September 1, 1939, was followed by the British declaration of war on September 3.

War came in 1939 because of mutual misunderstandings. Hitler was convinced that the democracies would not fight. The Allies still believed Hitler was reasonable and they were unable to recognize the horror of Nazism. Hitler did not prefer war at this time and the Allies never wished it. But, as in 1914, the world stumbled into war.

Using Reading 20

This reading details the early steps of Hitler's violation of the Treaty of Versailles.

Most historians believe the West unintentionally collaborated by resorting to actions of pacifism and policies of appeasement. Not until Hitler attacked Poland did the Allies take a stand. World War II had begun. Prior to undertaking the reading, the teacher might ask students to review "Excerpts From the Treaty of Versailles" and refer to a map of Europe to make the reading more understandable and purposeful.

Introduce the following terms for addition to the students' vocabulary list: *West, pacifism, appeasement, belligerent, annexation, rearmament, compensation.*

Students can discuss the fundamental differences between pacifism and appeasement. Pacifism is a rigid insistence on peace regardless of the circumstances. Pacifists actively resist war, military preparedness, or any acts of violence. Two celebrated pacifists of the 20th century were Mahatma Ghandi and Martin Luther King, Jr. Pacifism increased before World War II because of the disillusionment over World War I and its terrible loss of life. Appeasement is the act of making concessions to potential aggressors in order to maintain peace; its most celebrated proponent in this period was Neville Chamberlain. Appeasers were willing to satisfy Hitler's "legitimate" demands and they rationalized Hitler's takeover of the Sudetenland of Czechoslovakia because 3,000,000 Germans lived there. France agreed to this, despite a treaty obligation to protect Czechoslovakia.

Students could make a chart showing the dates, territories, justifications, and articles of the Versailles Treaty that were violated by Hitler's actions. Among the issues that might be raised with students are these: Is pacifism justifiable if Hitler invades your country? Would it be right to declare war on Hitler because he attacked another country? Is war ever justified? When?

The text about the Sudetenland of Czechoslovakia can be discussed using the following questions: What was Chamberlain's dilemma? Under what conditions would he not fight? When would he be willing to fight? Should a small nation be sacrificed in order to preserve peace?

Reading 21

Quotation

In his orders to march into Poland, Hitler told his generals:

Our strength is in our quickness and brutality. Ghengis Khan had millions of women and children killed by his own will and with a gay heart. History sees only in him a great state builder. What weak Western European civilization thinks about me does not matter.... I have sent to the east only my "Death Head units" with the order to kill without mercy all men, women and children of Polish race or language. Only in such a way will we win the vital space that we need. Who still talks nowadays of the extermination of the Armenians?[27]

According to John Weiss, the author of *The Fascist Tradition*, the British and French Conservatives failed to understand Hitler's need for conquest. Unless they joined with Russia against Hitler, there could be no real military threat. "The Non-Aggression Pact signed by Hitler and Stalin in August 1939," wrote Weiss, cancelled the Russian threat and "gave Hitler a free hand to attack France as well as Poland, as long as Stalin was granted his share of spoils. On September 1, 1939, then, the German and Russian armies invaded Poland."

Despite the objections of Hitler's military advisors, "Hitler instructed his generals to prepare for a new kind of war, a war between ideologies and races, a war which could only be properly fought by those who discarded obsolete Christian and humanitarian sentiments."

Citations

Chapter 4

[1] "Why Remember?" — introduction from *Never to Forget: The Jews of the Holocaust* by Milton Meltzer. Copyright © 1976 by Milton Meltzer. Reprinted by permission of Harper & Row, Publishers, Inc., pp. xiii, xiv.

[2] Louis Snyder, *Basic History of Modern Germany* (Van Nostrand, 1957).

[3] Paul Fussell, *The Great War and Modern Memory* (Oxford University Press, 1975) p. 8.

[4] Claude Lutz, *Fall of the German Empire* (Stanford University Press, 1953) pp. 268-269.

[5] Koppel Pinson, *Modern Germany* (New York: Macmillan, 1954) p. 349.

[6] Ibid., p. 398.

[7] Gerald Leinwand, *The Pageant of World History* (Boston: Allyn and Bacon, 1977) p. 508.

[8] Ibid., p. 508.

[9] Pinson, *Modern Germany,* p. 380.

[10] P.L. Jarmon, *The Rise and Fall of Nazi Germany* (New American Library, 1956) p. 119.

[11] Philip Scheidemann, *Making of New Germany* (Books for Libraries, Inc., 1923) pp. 261-263.

[12] John Rhodes, *Germany: A History* (New York: Holt, Rinehart, and Winston, 1964) p. 494.

[13] Alan Bulloch, *Hitler: A Study in Tyranny* (New York: Harper and Row, 1960) p. 325.

[14] Ibid., p. 355.

[15] Colt, Connelly, *Excerpts*.

[16] From *Hitler: Great Lives Observed,* edited by George H. Stein. © 1968 by Prentice-Hall, Inc. Published by Prentice-Hall, Inc., Englewood Cliffs, NJ 07632, pp. 97-98.

[17] Information from Meltzer, *Never to Forget,* pp. 16-17.

[18] From *History of Political Theory*, 3rd Edition, by George H. Sabine. Copyright © 1937, 1950 © 1961 by Holt, Rinehart and Winston, Inc. Renewal copyright © 1965 by George B. Sabine, Janet S. Kelkley, and Mary J. Sabine. Reprinted by permission of Holt, Rinehart and Winston. pp. 904-905.

[20] Meltzer, *Never to Forget,* p. 15.

[21] John M. Good, *The Shaping of Western Society* (New York: Holt Rinehart, and Winston, 1968).

[22] Pinson, *Modern Germany,* p. 452.

[23] Robert G.L. Waite, *Hitler and Nazi Germany* (New York: Holt, Rinehart, and Winston, 1969) p. 43.

[24] Pinson, *Modern Germany,* p.434.

[25] Alexander Baltzly and A. Williams Salomone, *Readings in Twentieth-Century European History,* (Appleton, Century, Crofts, 1950).

[26] From *Europe Since 1815* by Gordon A. Craig. Copyright © 1961 by Holt, Rinehart and Winston, Inc. Reprinted by permission of Holt, Rinehart and Winston, CBS College Publishing, p. 702.

[27] Pinson, *Modern Germany,* p. 523.

5 Nazi Philosophy and Policy

> One had no time to think.... There was so much going on. The dictatorship, and the whole process of its coming into being, was above all diverting. It provided an excuse not to think for people who did not want to think anyway.[1]

Overview

Germany entered the 1930s, a time of political, economic, and social stress, with a tradition of antisemitism and a pseudoscientific racial theory; Hitler, with paranoid delusions about World War I and his imagined powerful Jewish conspiracy, aroused a nation of citizens who accepted National Socialism mixed with German nationalism and racial policy. This chapter examines the theories and policies of totalitarian government, racism, and Lebensraum, which were key to Nazi philosophy.

The fundamental problem in attempting to explain Nazi philosophy and policy is that we are constantly dealing with irrationality, or, as George M. Sabine, author of *A History of Political Theory,* suggests in his analysis of fascism and national socialism, "Their so-called philosophies were mosaics of ancient prejudices, put together without regard for truth or consistency, to appeal not to common purposes but to common fears and hates." Because policies were not developed and implemented with consistency, and because of the irrationality of many of the policies and personalities of this period, it is imperative that one not seek simple explanations for this complex history, nor see it as inevitable.

In this investigation of genocide, we study how an entire society became absorbed in a genocidal process, step by step, where human life became expendable in the name of the fatherland. The bureaucracy, the individual, the group, the military, the churches were all willingly or unwillingly victim to the Nazi state and some became victimizers also.

In 1934, Hitler described his goal of creating a block for Germans in the middle of Europe. Surrounding European countries would be exploited for their food and labor while being politically subordinate to Nazi rule. In these occupied territories, he would create a slave people without independent political, social, economic, or cultural life. Extermination squads and famine would rid the area of all "dangerous" and "subhuman" populations, while the SS would populate the Reich with "racially pure" stock. To consolidate his power in the Reich, Hitler used terror, education, and biological selection within the totalitarian state to insure that his goals were carried out.

The antisemitism toward the Jews and the racism toward the Gypsies and Slavs contributed to the dehumanization policies that deprived populations of their rights to exist as human beings. Once these groups were categorized as "subhuman," the normal rules of civilized behavior didn't apply and they became victim to mass brutalization.

...The precondition for mass extermination was engineered dehumanization: the conversion of citizens into aliens, first by executive decree, then by legislative enactment, and finally by judicial consent. These legal and sociological events represent the precondition for the technical performance of genocidal policies of totalitarian states.[2]

The fact that the 20th century was the setting for this history is not to be passed over lightly. People were no longer isolated in their homes or villages. The opportunity to be affected by the messages and symbols of the state increased as people went to the factory, drove cars to the cities, listened to the radio, went to the cinema, or walked streets where the voices of the charismatic were amplified. All this demanded preparation for making different choices about new information, and new challenges. Sadly, the leadership and the masses were not prepared to choose or create plans for the protection of human rights and life in the name of survival; instead, the choices were made for survival at the expense of human life. The state chose to affect the decisions of the masses by playing on old hatreds, new fears, and their information about human behavior.

To paraphrase Irving Horowitz, a study of Italian Fascism and German Nazism in the 20th century dispels the myth that both systems, though closely related, made choices to take lives (not in war) through genocidal policies. Says Horowitz, this proves "that cultural variables are unique determinants of behavior in a social system." Finally, this study warns us not to label all fascist states as genocidal.

Reading 1

Behind the Policies Are the People

Life is almost always more complicated than we think. Behind the gleaming ranks of those who seem totalitarian robots stand men and women, various and diverse, complex and complicated, some brave, some cowardly, some brainwashed, some violently idiosyncratic, and all of them very human.[3]

Using Reading 1

Discuss with students how this quotation might anticipate the themes of this chapter. Often we are duped by labels into thinking that institutions are responsible for actions, when in fact the decisions are made by human beings. Policies were not made and implemented by the Reich, the leadership, the Nazis, the machine, the nations—they were made by individuals who had choices.

Reading 2

What Is a Fascist State?

In a fascist state, the state is organized to regulate labor and management. The bureaucracy grows larger than any other segment of society. The state organizes everything from education to the military in order to insure its own survival and expansion. "State preeminence creates conditions for authoritarian domination over vast populations, national and even international."[4]

Fascism in Italy during 1920-1943 and in Germany in 1933-1945 shared similar characteristics: "the one-party system, the permanent charismatic ruler, and the orchestrated mobilization of masses by state-controlled agencies. These are important categories in any discussion of fascism. Yet for those who had to (or rather could) make rational decisions about where to live in the 1930s, Rome in the Fascist period was far less austere and grim a place than Berlin in the Nazi period."[5]

The following list of "Elements in Fascism," taken from the "Fascist Characteristics of Parsons," and discussed by Irving Horowitz in *Taking Lives*, is characteristic of Germany in the 1930s.

- emergence of an emotional fanatical mass movement closer to religion than to political movements
- huge and sudden shifts in population and demographic patterns
- the emergence of nationalism
- the willingness of privileged classes to yield their prestige and power to newer, emerging classes

Many historians agree that a study of the Third Reich is a study of a 20th-century totalitarian state. It is important, though, not to isolate events and actions that led to Hitler's total control of the German citizenry from an understanding of the racial theories and policies espoused and implemented by the Fuehrer and the Reichsfuehrers. Nor would an interpretation of this history be adequate without the understanding of the policy of "living space." These themes of race, totalitarianism, and living space came together in all of the policies of the Third Reich.

Using Reading 2

Students share with historians the same question: "How could fascism take hold in Germany?" In class discussions students can anticipate many of the explanations presented here.

The following excerpts by scholars interested in this historiography indicate the social, political, economic, and psychological complexities involved in this question. Some historians look to "national character," some to fascism, some to Hitler, and others to psychology for an explanation of what happened in Germany.

William Shirer in *The Rise and Fall of the Third Reich* finds in the German character prior to Nazism, the roots for the policies of the Third Reich. He describes the tradition of Teutonic racism, German anti-semitism, power for the state, the submissive individual, and anti-democratic history rooted in the religious, literary, and intellectual heroes of German history. According to Shirer, militarism, efficiency at all costs, and obedience to authority were vital components of the Prussian rule before Nazism.

In *The Fascist Tradition*, J. Weiss offers an economic explanation for the appeal of National Socialism:

Any study of fascism which centers too narrowly on the Fascists and the Nazi alone may miss the true significance of right-wing extremism.... The radical right thrives in societies where older but still powerful conservative classes are threatened by rapid and modernizing social change; change which relates or gives strength to liberal and radical classes and groups antagonistic toward the old ways.... For without necessarily becoming party members or accepting the entire range of party principles themselves, aristocratic landlords, army officers, government and civil service officials and important industrialists in Italy and Germany helped bring Fascists and Nazis to power. In doing so, after the end of World War I, they were motivated by the fear that loss of their power, prestige, wealth, and values would shortly follow the new participation of the masses in full-fledged parliamentary democracy. The radical right was to constitute the last line of defense against the mounting liberal and radical agitation for land reform, social welfare measures, demilitarization, higher wages, and the socialization of the means of production. War, inflation and the Great Depression certainly polarized social attitudes into extremes of left and right and opened vast opportunities to the radical right; but the basic social climate was as old as the rise of liberalism.

Social psychologists look to the psychological condition of the German people to explain the appeal of National Socialism. They believe Nazism gave hope to those citizens of a country recently defeated in war, humiliated in the Versailles Treaty, and plagued by unemployment. "Nazism," Zebedei Barbri explains, "promised to solve the problems and give the people purpose and power."

Lucy S. Dawidowicz, in her book *The War Against the Jews 1933-1945*, writes that Hitler often decided suddenly to take action on a specific part of his program because the opportunity was right; later the practical work was improvised.

The grand design was in his head. He did not spell it out in concrete strategy. Nothing was written down. (On April 29, 1937, he advised NSDAP leaders: "Everything that can be discussed should never be put in writing, never!") ... The implementation of his plans was contingent on the opportunism of the moment or the expediency of the delay.

In order to understand what happened in Germany in the 1930s, writers explore two aspects of German culture in the 1920s and 1930s: that of the ordinary citizen and that of the academic and artistic community. One author, Otto Friedrich, who looks at the real lives of real people, states in *Before the Deluge: A Portrait of Berlin in the 1920s*, "The desire to live one's life as best one can, to do one's own work and raise one's own children, is not a contemptible emotion. And to understand the ordinary Berliner in 1933, one can only try to imagine what one might do in a similar situation."

Some writers examine the dynamics between life in the '20s and '30s and the rise of Nazism, and a few go beyond to attempt to find causes, cures, and conclusions. In William Sheridan Allen's *The Nazi Seizure of Power: The Experience of a Single German Town, 1930-1945*, he documents the causes and effects of Nazism in one community, Thalburg; it is a study of totalitarianism. In his final paragraph, Allen warns:

Each group saw one or the other side of Nazism, but none saw it in its full hideousness. . . . The problem of Nazism was primarily a problem of perception.

Hitler forecast in *Mein Kampf* the principles of Ein Volk, Ein Reich, Ein Fuehrer (one people, one government, one leader) upon which the Nazi party of the '30s would build. But scholars differ as to whether Hitler had a master plan for a totalitarian state or not. For example, the historian Milton Meltzer wrote, "he improvised hastily to meet each crisis, both in his rise to power and in his exercise of that power once he attained it." A.J.P. Taylor said, "Hitler ... did not seize power; it was handed to him."

Reading 3

No Time To Think

Milton Mayer went back to Germany after the war to interview the citizens who were once his friends, to ask how it could have happened. His friend the baker explained, "One had no time to think. There was so much going on."

People reported that they had become separated from their government with every new crisis or reform. Gradually they accepted decisions made in secret because they trusted Hitler and others who they felt knew more than they did.

The following is one man's description of how the dictatorship came into his life and why he didn't resist it.

So Much Activity

"...my Middle High German was my life. It was all I cared about. I was a scholar, a specialist. Then, suddenly, I was plunged into all the new activity, as the university was drawn into the new situation; meetings, conferences, interviews, ceremonies, and, above all, papers to be filled out, reports, bibliographies, lists, questionnaires. And on top of that were demands in the community, the things in which one had to, was 'expected to' participate that had not been there or had not been important before. It was all rigamarole, of course, but it consumed all one's energies, coming on top of the work one really wanted to do. You can see how easy it was, then, not to think about fundamental things. One had no time."

Too Busy to Think

"Your friend the baker was right," said my colleague. "The dictatorship, and the whole process of its coming into being, was above all diverting. It provided an excuse not to think for people who did not want to think anyway. I do not speak of your 'little men,' your baker and so on; I speak of my colleagues and myself, learned men, mind you. Most of us did not want to think about fundamental things and never had. There was no need to. Nazism gave us some dreadful, fundamental things to think about—we were decent people—and kept us so busy with continuous changes and 'crises' and so fascinated, yes, fascinated, by the machinations of the 'national enemies,' without and within, that we had no time to think about these dreadful things that were growing, little by little, all around us. Unconsciously, I suppose, we were grateful. Who wants to think?"

We Sensed Better

"Men like me... are the greater offenders, not because we knew better (that would be too much to say) but because we sensed better. Pastor Neimoller spoke for the thousands and thousands of men like me when he spoke (too modestly of himself) and said that, when the Nazis attacked the Communists, he was a little uneasy, but, after all, he was not a Communist, and so he did nothing; and then they attacked the Socialists, and he was a little uneasier, but still he did nothing. And then they attacked the Church, and he was a Churchman, and he did something—but then it was too late."

Waiting to React

"One doesn't see exactly where or how to move. Believe me, this is true. Each act, each occasion, is worse than the last, but only a little worse. You wait for the next and the next. You wait for one great shocking occasion, thinking that others, when such a shock comes, will join with you in resisting somehow. You don't want to act, or even talk alone; you don't want to 'go out of your way to make trouble.' Why not?—Well, you are not in the habit of doing it. And it is not just fear, fear of standing alone, that restrains you; it is also genuine uncertainty."

Uncertainty

"Uncertainty is a very important factor, and, instead of decreasing as time goes on, it grows. Outside, in the streets, in the general community, 'everyone' is happy. One hears no protest, and certainly sees none. You know, in France or Italy there would be slogans against the government painted on walls and fences; in Germany, outside the great cities, perhaps, there is not even this. In the university community, in your own community, you speak privately to your colleagues, some of whom certainly feel as you do; but what do they say? They say, 'It's not so bad' or 'You're seeing things' or 'You're an alarmist.'

"And you are an alarmist. You are saying that this must lead to this, and you can't prove it. These are the beginnings, yes; but how do you know for sure when you don't know the end, and how do you know, or even surmise, the end? On the one hand, your enemies, the law, the regime, the Party, intimidate you. On the other, your colleagues pooh-pooh you as pessimistic or even neurotic. You are left with your close friends, who are, naturally, people who have always thought as you have.

"But your friends are fewer now. Some have drifted off somewhere or submerged themselves in their work. You no longer see as many as you did at meetings or gatherings. Informal groups become smaller; attendance drops off in little organizations, and the organizations themselves wither. Now, in small gatherings of your older friends, you feel that you are talking to yourselves, that you are isolated from the reality of things. This weakens your confidence still further and serves as a further deterrent to—to what? It is clearer all the time that, if you are going to do anything, you must make an occasion to do it, and then you are obviously a troublemaker. So you wait, and you wait."

Small Steps

"But the one great shocking occasion, when tens or hundreds of thousands will join with you, never comes. That's the difficulty. If the last and worst act of the whole regime had come immediately after the first and smallest, thousands, yes millions, would have been sufficiently shocked—if, let us say, the gassing of the Jews in '43 had come immediately after the 'German Firm' stickers on the windows of non-Jewish shops in '33. But of course this isn't the way it happens. In between come all the hundreds of little steps, some of them imperceptible, each of them preparing you not to be shocked by the next. Step C is not so much worse than Step B, and, if you did not make a stand at Step B, why should you at Step C? And so on to Step D."

Too Late

"And one day, too late, your principles, if you were ever sensible of them, all rush in upon you. The burden of self deception has grown too heavy, and some minor incident, in my case my little boy, hardly more than a baby, saying 'Jew swine,' collapses it all at once, and you see that everything, everything, has changed and changed completely under your nose. The world you live in—your nation, your people—is not the world you were born in at all. The forms are all there, all untouched, all reassuring, the houses, the shops, the jobs, the mealtimes, the visits, the concerts, the cinema, the holidays. But the spirit, which you never noticed because you made the lifelong mistake of identifying it with the forms, is changed. Now you live in a world of hate and fear, and the people who hate and fear do not even know it themselves; when everyone is transformed, no one is transformed. Now you live in a system which rules without responsibility even to God. The system itself could not have intended this in the beginning, but in order to sustain itself it was compelled to go all the way."

Living with New Morals

"You have gone almost all the way yourself. Life is a continuing process, a flow, not a succession of acts and events at all. It has flowed to a new level, carrying you with it, without any effort on your part. On this new level you live, you have been living more comfortably every day, with new morals, new principles. You have accepted things you would not have accepted five years ago, a year ago, things that your father, even in Germany, could not have imagined.

"Suddenly it all comes down, all at once. You see what you are, what you have done, or, more accurately, what you haven't done (for that was all that was required of most of us: that we do nothing). You remember those early meetings of your department in the university when, if one had stood, others would have stood, perhaps, but no one stood. A small matter, a matter of hiring this man or that, and you hired this one rather than that. You remember everything now, and your heart breaks. Too late. You are compromised beyond repair."[6]

Using Reading 3

Consider with students the important role "thinking" has in this man's memory. How could thinking have made a difference? Consider also how this quotation by Leo Baeck, a victim of the Holocaust, relates to the reading.

Like the State, the servant of the State easily became something conceptual and mechanical—concepts can become machines.

At what point did the state take on so much power or the person give up so much power that human qualities were suppressed in the name of the fatherland?

Reading 4

"Do You Take the Oath?"

An employee in a defense plant remembers the day the "world was lost" for him, the day in 1935 when he took the oath to be faithful to the Fuehrer. That day he went against his conscience. He remembers his decision:

"I was employed in a defense plant (a war plant, of course, but they were always called defense plants). That was the year of the National Defense Law, the law of 'total conscription.' Under the law I was required to take the oath of fidelity. I said I would not; I opposed it in conscience. I was given twenty-four hours to 'think it over.' In those twenty-four hours I lost the world. . . .

"You see, refusal would have meant the loss of my job, of course, not prison or anything like that. (Later on, the penalty was worse, but this was only 1935.) But losing my job would have meant that I could not get another. Wherever I went I should be asked why I left the job I had, and when I said why, I should certainly have been refused employment. Nobody would hire a 'Bolshevik.' Of course, I was not a Bolshevik, but you understand what I mean. . . .

"I tried not to think of myself or my family. We might have got out of the country, in any case, and I could have got a job in industry or education somewhere else.

"What I tried to think of was the people to whom I might be of some help later on, if things got worse (as I believed they would). I had a wide friendship in scientific and academic circles, including many Jews, and 'Aryans,' too, who might be in trouble. If I took the oath and held my job, I might be of help, somehow, as things went on. If I refused to take the oath, I would certainly be useless to my friends, even if I remained in the country. I myself would be in their situation.

"The next day, after 'thinking it over,' I said I would take the oath with the mental reservation, that, by the words with which the oath began, 'Ich schwore bei Gott, I swear by God,' I understood that no human being and no government had the right to override my conscience. My mental reservations did not interest the official who administered the oath. He said, 'Do you take the oath?' and I took it. That day the world was lost, and it was I who lost it."

Although this man was able to save many lives by hiding fugitives in his apartment, he explains why taking the oath was evil.

"First of all, there is the problem of the lesser evil. Taking the oath was not so evil as being unable to help my friends later on would have been. But the evil of the oath was certain and immediate, and the helping of my friends was in the future and therefore uncertain. I had to commit a positive evil there and then, in the hope of a possible good later on. The good outweighed the evil; but the good was only a hope, the evil a fact. . . . The hope might not have been realized — either for reasons beyond my control or because I became afraid later on or even because I was afraid all the time and was simply fooling myself when I took the oath in the first place.

"But that is not the important point. The problem of the lesser evil we all know about; in Germany we took Hindenburg as less evil than Hitler, and in the end, we got them both. But that is not why I say that Americans cannot understand. No, the important point is — how many innocent people were killed by the Nazis, would you say? . . . Shall we say, just to be safe, that three million innocent people were killed all together? . . . And how many innocent lives would you like to say I saved? . . . Perhaps five, or ten, one doesn't know. But shall we say a hundred, or a thousand, just to be safe? . . . And it would be better to have saved all three million, instead of only a hundred, or a thousand? There, then, is my point. If I had refused to take the oath of fidelity, I would have saved all three million. . . .

"There I was, in 1935, a perfect example of the kind of person who, with all his advantages in birth, in education, and in position, rules (or might easily rule) in any country. If I had refused to take the oath in 1935, it would have meant that thousands and thousands like me, all over Germany, were refusing to take it. Their refusal would have heartened millions. Thus the regime would have been overthrown, or, indeed, would never have come to power in the first place. The fact that I was not prepared to resist, in 1935, meant that all the thousands, hundreds of thousands, like me in Germany were also unprepared, and each one of these hundreds of thousands was, like me, a man of great influence or of great potential influence. Thus the world was lost. . . .

"These hundred lives I saved — or a thousand or ten as you will — what do they represent? A little something out of the whole terrible evil, when, if my faith had been strong enough in 1935, I could have prevented the whole evil. . . . My faith. I did not believe that I could 'remove mountains.' The day I said, 'No,' I had faith. In the process of 'thinking it over,' in the next twenty-four hours, my faith failed me. So, in the next ten years, I was able to remove only anthills, not mountains.

"My education did not help me, and I had a broader and better education than most men have had or ever will have. All it did, in the end, was to enable me to rationalize my failure of faith more easily than I might have done if I had been ignorant. And so it was, I think, among educated men generally, in that time in Germany. Their resistance was no greater than other men's."[7]

Using Reading 4

Milton Mayer traveled to Germany after the war to interview the "average" citizen of Germany about the war and the exterminations. In this interview one professional recalls the day in 1935 when he said, "It was I who lost it [the world] and I will tell you how." In this interview there is reasoning about loyalty, responsibility, good, evil, and courage.

This reflection deals with complex moral issues; we suggest you read this aloud with the class before discussion. Ask students if they agree with this man that education failed him. Do students agree with him that taking the oath and saving hundreds was a mistake?

Reading 5

A Step Toward Creating a Totalitarian Government: Suspending the Constitution

This list of events, quotations, and readings provides a picture of a society no longer based on law — a society in which "Hitler is the law," and the themes of race, state, and living space combine to change the Germany of the Weimar Constitution into the Germany of the Third Reich. It is important to investigate also the social foundations of fascism. Keep in mind the question, who followed Hitler? as you read this list.

Political

1923 "Instead of working to achieve power by an armed coup, we will have to hold our noses and enter the Reichstag against the Catholic and Marxist members. If outvoting them takes longer than outshooting them, at least the result will be guaranteed by their own constitution."
Hilter "Democracy . . . is a rule of crazy brains. The German Republic is a monstrosity."
Suspend rights Weimar Constitution of 1919 provided a provision that allowed the president to scrap the entire Bill of Rights and Article 48. A dictator could rule by decree.

The Reich President may, if the public safety and order in the German Reich are considerably disturbed or endangered, take such measures as are necessary to restore public safety and order. If necessary he may intervene with the help of the armed forces. For this purpose he may temporarily suspend, either partially or wholly, the Fundamental Rights established in Articles 114, 115, 117, 118, 123, 124, and 153, without delay of all measures taken under Paragraph 1 or Paragraph 2 of this Article. On demand by the Reichstag the measures shall be repealed. . . .

Abolish title Legislature abolished by law the title of President and Hitler became known as the Fuehrer and Reich Chancellor, Head of State, and Chief of the Armed Forces.

Military

Oath Hitler moved early to consolidate power over the armed forces by replacing the old oath of allegiance with a new oath.

Old Oath:
I swear loyalty to the Constitution and vow that I will protect the German nation and its lawful establishments as a brave soldier at any time and will be obedient to the President and my superiors.

New Oath:
I swear by God this sacred oath, that I will render unconditional obedience to Adolf Hitler, the Fuehrer of the German Reich and people, Supreme Commander of the Armed Forces and will be ready as a brave soldier to risk my life at any time for this oath.

Total control With support of the military, and armed with a racial policy that planned for the breeding of more pure-blood Germans at the expense of other human lives, Hitler, Goering, Goebbels and Himmler moved to exercise their total control of the state.

- 1933—United all German police.
- Secret Police—Gestapo established as arm of the SS.
- Civil liberties suspended so police could silence and terrorize enemies of the State under the cloak of legality.
- 1935—Supreme Court ruled the laws and actions of the Gestapo were not subject to judicial review.
- 1936—"As long as the police carries out the will of the leadership, it is acting legally." Courts could not interfere with the activities of the secret police—they were above the law.

Judicial

No independent law The following is an explanation given to the judiciary by the Commissioner of Justice, Dr. Hans Frank, of their role as judges.

There is no independence of law against National Socialism. Say to yourselves at every decision which you make: "How would the Fuehrer decide in my place?" In every decision, ask yourselves: "Is this decision compatible with the National Socialist conscience of the German people?" Then you will have a firm iron foundation which, allied with the unity of the National Socialist People's State and with your recognition of the eternal nature of the will of Adolf Hitler, will endow your own sphere of decision with the authority of the Third Reich, and this for all time.

Citizenry

Total control The following list contains several examples of the areas of the citizen's life that were touched by the totalitarian dictatorship; race was an integral part of these totalitarian policies.

- Newspapers and journalists had to be politically and racially "clean" by law.
- Workers could not strike.
- Religions could not be a danger to "the moral feelings of the German race."
- Leisure time was controlled.
- Hissing at the dull movies provided for the cinema by Goebbels was "treasonable behavior on the part of cinema audiences."[8]
- The public show of dancing bears was forbidden and Italians who led monkeys on a leash had to flee Germany. The punishment for cruel treatment to animals was two years in prison. Also domestic animals could not be abandoned nor could dogs chase cats or pursue foxes.
- Citizens were told that "Ladies may not use makeup, smoke or otherwise display immoral ways. No modern music is allowed, only German folk music. Any public institutions such as Inns, Pubs, Restaurants, Hotels which do not display signs to that extent will be made public in newspapers."[9]

Executive

Hitler is law Finally on April 26, 1942, the Reichstag passed a law that made Hitler the law; he would have absolute power over every German and could suspend any laws that might stand in the way.

In the present war, in which the German people are faced with a struggle for their existence or their annihilation, the Fuehrer must have all the rights postulated by him which serve to further or achieve victory. Therefore, without being bound by existing legal regulations—in his capacity as Leader of the nation, Supreme Commander of the Armed Forces, Head of Government and Supreme Executive Chief, as Supreme Justice and Leader of the Party—the Fuehrer must be in a position to force with all means at his disposal every German, if necessary, whether he be common soldier or officer, low or high official or judge, leading or subordinate official of the party, worker or employer—to fulfill his duties. In case of violation of these duties, the Fuehrer is entitled, after conscientious examination, regardless of so-called well-deserved rights, to mete out due punishment and to remove the offender from his post, rank and position without introducing prescribed procedure.[10]

Using Reading 5

1. According to these laws, which ideas, individuals, and groups would become the new enemies of the nation according to the Nazis? Can an idea be considered an enemy? How?

2. According to the Commissioner of Justice, Dr. Frank, how should decisions about law be made? By judges? Juries? Companies? Lawyers? Adolf Hitler? The government? Individuals?

3. The oath of generals and officers was to Hitler, not to Germany or to the Constitution. According to William Shirer in *The Rise and Fall of the Third Reich*,

It was also a pledge which enabled an even greater number of officers to excuse themselves from any personal responsibility for the unspeakable crimes which they carried out on the orders of the Supreme Commander whose true nature they had seen for themselves ... One of the appalling aberrations of the German officer corps from this point on rose out of this conflict of "honor"—a word ... often on their lips .... Later and often by honoring their oath they dishonored themselves as human beings and trod in the mud the moral code of their corps.

Initally, the German generals who opposed Hitler opposed his threats to make war. His generals argued that the country was not ready for the war he proposed. Prominent German civilians tried to persuade the Allies to distinguish between Nazis and Germans and to stand firm for Czechoslovakia. By 1938, plans for a coup d'etat had been made and the conspirators were arguing whether Hitler should be murdered, tried, or declared insane. The two top commanders of the army were involved, but they vacillated. Must one fulfill his military duty—his personal oath to his Fuehrer—or his moral duty? Hitler's early successes in the war didn't help his opposition, nor did America's insistence that it was fighting a total war against all German people. In the course of the war, several German commanders were willing to aid the Allies in the hope that they could save lives, purge the country of its guilt, and save something for the future.

One German colonel, Claus von Stauffenberg, tried unsuccessfully to kill Hitler with a bomb. He said:

He who has the courage to do something must do so in the knowledge that he will go down in German history as a traitor. If he does not do it, he will be a traitor to his conscience.[11]

4. Discuss what the implications are for individuals and minority groups swearing an oath to an individual leader rather than to a country.

5. Milton Mayer wrote that there was a time in Nazi Germany when teachers could have made different decisions. Why was the decision of most teachers to take and obey the new oath to Hitler a crucial step toward totalitarianism?

6. The racial policies of the Nazi party, rooted in myth and psuedo-science about a superior Aryan race descended from Nordic stock, were adapted and transformed into government policies to legitimize abuses against the civil rights and human dignity of some citizens of Germany. After Hitler had consolidated his power and capitalized on political and economic events, he suspended those principles of the constitution that protected against the abuses of a totalitarian government. He created the SS, the SA, and the Gestapo, who were selected according to a strict racial policy, and who swore an oath of loyalty to Hitler—not to the constitution nor to the nation. These men often insured obedience through terror.

The defense used at Nuremberg related directly to this reading. (See Chapter 10.)

Reading 6 First Amendment Issues: Testing the Constitution

The preceding readings detailed how Germany's constitution was suspended gradually and replaced by the law of only one man. The struggle to understand how a constitution must be kept alive by its citizens and how this struggle is often controversial is illuminated by the Skokie case, a test of the First Amendment by Nazis in America who wanted to march in Skokie, Illinois.

The following is an explanation by the attorney for the American Civil Liberties Union, who describes why he defended "freedom of speech in

Skokie, Illinois," in 1977-78 for a "handful of people calling themselves 'Nazis'."*

The case began when the Nazis scattered requests to several Chicago suburbs seeking permits to hold a rally in their towns. Skokie was one of those towns.

Many of the towns that received the Nazis' request just ignored it. Skokie did not.

Skokie responded by obtaining a court order banning the rally, and by passing several local laws that in effect prohibited most political rallies, not only the Nazis.

The Nazis asked us to defend their right to hold the rally, and to challenge one of the laws prohibiting it. Though I detested their beliefs, I went into court to defend the First Amendment.

I've had a lot of experience with bans on speech like the one in Skokie. I've opposed them when they were used to block civil rights marches, and I've opposed them when they were used to ban antiwar demonstrators. At this very moment, I am representing the Martin Luther King, Jr., Coalition, which has been banned from Marquette Park, a hostile white neighborhood on the southwest side of Chicago, by a law very much like the Skokie laws.

But the Skokie case was quite different.

Skokie's population is predominantly Jewish, and includes a large number of concentration camp survivors. To allow people calling

*The information here is excerpted from a letter to American Civil Liberties Union members written by David Goldberger, the attorney who defended the Nazis in the Skokie march case.

themselves Nazis to parade in that town seemed to many an agony too much to bear.

I share that agony. All of us at the ACLU do.

The Executive Director of the ACLU, Aryeh Neier, is himself a survivor of Nazi Germany. He has more reason than most to despise what people calling themselves Nazis stand for.

But the Nazis are not the real issue. The Skokie laws are the real issue.

Very few people have actually seen the Skokie laws. They do not specifically prohibit Nazis from speaking. They don't even mention them.

The Skokie laws require anyone who wants to speak, parade or demonstrate to apply first for a permit, and they grant the village officials the power to deny a permit if in their opinion the proposed speech portrays a "lack of virtue" in others or "incites hostility."

Anyone who wants to speak must also post a $350,000 insurance bond. This requirement applies to everyone, not only the Nazis, and since insurance companies rarely will write such insurance, the requirement in effect prohibits everyone's free speech.

It is crucial that these kinds of laws and requirements be struck down, because there is no way to limit them. If they are not struck down, then towns everywhere will have the legal power to pass identical laws, and to use them to prohibit whatever they believe is offensive.

Think of such power in the hands of a racist sheriff, or a local police department hostile to antiwar demonstrators, or the wrong kind of President.

That is what was at stake in the Skokie case.

Yet many, understandably, did not see it that way. They felt that the Nazis' views were so reprehensible that they did not deserve the protection of the Constitution.

A few people even made personal threats against me and other members of the ACLU staff.

On May 22, 1978, the United States Court of Appeals struck down all three Skokie laws including the $350,000 insurance requirement. A short time later the United States Supreme Court refused to bar the Skokie demonstration.

We were relieved that the citizens of Skokie were spared yet another reminder of the horrors that Nazism represents. The Nazis chose to rally in Chicago when the ACLU persuaded the U.S. District Court to overrule the Chicago Park District's opposition.

Using Reading 6

One 8th grade student remarked that the Holocaust could never happen in the United States because we have the Bill of Rights. What do students think of this remark after reading this section on totalitarianism in Germany, viewing this cartoon, and reading about the ACLU decision to defend the Nazis in America?

For students who enjoy preparing a courtroom trial, this case explores important questions about the First Amendment.

Students might also discuss the protection our Constitution gives to the Ku Klux Klan.

"Skokie," a TV special, and the film "The Speaker" demonstrate the First Amendment issues for students.

In the following student responses, they reflect on the power the discussions of the Skokie case had for them.

When you first made the statement that there are no simple solutions to complex problems, I didn't really understand. But then the case of the Nazis in Skokie, Illinois, became the topic of many of our discussions. I could see it was a complex problem and knew there was no simple answer. If they were not allowed to march that would be morally right, but legally wrong according to the First Amendment. If they were allowed to march, that would be legally right and morally wrong.

We argued (among ourselves, without the idea of a teacher ... we've learned to have discussions on our own) about whether the Nazis had a right to march. It was in the Constitution that they had the legal right, but was it right to the people who had suffered the Holocaust for the Nazis to march in celebration of a man's birthday who had made them prisoners of the horrible memory.

Reading 7

Nazi Storm Troopers: Terror in the Totalitarian State (1930-1934)

Reading about the history of violent political groups in Germany after World War I makes one wonder, where were the police? Where were the traditional organizations such as the churches, schools, and businesses that could respond in an effort to curb the violence?

Police reports in 1930 indicate the magnitude of the problem that faced the police in curbing the violence that accompanied the rallies and demonstrations. In that year alone the police had to be present at 23,946 open-air rallies and demonstrations involving 25 million participants and 34,742 indoor meetings with 13.5 million participants.

The Berlin chief of police stated:

Ordinary brawls had given way to murderous attacks. Knives, blackjacks and revolvers had replaced political argument. Terror was rampant. Carefully prepared alibis helped the terrorists (both Nazis and Communists) to escape conviction.[12]

The Nazis and Communists were involved in 90 percent of the violent demonstrations and rallies, and, in response, the government placed a ban on their activities. When Chancellor von Papen took office in 1932, one of his first acts was to lift the ban against the Nazi storm troopers, which before had been designated as a "danger to the state." This action unleashed an onslaught of violence in the streets between the Nazis and Communists. Efforts of government officials to end the street warfare by banning "paramilitary uniforms and demonstrations" were overruled by President von Hindenburg.[13]

An irony of this history is that when the many local officials tried to take steps to prevent the violence, the higher government leaders seemed concerned only with appeasing the radical groups.

The storm troopers became strong between 1930 and 1932, yet they were not simply created by Hitler. "They had been nurtured by a full decade of paramilitary politics, and often came directly from other, similar organizations or from the rebellious ranks of organized youth."[14]

Using Reading 7

Students might discuss the power of a uniform and the crowd effect of a demonstration to disguise or promote certain feelings. The notion of "use and abuse" is certainly applicable in this discussion.

There were many paramilitary groups in the Weimar Republic:

- "It was not unusual for a young veteran or member of the post-war generation to join and spend much of his free time with one of these private armies."[15]
- The various paramilitary groups had much in common in terms of symbols of power.
- Military sports and voluntary labor service to the government were among their common interests.
- The intense rivalry and competition among the paramilitary groups helped them grow in size and military strength. For example, the Nazis needed the Communists to clash with in order to rationalize their own existence.
- The storm troopers were late-comers and many of their recruits were individuals who had become disenchanted with other paramilitary groups. The Nazis and their violent storm troopers became a major and growing force . . . "only from about 1929, when large numbers of converts, especially from the right, swelled the ranks of what had been a violent fringe group."[16]

The ideology of the storm troopers seems to reveal both a strong admiration for Hitler, the person, and an intense hatred of the Communists. But, according to Peter Merkl, individuals joined the storm troopers for the physcial struggle of the demonstrations themselves, rather than for an ideology or hope for a better society.

When a storm trooper put on his uniform and went to do his "service," he literally stripped off his humdrum worker's life, or meek bourgeois habit, and became a heroic superman to himself and his comrades. Marching and fighting in closed formation, in particular, he felt powerful and masculine beyond compare.[17]

- About one-third of the Nazis in 1933 were veterans who still longed for the comradeship of the war years, fighting against a common enemy. These men were shocked at the lack of public support for the military when they returned home.
- A large number of Nazi leaders were born abroad or had spent a great deal of time abroad, e.g., Rudolf Hess, Walter Darre, Alfred Rosenberg, Joachim Ribbentrop.
- Many Nazi storm troopers were from families that were "socially declining" and who moved constantly from place to place.
- Almost two-thirds of the storm troopers had previously been involved in political street violence before joining.
- Most storm troopers were young.
- The tactics of the storm troopers were not to control areas but simply to use the demonstrations as "heroic happenings." As one storm trooper writes:

SA men never give in. They answer the enemy in kind. They put up terror against terror. When the KPN (Communists) assaults a comrade, the SA smash the tavern where the murderous mob is known to be. And when the police arrest them by the hundreds during a propaganda campaign and drag them off to (Berlin police headquarters), they smash up the hall in which they are locked up. They smash the benches, throw the telephones through the breaking windows, and tear out the water lines so that the upset police have to call the fire brigade for help.[18]

- Individuals were not forced to join the storm troopers, for, as Peter Merkl reminds us,

Reconstructing the world of meaning as the storm troopers and party men saw it goes a long way toward explaining their decision to march and fight and proselytize, as long as we remember that it was still their free decision to join and work for the movement.[19]

By 1934 Hitler had become concerned about the strength of the storm troopers (SA) and that there was the possibility that an SA state could develop within the Nazi state. The SA posed a threat to Hitler's goal of complete totalitarian control. In June 1934, Hitler, Goering, and the SS conducted a purge of the SA throughout Germany, arresting and killing much of the SA leadership. The "disorderly storm trooper violence of 1933 was replaced by the quiet and deadly efficiency of the SS-guarded concentration camps. . . ."[20]

Reading 8

Steps Toward Terrorizing a Town

The description of the way the Nazis gained control of the town of Thalburg appears in William Allen's *The Nazis' Seizure of Power.* In this reading a high school student describes the major steps toward control through the practice of terror in the town. The term *takeover* is not appropriate for the initial stages of Nazi dominance for they were legally voted into office.

- The Nazis had a fifteen-seat majority on the city council, and the Socialist party (SPD) had five seats — enough to guarantee at least one Socialist on every committee formed. The Nazis persuaded a once vehemently anti-Nazi Socialist to change his status to "neutral."
- Instead of holding the council meetings in city hall, they were held in a large hotel room so that Nazi supporters from outside Thalburg could fill the room. The Socialist members received boos when they did speak.
- The Nazis were surprised by how easy it was to destroy the Socialist party. In fact, by June 27 1933, only a few months after gaining power, the Nazis had forced every Socialist off the council. Many Socialists felt it was safer to join the Nazi party than to continue to speak out against Nazism.

By mid-June the Nazis could start to gain full control over every facet of Thalburg life. The Enabling Act gave Hitler the power of a dictator, and ensured that the Nazis of Thalburg could not be stopped by law.
- The Nazi newspaper printed propaganda and made the truth hard to discover.
- The Socialists and anti-Nazis were terrorized.
- The punishment for the smallest crime, even criticizing the Nazis, was assignment to a concentration camp. No one knew who was a Gestapo agent. Therefore, it was dangerous to confide in your closest friend.
- To provide an excuse for the terror, the Nazis claimed communist insurgents were everywhere. The Nazis claimed that everyone and everything should be searched for weapons.
- The entire city had been terrified so much that the citizens avoided each other, fearing for their lives. The Nazis then began to bring the people together while still keeping up the fear.
- The Nazis managed to first unite the citizens by ordering boycotts of Jews. Although there were only 120 Jews in Thalburg and antisemitism didn't flourish, the boycott of the Jews, as ordered, made the townspeople feel secure.

- Soon the Nazis managed to unite all unions into the German Workers Front, and the clubs into one club.

Thus in less than a year, the Nazis had absolute and complete control over Thalburg.

Using Reading 8

Discuss what means the Nazis used to further their power. This reading reminds us that a constitution itself is not a protection; it is the responsibility of the citizens to make the proper choices.

Reading 9

A Major Step Toward Terrorizing a Nation

On November 9, 1938, the Nazis carried out what the German press called a "spontaneous demonstration" against Jewish property, synagogues, and people. Dr. Goebbels, the propaganda minister, claimed that the demonstration was in reaction to the shooting of a third-secretary of the German Embassy in Paris. A Jewish boy who had escaped from Germany to France because of the Nazi persecutions of Jews had planned to kill the ambassador because his father had been deported to Poland in a sealed boxcar.

Throughout Germany fires and bombs were used to destroy synagogues and shops, and store windows were shattered, leaving broken glass everywhere. That night became known as the night of the glass, or Kristallnacht.

Later, German documents showed that Kristallnacht had been carefully planned weeks in advance by the Nazis who were waiting for the right incident before carrying out their plans.

In Nuremberg, one German city, Jewish homes were destroyed with hatchets, because earlier at a rally of about 30,000 Nazis, a Nazi official made a speech that incited the crowd against the Jews. Each Nazi was given a hatchet and permission to do whatever he wanted to the Jews.

The following is one memory of that night:

I lived in Cologne, a city of about 100,000, on a street opposite an Orthodox synagogue, in a two-story apartment house. Next door was our small restaurant. My room was upstairs under the roof and the window faced the synagogue. About four houses away was the 4711 factory—a place that manufactured perfume. I woke up in the middle of the night hearing noises—as though heavy barrels were being rolled about. I climbed out of bed onto the slanted roof and thought I saw people at the factory.

Nazis were going in and out of apartments. Some Nazis rolled heavy kegs from the factory into the synagogue and put it on fire. I ran downstairs and woke my parents. We took a small amount of jewelry and ran back to my room, locked the door, and hid the jewelry on the roof. We heard lots of noise, both in the house and in the restaurant. Finally the Nazis left. We went downstairs. Everything in the apartment and restaurant was smashed to pieces, including my beautiful grand piano. It was over-turned and every single string had been cut. Sofas and chairs were upside down and books and valuables had been stolen. My father was taken by two Nazis and put in jail. . . .

Another first-hand report comes from a small town called Kassel. This girl was only fourteen years old when Kristallnacht occurred:

I was visiting my aunt nearby when my father came to get me. He was very upset for he had just seen freight trains packed with Jews. We went to our small home, and about two o'clock in the morning, my uncle from another village knocked on the door. He told us Nazis had come into his village and arrested all the Jewish men. He hid, and later walked 25 kilometers to our home. My cousin, who was seventeen years old, had been tied onto a horse and dragged about the village. The two large synagogues in my town were burned. At night I went back to stay with my aunt, because she was alone. She wept all night, and recited the Shema over and over. The next morning all the Jewish apartments in my town were ransacked. Featherbeds were torn and feathers scattered. When I returned home, nothing was left but the house. My mother and sister were in jail. Every piece of china had been smashed, every piece of clothing stolen. I thought of my two violins. One was new and the other an older, 3/4 child-size. The new one was gone and the 3/4 one smashed. I had a mama doll with a china head. The arms, legs, and head were torn off. The furniture had been hacked with saws and axes.

My father was sent to Buchenwald (a concentration camp) for five weeks. We had almost nothing to eat, and no one would sell us anything. My mother had a heart attack and the doctor refused to come. Jewish children were not allowed to go to public schools. At that time Jews could still be ransomed, and we finally were able to ransom my father. When he returned home, he had lost 60 pounds. Later, no one could be ransomed. We were fingerprinted and forced to wear a yellow star on the front and back of our clothing and on armbands. A large "J" was stamped on our passports. . . .

The following note was sent to all Gestapo (secret police) stations before Kristallnacht:

This teleprinter message is secret:
At very short notice Aktionen against Jews, especially against their synagogues, will take place throughout the whole of Germany. They are not to be stopped. . . .
Preparations are to be made for the arrest of about 20,000 to 30,000 Jews in the Reich. Wealthy Jews in particular are to be selected. More detailed instructions will be issued in the course of this night.[21]

Reading 10 **Kristallnacht**
In the following reading a German Catholic remembers the night the SA and SS came to his street to terrorize his Jewish neighbors.

The evening before (November 8), we all were unsuspecting. About 11:00 p.m., there began a terrible noise and commotion. SA and SS men in uniform, all personally known to us, appeared in front of our door and began to demolish the house of Loehnberg's across the street from us. Furniture and other articles were thrown into the street, and even the food that was found was thrown out and trampled upon. And these poor people had next to nothing to eat any more because the stores for some time were not allowed to sell to Jews. The two old ladies, Mrs. Loehnberg and Mrs. Lebenberg, both old and grey, were driven out of the house in a brutal way; scantily dressed, they ran crying pitifully up and down the street.

Many remember *Kristallnacht* as the night the violence against the German Jewish people began. Glass was shattered, synagogues were burned and many Jews were arrested and taken to concentration camps.

My father had already gone to bed and he woke up from the loud noise, looked out of the window, and when he saw what was happening, he began to shout and wanted to open the window to tell the Nazis to stop. My mother stood behind him. I can still see how she held him back, because she was afraid they would call us Jew-friends and would also attack us and demolish our house. My father got me out of bed—I was 13 years old at the time. He took me to the window so that I should witness it. He was crying. None of us had imagined anything so inhuman; and I think it was supposed to be a warning for all Germans who were not yet Nazis, that the same thing would happen to them if they would show resistance to the system. In Beckum, nothing was undertaken against these acts of violence; everybody feared for his own life and his property, and we all could not guess where all this would lead to.

I remember the day when Mrs. Terboch, another Jewish neighbor, came to say goodbye to us; she cried terribly. My father and grandfather were standing next to her, and she said, "You were our best neighbors; but don't forget, now it is the garlic and next comes the incense." I did not understand what she meant, and my father had to explain it to me. Mrs. T. meant that it was the Jews who suffered now, and then the Nazis would begin with the Catholics.

On the other end of Novd Street—and we could hear it—they had begun to demolish the synagogue. Books and religious objects were thrown into the street. The next morning on my way to school, I saw Erich Stein and a stepladder in front of the synagogue; with hammer and chisel he had to remove the Hebrew letters over the entrance which said,

"This house is a sanctuary for all peoples." I still see in my mind Mr. Stein standing up there; an SA man in uniform stood watch over him.

At this time the last remaining Jews in Beckum suffered from terrible persecution. They had to wear a yellow star on their clothing—the Star of David. They were allotted only a few food items and had to turn over all their valuables. They were not allowed to walk on sidewalks, only on the street, and had to greet every passing by Nazi Party member.

I remember very well the old gentleman, Louis Rose, who had stayed in Beckum, because like many others he just could not believe that the Germans could do such things. He also relied on the coveted military award which he had received when he had joined the army as a volunteer in the Chinese revolt in 1902; it was the Iron Cross 1st Class, the highest military award at that time, an award which Hitler had also received. He wore the Iron Cross next to the yellow star, but it did not help him. His house was also completely demolished, and he and his wife perished in the concentration camp at Theresienstadt.

The worst things happened on Novd Street in the house of Mr. Alex Falk, an old gentleman who lived alone. Part of the building was used by a grocery store, and the manager of the store, a young lady, lived upstairs. When this terrible destruction began, the 80-year-old man fled upstairs to call the lady for help. He found the door of her apartment locked, and it was there that the SS and SA found him. It was declared that he had tried to enter her bedroom and rape her—the insanity of it!

Right there and then he was beaten to death.

Three well-known Beckum men were responsible for the death of Mr. Falk, one of them, a neighbor. It is known that all three of them took their own life at the end of the war. The young woman was led through the city the next day with a sign hanging around her neck in front and in back reading: "I, a German woman, had a relationship with a Jew." Following this march, she had to stand for some hours on a flat truck, and was insulted by the Nazis. It is said that she later suffered from a nervous disease and left Germany.

The next day my father walked with me through the city to see the destruction. Everywhere we met people who were shocked and who told my father so—because they knew him. The streets were littered with splintered glass of all the many shattered windows. It glittered everywhere, and for that reason has come the name "Kristallnacht."

After this night the last remaining Jewish citizens disappeared from the streets. They stayed in their ruined houses. I am puzzled how they got something to eat and continued to exist. Shortly after that they must have been picked up secretly at night, because suddenly they were not there any more.

The Loehnberg house was standing as a ruin for several months or years. Then suddenly it was pulled down, because the "Aete Garde," the party members who had joined the Nazi Party before 1933, were expected on a visit to the city. They came riding through town in open trucks, flags were out, and the school children had to stand by and shout "Heil." Most of these men were terribly drunk, and it was more of a disgrace than a joy to have to watch something like that.

My father had been approached several times and was offered the purchase of Jewish houses. But he declined. I don't believe that he could ever think of it. His motto was always: "Unrecht gut gedeiht nicht"—There is no blessing in something gained dishonestly.

What did the citizens of Beckum and the people, in general, who were not Nazis, do to prevent the happenings and to protect the Jewish citizens?

Unfortunately, Hitler had found an existent anti-Semitism among the German people, stemming from the disastrous mistake in the thinking of the Christian religion. He took advantage of this and developed it up to the fatal culmination. For years he had spread the message: "The Jews are our misfortune!" — The Jews were made responsible for everything that was bad: the disastrous First World War, the inflation of the 20 years, etc. Added to that came the insane race politic! In the schools the children were indoctrinated with Nazi ideas by otherwise good teachers.

For instance, I had a professor in college, an avid Nazi who always came to class in his uniform. He judged the students by their service in the Hitler youth organization. As soon as he heard that a student was not enthusiastic about that, the student could expect a bad report card. It was practically the same for adults. City or government officials, for instance, had to be party members. Otherwise, they could not be promoted or were transferred to different places and inferior positions.

And so, slowly, everybody adjusted, partly from conviction, more likely out of fear and personal considerations.

I remember that my father withdrew from all his posts of honor. He was head of his trade guild. He left the voluntary fire department because he had to use the "German Salute." My mother, with her timid nature, was fearful because he continued expressing his opinion, and had already the reputation as grumbler.

And — not to forget — and unfortunately this will be the case with all peoples — one could trust almost nobody. Many people became traitors and sold their fellow men to the party organizations to gain advantages for themselves.

Only in this way can it be understood why the people remained silent in the face of the devastations and the inhuman acts. One simply feared for one's life, for one's family, and for one's position; or, and that is worse, through these years of propaganda one was already so brainwashed and indoctrinated that one really believed to do his fatherland a service by remaining silent.

Humans are simply no heroes — that proves true especially in such critical situations. So it was in the Kristallnacht in Beckum; the people who had to watch stood by, deep down shuddering, but silent; no one trusted the other, and each one thought only of his own safety.

But I give you my word of honor that at that time neither my parents nor anyone around us knew that there were already concentration camps in which death awaited these poor people.

One wanted, by all means, to expel the Jewish people from Germany and to slam the door between them and ourselves, not realizing that one had slammed the door suddenly between themselves and all humanity and that one stood alone outside.[22]

Using Reading 10

Kristallnacht, the Night of the Broken Glass, is a significant night in the history of Germany before the Holocaust. This story, from the memory of a Catholic child, gives one perspective. In Bea Stadler's *The Holocaust* and in Milton Meltzer's *Never to Forget*, other perspectives are described.

Reading 11

Peasants Oppose Nazi Terror

In the Catholic districts of Germany the Nazis repeatedly removed crucifixes from the religious schools and tried to replace them with swastikas. Peasants of the Bishropric of Munster demonstrated in protest.

No one spoke for hours, there was no shouting of slogans during this demonstration; there was nothing but the continual murmur of one word coming from all the people gathered. The crowd stood there, murmuring the word: "Crosses, crosses, crosses..." without interruption, for hours, "crosses, crosses, crosses...." In this single instance, the Nazis surrendered. They returned the crosses to the diocese. In almost every other place, they were victorious, for almost nowhere else did they meet with opposition.[23]

Using Reading 11

What if there had been more opposition to the Nazis earlier, when the consequences of such action were not so drastic? What if German citizens had opposed each new step instead of accepting it?

Now there is a really good example of sticking up for what you believe and the importance of not staying silent.
—an 8th grade student

The Catholic opposition was wonderful. They stopped being bystanders and were able to get their crosses put back into their churches. It shows if you stand up to people and voice your opinions you have more chance to win your case.
—an 8th grade student

Students could discuss the fact that there were incidents of citizen resistance to totalitarian policies, but that they were rare. This history is not about those who stood up for their neighbors as much as it is about those who did not.

Reading 12

Art as a Weapon in a Totalitarian State

The Reichskulturkammer, the Reich Chamber of Culture, was created in 1933 to control all public taste and culture by instigating a rigid ideological control over all the arts. The Reich Chamber for Fine Arts, for example, controlled the content, style, and authorship of all sculpture, interior decorating, painting, landscape gardening, art auctions, and publications about art. All artists had to be members.

Another special commissioner was responsible for artistic design of symbols for everything from postcards and stamps to billboards and statues.

All modern expressionist works of art were banned and many items were confiscated from private and museum collections. The Reich denounced artists such as Picasso, van Gogh, Chagall, Klee, and Kollwitz for producing "Jewish and Bolshevik art of disintegration and sedition." Hitler attacked the art of the Weimar period, calling it:

The degenerate art of charlatans who belonged either in insane asylums or prisons, the cubistic-dadaistic cult of primitivism, and the architecture designed by Bauhaus fools.[24]

On March 20, 1939, there was a public bonfire to burn 5,000 art works; others were sold or purchased for Goering's art collection.

Using Reading 12

Students will need to define *degenerate*. The control over the visual arts has been a necessary component of most modern dictatorships. This reading begins to describe the bureaucracy necessary to carry out control of all works of art, even the postage stamp. Sybil Milton, a scholar in the area of the social responsibility of the artist in Nazi Germany, wrote:

The fires of 1933 had burned books; those of 1939 consumed works of art; after 1941, the bonfires cremated human beings, many of them artists.

Documentation in film of the opening of the "House of German Art" by Hitler and footage of ideal art is shown in the film "Swastika," used later in this unit. It is interesting to note that the United States army has a large collection of the Nazi-sponsored art created by Hitler's artists to define and document the "Aryan" German. Recently the U.S. army showed the captured Nazi art in a show in cities in the United States. The audiences loved the grand canvases and "gargantuan figures." Many viewers commented that finally they were seeing "good art."

Reading 13

Two Artists Protest

Kaethe Kollwitz, a socialist, became an exile in her country under the Nazis. Her protest against Hitler in the March 1933 election led to her enforced resignation from the Prussian Academy of Arts and her removal from its teaching faculty and membership roster. She was banned from all public exhibitions and artistic activity. Despite Gestapo harassment, she attempted to continue a humanitarian graphic art and sculpture tradition.

Karl Schwesig (1881-1955) was an outspoken opponent of the Nazis and after 1940, was interned in the Vichy French camps of Gurs, Noe, and St. Cyprien. Schwesig was not Jewish but was probably a Communist. When the Nazis came to power he was arrested for "high treason" and his works were destroyed.

Reading 14

Herman Goering Describes Hitler

Herman Goering was Hitler's number-two man and although he was the most practical and the least consumed by ideology of the men close to Hitler, he had an "unreasoning" belief in Hitler's superhuman powers. He dictated this description of Hitler in 1933.

When the need was greatest the Lord gave the German people its saviour—an unknown soldier of the World War, a man of the people, without rank or property or connections, a plain, simple man, but one with an overwhelming genius and greatness of character. From the primordial force of the people itself Adolf Hitler arose and passed through all of Germany as the herald of German freedom and German justice, appealing, arousing, and inflaming the people like the incarnation of the German conscience itself. And then it seemed to all ardent, expectant Germans as if the beacon of the hidden German had illuminated the starless night of hopeless despair. The German heart was found again; with magic power it drew to itself and into itself the noblest German blood and poured it out again into the people (Volk) in countless screams of resolution and strength. . . .

Just as the Roman Catholic is convinced that the Pope is infallible in all matters of religion and morals, so we National Socialists believe with the same inner conviction that for us the Fuehrer is infallible in all political and other matters that concern the national and social interests of the people. What is the secret of his mighty influence on his followers? Is it his goodness as a person, his strength of character, or his unique modesty? Is it perhaps his political talent for divining and foreseeing the course that events will take? Or is it his exceptional courage or his extraordinary loyalty to his followers? I believe that, whatever one singles out, one will in the end arrive at the conclusion that it is not only the sum of all these virtues but also something mystical, inexpressible in this unique man, and he who does not feel it will not understand it. For we love Adolf Hitler, because we believe deeply and unalterably that he has been sent to us by God in order to save Germany.

And it is Germany's blessing that Hitler is that rare combination of penetratingly logical thinker, genuinely profound philosopher and iron man of action, tenacious to the extreme. How seldom are the gifts of genius united with the will to action! In Hitler they find a perfect union.[25]

Using Reading 14

Hitler is described as the German savior. What does Goering's description tell the reader about his passion and faith? Did other Germans accept Hitler "on faith"? What arguments could be used to debate this description? Would the arguments be based on reason or emotion?

Do testimonies, biographies, autobiographies, and diaries from people like Goering who helped plan Hitler's decisions shed some light on the development of Nazi policies?

Reading 15 **Two Views on How to Combat Totalitarianism**

I.F. Stone suggests that, in order to combat fascism, we must "keep alive the tradition of freedom; it needs to be freshly taught, explained and fought for in every generation." He was concerned with how to preserve freedom of thought and expression against the repression that arises in every generation. He makes a distinction between freedom of thought and "liberty." For "'liberty' is too vague and slippery," he wrote, "and it often includes the freedom to exploit others."

He writes further:

. . . That a society in which men are not free to speak their minds is not a good society, no matter what material benefits it may offer the few or the many . . . . The only absolute value I would affirm is freedom of the mind—without it there cannot be social justice, which is our duty to others.[26]

Hannah Arendt also writes about the freedom to think:

Thinking, an activity without space or time, paradoxically requires space and time. Of all the forms of political organization that do not permit freedom, only totalitarianism consciously seeks to crowd out the ability to think. Man cannot be silenced, he can only be crowded into not speaking. Under all other conditions, even within the racing noise of our time, thinking is possible.

Using Reading 15

I.F. Stone refers to "new excuses for repression" that "arise in every generation." Ask students if they agree that there are such excuses in today's generation. If so, what are they?

What does Stone mean by a distinction between freedom of thought and liberty?

What suggestions do students have for keeping the tradition of freedom alive?

Hannah Arendt argues that the freedom of the mind is critical to thinking. I.F. Stone argues that freedom of the mind is critical to social justice. Can you try to explain why they would see a connection between social justice and thinking?

Teachers might read *The Children's Story* by James Clavell, a powerful and controversial book about conformity and obedience.

Reading 16

Political Protection in the Human Community

Hannah Arendt was a philosopher who wrote and thought about totalitarianism. She believed that individuals and groups must engage in an active political life. This life would call for practicing speech and action in public by individuals who are at the same time displaying their freedom and insuring freedom for all the human community. Jews became victim, she writes, as did all Europe, to a system of values that led to totalitarianism when they "lost all freedom, and with it the capacity for action . . . ."

Even though Jews in the 19th century received legal emancipation and underwent economic and social assimilation, they were still separated from the real world of political action and freedom, and because the real world was still "race-oriented" Jews were "outlawed."

The Enlightenment of Europe promised in its ideals nations of laws, political citizenship, and the rights of man, but instead Europe got fascism and totalitarianism.

European Jews lacked the right to act in the political world. They were outlawed from practicing "free action and speech" in the human community.

"The 19th century equation of race and nation made it clearly less likely that Jews could become citizens, equal partners in any non-Jewish nation. They were always outsiders, no matter how assimilated . . . ."[27]

Using Reading 16

This reading is difficult. It is critical, however, for identifying the idea that a nation can decide whether to protect or make victim its minority groups. This reading further develops the issue of individual and group responsibility for this history. Discuss the meaning of a Human Community.

According to this reading, how do the policies of totalitarianism and racism outlined in this chapter relate to the German Jewish citizens living in Nazi Germany?

Discuss the following questions in relation to Hannah Arendt's views of totalitarianism and racism:

- Are there subtle, benign forms of discrimination against individuals or groups today?
- What does a "pariah status" mean?
- How can being active politically protect a minority group from abuse?
- What does the term *outlaw* mean in this reading?
- Why did Hannah Arendt believe that the precedent of outlawing a community or group was dangerous for all of Europe?
- Helen Fein, in *Accounting for Genocide*, and other scholars who write about genocide believe the defining of a group as "outside the community" is a significant precondition toward a policy of genocide in a nation. Is Arendt's "outlaw" the same as Fein's "outside the community"? Fein wrote, "The victims have previously been defined as outside the universe of obligation of the dominant group."
- What does Hannah Arendt mean by "social engineering?"
- For high school students who have studied the Enlightenment, Modern Europe, and the French Revolution, the thesis that the emancipation of the Jews in Europe was a precursor to their modern day persecution should be of great significance. These students should recognize the names of Robespierre and Dreyfus, and should be challenged to think about the quotation, "the era of Robespierre prepared the way for the era of Dreyfus."

The following excerpt from a recent review of Hannah Arendt's writings, by Leon Botstein, is included here for the educator who wishes to think more about Hannah Arendt's provocative ideas.*

Arendt's ideal political vision stems from her belief that the loss of the opportunity to engage in an active political life was the most adverse consequence of the segregation of the Jews in modern history. The tragedy of the Jews as "pariah" in modern Europe was the depoliticization of the Jews.

In the 19th century the exacerbation of this pariah status of the Jew came about in seemingly benign forms, such as legal emancipation and economic and social assimilation. These did not for Arendt compensate for the separation of the Jew from the real world of political action and freedom. To Arendt, economic and even social gains failed to pierce the fundamental illusion of assimilation and emancipation in the race-oriented modern world.

The fate of the Jews, the loss of political freedom, was really only a precursor of what race thinking and imperialism would eventually do after 1933 to all Europeans. As Arendt argues in the *Origins,* the ideals of a nation of laws, of political citizenship and of the rights of men—in the Enlightenment sense—were subverted. The 19th century bred fascism and totalitarianism, international movements which deprived men of their individuality and their capacity for freedom and action— precisely the Jewish experience. Modern history threatens to make

---

*According to a review by Geoffrey Barraclough of the book, *The Nazi Question: An Essay on the Interpretations of National Socialism (1922-1975)* by Pierre Aycoberry, the totalitarian model for examining the significance of the Nazi regime is artificial, although he acknowledges it opened new avenues for inquiry.

pariahs of us all. As she wrote in 1943, "... the outlawing of the Jewish people has been followed closely by the outlawing of most European nations...."

Since Arendt regarded the loss of the active life as the decisive dimension of the diaspora experience—her own experience—it is no accident that she chose as her lifelong guides the idealized ancient polis of free citizens and the Aristotelian view of man as a political animal. No wonder she parted ways with Marx on the political primacy of economics and "the social question" and continued to stress the autonomous political dimension of life. For it was this that the European Jews lacked. If the ultimate expression of man's potential nature was action and speech in a free political realm with ultimate ends in view— justice, virtue, freedom—then her interpretation of Marx's legacy as having undermined freedom, gloried labor (the process rather than the telos of life) appears not as a point within the conventional Marxist-nonMarxist ideological debate, but as a reflection of Jewish history. Her view of the desired direction for modern man, as offered in *The Human Condition,* points toward those virtues which the Jews were the first to be prevented from nurturing: free action and speech in the human community....

The social agenda of the French Revolution—its stress on equality and fraternity—led in Arendt's view, to social engineering as the priority of politics and race thinking as the basis of the nation-state. The stress on social and economic equality in politics highlighted the presumed social and economic privileges of the Jew and made him, despite legal political emancipation, a growing target of official and social hostility.[28]

Reading 17   **Defining Those "Unworthy" of Life**

If you tell a lie big enough and long enough, people will believe you.
— *Hitler*

Using Reading 17

In this section students read about the steps Hitler and the Nazi leaders took to carry out Hitler's social goals for the perfect Aryan superrace. Plans were made to affect the behavior of German citizens so that they would label certain groups as unworthy of life. In order to carry out the policies of dehumanization, plans were made to affect the social and psychological inhibitions toward protecting fellow human beings, while community life and national consciousness were destroyed.

Such policies were carried to the most terrible extremes by the Germans, yet they were not solely German policies. They were Fascist policies. Rumanian Fascists, for example, carried out murderous genocide policies against the Jews. Bulgarian Fascists attempted to eradicate Greek culture in eastern Macedonia, and strove to resettle at Greek expense thousands of Bulgarians. On a lesser scale, Italians, Austrians, and Lithuanians committed deeds which pale only by comparison with those of the Germans.[29]

These Nazi policies of racism effected the Gypsies, the people of Poland, the Belorussians, and all those labeled as subhuman. More detailed accounts of these victims of Nazi racism, imperialism, and war are described in the "Victims of Tyranny" chapter and accounts of the war within a war, the Holocaust of European Jews, are included in the chapter on the Holocaust. For more information, read *The Other Holocaust* by Bohdan Wytwycky.

Although there were, to be sure, differences in degree, circumstances and intent in the suffering imposed upon Jews, Gypsies, and Slavs, the effects of Nazi brutality have left an indelible mark on the collective memory of them all.

The struggle to critical distinctions about the universal and particular nature of this history begins here.

Reading 18

Racism: The Views of Hitler and the Nazi Party

The Nazi program of "cleansing" and "purifying" their nation of all "culture-bearing" and "culture-destroying" races went hand in hand with the restoration of German militarism. As the Nazis conquered groups of Poles, Russians, Slovaks, Yugoslavs, Greeks, Gypsies, and others, they were all labeled and categorized according to their status of "inferiority." The Nazi programs of relocation, deportation, starvation, torture, and killing affected millions of these people, but at times preferential treatment was given and the policy of "purification" was altered in favor of other priorities, such as the war effort. But the plan for total extermination of Jewish people was never deterred. The policy of extermination was pursued at all costs; it was in effect the ultimate irrationality.

Hitler's Views

Hitler described the Jewish people as the inferior semitic race. In *Mein Kampf*, Hitler attempted to outline his racial theory:

- Social progress results from a "struggle for survival in which the fittest are selected and the weak are exterminated." This selection process occurs within races as well as among races.
- "... intermixture of two races results in the degeneration of the higher race." "Racial mixtures" cause the decay of a civilization, but it is possible to "purify" a race because "hybrids tend to die off."
- Hitler divided all people into three types: a. the "culture-creating" or "Aryan race" (This race depends upon the "labor and services" of inferior races that have been subjugated by the Aryans.) "Dutifulness and idealism [honor] rather than intelligence are the Aryan's outstanding moral qualities." b. the "culture-bearing race" that can "borrow and adapt but cannot create." c. the "culture-destroying race"—all the people whom he considered inferior.[30]

According to Hitler, society was separated into three parts—the Leader, the elite, and the masses.

The Leader
- The Leader is the person "in whose name everything is done, who is said to be 'responsible' for all, but whose acts can nowhere be called in question."
- "He is the genius or the hero conceived as the man of pure race."
- The Leader is the "practical psychologist and an organizer—a psychologist in order that he may master the methods by which he can

gain the largest number of passive adherents, and organizer in order that he may build up a compact body of followers to consolidate his gains."

The Elite
- This ruling class provides the intelligence and vision needed to govern and lead the masses.
- This group will be formed out of the "struggle for power which is characteristic of nature."
- This group is the "racially fittest."

The Masses
- The masses are "capable neither of heroism nor intelligence."
- The masses are generally "inert." They "fear originality," "hate superiority, yet [their] highest desire is to find [their] leaders."
- The masses are fearful of change, and can be "swayed only by gross and violent feelings like hatred, fanaticisms, and hysteria."
- They must be presented with the "simplest arguments, repeated again and again." These arguments must be "fanatically one-sided and with unscrupulous disregard for truth, impartiality, or fair play."
- "In dangerous moments," Hitler writes, the masses become "rooted in the unity of blood" in order to preserve the survival of the nation.[31]

Nazi Party Views

The ideas of Volk, Aryan race, and antisemitism existed long before the policies of the Third Reich became a reality. But the Nazi racial theory ranked and labeled all human beings.

- Often *Volk* referred to the German people collectively as the source of civilization from whose spirit comes "mystically, art and literature, law and government, morals and religion all marked with the spiritual qualities of the national soul."[32]

The Nazis believed that a spirit of heroism and creativity distinguished the German people from all others but still they defined a hierarchy of "natural superiors and natural inferiors" among the German people.
- According to Wilhelm Marr, a race theorist of the 19th century, Aryans are those Teutonic or Nordic people such as the Germans, Austrians, Scandinavians, Dutch, English, and French.

The Nazis acknowledged that their racial philosophy was not logically developed. According to the Nazi theorist Alfred Rosenberg, "It is the construction of a mystical synthesis or activity of soul which cannot be explained by rational inferences or made comprehensible by exhibiting causes and effects . . . ."[33]

To racial science theorists who ascribed absolute superiority to the Aryan-Nordic race, "Teuton stood for good, true and beautiful. Non-German stood for bad, false and ugly." These views were not new. They had been passed down through legends, myths, and stories of ancient heroes. But the Nazis added their own brand of biology and anthropology to the Aryan myth:

[Theories and legends about racial hygiene] turned the Aryan myth into a reality only too easily adaptable to needs of a regime that made racial selection and military discipline overriding principles that legitimized every excess. This process was facilitated by the fact that these men distorting Darwin's theory of the survival of the fittest did not hesitate to

maintain that the struggle of the creative Teutonic-Aryan race boiled down to the struggle against the parasitic Semitic race....
The theory of the master race and of the "humanity of nature that exterminates the weak for the benefit of the strong," the belief that "in the old days the victor had the right to exterminate whole races and peoples," were thus Nazi ideas, rooted in German tradition, that were easily accepted by many Germans when Adolf Hitler attained power in 1933.... Thus the leaders of the Third Reich ... used the pretext of purifying the German race to initiate a process of planned reproduction on the one hand and extermination on the other hand.[34]

As Lucy Dawidowicz suggests, this was a period in German history where "conventional anti-Semitism" converged and was finally consumed by the "radical anti-Semitisms" of the Nazi program:

Generations of anti-Semitism had prepared the Germans to accept Hitler as their redeemer. Layer upon layer of anti-Semitism of all kinds—Christian church teachings about the Jews, Volkist anti-Semitism, doctrines of racial superiority, economic theories about the role of Jews in capitalism and commerce, and a half-century of political anti-Semitism—were joined with the solder of German nationalism, providing the structural foundation upon which Hitler and the National Socialist movement built.[35]

Using Reading 18

It is useful to define with the class the terms *Volk* and *Aryan*. Do not assume that students understand these terms as the Nazis transformed them or as they were energized by myths through time.

George Sabine sees the Nazi philosophy of the "heroic will" and creative capacity of Germans as an outgrowth of two characteristics often expressed in German history. As Sabine suggests, "It had been a cult of the folk or the people or the nation, and it had been a cult of the hero or the genius or the great man."

In Germany especially this cult of the *Volk* had been characteristic of literary romanticism.

The Nazis combined this idea of a hierarchy in society and the spirit of the German people with their pseudoscientific theory of a superior Aryan race. The meaning of the word *Aryan* had been debated long before Hitler formulated his notion of the superiority of the Aryan race. Max Muller wrote an answer to Wilhelm Marr's race theory:

It is but too easily forgotten that if we speak of Aryan and Semitic families, the ground of that classification is language and language only. There are Aryan and Semitic languages, but it is against all rules of logic to speak ... of an Aryan race, of Aryan blood, or Aryan skills, and to attempt ethnological classification on purely linguistic ground.[36]

Hitler and the Nazis were not concerned with rules of logic, for, as George Sabine states, "Purity of blood speaks louder than reason or fact."

Reading 19 **Traditions of Antisemitism and Racism in the United States in the 1920s and 1930s**

It is important to note that antisemitism was a cultural phenomenon not unique only to Europe in the 20s. Between 1920 and 1922, Henry Ford published a weekly magazine, *The Dearborn Independent*, and in a series of very antisemitic articles, the idea of a Jewish conspiracy was defined—his description was not unlike the analysis of social and economic ills given in *Mein Kampf*. Ford's biographers characterized this series, saying: "Its general thesis was that the international Jew, a secret Leadership of the race, was bent on disrupting all Gentile life by war, revolt, and disorder, and thus finally gaining world control of politics, commerce and finance." The editors of the *Dearborn Independent* explained their feelings about Jews by making distinctions between the Jewish people and the Jewish idea. We are reminded that ". . . one need not condemn 'the whole Jewish people' to qualify as an anti-Semite."[37]

The Jewish question is not in the number of Jews who here reside, not in the American jealousy of the Jews' success, certainly not in any objection to the Jews' entirely unobjectionable mosaic religion; it is something else, and that something else is the fact of Jewish influence on the life of the country where Jews dwell . . . . It is not the Jewish people, but the Jewish idea, and the people only as vehicles of the idea, that is the point at issue.[38]

When antisemitism became a race theory in the 19th and 20th century, it moved from a prejudice to a doctrine that pretended to explain movements of world history. Houston Stewart Chamberlain of Britain was instrumental at the turn of the century in propagating the new antisemitism that described the Jew as trying to acquire the Kingdom of God on Earth by conquering, not by working directly for it. Ezra Pound was influenced by Chamberlain's idea. When Pound described the entrepreneur or industrialist (Ford was his friend) and the financier as the nonworking ones who "take in credit from the public" or hatch plots to "worm" money from others, then he is articulating an antisemitic sentiment. "Although Pound pointed out in many cases that not all those responsible for financial trickery are Jews, the anti-Semitic style predominates as those non-Jews become 'non-Jewish kikes.' "

The following statement made by Ezra Pound on a radio broadcast for Mussolini expresses his antisemitic doctrine:

Don't start a pogrom. That is, not an old-style killing of small Jews. That system is no good whatever. Of course, if some man had a stroke of genius, and could start a pogrom at the top . . . there might be something to say for it. But on the whole, legal measures are preferable. The 60 kikes who started this war might be sent to St. Helena as a measure of world-prophylaxis, and some hyper-kikes or non-Jewish kikes along with them.[39]

Race theory, too, has a long history in the United States. A study of the literature about black people in the United States before the Civil War is full of racial theories not unlike the 1950s document that follows. In 1954 in the United States of America, a book was written by Tom P. Brady, later a justice of the Mississippi Supreme Court, titled *Black Monday*. The book claimed to document the basic inferiority of the Negro, the necessity of segregation, the historical reasons for the Court's decision, and the dire consequences that could follow court-ordered integration.

Why was it that the negro was unable and failed to evolve and develop? It is obvious that many rationalizations and explanations will be offered by minority group leaders and educators, but the fact remained that he did not evolve simply because of his inherent limitations. Water does not rise above its source, and the negro could not by his inherent qualities rise above his environment as had the other races. His inheritance was wanting. The potential did not exist. This is neither right nor wrong; it is simply stubborn biological fact.[40]

Using Reading 19

Students might speculate on what common themes can be found in the ethnic and racial theories presented in the readings. Also, students might think about what motivates the writers and the believers.

1. How different is this quotation and what it advocates from the quotations of European antisemitics?
2. The Nazis advocated a system of Judenrein in which cities and villages would be free of Jewish people. Look up the word "prophylaxis" to see if it relates to the German word *Judenrein*.
3. Does Mr. Pound argue that the pogrom is immoral or that it is ineffective? Are the words harmful?
4. To whom would racist and antisemitic arguments appeal in the United States?

The divisions in South Africa along lines of race were defined in the 1950 Population Registration Act; Every individual was to be one of four racial groups, "coloured," "Bantu," "White," and "Asian."[41]

Racism existed in South Africa from the time of its settlement by Europeans, but it operated in a sporadic and ill-defined manner until 1948 when the concept of apartheid was elevated to an ideology, a philosophy, and a systematic if inherently inconsistent governmental policy. The term, coined in 1929, literally means "separation" and is euphemistically called "parallel development."*

The following excerpt from the Epilogue of *The Other Holocaust* is relevant here:

Dehumanization may appear to be at the extreme end of a scale which also includes prejudice and racism. Though there is some insight here, this appearance is dangerously misleading. For prejudice and racism are in fact the psychological cornerstones of dehumanization. . . .

One of the effects of prejudice directed at whole categories of people is that it robs these people of their humanity. Made stereotypes of evil, stupidity and social disease, the victims are forced to travel the first leg of the journey to subhuman status. Made a depository of inferior or socially pathological traits, they receive a rude shove down the slippery slope to total dehumanization.

It is important to emphasize that prejudice and racism help to make mass brutalization possible, for it is easy — under normal historical circumstances — to acquire a false sense of security. The possibility of mass atrocities appears to be so remote that we are unlikely to pay serious attention to the budding of poisonous attitudes. However, given a sudden and traumatic shift in social conditions, dehumanization can easily develop its own deadly momentum if the ground for it is fertile.[42]

---

*The information about South Africa was provided in the playbill for the production *A Lesson from Aloes* by Athol Fugard presented at the Mark Taper Forum in Los Angeles, California, August 1981.

Reading 20 **Racial Policies and Nazi Bureaucracy**

In the following reading from *Education for Death,* Gregor Ziemer describes his visits to Nazi institutions: prenatal Nazi clinics, sterilization hospitals, schools for infants, schools for the feeble-minded, schools and institutions for boys and girls of all ages, including colleges and universities where the policies of Nazi race theory were being carried out.

One official explained to Mr. Ziemer, "there would be little use in driving out the impure Jews if Germany did not make a scientific effort to prevent undesirables from being born. Hitler wanted a super-race; this could only result from mating healthy individuals.... But soon there will be no puny, feeble-minded diseased children in Germany! The undesirables, the feeble-minded, those afflicted with incurable diseases, even the antagonistic in spirit would not have any more children." That was the wish of the Fuehrer, and Young Germany carried out his decrees.

The Nazi guide showed Mr. Ziemer the city hospital for women where women were being sterilized. He was informed "they were the mentally sick, women with low resistance, women who had proved through other births that their off-springs were not strong. They were women suffering from defects . . . some were sterilized because they were political enemies of the State."

"We are even eradicating color-blindness in the Third Reich.... We must not have soldiers who are color-blind. It is transmitted only by women."

"Who decides that the women are to be sterilized?" I asked.

"We have courts. It is all done very legally, rest assured. We have law and order."[43]

Lucy Dawidowicz also documents the killing of children and later adults who were diagnosed as "mentally deficient and physically deformed." Case reports were first collected from various health institutions and medical departments. Experts on the Reich Committee for Scientific Research of Hereditary and Severe Constitutional Diseases then reviewed each case and decided if "euthanasia" was necessary. This "euthanasia" program operated from about 1939 until 1944, and approximately 5,000 children were killed.

"Medical" murder was also carried out against adults. This program was camouflaged by the title T-4 and consisted of a network of various nursing homes, asylums, transportation organizations, "observation institutions," and "euthanasia" centers. Unlike the individual injections given to the children, carbon monoxide was generally used to kill groups of adult patients. Public awareness and finally public pressure forced Hitler to "stall" this "euthanasia" program in August 1941. By that time between 80,000 and 100,000 people had fallen victim to the T-4 program.[44]

The following bureaucracies were set up to implement "racial purity."[45]

• The Lebensborn — The aim of these institutions was the breeding of a Nordic super-race with the aid of men and women carefully selected in accordance with the racial principles of the Third Reich; they were established by Himmler. One of the activities was to set up special maternity homes to turn out Nordics. ". . . all over Europe the Germans had kidnapped thousands of 'racially valuable' children from their families to Germanize them. That was one of the ways of helping the

The poster art during the Nazi era reflected the racial policies of the Reich.

super-race to be fruitful and multiply...." After Himmler was appointed Reichsfuehrer SS, the whole nation would be subjected to the principles of selection for the authentic Teuton. Hans Gunther, official party theorist, gave the following specifications of the authentic Teuton: "tall, long head, narrow face, well-defined chin, narrow nose with very high root, soft fair (golden-blond) hair, receding light (blue or grey) eyes, pink white skin color."
• Racial science doctors—"These doctors screened volunteers for genuine descendents of the Indo-European tribes that had emigrated from Jutland (Denmark) and been settled in Germany since the third century B.C. These were to be the stock from which the new Teutonic race was to be bred and the SS to be recruited."
• Offices for Race and Settlement, and Race Examiners were created.
• SS—In order to join the SS, initially, one had to certify that he was of Aryan origin dating back to 1750, have perfect movement and physique and have "no filled teeth." The Reichsfuehrer or "the chiefs of the race offices inspected photographs of every applicant to make sure his face bore no sign of taint, such as 'orientally' prominent cheekbones, 'mongolian slit eyes, dark curly black hair, legs too short in relation to

the body, a body too long in relation to the arms, a bespectacled Jewish intellectual look.'" Himmler had decided that man was no longer to be descended from the ape, but from the SS.

Ministries of the Reich tried to tone down Himmler's Nordic ardor. In view of the predominance of the dark over the fair, and of the short over the tall, among the German population at large, memoranda were from time to time circulated asking for less public emphasis to be laid on Nordic superiority in relation to the rest of the population.

Using Reading 20

Often students want to believe that the Holocaust happened because no one knew about it or only Hitler was responsible. But behind these bureaucracies were people making choices.

Reading 21

Time Line of Racial Policies Toward the Jews

When Hitler became the leader of Germany in 1933 he immediately began to carry out his policy of discrimination toward people he regarded as inferior and troublesome. Total discrimination toward Jewish people was basic to his racial policy. In 1938 there were a half million Jewish people in Germany who made up less than one percent of the population.

1933
In April, by order of the Reich government, civil servants who were not of Aryan descent were to be retired. If they were honorary officials, they were to be dismissed from official status.[46] A general boycott of all Jewish-owned businesses was ordered and Jews were dismissed from civil service (bureaucracy) jobs and excluded from journalism, radio, farming, teaching, the theater, and films.[47]

The first concentration camps at Dachau and Orainenburg were set up in the spring of 1933. In May books written by Jews and others considered opponents of the Reich were burned. By the end of the year over 37,000 Jews had left Germany.

1934
Jewish people were dismissed from the army. In practice Jewish people were excluded from the stock exchanges, law, medicine, and business. Legal discrimination did not come until 1938.

1935
In the summer of 1935 *Juden Verboten* (No Jews) signs were found more frequently outside towns, villages, restaurants, and stores. These signs were removed for the Olympic Games in the summer of 1936. In September the Nuremberg Laws were passed by the Nazi government "for the protection of German blood and honor." Marriages between Jews and German citizens were forbidden, as were extramarital relations between Jews and Germans. Jews could not employ German servants under forty-five in their households. They were forbidden to raise the national flag, the swastika. They were permitted to raise the racial flag. Violations of the articles about marriage, sexual relations, and the employment of servants were punishable by imprisonment at hard labor. Raising the wrong flag was punishable by "simple imprisonment."

[*The Nuremberg Laws*] *took away the citizenship of Jews born in Germany and turned them into "subjects." A citizen of a country has status, he belongs to the country. But a subject has no rights and is not a particularly welcome person. Certainly a subject has much less value than does a citizen. That was exactly the feeling Hitler wanted the Germans to have about the Jews—that Jews were untermenschen (subhumans). . . .*

Jewish businesses were taken away from their owners by the Nazis and placed in the hands of German "trustees." These included huge department stores and little family shops. If people could not practice their professions or work in stores or own businesses, they could not earn a living.

In addition, signs saying "Jews Not Admitted" were placed on the doors of stores, theaters, parks, and hotels. Jews were not permitted to even walk or ride on certain streets. The name Israel was added to the identity card of each Jewish male and the name Sarah was added to that of each Jewish female. Jewish children were no longer permitted to go to public schools.[48]

The Nuremberg Laws defined not only the status of Jews, but part-Jews, for example, a "Mischling, second degree," was a person with a Jewish grandparent.

In November 26,000 Jewish people were arrested and sent to concentration camps and Jewish children were expelled from German schools.

1939

All Jewish people were ordered to hand in their radio sets, and other laws forbade Jews to leave their homes except for a few hours a day. Jews were forced to deposit all their money in banks. Then laws were enforced that forbade them to take the money out. The money was confiscated by the Nazis. Jews were forced to turn over their radios to Nazi authorities. Telephones were taken away from them. Gradually, everything but the clothes on their backs was taken from them.[49]

By spring of 1939 about 250,000 Jewish people had left Germany, leaving all their belongings. (Total Jewish population in Germany was about 600,000.)

Jewish people found it difficult and sometimes impossible to buy food because stores refused to sell to them. Pharmacies would not sell them medicine and hotels closed their doors. Signs appeared everywhere: "Jews Strictly Forbidden in This Town," "Jews Enter This Place at Their Own Risk," or "Jews Not Admitted." At a sharp bend in the road near the town of Ludwigshofen was a sign, "Drive Carefully! Sharp Curve! Jews 75 miles an hour!"[50]

1940

Clothing coupons to Jews were discontinued.

1941

In July all frontiers were closed to Jews so that they could no longer leave. In September all Jewish people over six years old were forced to wear a yellow star with the word "Jew" inscribed in the center. By autumn transports of Jews were sent to the Theresienstadt concentration camp. In October Jews needed permission slips to leave their houses or use public transportation. The government took (confiscated) possessions of Jews who had left Germany.

1942
Jews were forced to display "star of Judah" on their houses. Jews were not allowed to keep cats, dogs, birds, or other pets. Jews were not allowed to use public transportation. Jews were forced to give up "all available clothing." All well-known Jews were sent (deported) to the East. Jewish children were not allowed to attend any schools, even Jewish schools. Jews and other prisoners (Gypsies, Russians, etc.) were handed over to secret police (SS) for "destruction by work."

1943
Jews were arrested when they came to their places of work and Jews were not allowed to defend themselves in police courts.[51]

Using Reading 21

This time line describes the total policy of discrimination toward a selected minority. Before using this time line, the teacher may want to introduce some of the following statements by Milton Meltzer:

Another charge made by the Nazis was that the German government had been "riddled" with Jews. But in the 19 cabinets of the Weimar Republic, up to 1932, of a total of 237 ministers, only three had been Jews; four were described as "of Jewish descent." The last few governments preceding Hitler's had no Jewish ministers. In the federal states, the picture was the same....

The truth was the opposite of what Hitler said it was. Rather than an all-powerful threat, the Jews of Europe were the weakest enemy Hitler could have chosen. They had no land of their own, no government, no central authority, no allies, no political weight. They were divided in every possible way. In faith they ranged from devout believers to atheists or converts to Christianity; in income they were rich, poor, and in-between; in politics they included conservatives, liberals, and radicals. If they had been united and highly organized, the way the Nazis said they were, then millions more of them might have been saved....

The Nazis ignored how few Jews there were and instead charged that they dominated industry, government, and finance.

Not one of the most powerful German industries—Krupp, Klochner, Siemens, Stinnes, I.G. Farhen, Hugenberg, Vereinigte Stahlwerke, Hapag, Stumm, Nordlloyd—was in Jewish hands. And the international cartels which German industries were part of—oil, iron, potash, chemicals, shipping—Jews had no influence in them, either as owners or directors. Tick off the most powerful families in the country: not one was Jewish.[52]

Reading 22 **Living Space**

When Hitler came to power in 1933, he concentrated on consolidating his position within Germany. With the tools of totalitarianism and terror he suppressed the political freedoms of the citizen and the institutions of the Weimar Republic. By 1936, he turned to foreign affairs and his plans for war.

His ideology envisaged war as the necessary strategy to destroy world Jewry and Bolshevism and, at the same time to seize Russian territory to provide the Lebensraum—living space—which, according to his world outlook, Germany required for its existence and deserved because of its racial superiority.[53]

The race policy instituted by Himmler demanded "living space" for the pure-blood Germans whose numbers would be increasing steadily because of the policies of breeding through racial rules and regulations, kidnappings of foreign children of Aryan specifications, and war. Resettling, expelling, and extermination, then, are directly related to the need for "living space."

With the attack on Poland in 1939, the Third Reich, armed with its propaganda and the obedience of the army, intertwined its policy of race and living space to produce the new fatherland—one people, one government, one leader—which would rule for 1,000 years. This war, though, took on dimensions previously unknown to the modern world; 35 million combatants and civilians were killed.

Our explanations are too simple. Hitler did not take more because no one stopped him from taking less, or because appeasement increases appetite. He took more because he had to have more to reach his implicit social goals.[54]

Hitler blamed Jews for the Treaty of Versailles, which took away German colonies and ships, and made Germany pay reparations and deliver coal to France and the low countries. He felt, because of Germany's population, that they had a right to land held in the east by Russia and others. Later this drive for land combined with the racial ideas and promised, in Hitler's mind, the answer to the survival of the Aryan race. He wrote in Mein Kampf that war was inevitable. "War is life. War is the origin of all things." It was in Mein Kampf that Hitler first expounded his theory of Lebensraum:

The foreign policy of the Volkist state must safeguard the existence on this planet of the race embodied in the state, by creating a healthy, viable natural relation between the nation's population and growth on the one hand and the quantity and quality of its soil on the other.

Hitler believed that Germany was entitled to more land, not only because its people would have "the courage to take possession of it, the strength to preserve it, and the industry to put it to the plough," but because Germany was the "mother of life," not just "some little nigger nation or other." Furthermore, according to Lucy Dawidowicz, Germany's leaders were justified in shedding even German blood to attain that goal:

. . . We National Socialists must hold unflinchingly to our aim in foreign policy, namely, to secure for the German people the land and soil to which they are entitled on this earth. And this action is the only one which, before God and our German posterity, would make any sacrifice of blood seem justified. . . . The soil on which someday German generations of peasants can beget powerful sons will sanction the investment of the sons of today, and will someday acquit the responsible statemen of blood-guilt and sacrifice of the people, even if they are persecuted by their contemporaries.[55]

Initially the Lebensraum plan envisioned that the population of the Eastern European countries would become slave to the new German colonists. However, because of labor shortages many of those labeled "undesirables" from the East were deported into Germany to work.

Polish workers, men and women, in Germany were made to wear a label "P." These workers were to be isolated. "No German may say he knows a decent Pole. There are no decent Poles, just as there are no decent Jews."[56]

Originally the workers of the Ukraine were duped into volunteering to go to the Reich by ads and promises, but almost immediately the pretense was dropped and millions of Eastern Europeans were forced under terror and penalty of death to obey the deportation orders. The workers from the eastern occupied areas called Ostarbeiter were victims to both the Nazi racist policy and policy for living space.

Using Reading 22

The idea of living space, mass hostages, and mass deportations has not been exclusively German. These ideas have been the basis of government policy for many countries throughout history. They were part of German foreign policy prior to the outbreak of World War I.

Before World War I began, Baron von Wangenheim, the German ambassador to Turkey, stated, "There are only three great countries.... Germany, England, and the United States. We should get together; then we could rule the world."[57] Wangenheim believed that Germany would become the "great merchant nation." This plan would involve creating coaling stations "every where" in the world; building the Berlin to Baghdad railroad in order to gain economic advantages in the Middle East; and acquiring control and privileges throughout South America and Africa.[58] The policy of holding hostages on a large scale, closely related to the German designs in World War I, is expressed in the following excerpts from Henry Morgenthau's memoirs.

If England attempted to starve Germany, said Wangenheim, Germany's response would be a simple one: she would starve France. At that time, we must remember, Germany expected to have Paris within a week, and she believed that this would ultimately give her control of the whole country....[59]

Any one who has read even cursorily the literature of Pan-Germania is familiar with the peculiar method which German publicists have advocated for dealing with populations that stand in Germany's way. That is by deportation. The violent shifting of whole peoples from one part of Europe to another, as though they were so many herds of cattle, has for years been part of the Kaiser's plans for German expansion. This is the treatment which, since the war began, she has applied to Belgium, to Poland, to Serbia; its most hideous manifestation, as I shall show, has been to Armenia. Acting under Germany's prompting, Turkey now began to apply this principle of deportation to her Greek subjects in Asia Minor.[60]

The following are vocabulary words related to a study of Lebensraum and racism in Nazi policies.

Drang nach Osten (push to the east) — the slogan used to represent Germany's expansionist ambitions toward Eastern Europe.

Lebensraum (living space) — the concept used to express the rationale for Nazi imperialism; i.e., Lebensraum was the object of Drang nach Osten.

Ostarbeiter (eastern workers) — the name applied to the slave laborers taken from the Ukraine, Belorussia, and Russia.

Untermensch (subhuman) — name applied by the Nazis to virtually all of

the undesirable peoples at one time or another, but most often used in reference to the Slavs living in the Soviet Union.
Volksdeutsche (ethnic Germans living outside of Germany proper or Austria).

Reading 23

Lost Territories and New Soil

Hitler believed that "living space" for Germany would come from "lost territories and new soil." The "lost territories" were the lands that would soon become part of Greater Germany—Austria and western Czechoslovakia—and which would have to be won back by war, "back to the bosom of a common Reich, not by flaming protests, but by a mighty sword."

The "new soil" that would give Germany its Lebensraum could be "only in the East." Hitler spelled it out in *Mein Kampf:* "If we spoke of soil in Europe today, we can primarily have in mind only Russia and her vassal border states."[61] Germany would make a historical claim for Russia because of early colonies and because, according to Alfred Rosenberg, a leading Nazi ideologist, Jews controlled Russia.

Hitler's plans for the Third Reich included conquering new land for Germany in Eastern Europe up to the Ural Mountains and deep into Russia and repopulating the territory with racially superior "Aryans." Hitler wanted an empire that would rival the United States or China in size and population. Unlike England with its colonies scattered around the world, Hitler's new Germany would be a huge land power that would rule all Europe from the Atlantic to Asia.

After the early victories of the war, Hitler made northern France, Holland, Belgium, and the Scandinavian countries provinces of Germany, politically and economically dependent on Germany. In the east, Hitler immediately annexed Austria, Czechoslovakia, and western Poland. Further east, in a band running south through Latvia, Estonia, and Lithuania to the Ukraine of Russia, the Nazis began a program of eliminating the local population to prepare the land for large-scale German colonization. The area of Russia beyond Moscow to the Ural Mountains was intended as an area for future colonization for the 1000-year Reich.

In Russia the most terrible extremes of inhumanity became matters of mundane social policy. When detected, Communist officials and party members, as well as Jews, were shot out of hand—often enough by the army. Deliberate starvation policies were carried out. Eventually, the population was to be lowered by tens of millions, and the bulk of the miserable survivors were to be pushed hundreds of miles beyond the Urals. Not even a Nazi Russia could be allowed to exist. As Erich Koch, the prime executor of this program put it, "If I find a Ukranian worthy of sitting at the same table with me, I must have him shot." Even beyond the Urals, the displaced Russians were to be subject to terrible SS punitive raids, designed to destroy by terror and force any seeds of potential community spirit or evidence of its practice. These raids would also, it was hoped, maintain the biological purity of the SS itself through selection by battle. Goering, Frank, Koch, and Hitler agreed: 20 or 30 million must die by whatever means during the first two years of German occupation. Hitler ordered Leningrad wiped off the map with Moscow and Stalingrad to follow.

There was never again to be a Russian culture. "They shall do no brain work," Hitler insisted, "or else we shall rear thereby our most determined enemy. . . ." The army played an important role in wiping out whole villages and towns where partisan activity was suspected. Unarmed peasants and women and children were simply shot down on such pacification raids. The military and the SS totally destroyed literally thousands of towns, villages, and cities together with their populations.[62]

Using Reading 23

The Reich came to power in Germany in answer to their complex internal problems of the 1920s and 1930s. And the identification of the enemies from within and from without, combined with racism and antisemitism, helped to consolidate power among the citizens of Germany and in the collaborating peoples of the occupied nation.

In the following statement by the Nazi ruler of Russia, on reads the result of the policies of racism, war, and living space.

We are the master race. We must remember that the lowliest German worker is racially and biologically a thousand times more valuable than the population here."[63]

Reading 24

Hitler Combines the Policies of Lebensraum, Racism, and War Against the Jews and Russia

In Germany, before the outbreak of the war, the non-Aryan most exposed was the Jew. Jews were denied their citizenship, stripped of their jobs, and their funds; their properties were confiscated and used in the initial preparations for war. Those German Jews who did not or could not escape or pay randsom before 1938 were isolated, resettled, concentrated, used as free labor, used for Reich propaganda and were finally exterminated by a totalitarian bureaucracy looking for solution to its Jewish problem. In the war antisemitism became translated into a policy of race-murder.

According to Lucy Dawidowicz, the war for living space was closely associated in Hitler's mind with the war against the Jews.

War, the Jews, and racial utopia were all interrelated in Hitler's mind. In 1935 he referred to war as a cover for planned murder, when he told Gerhardt Wagner, the NSDAP's top medical officer, that if war came, he would pick up and carry out this question of euthanasia, for then such a program could be put into effect more smoothly and readily and in the general upheaval public opposition would be less likely.

Often in discussing foreign-policy matters, Hitler shuttled back and forth between a real world of nations and armies and a phantasmagoric universe ruled by the Jews.[64]

Using Reading 24

Hitler believed that the real enemy to Germany was Bolshevism and that a war against Russia would be a war also against Jewish leadership, and would ultimately provide Germany with Lebensraum.

Hitler believed he was in a "holy war" against Jewish Bolshevism. Hitler's fanaticism is also described by Lucy Dawidowicz in another source:

The widespread acceptance by the German people of antisemitism as a common political dogma paved the way for Hitler's rise to power. Without Adolf Hitler, however, the Final Solution would not have been planned and would not have been carried to its irrevocable end. The idea of destroying the Jews had inhabited the deranged minds of antisemites long before Hitler, but only Hitler turned the fantasy into reality. Only Hitler achieved the political power, commanded the economic and technological resources, and maintained the military advantage to carry out that destruction. All his life he was obsessed by the thought of a holy war against the Jews, whom he saw as the Host of the Devil and as the Children of Darkness. He never swerved from his single-minded dedication to the goal of their destruction.

The history of the German war in Russia is a history of atrocity. According to Lucy Dawidowicz,

One cannot begin to understand contemporary Soviet policy, economic and foreign, without taking into account the effect the war had on its people. Russia suffered the loss of almost one-quarter of her population, and the destruction of her great cities and towns, to defeat Hitler's German Army.[65]

Reading 25 Planning Genocide

Based on the policies of racism, Lebensraum, and totalitarianism, the bureaucrats made plans to take lives. Hitler told the Reichstag, in his "peace plan" speech of October 6, one of the six German cardinal aims in the Eastern area was that all minority problems should be solved and the living space organized according to nationalities. An experiment would therefore be made in regulating and organizing the Jewish problem in Poland.

Hitler as the Reich Commissioner for the Strengthening of German Folkdom . . . was to bring back to the Reich all racial Germans living under foreign governments, to eliminate all alien influence in Reich territory, and to create new German colonies in occupied territory by the resettlement of racial Germans or Volksdeutsche returning from abroad.

In his orders to invade Poland, Hitler made clear to his generals that they should show no mercy in Eastern Europe.

Alfred Rosenberg designed a plan for conquering the East based on "historical and racial conditions . . . which would Germanize the racially assimilable Balts and banish the undesirable elements." In Latvia and Estonia, "banishment on a large scale will have to be envisaged. Those driven out would be replaced by Germans, preferably war veterans."

The job of feeding the German people stood at the top of the list of Germany's claims on the East. The Southern (Russian) territories would have to serve . . . for the feeding of the German people.

By May 23, 1941, surplus food from Russia's black- earth belt in the South was not to be diverted to the people in the industrial areas, where, in any case, the industries would be destroyed. The workers and their families in these regions would simply be left to starve—or, if they could, emigrate to Siberia. Russia's great food production must go to Germans.

There was no doubt, a secret memorandum of the conference

declared, "that as a result, many millions of persons will be starved to death if we take out of the country the things necessary for us."

These plans were not merely wild and evil fantasies of distorted minds and souls of men such as Hitler, Goering, Himmler and Rosenberg. For weeks and months, it is evident from the records, hundreds of German officials toiled away at their desks in the cheerful light of the warm spring days, adding up figures and composing memoranda which coldly calculated the massacre of millions. By starvation, in this case, Heinrich Himmler, the mild-faced ex-chicken farmer, also sat at his desk at SS headquarters in Berlin those days, gazing through his pince-nez at plans for the massacre of other millions in a quicker and more violent way." [66]

Using Reading 25

The above quotations relate to the particularly brutal and violent ways in which the concept of Lebensraum became a reality as Hitler moved to conquer the East. This German imperialism mixed with race theory made the population of Eastern Europe victim to atrocities that included starvation, mass shooting, gas vans, and military brutality. In order to put down any resistance to German control in the East, special army orders and death squads searched out all Jews, Russian officials, Communist party members, and others seen as a threat to the Third Reich.

Citations

Chapter 5

[1] Reprinted from *They Thought They Were Free* by Milton Mayer by permission of The University of Chicago Press. Copyright © 1955 by the University of Chicago Press. p.167.

[2] Published by permission of Transaction, Inc. from *Taking Lives: Genocide and State Power* by Irving Louis Horowitz. Copyright © 1980 by Transaction Books. p. 27.

[3] Ilse Koehn, *Mischling, Second Degree: My Childhood in Nazi Germany* (Greenwillow Books, 1977).

[4] Horowitz, *Taking Lives*, p. 24.

[5] Ibid.

[6] Mayer, *They Thought They Were Free*, pp. 166-172.

[7] Ibid., pp. 177-181.

[8] Lucy S. Dawidowicz, *A Holocaust Reader* (Behrman House, 1976) pp. 38-53; and William L. Shirer, *The Rise and Fall of the Third Reich: A History of Nazi Germany* (Simon and Schuster, 1960) pp. 231-276.

[9] "Das Reich No. 4, 1933," *Time Magazine*, translated by Elizabeth Dopazo.

[10] Shirer, *The Rise and Fall of the Third Reich*, p. 867.

[11] Ibid.

[12] Peter H. Merkl, *The Making of a Storm Trooper* copyright © 1980 by Princeton University Press. Reprinted by permission of Princeton University Press, p. 95.

[13] Ibid., p. 26.

[14] Ibid., p. 30.

[15] Ibid., p. 86.

[16] Ibid., p. 100.

[17] Ibid., p. 231.

[18] Ibid., p. 165.

[19] Ibid., p. 308.

[20] Ibid., p. 183.

[21] Selection from *The Holocaust: A History of Courage and Resistance*, copyright 1973 by Bea Stadtler, revised 1974; Published by Behrman House, Inc., New York, used with permission.

[22] Source unknown.

[23] Erika Mann, *School for Barbarians* (Modern Age, 1938) (out of print).

[24] From draft of speech: "Artists Versus Hitler; the Social Responsibility of the Artist in Germany." This paper was presented at the International Conference on the Lessons of the Holocaust; Philadelphia, October 1978. Footnotes regarding related materials are included in Sybil Milton's original speech.

[25] From *Hitler: Great Lives Observed,* edited by George H. Stein. © 1968 by Prentice-Hall, Inc. Published by Prentice-Hall, Inc., Englewood Cliffs, NJ 07632, p. 105.

[26] "Izzy on Izzy," *New York Times Magazine,* January 22, 1978.

[27] Leon Botstein, "Hannah Arendt: The Jewish Question," *New Republic,* October 21, 1978, p. 34. Reprinted by permission of *The New Republic,* copyright 1978, The New Republic, Inc.

[28] Ibid.

[29] J. Weiss, *The Fascist Tradition* (Harper and Row, 1967) p. 125.

[30] George H. Sabine, *A History of Political Theory* (New York: Holt, Rinehart and Winston, 1973) p. 906.

[31] Ibid., pp. 903-904.

[32] Ibid., p. 889.

[33] Ibid., p. 896.

[34] From *Of Pure Blood* by Marc Hillel and Clarissa Henry. Copyright © 1976 by Marc Hillel and Clarissa Henry. Used by permission of McGraw-Hill Book Company, p. 23.

[35] From *The War Against the Jews* by Lucy S. Dawidowicz. Copyright © 1975 by Lucy Dawidowicz. Reprinted by permission of Holt, Rinehart and Winston, Publishers. p. 220.

[36] Paraphrased from Milton Meltzer, *Never to Forget: The Jews of the Holocaust* (New York: Harper & Row, 1976) p. 7.

[37] Charles Brezin, "Poetry and Politics in Ezra Pound," *Partisan Review,* 1981, p. 264.

[38] Ibid.

[39] Ibid., p. 265.

[40] Florence Mars, "The Roots of War," *Witness in Philadelphia* (Louisiana State University Press, 1977) p. 54.

[41] Athol Fugard, *A Lesson from Aloes* (Random House, 1981).

[42] Bohdan Wytwycky, *The Other Holocaust: Many Circles of Hell,* (The Novak Report, 918 F Street, N.W. Washington, D.C. 20004, 1980) pp. 82-83.

[43] Gregor Ziemer, *Education for Death: The Making of the Nazi* (Oxford University Press, 1941). Reprinted by permission of the author.

[44] Dawidowicz, *The War Against the Jews,* pp. 177-179.

[45] Hillel and Henry, *Of Pure Blood,* pp. 24-26.

[46] *The Record: The Holocaust in History 1933-1945* (The Anti-Defamation League of B'nai B'rith, 1978) p.5.

[47] Shirer, *The Rise and Fall of the Third Reich,* pp. 233-234.

[48] Stadtler, *The Holocaust: A History of Courage and Resistance,* pp. 19-21.

[49] Shirer, *The Rise and Fall of the Third Reich,* pp. 233-234.

[50] Schools Council General Studies Project, *Anti-Semitism in Practice* (Longman Group Ltd. Resources Unit, 1972) pp. 1-2.

[51] Zeimer, *Education for Death.*

[52] From *Never to Forget: The Jews of the Holocaust* by Milton Meltzer. Copyright © 1976 by Milton Meltzer. Reprinted by permission of Harper & Row, Publishers, Inc., p. 32, 31.

[53] Dawidowicz, *The War Against the Jews.*

[54] Weiss, *The Fascist Tradition,* p. 120.

[55] Dawidowicz, *The War Against the Jews,* p. 120.

[56] Wytwycky, *The Other Holocaust,* p. 77.

[57] Henry Morgenthau, *Ambassador Morgenthau's Story* (New Age Publishers, 1919) p. 90.

[58] Ibid., p. 92.

[59] Ibid., p. 93.

[60] Ibid., p. 49.

[61] Dawidowicz, *The War Against the Jews,* pp. 121-122.

[62] Weiss, *The Fascist Tradition,* pp. 125-126.

[63] Ibid., p. 127.

[64] Dawidowicz, *The War Against the Jews,* pp. 122-123.

[65] Massachusetts Teachers Association and WNAC-TV, "The Unknown War," *Study Guide.*

[66] Shirer, *The Rise and Fall of the Third Reich,* p. 834.

6

Preparing for Obedience

I felt—and feel—that it was not German Man that I had met, but man. He might under certain conditions, be I.
—Milton Mayer[1]

Overview

Obedience is one of the critical ingredients of a totalitarian society. Like other dictators, Hitler depended on obedience to implement his grand plan for a new order. Although a major portion of the readings in this chapter concentrate on the education of youth in Nazi Germany, the broader focus relates to questions of obedience, conformity, and responsibility. And even though this chapter documents the propaganda, training, and bureaucracy of the Nazi regime we are left with no simple explanation for the human behavior.

When students investigate the role of propaganda in translating the Nazi ideology to the elite and the leadership, and as they learn about the effect of the totalitarian policies upon the masses, they begin to think about how a nation moves toward carrying out policies of mass extermination.

When the ruling elite decides that their "continuation in power transcends all other economic and social values, at that point does the possibility, if not the necessity, for genocide increase qualitatively.... Genocide is always a conscious choice and policy. It is never just an accident of history or a necessity imposed by unseen economic growth requirements. Genocide is always and everywhere an essentially political decision.[2]

The Nazi leadership, then, used the tools of the modern state as much to silence opposition as they used them to create believers.

Some of the major choices for the average citizen in the 1920s and '30s included (1) joining the SA (in its early stages made up of radical paramilitary groups from the right and left, and only later, after the purge, more "disciplined" as the newly created SS), (2) obeying, conforming, or believing in the propaganda of the totalitarian machine, or (3) resisting and combating these influences.

Without strong democratic leadership and the cooperation and support of the major institutions, such as the Church, the chance to confront antisemitism and racism, and to educate the public to an understanding of the onslaught of change brought on by the Industrial Revolution, the organized and individual resistance to hate was small and ineffectual.

And as the state promoted its racist ideas by allying racism with cleanliness, honesty, family, and hard work, familiar virtues of the church and middle class, the masses chose to follow. Instead of seeing that all individuals and groups could be victim to racism, the masses chose not to cooperate to oppose the early policies of racism that later led to genocide. For some, according to Irving Horowitz, the very "momentousness of genocide as a state practice made it difficult to recognize."

In the early stages of the totalitarian consolidation of power, the state demanded that the people give up their belief in law and recognize instead a "higher law" of nature, divinity, or history. Later when the state policies toward taking lives in the Holocaust began, the legal protection for human life was not an issue for the Reich.

It is important to consider that some citizens, also in a fascist state, chose not to follow a path toward genocide. Between 1938 and 1943, the Italians representing many classes rejected the Fascist regime. When antisemitism became official state policy, a policy related in content and intent to the Nazi racist ideas, the Italian Fascists began to lose the masses. Irving Horowitz calls Fascist Italy an incarceration society with an absence of mass murder while Nazi Germany became a genocidal society.

Reading 1 Quotation and Reading

Thinking, an activity without space or time, paradoxically requires space and time. Of all the forms of political organization that do not permit freedom, only totalitarianism consciously seeks to crowd out the ability to think. Man cannot be silenced, he can only be crowded into not speaking.[3]

So much of the Nazi propaganda machine was aimed at suppressing thinking. The machine competed for control of the time and place where thinking happens. "The object of propaganda has little to do with truth," said Leni Riefenstahl, Hitler's filmmaker. "Its object is to make people lose their judgment." Propaganda must be addressed to the emotions and not to the intelligence, said Adolf Hitler. "It must concentrate on a few simple themes, presented in black and white." "Propaganda consists in attracting the crowd, and not in educating those who are already educated." Hitler's statement that whoever has the youth has the future is particularly relevant to a study about obedience.

Using Reading 1

Students should speculate on the meaning of these quotations.

Later in this chapter when today's students compare their education with that planned for the Hitler youth, they struggle to understand the reasoning of those who resisted and those who obeyed. These notions of conformity and obedience are powerful—so powerful, in fact, that most students describe thinking about obedience as their most important, and often frightening, memory of the curriculum.

Activity 2 Film: *The Hangman*

The following quotations by Pastor Martin Neimoeller and by Thomas Paine anticipate the content of the film *The Hangman*.

In Germany, the Nazis came for the Communists, and I didn't speak up because I wasn't a Communist. Then they came for the Jews, and I didn't speak up because I wasn't a Jew. Then they came for the trade unionists, and I didn't speak up because I wasn't a trade unionist. Then they came for the Catholics, and I didn't speak up because I was a Protestant. Then they came for me, and by that time there was no one left to speak for me.

Pastor Martin Niemoeller was a Lutheran minister who opposed Hitler and was thrown into Theresiendstadt, a Nazi concentration camp.

He that would make his own liberty secure, must guard even his enemy from oppression, for if he violates this duty, he establishes a precedent that will reach to himself.

Thomas Paine lived from 1739 to 1809 and wrote to influence the political thinking of the leaders of the American Revolution.

Using Activity 2

This film provides an effective way to introduce the themes of this chapter. This short animated film may be difficult to understand after only one viewing. Some students will be able to guess at the message of the film: "He who serves me best," said he, "shall earn the rope on the gallows-tree." Discuss the questions:
• What is happening in the town?
• How did the townspeople respond to the Hangman?
• What does the Hangman represent?
• Who was hung on the gallows?
• What do the contracts represent?
• Can you identify some of the symbols and the meanings they suggest?

For example, the gallows-tree takes root; the animated people become paper dolls; the shadow grows on the courthouse wall. The symbolism in the film provides for an effective lesson on metaphors and the technique of comparing unlike things.
• How does this film relate to what we are studying? Obedience—obligation—responses—group behavior—fear?

The Hangman *was to me strange. The "hidden message" of this is harder to find than any other movie or section we have seen so far. I understand, now, that instead of standing as a bystander all the time, I should voice my opinion before it is worthless.*
—an 8th grade student

I guess most people would be like the man who stood by and watched the townspeople being hung. I mean who would really have the guts to stand up and say "stop". . . especially if you got no support from the crowd. I don't think I could. . . . This is a good film. It really makes you think.
—an 8th grade student

Reading 3

"You Will Do as Directed"[4]

This is the story of a teacher, Ron Jones, who tried an "experiment" about obedience with his class. The results were frightening!

For years I had kept a strange secret. Two hundred students shared this secret with me. Yesterday I ran into one of them by chance, and for a moment it all rushed back.

Steve McDonald had been a student in my World History class. As he came running down the street shouting, "Mr. Jones! Mr. Jones!" I had to stop for a minute to remember: Who is this young man hugging me? Steve sensed my doubt and backed up, then smiled, and slowly raised a hand in a cupped position. My God! He's a member of the Third Wave. It's Steve—Steve McDonald. He sat in the second row—a sensitive and bright student, played guitar and enjoyed drama.

I unconsciously raised my hand in the same salute: two comrades meeting long after the war. "Mr. Jones, do you remember the Third Wave?" I sure do: one of the most frightening events I have ever experienced in the classroom.

We talked and laughed about our secret, the Third Wave, for the next few hours. Then it was time to part. Steve turned and gave the salute without a word. I returned the gesture.

The Third Wave. Well, at last it can be talked about. The nightmare must finally be waning, after three years. I think it was Steve who initiated it all with a question.

We were studying Nazi Germany, and in the middle of a lecture he asked: How could the German people claim ignorance of the slaughter of the Jews? How could railroad conductors, teachers, doctors, know nothing about concentration camps and human carnage? How could neighbors and even friends of a Jewish citizen say they weren't there when it happened? I didn't know the answer.

There were several months to go in the school year and we were already at World War II, so I decided to take a week and explore the issue.

Strength Through Discipline

On Monday I introduced my class to one of the key experiences of Nazi Germany—discipline. I talked about the beauty of discipline: how an athlete feels having worked hard and regularly to be successful at a sport; how a ballet dancer or painter perfects a movement, or a scientist pursues an idea. It's discipline, self-control, the power of the will, the tolerance of physical hardship for superior mental and physical ability. The ultimate triumph.

To demonstrate the power of discipline, I invited the class to try a new sitting posture. I described how proper posture assists concentration and strengthens the will. In fact, I commanded them to adopt this posture: feet flat on the floor, hand placed flat across the small of the back to force a straight alignment of the spine. "There. Can't you breathe more easily? Don't you feel better?"

We practiced this new position over and over. I walked up and down the aisles making small improvements. Proper sitting became the most important aspect of learning. I would allow the class to leave their desks, then call them abruptly back to sitting at attention. In speed drills, I concentrated on the feet being parallel and flat, ankles locked, knees bent at 90 degrees, hands flat and crossed against the back, spine straight, chin down, head forward. After repeated drilling, the class could move silently from outside the room to sitting at attention at their desks in five seconds.

It was strange how quickly the students took to this code of uniform behavior. I began to wonder just how far they could be pushed. Was this display of obedience a temporary game we were all playing, or was it something else? Was the desire for discipline and conformity a natural need, a social instinct we exercise subliminally inside a world of franchise restaurants and TV programming?

I decided to stretch the class's tolerance for regimented action. In the final 25 minutes I introduced some new rules: students must be sitting at attention before the late bell; all must carry pencils and paper for note taking; when asking or answering questions, students must stand at the side of their desks; the first words of what they say must always be "Mr. Jones." We practiced questions and answers to achieve promptness and respect. Eventually the intensity of the response became more important than the content. To accentuate this, I demanded answers of three words or less. Students were rewarded for effort, and for a crisp and attentive manner. Soon everyone began popping up with questions and answers, even formerly hesitant speakers. The entire class seemed more involved—listening more intently, speaking out more openly, offering greater support. There was even a marked improvement in the quality of answers.

As for my part, I had nothing but questions. Why hadn't I thought of this exercise before? Students were reciting facts and concepts more accurately, asking better questions and treating each other with more compassion. How could this be? Here I was creating an authoritarian environment and it was turning out to be highly productive. I began to ponder not just how far this class could be pushed but how much I would alter my belief in the open classroom and self-directed learning. Was my faith in Carl Rogers to shrivel away? Where was this experiment leading?

Strength Through Community

On Tuesday, the second day, I entered the classroom to find everyone sitting silently at attention. Some of their faces were relaxed with smiles that come from pleasing the teacher. But most of the students were looking straight ahead earnestly—neck muscles rigid, no sign of a smile or a thought. To release the tension I went to the board and wrote in big letters: STRENGTH THROUGH DISCIPLINE. Below this I wrote a second law: STRENGTH THROUGH COMMUNITY.

While the class sat in stern silence, I began to talk—lecture, sermonize—about the value of community. Inwardly I was debating whether to stop the experiment or continue. I hadn't foreseen such intensity or compliance. In fact, I was surprised to find my ideas on discipline acted out at all. I talked on and on, making up stories from experience as an athlete, coach and historian. It was easy. Community is that bond between individuals who work and struggle together. It's raising a barn with your neighbors, feeling that you are part of something beyond yourself—a team, a cause, *la raza*.

It was too late to go back. I now can appreciate why the astronomer returns relentlessly to the telescope. I was probing deeper into my own conceptions and into the motivations for group and individual action. There was much more to see and understand. Why did the students accept the authority I was imposing? Why didn't they question this martial behavior? When and how would this end?

I told the class that community-like discipline must be experienced to be understood. I had them chant in unison: "Strength Through Discipline. Strength Through Community." It was fun. They began to look at each other and sense the power of belonging; everyone was capable and equal. For the entire period we developed this simple activity.

What's more, I began to think of myself as part of the experiment, a willing subject of the group's momentum and identity. As the period was ending, and without forethought, I created a salute for class members only. To make it you brought your right hand up toward the right shoulder in a curled position. I called it the "Third Wave" salute because the hand resembled a wave about to top over; the beach lore has it that waves travel in series, the third wave being the last and largest. I made it a rule to salute all class members outside the classroom. When the bell sounded, with everyone sitting at attention, I slowly raised my arm and with a cupped hand saluted. It was a signal of recognition. Without command the entire group returned the salute.

Throughout the day, around the school, students from the class exchanged this greeting. I would be walking down the hall when suddenly three classmates would turn and flash a quick salute. In the library or in gym, they'd be seen giving this signal of recognition. The mystique of 30 individuals making this strange gesture soon called attention to the class and its exploration of the Nazi German personality. Many students outside the class asked if they could join.

Strength Through Action

On Wednesday I decided to issue membership cards to everyone who wanted to continue what I called "the experiment." Not a single student elected to leave the room. There were now 43 in the class; 13 had cut other classes to join us. While the students sat at attention, I gave them a card. I marked three of the cards with a red X and informed the recipients that they had a special assignment: to report any members not complying with class rules. I then explained how discipline and community were meaningless without action. I discussed the beauty of taking full responsibility, for believing so thoroughly in yourself and your community or family that you would do anything to preserve and protect them. I stressed how hard work and allegiance to each other would accelerate learning. I reminded students what it felt like to be in classes where competition caused pain and degradation, the feeling of never acting wholeheartedly, never supporting each other.

At this point, people began to volunteer testimonials: "Mr. Jones, for the first time I'm learning lots of things." "Mr. Jones, why don't you teach like this all the time?" I had been pushing information at them in an extremely controlled setting, and the fact that they liked it was shocking. It was equally disconcerting to realize that the complex, time-consuming homework on German life was being completed and even enlarged on by students. I began to think they might do anything I assigned, and I decided to find out.

To create the experience of direct action I gave each individual a specific assignment: "It is your task to design a Third Wave banner...to stop any student who is not a Third Wave member from entering this room...to memorize the name and address of every Third Wave member...to convince at least 20 children in the elementary school that our sitting posture is necessary for better learning." I also asked each student to give me the name and address of one reliable friend who might want to join the Third Wave. I announced that once recommended, new members would receive a card and must pledge obedience to our rules.

By this time the whole school was alive with rumor and curiosity. Our principal came into an afternoon faculty meeting and gave me the Third Wave salute. The librarian thanked me for the 30-foot banner on learning, which she placed above the library entrance. By the end of the day, over 200 students were admitted into the order. I felt alone and a little scared.

Most of my fear came from the incidence of tattletaling. Although I appointed only three students to report deviate behavior, about 20 came to me with reports of Allan's not saluting, or Georgene's criticizing our experiment. This meant that half the class now considered it their duty to observe and report on other members.

By the end of the third day I was exhausted; I'd lost the balance between role playing and directed behavior. Many of the students were completely absorbed in being Third Wave members. They demanded strict obedience and bullied those who took the experiment lightly. Others simply fell into step and assigned themselves roles. I particularly remember Robert, big for his age and an academic drudge, though he tried harder than anyone I know to be successful. Like so many kids in school who don't excel or cause trouble, Robert was invisible. The only reason I came to know him at all was that I usually found him eating lunch in my classroom, alone.

The Third Wave gave Robert a place. At last he was equal to everyone; he could take part. Wednesday afternoon I found him following me and asked what in the world he was doing. He smiled (I don't think I'd ever seen him smile) and announced: "Mr. Jones, I'm your bodyguard. I'm afraid something will happen to you. Can I do it, Mr. Jones, please?" Given that assurance and smile, I couldn't say no. For the rest of the day Robert remained at my side, opening and closing doors for me, smiling at and saluting other class members. In the faculty room he stood silently at attention while I gulped coffee. When accosted by another teacher for being in the teachers-room, he just smiled and informed the faculty members that he wasn't a student, he was a bodyguard.

Strength Through Pride

By Thursday I was ready to wind things up. Many students were over the line; the Third Wave was dominating their existence. I myself was acting instinctively as a dictator, however benevolent. I played the role more and more, and had trouble remembering its pedagogic origin and purpose. I wondered if this happens to many people. We get or take a role and then bend our lives to fit it. Soon the role is the only identity other people will accept. I worried about students doing things they would regret, and I worried about myself.

Once again I debated closing the experiment immediately or letting it go its own course. Both options were painful. If I stopped, a great number of students would be left hanging. They had committed themselves in front of their peers to radically new behavior patterns. If I suddenly jolted them back, I would face a deeply confused student body for the rest of the year. It would be especially demeaning for people like Robert to be suddenly thrust back and told it's just a game in front of bright students who had participated in a more deliberate, cautious way. I couldn't let the Roberts lose again.

On the other hand, things were already getting way out of control. Wednesday evening a father of one of my students had broken in and ransacked the room. He was a retired Air Force colonel who had spent time in a German prison camp. Upon hearing of our activities, he had simply gone berserk. I found him next morning propped up against the classroom door. He told me about his buddies killed in Germany. Holding on and shaking me, he pleaded brokenly that I understand and get him home. Later we spent hours talking about what he had felt and done, but at that moment I was more concerned with what was happening at school.

The Third Wave was affecting the faculty and other students and disrupting normal learning. Students were cutting class to participate, and the school counselors were beginning to question every student in the class. With my experiment threatening to explode, I decided to try an old basketball strategy; when you're playing against all odds, try the unexpected.

By now the class had swollen to over 80. A strange calm takes effect in a room full of people sitting at perfect attention. I talked ringingly about pride. "Pride is more than banners or salutes. Pride is something no one can take from you. Pride is knowing you are the best. It can't be destroyed." In the midst of this crescendo I abruptly lowered my voice to announce the real reason for the Third Wave. "The Third Wave isn't just an experiment or classroom activity. It's far more important. The Third Wave is a nationwide program to find students willing to fight for political change. That's right. What we've been doing has been practice for the real thing. Across the country teachers have been recruiting and training a youth brigade capable of demonstrating a better society through discipline, community, pride and action. If we can change the way school is run, we can change the way factories, universities and all other institutions are run. You are a selected group of young people chosen to help in this cause. If you will display what you have learned in the past four days, we can bring this nation a new sense of discipline, community, pride and action. Everything rests with you and your willingness to take a stand."

To show my seriousness I turned to three people who I knew had questioned the Third Wave, and demanded that they leave the room. I assigned four guards to escort them to the library and keep them from entering class on Friday. Then dramatically I announced a special noon rally on Friday—a rally for Third Wave members only.

It was a wild gamble. I just kept talking, afraid that if I stopped someone would laugh or ask a question and the grand scheme would dissolve. I explained how at noon Friday a national candidate for president would declare a Third Wave Youth Program. Simultaneously, over a thousand youth groups from every part of the country would stand up in support of the movement. I confided that the students in my class had been selected to represent their area, and I asked if they would make a good showing, because the press had been invited. There was no laughter, no murmur of resistance. Quite the contrary. Feverish excitement swept the room. "We can do it!" "Should we wear white shirts?" "Can we bring friends?"

"It's all set for tomorrow," I said. "Be in the auditorium ten minutes before noon. Be seated, ready to display the discipline, community and pride you have learned. Don't talk to anyone about this. This rally is for members only."

Strength Through Understanding

I spent most of Friday morning preparing the auditorium for the rally. At 11:30 students began to show up—at first a few scouting the way and then more. Row after row filled up in hushed silence. Third Wave banners hung like clouds over the assembly. At 12 sharp I sealed the room and placed guards at each door. Several friends of mine posing as reporters and photographers began to interact with the crowd, taking pictures and jotting down notes. A group photograph was taken. The room was crammed with over 200 students: athletes, social stars, student leaders, loners, kids that always left school early, bikers, the pseudo hip, a few representatives of the school's Dadaist clique. But they all looked like one force as they sat at attention, focused on the TV set at the front of the room. It was as if we were all witnesses to a birth; the tension and anticipation were hard to believe.

"Before turning on the national press conference, I want you to demonstrate the extent of our training." With that, I gave the salute, and automatically 200 arms stabbed a reply. I then pronounced the words "Strength Through Discipline," and the chorus replied. The photographers were still covering the ritual but by now no one noticed them. Again the room rocked with the guttural cry, "Strength Through Discipline!"

At 12:05, I turned off the lights and walked to the TV. The air in the room seemed to be drying up; it felt hard to breathe and even harder to talk. I switched the set on and stood next to it, facing the people. The machine came to life, producing a field of light. The only light in the room, it played against the faces of the crowd. Their eyes strained and pulled toward it, but the blank screen didn't change. The room stayed deadly still; there was a mental tug of war between the people and the television. Yet the white glow didn't snap into an image of a political candidate; it just hummed on. Still the viewers persisted — there must be a program coming on; where is it? This trance continued for what seemed like hours. It was 12:07 . . . Nothing . . . Anticipation turned to anxiety and then to frustration. Finally someone stood up and shouted: "There isn't any leader, is there?"

Everyone turned in shock, first to the desperate student and then back to the television. Their faces filled with disbelief. In the confusion of the moment I moved slowly toward the set and turned it off. Immediately I felt air rush back into the room; the room remained silent, but people were breathing again, bringing their arms from behind their chairs. Instead of a flood of questions, there was intense quietness. I began to speak.

"Listen closely; I have something important to tell you. . . . There is no leader! There is no such thing as a national youth movement called the Third Wave. You've been used, manipulated, shoved by your own desires to where you now find yourself. You're no better or worse than the German Nazis we have been studying.

"You thought you were the elect — better than those outside this room. You bargained your freedom for the comfort of discipline. You chose to accept the group's will over your own convictions. Oh, you think you were just going along for the fun, that you could extricate yourself at any moment. But where were you heading? How far would you have gone? Let me show you your furture."

With that I switched on a rear screen projector, which lit up on a white cloth behind the TV. Large numbers appeared in a countdown; then the roar of the Nuremberg rally blasted into vision. My heart was pounding. In ghostly images the Third Reich paraded into the room: discipline, super race, the big lie, arrogance, violence, terror. People being pushed into vans, the visual stench of death camps, faces without eyes. The trials, the plea of ignorance, "I was only doing my job." As abruptly as it started, the film froze on a single written frame: "Everyone must accept the blame. No one can claim that they didn't in some way take part."

In the dark the last footage flapped against the projector. I felt sick to my stomach. No one moved. As if awakening from a deep dream, the whole room took one last look back into their minds. Several minutes went by, then questions began to emerge. With the room still dark I admitted my sickness and remorse. Feeling myself shift from participant to the easier role of teacher, I began to decribe what had happened.

"In the past week we have all tasted what it was like to live and act in Nazi Germany. We learned what it felt like to create a disciplined social environment, pledge allegiance to that society, replace reason with rules. Yes, we would all have made good Nazis. We would have put on the uniform, turned our heads as friends and neighbors were cursed and then persecuted, pulled the locks shut, worked in the "defense" plants, burned ideas. We now know in a small way what it feels like to find a hero, to grab quick solutions, to control our destiny. We know the fear of being left out, the pleasure of doing something right and being rewarded. Perhaps we have seen what these actions can lead to.

"Over the past week we have seen that fascism is not just something those other people did. It's right here in this room, in our own personal habits and way of life. Scratch the surface and it appears; we carry it like a disease: the belief that human beings are basically evil and therefore demand a strong leader and discipline to preserve social order.

"This is the crucial lesson, which started our plunge into Nazi life. Do you remember the question? It went something like this: How could the German soldier, teacher, railroad conductor, nurse, tax collector, the average citizen claim afterwards that they knew nothing of what was going on? How could they be part of something and then say at the end that they were not really involved? What causes people to blank out their own history? In the next few minutes and perhaps years, you'll have the chance to answer this question.

"If our enactment of the fascist mentality is complete, not one of you will ever admit to being at this Third Wave rally. You won't allow your friends and parents or even yourself, to know you were willing to give up individual freedom to the dictates of order and unseen leaders. You won't admit to being manipulated, to accepting this madness as a way of life. You will keep the Third Wave and this rally a secret. It's a secret I shall share with you."

I took the film from the news cameras and exposed it to the light. The Third Wave ended.

Students slowly rose from their chairs and without talking began to file outdoors. Robert was sobbing. I walked over and threw my arms around him. We stood in the stream of students, some of whom swirled back to hold us for a moment. Others were crying or moving toward the door and the world outside.

For a week in the middle of a school year we had shared something fully. In the four years I taught at Cubberly High School, no one ever spoke of the Third Wave rally. Certainly we thought over what we'd done. But the rally itself, everyone wanted to forget.

Using Reading 3

The following account by a classroom teacher documents the powerful effect this reading had on her students:

Electrifying. I read "You Will Do as Directed" from the teacher's guide, slowly and stopping for analogies. I couldn't believe the intensity in the room—kids kept moving chairs closer. They were spell-bound. Most felt they would have joined the Third Wave; they used phrases like "the power of belonging" and we discussed the vulnerability in us that makes us want to be part of a group, expecially if it's elite. I feel comfortable already that they know it's not just a Jewish-German issue we're dealing with. One girl who rarely connects because she's so busy passing notes, was making fascinating obervations like, "To stop a movement like that you must do it at the beginning because it multiplies rapidly, and they will only listen to their leader not the voice of reason." They made analogies to Hitler—the symbols and trappings of power, the discipline, the rallies. We talked about how great it felt to be part of a movement and that was relevant because many had been part of the March on Hunger and enjoyed the camaraderie. They began to argue among themselves about whether the teacher had done a good thing. Some said he had no right, but that the kids were lucky he knew when to stop. Most felt that the teacher was doing them a favor—showing them how easily they could be drawn into the situation, thus helping assure that they wouldn't be. One child said that the more you had been pulled in (like the bodyguard) the more humiliated you'd feel afterwards.

The following student responses attest to the power of the content:

I'm shocked. Right up to the end I was going along with the Third Wave group. I hadn't realized that there could be anything wrong with this, but when the so-called Mr. Jones put it in a different perspective, I realized I was the same as those kids.

It's scary to think that within each of us is the (hidden?) desire to bargain away our freedom for "the comfort of discipline." While reading it I kept wondering how those high school students could let themselves be manipulated so blatantly by their history teacher. Could I have been a Nazi? Only knowing what I know now or, more importantly, feeling the way I do now, I would have to say NO.

Recently an adaptation of this story was shown as an ABC TV special.

A warning about the abuse of simulation games is warranted here. Some teachers use certain readings, writings, or class activities to "grab" students, engage them "emotionally," or stimulate affective experiences and learning. Without the cognitive component such lessons become only games. Students will remember the game long after they forget the meaning of the point being introduced or developed.

With simulation games comes a tendency to oversimplify the actual event or events and often students are left with simple generalizations and inaccurate history. To imply to students that they can "experience the existence of a person victim to the Holocaust" is unfair, and to try to recreate feelings of the participants of this history without carefully preparing students in perspective taking could reinforce stereotypes instead of break them. It might be helpful to keep in mind the comments of one boy who wrote in Auschwitz: "If heaven was full of paper and the oceans full of ink—I could not express my pain."

In a curriculum on the Holocaust, some students play the game "Gestapo," and they report a glorification of Nazism and increased fascination with the power of the SS.

Activities that encourage role taking and widening of perspective have different goals and outcomes than simulation games.

If simulation activities are to be used, the teacher must be confident that he or she understands possible ramifications for the class. Teachers should also secure the students' approval for participating in such an experiment. Some simulation activities build on the concepts of ridicule, discrimination, fear, and insecurity. Inherent in these experiments is the blind faith students demonstrate in their teachers and classroom situation that makes them obey and join the activity. This blind obedience is in itself worthy of class discussion. One teacher, aware of the abuse of simulation games, used the "Judenrat" games with her students. The teacher stated that "the learning experience derived from the simulation exercise was valuable in its own right." However, it did put a strain on the efforts of the class to "establish a sense of communinty."

In "The Pathology of Imprisonment" published in *Transaction Society,* April 1972, Philip G. Zimbardo describes a simulation experiment conducted at Stanford University on what it means psychologically to be a prisoner or a prison guard.

... In the end, I called off the experiment not because of the horror I saw out there in the prison yard, but because of the horror of realizing that I could have easily traded places with the most brutal guard or become the weakest prisoner full of hatred at being so powerless ....

Activity 4

Film: *Milgrim Experiment, a Study in Obedience*

"How do average, even admirable, people become dehumanized by the critical circumstances pressing in on them?" asks Hannah Arendt. With this film students further explore the nature of obedience.

This black and white film documents the experiments of Dr. Stanley Milgrim at Yale in the 1950s. In these experiments people followed orders even when the orders resulted in pain, if they perceived the order-givers as superiors or holders of the authority.

The information about obedience in America provided by these experiments shocked even the professor.

One of his conclusions stands as a warning for us today: the more fragmented and bureaucratic our lives become the less responsibility we feel for our actions.

Using Activity 4

For many this film is an introduction to experiments involving human subjects. Class discussions revolve around questions of what is "fair" or "unfair" about the experiments.

Since the overall experiment is not revealed until well into the film, students need to have a complete introduction and summary before viewing it. Statistics and statements toward the end of the film, although extremely interesting, may lead to drawing simple conclusions.

Throughout the course, students will continue to refer to the questions of human behavior raised in this film. The following are samples of 8th grade students' responses:

This film is scary. Those are just regular people.

Sometimes I really wonder why everyone went with Hitler. I know a few reasons that might be, but I still don't really understand. I'm not trying to say that all the people are stupid and bad. I'm just trying to say that if this ever happened again, I would try anything I could think of to try and stop him/her from doing ANYTHING. Maybe that's why I'm so against the Nazi march.

The best film of the year was the one about how people act when they are given a command against their conscience. From this film and the dis-

cussion afterwards, I understood more about how Hitler got people to follow him and abide by his ways.

Many things I learned this year I found very scary, expecially the movie Obedience. It showed me that we, humans, have more power than we think and that if someone who was power-hungry abused it, it could hurt many people.

Reading 5

The Minister of Propaganda

Joseph Goebbels was Minister of Propaganda for the Third Reich. His job was to create faith in Hitler, arouse fear and hatred of Jews and foreigners, and convince the German people that the Third Reich was acting in their best interests and that they should obey.

In his diary Goebbels said:

That propaganda is good which leads to success, and that is bad which fails to achieve the desired result, however intelligent it is, for it is not propaganda's task to be intelligent; its task is to lead to success. Therefore, no one can say your propaganda is too rough, too mean; these are not criteria by which it may be characterized. It ought not be decent nor ought it be gentle or soft or humble; it ought to lead to success. If someone says to me, "Your propaganda is not at a well-bred level," there is no point in my talking to him at all. Never mind whether propaganda is at a well-bred level; what matters is that it achieves its purpose . . .

"Once the war began, the government could do anything 'necessary' to win it; so it was with the 'final' solution of the Jewish problem, which the Nazis always talked about but never dared undertake, not even the Nazis, until war and its 'necessities' gave them the knowledge that they could get away with it."[5]

Using Reading 5

Defining the word *propaganda*: This lesson is necessary before students can begin to speculate on the role of propaganda in the daily life of Nazi youth. The teacher might refer to the word *abuse*, which was introduced in the introductory lesson in relation to the meaning of propaganda. A working definition of *propaganda* might include *pro* meaning *for something* and *ganda* meaning *to reproduce*. The terms *persuade* and *indoctrinate* need to be defined. Students should add these words to their vocabulary lists.

Suggested questions for exploration:
- If you were the Minister of Propaganda, how would you build your appeal to the German people? What would you say and do? What reasons would you give so people would follow your orders? What would you have to know about human behavior? The lesson might reflect on discussions and diagrams about security, the in-group, peer pressure, fear, etc., which were presented earlier.
- If you were given the chance to present your views, which were in direct opposition to the views of Goebbels' plan, on what would you base your appeal? What would you want the German people to do and think? What arguments, facts, and ideas would you use to convince others that you were right?
- Since loyalty is a quality that we cherish in an individual and value in a citizen of the United States, how do we guard against abusing it?

• A study of the response of American citizens to the Japanese-American during World War II is illuminating for those students who believe "Americans" would stand up to fear, prejudice, and propaganda. In fact there was little resistance to the "re-locating" of Japanese-Americans to camps. The Bill of Rights was tested here too! Documentary Photo Aids reveal the racism and discrimination toward Japanese-American citizens in America, and *Farewell to Manzanar* by Jeanne Wakatsuki and James Houston describes one person's experience in the internment.

Reading 6

Language and Propaganda

George Orwell once wrote in an essay about politics and the English language, "If thought corrupts language, language can also corrupt thought." This quotation is relevant to a study of propaganda.

A special vocabulary was used in connection with the enemies of the state, words such as *enemy, removal, elimination, cleaning up,* and *expulsion*. In the process of the dehumanization of the Jewish people, the language of Nazi propaganda was especially powerful. The labels referred to Jews as usurers, profiteers, exploiters, big capitalists, international money power communists, Social Democrats, revolution criminals, aliens, and foreigners.[6]

When it came to determining responsibility for deeds planned and carried out by individuals of the Reich, the use of language was critical to the cover up. Responsibility was diffused; orders seemed to come from institutions or organizations, not people. "Orders from the top!" Euphemisms were used to disguise events, to separate words from truth, as with "the final solution, the settlement of the Jewish Problem."

Words were used to mystify, not clarify.

Using Reading 6

One goal of these lessons is to prepare students to be discriminating viewers, listeners, and readers. By concentrating on the abuse of persuasion perhaps students can gain the critical perspective necessary to protect against indoctrination through propaganda.

Reading 7

Jews and the Propaganda Machine

The antisemitic campaign against the Jews was designed to create hate. The following statements reflect the extent of the planning. Hitler wrote:

If the Jew did not exist . . . . we should invent him."[7]

These instructions were given to trusted agents:

. . . Bring up the Jewish question again and again and again, unceasingly. Every emotional aversion, however slight, must be exploited ruthlessly. As a basic rule among the education professions the Jewish questions should be discussed from the standpoints of the findings of the science of race, of higher ethics, etc. While among members of the labouring classes one must seize on the purely emotional; the emotional aversion to Jews is to be heightened by all possible means.[8]

Hitler wrote in *Mein Kampf*:

The energies and the emotions of the masses ... can be harnessed and heightened to their highest pitch by holding up before them the image of a single enemy implacable, terrifying and lusting after their lives.[9]

The following was excerpted from a secret party circular on the antisemitic campaign:

... Increase and intensify the antisemitic Enlightenment of the populace ... the Jewish questions had been rather neglected in propaganda since the outbreak of war.... such neglect was "false and dangerous," for the Jewish question "must ... remain ... at the core of our political attitude." Above all the propaganda should harp on the theme that the "Jews had instigated the war ... the Jews are to be blamed for the war. They are therefore to be blamed also for all the distress, sadness, discomfort, privations, burdens and strains that the war brings. But the end of the suffering and of Jewry is not far off."[10]

The following questions might be helpful as one considers how racism turned neighbor against neighbor and citizen against citizen, in order to "break the moral backbone of a citizenery."*

1. What is prejudice?
2. Is there a connection between social custom and prejudice?
3. Are education, propaganda, indoctrination, and conditioning more important for creating prejudice or fighting it?
4. Are irrational beliefs and myths more easily acceptable than rational beliefs?
5. Why did people need scapegoats?
6. How can frustration cause prejudice?
7. Why are some minorities selected for scapegoats and others ignored?
8. Is there a connection between patriotism and prejudice?
9. What is a demogogue?
10. Is it true that people do not want to be confused with facts?

The Jews as a group, although a minority and politically powerless, would serve as the target for social and economic frustrations. In the fight between the forces of good and evil, the Jew would be used to embody all that was evil. The propagandists used the Jewish conspiracy theory to energize the Nazi party.

In this simple explanation for all history of the human race, there is war between races in which the Jews want to dominate the world. In this theory the Jews are dispersed among nations and seek to rule and exploit. They are well organized and secret using devilish techniques. The Jews hold sway over a people while hiding behind a facade.

The terrifying imagery had a great emotional appeal, especially for the "minds of men suffering in a world whose vastness and working they couldn't understand." Goebbels describes the Jews as "the world enemy, the destroyer of civilization, the parasite among nations, the sons of chaos, the incarnation of evil, the germ of decomposition, the plastic demon, the decay of humanity."[11]

---

*These questions are adapted from "Questions for Classroom Discussion" for "The Nazi Holocaust" documentary photo aids.

Using Reading 7

One of the functions the Jew held for the totalitarian state was to embody all the evil things made taboo by the state.

Almost all that the regime desired to be eradicated from German life, all that it deemed inimical to its purpose was said to be either the direct work of Jewry, to proceed secretly from it or to be impregnated with it. The adjective Judish *ceased to refer only to Jews proper but was expanded to embrace the whole forbidden realm. All forms of art, architecture, all ideas and philosophical systems that contradicted the Nazi creed were pronounced to be verjudet (Jewified). Germans who refused to bend their minds to the new myth-orthodoxy were denounced as Gesinnungsiuden (Jews in mind).*

The Jew hatred could function to bridge classes and therefore to attract followers from all social levels; it could be used as a tool of foreign policy to weaken the enemy's morale.

According to Professor Erich Goldhagen of Harvard University:

The Nazi leaders held a genuine belief in antisemitism although they often consciously lied in order to use antisemitism for their purposes. [They were in] revolt against the foundations of Western civilization. They strove to eradicate from within Germany what is loosely called the Judeo-Christian morality together with the intellectual traditions of the Enlightenment and the socio-political ideals of the French Revolution— those stupid, false and unhealthy ideals of humanity. They condemned pity as a base emotion, preached the duty of killing the feebleminded and the infirm, denounced the demand for the moral equality of all human beings as contrary to the Laws of Nature, spurned Reason as the work of Jewry who had brazenly claimed sovereign power over the minds of men; she must be kicked away and replaced by the vice of blood, the pure Aryan Blood, murmuring discreetly its superior wisdom.[12]

Goldhagen labels the obedience of the German people to Hitler as a time of lapse of reason. Hitler replaced the old moral code with a social Darwinian ideology—

. . . that the fittest survive. He could show that it was contrary to the laws of nature to help handicapped, infirm or insane people, and in doing so he opened the flood gates of murder. When he began executing the feeble and insane a panic spread among the Germans. People feared having an X-ray because they might be found unhealthy. There were mass demonstrations against Hitler's killing of these Germans and so he stopped, but no similar protests occurred when he began killing the Jews.[13]

Reading 8

Indoctrinating the People

The propaganda machine was used to consolidate support for war and racism and to prepare the way for state decisions of genocide.

" . . . One lesson to be learned from the Nazis is how easily an old system of values can be overthrown and replaced by its opposite—how vulnerable man is to indoctrination. And by creating mass enthusiasm for their ideologies, which were nonrational and inconsistent, the Nazis distracted the people from the major contradictions in the ideology. Consider the following two contradictions:

Preparing for Obedience **161**

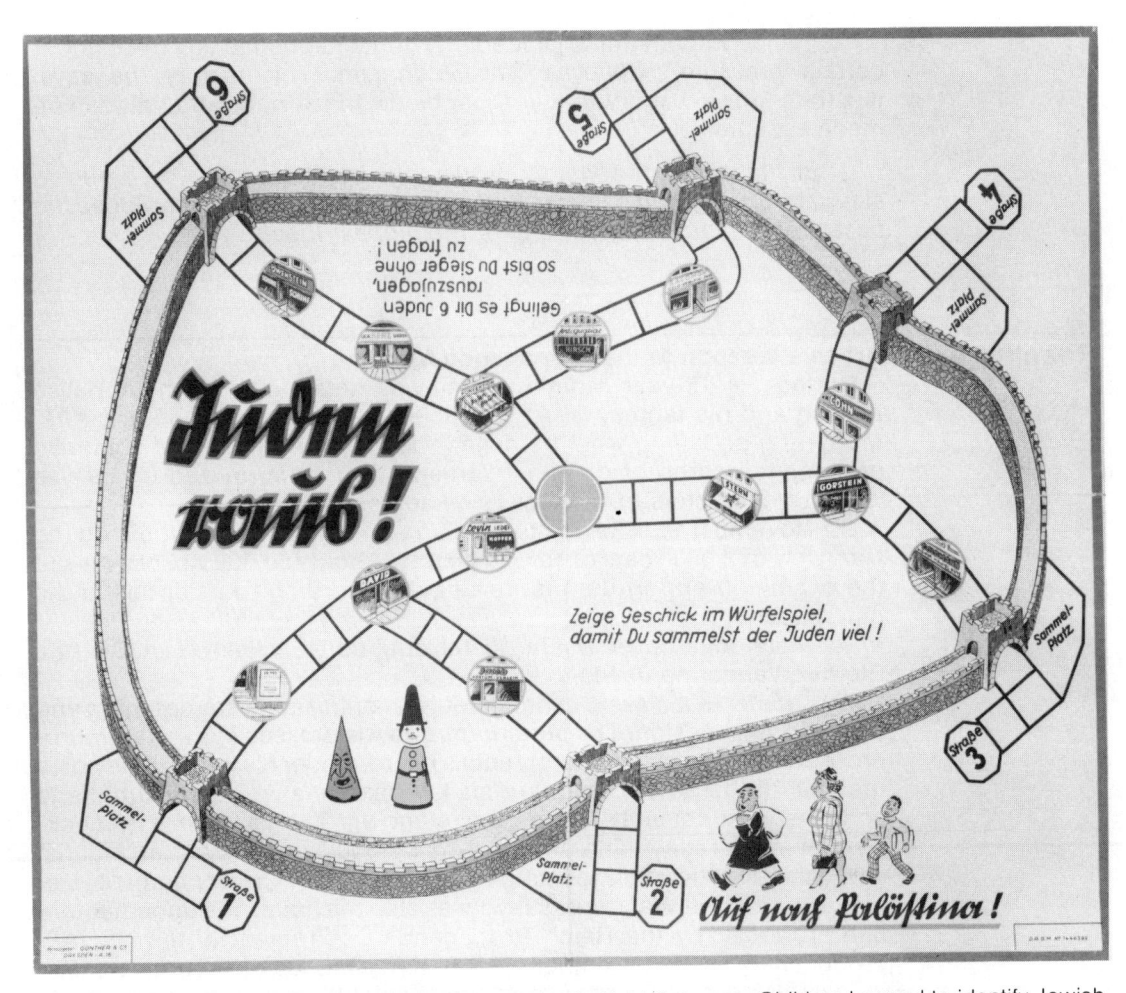

This board game was popular in Nazi Germany. Children learned to identify Jewish businesses and neighborhoods.

Ideology demanded that the Nazis prefer the Nordic, but their world view required that they recruit others. Thus, while they tended to exclude non-Germans from policy discussions, they allied themselves with the Japanese and raised SS units in every European country. On the one level they denounced them as "vermin," totally inferior, who were to be exterminated by gas. On another level they saw them as "devils," a group of extraordinary power, who if not exterminated would take terrible vengeance.[14]

Using Reading 8

The following quotation will stimulate discussion about indoctrination:

How easily Germans were converted from petit bourgeosie into ferocious, sadistic brutes. How easy it is to unlock the ferocity that dwells within man and then suddenly to hide it behind the facade of a quiet, humdrum existence. It is a mistake to think of the Nazis as brutes from the fringes of society who were particularly predisposed to cruelty. . . . Man's aggressive instincts find social sanction in war . . . .[15]

" . . . A fall into an immoral ideology could happen to any of us under certain pressure," believes Dr. Goldhagen. This history, he says, illustrates the savagery that lies just below the surface and that can be made acceptable.

. . . in the name of a visionary ideology *men would be prepared to slaughter on a grand scale. In killing for a* noble vision *they unloose the basest of instincts in the name of the highest ideals . . .*[16]

Reading 9	**Art as a Weapon in the Propaganda Machine**

During his 12-year regime, Hitler was determined to memorialize himself and his fantasy of Aryan racial supremacy through art. After murdering or exiling what he called "degenerate" artists, he created a propaganda corps of obedient "artists" who immortalized on canvas "heroic" characters of his racist, ideological charade.

On November 8, 1837, in Munich, an art exhibit opened showing the Nazi view of 2,000 years of Jewish history. About 150,000 visitors viewed the exhibition during the first few days, according to an article in the newspaper.

The catalogue cover was a poster entitled DER EWIGE JUDE (the Eternal Wandering Jew).

This poster is a classic example of Nazi antisemitic stereotyping and of Nazi poster design. The stereotyped Jew is dressed in a kaftan, with a crooked nose and an unkempt rabbi's beard. Under his left arm, he holds the map of the Soviet Union; in his left hand is a whip. His right hand contains gold coins at which he is glancing. The letters are in mock-Hebrew calligraphy. The Jew is simultaneously portrayed as Marxist and capitalist, two themes common to much of NS-propaganda. *Der Ewige Jude* (The Wandering Jew) was also the name of a documentary film produced by the Reich Propaganda Department of the NSDAP, produced by Dr. Fritz Hippler. This film was made in 1940 and released in several versions; it shows the poverty and filth of poor ragged Jews in the ghettos of Poland. This film was shown to SS units, concentration camp guards, and native populations prior to deportations of Jews. Poster and cinema had a major impact on mass consciousness, reinforced by the legal restrictions, internment, deportation, and annihilation of Jews in Germany and occupied Europe. Nazi art was an integrated and calculated part of the system of indoctrination that led to the implementation of the "final solution." Popular education, museum exhibitions, poster designs, and films were related directly to every facet of life in Nazi-occupied Europe.

Similar stereotypes were used to indoctrinate young Germans in a series of Stuermer children's books entitled *Trust No Fox and No Jew*, written and illustrated by Elwira Bauer in 1936, and *The Poisoned Mushroom*, written by the chief editor of the Stuermer. The stereotyped text and illustrations show the Jew as sex-fiend, capitalist swindler, communist orator, dishonest doctor and lawyer, and criminal.[17]

Using Reading 9	Today, remnants of Nazi propaganda art are being preserved for posterity by the United States Army and shown in museums to be viewed by thousands of Americans. After the war, the Allies agreed that the art would never be utilized to glorify the Nazi ideals.

Consider with students: Has Hitler managed to triumph? Should the art have been destroyed in 1947? Do we have the right to destroy it now? Can we disregard the newsreel shots of Nazi bookburning sprees? Dare we emulate the very actions we so detested?

Destroy or display—are both courses of action immoral?

Reading 10

Lessons on Propaganda Posters[18]*

Goebbels said, "Nothing is easier than leading the people on a leash. I just hold up a campaign poster and they jump through it."

Historically, man has relied on the arts for knowledge, revelation, and understanding. The effect of art and its influence on large numbers of people are important parts of any historical study.

When we view a propaganda poster we are able, for a brief moment, to more acutely sense the political and social atmosphere of another place and time: it is important for us to be aware of the personal reactions to materials, and to share with others the ways in which the material effects us. According to Max Gallo, author of *The Poster in History*:

The function of the poster today is to appeal to our subconscious feelings and our barely conscious needs and then channel them so that we do what the sponsor of the poster wants us to do. To discover not the literal but the implicit intention of posters is to examine human behavior and history.

The following terms are helpful when viewing posters.

Empathy—a feeling "into," becoming what you see or hear; "tuned in," "turned on," deeply involved; to identify with the object or character that interests you.

Psychic distance—a mental or emotional distance from what we see or hear; it can be very close or very far. It is a term used to describe the amount of empathy aroused.

Using Reading 10

Art is never an objective set of materials, of specific dimensions and conformations; art is subjective, it forces people who view it to adjust their ways of seeing in order to make decisions about the value and meaning of what they see.

In order to make the study of any subject meaningful, a student must be able to relate it in some way to his or her own life, to connect it, in a very personal way, to a particular situation, time, and/or stage of development. Art activities can help students express, test, consider, create, and/or redefine their ideas of order, organization, and purpose, both within their own world and the larger world that is examined in this unit. The value of direct experience in art with these materials, and the corresponding immediacy of feelings, allows students to gain insight into the past through aesthetic experiences in the present; these are valuable components in this curriculum as students struggle to comprehend the issues surrounding the Holocaust and their relevance to their own daily lives.

*These lessons on art and propaganda posters presented here and on monuments in the last chapter were adapted from Barbara Travetti Hearn's complete lessons on art, available at the Facing History and Ourselves Resource Center. A project prepared by Nancy Crasco for Lesley College on using art to enhance the teaching of *Facing History and Ourselves* in an Arlington, Mass., public school is available at the Resource Center.

Ask students if they agree with the statement "a picture is worth a thousand words"?

What can pictures do that words cannot do?

What makes a stronger impression on you, something you read or something you see?

Which do you remember longer, a picture or something you read or hear?

Have students make a list of places they have seen posters, and think about how a person might avoid going to hear a political speech or reading a political pamphlet, and whether a poster can be avoided in the same manner?

There are many ways of organizing a slide presentation on propaganda art. One can select posters from several different categories: historical examples before World War I, including World War I, Nazi posters used in Germany before Hitler's takeover and after Hitler came to power, Nazi posters used in countries of occupation, and Allied posters from the United States, England, or Russia. Posters can be used from both sides that deal with specific issues, such as giving information to the enemy, the civilian contribution to the war effort, posters aimed at inspiring hatred for the enemy, posters that use a similar gesture (the raised fist, for example, to show how many sides and causes used the same gesture or symbol), and posters from more recent times that deal with world peace, drugs, pollution, and other topics.

The comparison of images and messages, the formal arrangement of art elements in posters made at different times by differing ideologies will help sensitize students to the subtle messages implicit in the art form and the way they affect human behavior.

When showing slides of propaganda posters there are three important steps students should go through in looking at each slide as active observers:

1. Ask the students to look carefully at the image and describe it exactly as they see it. Defer interpretation and judgment.

2. Ask students to analyze the formal relationships of color, shape, space, and the use of perspective in understanding how the artist designed the impact of the image.

3. Then ask students to interpret the message with regard to the visual and verbal information present in the poster, along with any historical information they might have. Apply concepts from class content. Identify symbolism. Listen to differing perceptions.

It is a good idea to ask the group to decide what parts of the poster they can accept as fact and what parts are more open to interpretation. A World War I poster titled "Red Cross or Iron Cross" was particularly difficult to interpret. Students were not familiar with either term and therefore were unable to reach any real conclusions. We then talked about the context in which a poster is made, and that when we look at them in a classroom we are taking them out of context and it is confusing. One boy said, "Oh, I know what you mean, it's just like Star Wars posters. Years from now no one will understand what they were really about unless they remember the movie."

Questions such as who is sending the message and who is it for are good ways to start the discussion of interpretation. What did the artist do to appeal to a specific group or audience? What is the emotion? What does the artist do to appeal to people's emotions? What symbols does he or she use? All these questions should start students thinking about human behavior and how they personally react to certain messages.

The German Nazi posters that we saw today were to me very spooky. I cringed every time I looked at them reaching out saying that they were friends.

When I was in art we did something to relate to the Holocaust, and to me I got a lot out of that. It brings out feelings you can't say in words, but you can say in what you make. It's very important to do that, because you can't always express feelings in words but the things you make show your feelings; for some people that's easier to do.

Activity 11

Film: Swastika

This documentary film uses Nazi-photographed material to present a montage of the reality created by the Nazis from 1933 to 1939. It includes color home movies of Adolf Hitler and Eva Braun at their country villa.

This film is comprised of carefully edited, authentic footage taken from newsreels, propaganda, and home movies.

Hitler used the film-making expertise of Leni Reifenstahl, who served as his personal film maker. "Propaganda must be addressed to the emotions and not to the intelligence," she said. She created scenes of German folk life, German youth, rallies, and Hitler that were made to glorify the people and plans of the Third Reich. Her films give insight into the "blind and fanatical loyalty and obedience" that many felt for the state. Chapter 10 on judgment describes distinctions made between loyalty and blind obedience.

Using Activity 11

How does the film maker use visual images to touch the emotions, not the reason, of the viewer?

Oh, now I understand the power of propaganda. Maybe I, too, would believe if I saw these films.
—an 8th grade student

Today we saw the first reel of the movie, Swastika. It was very nationalistic and a little frightening. One sees well-dressed middle-class people praising Hitler. I, myself, was moved by Hitler when Wagner's music was played. It sounded almost like a national anthem. At some point in the film I began to feel angry, knowing as I did what was going to take place. I kept seeing pictures of Hitler playing kindly with young children. It seemed horribly ironic for Hitler, a serious and brutal man, to smile and even laugh. I believe that the national pride he gave to the people was extremely important. Unfortunately, some nationalism led to temporary blindness. I know what national pride feels like. Last night I was watching the Olympics on TV, thinking how great my country is.
—a high school student

A trying and confusing movie. I'm ashamed because I actually felt a sort of triumphant feeling after watching this movie. I now understand why so many Germans fell helplessly into the hands of Hitler. At times I felt like getting up and marching with the German soldiers.
—a high school student

Reading 12 — Goals of Education

Before learning in more detail about the education of the Nazi youth, it is useful to think about the goals of parents, teachers, and students for their own education in America today. Consider these questions:
- What do educators want students to learn?
- What do parents want their own children to learn?
- What do you think American students should learn?
- What is the role of education in American society?

The following message written by a school principal states his goal for education. He sent this letter out on the first day of the new school year to all the teachers.

Dear Teacher:
I am a survivor of a concentration camp. My eyes saw what no man should witness:
Gas chambers built by learned engineers.
Children poisoned by educated physicians.
Infants killed by trained nurses.
Women and babies shot and burned by high school and college graduates.
So, I am suspicious of education.
My request is: Help your students become human. Your efforts must never produce learned monsters, skilled psychopaths, educated Eichmanns.
Reading, writing, arithmetic are important only if they serve to make our children more humane.[19]

Using Reading 12

Students should think about what they think *others* want them to learn. Then they can check their hypotheses in actual interviews with parents, teachers, and administrators. Help students to put themselves into the role of the curriculum writer, the teacher, and the school principal. Whose values prevail if there is a conflict over the goals of education? Share curriculum guides with students. Look at goals and objectives. Research the views of Mr. and Mrs. Gabler who object to many textbooks now being used in this country.

If a parent responded "students should learn the history of the United States," then what types of classroom activities or materials should be used to attain this goal? Lectures? Should students be given choices as to what aspects of history they study? Should students be presented with materials that develop negative interpretations of our country's policies? Should discussions and debates be allowed?

Does our system of education attempt to create a certain type of person? Does it attempt to create a person who has mastered certain types of skills? Does there seem to be a "grand plan" of this type of education? Challenge students to reach some sort of consensus regarding the purpose of our schools and what students should learn. Since many of the responses collected from students, parents, and educators will be varied and often contradictory, a class consensus will be difficult, but it provides an important springboard for the next lessons on Nazi education.

Reading 13 Burning Books

Anatoli Kutznetsov wrote in *Babi Yar:* . . . burning books is the first sign of trouble.

. . . if books are burned, that means things are going wrong. It means that you are surrounded by force, fear and ignorance, that power is in the hands of barbarians.

The obvious question is, "Why are books burned?"

Reading 14 Preparing Nazi Youth

Readings 15 through 27 describe those school systems in regions of Germany where the Nazis had strong influence and control.* The readings describe the goals and programs of Nazi education for teachers and students, yet the extent to which this was implemented in the German schools varied from town to town.

Speaking of youth, Hitler said:

In my great educative work, I am beginning with the young. We older ones are used up. Yes, we are old already. We are rotten to the marrow. We have no unrestrained instincts left. We are cowardly and sentimental. We are bearing the burden of a humiliating past, and have in our blood the dull recollection of serfdom and servility. But my magnificant youngsters! Look at these young men and boys! What material! With them I can make a new world.[20]

Using Reading 14

All the power of the regime—all its cunning, its entire machine of propaganda and discipline—is directed to emphasize the program for German children. According to Hitler's plans as set out in *Mein Kampf:*

Beginning with the primer, every theater, every movie, every advertisement must be subjected to the service of one great mission, until the prayer of fear that our service of one great 'Lord, make us free,' shall be changed in the mind of the smallest child into a cry: "Lord, do thou in future bless our arms."

. . . All education must have the sole objective of stamping the conviction into the child that his own people and his own race are superior to others.

No German group was more stringently effected by the changes of the dictatorship than the children. An adult German must be first a National Socialist, but he can—by now—be, in the second place, a shopkeeper or a manufacturer, without his shop or factory belonging to the state; but the German child is a Nazi child, and nothing else.

Reading 15 Through the Nazi Streets Walks the Nazi Child

Every child says "Heil Hitler!" from 50 to 150 times a day, immeasurably more often than the old neutral greetings. The formula is required by law; if you meet a friend on the way to school, you say it; study periods

---

*These descriptions and lessons about Nazi education were excerpted from *Education for Death* by Gregor Ziemer and *School for Barbarians* by Erika Mann.

Much of the Nazi propaganda was directed at German children.

are opened and closed with "Heil Hitler!" "Heil Hitler!" says the postman, the streetcar conductor, the girl who sells you notebooks at the stationery store; and if your parents' first words when you come home to lunch are not "Heil Hitler!" they have been guilty of a punishable offence, and can be denounced. "Heil Hitler!" they shout, in the Jungvolk and Hitler Youth. "Heil Hitler!" cry the girls in the League of German Girls. Your evening prayers must close with "Heil Hitler!" if you take you devotions seriously.

Officially—when you say hello to your superiors in school or in a group—the words are accompanied by the act of throwing the right arm high; but an unofficial greeting among equals requires only a comparatively lax lifting of the forearm, with the fingers closed and pointing forward. This Hitler greeting, this "German" greeting, repeated countless times from morning to bedtime, stamps the whole day.

Heil really means salvation, and used to be applied to relations between man and his God; one would speak of ewiges Heil (eternal salvation), and the adjective "holy" derives from the noun. But now there is the new usage.

You leave the house in the morning, "Heil Hitler" on your lips; and on the stairs of your apartment house you meet the Blockwart. A person of great importance and some danger, the blockwart has been installed by the government as a Nazi guardian. He controls the block, reporting on it regularly, checking up on the behavior of its residents. It's worth it to face right about, military style, and to give him the "big" Hitler salute, with the right arm as high as it will go. All the way down the street, the flags are waving, every window colored with red banners, and the black swastika in the middle of each. You don't stop to ask why; it's bound to be some national event. Not a week passes without an occasion on which families are given one reason or another to hang out the swastika. Only the Jews are excepted under the strict regulation. Jews are not Germans; they do not belong to the "Nation," they can have no "National events."

You meet the uniforms on the way to school; the black SS men, the men of the Volunteer Labor Service, and the Reichswehr soldiers.

There are more placards as you continue past hotels, restaurants, indoor swimming pools, to school. They read "No Jews allowed"—"Jews not desired here"—"Not for Jews." And what do you feel? Agreement? Pleasure? Disgust? Opposition? You don't feel any of these. You don't feel anything, you've seen these placards for almost five years. This is a habit, it is all perfectly natural, of course Jews aren't allowed here. Five years in the life of a child of nine—that's his life, after four years of infancy, his whole personal, conscious existence.

Through the Nazi street walks the Nazi child. There is nothing to disturb him, nothing to attract his attention or criticism. The stands sell Nazi papers almost exclusively; all German papers are Nazi; foreign papers are forbidden, if they do not please the men at the top. The child won't be surprised at their huge headlines: "UNHEARD-OF ACT OF VIOLENCE AGAINST GERMANY IN CZECHOSLOVAKIA! " "JEWISH GANGSTERS RULE AMERICA!" "THE COMMUNIST TERROR IN SPAIN SUPPORTED BY THE POPE!" "150 MORE PRIESTS UNMASKED AS SEXUAL CRIMINALS!"

That's how it is in the world, the child thinks. "What luck we're in, to have a Fuehrer! He'll tell the whole bunch—Czechs, Jews, Americans, Communists and priests—where to get off!"

Using Reading 15

Discuss with students how discrimination can become a habit.

Reading 16   **The Home is Not the Most Important Place**

The break-up of the family is no by-product of the Nazi dictatorship, but part of the job that the regime had to do if it meant to reach its aim—the conquest of the world.

If the world is to go to the Nazis (for no one else, in Hitler's eyes, is German), the German people must first belong to them. And, for that to be true, they can't belong to anyone else—neither God, nor their families, nor themselves.

Today every member of the nation—man, woman, and child—must belong to at least one Nazi organization: to the Party, to a professional union, a Women's or Mothers' union, the Hitler Youth, the young people, or to the League of German Girls. These take all the time left after one's profession, housework, or school. Even without a deeper reason, it would be impossible for anyone to devote himself to family problems, just for lack of time.

Now: the head of a family comes home; no one is in, but there is a note on the library table that says: "Am at a meeting of the National Socialist Women's Union. Will be home late.—Mother." So he scribbles an answer and leaves it beside the other: "Going to a Party meeting. Will be back late—Father." The next in is the son, who leaves a note: "Night practice. Won't be home till morning.—Fritz." Hilda, the daughter, is last, and she writes: "Must go to a meeting of the Bund of German Girls.—Hilda."

At about two in the morning, the family gets home, to a bare apartment from which everything movable has been stolen; but there is a fifth note on the table: "We thank our Fuehrer. Heil Hitler!—The Gang."

Using Reading 16

Discuss the subtle measures used to destroy the family. Destruction began only when, within the family itself, mutual suspicion grew great. It was not until father became suspicious of mother, mother of daughter, daughter of son, and son of father, that the family was really endangered. From the moment when no one dared speak, because every word might be reported, every gesture misunderstood and denounced, the family lost its meaning. Life within it became senseless. Parents who were members of a society of Bible students in Waldenberg were both accused of having infected their children with pacifist ideals and of influencing them against the Nazi regime. The father declared in court that he exercised no influence whatsoever upon his children, and the answer given him was that whether or not his statement was true, the atmosphere in the home of Bible students could not be anything but poisonous for children; no one could live in it without becoming an enemy of the state. The father admitted a previous conviction for having failed to send his children to some National Socialist school festival. He assured the court that the children had not wanted to go. But the court's opinion was that this in itself showed the harmful effect of the parents' influence.

And so the children were taken from their parents, not for a crime proved or committed or even contemplated, nor for expressed opinions, but solely because the atmosphere of such a home could not bring these children of the Bible students up to revere the state.

One thing was clear to the men in power: an example had to be made. All parents had to be warned: surely, from now on, everyone who had children would avoid Bible groups and pacifist ideas.

Reading 17   **The Birthday Party**

One boy's family gave their child a birthday party, with ordinary, normal, "civilian" presents: a paintbox, a picture puzzle, a shining new bicycle—and lit twelve candles on his birthday cake. How they looked forward to that party! And it went off like a political conference. Six boys had been invited, and five of them came right on time.

"Who's missing?" the mother asked.

"Can't you see?" said the boy. "HE's missing—Fritzekarl!"

"What a pity!" she answered. That it should be just Fritzerkarl! Two years older than her son, he was the leader in the Jungvolk, and his presence at the party was of great importance. If he did not appear, it was a sign of disfavor; the whole thing would be spoiled.

The boys, in their Hitler Youth uniforms stood around the birthday table, not knowing quite what to do with the toys. The bicycle pleased all of them, with its bell (which they took turns ringing) and its rubber tires, which were so hard to get nowadays, and which the father had finally been able to obtain after using all of his contacts in the Party, paying a high cash price, and emphasizing the fact that this was a wheel for a boy, a Jungvolk boy, and not for a girl who would never go to war! Now it stood there, complete with instructions and a copy of the *German Cyclist*, saying "Boys on bicycles must try to remember the names of towns, rivers, mountains and lakes as well as the material and type of architecture of bridges, etc. They may be able to make use of this knowledge for the good of the Fatherland."

The bell rang, and the son dashed to the front door. A sharp voice came through, crying "Heil Hitler!" and the five boys at the table turned on their heels as the answer came in a voice already breaking, "Heil Hitler!" Their superior officer was received with the "German salute," five hands raised, great composure, solemn faces. Solemnly, Fritzekarl gave the host his birthday present—a framed photograph of the Leader of the Reich Youth, Baldur von Schirach, with a facsimile autograph! The son clicked his heels as he received it.

"I wish to speak to your father," Fritzekarl said curtly.

The mother answered in her friendly voice, "My husband is not free just now—he's upstairs working."

Fritzekarl attempted to keep the note of military command in his shrill young voice. "Just the same, madam, I should prefer to speak to your husband for a moment . . . in the interest of your son."

His manner was correct, in spite of his tone. He bowed slightly to the mother as he finished his masterful little speech.

"Fourteen years old!" she thought, "but the mechanism of power backs him up, and he knows it."

The son was blushing violently, "For goodness' sake call him!" he said, stepping toward his mother.

The father came down at once.

"Heil Hitler!" cried Fritzekarl.

"Heil Hitler!" repeated the man. "What can I do for you, Lieutenant?"

"Pardon me," says Fritzekarl, who doesn't get the joke, and retains his martial stare, "but your son was absent from our last practice exercises."

"Yes, I know," the father interrupts at this point, "he had a cold."

"It was at your suggestion that he absented himself," Fritzekarl continues, his voice breaking and going hoarse over the phrase, "You wrote me some sort of excuse, to say that he was staying home at your wish."

The father puts his weight first on one foot and then on the other. "As a matter of fact, it is my wish that he stay home when he has such a severe cold."

"Oh, I didn't have such a bad cold at all," the son breaks in. He is leaning on the handle-bars of the bicycle that his father had to fight for. "I could have gone, perfectly well."

The man looks at his son, a long look of surprise and pain and the resignation he has learned. "Well," he says, and moves toward the door.

But Fritzekarl stops him. "A moment, please," he insists, but politely. "Your son was in school on that day and the following day. So he cannot have been really ill. Let me call your attention to the fact that he should have been present at practice and that it is my duty to report the absence!"

"Oh, please—" the boy was speaking for his father, quickly, bargaining, "—don't do that, please! It won't ever happen again—will it father?—really, never again!"

The father wanted to protest; he felt the despairing look of his wife, the outrage and embarrassment of the scene. "How dare you speak to me like that!" was what he was repeating in his mind. But he knew the consequences of such an argument, for himself, and for his son. Even if he could convince the Nazi authorities of his own part and Fritzekarl's rudeness, his son would still have to face the Jungvolk, paying for his father's moment of "courage." And so he only said hesitatingly and stiffly, "No—it certainly will never happen again!"

"I thank you," replied the fourteen-year-old superior of the treasonable son. The father was dismissed.

He cannot air his resentment; he has to expect eavesdroppers and spies everywhere. His wife tells their son everything—not out of malice, but in the mistaken hope of reclaiming him this way. And the new maid is a person to be feared. She listens at doors, reads everything that's lying around the house, and she happens to be having an affair with a Blockwart; he could destroy a family singlehanded. The boy would hardly denounce his own father, the man reflects, but if he repeats some remark to the maid, she will run to her Blockwart, the Gestapo (Secret State Police) will have it right away, and the doom will begin to move on them. Or, if they decide to dismiss the maid, her vengence hanging over their heads may be even worse.

Using Reading 17

One boy, after reading this story, remarked, "This is like a world upside down—the children have the power."
Would students want to have such power now?

Reading 18   **The Training of a Nazi: Before the Grand Plan of Nazi Education**

Until recently, German schools had the world's respect: the relationship between teachers and pupils, especially just after the War, was human and dignified, and the teachers themselves were distinguished for thoroughness, discipline, and scientific exactness. The grammar schools and Gymnasium (high schools), colleges and universities, were open to all, and their moderate tuition fees were cancelled for talented students of limited means. There were some, like the best American boarding schools, in beautiful, healthful places, whose modern methods allowed teacher and pupils to sit in the garden and have lessons that were remembered as stimulating conversation, or to make excursions over the hills and fields. There were performances in the school theaters, and films shown to supplement courses in natural science, history, and geography.

One subject, political propaganda, was missing from the curriculum. The German Republic refused to influence its citizens one way or the other, or to convince them of the advantages of democracy; it did not carry on any propaganda in its own favor. This seems to have been an error; and its atonement has been a terrible error. Whatever its cause, modesty or the waverings of a young and confident Republic, the error stands. What the Republic did toward education was done as a matter of course. Civic buildings, for peacetime use, were put up, and of these many were schools—airy, spacious, and happily adequate. They were set into service without propaganda or hullabaloo. The state was the people's servant; it served in quiet, believing that its master, the people, would be thankful. But the state was wrong.

Had the "old fashioned" educators tried to make civilized human beings of the children in their care? Had they encouraged them in their search for truth? Left youth as much personal freedom as they thought compatible with discipline? Taken them to theaters and movies to serve educational purposes? Had they done all of this? It must all go, according to the Nazis, immediately and radically. Morals, truth, freedom, humanitarianism, peace, education—they were errors that corrupted the young, stupidities with no value to the Fuehrer. "The purpose of our education," he was crying, "is to create the political soldier. The only difference between him and the active soldier is that he is less specially trained."[21]

Using Reading 18

Nazi education was to transcend old-fashioned pedagogy. Education in Hitler's schools was to stem from political conflict and victory.

"Students who are unable to produce required results or who betray any weakness, are to be kept out of the secondary school," states the iron Minister of Education to his iron-minded teachers on page one of his ironclad manual.

The regime draws a sharp distinction between girls, inherently weak, and boys, natural exponents of strength. Boys and girls have nothing in common. Their aims, their purposes in life, are fundamentally different. Boys will become soldiers; girls will become breeders. Co-educational schools are manifestations of decadent democracies and hence are taboo.

Reading 19 **Grand Plan for Nazi Education**

The Nazi Minister of Education reminded his instructors:

The chief purpose of the school is to train human beings to realize that the State is more important than the individual, that individuals must be willing and ready to sacrifice themselves for Nation and Fuehrer.

It matters little if boys and girls carry away only scraps of formal concrete knowledge from school.... The fundamental principle to keep in mind is that we are not striving to inculcate as much knowledge as possible into the minds of our students. If students have learned to submit to authority, if they have developed a willingness to fit into that particular niche chosen for them by the Party, then their education has been successful.

The German character can be formed only if there are many obstacles. Knowledge widens the view only if it promotes the feeling of power, if it promotes obedience and modesty in the individual.

A wide cultural knowledge, a broad education in various phases of learning, dulls the senses; a general assortment of information weakens, does not strengthen; too much universal learning tires the mind, paralyzes the will power and the ability to make decisions.

Discipline is to be rigorous. "The new school will subject all students to a severe training of spirit.... It will not hesitate to make them hard in body and mind, through coercion if necessary; it will expect of them mastery of hard facts, rules, numbers."

Every girl must learn the duties of a mother before she is sixteen, so she can have children. Why should girls bother with higher mathematics, or art, or drama, or literature? They could have babies without that sort of knowledge.

Hitler devotes thirty pages of *Mein Kampf* to the education of boys. Seven lines he grants to the girls.

The Nazi mother dedicates her son to Hitler before he is born. When the child is six years old, he takes the first oath to give up his life for the Fuehrer; he repeats it when he is ten, and again when he is fourteen.

A similar oath is expected of him when he begins his compulsory labor year. His education for death is nearly completed as he finally enters the army, the profession that not only prepares him to die but to kill, with the following words:

"I swear by God this holy oath, that I will unconditionally obey the Fuehrer of the German Reich and the German people, Adolf Hitler, Commander in Chief of the Army; as a brave soldier I will forever defend this oath at the cost of my own life."

Using Reading 19

According to one American observer in Germany during this time the education was so different from the normal education of American youth that any comparison would be "inane" and any evaluation extremely difficult.

Hitler is making Nazis who are eager for action, eager for conquest, ready to die for him and his ideals. They respect authority and are not afraid to work. They would dig their own graves if he asked them to.

Reading 20 **The Nazi School**

According to the Nazi government manual, the teacher is to be an iron disciplinarian who commands instead of instructs and who, if necessary, would use force. They are to encourage physical education and to teach the Nazi philosophy that inspires them. National Socialistic ideology is to be a sacred foundation. It is not to be degraded by detailed explanation or discussion. It is a holy unit that must be accepted by the students as a holy unit. It must be taught by teachers who fully comprehend the true meaning of our sacred doctrines.

The teacher is to be a miniature Hitler and Fuehrer in his own classes. His role is to brook no opposition, and demand blind obedience.[22]

Teachers are to lecture, because in class discussion youth tends to abuse freedom by criticizing or finding fault. Erika Mann wrote about the Nazi goal for education:

... Too much detail, too much delving into particulars make minds too critical and analytical.[23]

Curriculum and classes had to be flexible in order to accommodate last-minute military parades or special duties and new state enemies and geography. For example, changes had to be made in history classes because Russia was at one time the enemy, then the ally, and then the enemy again.

Using Reading 20

This information will be valuable as students investigate and compare their education Nazi to education.

Reading 21 **Pimpf: A Boy's Education**

At the age of six a young boy became a member of the Pimpf (little fellow) organization. He kept a record book of his development in physical education, ideological growth, and military ability. He had to prove a knowledge of Hitler songs, oaths, holidays, and biography, plus names of the territories lost in the Treaty of Versailles.

At the age of ten he graduated to the Jungvolk where he was ready to die for Hitler. Later he would be ready for the Hitler Youth.

Young boys marched an average of 12-1/2 miles a day. The following story is about a boy who, ready to die for Hitler, made the hard march.

"Here's my young patient. Age nine, pneumonia."

On a cot lay the restless form of a boy with an emaciated face. The doctor touched the boy's wrist to take his pulse. The boy tore his hand away, shot it high and shouted in a delirious, unnatural voice, "Heil Hitler."

"If only they had not made him march," she said hoarsely. "They knew he was not well. But they said he had to march. It took days to get down to Leuchtenburg by Kahla, in Thuringia, where they were going to promote him to Jungvolk. His father is a storm trooper. He said the boy had to go. He did not want a weakling for a son. And now—"

From the cot came words—shrill, penetrating. "Let me die for Hitler. I must die for Hitler!" Over and over, pleading, accusing, beseeching, fighting against life, fighting the doctor, fighting to die.

"They told him at the ceremony that he had to die for Hitler," the mother continued. "And he's so young..."

She broke then, sobbing. His right hand was straight up now, stiff and unyielding. His lips kept forming the words his burning soul prompted him to utter:

"I must die for Hitler!"

"His father says if he dies, then he dies for Hitler," the mother said tonelessly.

"He wants to die. What is this strange ideology that can even pervert instincts?"

Using Reading 21

The mother asks, "What is this stange ideology. . .?" Discuss with students why children are so vulnerable.

Reading 22 **Boys in a Geography Class**

Children were taught that nature respects only the strong, the aggressors, and victors, not the victims who were to be dominated.

In one geography class, the teacher explained that Germany was powerful now because of the doctrine of race purity. He asked his students to name the countries that were declining because of racial sins.

They mentioned Russia, England, France. The teacher was not satisfied.

"Well, which country has always called itself the 'melting pot' of all other nations? Jungens, that you must know."

Then came the chorus, "Amerika."

The teacher launched into a devastating diatribe that made short shrift of the United States, that country which had joined the last war just to make money. He worked himself into an emotional fervor.

He explained how during the centuries there had been many men and women who could not get along in Europe. Most of them were criminals and crooks, reprobates and renegades. They were the undesirables. Whenever they tangled with the law in Germany, or any other European country, they got on a boat and went to the United States. There they married each other. And now the children—well, any German boy with intelligence could see what the result would be. The citizens of the United States were sinking lower and lower.

"There are many other weaknesses as a result of this lack of racial purity," he continued. "Their government is corrupt. They have a low type of government, a democracy. What is a democracy?"

"A democracy is a government by rich Jews."
"A democracy is a form of government in which people waste much time."
"A democracy is a government that will be defeated by the Fuehrer."
"Das so wie so". The teacher grinned. "That in any case." He expressed the conviction that the democratic form of government could not last long in a world where National Socialism was fast getting the upper hand. Democracies had too many flaws.

"Look at the United States," he said. "It is the richest country in the world. It has almost all the gold in the world. But it also has the largest number of unemployed of any country. Look at some of these pictures."

He had pictures, cut from German illustrated weeklies, purporting to depict starving men along sidewalks and wharves in American cities.

Moreover, the United States was abusing its minorities. The American Indian was almost exterminated; the Negro was lynched on the nearest tree.

The lot of the laboring man was especially unenviable. He reminded the boys of the benefits their fathers were deriving from the labor front, the Nazi Arbeitsfront, which provided pensions, free vacations, trips to the Mediterranean. But in America capital and labor were engaged in an eternal struggle. As a result there were innumerable strikes.

The boys, most of them nine years old, did not know what strikes were. There had not been any in Germany since 1933. The teacher explained, and used more pictures, allegedly of American strikes.

The reactions were written clearly on the faces of the listening boys. A country where such things could be need not be respected, much less feared.

The teacher had one parting shot, "And the leader of the United States? Who is he?"

"Roosevelt," somebody said.

The teacher's voice got mysterious. "Roosevelt he calls himself. But his real name is Rosenfeldt. What does that show you?"

"He's a Jew," shouted the class.

A bell rang. . . .

Using Reading 22

This reading describes "indoctrination." Discuss the power of the teacher and explore which type of education guards against such practices the most.

Reading 23

Young Girls

Before girls were fourteen, they were called Jungmaedel and were minimally educated except in matters relating to childbirth. These girls went to school Monday through Saturday but they had no textbooks and no homework. Although most of their class time was devoted to physical education and the science of being a homemaker, they too had to learn geography, history, and songs about the Nordic race. After sports in the afternoons, these young girls had special evening instruction.

The Fuehrer wanted the girls to feel that their bodies were more important than their minds. In *Mein Kampf*, Hitler wrote:

It is in the interest of the nation that those who have a beautiful physique should be brought into the foreground, so they can encourage the development of beautiful bodily form among the people in general.

In one class on morals girls learned that, "there was no such thing as a problem of morals in Hitler's Germany. The Fuehrer wanted every woman, every girl, to bear children—soldiers."

Using Reading 23

Ask students to compare the Nazi education for boys and for girls. Imagine the girl who did not want to go along or the boy who resisted the structure. How different was Harrison Bergeron?

Reading 24

An Arithmetic Lesson

The following problems appeared in the *National Political Practice in Arithmetic Lessons*:

1. Germany had, according to the Versailles Treaty, to surrender all her colonies. (An enumeration of colonies and mandates, with estimates of population and area is given.)
   a. What was Germany's total loss in population and territory?
   b. How much did each mandatory power receive in territory and population?
   c. How many times greater is the surrendered territory than the area of Germany?
   d. Compare the population of Germany with the population of the lost territories.
2. A bombing plane can be loaded with one explosive bomb of 35 kilograms, three bombs of 100 kilograms, four gas bombs of 150 kilograms, and 200 incendiary bombs of one kilogram.
   a. What is the load capacity?
   b. What is the percentage of each type of bomb?
   c. How many incendiary bombs of 0.5 kilograms could be added if the load capacity were increased 50%?
3. An airplane flies at the rate of 240 kilometers per hour to a place at a distance of 210 kilometers in order to drop bombs. When may it be expected to return if the dropping of bombs takes 7.5 minutes?

Another textbook, *National Political Application of Algebra,* by Otto Zoll, achieves the same objectives as the *Practice.* "How many people can seek protection in a bomb-proof cellar, length 5 meters, width 4 meters, and height 2.25 meters? Each person needs 1 cubic meter per hour, and they remain there for three hours."

In his book *Aerial Defense in Numbers*, Fred Tegeder asks the same kind of question: "If the speed of an airplane is 175 kilometers per hour, how many hours does it take for a plane to reach Moscow, 1,925 kilometers from Berlin; Copenhagen, 481 kilometers from Berlin; and Warsaw, 817 kilometers from Berlin?" In the problem the 7.5 minutes that, as everyone knows, a "passenger plane" needs to drop its bombs, are not mentioned.

Another book, *Germany's Fall and Rise—Illustrations Taken from Arithmetic Instruction in Higher Grades of Elementary School*, which in 1936 had reached a circulation of 715,000 copies, asks: "The Jews are aliens in Germany—In 1933 there were 66,060,000 inhabitants of the German Reich, of whom 499,682 were Jews. What is the percentage of aliens?"

Using Reading 24

Students can easily identify how education was used to teach the objectives of the Nazi state in all curriculum areas.

Reading 25 — A Lesson in Racial Instruction

The German schools consider no method that may carry out [the] wish of the Fuehrer too superstitious, too brutal, or clumsy.

Professor Ernst Dohers wrote in his book *The Jewish Question — Material and its Treatment in Schools*:

How do we wish our people to look? We place two groups of pictures side by side: on the one hand, Nordically classified bodies and faces, sportsman types, Olympic athletes, soldiers, typical officer leaders; on the other hand, we present a group of Jews.... It will naturally result that the children will feel kinship with the one side, and quite naively, passionate rejection on the other; that is a matter of course, it is then the object of the spoken pedagogical word constantly to strengthen and to build up with knowledge and perception this consciousness of the German child's own nature and the complete foreignness of the other.[24]

Using Reading 25

Racial instruction was given in all classes. The belief was that if students were "educated" at a very early age in the new Nazi science of race, then they would be convinced of the necessity of pure blood.

Reading 26 — Grand Plan of Racial Purity

The undesirables, the feeble-minded, those afflicted with incurable diseases, even the antagonistic in spirit would not have any more children. That was the wish of the Fuehrer, and Young Germany carried out his decrees.

The mentally sick, women with low resistance, women who had proved through their own births that their offspring were not strong: They were women suffering from defects.

"We are even eradicating color-blindness in the Third Reich. We must not have soldiers who are color-blind. It is transmitted only by women."[25]

Using Reading 26

Discuss how these early policies could be preconditions for genocide. Ask students to think about those who were made the objects of the racism. What responses were possible?

Reading 27 — The Training of a Nazi: Chemistry and Drawing Lessons

The lessons in chemistry and drawing reflected the repetition of the Nazi goals.

According to Dr. Walter Kintoff's book, *School Experiments in the Chemistry of Fighting Materials*, children from fifteen to eighteen had to be trained in the problems of defense. Lessons were prepared on experimenting with incendiary materials although there was the "regrettable" chance of danger for the students. "Fire has a double mission in matters related to war," Kintoff wrote. "On the one hand, it is supposed to cause considerable damage, and on the other, to wear the population out morally, that is, to break its power of resistance."

In the art classes students had to study motion, especially as it related to aerial defense. Teenage boys would experience motion in parachutes, jumping, explosions, searchlights, and burning houses. Motionless forms, such as the houses of a city, for example, were

Hitler with young boys of the Pfimpfen.

considered no more than meaningless scenery, and as such could often be omitted.

In a fourth grade art class students would draw a bomb-proof cellar, stressing the dramatic impact of a bomb hitting nearby. The upper classes practiced drawing the human head by using the form of a gas mask.

There is one thing rightfully demanded of a German compositon: an avowal of the spiritual forces of reason, will, and emotion latent in man; and it is exactly the same thing that we demand of the instruction in drawing. Namely: the training of imitative power, the cultivation of the sense of beauty, and a single-minded point of view toward all that is false — these are the permanent values given Youth on its way through life."[26]

Using Reading 27

Students should develop diagrams for the Nazi youth similar to those in the chapter "Society and the Individual." As each topic about the education and training of the Nazi youth is read and discussed, students should gradually develop their diagram of an individual youth in a Nazi society.

What is the end product of this Nazi education? What could a student be like? Is it easier to describe the end product of Nazi education or that of our own system of education? Most of our students conclude that, since our system is more decentralized in terms of educational goals and activities, the end product is more varied than in Nazi Germany and more representative of the variety of beliefs and traditions in our country. Have students write a clear description of what they think is the Grand Plan of Nazi education.

How did the Nazis prepare their youth? What techniques were used? What were the specific aspects of Nazi society that affected the daily routine of the German child? Since the preparation of Nazi youth was something that was nurtured over a decade, the class might speculate as to how a society (or a society of nations) "turns off" this process.

Students should examine different textbooks and resources from their various classes. The type of problems and questions from math, science, and foreign language resources should be analyzed. Challenge students to clarify the underlying messages of student materials and teacher guides. A group of students might explore where and by whom school materials are published. What types of objectives are used in some teacher guides? What are some of the educational policies (goals) of the school administration or school committee? The conclusions that result from studying these materials, objectives, and policies should be compared to the Nazi system of education. A large chart listing these conclusions might be posted in the classroom.

What happens to individual students and teachers who do not want to go along with a certain type of educational system? How are rebellious teachers and students silenced? Students might remember lessons from *The Bear That Wasn't,* which dealt with the effect of society on an individual.

Reading 28 Growing Up in Nazi Germany: A Jewish Family

The following excerpt, describes some of the difficulties Jewish children had in their families and in school in the early 1930s. These views of the Jewish child in Nazi Germany reflect how painful it was to grow up with hate and lies.

If life in the family has fallen to such small importance for the average German child, it is infinitely more difficult for the child of Jewish or "non-Aryan" descent. All the misery of the pariah—of being outside and despised—he must suffer because of his parents.

"If only I had other parents, 'Aryan' parents," the child thinks, "I could be happy, like the others—belong to them, go marching and sing their songs. I would be a human being—not an *Untermensch,* an 'enemy of the German people,' a 'misfortune.' 'The Jews are our misfortune,' they tell us in school—my parents are Jews, and they are my misfortune. If only I had some other parents!"

Many Jewish children will look around the dinner table and think that. Others will look for protection at home from the persecutions they find outside; but their home is unable to give them that refuge, and the child feels, "They are good, but helpless. Just as I am, they are hit by this misfortune." Home cannot make up for what happens outside; they are all defenseless, and tragically aware of it.

The Jewish child, in contrast to the "Aryan," has leisure; he has time to think about himself. The Hitler Youth is closed to him.

That child, too, sits at home, whose father is Jewish, but whose "Aryan" mother would be taintless, if she had not followed him into an infatuation contrary to her "duties to the race." She has heard stories of half-Jews who were declared "Aryan" after their mothers took an oath that they were not the issue of the Jewish husband, but of an adulterous liaison with an "Aryan."

This devastation has entered the souls of children. If the "Aryan" child suffers objectively through the destruction of the family, the "non-Aryan" child received the full subjective impact: he knows how great the damage is. He knows the grief of his parents because they are Jews and their chances of making a decent living have been taken from them. He sees one Jewish parent going about like a criminal, and the growing hatred or the tragic pity that the "Aryan" parent feels for the other. And he loves both his parents; perhaps, however, he adores the Fuehrer; and his deepest wish is to "belong"—to be a "pure Aryan."

The quarter-Jews are in the strangest situation of all; those children having (according to the Nuremberg laws) one Jewish grandparent are treated almost like "Aryans" in school; they are good enough to be *aufgenordet* (Nordified), and it will be their duty in time to marry a "pure Aryan." For their part, "Aryans" are permitted to marry quarter-Jews— indeed, some of them will have to, to bring about the state's "Nordification." At home, the child must resign himself to the fact that one of his parents is a half-Jew. Some of these children have been given the businesses of their half-Jewish fathers, and taught that, whether the father has founded it and brought it to success or not, it actually belongs to the child, and the father is countenanced as manager by him and his mother. The Fuehrer wills it.

These shattered "mixed" families are the exception, however. A much larger group of "mixed" families have retained dignity and pride, and have not been broken by the degradations they suffer under National Socialism. Whether by regarding themselves as a nation which they hope to see united into a national Jewish State, or by a standard of reason and humanity which is out of place in modern Germany, they stand with the opposition made up of millions of Catholics, Protestants, liberals and ordinary decent human beings. And if their children have been kept out of the Nazi schools and put in the Jewish ones, they feel personal pride and the distinction of belonging in this "camp." They have a chance of organizing because they live harmoniously in closed groups. And, through all the danger, they are far more *gemutlich* than any Nazi—or apparently Nazi—family can be today.

Of course, many "non-Aryan" families have been reduced or destroyed under National Socialism. Robbed of a future, children were sent abroad to school or emigrated, if they could, to start life again in England or America or Palestine. The parents, alone in Germany, often do not dare to correspond with them, and many have died, without seeing their emigrant children. Often months pass before the children learn of the death of these parents.

The life of the "non-Aryan" family has been altered in the dissolution. The "non-Aryan" child of a "mixed" family cannot face his relatives openly any more. He feels his situation as a problem to them, even to those whose sympathies lie with the Jewish members of the family.

The separation which exists throughout Germany in the lives of adults and children—a separation between official and private life (such as it is), between controllable and secret activities—makes schizophrenics of many children. Bewildered and torn, forever at odds with themselves, they turn inward in tragic confusion.

Association between "Aryan" and Jewish children, of course, is absolutely forbidden.

They don't concern themselves about their state of mind; all efforts are made so that the children of Germany shall not worry, for the country has become a powder-keg; thoughts might set it off.

The so-called "quarter Jews," who have only one Jewish grandparent, will not be included in the separate schools. A separate Jewish elementary school is to be established wherever a sufficient number of Jewish children are to be found in one community or within the area of one urban or rural educational district. It will be necessary, in this case, to put children of different school ages in one classroom, because, for the establishment of these separate Jewish schools, twenty school children are to be considered as a sufficient number.

The Nazis, of course, place no funds whatever at the disposal of such schools, and it is often as a result of this lack of money that "children of foreign blood" are subjected to the martyrdom of Nazi instruction. In the Nazi schools, they are used to the same end as everything else. They are living examples in "Racial Science." The Jewish child is called forward by the teacher; she stands on the platform, defenseless and trembling before her schoolmates (who are not allowed to be her playmates) while the teacher demonstrates the "distinctive marks of the Jewish race." "What do you see in this face?" the pupils are asked; and, whatever the face shows, the children answer what they have learned from the Sturmer: "A gigantic nose, negroid lips, inferior frizzy hair." And the tears in those dark eyes, the scarred spirit!—the scar that can never be explained or atoned for! "What else do you see?" asks the teacher; and when the pupils are silent, feeling that there is a boundary to cruelty, the teacher adds at last: "You see, besides, a cowardly and disloyal facial expression."

"Aryan" pupils learn from living examples and are taught not only "racial characteristics" but how to treat these types.

During the morning recess, all the children lined up at the door of the canteen for a cup of milk and a piece of bread. Whenever a little Jewish girl reached her turn, the teacher in charge held up the cup, and cried, "Run along, Jewess! Next, please!" And this was repeated daily. The little Jewish children were never spared the necessity of standing in line and reaching for the cup they were never given. The Christian children had to witness this scene daily, to learn how to treat a hungry Jewish child.

The mark of this treatment on the lives of the Jewish children is frightful, of course; but the results are terrible also for the "German," the "Aryan" children—for while the Jews are only tortured, they are corrupted, deeply corrupted. Some of the strongest of the "non-Aryans" may come through, and leave childhood with toughened nerves. But the "Aryans" are in peril, for their sense of justice and humanity is being stolen from them. And unless they meet other influences, they will lose all sense of truth—the sense which balances us and allows us to walk through the world.[27]

For further information read *Mischling, Second Degree* by Ilse Koehn.

Reading 29

Childhood Memories

Elizabeth Dopazo* grew up in Nazi Germany. In the following excerpt she remembers her childhood:

It seems . . . you convince yourself in your mind that it really did not happen to you—you read it somewhere, you saw it in the movies, but it really didn't happen to you. You don't want it and you try to dismiss it from your mind and it all becomes a little vague and hazy until you're confronted by something that reminds you. After I spoke about it to the classes a few times and started dwelling on it in my mind and it became real, then it was really a nightmare. I didn't want to talk about it but I thought, "Why don't I once and for all relive the whole thing and then maybe I'll feel a little more at peace," although you never do.

I was born in 1929, so things were fairly peaceful then. I was born in Saxony which is now the Russian part of Germany. My father had a hairdresser business, but he was very often not at home because he was a representative of the Watchtower Society (we were Jehovah's Witnesses) so he used to go pick up the literature in Leipzig and distribute it around the countryside on his bicycle. We had a lot of friends and meetings in our home. Things were very nice.

As time went on, the first thing I remember was when I was four years old. That was in 1933, the year Hitler came to power and people started this nationalistic fever. Our neighbors would go to the police and say, "These people are holding meetings and many people come to the house and who knows what they're plotting." Right away it started. My father was arrested for the first time in 1934. He had to go to a stone quarry prison. The prisoners used to walk by our house, and he was one of them, and my mother . . . they were only in their twenties then, and we were little.

My father wouldn't join the Nazi party because of his religious convictions; it was totally against the principles of the Bible to be militaristic. My family was very close-knit. We had a huge shelf and a globe and just two comfortable chairs where my mother and father would sit and read and we had just little stools, my brother and I. Mostly we read and talked. My father spoke five languages. He also corresponded with people all over the world and that already made you suspect. That period ended when my father was arrested in 1936 and that's the last time we saw him. We had breakfast one morning and the Gestapo came in and arrested him at gunpoint. I was seven. Well, then my mother was arrested too—right after. They already told her when they came for my father that they would come for her too. The arresting women officers took us and my mother by train to North Germany to deliver us to my grandparents' doorstep. My mother wasn't allowed to go in or anything. She got a two and a half year sentence with six months in solitary. She was considered less subversive than my father.

We had letters from her, and even from my father in the beginning because he was in various prisons. When he was transferred to the concentration camp we didn't hear from him again. He died in 1941. Unlike Jewish people, German citizens were notified of death, so we do have a telegram saying that my father had passed away of heart failure at the

---

*Ms. Dopazo is a Brookline parent who speaks to classes about her experiences. Video tapes of Ms. Dopazo are available at the Resource Center. Oral History prepared by Barbara Perry.

age of thirty-five. On the back it said that due to persistent stubbornness of this prisoner he couldn't be released. You see, German political prisoners like Jehovah's Witnesses did have an opportunity every six months to sign papers saying they would obey the laws of the fatherland and join the army and then they would be released, but my father *could not*. It was totally against our belief to take up arms against anyone.

I had met my grandparents once before. It was very difficult for my brother and me. I was seven at this point and he was six, and we spoke a dialect much as if Southern children would come up here and people made fun of them because of how they look and sound and what their parents stand for. My grandparents were Jehovah's Witnesses too, but not as strong. They stopped going to meetings when we came because they felt they would be arrested too and then what would happen to us? So they kept a very low profile.

We had to quickly change our way of speaking so maybe we wouldn't be so noticeable. In school right away it started, you see. We had to raise our right arm and say "Heil Hitler" and all that sort of thing and then we didn't do it a few times. A few times was all right. You can drop a handkerchief, you can do a little something, but quickly they look and they say, "Ah, you're different and you're new in the school." So you're watched a little more closely. You might get one or two children who'd tell on you but it was rare. The teacher would bring you to the front of the class and say "Why don't you say Heil Hitler?" and you were shaking already because you knew, unlike other children, if you told them the real reason there'd be trouble. For us to say "Heil Hitler" and praise a person would be against our belief. We shouldn't, because we had already pledged our allegiance to God and that's it. So, we could stand and be respectful to the government, but we were not to participate in any adulation for political figures.

We didn't want to offend God. We thought we could die, but that doesn't mean much, but if we offend God then we lose out altogether. That much we knew, but then we didn't want to explain why because we were afraid that by the time we got home our grandparents wouldn't be there and we would be put in an institution, so we used to make little excuses but you can't do that every day. So in no time at all we also said it, because we were just too afraid.

My brother and I talked about all these things at home after school. We had a little attic we used to go in and discuss what would be best. We grew up very fast. We never really had a childhood.

When my mother was released from prison in 1940 she had to sign papers that she would not divulge anything she heard or saw or anything that went on in prison. She had to report to the police once a week. She never spoke of it even to her mother until after the war, because even without meaning to, if someone said something . . . you just couldn't trust anybody at all. You couldn't really trust your family.

My mother came out of prison and she had to work in a factory and then the bombing started. By this time we were in Lubeck, which was one of the first cities to be bombed by the British and those were phosphorus bombs . . . everything went up in flames, fire, and we lost our apartment. By sheer coincidence, this night we were with my grandparents outside the city. If we had not been I wouldn't be here now, because over three thousand people died that night from the falling buildings, heat and fire. People in streets, trying to escape—the asphalt gets soft and you stick to it. It was the most ghastly sight. For three days the fires burned. When we were able to go in we couldn't even find the place where we had lived.

Later, around age twelve or thirteen, we joined the Hitler Youth, which we actually didn't want to do, but the Gestapo came to my grandparents' house, just like you've seen it in the movies with the long leather coats on and they stood at the front door and they were saying, "Your grandchildren have to join the Hitler Youth and if they don't by Thursday we will take stronger measures." After they'd left we told our grandparents we'll join tomorrow, even if we hate all that stuff. They agreed we'd better do it and we very quickly donned those uniforms and just went right along with it.

As time went on, my brother, when he was thirteen or fourteen, sort of was swayed. You know, you have to believe in something. He wanted to be a German officer and said our father had been wrong all along and that we went to the dogs for our father's beliefs. He died for his ideals and where are we? He was very angry. I was too, but not as much. I was torn between what would be the good thing to do and what would not.

In fact, just before the war ended, we were afraid my brother would denounce—that he would go to the authorities and say that my family is against the regime and I don't want anything to do with them anymore; I want to join the army and I don't want my family hindering me in getting ahead because they've done that enough as it is. We were not allowed to go to higher education because we were a detriment to others. So you can imagine how he felt when the war finished. He was all disillusioned and shattered.

During the war, we children were sent to Austria for six months as evacuees to get away from the mental anguish of the daily, daily, daily bombings. We spent more time in the cellar of our school than in the classroom. By this time I was in the Hitler Youth and we used to march and sing those stupid songs and in the morning we had to raise the flags. I would drop the flag and hope that the kids would laugh—silly things like that. I felt I did a little something.

There was a boy I knew from home who went to a different school than I, so when I went to Austria we would write to each other and we were friends. His family also were political dissidents. They were not Jehovah's Witnesses but they were against the regime so they were hassled too. It's funny how you stick together. So we wrote to each other. At this time I was fourteen and he was fifteen. He had left school for a year to make some money to help his family. Where he was working in some type of storehouse, he had access to food including candy which you never, ever saw. So he sent me periodically, a parcel of marzipan and I was immediately, when I received the parcel, so afraid. I thought, "Oh, where does this come from? Where did he get this?" Something had to be wrong because candy had to be obtained from some source that wasn't legal. Everything had to do with what is legal and not legal—rules for everything. Things were very orderly.

He said in his letter, "Don't mention the candy when you write to me," so that was an added factor. I wanted so desperately to let him know I didn't want the candy. *I didn't want it!* I was afraid that if my teacher or the other children found out I had candy they'd want to know where it came from and then they would write to his parents or something. As a child you magnify in your mind what can happen.

So he sent a second parcel. By this time I knew when we were going home. By the time we got home he had already committed suicide. One day, when he was at work, the Gestapo came into his establishment. At that time you knew the difference between Gestapo and police. You thought, "Gestapo...no, it couldn't be." The Gestapo wouldn't really be interested in candy stealing. That would be more the normal police. The next day, police came. He thought they'd found out that he stole candy and they had come to take him away to prison. So he decided to end it all and he jumped in front of a fast moving train from a bridge.

The police were not coming to get him. That was the first funeral I ever went to. I remember it so well. It was a cold, cold day, in winter and I borrowed my aunt's coat. I just couldn't believe it. I felt responsible and his parents were very cool to me afterwards. I felt, indirectly, they blamed me also and I already blamed myself. He meant well. The system did that to us.

Using Reading 29

Mrs. Dopazo visits classrooms to work with students as they think about the power of propaganda and as they struggle to yield their simple explanations about this history. The following responses from students indicate the power of her presence:

In schools the Jews were taught to hate themselves. When I read what Mrs. Dopazo experienced, I was particularly touched when she mentioned that you couldn't even trust family. If you can't trust your own family, who can you trust?
—an 8th grade student

This woman's life is scary. I can't imagine what it must be like to have the Gestapo walk into my breakfast time and arrest my father right in front of my eyes.
—an 8th grade student

Mede von Nagel also lives in America today. She remembers her childhood as a nightmare.

She was born in the town of Mannheim in 1933. Her birth was a great disappointment to her father, who wanted sons to serve Hitler and the nation. Of even greater disappointment was the fact that Mede did not have any of the Aryan traits of her blonde older sister. Instead, Mede says she was "cursed with auburn hair and dark brown eyes."

It was not until the fourth child that the father was rewarded with a blond, blue-eyed son. "At last," he said, "the child I wanted."

Mede's parents taught her to believe in Hitler as a "super god" and in Germany as the superior country. She and her sister were trained to be the "unquestioning helpmates of men." Failure to perform as this "model of obedience" could result in public humiliation.

Mede was exposed to the massive Nazi rallies in Munich when her grandfather forced her to stand for hours "between thousands of black boots" and listen to the screaming crowd.

When Germany began to collapse, Mede's world was "turned upside down." Hunger, air raids, death, and destruction were impossible for a country that was supposed to be superior. Her "super god" had been branded a "fanatical murderer," and all Germans, including the youth, had also been labeled as murderers. "What we had thought was good now was bad, and bad now became good."

Confused and angry, Mede tried to search for answers in postwar Germany, but all she found was a "deathly silence . . . nobody talked." For years Mede felt a "shame" for her upbringing and her parents. "We children were the forgotten victims who did not get liberated."[28]

Citations

Chapter 6

[1] Reprinted from *They Thought They Were Free* by Milton Mayer by permission of The University of Chicago Press. Copyright 1955 by the University of Chicago Press.

[2] Irving Horowitz, *Taking Lives: Genocide and State Power* (Transaction Books, 1980), pp. 37, 38.

[3] Hannah Arendt, *The Life of the Mind: Thinking*, Volume I (New York: Harcourt Brace Jovanovich, 1971

[4] From *No Substitute for Madness* by Ron Jones, published by Island Press, Covelo, CA 95428. © 1981 by Ron Jones. Used with permission.

[5] Milton Mayer, *They Thought They Were Free*.

[6] From *The War Against the Jews* by Lucy S. Dawidowicz. Copyright © 1975 by Lucy S. Dawidowicz, Reprinted by permission of Holt, Rinehart and Winston, Publishers, pp. 203-205.

[7] Erich Goldhagen, "Obssesion and Realpolitik in the Final Solution," *Patterns of Prejudice*, Vol. 12, January-February 1978.

[8] Ibid., p. 4.

[9] Ibid., p. 3

[10] Ibid. (Secret Party circular on the antisemitic campaign and the "Jews and The War," 1943.)

[11] Ibid., p. 3.

[12] Ibid., p. 9.

[13] Ibid., p. 2.

[14] Henry Friedlander, "Toward a Methodology of Teaching about the Holocaust," (original paper), 1978, p. 19.

[15] Erich Goldhagen: Report for the Facing History and Ourselves Project at a Brookline Teachers' Meeting, Oct. 5, 1977, p. 1.

[16] Ibid.

[17] Sybil Milton, "Artists versus Hitler; The Social Responsibility of the Artist in Nazi Germany," paper presented at the International Conference on the Lessons of The Holocaust, Philadelphia, October 1978.

[18] Barbara Traietti Hearne, *Lessons on Propaganda Posters*, (Facing History and Ourselves Project).

[19] Haim Ginott, *Teacher and Child* (New York: Macmillan, 1972).

[20] Schools Council General Studies Project, "Nazi Education" (Longman Group Ltd. Resources Unit, 1972), p. 4.

[21] Erika Mann, *School for Barbarians* (Modern Age, 1938).

[22] Gregor Ziemer, *Education for Death: The Making of a Nazi* (Oxford University Press, Copyright© 1941). Reprinted by permission the author.

[23] Erika Mann, *School for Barbarians*.

[24] Erika Mann, *School for Barbarians*.

[25] Gregor Ziemer, *Education for Death*.

[26] Erika Mann, *School for Barbarians*.

[27] Ibid.

[28] Mede von Nagel, "The Nazi Legacy—Fearful Silence for Their Children," *Boston Sunday Globe*, Boston, Massachusetts, October 23, 1977.

7

Victims of Tyranny

Perhaps we universalize the Holocaust because it seemed to kill off the Enlightenment; it acquainted us with guilt; it testified to inhuman possibility; there aren't any civilians anymore and we are capable of anything. That is a great deal to assimilate....[1]

Overview

In the next two chapters students begin to learn about the victims of the expulsions, resettlements, transports, ghettos, labor camps, factory camps, and crematoriums. The "final solution" resulted in the systematic extermination of almost all Jewish people in Europe.

This chapter is about the civilians of Europe who were selected by official Nazi policy for destruction independent of war. Millions of people such as Poles, Gypsies, Ukrainians, and Belorussians who fell victim to the Nazi policies of genocide, "were not soldiers or accidental victims of the war," wrote Michael Novak, "these were civilians chosen for racial, religious, cultural or political reasons for destruction along with the Jews."[2]

It is estimated that one-quarter of all Gypsies in Europe were killed, along with one-quarter of all Polish civilians, one-fifth of the Ukrainian civilians and one-quarter of all Belorussians.

But treatment of other people remained relatively random in contrast to the highly rationalized and total destruction of Jews under Nazi occupation.[3]

One-third of the Jewish people in the world were hunted down and exterminated by an elaborate organization of citizens, military, and government bureaucracy.

While planning the invasion of Poland in 1939, Hitler promised the destruction of what he called the Jewish race in Europe. In the first stage of the "final solution," Jews were concentrated in ghettos where they died of hunger, disease, cold, and exhaustion.

Although the initial plans for the "final solution" were kept secret, those involved in the carrying out of the early stages of concentration and mass shootings were witnessing the development of the practices of the mass murders, later to become a "war within a war," the Holocaust,* against all Jews. The victimizers used a special bureaucratic language to cover their actions. Often these euphemisms masked the reality of the

---

*The following definition of the word *Holocaust* is found in *Never To Forget* (p. xv) by Milton Meltzer: "A complete or thorough sacrifice or destruction, especially by fire, as of large numbers of human beings. The word derives from the word *olah* in the Hebrew Bible. It had the religious meaning of a burnt sacrifice. In the Greek translation of the Old Testament the word became *holokauston*. The English definition made it 'an offering wholly consumed by fire." We have found it helpful to use Lucy Dawidowicz's concept of a "war within a war" to describe the war against the Jews, the Holocaust.

order. The word *Endlosung* (final solution) was used to cover the real decision to murder all Jews. *Aktion* (action) was used to describe a mass extermination in a certain time. *Judenrein* (free of Jews) meant the murder of all Jews in an area. Even the gas chambers, *Spezialeinrichtunger* were called "special installations" or *Badeanstalka,* which meant bath houses.

According to Lucy Dawidowicz:

The Final Solution grew out of a matrix formed by the paranoid delusions that seized Germany after World War I and the emergence of Hitler and the National Socialist movement.[4]

The policies of race, imperialism, living space, and the milieu of traditional and radical antisemitism all combined to deny the Jewish people their citizenship, their jobs, their homes, their nation, their humanity, and finally their right to live.

As Hitler moved from "the internal domestic stage to the second phase—aggression and war," he combined the mission to annihilate the Jews with the destruction of Bolshevism. And "Hitler's mission to annihilate the Jews within the tradition of antisemitism by which the Germans sought self-definition grew as his organization and propaganda spread."[5]

Hitler's attempt to murder all Jewish people became fully integrated with his international policy of war. Again Dawidowicz suggests that:

In his mind, the destruction of the Jews was the way to restore Germany to its virile Germandom. But once he encountered Alfred Rosenberg, Hitler's political horizons expanded; he began to see the Jews primarily as an international group whose destruction demanded an international policy. . . .[6]

Rosenberg further showed Hitler the possibilities of exploiting Russia as the political locus of international Jewry, thus providing him with the eventual major theater of operations for his war against world Jewry.

Hitler combined the annihilation of the Jews with the destruction of Bolshevism, both of which could be accomplished by an invasion of Russia. The whole was supported in racial terms: the innate racial superiority of the Aryans whose culture justified their need for Lebensraum. . . .[7]

Throughout the war, as each new country was conquered, orders were made regarding the treatment of Jews in the occupied areas. Antisemitic decrees imposed on the Jews included: the wearing of a special badge, forced labor, looting of Jewish property, and expulsion to labor camps. Infectious diseases, starvation, and over-crowding killed many people before mass selections were made for extermination. Ghettos were established as a transitional stage in the solution of the Jewish problem, and Jews were isolated in overcrowded, unsanitary conditions.

Within these ghettos Jewish institutions were set up to govern welfare and life in the ghetto. Various forms of physical and spiritual resistance helped Jews to survive for a while under these conditions: political parties continued, education was carried on, supplies and food were smuggled, newspapers were printed, and radios were turned to Allied radio broadcasts. At the same time the process of concentration, death, and the "final solution" spread. In 1942 the Wannsee Conference drafted plans for the extermination of eleven million Jews, and in 1943 all ghettos, except Lodz, in the USSR and Poland were liquidated.

Even when the German military position began to deteriorate in the East, the top priority remained the "final solution." Although military supplies and soldiers were needed for the Eastern Front, railroads transported Jews to annihilation camps. Even Slavs were given permission to fight beside the German army in order to save the war. When plans were made by the army for Jews to labor for the war effort, the SS refused to delay the "final solution." The carrying out of the extermination of the Jews tolerated no delays even in the name of principle, economics, or military strategy.

When in 1943, a time of German military defeats, Himmler ordered the expansion of the plan to colonize the East to include the Baltic countries, White Russia, and the Crimea, "Hitler became the realist.... But the final solution did not fall into this category. Its completion was urgent...."[8]

Reading 1

A Question of Numbers

"We are not in a contest to measure pain or degree of victimization,"[9] and yet we cannot escape estimates about the numbers of civilians selected to be murdered independent of the enormous amount of killing in World War II.

... Figures dull the mind, unless one tries to visualize the faces of the old and young, men and women, intellectuals and peasants, and all the days of sunshine and rain they would have seen had their lives not been wrenched from them.[10]

The following statement by Eva Fleischner, a Catholic theologian and educator, warns us not to avoid the struggle with numbers, no matter how odious, because the confrontation with the particular victims gives the Holocaust its meaning:

There is something odious about playing the numbers game. Every single human life is precious, as the rabbis of old remind us. But we can attain universality only through particularity; there are no short cuts. The more we come to know about the Holocaust, how it came about, how it was carried out, etc., the greater the possibility that we will become sensitized to inhumanity and suffering whenever they occur. If we take shortcuts we are in danger of losing all distinctions, of what Yosef Yerushalmi calls the "debasement of our vocabulary." We may soon, then, have simply one more word which for a short time was a new and powerful symbol, but which quickly became emptied of all meaning."[11]

Using Reading 1

The author of *The Other Holocaust*, Bohdan Wytwycky, has tried to document the history of the millions who were exterminated along with the Jews. He wrote about the question of numbers:

So many were killed so recklessly, with such criminal intent and such thoroughness, that for many no records were kept and no witnesses have survived. On the other hand, such vast mountains of material remain to be sifted that no single human being could acquaint himself with all of it.... Estimates are inescapable.[12]

Teachers and students struggle to grasp the meaning of the numbers of human lives exterminated. Our numbers, like our vocabulary, cannot help us to make the leap in imagination necessary to be able to imagine the lives lost in the extermination. One teacher describes how the collective numbers took on new meaning for her. She describes holding the hundreds of responses to an ad placed by Yad Vashem, the Holocaust museum in Israel, in American newspapers. The ad asked for testimony about any Jewish person exterminated in the Holocaust.

I felt I was touching sacred papers. I was overwhelmed—it was another one of those moments—each page gave life through memory to somebody's mother, father, sister, brother, son and daughter—I felt compelled to sit until I had read every page—every testimony. In some sense I was witnessing the dissolving of the collective number—6 million—and the birth of a memory for each family member for whom life was so precious and unique.

Teachers might prepare a lesson using the Yad Vashem forms in order to inquire about the purpose, the person remembered, and the surviving family member. Teachers and students might discuss the children of survivors and the meaning this experience might have for the Jewish person today.

Activity 2

Filmstrip: *The Camera of My Family*

The first targeted Jews of the Nazi racial policy were the German Jews. The Jews of Germany, most often assimilated into the German nation and difficult to identify, didn't easily fit into the "race-hate." The Nuremberg Laws had to be defined to distinguish the German Jewish Citizens from the "other" German citizens.

The following time line, adapted from *Taking Lives* by Irving Horowitz, details the stages of the Nazi program.

1933—"The Jews are our misfortune," the Jewish problem is uniquely a German curse.
1935-37—Only Aryans or persons of German blood could be citizens—Nuremberg Laws.
1938-39—Anti-Jewish riots, first concentration camp opened at Buchenwald.
1939-40—War, ghettos sealed and made into concentration camps.
1942-44—Liquidation of all ghettos, Jews exterminated.
1945—Destroy all Jewish remnants and clean the Third Reich of all the activities of the previous stages.[13]

Since many of the visuals used in this curriculum are actual propaganda films made by the Nazis, we are victims, consciously or unconsciously, to the power of the visuals. The filmstrip *The Camera of My Family* helps destroy the stereotypical image of the Jews so powerfully designed and perpetuated by the Nazi propaganda machine.

The answer to the question, Who were the European Jewish people, should include a variety of images.

The filmstrip is the personal account of Catherine Noren's search for her German roots. She documents the world of her family until it disappeared in the Holocaust.

Using Activity 2

In Chapter 3, Roman Vishniac's slide tape depicts the Jews of the small eastern European villages and towns. *The Camera of My Family* depicts another group of Jews living a more "modern life." Both the Jews of the traditional world of tribal hates and little education, and the Jews of the modern world of complex institutions, and modern inventions fell victim to the power of prejudice, racism, and hate. There were no protections.

The following, adapted from Henry Feingold's thesis, is included here to provoke more thinking about the questions, Who were the Jews? and Why did this happen to the Jews of Europe? Since the earlier chapters introduced information about historical antisemitism, it is also important to include information on other dimensions of history that came together in a particular setting to produce the Holocaust.

Feingold describes a "modernizing elite" of European thinkers who had a belief in change and an "optimistic view of what the world might become." Among the "universalizing elite" were a large number of Jewish thinkers who belonged to their nations, and according to Feingold, were often the "most avid generators and carriers of the national culture." But because they were involved in international activities and were seeking ways to confront the social, economic, and personal problems of the emerging modern societies, they were seen as a threat. Although these thinkers were only a small percentage of the Jewish masses and were dispersed across Europe, vulnerable and in need of protection, their influence in spreading the ideas of the enlightenment, equality, and hope for all humanity were seen as dangerous. They hoped for a modern scientific world where change would help destroy traditional hates and bring people together.

As the Jewish thinkers watched a society that had not truly accepted them they could identify and criticize the failings of the governments while hoping for improvement. They joined international agencies, became international lawyers and businessmen, joined peace movements and supported the World Court, the League of Nations, and the United Nations.

This universalism, wrote Feingold, was one "that did not so much reject national loyalties as it refused to be contained by them."*

Reading 3

The Ghettos—1939-1945

The process of deportation, opening and liquidating ghettos, and building extermination facilities was going on at different paces and with different support at various times all over Europe. On October 10, 1939, western Poland was annexed by the Third Reich. In September, Heydrich ordered that ghettos be established in occupied Poland. In November of 1939, Jews in Central Poland were told to wear an identifying armband. And on November 28, 1939, the first Polish ghetto was established at Piotrokow. One year later, on November 15, 1940, the Warsaw Ghetto was sealed off from the rest of Poland. And by August 17, 1940, there were mass demonstrations by starving people in the Lodz Ghetto. By December 1940, secret archives called the "Oneg Shabbat"

---

*This material was adapted from "Determining the Uniqueness of the Holocaust: The Factor of Historical Valence" by Henry L. Feingold, *Shoah*, Spring 1981.

were begun in the Warsaw Ghetto to record the events. In October 1941, the Theresienstadt Ghetto was established in Czechoslovakia. By September 13, 1942, 300,000 Jews of the Warsaw Ghetto had been deported to Treblinka Extermination Camp in a large scale *Aktion* and 40,000 from the Lwow Ghetto had been deported to other extermination camps. In the *Aktion* of Bialystock Ghetto of February, 1943, 1,000 Jews were killed on the Stok and 10,000 deported to Treblinka. Finally, the Warsaw Ghetto was liquidated from February 16 to May 1943.[14]

Using Reading 3

For some students it is useful to construct a time line of the events of the steps up to the "final solution." It has been our experience that students have a tendency to lump all the camps and ghettos into one symbol, into one country, and into one time, which distorts the reality of the experience. When students realize, for example, that ghettos, work camps, and concentration camps existed mostly in eastern occupied Europe, not in Germany, they are surprised. When they learn that there were thirty-nine concentration camps in France they are also surprised. Victims of the ghettos and later of extermination and work camps spoke many different languages, came at different times, in different years, and were often shipped from camp to camp if they had survived a selection to the gas chamber and crematorium, the disease and starvation, the dehumanization techniques, the medical experiments, the hard labor, the long marches, and the arbitrary random killings.

As the power of this information begins to break the simple notions and concrete images commonly held, even by those attempting to "understand" this part of the history, the students are truly changed by the enormity of these events. Just the bureaucratic decisions that had to be made to carry out the transfers, to build the crematoriums, to purchase the gas, to purchase the one-way railroad tickets dispel long-held myths about this history.

The following is an account of the terror in a Polish town before the ghetto was established, written by Jacob Birnbaum.

On September 1, 1939, the Germans launched an all-out attack on Poland. The next day, Saturday, September 2, at 8:30 in the morning, Piotrkow was heavily bombed, resulting in many casualties. The heavy bombing continued through the following day, destroying a number of public buildings, including the city hall, police headquarters, the State Bank, the post office, and the city's water system. On Tuesday, September 5, at 4:00 in the afternoon, German ground troops entered Piotrkow and conquered the city after two hours of street fighting. That same day they set out on a search for Jews in the almost deserted city, found twenty, among them Rabbi Yechiel Meir Fromnitsky, and shot them in cold blood. Thus it began.

The next day, September 6, the Germans set fire to a few streets in the Jewish quarter and shot Jews trying to escape from their burning homes. Only those who ran unnoticed over a narrow "Dead Lane," which was discovered at a later date, managed to survive. In light of the German atrocities, those Jews still hidden in their homes were panic stricken. They soon noticed that the Germans were interested primarily in their property. Both individually and in groups the Germans invaded the Jewish community and stole virtually everything they feasibly could—clothes, linen, furs, carpets, valuable books. They often invited the Poles on the streets to take part in the looting, after which they would fire bullets into the air in order to give the impression that they were driving away the Polish "thieves." These scenes were photographed by the Germans to demonstrate for all that they were protecting Jewish property from Polish criminals.

Jews, many of them elderly, were kidnapped and sent to forced labor camps where they were tortured and beaten — often to the point of loss of consciousness. These kidnappings took place during the days preceding Rosh Hashanah, as well as on the holy day itself. Jewish men hid themselves in cellars, attics, and elsewhere, yet most were caught. The worst fate was that of the Jews sent to the SS Precinct. The main objective of the work there was torture, not productivity. Jews were forced, for instance, to do "gymnastics" while being beaten and subjected to various other forms of humiliation. . . .

One common insult suffered by the Jews during the early days under the new regime was their being chased away or beaten as they tried to wait in line for food together with other citizens. All Jews who attempted to resist were gunned down immediately.

During the holy days of Rosh Hashanah, as Jews hurriedly gathered to pray in the synagogues and private homes, still more torture was inflicted upon them. Several German officers entered the Great Synagogue stirring up much confusion among the worshipping Jews, many of whom attempted to escape. Twenty-nine worshippers were beaten brutally and taken away to prison, among them the lay leader of the congregation. The news of this event spread rapidly through the city, causing a great deal of fright, consternation, and anxiety. There were no worshippers in the synagogue on the second day of Rosh Hashanah.

Two days before Yom Kippur, German officers and troopers entered the shut synagogue, broke up the furnishings, and completely demolished the beautifully ornamented eastern wall. . . .

An order to erect a ghetto in Piotrkow (for the first time officially labelled a "ghetto") was issued on October 8, 1939, by the city commissar, Oberburgermeister Hans Drexel. This was the first ghetto in the occupied areas of Poland. According to the decree, Jews from all parts of the city had to leave their belongings in their former dwellings and move to a small area designated as the official Jewish ghetto — only their pillows and blankets were they allowed to take with them. Thus, with one stroke of legislation, hundreds of Jewish families were uprooted and forced into poverty. Only three Jews were allowed to live outside the ghetto: old Dr. Shantser, who had been an apostate for sixty years, Jacob Witorsh, who was a Turkish citizen, and an Egyptian named Kam. These exceptions proved only temporary; during the "Action" (liquidation) they were to be transferred to the ghetto and from there, together with the remaining Jewish population of Piotrkow, to Treblinka and the gas chambers.

The city's German commissar ordered all Jews to wear on their right forearm yellow badges bearing the inscription *Jude* (Jew). The order included not only those who would call themselves Jews but also those Christians who had even one Jewish parent even if the parent had converted. Anyone found without such a badge faced death. There soon followed a rapid series of orders which were to become the standard for ghettos throughout the German occupied territories. The decrees, which purported to legally expropriate Jewish property, ruled that no Jew was permitted to possess more than 2,000 zloty ($400) or any gold and pieces of jewelry. Jews were forbidden to work in industry or in public and governmental institutions; they were not allowed to bake bread for Aryans nor to engage in trade with them. They were neither permitted to heal Aryan patients nor to be treated by Aryan physicians. Furthermore, Jews were not allowed to leave the city without a permit nor to ride on a train. An even greater burden was the demand for frequent "contributions" by the local authorities on their own initiative or, more frequently, on the orders of the Governor-General. The demands were simply impossible to fulfill. . . .

Not only the German police saw to it that the new decrees were executed; to keep the ghetto population in constant terror, the German authorities established a Jewish Community Council, ordering it to deliver 1,000 workers daily for the task of erecting barracks which were designed to house masses of displaced Jews from the neighboring towns and villages. This marked the beginning of the second phase in the German plan to exterminate the Jews.

In a short time, the displaced Jews started streaming in enlarging the number of Jews in Piotrkow to 25,000 — a figure representing one-half of the entire general population of Piotrkow. To make matters worse, the Gestapo gave orders to reduce the size of the ghetto, making the conditions barely livable. Arrests and executions became daily occurrences during this phase of the extermination process. It was obvious to the Piotrkow Jews that the Germans were preparing for an imminent "Action," but surrounded by the hostile community, they felt helpless to react. The tension reached its climax on October 13, 1942, when the tragic news spread that the "Action" was to begin on the following day.

By 2:00 a.m. the Ukrainian SS police together with the "navy blue" Polish police had surrounded the ghetto. In the dark hours before dawn, the first shots were heard as the German SS entered the ghetto and chased the terrified Jews from their homes toward the assembly point. Those assembled on the square were arranged in two columns. The right column was to wait for a future selection (these were mainly individuals who worked in German firms and who carried "good" worker cards stamped with a swastika), while the left column was destined for the deportation to Treblinka. Many families were broken up: Children were torn away from their mothers and wives from their husbands. The cries and screams of the children were silenced by the German with kicks from their boots or blows from their whips. Often parents or children who qualified for the "right" column shifted over to the other group in order to go to their deaths together with their families. The children from the orphanage were deported together with the orphanage staff. In the presence of the Gestapo the Ukrainians walked between the rows of assembled Jews, emptying their pockets of everything they found. So many Jews were forcefully deported that the "Action" required eight days. It was completed on Wednesday, October 21. Five thousand Jews were deported to Treblinka every other day, squeezed into fully packed freight-cars with 150 people in each. Before the Jews entered the cars, they were ordered by the Germans to remove their clothing and shoes. Old, sick, or weakened people were shot on the spot and dead bodies were strewn out along the whole route. In total, over 20,000 Jews were deported, including many from outside of Piotrkow. The Jews who were shot during the deportation, most of them old or sick, numbered roughly 1,000.

After the "Action" about 2,000 "legal" Jews remained in Piotrkow, the majority working in German factories or serving as policemen and community officials. Besides those employed, the small ghetto also contained non-employed "illegals" who either came out of their hiding places after the "Action" or returned from the "Aryan side" because of their treatment by the civilian population there. These "illegals," most of them young men, would steal into the "small ghetto" during the night and were often shot while trying to slip through the barbed wire. Within a short period of time, the number of inhabitants of the ghetto grew to 4,000. The German authorities took note of this and decreed that no more than 2,000 workers would be allowed to remain.

A series of "Actions" against the "illegals" took place between November and December 1942. They were herded into the empty synagogue in large groups and then marched to the Rakow forest where they were shot and left in mass graves.

On November 25, at the urging of the Gestapo, the head of the Judenrat appealed by means of posters to all "illegals" to come out and register in order to become legalized. In response to the appeal, most of those hidden in the bunkers complied and came forth to register; but, on November 30, an "Action" was carried out against these newly-registered "illegals." They were arrested at the gathering place on the ghetto's main street and brought to the synagogue.

In spite of what had already transpired, the community was not prepared for what happened next. The Ukrainian SS police surrounded the building and fired their bullets into the synagogue through the windows. An eyewitness, Richard Chentzinski, later described the macabre spectacle. A group of Ukrainians, headed by Oberleutenant Lukner, took eight children out of the synagogue and burned them in basins on a bonfire in front of the synagogue. The torture lasted for several days.

Conditions in the synagogue were terrible. The people were crowded together, without light, without food, and without water. The cries of children and old people and the stench of human excrement filled the air. The dead lay all about. On Saturday, December 19, 42 survivors were taken out of the synagogue and led along the road leading to the Rakow forest. There they found the Gestapo waiting for them with a truck and tools. They were given spades and shovels and ordered to dig five long ditches. At 3:30 p.m. an enforcement of Germans and Ukrainians arrived. The Jews refused to obey the command to take off their clothes. Some of them attacked the enemy and a few even managed to escape. All the rest, however, were shot. That night, the last Jews remaining in the synagogue were taken out in groups of 50 and led to the Rakow forest. Aware of the newly-dug graves, some Jews tried to escape. The Germans opened fire and killed many of the Jews, leaving their bodies lying near the synagogue. The Jews marched to Rakow through the darkness, weeping, reciting psalms, and pronouncing the "Shema Israel" as they went to their own funerals. Five hundred and sixty Jews were shot in the Rakow forest that night. Those who were wounded— but not fatally so—were buried together with the dead in the mass graves. More was to come. Always the survivors thought the Nazi pogrom would end as others had. It was not to be.

The Germans found out through informers that a group of Jews succeeded in obtaining Aryan documents in preparation for their anticipated escape from the ghetto. This denunciation elicited another mass execution in the Jewish cemetery, on April 21, 1943, a day that coincided with the first days of the Warsaw Ghetto Uprising. But for Piotrkow a heroic end was not to be. The current policy of the Germans at that time was to collect all the remaining Jews from the occupied territories into SS concentration camps. The small ghetto of Piotrkow, like many others throughout Eastern Europe, was doomed to liquidation. The last remnants were shipped to their deaths in July 1943. A sign was put up on the railway station which read: *Petrikau ist Judenrein* (Piotrkow is clean of the Jews).

After the termination of World War II, the approximately 1,400 survivors from Piotrkow, those who had somehow survived the camps or partisan warfare in the Rakow forest, tried to reestablish their lives. The majority of them joined with other survivors in the occupied zones of Germany and Austria and participated in the "illegal" immigration to Palestine, where, after settling, they fought in the underground organizations and later in Israel's War of Independence. Some emigrated to Canada, the United States, and South America. Approximately 400 survivors felt a strong urge to return to Piotrkow and fulfill a promise they made to each other during the Nazi persecution. They recovered the remains of the Jews from the mass graves in the Rakow forest and gave them a proper Jewish burial in the Jewish cemetery. They started to restore the Great Synagogue . . . . that was until they were shocked by the brutal murder of three Jewish women who had tried to reclaim their property from their Polish neighbors. This tragic event was far from unique. The vicious antisemitic reaction to their attempted resettlement convinced the survivors that the hatred of the Jews had not died with the Nazis, that Jewish life in Piotrkow was no longer possible. They left, never to return. Today there is but one Jew remaining in Piotrkow—a childhood friend and playmate of mine—Ruben Hipsher."*

This detailed account is included because it gives background information about the ghetto, which helps explain many of the events documented in the film *Warsaw Ghetto*. For teachers who cannot obtain the *Warsaw Ghetto* film, this reading can be used.

Activity 4 **Film: *Warsaw Ghetto*****

This documentary was made by the BBC using actual Nazi propaganda films and photographs. Many of the photos are from Himmler's private collection. The Nazi photographer had been instructed to capture the effects of malnutrition and disease on the faces of individuals who could be followed from year to year. These photos, Himmler felt, would document the existence of inferiors before the superrace of the Third Reich was complete. It is a difficult movie to watch. The visual images are so powerful that sometimes it is difficult to remember that these films are propaganda films designed to create stereotypes of the subhuman, yet the victimizers are the ones we do not see and they created the malnutrition, disease, and death that these photos are documenting. It is also hard to imagine that the horror in this film is a ghetto; imagining the extermination camp and the "living hell" of the labor camps is impossible.

---

*The complete story of the Piotrkow Ghetto written by Jacob Birnbaum of Newton, Mass., is available at the Resource Center.

**It should be noted that there has been criticism by Lucy Dawidowicz as to the appropriateness of showing this film. One fear is that this film will reinforce stereotypes.

Using Activity 4

A teacher remembers:

After viewing the films made in the Warsaw Ghetto and films of the concentration and extermination camps, some students wanted silence — others demanded discussion.

One student bent her knees to her chest, wrapped her arms around her knees and peered out at me for a long silent time. Finally, she raised her head high and said, "Mrs. Strom — I think these pictures are going right through me — I can't understand or believe what I see." In class, we talked about how we have no vocabulary for these horrors and atrocities.

Preview this film with a student or small group of students and prepare the class for the violence and sadness they will see. Locate Warsaw, Poland, on the map. Review *The Life That Disappeared*, by Roman Vishniac, and *Boy of Old Prague*. Discuss the power of the visual images and stereotypes.

The following are questions about the film to explore with students.

• What does it mean to have to move through the streets with all that you care about in your hands? What do you take with you? Can we adapt so quickly to such forced change? What happens to traditions, values, beliefs, routines, and the roles of women, men, and children? The attempt to carry on a "normal" life was resistance for some.
• Students might need to clarify the concepts of a ghetto. Do you have to have a physical boundary like a wall to be in a ghetto?
• What examples of hope are seen in the ghetto? Of educating the children? Of carrying on the traditions of religion? Of organization and planning designed to keep hope?
• What does it mean to *have to* wear an armband?
• Actual film footage and photographs are part of Himmler's private scrapbook. What does this say about Himmler's motivation? Why did the cameraman follow the same faces month after month?

The Jewish Council's role and that of the Jewish Police are topics for students exploring the complex social, political, and economic structure of the ghetto. The dilemmas these people faced were extremely complex.

Creating lessons and evaluation activities for this history sometimes seems impossible. Ultimately the Holocaust must be a part of the curriculum and therefore subject to evaluation. The teachers, though, find they prepare activities carefully and creatively!

One teacher assigned a one-paragraph response to a specific topic.

The detailed paragraph was to contain the following elements:
• A topic sentence that states what the topic is.
• One or more sentences of facts, giving the "basic details" about the topic.
• Which *issue* at the end of our curriculum — the issue of *obedience* or the issue of *responsibility* — comes through the stronger to you when you think about this topic? Choose one and explain how it is related to this topic. Use two or three sentences.
• What *implication(s)* exist for our own lifetimes when we study and think about this topic? Use one or two sentences.

As a model for this assignment, the teacher wrote his own paragraph in response to this topic.

Included here is his paragraph:

It is a fact that Hitler and his assistants ordered that detailed filmed records — movies and still photographs — be kept of the concentration camps, executions, the Warsaw Ghetto, etc. Perhaps the reason for this can be found in Herman Goering's testimony at the Nuremberg trials — that someday, his own statue would appear in all German schools — that Nazi deeds would be a great source of pride in future generations.

I see the issue of responsibility here, especially when I think about the soldier taking pictures on the film, Joseph Schultz. To me, that photographer is as guilty of the murders which took place as the soldiers, standing by coldly, perhaps proudly, watching and recording the deeds of his fellow-soldiers. In our own lives, we face many situations where, although we are not committing any crimes or injustices against another person, we may be standing by, in a position to do something, if only to "tell" someone else without jeopardizing yourself. For example, suppose a Nazi photographer had smuggled out pictures of what was really taking place in the concentration camps when they were first starting, since so many people around the world could not believe that the rumors of gas chambers they heard were true? Sometimes, even a small act of "resistance" by a small person can make a difference, then, or now.

The following are student responses to *Warsaw Ghetto:*

I think for once the enormity of the things that went on really hit me. I imagined all those people who had families and little problems of life just being killed.

I was frustrated that I myself could not believe or accept that what I was seeing really happened.

It was awful. Those were people and other people did that to them. How? No matter what kind of teaching they had, training or whatever. Didn't they ever stop to think that the people in the Warsaw Ghetto were people?

When I saw movies like this I felt like crying, but I never did — I just looked somewhere else or closed my eyes. Movies, like that, like the Holocaust, I think I learned much more than from other movies that weren't really real.

Like we can't always learn only the good things that happened in life, we also have to learn about the bad things too. Because if we only learned the good things, then we wouldn't know anything that happened a long time ago and we wouldn't then have any history of the world. It isn't because everything in the world is bad, but it's just that there are good and bad things.

During the year we saw a film called The Warsaw Ghetto. *Some people in the class were effected very much by this film. I was not effected at all. At first I felt guilty, but then I thought that I shouldn't feel guilty because there's nothing I could have done about it. I must admit though it did leave a mark on me. I think you should show this film as long as you teach the Holocaust, I think that it is very important for me to realize not for me to feel guilty about my opinion about the movie. I thank you for helping me see this.*

Activity 5

Filmstrip: *The Warsaw Ghetto* — One Type of Resistance*

With all these obstacles, isn't it a wonder that there was Jewish resistance at all? What is astounding is not that there was so little resistance, but that there was so much![15]

Since the subject of resistance is so complicated we have included a variety of examples of resistance, some passive, some active. This filmstrip documents one famous incident of resistance. For many, remembers Saul Nitzberg, "Resistance took the form of outsmarting the Germans by living another day."

The counterattack of the Jews in the Warsaw Ghetto in April and May of 1943 is well documented. In fact, Himmler's own documentation of the Warsaw Ghetto includes films of the fierce fighting between the German army tanks and the surviving men and women of the Warsaw Ghetto who fought from rooftops and sewers as the ghetto was burned by the Germans building by building. The destruction of the Warsaw Ghetto had been promised for Hitler's birthday.

Using Activity 5

This filmstrip, narrated by Theodore Bikel, is one introduction to the subject of resistance. The narration describes spiritual and armed resistance in general and the experience of an underground resistance survivor. Milton Meltzer's *Never To Forget* and Albert Friedlander's *Out of the Whirlwind* introduce the complexities of the subject of resistance. (For further suggestions on the topic of resistance see the Bibliography available at the Facing History Resource Center).

On May 14, 1943, twenty-five days after the beginning of the uprising, the SS general complained:

The Jews have a new strategy: they clamber up to high places and conceal themselves in space amidst the rubble, which they render totally inaccessible to us. From there they ambush us with grenades and gasoline bottles, as in the early days of the battle. It appears that even destroying the house is not enough to rid the Ghetto entirely of Jews.

They dug bunkers, made tunnels, lived in sewers, attacked with knives, acid, clubs, and a few weapons.[16]

General Stroop's report of the Jewish Ghetto was written in May 1943 and described the unexpected, unusually strong Jewish Resistance as a great surprise. Later, after the war, General Stroop's sole printed page report was used at the International Tribunal at Nuremberg. According to the report, there were 9 German dead and 86 wounded in the attack that "eliminated 56,065 people . . . not counting others killed through blasting, fire, etc." The following excerpt is from the Stroop report:

The resistance put up by the Jews and bandits could only be suppressed by energetic actions of our troops day and night. The Reich Leader—SS (Himmler) ordered therefore on April 23, 1943, the cleaning out of the ghetto with utter ruthlessness and merciless tenacity. I therefore decided to destroy and burn down the entire ghetto. . . . Jews frequently remained in the burning buildings, and jumped out of the windows only when the heat became unbearable. They then tried to crawl with broken

---

*Available at the Resource Center under title of: *The Warsaw Ghetto: Holocaust and Resistance.*

bones across the street into buildings which were not on fire.... Life in the sewers was not pleasant after the first week.... Tear gas bombs were thrown into the manholes, and the Jews driven out of the sewers.... Countless numbers of Jews were liquidated in sewers and bunkers through blasting. The longer the resistance continued, the tougher became the members of the Waffen-SS, Police and Wehrmacht, who always discharged their duties in an exemplary manner.*

Other resistance has been documented from the Vilna Ghetto in a manifesto for Jewish resistance and in stories of individual courage. The fighters near the Russian city of Novgorod destroyed power stations, railroad terminals, and food supplies. They lived in the woods without food, arms, or shelter.

Reading 6

Two Accounts from the Warsaw Ghetto

A Jewish Fighters' Organization manifesto stated:

...We—the besieged in the Ghetto—send you heartfelt, brotherly greetings.

Every threshold in the Ghetto has been and will remain a fortress.... At the cost of our lives, we shall not surrender. Along with you, we aim to punish our common foe for all the crimes.... This is a struggle for our common freedom, for common human and social dignity and honor!

We shall avenge the crimes committed in Auschwitz, Treblinka, Belzhetz and Maidanek!

Long live liberty.... Long live the moral struggle against the occupier![17]

In 1942 Chaim Kaplan, inside the Warsaw Ghetto, kept a diary in which he recorded his life there. He wrote:

The whole nation is sinking in a sea of horror and cruelty.... Anyone who keeps such a record endangers his life, but this doesn't alarm me. I sense within me the magnitude of this hour and my responsibility to it. I have an inner awareness that I am fulfilling a National obligation.... My record will serve as a source material for the future historian.

He also wrote:

This journal is my life, my friend and my ally. I would be lost without it. I pour my innermost thoughts and feelings into it and this brings relief. When my nerves are taut and my blood is boiling, then I am full of bitterness. In my helplessness I drag myself to my diary and at once I am enveloped by a wave of creative inspiration, although I doubt whether the recording that occupies me deserves to be called "creative." Let it be edited at some future time as it may be. The important thing is that in keeping this diary I find spiritual rest. That is enough for me.[18]

Using Reading 6

The resistance leadership came from a variety of backgrounds: engineer, agricultural specialist, typesetter. Without arms, the Jews resisted as their houses were systematically destroyed block by block.

---

*The full Stroop report in the original German covers 66 printed pages. It is reproduced as Document 1061-PS, Exhibit USA-275, in the official printed record of the trial, vol. 26, pp. 628-694. It lists the casualties on the German side as 8 dead and 86 wounded.

A wall was built around the Warsaw Ghetto.

Finally, many took poison if they had it or leaped from burning buildings to their deaths. Finally a Nazi official could report, "As of today there is no Jewish district in Warsaw."

Reading 7

On Resistance

Before the summer of 1942, Jews did not know the truth about the extermination camps. Until then, Jewish mothers, fathers, and children did everything possible to "resist" the Nazi efforts to dehumanize and to starve them; they fought to survive—many Jews hoped for an early German defeat. One Warsaw Ghetto educator wrote:

The eyes of the world are turned to America and its leader Roosevelt. Will they allow . . . all of Europe . . . to become Nazi-Fascist? . . . Thus the war is destined to become worldwide. And in a world war, the defeat of Germany and Italy is certain.[19]

While many hoped for an early German defeat, the daily acts of resistance continued. Victims chose to control their lives by such acts as continuing their religious practices at the risk of immediate death, listening to a short-wave radio for Allied announcements, smuggling food, infiltrating the SS, following a command in order to survive to tell the story, educating the children. "Some bore children as if to say, No matter what you do, the generations will go on." Others fought desperately to stay with their children.

For many Jews, who were locked in ghettos and camps without arms or a way to escape, hope of surviving and preserving human dignity were their goals. Conditions for armed resistance were available to the non-Jewish resistance. Non-Jewish had mountains and forests to escape to and smuggled weapons with which to fight for their goals, political freedom, and their homeland. Jews could not count on the Poles, Czechs, and other resistance fighters to help them fight.

That very decision — whether to stay in the ghetto with the mass of Jews or to escape and fight outside — was an agonizing one to make. Many passionate debates took place over the moral issue. Usually they ended with the resistance forces staying inside. They helped the inmates of the ghetto struggle against oppression and then led the fight against deportation to the death camps. They left only when there was no longer any chance to be useful in the ghetto.[20]

Under such conditions, those who conducted an organized and armed resistance were a minority. That even such a minority existed was a miracle. The right question to ask, Elie Wiesel has said, is not, Why didn't all the Jews fight? but, How did so many of them?[21]

But, when they could, Jews did take part in national resistance movements, fought in national armies, and joined resistance movements. Acts of resistance, when possible, presented dilemmas that remind us that this history of the Holocaust defies simple explanations. For example, during the Nazi occupation in Europe, a resistance movement developed. The resistance movement would ambush German patrols and carry out acts of sabotage. The Germans adopted the following response policy: for any act of sabotage or killing of German soldiers, they would kill fifty men in the nearest city or village. Every additional act of sabotage in that area would increase the number of men that they would execute.

When escape was made, Jews were not always welcome to join other non-Jewish resistance. For example:

When some 3,000 of Tuczyn's 6,000 Jews fled to the forests nearby, their Ukrainian neighbors turned in between one-third and one-half of them within a few days. Most of the rest were killed by the Ukrainians themselves, and some were caught by the Germans; exactly 15 survived. Similarly, Don Ben-Yakov, a former partisan who now lives in Israel, reports that of the ghetto fighters who escaped from his one-time home of Czestochowa in Poland, most were murdered by Polish partisans.[22]

Acts of resistance were countered by the Nazis with a violence beyond belief. In 1941, a group of Dutch Jews dared to attack German police in Amsterdam. Hannah Arendt reports their punishment:

Four-hundred-thirty Jews were arrested in reprisal and they were literally tortured to death, first in Buchenwald and then in Mauthausen. For months they died a thousand deaths, and every single one of them would have envied his brethren in Auschwitz and even in Riga and Minsk. There exist many things considerably worse than death, and the SS saw to it that none of them was ever very far from their victims' minds and imaginations.

In the ghettos, Jewish Councils, *Judenrat*, were set up to work with and sometimes for, the Nazis, to govern the ghetto, to meet the increasing demands for labor and lives.

The ghetto Councils, faced with the choice — to resist or not to resist — did not act on a rigid pattern. There were variations, but the end remained the same. In Vilna, the Judenrat did whatever the Germans asked. . . . In Kovno, while the Council seemed to be carrying out Nazi orders, its leader worked secretly with the resistance, and the Jewish police chief doubled as a resistance leader. In Lvov, two Council heads heroically refused to collaborate with the Nazis.[23]

Adan Czerniakow, the leader of a Judenrat, committed suicide. The following is one response to his choice:

. . . Did he choose death rather than sanction any further murder of his people? Whatever his motives or intention, his death did not help us. We felt it was desertion, not leadership. Czerniakow failed to sound the alarm and summon his people to resistance. If he had been given a glimpse of the bottomless abyss to which we were consigned, he did not pass his knowledge on to us. His suicide only intensified our despair and our panic. If it bore witness to his personal integrity, it did not attest to his greatness.[24]

Using Reading 7

The subject of resistance under such conditions of extremity as the ghetto, the concentration camp, and the death camp demands careful and thoughtful scrutiny. Most Jewish resistance fighters did not survive and, until very recently, historians had little documentation of resistance; now memoirs, trial depositions of witnesses, records of trials, and thousands of oral interviews with survivors are providing important information, from which we learn that resistance encompassed the entire range of human responses.

For documenation of responses of individuals, nations, and institutions that chose to resist the Gestapo order to round up and deport Jewish citizens, see Chapter 9.

Reading 8

Janusz Korczak

This is the story of the deportation of Janusz Korczak and the children of the Orphaned Child's Home. It is taken from *The Holocaust Kingdom* by Alexander Donat.

It was Wednesday, August 5, 1942 when the Nazis came for the children in Korczak's charge. It was not clear whether Korczak told the children what they might expect or exactly where they were going; but his staff of teachers and nurses had the two hundred orphans ready for the Nazis when they raided the orphanage at 16 Sienna Street. The children had been bathed, given clean clothing, and provided with bread and water to take with them. The Nazis burst in, but the children, though frightened, did not cry out or run and hide. They clung to Korczak, who stood between them and the Germans.

Bareheaded, he led the way, holding a child by each hand. Behind him were the rest of the two hundred children and a group of nurses clad in white aprons. They were surrounded by German and Ukrainian guards, and the Ghetto police. One could see how weak and undernourished the children were. But they marched to their deaths in exemplary order, without a single tear, in such a terrifying silence that it thundered with indictment and defiance.

When the Judenrat heard of what was happening in the orphanage, everyone there tried desperately to telephone, to do something, but they tried only to save Janusz Korczak, not the two hundred children. Korczak was told of their efforts in his behalf, but refused aid; instead, he chose to go with the children to the *Umschlagplatz*.

Other orphanages besides Korczak's, some of them larger, were liquidated by the Nazis in the very same manner, and there were many other nurses and teachers who refused to leave their charges but heroically went with them to their deaths. Korczak became a model of heroism and humanity in the sight of barbarism.

Long before the time of murder, Korczak had written, "There is no greater mishap than to be born a man." He died, as he had lived, simply and with dignity. "Oh, how difficult is life, how easy death!" he wrote in his Ghetto diary and in his death he became a monument to the 100,000 murdered Jewish children of Warsaw.

Their deaths also gave the Ghetto its first insight into the true significance of resettlement. Why had the Judenrat tried to save Korczak? If the two hundred children were really going to be resettled somewhere in the East, wasn't it perfectly natural for their teacher and shepherd to go along with them? What we had suspected all along — but could not or did not want to beleive — was now confirmed. What we had dismissed as the hysterical outpourings of morbid imaginations was now reality. This was not resettlement; this was deportation to death. Moreover, the Judenrat knew, the heads of the Jewish police knew, and they had not told us.[25]

Using Reading 8

Again the Jewish Councils are mentioned. Their role as peace keepers is very complicated. One fictionalized view of the Judenrat is portrayed in *The King of the Jews,* by Leslie Epstein. The controversy over his portrayal of the dilemmas these councils faced each day reminds us not to rush to judge the victims, but to remember to ask why the victimizer created such extreme situations under which normal choices for human beings were abandoned.

Reading 9

Two Stories of Resistance: Choiceless Choice
The Holocaust Kingdom documents deportation.

I saw a young mother run downstairs into the street to get milk for her baby. Her husband, who worked at the *Ostbahn,* had as usual left earlier that morning. She had not bothered to dress, but was in bathrobe and slippers. An empty milk bottle in hand, she was headed for a shop where, she knew, they sold milk under the counter. She walked into Operation Reinhard. The executioners demanded her *Ausweis*. "Upstairs . . . *Ostbahn* . . . work certificate. I'll bring it right away."

"We've heard that one before. Have you got an *Ausweis* with you, or haven't you?"

She was dragged protesting to the wagon, scarcely able to realize what was happening. "But my baby is all alone. Milk . . ." she protested. "My *Ausweis* is upstairs." Then, for the first time, she really looked at the men who were holding her and she saw where she was being dragged: to the gaping entrance at the back of a high boarded wagon with victims already jammed into it. With all her young mother's strength, she wrenched herself free, and then two, and four policemen fell on her, hitting her, smashing her to the ground, picking her up again, and tossing her into the wagon like a sack. I can still hear her screaming in a half-crazed voice somewhere between a sob of utter human despair and the howl of an animal.[26]

Another young woman I knew, after much trouble, finally persuaded a friend of her husband's, a man who managed a shop, to register her with his firm so that she could have an *Ausweis*. "I'm doing it for you because you're Leon's wife," the man told her, but it cost her every penny of what remained of the possessions she and her husband had owned when he had left in September 1939. "You know I'm not taking this for myself. You understand, don't you? It's because of the others. . . ." Then he explained to her how the very next day she must move to the shop area and bring her eight-year-old boy with her. There she would be safe. She needn't worry about having no money or about leaving her apartment; she must bring only the absolute necessities with her, no more than the apartment house janitor's wheelbarrow could carry in one trip; but everything would be all right.

And, indeed, she was reassured. Calmly, she went about doing what she had to do, fighting for the life of her child. Her husband, she knew, would be proud of how well she had managed. Holding her little boy's hand, she told him, "Now, you mustn't be afraid. Mother is looking out for you." As she was turning the corner into the street where they lived, the little boy ran ahead, as children do. He skipped around the corner before she got to it. Why had she let him do it? How could she have let her sense of danger relax even for an instant? The street seemed so calm. When she heard him scream, "Mama! Mama!" she sped around the corner and had just time enough to see a little body with a familiar striped sweater disappearing among the mass of other bodies in the wagon surrounded by police. She thanked God that she was in time to explain, that she had an *Ausweis*.

"But Madam," the police said, "how can we be sure that this is *your* child?"

She had not, it seems, quite understood. No more than any of us did at first. And when she finally did understand, she was beaten brutally "for resisting the authorities," but not a sound, not a sob escaped her. The policemen showed that they were not, after all, completely heartless. By surrendering her *Ausweis* to them—a commodity more valuable than gold at that point—she was permitted to get into the wagon, too, to accompany her son to the *Umschlagplatz*, and what lay beyond.

As the wagon began to move away, anyone within earshot could hear the voice of an old woman coming from beyond the boards of the van, repeating monotonously, "Tell Zalme Katz his mother was taken away . . Tell Zalme Katz his mother was taken away."[27]

Using Reading 9

One of the deterrents to mounting early armed resistance was the inability of the Jewish families to recognize just when the Germans would recall a policy of protection. For example, the victims had confidence in documents that were at first respected by the Nazis but later recalled.

For the victims and the victimizer, the early stages of the genocide were not recognized as such. For example, these two stories tell of the confidence ghetto victims had in the *Ausweis* as a guarantee of security against "resettlement."

The following passage gives us some insight into the complexities of the question, Who resisted and why?

The basic factor in the Ghetto's lack of preparation for armed resistance was psychological; we did not at first believe the Resettlement Operation to be what in fact it was, systematic slaughter of the entire Jewish population. For generations, East European Jews had looked to Berlin as the symbol of law, order and culture. We could not now believe that the Third Reich was a government of gangsters embarked on a program of genocide "to solve the Jewish problem in Europe." We fell victim to our faith in mankind, our belief that humanity had set limits to the degradation and persecution of one's fellow man. This mentality underlay the behavior of the Jewish leadership at the very beginning of the Resettlement, when the overwhelming majority voted against armed resistance. Some felt we ought to wait for a joint rising with the Poles. Others were resigned to sacrificing 70,000 Jews rather than jeopardizing the entire community of 400,000—the Nazi policy of collective responsibility was very much alive in our memories. Still others were religious Jews, committed to the tradition of *Kiddush Hashem:* that is, a martyr's death in the name of God. They believed that, when the enemy came for us, we should be dressed in our prayer shawls and phylacteries, pouring over the holy books, all our thoughts concentrated on God. In that state of religious exaltation, we should simply ignore all Nazi orders with contempt and defiance; resistance, violence, only desecrated the majesty of martyrdom in sanctification of the Lord's name. I heard the following unexpected argument in favor of nonresistance.

"Try to imagine Jesus on the way to Golgotha suddenly stooping to pick up a stone and hurling it at one of the Roman legionnaires. After such an act, could he ever become the Christ? Think of Gandhi and Tolstoy, too. For two thousand years we have served mankind with the Word, with the Book. Are we now to try to convince mankind that we are warriors? We shall never outdo them at that game."

Lastly, there was the fact that there can be no struggle without some hope. Why does the man unjustly condemned to death fail to turn on his guards as he is led to the gallows? Why did the three thousand Turkish prisoners Napoleon ordered drowned put up no resistance? Why did fifty thousand French Huguenots permit themselves to be slaughtered in a single night by French Catholics? And what of the Armenians?

There is no precedent for the eventual uprising of the Warsaw Ghetto because it was undertaken solely for death with dignity, and without the slightest hope of victory in life.[28]

Reading 10 Einsatzgruppen—Nazi Killing Units

The Einsatzgruppen carried out the early stages of the "final solution." Three thousand men were to make up four killing groups, which were instructed that Jews were Bolsheviks, and that both were enemies of Germany. The mass exterminations began in occupied Soviet territory with the murders of all Jews, and certain Communist leaders and members of the Red Army. The Einsatzgruppen came directly behind the German attack into Russia in 1941. Two million Jews were killed by these special units. They would, according to Otto Ohlendorf, Chief of Einsatzgruppe D:

... enter a village or a city and order the prominent Jewish citizens to call together all Jews for the purpose of resettlement. They were requested to hand over their valuables to the leader of the unit and shortly before execution to surrender their outer clothing. The men, women and children were led to a place of execution which in most cases was located next to a more deeply excavated anti-tank ditch. Then they were shot, kneeling or standing, and the corpses thrown into the ditch.[29]

The procedures of Einsatzgruppe A were described by SS Colonel Jager:

The decision to free each district of Jews necessitated thorough preparation of each action as well as acquisition of information about local conditions. The Jews had to be collected in one or more towns and a ditch had to be dug at the right site for the right number. The marching distance from collecting points to the ditches averaged about three miles. The Jews were brought in groups of 500, separated by at least 1.2 miles, to the place of execution. The sort of difficulties and nerve-scraping work involved in all this is shown by an arbitrary chosen example:

In Rokisis, 3,209 people had to be transported three miles before they could be liquidated. . . .

Vehicles are seldom available. Escapes, which were attempted here and there, were frustrated solely by my men at risk of their lives. For example, three men of the commando at Nariampole shot 38 escaping Jews and communist functionaries on a path to the woods, so that no one got away. Distances to and from actions were never less than 90-120 miles. Only careful planning enabled commandos to carry out up to five actions a week and at the same time continue the work in Kovno without interruption.

Kovno itself, where trained Lithuanian (volunteers) . . . are available in sufficient numbers, was comparatively speaking a shooting paradise.[30]

According to Ohlendorf, the order to kill the Jews came verbally from Heydrich, although Himmler was given the orders directly by Hitler.

Himmler transmitted the orders for the "final solution" from Hitler to the Einsatzkommandos at Nikolayer:

He repeated them the liquidation order, and pointed out that the leaders and men who were taking part in the liquidation bore no personal responsibility. The responsibility was his alone, and the Fuehrer's.[31]

Later, in a letter, Himmler wrote:

The occupied Eastern territories are to become free of Jews. The execution of this very grave order has been placed on my shoulders by the Fuehrer. No one can deny me the responsibility anyway.[32]

Using Reading 10

The men who made up the special killing groups came from the SS, SD, Gestapo, the State Police, and the Waffen-SS. Later, they were aided by Ukrainians, White Russians, Letts, and Lithuanians. Erich Goldhagen suggests some of the "forces" that motivated these killing units:

After the extermination of a Jewish community in the region of Nemel, the commanding officer of the massacre was convinced that he had just contributed toward the fulfillment of an historical mission; and to his men who stood bewildered and shaken — a state that attended many of the murderers after their first massacre — he exclaimed: "Men! Damnit! A generation must perservere in it so that our children may have peace."

Hitler was no doubt the author of the Final Solution. Driven by his consuming hatred of the Jews, he ordered that all, without exception, be killed. To accomplish this aim, he employed a small army of murderers — executioners and sundry auxiliary bureaucrats and officials. That small army pursued the extermination of the Jews with efficiency, energy and in many cases, even with zeal. Manifold were the motives that moved the executioners and those that directed and aided them from behind neat desks in quiet offices . . . fidelity and fantasy, praetorian duty and ideological frenzy were the main twin driving forces of the murders of European Jewry.[33]

Reading 11 Inciting the Local Population to Start the Killing

To break Russian resistance to Hitler's policy of living space and racial purity, all Jews and Communist leaders were to be killed. The Einsatzgruppen were, when possible, to stir up native antisemitic forces by starting pogroms against Jews. One report describes an attempt in Riga, the capital of Latvia, to stir the local population against their own fellow human beings. Before the Security Police put in an appearance, the leader of a Lithuanian pro-German partisan unit was to make the start of the pogrom appear as a spontaneous local outburst. In this way, no German order or instigation would be noticed from the outside. During the first pogrom in the night from 25 to 26 June 1941, the Lithuanian partisans did away with more than 1,500 Jews, set fire to several synagogues, and burned down a Jewish district of about 60 houses. During the following night, about 2,300 Jews were made homeless in a similar way. In other parts of Lithuania, similar actions followed the example of Kovno, though smaller and extending to the Communists who had been left behind.

Another report, prepared in October 1941, complained that Einsatzgruppen operating in Estonia could not "provoke spontaneous anti-Jewish demonstration with ensuing pogroms" because "adequate enlightenment was lacking" so that the killings had to be done "under the direction of the Einsaztgruppe. . . ."[34]

After the war, at the American Tribunal at Nuremberg, twenty-three Einsatzgruppen leaders were put on trial "to answer the charge of destroying over one million of their fellow human beings." Most of the victims were Jews.

The defense claimed that: ". . . especially in the Baltic area, virulent antisemitism was widespread and that local groups there participated and, in fact, often started the massacres.*

The Tribunal concluded that:

. . . Whatever predisposition may have previously existed, a pogrom mentality was deliberately fostered among the local population by the invaders; and that indoctrination, the Judgment added, was designed to

---

*For further information on judgement and the war crimes trials at Nuremberg refer to Chapter 10.

"bear continuous fruit," even after the war and regardless of the war's outcome. Certain Einsatzkommandos (sub-groups of those units) committed a crime which, from a moral point of view, was perhaps even worse than their own directly committed murders, that is, their inciting of the population to abuse, maltreat, and slay their fellow citizens. To invade a foreign country, seize innocent inhabitants, and shoot them is a crime, the mere statement of which is its own condemnation. But to stir up passion, hate, violence and destruction among the people themselves, aims at breaking the moral backbone even of those the invader chooses to spare. It sows seeds of crime which the invader intends to bear continuous fruit, even after he is driven out.[35]

Using Reading 11

This reading reports that the killing units in Estonia could not incite demonstrations and pogroms because "adequate enlightenment was lacking." Discuss what is meant by "adequate."

What, according to the tribunal of judges, could the killing units have done "even worse" than the murders?

This distinction between the act of shooting innocent victims and the act of stirring up passion, hate, violence, and destruction, aimed at breaking the moral backbone of a citizenry, is important to discuss with students.

Reading 12

Rivka Yosselevscka Describes the Killing Units

In the town of Zagrodsi, in the Pinsk district, lived some 500 Jewish families. A killing squad arrived in mid-August 1942. The Jews were to leave everything in their houses, take only their children, and come out to the square for a rollcall. Trucks rolled up, and the Jews were jammed aboard. There wasn't room for everyone, so the rest were ordered to run after the trucks. A young mother, Rivka Yosselevscka, was among them. After the war, she told a court what happened:

Q: And you ran with your daughter?
A: I had my daughter in my arms and ran after the truck. There were mothers who had two or three children and held them in their arms— running after the truck. We ran all the way. There were those who fell— we were not allowed to help them rise. They were shot right there— wherever they fell.... When we reached the destination, the people from the truck were already down and they were undressed—all lined up. All my family was there.
Q: Where was that?
A: This was some 3 kilometers from our village.... There was a kind of hillock. At the foot of this little hill, there was a dugout. We were ordered to stand at the top of the hillock and the four devils shot us—each one of us separately.
Q: Now these four—to what German unit did they belong?
A: They were SS men—the four of them. They were armed to the teeth. They were real messengers of the Devil and the Angel of Death.
Q: Please go on—what did you see?
A: When I came (to) the place—we saw people naked lined up. But we were still hoping that this was only torture. Maybe there is hope—hope of living. One could not leave the line, but I wished to see—what are they doing on the hillock? Is there anyone down below? I turned my head and saw that some three or four rows were already killed—on the ground.

There were some twelve people amongst the dead. I also want to mention that my child said, while lined up in the ghetto, she said, "Mother, why are we waiting, let us run!" Some of the young people tried to run, but they were caught immediately, and they were shot right there. It was difficult to hold on to the children. We took all children not ours, and we carried — we were anxious to get it all over — the suffering of the children was difficult; we all trudged along to come nearer to the place and to come nearer to the end of the torture of the children. The children were taking leave of their parents, and parents, of their elder people.

Presiding Judge: How did you survive through all this?

Attorney General: She will relate it.

A: We were driven; we were already undressed; the clothes were removed and taken away; our father did not want to undress; he remained in his underwear. We were driven up to the grave. . . .

Attorney General: And these garments were torn off his body, weren't they?

A: When it came to our turn, our father was beaten. We prayed, we begged with my father to undress, but he would not undress; he wanted to keep his underclothes. He did not want to stand naked.

Q: And then they tore them off?

A: Then they tore the clothing off the old man and he was shot. I saw it with my own eyes. And then they took my mother and shot her too; and then there was my grandmother, my father's mother, standing there; she was eighty years old and she had two children in her arms. And then there was my father's sister. She also had children in her arms, and she was shot on the spot with the babies in her arms.

Q: And finally it was your turn?

A: And finally my turn came. There was my younger sister, and she wanted to leave; she prayed with the Germans; she asked to run, naked; she went up to the Germans with one of her friends; they were embracing each other; and she asked to be spared, standing there naked. He looked into her eyes and shot the two of them. They fell together in their embrace, the two young girls, my sister and her young friend. Then my second sister was shot and then my turn did come.

Q: Were you asked anything?

A: We turned towards the grave and then he turned around and asked, "Whom shall I shoot first?" We were already facing the grave. The Germans asked, "Who do you want me to shoot first?" I did not answer.

I felt him take the child from my arms. The child cried out and was shot immediately. And then he aimed at me. First he held on to my hair and turned my head around; I stayed standing. I heard a shot, but I continued to stand. Then he turned my head again and he aimed the revolver at me and ordered me to watch, and then turned my head around and shot me. Then I fell to the ground into the pit amongst the bodies, but I felt nothing. The moment I did feel, I felt a sort of heaviness, and then I thought — maybe I am not alive anymore, that this was the feeling which comes after death. Then I felt that I was choking; people falling over me. I tried to move and felt that I was alive and that I could rise. I was strangling. I heard the shots and I was praying for another bullet to put an end to my suffering, but I tried to save myself, to find some air to breathe, and then I felt that I was climbing towards the top of the grave above the bodies. I rose, and I felt bodies pulling at me with their hands, biting at my legs, pulling me down, down. And yet with my last strength I came up on top of the grave, and when I did, I did not know the place, so many bodies were lying all over, dead people; I wanted to see the end of this stretch of dead bodies, but I could not. It was impossible. They were lying, all dying, suffering; not all of them dead, but in their last sufferings; naked; shot, but not dead. Children crying "Mother," "Father"; I could not stand on my feet.

Presiding Judge: Were the Germans still around?

A: No, the Germans were gone. There was nobody there. No one standing up.

Attorney General: And you were undressed and covered with blood?

A: I was naked, covered with blood, dirty from the other bodies, with excrement from other bodies, which was poured on me.

Q: What did you have in your head?

A: When I was shot, I was wounded in the head.

Q: Was it in the back of the head?

A: I have a scar to this day from the shot by the Germans; and yet somehow I did come out of the grave. This was something I thought I would never live to recount. I was searching among the dead for my little girl, and I cried for her—Merkele was her name—"Merkele!" There were children crying "Mother!" "Father!"—but they were all smeared with blood and one could not recognize the children. I cried for my daughter. From afar I saw two women standing. I went up to them. They did not know me. I did not know them, and then I said who I was and then they said, "So you survived." And there was another woman crying, "Pull me out from amongst the corpses. I am alive, help!" We were thinking how could we escape from the place. The cries of the woman, "Help, pull me out from the corpses!" We pulled her out. Her name was Mikla Rosenberg. We removed the corpses and the dying people who held on to her and continued to bite. She asked us to take her out, to free her, but we did not have the strength.

Attorney General: It is very difficult to relate, I am sure. It is difficult to listen to, but we must proceed. Please tell us now: after you hid?

A: And thus we were there all night, fighting for our lives, listening to the cries and the screams, and all of a sudden we saw Germans, mounted Germans. We did not notice them coming in because of the screamings and the shoutings from the bodies around us.

Q: And then they rounded up the children and the others who had got out of the pit and shot them again?

A: The Germans ordered that all the corpses be heaped together into one big heap and with shovels they were heaped together, all the corpses, amongst them many still alive, children running about the place. I saw them. I saw the children. They were running after me, hanging on to me. Then I sat down in the field and remained sitting with the children around me. The children who got up from the heap of corpses.

Q: Then the Germans came again and rounded up the children?

A: Then Germans came and were going around the place. We were ordered to collect all the children, but they did not approach me, and I sat there watching how they collected the children. They gave a few shots and the children were dead. They did not need many shots. The children were almost dead, and this Rosenberg woman pleaded with the Germans to be spared, but they shot her.

Attorney General: Mrs. Yosselevscka, after they left the place, you went right next to the grave, didn't you?

A: They all left—the Germans and the non-Jews from around the place.

214 Facing History and Ourselves

They removed the machine guns and they took the trucks. I saw that they all left, and the four of us, we went onto the grave, praying to fall into the grave, even alive, envying those who were dead already and thinking what to do now. I was praying for death to come. I was praying for the grave to be opened and to swallow me alive. Blood was spurting from the grave in many places, like a well of water, and whenever I pass a spring now, I remember the blood which spurted from the ground, from that grave. I was digging with my fingernails, but the grave would not open. I did not have enough strength. I cried out to my mother, to my father, "Why did they not kill me? What was my sin? I have no one to go to." I saw them all being killed. Why was I spared? Why was I not killed? And I remained there, stretched out on the grave, three days and three nights.[36]

Using Reading 12

The testimony of Rivka Yosselevscka was given at the Eichmann trial in Israel. It is helpful at this point in the curriculum to think about how we hear and think about the survivor's tale.

Larry Langer reminds us that the literature of survival is just that, the stories of surviving. The Holocaust is not a history of survival; it is instead a history of mass extermination, and that is one of the dimensions of this history that makes the knowing finally impossible.

One chapter of D. M. Thomas's *The White Hotel** forces a confrontation with the "reality" of Babi Yar, the site of mass shootings of Jewish villagers near Kiev in the Ukraine. Many Gypsies died there also. Today the monument at Babi Yar does not mention the word *Jew*. For the Soviet Union their suffering is only to be seen as part of the war against facism. The Jewish victim is ignored.

The experience lies beyond our reach. Ask any survivor; he will tell you, he who has not lived the event will never know it. And he who went through it will not reveal it, not really, not entirely. Between his memory and his reflection there is a wall—and it cannot be pierced. The past belongs to the dead, and the survivor does not recognize himself in the words linking him to them. . . . Only the survivor can—bear witness, transmit a spark of the flame, tell a fragment of the tale, a reflection of the truth.
—Elie Wiesel[37]

What does Elie Wiesel mean when he writes, "Between his memory and his reflection there is a wall"?

The following are student reactions to the readings in this chapter:

This was by far the most emotional and incredible section we have had to read. I can't bring myself to think about soldiers lining people up and shooting them like those little ducks you see in amusement parks. . . .

There are times when I hate this course . . . and this is one of them. Reading about what happened to people makes me know that I would rather have been killed than watch my family, friends and even strangers being shot left and right.

---
*Although *The White Hotel* by D.M. Thomas (Viking, 1981) is not appropriate reading for junior high school students, teachers might refer to it for one of the most powerful descriptions of the stages of the "final solution."

Reading 13 **We Have No Vocabulary of Annihilation**

Do you know how one says "never" in camp slang? "Morgen fruh," tomorrow morning.
—*Primo Levi*

No one has yet invented a vocabulary of annihilation, though the Nazis created a long list of euphemisms to deflect the imagination from its concrete horrors. For this reason, we must bring to every "reading" of the Holocaust experience an intense consciousness of the way in which "free words" and euphemisms can distort the facts and transform them into more manageable events. . . . Our entry into the world of the Holocaust, our sense of its meaning, depends not only on who tells the tale, but on how he or she chooses to tell it. And how we choose to interpret what is told. Perhaps this is what Primo Levi, himself a survivor, was trying to say in *Survivial in Auschwitz* when he wrote of the use of language in the death camps:

Just as our hunger is not that feeling of missing a meal, so our way of being cold has need of a new word. We say "hunger," we say "tiredness," "fear," "pain," we say "winter" and they are different things. They are free words, created and used by free men who lived in comfort and suffering in their homes. If the Lagers (camps) had lasted longer, a new, harsh language would have been born; and only this language could express what it means to toil the whole day in the wind, with the temperature below freezing, and wearing only a shirt, underpants, cloth jacket and trousers, and in one's body nothing but weakness, hunger and knowledge of the end drawing near.

We suffer from an absence of analogies, and fall back on familiar vocabulary in our efforts to describe this unprecedented event.

This creates a difficulty for those who would write honestly about the Holocaust. All survivor accounts, and all narratives about survivors, are limited by having to speak of a world where the values cherished by western civilization were extinct, and to a world where those values presumably remain intact. But orthodox verbal scaffolds cannot support the unorthodox fates of the victims. This crucial observation leaves us with a profound dilemma, since the language of "free words" is the only one we possess.[38]

Using Reading 13

The dilemma for the reader is how to "know the Holocaust," when we know our language can't tell us. We cope instead of confront the event unless we make a leap in our imaginations to absorb the many dimensions of the experience.

Lawrence Langer writes about the literature of the Holocaust:

Since the way in which language is used to describe the Holocaust shapes our reponses and determines the image of atrocity which will be engraved on our imaginations, we must approach each written evocation of the event with a receptive but wary mind, prepared to hear many voices before we begin the arduous task of reconstructing a vision of the death camps that will satisfy our personal desire for authenticity. Certain words and expressions that have consoling associations in the world we are familiar with may sound like verbal formulas when applied to the experience of extermination. Consider Viktor Frankl's conclusions in *Man's Search for Meaning* (while remembering that Frankl himself is a survivor of Auschwitz): "When a man finds that his destiny is to suffer, he will have to accept his sufferings as his task." What comfort would these words offer to a mother and daughter who are about to be herded into a gas chamber? Words like "destiny" and "suffering," which we identify with a long tradition of religious martyrdom and tragic experience, may be less appropriate when applied to the ordeal of extermination. . . .

The language available to us has difficulty absorbing the abrasive contradiction between the fact of suffocation in the gas chamber and consoling descriptions of the event which speak of "tragic insight" or "salvation gained through suffering."[39]

Larry Langer indicates the depth of the dilemma in regard to Holocaust literature:

Heroic defiance, growing into tragic insight, needs a vision of moral order to nourish it, and this is precisely what the Holocaust universe lacks. The Holocaust is a saga without a controlling myth, opening out into an unending vista of chaos. Sporadic gestures of compassion or support within the death camps, which often saved one life at the cost of another, cannot change this. Clearly the usual notion of tragedy, with the hero or heroine caught between difficult choices, but free to embrace an attitude toward the consequences, and hence to preserve his or her moral stature, does not apply to men and women dying in the gas chambers or struggling for life in their vicinity. Agamemnon's dilemma as father and warrior, Clytemnestra's grief and later her rage, Iphegenia's very helplessness as the victim of a greater struggle, all achieve grandeur of expression by the controlling myth that lifts them into a timeless statement about human destiny and divine will. But how are we to portray the Greek Jewish mother of three children who was told by the Nazis that she might save *one* of them from execution? She was free to "choose," but what civilized mind could consider this an example of moral choice, or discover in modern history or Jewish tradition a myth to dignify her dilemma? The alternatives are not difficult, they are impossible, and we are left with the revelation of a terrifying question posed by a universe that lacks a vision to contain it. How is a character to survive any decision in such a situation, and retain a semblance of human dignity? What can one do but echo the weary refrain of the young girl who survived her family: "But, here I am and I have to live; what for?"[40]

Reading 14 Isabella Remembers

The following reading, excerpted from *Fragments of Isabella*, gives us a glimpse of part of the world for Isabella Leitner's Hungarian family before and during their deportation.

My father left Hungary for America. . . . "Give me immigration papers for my precious seven, so they can come here and live. Don't let them be murdered."

And they gave him the papers, *finally*.

But the clock ticked faster than the hands of bureaucracy moved. We received the necessary documents with instructions to be at the

American consulate in Budapest on a certain Monday morning. My mother, Chicha, and I arrived in Budapest on Sunday. We were good and early, for on Monday morning we had an appointment with life!

We were at a friend's house, chatting happily about the appointment, listening to music on the radio. There was a sudden interruption. The music stopped.

There was no appointment at the American consulate on Monday morning. It was December 8, 1941. Hungary had declared war against the United States. . . .

"Give me papers for Israel. . . ."

And they gave him the papers, *finally*.

And we received them . . . four weeks after Hitler had occupied Hungary. . . .

But mostly I remember the conversations my mother used to have with the many adults who came to visit us from other parts of Europe—business people, friends, relatives. The six kids stood around drinking in those very big words, those very big subjects—politics, art, books, and always *man's inhumanity to man*. Sometimes I was resentful. Must she care about everyone in this world? Look at me! Praise me! I want to be the most important! Why do you care so much about so many things?

But now, so many years later, I say: Thank you, Mother, for being what you were, for trying to develop me in every way.

Kisvarda was just a little town. It's where I began, where I yearned to be away from. I didn't think I could take a large enough breath there. Yet the memories of my teens are crowded not only with teen pains but also with precious hours spent with dear friends in a house alive with interests, thoughts, activities, conversations, dancing, playing, and falling in and out of love that my house—the whole town—seemed to be bursting apart.

But there were other things, too—bad things. I cannot count the times I was called a "dirty Jew" while strolling down Main Street, Hungary. Sneaky whispers: "Dirty Jews." No, "Smelly Jews"—that's what I heard even more often. Antisemitism, ever since I can remember, was the crude reality. It was always present in the fabric of life. It was probably so everywhere, we thought, but surely so in Hungary—most certainly in Kisvarda.

They really hate us, I would think. It certainly felt that way. You couldn't hide from it. You couldn't run from it. It was everywhere. It was thinly veiled, when it was veiled at all. It was just under the skin. It was hard to live with.

You, my former neighbors, I cannot live with you again. You could have thrown a morsel of sadness our way while we were dragging ourselves down Main Street. But you didn't. Why?

Please take me away from here. I don't know these people. I don't ever want to know them. I can't detect the difference between them and the SS, so I'll go with the SS.

Soon we are packed into the cattle cars . . . cars with barred windows, with planks of wood on the bars, so that no air can enter or escape . . . 75 to a car . . . no toilets . . . no doctors . . . no medication.

It is Sunday, May 28, my birthday, and I am celebrating, packing for the big journey, mumbling to myself with bitter laughter—tomorrow is deportation. The laughter is too bitter, the body too tired, the soul trying to still the infinite rage. My skull seems to be ripping apart, trying to organize, to comprehend what cannot be comprehended. Deportation? What is it like?

A youthful SS man, with the authority, might, and terror of the whole German army in his voice, has just informed us that we are to rise at 4 a.m. sharp for the journey. Anyone not up at 4 a.m. will get a *Kugel* (bullet).

A bullet simply for not getting up? What is happening here? The ghetto suddenly seems beautiful. I want to celebrate my birthday for all the days to come in this heaven. God, please let us stay here. Show us you are merciful. If my senses are accurate, this is the last paradise we will ever know. Please let us stay in this heavenly hell forever. Amen. We want nothing—nothing, just to stay in the ghetto. We are not crowded, we are not hungry, we are not miserable, we are happy. Dear ghetto, we love you; don't let us leave. We were wrong to complain, we never meant it.

We're tightly packed in the ghetto, but that must be a fine way to live in comparison to deportation. Did God take leave of his senses? Something terrible is coming. Or is it only me? Am I mad? There are seven of us in nine feet of space. Let them put fourteen together, twenty-eight. We will sleep on top of each other. We will get up at 3 a.m.—not 4—stand in line for ten hours. Anything. Anything. Just let our family stay together. Together we will endure death. Even life.[41]

Using Reading 14

In Hungary the government handed over 20,000 Jewish, Polish, and Russian citizens to be deported and murdered. Eichmann applied the policy of extermination in 1944 and 400,000 Hungarian Jews were deported to Poland to be murdered en masse at Majdanek and Auschwitz. The majority of the Jews, including children and aged were sent directly to the gas chambers.[42]

Raul Hilberg documents an attempt to ransom Jews:

A few days after the beginning of the Hungarian deportations, a Jewish delegate from Budapest arrived in Istanbul, Turkey, with a Gestapo offer to release the remaining one million Jews under German control in return for ten thousand trucks. The emissary, Joel Brand, was a member of the Jewish rescue committee in Hungary, and as further authorization he carried a letter signed on May 16, 1944, by Court Counselor Stern, chairman of the Jewish Council, and Philipp von Freudiger.

Brand had been talking to Eichmann in Budapest, and the proposal he was transmitting to the Allies had been considered by some of the highest strata in the SS and the Foreign Office in Berlin. Under the terms of the offer, the Germans were prepared to free the first 100,000 for the next thousand, and so on. Meanwhile, the killings would continue.

Both Germans and Jews were waiting for a reply. The Germans promised to use the vehicles only on the eastern front, and they were actually thinking of motorizing the Eighth SS-Cavalry Division Forian Geyer and Maria Theresia, both assigned to Hungary. The Jewish rescue committee was anxious for some move or sign of Allied acceptance which would give pause to the Germans or at least slow them down. The British, the first Allied power to receive word of the ransom attempt, summarized their attitude in a memorandum of June 5, 1944, to the United States. The Germans, in the meantime, went on with their killings.[43]

Reading 15

Searching for Parallels and Recognizing the Particular Victim

As it is our aim to study man and society we cannot escape searching for parallels . . . comparisons are essential if we are to think about the lessons posed by the Holocaust . . . we have seen that the impulse to exterminate is old and pervasive; we only have to read the newspapers to know that it still exists. . . . Of course, no single historical event duplicates the Nazi deed, but many share different aspects of the process that led to the death camps.[44]

The history of the genocide of the Armenian people after World War I and the testimonies of those survivors are stark reminders that the impulse to carry out policies of genocide are not unique to the Third Reich. The experiences of the Japanese-Americans and the native-Americans remind us that the protection of democracy is not always complete. The process of stripping selected citizens of their political, economic, and social rights and confining others in Soviet labor camps, shares similar content with the Holocaust.

And Auschwitz is linked, although not exclusively, to a cultural tradition of slavery "which stretches back to the Middle Passage from the coast of Africa, and beyond, to the enforced servitude in Ancient Greece and Rome. If we ignore this linkage, warns Richard Rubenstein, we ignore the existence of the sleeping virus in the bloodstream of civilization, at the risk of our future.[45]

The highest moral standards of a nation and citizen are tested in war. Human behavior in war often challenges our notions of good and evil and morality. The Milgram Experiment, the accounts of atrocities in My Lai, Viet Nam and Cambodia, and the confessions of Phil Caputo in *Rumors of War* raise questions about obedience and morality similar to the questions we raise about the Nazis, the German citizens, and the soldiers. In *Rumors of War*, for example, Phil Caputo describes his transformation from a "civilized" American to an American soldier who in another environment commits acts of violence he never thought possible.

What is unique about the Holocaust is that the Nazis used the tools of modern technology and the bureaucracy of a modern nation with the cooperation of citizens, army, and industry to commit genocide. The Holocaust was carried out without any compromising of policy, no matter if it threatened the nation's survival or success. A more complete discussion of the unique and universal aspects of this history is found in the overview to this curriculum.

Using Reading 15

Richard Rubenstein in his book *The Cunning of History* reminds the students of the Holocaust to recognize the uniqueness of the event but also to consider the connections the history has to Western history, especially to the dehumanization of slavery.

What is Rubenstein calling "the sleeping virus in the bloodstream of civilization"? Since most students have studied the history of Greece and Rome before this, it would be instructive to construct a continuum of slavery based just on the information and countries listed here.

Do you agree with the notion that:

It is not necessary that the analogy be perfect for a young person to hurl himself into peaceful combat against what he regards as barbarism. For him that war in Vietnam or that instance of racial injustice is his Holocaust of the moment.[46]

Reading 16 The Many Circles of Genocide

In his book *The Other Holocaust: Many Circles of Hell,* Bohdan Wytwycky writes, "the most desperate circle in the Nazi hell was undeniably the Jews." It is estimated that between 65 and 70 percent of all Jews living in Europe were killed.

The following readings detail some of the Nazi policies against other groups that fell victim to the extermination camps planned for the Jews.

Reading 17 Nazi Policy Against the Gypsies

The fate of the Gypsies was close to that of the Jews. The Nazis killed between a fourth and a third of all Gypsies living in Europe, and as many as 70 percent in those areas where Nazi control had been established the longest. Between 400,000 and 600,000 were killed.[47]

For years in Europe, the Gypsies had been labeled as primitive and unworthy. The Nazi labels of "labor shy," "asocial", and "alien blood" singled them out as enemies of the state to be resettled and later exterminated. In 1937, "Laws Against Crime" defining "asocial" were enacted under which Gypsies were sent to Buchenwald.

The law against the Gypsies, called the "Fight Against the Gypsy Menace," was passed to force registration of all Gypsies with the police. In 1938, "experience gained in the fight against the Gypsy menace and the knowledge derived from race-biological research have shown that the proper method of attacking the Gypsy problem seems to be to treat it as a matter of race . . .".[48] In 1939, all Gypsies in Germany and Poland were to be reported and forbidden to leave their homes and campsites. In 1940, a roundup and deportation of Gypsies lasted from May through October, when there was a shortage of transports. They were interned. In 1942, special laws pertaining to work, marriage, and education considered Gypsies the same as Jews. The decision to work to death persons under protective arrest was made by Himmler. Gypsies were sent to Auschwitz. From 1939 through 1943, Gypsies in other European countries were persecuted and arrested. Gypsies, along with Jews and Serbs, were slaughtered en masse near their homes and the survivors were shipped to labor and death camps.

"Wherever the conditions were suitable, i.e., where the administrative area was small and the Gypsies were easy to identify and isolate, for example in Estonia, the annihilation of the Gypsy population is estimated to have been complete."[49] When the Einsatzgruppen entered the Soviet Union, they eliminated the Gypsies as real or potential enemies of the Reich.

The Gypsies were brought to Auschwitz in large numbers at the end of 1942; then in 1943, the Nazis created a separate camp that lasted 16 months. They wore black triangles designating them as asocials. On families who weren't gassed immediately, Dr. Mengele performed his medical experiments.

In 1944, the Gypsy camp was liquidated and from then on Gypsies were gassed on arrival. When Gypsies came from Buchenwald to Auschwitz, the 800 children and 200 adults were immediately gassed.

Using Reading 17

The Association of German Gypsies claims that persecution of their people continues in West Germany today. According to Alfous Heck[50] in his article "West Germany's Gypsies: Justice Denied?" their refusal to be assimilated into West German society, "as well as their stubborn insistence on putting loyalty to clan above allegiance to host country," has led to constant harrassment from government officials and local townspeople.

In 1956, the West German Federal Supreme Court decided that "until May of 1943 most deportations of Gypsies were carried out for 'military' or 'crime-preventing' reasons, not on racial grounds." As a result, only token restitution has been granted by the German government (about $3.00 for each day spent in a death camp).

Reading 18

Nazi Policy Against the Poles

Six million Polish citizens, three million Polish Christians, and three million Polish Jews were killed by the Nazi machine by starvation, in slave labor camps, by torture, and by extermination. Poland's educated classes, its priests, its Jews, and its peasants were to be victim to the new German Empire.

Knowledge about the Nazi racist attitudes toward the Poles, Ukrainians, Belorussians, and Russians is inadequately understood. But we do know that the Nazi war against Poland was a declaration of war against the Polish people and Polish nationhood. The Nazi army attacked civilian targets, they invaded and killed civilians, and bombed residential areas.

The Nazis divided Poland as follows:
- All of western Poland and sections of central and southern Poland were annexed to the Reich.
- The rest of the Polish territories to be administered was an occupied zone, called "General Government."

The Nazis used four strategies for Germanization:
1. terror to stifle and paralyze resistance
2. expropriation of land and possessions
3. deportation
4. enslavement

A Nazi official said about the annexation of Poland and the plan to Germanize all the territory:

... In ten years there will not be a single point of land that is not German, nor a single farm in the possession of anyone but our own colonists. Already they are coming from all the provinces of the Reich to estabish themselves in these regions. Each and every one of them comes to engage in a relentless struggle against the Polish peasant. ... If God exists — it is He who has chosen Adolf Hitler to drive this vermin hence.[51]

The key rationalization required for genocide is the development of an attitude on the part of those to carry it out that its victims are less than human. A Nazi propaganda circular issued in January 1940 contained instructions for the German press:

... The attention of the Press is drawn to the fact that articles dealing with Poland must express the instinctive revulsion of the German people against everything which is Polish. Articles and news items must be drawn up in such a way as to transform this instinctive revulsion into a

lasting revulsion. This should be done, not by special articles, but by scattering phrases here and there in the text.

Similarly, it must be suggested to the reader that Gypsies, Jews and Poles ought to be treated on the same level.[52]

Using Reading 18

Although there were similarities between the Nazi policy toward Jews and toward Slavs, there were also critical distinctions, according to Bohdan Wytwycky:

• The policy to eliminate all Jews, "the war within a war," took precedence even over the war against the Allies.
• "Whereas the Slavs as a people were slated to suffer the decapitation of each nation's leadership and then the subjugation of others to slavery, the Jews were condemned to total and unequivocal annihilation."
• About 4.5 million of the total 6 million Jews who were killed perished in the Nazi gas chambers. The majority of the 10 million Slavs were shot, starved, or worked to death outside the concentration camps. About one million Slavs were killed in the camps.

Reading 19

Jehovah's Witnesses

In 1933 there were about 19,000 Jehovah's Witnesses living in Germany and they, too, became victims of Nazi terror and murder. In a letter to Hitler, the Jehovah's Witnesses stated their position: "We have no interest in political affairs, but are wholly devoted to God's kingdom under Christ his King. . . ."

In an article entitled "They Too Were Victims of Nazi Terror," Gary Nelson reports on the Jehovah's Witnesses:

. . . They would not join the Nazi Party, salute the Nazi flag, or join the army. [They practiced neutrality.]

Jewish people were murdered because they were born; Jehovah's Witnesses were murdered because they chose certain beliefs—and when the Nazi persecution of the Witnesses became "more and more hateful," they continued to choose to be Witnesses. They could have avoided the torture and death by choosing to disavow their beliefs.

The experience of Emil Wilde and Friedrich Frey are only two examples. In 1937 the Gestapo searched Emil's home, questioned his children, and threw him and his wife in prison. Emil could hear the screams of his wife as she was beaten from one o'clock in the afternoon to one o'clock that night. He asked the police official why his wife was being beaten. The official denied that it was his wife but rather another woman who had misbehaved. The screams would not end, and Emil continued to call the official until finally he was told that unless he remained quiet he would receive the same treatment as his wife. She was finally taken to a "nerve clinic," where she died.

Friedrich Frey survived Dachau and remembers the torture and punishment which he endured. After "eating a couple of dry crumbs of bread during working hours," Friedrich [was beaten by a guard] and then hung on a pole with his arms chained behind him. The pain was unbelievable. As the guard swung Friedrich's legs back and forth, he yelled, "Are you still one of Jehovah's Witnesses?"

As with many other groups of people, the Witnesses were victims of the Nazis, yet they were not destroyed. By 1948 there were more than 27,000 living in Germany.[53]

Using Reading 19

Other groups that were caught in the Nazi plan of extermination and concentration camps included:
- over 30 different nationalities at Auschwitz alone
- 10,000 Spaniards who had opposed Franco and were living in France at the time of the Nazi invasion
- religious dissenters such as Jehovah's Witnesses
- German criminals
- homosexuals
- *Volksdeutsche* who were persons of partial German ancestry and who lived outside Germany and Austria prior to the outbreak of the war. Although these people were considered by the Nazis as superior to the non-Germans who lived in these areas, they "somehow managed to run afoul" of the Nazi government.

I think that the Holocaust was a lot more than the Nazi's reign of terror against the Jews, Poles, and Gypsies. A study in human behavior showed man's ability to be cruel to others.
—*an 8th grade student*

Reading 20

Nazi Policy Against the Slavs

According to Bohdan Wytwycky, Slavs, specifically Poles, Ukrainians, Belorussians, and Russians were designated by the Nazis as "an inferior breed of people whose alleged historical destiny was to serve as slaves" for the German Reich. Between nine to ten million of these people were killed or sent to concentration camps. Part of the Nazi plan was to eliminate all "leading intelligentsia" of the Slavic peoples.
- About 3 million Polish Christians and 3 million Polish Jews were killed. Out of this total, some 600,000 died while fighting for the Polish armed forces.
- Over half of Poland's educated people were killed, including over 2,600 Catholic priests.
- A minimum of 5.5 million Ukrainians were killed; 3.9 million of these people were civilians (900,000 were Jewish civilians).
- By the end of the war, Belorussia was described by many as a "wasteland." Some 200 towns and 9,200 villages were completely destroyed. About 2.3 million citizens out of a total population of 9.2 million Belorussians were killed.
- Hitler stated that the war in the East was not a conventional war, but rather a war of extermination. As a result, about 3 million Soviet prisoners of war were killed, mostly through starvation.
- Slave laborers used in German agriculture and industry amounted to about: 1.5 million Poles, 2.4 million Ukrainians, and 400,000 Belorussians.

Ukrainians

Two out of the four Einsatzgruppen operated in the Ukraine. When they marched into the East all "undesirables"—Jews, civilian elite, intelligentsia—were their victims. Dehumanization of all Slavs was due, according to race theory, to racial origins and to closeness to Soviet rule. "Ukrainians and Russians were claimed to be semi-savage inferiors, incapable of reason, more closely resembling machines or animals than human beings. Nazi officials referred to the local population in occupation zone Ukraine as helots, subhumans, and half-monkeys."[54]

The Nazi Commissioner in the Ukraine, Eric Koch, is reported to have said that the Ukrainians are "far below us . . . and strictly speaking, we are here among Negroes."[55] He ordered anyone with a sign of intelligence to be shot on the spot.

Most of the concentration camps set up in the Ukraine were for Jews. Throughout the occupation, Ukrainian villages were terrorized, and their civilian population randomly shot en masse and starved.

The Ukrainians were never slated for total annihilation, as were the Jews and the Gypsies, and the Nazis never articulated a clear positive program of genocide. Nevertheless, a racist ideology shaped and directed thought and action. Ukrainians and other Slavic nationalities were said not to constitute a people at all but rather an "indefinable mixture" (Koch) or a "conglomeration of animals." Of the 3.9 million civilian Ukrainians dead, .9 were Jews."[56]

Belorussians

The first targets of the Einsatzgruppen were the Belorussian Jews. The Belorussians were considered subhuman because they had been under Soviet rule. The plan for depopulating the area called for the elimination of 75 percent of the Belorussians.

Many Belorussians fled to the forests and many took part in partisan guerrilla warfare although the Nazi retribution for attacks was vicious. Of an estimated 2.3 million citizens lost, an estimated 250,000 Belorussian Jews were killed.

Soviet prisoners of war were not considered by the Nazis in military service and therefore they were mixed with the civilians in the camps in the Ukraine and Belorussia, where they were starved to death. Later in Poland alone after work camps and liquidation, one-half million Soviet prisoners of war had perished. After the war, Stalin considered the Soviet prisoners of war as traitors since they had fallen into Nazi hands. His orders for soldiers were to fight to the death or commit suicide. Many of these men either were sent to Siberia or died in Soviet concentration camps.

Citations

Chapter 7

[1] John Leonard, "Book Review of *The Holocaust and The Historians*," *The New York Times*, September 3, 1981.

[2] Michael Novak, "Publisher's Preface" to *The Other Holocaust: Many Circles of Hell* (The Novak Report, 918 F Street N.W., Washington, D.C. 20004, 1980) p. 9.

[3] Irving Horowitz, *State Power and Mass Murder* (Transaction Books, 1977) p. 25,

[4] From *The War Against the Jews* by Lucy S. Dawidowidowicz. Copyright © 1975 by Lucy S. Dawidowicz. Reprinted by permission of Holt, Rinehart and Winston, Publishers, p. 219.

[5] Ibid., p. 219.

[6] Ibid., p. 208.

[7] Ibid., p. 209.

[8] Ibid., p. 192.

[9] Henry Feingold, "Determining the Uniqueness of the Holocaust,—The Factor of Historical Valence," copyrighted by *Shoah: A Journal of Resources on the Holocaust* published by the National Jewish Resource Center, 250 West 57 St., New York, New York 10107. Spring 1981, p. 10. Reprinted by permission.

[10] Bohdan Wytwycky, *The Other Holocaust: Many Circles of Hell* (The Novak Report 1980) p. 64.

[11] Eva Fleischner, ed., *Auschwitz: Beginning of a New Era?* (KTAV Publishing House, 1977) pp. 288-229. Reprinted by permission of The Cathedral of St. John the Divine, New York City and KTAV Publishing Company, New York City.

[12] Wytwycky, *The Other Holocaust,* p. 10.

[13] *Taking Lives: Genocide and State Power* Adapted from Irving Horowitz (Transaction Books, 1980) pp. 25, 26.

[14] Information from Yad Vashem, *The Holocaust* (Martyrs' and Heroes' Remembrance Authority, 1975).

[15] Jack Porter, "Resistance," *Genesis Two,* p. 3.

[16] Hyman Bass, "A Day of Remembrance," *The Warsaw Ghetto Uprising,* (Congress for Jewish Culture, 1973) p. 6.

[17] Ibid.

[18] *The Warsaw Diary of Chaim A. Kaplan,* introduction by Abraham Katsh (Macmillan, 1973).

[19] Source unknown.

[20] From *Never to Forget: The Jews of the Holocaust* by Milton Meltzer. Copyright © 1976 by Milton Meltzer. Reprinted by permission of Harper & Row, Publishers, Inc., p. 145.

[21] Ibid., pp. 138, 139.

[22] Yehuda Bauer, *They Chose Life* (The American Jewish Committee, 1973) p. 49.

[23] Meltzer, *Never to Forget,* p. 138, 145.

[24] From *The Holocaust Kingdom* by Alexander Donat (Holt, Rinehart and Winston). Selections here reprinted in *Out of the Whirlwind,* Albert Friedlander, ed. (Schocken Books, 1968) pp. 165, 166.

[25] Ibid., pp. 175, 176.

[26] Ibid., p. 167.

[27] Ibid., pp. 167, 168.

[28] Ibid., pp. 176-180.

[29] Dawidowicz, *The War Against the Jews,* p. 170.

[30] Ibid., p. 171.

[31] Ibid., p. 173.

[32] Ibid., p. 173.

[33] Erich Goldhagen, "Obsession and Real Politik in the Final Solution," unpubished paper, Harvard University, 1981.

[34] John Fried, *Trial at Nuremberg: Freedom and Responsibility,* National Project Center for Film and Humanities and the Research Foundation of the City University of New York, 1973.

[35] Ibid.

[36] Raul Hilberg, ed., "Open-Air Killings in Russia," *Documents of Destruction* (Quadrangle Books, 1971). Reprinted by permission of the New York Times Book Company, pp. 59-66.

[37] Elie Wiesel, "Art and Culture After the Holocaust," in *Auschwitz: Beginning of a New Era,* Eva Fleischner, ed., (KTAV Publishing House, 1977) p. 405.

[38] This material in slightly altered form is taken from Lawrence Langer's *Versions of Survival: The Holocaust and the Human Spirit* (to be published in the March 1982).

[39] Ibid.

[40] From a paper presented to the third meeting of the ZACHOR Holocaust Studies Faculty Seminar, January 23, 1979.

[41] Excerpts from pages 3-4, 8-9, and 11-13 of *Fragments of Isabella: A Memoir of Auschwitz* by Isabella Leitner, edited and with an Epilogue by Irving A. Leitner. (Thomas Y. Crowell, Publishers) copyright © 1978 by Isabella Leitner and Irving A. Leitner. Reprinted by permission of Harper & Row, Publishers, Inc.

[42] Information taken from *The Holocaust* (Yad Vashem, 1977).

[43] Hilberg, *Documents of Destruction,* pp. 199-200.

[44] Henry Friedlander, "Toward a Methodology of Teaching about the Holocaust," (original paper, 1978).

[45] William Styron, "Hell Reconsidered," a book review of *The Cunning of History,* by Richard Rubenstein, *New York Review of Books,* June 29, 1978.

[46] Ibid.

[47] Wytwycky, *The Other Holocaust,* p. 89.

[48] Ibid., p. 31.

[49] Ibid., p. 55.

[50] Alfous Heck, "West Germany's Gypsies: Justice Denied?" *World View,* Winter 1980.

[51] Wytwycky, *The Other Holocaust,* p. 41.

[52] Ibid., pp. 45, 46

[53] Gary Nelson, "They Too Were Victims of Nazi Terror," *Quad City Times,* April 14, 1978.

[54] Wytwycky, *The Other Holocaust,* p. 55.

[55] Ibid., p. 55.

[56] Ibid., p. 64.

[57] Ibid., pp. 64-76.

8 The Holocaust

At Auschwitz...we sometimes had riots and difficulties. Very frequently women would hide their children under their clothes but of course when we found them we would send the children in to be exterminated.[1]

Overview

In this chapter students confront the results of the Nazi state policy of genocide. And in this confrontation they feel the inadequacy of any simple explanation for how this event could have happened; no reciting of an ideology, no understanding of racism and prejudice, no preparation for obedience prepares one for the unbelievable truth of the Holocaust—ordinary people, "methodically and systematically slaughtered their fellow human beings, not for anything they had done but for who they were."

As students make the leap in their imagination to confront the Holocaust, their vocabulary of morality fails them and their vision of a normal world is forced to expand to take in the most divergent visual and written images. As Irving Horowitz points out:

[The total number of Jews] slated for extermination was eleven million. The Nazi war machine fell short of realizing this number by approximately one half, since the bulk of Soviet Jewry survived the war, and nations like England and Switzerland were never occupied, and hence fell outside the Nazi sphere of influence. Even so, available data indicate that nearly six million Jews were arbitrarily executed between 1939 and 1945 at the hands of the Nazis. This figure does not include other groups which also died in concentration camps, such as Poles, Gypsies, and other undesirables. But treatment of other peoples remained relatively random in contrast to the highly rationalized and total destruction of Jews under Nazi occupation. One-third of world Jewry was exterminated during Hitler's rule. The sixteen million Jews of 1939 were reduced to eleven million by 1945.[2]

Plans for the non-Jews who were slated for genocide were never fully initiated. However the extermination of approximately four million people just at Auschwitz included "three-quarters of a million—or approximately a fifth of the total" in the Nazi category of Aryan. This was at Auschwitz alone. Multitudes of innocent civilians were murdered elsewhere."[3]

Reading 1

Choiceless Choice Situations

The victimizers created the "choiceless choice" situations for the victim; saving one life meant sacrificing another. The following example of the choiceless choice offers the victim no real options.

A mother arrives at a concentration camp with her three children. The guard says she and one of her children can be saved, the other two are to be executed. How can she choose? What is her choice?

Using Reading 1

In the absence of humanly significant alternatives—that is, alternatives enabling an individual to make a decision, act on it, and accept the consequences, all within a framework that supports personal integrity and self-esteem—one is plunged into a world of moral turmoil that may silence judgment, as in the above example, but cannot completely paralyze action, if one still wishes to remain alive. As one wavers between the dreadful and the impossible, one begins to glimpse a deeper level of reality in the death camps, where moral choice as we know it was superfluous, and inmates were left with the futile task of redefining decency in an atmosphere that could not support it.[4]

In the paragraph above Professor Lawrence Langer pushes the reader to make distinctions between those memoirs by survivors that help the learner to cope and those writings that encourage confrontation with the Holocaust experience. Langer warns us that "normal standards for judging behavior will not apply to the 'choices' of victims."

Reading 2

A Memory of Choice

Consider the following passage by Viktor Frankl; he describes choice. Langer believes Frankl helps the reader cope, not confront.

We who lived in concentration camps can remember the men who walked through the huts comforting others, giving away their last piece of bread. They may have been few in number, but they offer sufficient proof that everything can be taken from a man but one thing: the last of the human freedoms—to choose one's attitude in any given set of circumstances, to choose one's own way.

And there were always choices to make. Every day, every hour, offered the opportunity to make a decision, a decision which determined whether you would or would not submit to those powers which threatened to rob you of yourself, your inner freedom; which determined whether or not you would become the plaything of circumstance, renouncing freedom and dignity to become molded into the form of the typical inmate.[5]

According to Professor Langer, accounts of the behavior of the victims in a final selection in an extermination camp:

... cannot be viewed through the same lens we used to view normal human behavior since the rules of law and morality and the choices available for human decisions were not permitted in these camps for extermination. As important as it is to point out situations of dignity and morality which reinforce our notions of normal behavior, it is all the more important here to try to convey the "unimaginable," where surviving in extremity meant an existence that had no relation to our system of time and space and where physical survival under these conditions resulted in "choice-less choices!" Primo Levi in Survivor in Auschwitz *reminds the reader that our vocabulary and our standards for behavior are not sufficient tools with which to imagine this history.[6]*

The following episode was narrated by a survivor, a nurse who was deported to Auschwitz with 197 other Jewish women. After three weeks eighteen of them were still alive. This passage reminds us that we must make a leap in our imagination to conceive the reality of the death camps, and that moral choice as we know it didn't exist.

Two days after Christmas, a Jewish child was born on our block (i.e., in the prisoner barracks). How happy I was when I saw this tiny baby. It was a boy, and the mother had been told that he would be taken care of. Three hours later, I saw a small package wrapped in cheese cloth lying on a wooden bench. Suddenly it moved. A Jewish girl employed as a clerk came over, carrying a pan of cold water. She whispered to me, "Hush! Quiet! Go away!" But I remained, for I could not understand what she had in mind. She picked up the little package—it was a baby, of course—and it started to cry with a thin little voice. She took the infant and submerged its little body in the cold water. My heart beat wildly in agitation. I wanted to shout "Murderess!" but I had to keep quiet and could not tell anyone. The baby swallowed and gurgled, its little voice chittering like a small bird, until its breath became shorter and shorter. The woman held its head in the water. After about eight minutes the breathing stopped. The woman picked it up, wrapped it up again, and put it with the other corpses. Then she said to me, "We had to save the mother; otherwise she would have gone to the gas chamber." This girl had learned well from the SS and had become a murderess herself.[7]

Langer comments on this episode:

How is one to pass judgment on such an episode (which may be extreme, but is not uncharacteristic of Auschwitz, where saving one life frequently meant surrendering another)? How are we to relate it to the "inner freedom" which many commentators on the death camp experience celebrate as the last dignity available to the victim or survivor? Does moral choice have any meaning here? The drama involves the helpless infant, whose fate is entirely in someone else's hands (and the fate of the infant Oedipus only reminds us how far life in Auschwitz has drifted from the moral order, and even the moral ironies, of art); the absent mother, who may or may not have approved of the action; the "agent" of death, who coolly sacrifices one life to preserve another, as a deed of naked necessity, without appeal, not of moral choice; and the author, sole witness to a crime that is simultaneously an act of kindness and perhaps of literal secular salvation to the mother. Vocabulary limps through this situation that allows no heroic response, no acceptable gesture of protest, no mode of action to permit any of the participants, including the absent mother, to retain a core of human dignity. The situation itself forbids it together with the "law" stating that mothers who refuse to surrender their newborn infants to death must accompany them to the gas chamber.

Reading 3

Victimizers

The Nazi victimizers set up the situation; the victims had no choices. The decisions made were between one abnormal response and another imposed by the victimizer. Heinrich Himmler, head of the Nazi SS, in Posen in 1943, spoke to his SS subordinates in a closed session:

... Most of you know what it means to have seen 100 corpses together, or 500 or 1000. To have made one's way through that, and ... to have remained a decent person throughout, that is what made us hard. This is a page of glory in our history. ... In sum we can say that we fulfilled the heaviest of tasks [destroying the Jews] in love to our people. And we suffered no harm in our essence, in our soul, in our character.[8]

The following report of one survivor describes her choice:

A woman ... naked and wounded, had managed to escape from the ditch, the mass grave in which all the Jews of her town were mowed down by German machine-guns. That woman returned to the ditch after a little while to rejoin the phantasmagoric community of corpses. Miraculously saved, she still could not accept a life which in her eyes had become impure.... Guilt was not invented at Auschwitz, it was disfigured there.

The Nazis created the impossible situation.

Reduced to a mere number, the man in the concentration camp at the same time lost his identity and his individual destiny. He came to realize that his presence in the camp was due solely to the fact that he was part of a forgotten and condemned collectivity. It is not written: I shall live or die, but: someone — today — will vanish, or will continue to suffer; and from the point of view of the collective, it makes no difference whether that someone is I or another. Only the number, only the quota counts.[9]

Using Reading 3

Philip Hallie suggests that Himmler was pleading for a program that outlasted momentary sentiment.

He was pleading for the program, for institutionalized destruction... a commitment that overrides all sentimentality, tranforms cruelty and destruction into moral nobility, and commitment is the life-blood of an institution.... [This institutional cruelty] is the subtlest kind of cruelty.[10]

Consider the choices the victimizers had in the following situations:

Prominent guests from Berlin were present at the inauguration of the first crematorium in March 1943. The "program" consisted of the gassing and burning of 8,000 Cracow Jews. The guests, both officers and civilians, were extremely satisfied with the results and the special peephole fitted into the door of the gas chamber was in constant use. They were lavish with their praise of this newly erected installation ....[11]

It should be remembered that German companies and technical engineers competed with each other for contracts from the government to design the gas chambers and crematoriums at Auschwitz.

Topf and Company of Erfurt won the contract to design:
- a "processing unit" that could "dispose" of 2,000 bodies every 12 hours.
- a tall chimney large enough to draft 5 furnaces.
- a plan that could use body fat for fuel.

German Armaments, Incorporated, won the contract to design:
- "Corpse Cellars" (gas chambers) with gas-proof doors and a double 8-millimeter glass observation window.

German Vermin Combatting Corporation won the contract to supply:
• a commercial pesticide, Cyklon-B that was placed in the "Corpse Cellars" to kill people.[12]

Reading 4

Taking Lives at Auschwitz

The following description of the "Extermination Procedure in Auschwitz" was written by Rudolf Hoess, the Nazi commandant of Auschwitz.

The extermination procedure in Auschwitz took place as follows: Jews selected for gassing were taken as quietly as possible to the crematoriums, the men being separated from the women. In the undressing rooms, prisoners of the Special Detachment, detailed for this purpose, would tell them in their own language that they were going to be bathed and deloused, that they must leave their clothes neatly together and above all remember where they had put them, so that they would be able to find them again quickly after the delousing. The prisoners of the Special Detachment had the greatest interest in seeing that the operation proceeded smoothly and quickly. After undressing, the Jews went into the gas chambers, which were furnished with showers and water pipes and gave a realistic impression of a bathhouse.

The women went in first with their children, followed by the men who were always the fewer in number. This part of the operation nearly always went smoothly, for the prisoners of the Special Detachment would calm those who betrayed any anxiety or who perhaps had some inkling of their fate. As an additional precaution these prisoners of the Special Detachment and an SS man always remained in the chamber until the last moment.

The door would now be quickly screwed up and the gas immediately discharged by the waiting disinfectors through vents in the ceilings of the gas chambers, down a shaft that led to the floor. This insured the rapid distribution of the gas. It could be observed through the peephole in the door that those who were standing nearest to the induction vents were killed at once. It can be said that about one-third died straight away. The remainder staggered about and began to scream and struggle for air. The screaming, however, soon changed to the death rattle and in a few minutes all lay still. After twenty minutes at the latest no movement could be discerned. The time required for the gas to have effect varied according to the weather, and depended on whether it was damp or dry, cold or warm. It also depended on the quality of the gas, which was never exactly the same, and on the composition of the transports which might contain a high proportion of healthy Jews, or old and sick, or children. The victims became unconscious after a few minutes, according to their distance from the intake shaft. Those who screamed and those who were old or sick or weak, or the small children, died quicker than those who were healthy or young.

The door was opened half an hour after the induction of the gas, and the ventilation switched on. Work was immediately begun on removing the corpses. There was no noticeable change in the bodies and no sign of convulsions or discoloration. Only after the bodies had been left lying for some time, that is to say after several hours, did the usual death stains appear in the places where they had lain. . . .

Major Concentration Camps

(Map showing: Neuengamme, Ravensbruck, Stutthof, Bergen-Belsen, Sachsenhausen, Chelmno, Treblinka, Mittelbau Dora, Gross Rosen, Sobibor, Buchenwald, Maidanek, Auschwitz, Belzec, Plaszow, Flossenberg, Natzweiler, Dachau, Mauthausen; countries: France, Germany, Czechoslovakia, Poland, Austria, Hungary, Rumania, Lithuania, U.S.S.R.; North Sea, Baltic Sea)

The special detachment now set about removing the gold teeth and cutting the hair from the women. After this, the bodies were taken up by elevator and laid in front of the ovens, which had meanwhile been stoked up. Depending on the size of the bodies, up to three corpses could be put into one oven retort at the same time. The time required for cremation also depended on this, but on an average it took twenty minutes.

During the period when the fires were kept burning continuously, without a break, the ashes fell through the grates and were constantly removed and crushed to powder. The ashes were taken in trucks to the Vistula, where they immediately drifted away and dissolved.[13]

Using Reading 4

This indicates how one student confronted the material:

This was a very depressing section to read.... The descriptions... are disgusting and revolting. Now that I think about it, I think everyone should study the Holocaust. It makes you realize the effect of brutality on people's lives. It reminds me of the "poem" [that said] "Your efforts must never produce learned monsters, skilled psychopaths, educated Eichmanns...." I think that learning about the Holocaust will really help everyone. Maybe there will now be 19 less psychopaths!

Racial-biological "eugenics" were at first not applied to the Jews but to the elements in the German people itself. The "Law for the Prevention of Progeny with Hereditary Disease" was proclaimed on July 14, 1933. At that time the "Euthanasia Program" was a top secret program implemented by the staff of Hitler's private chancellery. The action included the concentration of mental patients chosen for "merciful death" and their transportation to the nearest euthanasia station, short medical investigations of each patient, mainly in order to decide on the most plausible fictitious cause of death, and then gassing of 20 to 30 people at one time in hermetically shut chambers disguised as shower rooms. Cremation took place in the crematorium-annex after gold teeth had been broken off and some of the brains secured for "medical research."

Between 1940 and August 1941, 70,273 German people were killed in five euthanasia institutions by this *sonder behandlung* (special treatment). The carbon monoxide gas was provided compressed in steel containers and released through pipes into the gas chamber. People were dead after 6-7 minutes. The first experiment was done by Kriminal-Kommisar Christian Wirth; later a specially trained chemist, Dr. Kallneyer, became responsible for the whole gassing process. In August 1941 Hitler called the program off officially following the evolving unrest in the population, legal complications, and mounting protests especially by the churches. In fact, the institutions continued to function until 1944, but death was administered partly by gas, partly by injections, and partly by gradual starvation. Also put to death were the chronically ill, Gypsies, foreign forced laborers, Russian prisoners of war, children of mixed marriages, and others "unworthy of life."[14]

Reading 5

A Description of Auschwitz

This description by Rudolf Hoess, written in 1946, recounts what Heinrich Himmler said to him in the summer of 1941.

"The Fuehrer has ordered that the Jewish question be solved once and for all and that we, the SS, are to implement that order.

"The existing extermination centers in the East are not in a position to carry out the large actions which are anticipated. I have therefore earmarked Auschwitz for this purpose, both because of its good position as regards communications and because the area can easily be isolated and camouflaged. At first I thought of calling in a senior SS officer for this job, but I changed my mind in order to avoid difficulties concerning the terms of reference. I have now decided to entrust this task to you. It is difficult and onerous and calls for complete devotion notwithstanding the difficulties that may arise. You will learn further details from Sturmbannfuehrer Eichmann of the Reich Security Head Office who will call on you in the immediate future. . . .

"The Jews are the sworn enemies of the German people and must be eradicated. Every Jew that we can lay our hands on is to be destroyed now during the war, without exception. If we cannot now obliterate the biological basis of Jewry, the Jews will one day destroy the German people."

On receiving these grave instructions, I returned forthwith to Auschwitz, without reporting to my superior at Oranienburg.

Shortly afterward Eichmann came to Auschwitz and disclosed to me the plans for the operations as they affected the various countries concerned. I cannot remember the exact order in which they were to take place. First was to come the eastern part of Upper Silesia and the neighboring parts of Polish territory under German rule, then, depending on the situation, simultaneously Jews from Germany and Czechoslovakia, and finally the Jews from the West: France, Belgium, and Holland. He also told me the approximate numbers of transports that might be expected, but I can no longer remember these.

We discussed the ways and means of effecting the extermination. This could only be done by gassing, since it would have been absolutely impossible by shooting to dispose of the large numbers of people that were expected, and it would have placed too heavy a burden on the SS men who had to carry it out, especially because of the women and children among the victims.

Eichmann told me about the method of killing people with exhaust gases in trucks, which had previously been used in the East. But there was no question of being able to use this for these mass transports that were due to arrive in Auschwitz. Killing with showers of carbon monoxide while bathing, as was done with mental patients in some places in the Reich, would necessitate too many buildings, and it was also very doubtful whether the supply of gas for such a vast number of people would be available. We left the matter unresolved. Eichmann decided to try and find a gas which was in ready supply and which would not entail special installations for its use, and to inform me when he had done so. We inspected the area in order to choose a likely spot. We decided that a peasant farmstead situated in the northwest corner of what later became the third building sector of Birkenau would be the most suitable. It was isolated and screened by woods and hedges, and it was also not far from the railroad. The bodies could be placed in long, deep pits dug in the nearby meadows. We had not at that time thought of burning the corpses. We calculated that after gas-proofing the premises then available, it would be possible to kill about 800 people simultaneously with a suitable gas. These figures were borne out later in practice.

Eichmann could not then give me the starting date for the operation because everything was still in the preliminary stages and the Reichsfuehrer SS had not yet issued the necessary order. Eichmann returned to Berlin to report our conversation to the Reichsfuehrer SS.

A few days later I sent to the Reichsfuehrer SS by courier a detailed location plan and description of the installation. I have never received an acknowledgment or a decision on my report. Eichmann told me later that the Reichsfuehrer SS was in agreement with my proposals.

At the end of November a conference was held in Eichmann's Berlin office, attended by the entire Jewish Section, to which I, too, was summoned. Eichmann's representatives in the various countries reported on the current stage of the operation and the difficulties encountered in executing it, such as the housing of the prisoners, the provision of trains for the transports and the planning of time tables, etc. I could not find out when a start was to be made, and Eichmann had not yet discovered a suitable kind of gas.

In the autumn of 1941 a secret order was issued instructing the Gestapo to weed out the Russian *politruks*, commissars, and certain political officials from the prisoner-of-war camps, and to transfer them to the nearest concentration camp for liquidation. Small drafts of these prisoners were continually arriving in Auschwitz and they were shot in the gravel pit near the Monopoly buildings* or in the courtyard of block II. When I was absent on duty my representative, Hauptsturmfuehrer Fritsh, on his own initiative, used gas for killing these Russian prisoners of war. He crammed the underground detention cells with Russians and, protected by a gas mask, discharged Cyclon B gas into the cells, killing the victims instantly.

Cyclon B gas was supplied by the firm of Tesch & Stabenow and was constantly used in Auschwitz for the destruction of vermin, and there was consequently always a supply of these tins of gas on hand. In the beginning, this poisonous gas, which was a preparation of prussic acid, was only handled by employees of Tesch & Stabenow under rigid safety

---

*Buildings in the base camp where articles of clothing and equipment for the SS were stored.

precautions, but later some members of the Medical Service were trained by the firm in its use and thereafter the destruction of vermin and disinfections were carried out by them.

During Eichmann's next visit I told him about this use of Cyclon B and we decided to employ it for the mass extermination operations.

The killing by Cyclon B gas of the Russian prisoners of war transported to Auschwitz was continued, but no longer in block II, since after the gassing the whole building had to be ventilated for at least two days.

The mortuary of the crematorium, next to the hospital block, was therefore used as a gassing room, after the door had been made gasproof and some holes had been pierced in the ceiling through which the gas could be discharged.

I can however only recall one transport consisting of nine hundred Russian prisoners being gassed there and I remember that it took several days to cremate their corpses. Russians were not gassed in the peasant farmstead which had now been converted for the extermination of the Jews.

I cannot say on what date the exterminatoin of the Jews began. Probably it was September 1941, but it may not have been until January 1942. The Jews from Upper Silesia were the first to be dealt with. These Jews were arrested by the Kattowitz Police Unit and taken in drafts by train to a siding on the west side of the Auschwitz-Dziedzice railroad line where they were unloaded. So far as I can remember, these drafts never consisted of more than 1,000 prisoners.

On the platform the Jews were taken over from the police by a detachment from the camp and were brought by the commander of the protective custody camp in two sections to the bunker, as the extermination building was called.

Their luggage was left on the platform, whence it was taken to the sorting office called Canada situated between the DAW* and the lumberyard.

The Jews were made to undress near the bunker, after they had been told that they had to go into the rooms (as they were also called) in order to be deloused.

All the rooms, there were five of them, were filled at the same time, the gasproof doors were then screwed up and the contents of the gas containers discharged into the rooms through special vents.

After half an hour the doors were reopened (there were two doors in each room), the dead bodies were taken out, and brought to the pits in small trolleys which ran on rails.

The victims' clothing was taken in trucks to the sorting office. The whole operation, including assistance given during undressing, the filling of the bunker, the emptying of the bunker, the removal of the corpses, as well as the preparation and filling up of the mass graves, was carried out by a special detachment of Jews, who were separately accommodated and who, in accordance with Eichmann's orders, were themselves liquidated after every big action.

While the first transports were being disposed of, Eichmann arrived with an order from the Reichsfuehrer SS stating that the gold teeth were to be removed from the corpses and the hair cut from the women. This job was also undertaken by the Special Detachment.

---

*After Auschwitz had been built, the German Armaments Works (DAW) built a branch factory inside the camp where a labor force of up to 2,500 prisoners was employed.

The extermination process was that time carried out under the supervision of the commander of the protective custody camp or the *Rapportfuehrer*. Those who were too ill to be brought into the gas chambers were shot in the back of the neck with a small-caliber weapon.

An SS doctor also had to be present. The trained disinfectors (SDG's) were responsible for discharging the gas into the gas chamber.

During the spring of 1942 the actions were comparatively small, but the transports increased in the summer, and we were compelled to construct a further extermination building. The peasant farmstead west of the future site of crematoriums III and IV was selected and made ready. Two huts near bunker I and three near bunker II were erected, in which the victims undressed. Bunker II was the larger and could hold about 1,200 people.

During the summer of 1942 the bodies were still being placed in the mass graves. Toward the end of the summer, however, we started to burn them; at first on wood pyres bearing some 2,000 corpses, and later in pits together with bodies previously buried. In the early days oil refuse was poured on the bodies, but later methanol was used. Bodies were burned in pits, day and night, continuously.

By the end of November all the mass graves had been emptied. The number of corpses in the mass graves amounted to 107,000. This figure not only included the transports of Jews gassed up to the time when cremation was first employed, but also the bodies of those prisoners in Auschwitz who died during the winter of 1941-42, when the crematorium near the hospital building was out of action for a considerable time. It also included all the prisoners who died in the Birkenau camp.

During his visit to the camp in the summer of 1942, the Reichsfuehrer SS watched every detail of the whole process of destruction from the time when the prisoners were unloaded to the emptying of bunker II. At that time the bodies were not being burned.

He had no criticisms to make, nor did he discuss the matter. Gauleiter Bracht and the Obergruppenfuehrer Schmauser were present with him.

Shortly after the visit of the Reichsfuehrer SS, Standartenfuehrer Blobel arrived from Eichmann's office with an order from the Reichsfuehrer SS stating that all the mass graves were to be opened and the corpses burned. In addition the ashes were to be disposed of in such a way that it would be impossible at some future time to calculate the number of corpses burned.

Blobel had already experimented with different methods of cremation in Culenhof and Eichmann had authorized him to show me the apparatus he used.

Hossler and I went to Culenhof on a tour of inspection. Blobel had had various makeshift ovens constructed, which were fired with wood and oil refuse. He had also attempted to dispose of the bodies with explosives, but their destruction had been very incomplete. The ashes were distributed over the neighboring countryside after first being ground to a powder in a bone mill.

Standartenfuehrer Blobel had been authorized to seek out and obliterate all the mass graves in the whole of the eastern districts. His department was given the code number "1005." The work itself was carried out by a special detachment of Jews who were shot after each section of the work had been completed. Auschwitz concentration camp was continuously called upon to provide Jews for department "1005."

On my visit of Culenhof I was also shown the extermination apparatus constructed out of trucks, which was designed to kill by using the exhaust gases from the engines. The officer in charge there, however, described his method as being extremely unreliable, for the density of the gas varied considerably and was often insufficient to be lethal. . . .

Originally all the Jews transported to Auschwitz on the authority of Eichmann's office were, in accordance with orders of the Reichsfuehrer SS, to be destroyed without exception. This also applied to the Jews from Upper Silesia, but on the arrival of the first transport of German Jews, the order was given that all those who were able-bodied, whether men or women, were to be segregated and employed in war work. This happened before the construction of the women's camp, since the need for a women's camp in Auschwitz only arose as a result of this order.

Owing to the extensive armaments industry which had developed in the concentraction camps and which was being progressively increased, and owing to the recent employment of prisoners in armaments factories outside the camps, a serious lack of prisoners suddenly made itself felt, whereas previously the commandants in the old camps in the Reich had often had to seek out possibilities for employment in order to keep all their prisoners occupied.

The Jews, however, were only to be employed in Auschwitz camp. Auschwitz-Birkenau was to become an entirely Jewish camp and prisoners of all other nationalities were to be transferred to other camps. This order was never completely carried out, and later Jews were even employed in armaments industries outside the camp, because of the lack of any other labor.

The selection of able-bodied Jews was supposed to be made by SS doctors. But it repeatedly happened that officers of the protective custody camp and of the labor department themselves selected the prisoners without my knowledge or even my approval. This was the cause of constant friction between the SS doctors and the officers of the labor department.

. . . The Reichsartz SS, who laid down the policy of selection, held the view that only those Jews who were completely fit and able to work should be selected for employment. The weak and the old and those who were only relatively robust would very soon become incapable of work, which would cause a further deterioration in the general standard of health, and an unnecessary increase in the hospital accommodation, requiring further medical personnel and medicines, and all for no purpose since they would in the end have to be killed.

The Economic Administration Head Office (Pohl and Maurer) was only interested in mustering the largest possible labor force for employment in the armaments industry, regardless of the fact that these people would later on become incapable of working. This conflict of interests was further sharpened by the immensely increased demands for prisoner labor made by the Ministry of Supply and the Todt Organization. The Reichsfuehrer SS was continuously promising both these departments numbers which could never be supplied. Standartenfuehrer Maurer (the head of department DII) was in the difficult position of being able only partially to fulfill the insistent demands of the departments referred to, and consequently he was perpetually harassing the labor office to provide him with the greatest possible number of workers.

It was impossible to get the Reichsfuehrer SS to make a definite decision in this matter.

I myself held the view that only really strong and healthy Jews ought to be selected for employment.

The sorting-out process proceeded as follows. The railroad carriages were unloaded one after the other. After depositing their baggage, the Jews had to pass individually in front of an SS doctor, who decided on their physical fitness as they marched past him. Those considered capable of employment were immediately taken off into the camp in small groups.

Taking an average of all the transports, between 25 and 30 percent were found fit for work, but this figure fluctuated considerably. The figure for Greek Jews, for example, was only 15 percent, whereas there were transports from Slovakia with a fitness rate of 100 per cent. Jewish doctors and administrative personnel were without exception taken into the camp.

It became apparent during the first cremations in the open air that in the long run it would not be possible to continue in that manner. During bad weather or when a strong wind was blowing, the stench of burning flesh was carried for many miles and caused the whole neighborhood to talk about the burning of Jews, despite official counterpropaganda. It is true that all members of the SS detailed for the extermination were bound to the strictest secrecy over the whole operation, but, as later SS legal proceedings showed, this was not always observed. Even the most severe punishment was not able to stop their love of gossip.

Moreover the air defense services protested against the fires which could be seen from great distances at night. Nevertheless, burnings had to go on, even at night, unless further transports were to be refused. The schedule of individual operations, fixed at a conference by the Ministry of Communications, had to be rigidly adhered to in order to avoid, for military reasons, obstruction and confusion on the railways concerned. These reasons led to the energetic planning and eventual construction of the two large crematoriums, and in 1943 to the building of two further smaller installations. Yet another one was planned, which would far exceed the others in size, but it was never completed, for in the autumn of 1944, the Reichsfuehrer SS called an immediate halt to the extermination of the Jews.

The two large crematoriums I and II were built in the winter of 1942-43 and brought into use in the spring of 1943. They had five three-retort ovens and could cremate about 2,000 bodies in less than twenty-four hours. Technical difficulties made it impossible to increase their capacity. Attempts to do this caused severe damage to the installations, and on several occasions put them out of action altogether. Crematoriums I and II both had underground undressing rooms and gas chambers in which the air could be completely changed. The bodies were taken to the ovens on the floor above by means of an elevator. The gas chambers could hold about 3,000 people, but this number was never reached, since the individual transports were never as large as that.

The two smaller cematoriums III and IV were capable, according to calculations made by the constructional firm of Topf of Erfurt, of burning about 1,500 bodies within twenty-four hours. Owing to the wartime shortage of materials the builders were compelled to economize during the construction of crematoriums III and IV and they were therefore built aboveground and the ovens were of a less solid construction. It soon became apparent, however, that the flimsy construction of these two four-retort ovens did not come up to the requirements. Number III failed completely after a short time and later ceased to be used altogether. Number IV had to be repeatedly shut down, since after its fires had been burning for from four to six weeks, the ovens or the chimneys burned out. The gassed bodies were mostly burned in pits behind crematorium IV.

Crematorium II, later designated bunker V, was used up to the last and was also kept as a stand-by when breakdowns occurred in crematoriums I to IV. When larger numbers of transports were being received, gassing was carried out by day in number V, and number I to IV were used for those transports which arrived during the night. The capacity of number V was practically unlimited, so long as cremations could be carried out both by day and night. Because of enemy air attacks, no further cremations were permitted during the night after 1944. The highest total of people gassed and cremated within twenty-four hours was rather more than 9,000. This figure was attained in the summer of 1944, during the action in Hungary, using all the installations except number III. On that day, owing to delays on the line, five trains arrived, instead of three, as expected, and in addition the carriages were more crowded than usual.

The crematoriums were erected at the end of the two main thoroughfares in Birkenau camp, first, in order not to increase the area of the camp and consequently the safety precautions required, and second, so that they would not be too far from the camp, since it was planned to use the gas chambers and undressing rooms as bathhouses when the extermination actions came to an end.

The buildings were to be screened from view by a wall or hedges. Lack of material prevented this from being done. As a temporary measure, all extermination buildings were hidden under camouflage nets.

The three railroad tracks between building sector I and II in Birkenau camp were to be reconstructed as a station and roofed in, and the lines were to be extended to crematoriums III and IV, so that the unloading would also be hidden from the eyes of unauthorized people. Once again shortage of materials prevented this plan from being carried out.

Because of the increasing insistence of the Reichsfuehrer SS on the employment of prisoners in the armaments industry, Obergruppenfuehrer Pohl found himself compelled to resort to Jews who had become unfit for work. The order was given that if the latter could be made fit and employable within six weeks, they were to be given special care and feeding. Up to then all Jews who had become incapable of working were gassed with the next transports, or killed by injection if they happened to be lying ill in the sick block. As far as Auschwitz-Birkenau was concerned, this order was sheer mockery. Everything was lacking. There were practically no medical supplies. The accommodations was such that there was scarcely even room for those who were most seriously ill. The food was completely insufficient, and every month the Food Ministry cut down the supplies still further. But all protests were unavailing and an attempt to carry out the order had to be made. The resultant overcrowding of the healthy prisoners could no longer be avoided. The general standard of health was thereby lowered, and diseases spread like wildfire. As a result of this order the death rate was sent up with a jerk and a tremendous deterioration in the general conditions developed. I do not believe that a *single* sick Jew was ever made fit again for work in the armaments industry. . . .

"Action Reinhardt" was the code name given to the collection, sorting and utilization of all articles which were acquired as the result of the transports of Jews and their extermination.

Any member of the SS who laid hands on this Jewish property was, by order of the Reichsfuehrer SS, punished with death.

Valuables worth many millions of dollars were seized.

An immense amount of property was stolen by members of the SS and by the police, and also by prisoners, civilian employees, and railway personnel. A great deal of this still lies hidden and buried in the Auschwitz-Birkenau camp area.

When the Jewish transports unloaded on arrival, their luggage was left on the platform until all the Jews had been taken to the extermination buildings or into the camp. During the early days all the luggage would then be brought by a transport detachment to the sorting office, Canada I, where it would be sorted and disinfected. The clothing of those who had been gassed in bunkers I and II or in crematoriums I to IV was also brought to the sorting office. . . .

Clothing and footwear were examined for hidden valuables (although only cursorily in view of the quantities involved) and then stored or handed over to the camp to complete the inmates' clothing. Later on, it was also sent to other camps. A considerable part of the clothing was passed to welfare organizations for resettlers and later for victims of air raids. Large and important munition plants received considerable quantities for their foreign workers. . . .

When the sorting-out process that followed each major operation had been completed, the valuables and money were packed into trunks and taken by truck to the Economic Administration Head Office in Berlin and thence to the Reichsbank, where a special department dealt exclusively with items taken during actions against the Jews. Eichmann told me on one occasion that the jewelry market was dominated by these sales.

Ordinary watches were likewise sent in the thousands to Sachsenhausen. A large watchmaker's shop had been set up there, which employed hundreds of prisoners and was directly administered by Department DII (Maurer). The watches were sorted out and repaired in the workshop, the majority being later dispatched for service use by front-line SS and army troops.

Gold from the teeth was melted into bars by the dentists in the SS hospital and forwarded monthly to the Sanitary Head Office.

Precious stones of great value were also to be found hidden in teeth that had been filled.

Hair cut from the women was sent to a firm in Bavaria to be used in the war effort.

Unserviceable clothing was sent for salvage, and useless footwear was taken to pieces and remade as far as possible, what was left over being converted into leather dust.

The treasures brought in by the Jews gave rise to unavoidable difficulties for the camp itself. It was demoralizing for the members of the SS, who were not always strong enough to resist the temptation provided by these valuables which lay within such easy reach. Not even the death penalty or a heavy prison sentence was enough to deter them.

The arrival of these Jews with their riches offered undreamed-of opportunities to the other prisoners. Most of the escapes that were made were probably connected with these circumstances. With the assistance of this easily acquired money or watches and rings, etc., anything could be arranged with the SS men or the civilian workers. Alcohol, tobacco, food, false papers, guns, and ammunition were all in the day's work. In Birkenau the male prisoners obtained access to the women's camp at night by bribing some of the female supervisors. This kind of thing natually affected the whole camp discipline. Those who possessed valuables could obtain better jobs for themselves, and were able to buy the good will of the Kapos and block seniors, and even arrange for a lengthy stay in the hospital where they would be given the best food. Not even the strictest supervision could alter this state of affairs. Jewish gold was a catastrophe for the camp.

In addition to Auschwitz there existed, so far as I am aware, the following extermination centers for Jews:

Culenhof, new Litzmannstadt	Engine exhaust gases
Treblinka on the Bug	" " "
Sobibor near Lublin	" " "
Belzec near Lemberg	" " "
Lublin (Maidanek)	Cyclon B

I myself have only seen Culenhof and Treblinka. Culenhof had ceased to be used, but in Treblinka I saw the whole operation.

The latter had several chambers, capable of holding some hundreds of people, built directly by the railroad track. The Jews went straight into the gas chambers without undressing, by way of a platform which was the height of the cars. A motor room had been built next to the gas chambers, equipped with various engines taken from large trucks and tanks. These were started up and the exhaust gases were led by pipes into the gas chambers, thereby killing the people inside. The process was continued for half an hour until all was silent inside the rooms. In an hour's time the gas chambers were opened up and the bodies taken out, undressed and burnt on a framework made of railroad ties.

The fires were stoked with wood, the bodies being sprayed every now and then with oil refuse. During my visit all those who had been gassed were dead. But I was told that the performance of the engines was not always uniform, so that the exhaust gases were often insufficiently strong to kill everyone in the chambers. Many of them were only rendered unconscious and had to be finished off by shooting. I heard the same story in Culenhof and I was also told by Eichmann that these defects had occurred in other places.

In Culenhof, too, the Jews sometimes broke the sides of the trucks in an attempt to escape.

Experience had shown that the preparation of prussic acid called Cyclon B caused death with far greater speed and certainty, especially if the rooms were kept dry and gastight and closely packed with people, and provided they were fitted with as large a number of intake vents as possible. So far as Auschwitz is concerned, I have never known or heard of a single person being found alive when the gas chambers were opened half an hour after the gas had been inducted . . . .[15]

Using Reading 5

Henry Friedlander describes the establishment of concentration camps:

Almost immediately after the seizure of power in January 1933, the Nazis created the concentration camps (Konzentrations lager, officially abbreviated as KL and unofficially as KZ). The earliest camps were *ad hoc* creations by the brownshirted SA Storm Troopers. Located in jails, offices, factories and other make-shift locations, they were places where the Nazis settled accounts with their political enemies. All were dissolved after several years. The first permanent camp established by the SS in 1933, was KL Dachau near Munich. After the SS seized control of all camps, and moved to regularized the system, Dachau became the model for all other camps, the training ground for generations of camp commanders. At first, expansion was slow: KL Sachsenhausen was established near Berlin 1936, KL Buchenwald near Weimar in 1937. During 1938-39 more were added: KL Mauthausen in annexed Austria, KL Nevengame near Hamburg, and the women's KL Ravensbruck near Berlin. Early in the war, more camps were established: in 1941-42 KL Gross-Rosen in Silesia, KL Stutthof in West Prussia, and KL Natzweiler in Alsace: in 1944 KL Dora-Mittelbau in Saxony. These were the main concentration camps, the so-called *Stammlager*.

At first the camps contained only the political enemies of the regime; to these were soon added non-political groups: professional criminals, homosexuals, religious dissenters, and other so-called asocial elements. Jews were incarcerated only if they also belonged to one of these groups; as Jews they entered the camps in large numbers only after *Kristallnacht* in 1938, but most of these were eventually released and forced to leave Germany. The Gestapo and the criminal police (later part of the central office for national security, the RSHA) delivered the prisoners to the camps; the administration of the camps was under the KL Inspectorate, and the guards came from the SS death head units. Theodor Eicke, the first Dachau commander, served as inspector and developed the system. Its aim was punishment and "reeducation," labor was used as a form of torture. The system was based on extreme brutality, and a total disregard of human life. . . .

During the war this changed. Political opponents and resistance fighters from all European countries swelled the camp population; Jews who at first were confined to the ghettos, labor camps, and killing centers of the East later also flooded the camp system. While the size made the camps less manageable, the needs of the war economy made the labor of the inmates more valuable. . . . Each Stammlager eventually headed numerous subsidiary camps; these covered Germany and a simple list fills a massive volume. The camps became a world apart; the French called them *l'universe concentrationaire*.

This system spawned the killing centers. They were staffed by death head units and commanded by Eicke's students. The three large camps in eastern Poland—Treblinka, Belzec, Sobibor—were operated by the local SS and Police Chief Odilo Globocnik as part of Operation Reinhardt; the one in western Poland—Chelmno (Kulmhof)—was run by a special *Einsatzkommando*. The techniques they used came from the experiences of the commandos that murdered the Jews in Russia and had killed the ill in the so-called Euthanasia Program. But the methods of running the camps came from the concentration camp system established in 1933. This explains why the procedure of death by gas, introduced not only for efficiency and speed but also because it was considered more "humane" than shooting, was everywhere accompanied by dehumanization and brutality.

The death camps were surrounded by many smaller camps. These were *ad hoc* installations where conditions varied; some were labor camps and some smaller killing centers: the Janowska camp in Lemberg and camp Trawniki near Lublin are good examples. No such camps existed in the West; but there the Nazis extablished transfer camps, antechambers for killing centers: Westerbork in Holland; Malines in Belgium; Drancy and Pithiviers in occupied France. The worst conditions obtained in the camps operated by the French authorities in Vichy France at Les Milles, Rivesaltes, and Gurs.

Two death camps — KL Auschwitz-Birkenau and KL Lublin-Maidanek — were administrated by WVHA and became an integrated part of the concentration camp system, combining in perfect balance the methods of total control with the procedures of mass murder. The most important of these, the largest of all extermination and concentration camps, was Auschwitz in Upper Silesia. Established as a concentraction camp in 1940 with the function of killing center added in 1941, it eventually became a huge enterprise, the center of many subsidiary camps. Divided into three parts, it swallowed millions of victims. Camp I was the Stammlager at Auschwitz; camp II was the killing center at Birkenau; camp III was the BUNA industrial complex at Monowitz."[16]

Reading 6

A Survival, Viktor Frankl

There would be no need or reason to question the behavior of human beings in such extreme situations had there been no victimizers to set up the situation. The question for Larry Fuchs, professor at Brandeis University is not about the victim but about the victimizer: "Why did so many enthusiastically, not just willingly, but enthusiastically, choose evil in their daily lives?"

The following passage is from Viktor Frankl's memories of survival published in *Man's Search for Meaning*.

... A very trifling thing can cause the greatest of joys. Take as an example something that happened on our journey from Auschwitz to the camp affiliated with Dachau. We had all been afraid that our transport was heading for the Mauthausen camp. We became more and more tense as we approached a certain bridge over the Danube which the train would have to cross to reach Mauthausen, according to the statement of experienced traveling companions. Those who have never seen anything similar cannot possibly imagine the dance of joy performed in the carriage by the prisoners when they saw that our transport was not crossing the bridge and was instead heading "only" for Dachau.

And again, what happened on our arrival in that camp, after a journey lasting two days and three nights? There had not been enough room for everybody to crouch on the floor of the carriage at the same time. The majority of us had to stand all the way, while a few took turns at squatting on the scanty straw which was soaked with human urine. When we arrived the first important news that we heard from older prisoners was that this comparitively small camp (its population 2,500) had no "oven," no crematorium, no gas! ...

When we new arrivals were counted, one of us was missing. So we had to wait outside in the rain and cold wind until the missing man was found. He was at last discovered in a hut, where he had fallen asleep of exhaustion. Then the roll call was turned into a punishment parade. All through the night and late into the next morning we had to stand outside, frozen and soaked to the skin after the strain of our long journey. And yet we were all pleased! There was no chimney in this camp and Auschwitz was a long way off. . . .

We were grateful for the smallest of mercies. We were glad when there was time to delouse before going to bed, although in itself this was no pleasure, as it meant standing naked in an unheated hut where icicles hung from the ceiling. But we were thankful if there was no air raid alarm during this operation and the lights were not switched off. If we could not do the job properly, we were kept awake half the night.[17]

Using Reading 6

So often students and adults want to question the behavior of the victim, instead of think about those who made the situations happen. When confronted with this notion, one student offered the following explanation: "Perhaps we are too close to being the victimizer or knowing what we would do to survive so we ask about the victims."

Students can be reminded that each person's memories are different from another's. Ask what effect the backgrounds of the survivors might have on how they adapted and remembered their experiences.

It would be appropriate at this time to encourage students to choose books from the annotated bibliography, which report a survivor's story. Studies are being conducted now on the behavior of men and women in camps. Should studies be done on the difference age, town, language, culture, country, etc. have on behavior in such extremity?

Finally, do students believe studies should be done on concentration camp behavior? What do researchers expect to learn? Can the lessons be applied?

Reading 7

The Killing Camps

There were many extermination camps in addition to Auschwitz. The following information on some of these camps gives us an indication of the massiveness of the extermination operations. The map gives additional information about the locations of the many camps. Notice in which countries most of the camps are located.

Treblinka

In 1942 the Nazis chose Treblinka, a small village northeast of Warsaw, as the site for a model death camp—the first of its kind, a camp that would exist only to mass-produce death, a camp in which no work was done but the labor of death. During a single year no less than 750,000 persons were exterminated in this place.

The rail siding at Treblinka was named "Potemkin" by the Nazis and camouflaged as a quaint rural station. Time tables and advertisements were posted on the walls in a kind of gruesome joke. From across the continent of Europe freight trains came to deposit their victims at the "Potemkin" station.

Then, in the summer of 1943, a small group of Jewish prisoners planned and led an armed rebellion, killing the SS guards and destroying the compound. . . .

Some time after the revolt the camp at Treblinka was razed and the land plowed. All the documents were destroyed. Only 40 men and women of the 600 who managed to escape during the revolt were alive on V-E Day.[18]

Dachau
Dachau, ten miles outside of Munich, the city of Hitler's first attempt at power in 1923 and later the huge Nazi rallies, was the camp of the "medical experiments."

Chelmo
In 1941 the Chelmo extermination camp opened near Lodz, and by April 1943, 360,000 Jews had been murdered here. The children of the Lodz Ghetto orphanage were sent to the Chelmo/Kulmlief death camp in September of 1942. The extermination began at Sobibor and by October 1943, 250,000 Jews had been murdered there. Extermination began at Belzec and by the end of 1942, 600,000 Jews had been murdered there. And in June the Treblinka extermination camp was opened where 700,000 were murdered by August 1943. Also in 1942, 600,000 Slovakian Jews were sent to Auschwitz and Maidanek. During 1942 partisan organizations within the Vilna, Warsaw and Kovno Ghettos and in Czech and Belorussian areas were operating.

In 1943, 7,000 Danish Jews were evacuated to Sweden by the Danes while revolts in the Ghettos of Treblinka, Warsaw, Bialystock and Vilna increased. Finally in May of 1944, 380,000 Hungarian Jews were sent to Auschwitz and the death marches began. "The Nazi pretense and camouflage were successful in deceiving the Jews until the very last moment. Rumors about the death camps were met with skepticism; no one could believe such rumors."[19]

Using Reading 7

For many survivors of the Holocaust and for many historians, the Holocaust "started in Germany on January 30, 1933, with the accession of the Nazis to power, and ended on May 8, 1945, with the unconditioned surrender of Nazi Germany."[20] "The 12 years of the Nazi anti-Jewish *Aktion* (1933-44) constitute an uninterrupted progression toward an ever-increasing radicalization of objectives and barbarization of methods in constantly expanded territories under direct Nazi control or under decisive Nazi influence, to the accompaniment of vicious, sometimes obscene anti-Jewish propaganda."[21]

Reading 8

Slave Labor in the World of Total Domination

At Auschwitz SS doctors examined the incoming transports of people, mostly Jews. The doctors would view the marching survivors from the trains and would decide on the spot who would live for a while to work and who would die immediately.[22]

Children of tender years were invariably exterminated since by reason of their youth they were unable to work.[23]

Viktor Frankl describes his "first selection":

Nearly everyone in our transport lived under the illusion that he would be reprieved, that everything would yet be well. We did not realize the meaning behind the scene that was to follow presently. We were told to leave our luggage in the train and to fall into two lines — women on one side, men on the other — in order to file past a senior SS officer. Surprisingly enough, I had the courage to hide my haversack under my coat. My line filed past the officer, man by man. I realized that it would be dangerous if the officer spotted my bag. He would at least knock me

Most of the new arrivals at extermination camps were selected for immediate death.

down; I knew that from previous experience. Instinctively, I straightened on approaching the officer, so that he would not notice my heavy load. Then I was face to face with him. He was a tall man who looked slim and fit in his spotless uniform. What a contrast to us, who were untidy and grimy after our long journey! He had assumed an attitude of careless ease, supporting his right elbow with his left hand. His right hand was lifted, and with the forefinger of that hand he pointed very leisurely to the right or to the left. None of us had the slightest idea of the sinister meaning behind that little movement of a man's finger, pointing now to the right and now to the left, but far more frequently to the left.

It was my turn. Somebody whispered to me that to be sent to the right side would mean work, the way to the left being for the sick and those incapable of work, who would be sent to a special camp. I just waited for things to take their course, the first of many such times to come. My haversack weighted me down a bit to the left, but I made an effort to walk upright. The SS man looked me over, appeared to hesitate, then put both his hands on my shoulders. I tried very hard to look smart, and he turned my shoulders very slowly until I faced right, and I moved over to that side.

The significance of the finger game was explained to us in the evening. It was the first selection, the first verdict made on our existence or non-existence. For the great majority of our transport, about 90 percent, it meant death. Their sentence was carried out within the next few hours. Those who were sent to the left were marched from the station straight to the crematorium. This building, as I was told by someone who worked there, had the word "bath" written over its doors in several European languages.

We who were saved, the minority of our transport, found out the truth in the evening. I inquired from prisoners who had been there for some time where my colleague and friend P—had been sent. "Was he sent to the left side?" [they asked]. "Yes," I replied. "Then you can see him there," I was told. "Where?" A hand pointed to the chimney a few hundred yards off, which was sending a column of flame up into the grey sky of Poland. It dissolved into a sinister cloud of smoke.

"That's where your friend is, floating up to Heaven," was the answer. But I still did not understand until the truth was explained to me in plain words.[24]

Using Reading 8

Richard Rubenstein, author of *The Cunning of History*, sees Auschwitz as the "arch-creation of the Nazi genius." To him the extermination camps are a more permanent threat to the human future because they also functioned to create a world of the "living dead."

As Rubenstein says in an important passage:

The death-camp system became a society of total domination only when healthy inmates were kept alive and forced to become slaves rather than killed outright.... As long as the camps served the single function of killing prisoners, one can speak of the camps as places of mass execution but not as a new type of human society. Most of the literature on the camps has tended to stress the role of the camps as places of execution. Regrettably, few ethical theorists or religious thinkers have paid attention to the highly significant political fact that the camps were in reality a new form of human society.[25]

William Styron, in a review of *The Cunning of History*, wrote about the camp:

...There was ultimately systematized not only mass murder on a scale never known before but mass slavery on a level of bestial cruelty. This was a form of bondage in which the victim was forced to work for a carefully calculated period (usually no more than three months) and then, through methods of deprivation calculated with equal care, allowed to die.

Slaving at the nearby factory of I.G. Farben or at the Farben coal mines (or at whatever camp maintenance work the SS were able to contrive), the thousands of inmates initially spared the gas chambers were doomed to a sick and starving death-in-life perhaps more terrible than quick extinction, and luck was more often than not the chief factor involved in their survival....

Only in a situation where human bodies were endlessly replaceable could such a form of slavery attempt to be efficient—but the Nazis, who aspired to be among the century's leading efficiency experts, had no cause for concern on this count, supplied as they were with all the Jews of Europe, besides thousands of Poles, Russian prisoners of war, and others. And although the concept was not entirely unique in the long chronicle of bondage (for a period in the West Indies the British, with a glut of manpower, had no qualms about working slaves to death), certainly no slaveholders had such a scale and with such absolute ruthlessness made use of human life according to its simple expendability. It is this factor of expendability, an expendability which in turn derives from modern attitudes toward the stateless, the uprooted and rootless, the disadvantaged and dispossessed—which provides still another essential key to unlocking the incomprehensible dungeon of

Auschwitz. The matter of population declared to be surplus (whether by Nazi Germany or other superstates, past and future) which Rubenstein touches upon [in his book] again and again haunts this book like the shadow of a thundercloud.[26]

Activity 9	**Filmstrip:** *The Holocaust* Part I of this filmstrip details the Holocaust in the words of those who experienced it. Historical photographs and excerpts from diaries, poems, and testimony at Nuremberg are used. Part II attempts to analyze the "how" and "why" of the Holocaust.
Using Activity 9	The first part of this media kit helps students differentiate between ghettos, extermination camps, and other methods of dehumanization and killing.
Reading 10	**Two Survivors Remember: Rose Murra and Viktor Frankl** *Survivors do not bear witness to Guilt, neither theirs nor ours, but to objective conditions of evil. In the literature of survival we find an image of things so grim, so heartbreaking, so starkly unbearable, that inevitably the survivor's scream begins to be our own.* —Leonard Tushnet, Pavement to Hell

Rose Murra

Rose began—"It went by 35 years, really 35 years, since we were liberated. All this time we're living with it, sleeping with it, dreaming all about being by the Nazis for six long years—things like you never talked out loud. Maybe we were too depressed. I always have to cry when I talk about it.

"I'm ready to talk now. . . . I don't think I'm ever going to be ready to talk . . . to talk like whole talking . . . I'll never be ready because really it's too close to my heart.

"I lived in my house next to our store—the house was 150 years old—my grandfather's grandfather's grandfather. . . . It was a happy and noisy house. I mean everybody was there.

"So then the war broke out which I didn't understand too much—war was like a game. I was reading in history books about wars—I didn't think war is going to be right here—my house. I was thinking the war's gonna be some other place. I remember my mother crying when the war broke out. She said war is awful. My mother was really afraid for the war, she was really afraid.

"Our whole life changed overnight. It's just like a real bad dream—I don't know what it is—it never looks real—I can't believe it—I just can't believe it—why me? It's so hard to understand. . . . I can maybe understand they come in and take our country—maybe, if they would take people of politics, or someone didn't want to obey their rules—okay maybe I could fathom this. . . . But for nothing—for nothing they did all those things.

"I had a little brother—he was so good—he was so fine—why me? And my parents—such hard working people. They tried to raise their kids the best they could—we weren't hoodlums—we didn't destroy anything—we wouldn't do any damage. Why us? Because we were

Jewish and I hope this story I'm gonna tell—never to do a thing like this to no nation, no people—because they're different."

That night Rose told us about her Judenrein city—about living in the forest at night—about the knapsacks her mother packed to be ready for escape—about the night her father, uncle and brother were killed—she listened to her brother's last breath after he was shot by the Nazis—she and her mother hid in a haystack—until the farmer felt the warmth of their bodies radiating from within. . . .

[Rose remembers this] conversation she had with her mother while in the cattle car to Maidanek . . . .

". . . When the cattle cars arrived at Maidanek . . . to go to work and the doors opened, a lot of people really jumped out right away. I really wanted to jump—I don't know what came over me. There were a few boys and girls who want to jump and I want to jump with them. Mother said, 'No, don't jump—you're gonna get killed—you know how to jump from a train? You ever jump from a train? You ever jump from a train? You get killed.'"

Rose halted her story—"You know how it is when you have a mother—you're still a kid—the minute I lost my mother I became old—an old person."

She continued the story—"Mother wouldn't let me jump—'Don't jump, please. Do me a favor.' So I said to myself:

"'First of all I didn't go away without my mother no place. I was everytime with my mother. When my cousins and my boyfriend said come with me—I said No, I'm not going to leave my mother. What's gonna be with my mother—listen my father is dead—my brother is dead and with whom I'm gonna leave my mother? To die?'" Rose paused in her story again—"See, it's one thing—I'm so easy in my heart—what I did for my mother."

She resumed—"So, I said no, I'm not going to leave my mother—you—go—try to rescue yourself. Maybe you're gonna be one to live through to tell the story. I'm not gonna be there.

"So, I said—Okay—Ma—I'm not gonna jump—Ma, I said, You jump—I jump. 'No,' my mother said, 'I'm too old to jump. And let's say you jumped. Where are you gonna go? Who you know? Who is gonna rescue you? You gonna start wandering around and get shot—I mean either way—the same thing.'

"So we're sitting in the wagon and I was talking to my mother, I said, 'Ma, listen we gonna go to a camp—I don't know they're gonna kill me. They're gonna kill you? Who gonna get killed first?

"'Listen don't cry over me—if I be killed—because that's the way of life—that's gonna be—don't cry—your little boy got killed—your husband—everybody died already—so what you think—we have to be the chosen ones—we don't have to be the chosen ones—we're gonna die too. So take it nice and easy. Death is not so bad. After death there's nothing to remember no more—so maybe death is the solution of it. I mean suffering—even more—look Ma—we went through typhus and hunger—the cold and the hiding—How much more can you take of this?'

"So my mother said—'Okay my child, I was thinking—okay—I would die—at least I want you to live. Somebody—somebody from the family should live and survive.'

"I said, 'Listen—a lot of families are killed already—nobody left already from a family.'

"In case you live through — don't ever forget to tell the story what your family went through.'

"I said, 'If I come through — which I know I'm not, well, I tell, I tell.' So that's what it is!

"When we entered Maidanek — the young went to one side — the old to another side — I was going with my mother — we came closer to the soldier and he told my mother to go to this side — 'You mean this side' — my mother said — 'I'm still young. I can work.'

"The soldier said — 'If you don't shut up your mouth — I'm gonna beat you to death.' And that's the last I saw of my mother — she just like disappeared!"*

Viktor Frankl

Fifteen hundred persons had been traveling by train for several days and nights: there were eighty people in each coach. All had to lie on top of their luggage, the few remnants of their personal possessions. The carriages were so full that only the top parts of the windows were free to let in the gray of dawn. Everyone expected the train to head for some munitions factory, in which we would be employed as forced labor. We did not know whether we were still in Silesia or already in Poland. The engine's whistle had an uncanny sound, like a cry for help sent out in commiseration for the unhappy load which it was destined to lead into perdition. Then the train shunted, obviously nearing a main station. Suddenly a cry broke from the ranks of the anxious passengers, "There is a sign, Auschwitz!" Everyone's heart missed a beat at that moment. Auschwitz — the very name stood for all that was horrible: gas chambers, crematoriums, massacres. Slowly, almost hesitatingly, the train moved on as if it wanted to spare its passengers the dreadful realization as long as possible: Auschwitz!

With the progressive dawn, the outlines of an immense camp became visible: long stretches of several rows of barbed wire fences; watch towers; search lights; and long columns of ragged human figures, gray in the grayness of dawn, trekking along the straight desolate roads to what destination we did not know. There were isolated shouts and whistles of command. We did not know their meaning. My imagination led me to see gallows with people dangling on them. I was horrified, but this was just as well, because step by step we had to become accustomed to a terrible and immense horror.

Eventually we moved into the station. The initial silence was interrupted by shouted commands. We were to hear those rough, shrill tones from then on, over and over again in all the camps. Their sound was almost like the last cry of a victim, and yet there was a difference. It had a rasping hoarseness, as if it came from the throat of a man who had to keep shouting like that, a man who was being murdered again and again. The carriage doors were flung open and a small detachment of prisoners stormed inside. They wore striped uniforms, their heads were shaved, but they looked well fed. They spoke in every possible European tongue, and all with a certain amount of humor, which sounded grotesque under the circumstances. Like a drowning man clutching a straw, my inborn optimism (which has often controlled my feelings even in the most desperate situations) clung to this thought: These prisoners look quite well, they seem to be in good spirits and even laugh. Who knows? I might manage to share their favorable position.

---

*Based on a narrative by Rose Murra, in an interview with Margot Strom.

In psychiatry there is a certain condition known as "delusion of reprieve." The condemned man, immediately before his execution, gets the illusion that he might be reprieved at the very last moment. We, too, clung to shreds of hope and believed to the last moment that it would not be so bad. Just the sight of the red cheeks and round faces of those prisoners was a great encouragement. Little did we know then that they formed a specially chosen elite, who for years had been the receiving squad for new transports as they rolled into the station day after day. They took charge of the new arrivals and their luggage, including scarce items and smuggled jewelry.[27]

Using Reading 10

A student responds:

The "Rose" story is very depressing. I can't imagine wanting to remember the death of my family after they have been killed mercilessly.... It makes me feel angry, sad, and weak, but also happy that she can share her grief with me and all of us who read that story.

Kitty Returns to Auschwitz is aired on PBS and national networks. The tape documents the trip that one survivor made back to Auschwitz with her son, now a medical doctor. It might be used at the end of this chapter when students read "Where are the camps now?"

Although the tape is long, teachers have reported using it in a variety of ways; One teacher divided it into 20-minute viewings, another showed it at one sitting. Decisions about how much time a teacher will take to explore one aspect of the Holocaust will depend on the teacher's goals, the particular student group, and the flexibility of his or her class schedule. Sometimes the visit to the class by a survivor with readings chosen from the chapter will suffice. Other times students demand to know more. In one class, students asked to see *Night and Fog* although it is not a part of the suggested films for junior high students. The teacher arranged a special showing for students after class and other adults were invited to come.

Night and Fog is a film made about the concentration and extermination camps. It is stark and painful. It never mentions the word Jew. It is in French with English subtitles.

The question of how much "horror" to show, with which class, and when depends very much on open class discussion. Finally, however, the decision belongs to the individual teacher. What is comfortable for a teacher one year may be uncomfortable another. And those who teach this history to many separate classes in a day report that each class differs so much that what is used in one class may not be used in another.

The following is a description of the film and how one high school teacher used it for both students and their parents.

Night and Fog is a French film of enormous power produced and directed by Alain Resnais. There is a terrible finality to it, a relentless visual beauty that is all the more incongruous because of its subject matter: scenes of the abandoned death camps as they are today juxtaposed with explicit Nazi and Allied documentary film footage of Nazi atrocities. "Who is responsible for them?" asks the narrator.

Some students replied in sorrow, others with indignation.

I can say who is responsible. All those who physically put the Jews on the train, all those who killed them in camps, all those who knew even if they lied to themselves and said they didn't. Those people are to blame for their apathy, those who knew but didn't rise up and help the persecuted people.

On the morning that we watched *Night and Fog*, the entire class was present. All of them had received permission to be absent from the various classes that followed in order that we might have two full periods together to see and assimilate the film.

When it was over, there was silence—five or ten minutes worth. There were some tears, quiet ones. We seemed unable to look at each other. When the curtains were finally opened the sun streamed in and you could hear birdsong outside, very strong, very close to the window. For one instant I felt guilty for inviting those warm yellow ribbons of light into the room. For the next I felt morally obligated to do so. The year before a student had written of just such a paradox: "To be grateful," she said, "not grateful that it wasn't me who died but grateful that the spring still comes is not only my conscious wish but also my duty. Anything less makes a mockery of life; the life that was robbed from eleven million people."

At this point the traditional language of student response becomes increasingly inadequate. Again the paradox. In the metaphor, touch, or silence itself. And even as we apply ourselves to that search we are reminded of the theorem that "all true feeling is in reality untranslatable. To express it is to betray it.*"

In most cases students' written responses to the films *Night and Fog*, *Warsaw Ghetto*, and *Genocide* were somewhere in between prose and poetry.

Silence—who dares to speak?
I for one am afraid
I can't watch what's before me
But my mind keeps wandering:
Political primaries, the G.O.P.
Am I guilty?
Here I am drawing—
I'm afraid of acting intelligent
I can't—afraid of being seen.
Who is responsible?
Everyone is involved
What's for lunch?

I'm feeling overwhelmed. My thoughts are unclear.
Should we have intervened in Nazi Germany?
What could we have done? What can I do?
   I'm confused.
Yes, the movie was extremely powerful although
I just couldn't cry. It's so hard to cry for others
and I'm naturally self-centered.
   But can I change?
I'm beginning to think that change is necessary.
I have to stick behind my beliefs. I want to help
But I feel so small. Far too often I'm wrapped up
   within myself.
How can some people survive such horrors?

*Antonin Artaud

*How could someone survive in a concentration camp?
I'm so frail I couldn't last
    more than a day.
It's not easy to forget those staring eyes of corpses.
The number of people who died during the Holocaust.
I'm beginning to see that those who died were actually
    human—just like me.
Six million just like me were slaughtered.
How can such an event happen?
We are obsessed with fear. We are afraid to break
Our time tables—to break our routines. Train operators
drove people, actual human beings, to their deaths.
The job becomes easier after the first load.*

Looking at those bodies. They were so destroyed. I kept saying to myself—people loved those lifeless rubber bodies. They had parents, relatives, friends, and lovers.

I don't understand it. I don't want to understand it. It's hard to think of any of these people as human. It's cold, merciless, like cattle being herded, shot, killed, slaughtered. Mass slaughter. I can't see any of it. It takes away all humanity. It steals your emotion.

I feel as if I've just seen something with such a message, so powerful and with such impact that I should feel something and do something. But I don't know what to do.

Interested parents of students in the course were invited to view *Night and Fog* on either one of two nights during the week that their children had seen it. The father of one student sat quietly for a long time after the film before he said wistfully, "If only we could draw a line around our kids' lives; separate them from all sadness. Maybe if no one ever knew about the bad things in life then they would never happen again." His wife leaned over to touch him and said, "But you can't do that, kids have to find it out." "I know," replied the father, "I know."

Students continued to write about this unit even after we had finished it. They also continued to connect it to other readings and films and to their lives.

I can't believe that human beings could do that to each other. It isn't like obedience and yet—at the same time—it is.

Reading 11   A Survivor Visits Classrooms

Harriet Wacks wrote the following description of her friend, Sonia Weitz, a survivor.

No one would ever suspect that Sonia Weitz spent her formative teen-age years in a ghetto and five concentration camps.

The unknowing listener would probably attribute the slight trace of a European accent to a French finishing school or the Sorbonne. Yet Plashow, Auschwitz, Bergen-Belsen, Venus-berg, and Mauthausen (all Nazi concentration camps) are her only alma matae.

Sonia Weitz is a very remarkable woman. She managed to overcome the scars of her youth to lead a full and rewarding life as a wife, mother, grandmother, and educator.

But Sonia has never forgotten the Nazis' mass murders of the European Jews, including over 80 members of her family.

Like many survivors of the Holocaust, for many years after liberation Sonia was unable to speak about the nightmares of her past. She turned to writing poetry and painting to express her repressed feelings.

"And then when I was ready to speak, no one wanted to hear me," says Sonia. "Times are changing and I think that people are now ready to take an honest look at this period of history."

"About two years ago I was asked to speak of my experiences in the camps to a group of local teen-agers. After much soul searching, I agreed to go. For days before and after I couldn't sleep."

Sonia was received with much enthusiasm and interest and now speaks frequently. "It is a compulsion," she explains. "To forget would be an injustice to those who perished."

"I have always had another fear," Sonia confides, "the fear that when the last eyewitness is no longer here to tell the tale of man's inhumanity to man, nothing will prevent the world from forgetting."[28]

The following poems* are about Sonia's memories of the Holocaust. She and her sister were the only two to survive out of a family of eighty-four.

In Memory to Father
Did the suffering
Drive you wild?
Did you think of me,
Your child?
Did you cry?
I know, you'd rather
spare me the gory truth . . .
Oh, Father!

No, the details
Matter not!
But, Dear God—
You forgot
A man who wept . . .
And begged for life,
Not for himself-
But for his wife . . .

You saw a father's
Tear-stained face,
But showed no mercy!
Not a trace;
You watched the pain—
'til his brothers
Were all slain . . .

And still my faith
In you is great,
And still I trust you—
Without hate;
For when he prayed
His dying word:
To save his daughters
—you heard!

Jahr-Zeit
Somewhere, behind the heavenly portal...
Her body destroyed, but her soul immortal,
Through cloudy skies, she's looking down;
A furrowed brow...An anxious frown...
Her love still warm, below her breast -
Her martyred heart won't let her rest,
With anguish—only a mother has known
When torn from her child—before it has grown
The clouds will soon pass, so she may find,
The little girl—she left behind...
She had such hopes for her, such dreams—
The years to give so few! It seems
They fluttered by like a gentle dove....
But she bequeathed a wealth of love,
Of faith, of truth, of will to live
In such a little time to give...
 (So helplessly she departed ...
When my life had barely started!)

*Copyright 1981, Sonia Weitz.

After Sonia read about the recent hangings of Jews in Baghdad she wrote a poem, *From Plashow to Baghdad*. The hangings reminded her of the hanging she was forced to witness in the public square as a child in a Nazi concentration camp. The last stanza, which is excerpted here, describes those who take no action. Sonia and her sister were the only two people to show up at a Boston Common protest against the Baghdad hangings.

Twenty-five years passed
but much has not changed;
once more Jews are hanging
in a public square,
executioners cheer . . .
and the bloody sun
glares undisturbed
'pon this callous planet,
this world that really
doesn't give a damn,
this human race;
just a bit embarrassed
and a little sad —
swiftly turning
to something less upsetting,
more pleasant,
more trivial . . .

Using Reading 11

Students asked survivors about revenge, hate, forgiving, and faith. They asked why those survivors who visited our class seemed so hopeful, so thankful.

One 13-year-old remembers a visitor to his class, who spoke about his life in a concentration camp and his liberation and about his love for America. The student asked, "Do you know something about freedom that we don't know?" Another asked, "How old are you?" Mr. Bonovika replied, "I was born in 1945" — when the meaning of that date came clear — you could have heard the silence in the room.

And another student remembers the visit of a survivor of Auschwitz. At one point while speaking, his eyes filled up and his voice choked and he said he was unable to go on. There was total silence, total respect . . . .

The following is a description of how the teachers and the students responded to the visit of Mr. and Mrs. Bork, survivors of the Holocaust, to a class of senior high school students.

"Towards the end of the semester, Mr. and Mrs. Bork, survivors of the ghetto, the deportation trains, and Auschwitz, came to school. Theirs was an unremitting and detailed naming of the parts of a journey so brutal as to be beyond comprehension.

Student response to the Borks was powerful and varied. A few felt anger, all felt an unutterable sadness and were grateful beyond measure that these two had "brought the Holocaust closer, maybe closer than we wanted it." Some seemed to be waiting for Mr. and Mrs. Bork to present a strategy, a skill or implement that might help us to adapt or convert their relentless lament into a lesson learned, an explanation, some sort of consoling aphorism about the triumph of the human spirit. None was forth-coming. Their history was without euphemism, without metaphor. And perhaps, finally, that was their gift to us. For the very first time we could fully perceive what Lawrence Langer had meant when he said in the Facing History curriculum, "All survivor accounts and all narrative about survivors are limited by having to speak of a world where the values cherished by Western Civilization were extinct, and to a world where those values presumably remain intact."

I feel so lonely with this terrible knowledge.

Oh, there is so much more to be learned about humans than what is found in textbooks. So much happened to the Borks that they could never tell it all. They can try to help us see but we never really can unless, God forbid, we live through it ourselves. They know so much more about life than I do and I want to understand their knowledge but I know that if I had to live through what they had to then I wouldn't really want their knowledge, but I do. I guess I want it for free. Does that make sense?

I realize how sheltered my life is, how little I have experienced. I'm not a survivor of the Holocaust or even of Vietnam. I am just a kid who spent the last twelve years studying, trying to comprehend what other people have been through.

Once again I addressed the question: are people all evil? And once again I decided that many are not, and the most important thing is that I keep myself from being evil like this, even on the smallest scale. And also I must do whatever is possible to keep others from committing these evils, because I know that deep down they do not want to.

When the Borks walk out of here and everywhere they go it must stick to them, it's there; a shadow hovering inside and outside. They live with it day in and day out. They are perpetually reminded and aware of a brutality of people. I can hope that it is not contaminating, that there will be peace and goodness; that things will change and get better.

Last Tuesday after talking to Mr. and Mrs. Bork, Anne and I hurried to English class. We were breathless when we arrived and the teacher asked us where we had been. We told him whom we had been talking to and he asked us what it was like and what we had talked about. Anne and I couldn't reply. We were so—I don't know the right word. We just couldn't talk about it.

Death is final. I guess I was reminded of that, too. There's no second chance. How many times I have just trucked through the day staring at my watch or counting the days left until school's out. The Borks had no idea of when they would "get out" or if they ever would. Every day each second was a matter of survival. I wonder if I could make my body do it.

What was it that saved you? I only wish I had the courage to ask some questions. I have so many questions ... often they are difficult to form in my own mind. Seeing you who have been through so much in real life has left an impression that I will not forget. I respect you for sharing something so painful in order to teach a handful of students. We learned. Thank you.

I have learned from you, Mr. and Mrs. Bork, more than I could have using every book, magazine article, and movie related to the Holocaust ... you have forced me to sit for an hour and a half and listen to accounts that I did not want to hear. There were moments when I did not want to listen.

I wanted to let my mind wander but you would not let me. After listening to you I was speechless. I could not talk to friends about your story. I doubt they would understand.

Reading 12

Liberation Day for Viktor Frankl

Survivors remember the day their camp was liberated in a variety of ways. Some remember those who died because they were fed too much food too quickly and their starved bodies couldn't adjust. Others remember the typhus that continued to kill even after liberation. Some remember the new rules set up by their particular liberators or the difficult decisions about revenge and retribution. One survivor remembered how his senses of touch and smell were heightened as he was hugged by Russian soldiers dressed in rough wool jackets. The following is one survivor's memory of liberation.

Our last day in camp arrived. As the battlefront came nearer, mass transports had taken nearly all the prisoners to other camps. The camp authorities, the Capos and the cooks had fled. On this day, an order was given that the camp must be evacuated completely by sunset. Even the few remaining prisoners (the sick, a few doctors, and some "nurses") would have to leave. At night, the camp was to be set on fire. In the afternoon the trucks which were to collect the sick had not yet appeared. Instead, the camp gates were suddenly closed and the barbed wire closely watched, so that no one could attempt an escape. The remaining prisoners seemed to be destined to burn with the camp....

Many weeks later we found out that even in those last hours fate had toyed with us few remaining prisoners. We found out just how uncertain human decisions are, especially in matters of life and death. I was confronted with photographs which had been taken in a small camp not far from ours. Our friends who had thought they were traveling to freedom that night had been taken in the trucks to this camp, and there they were locked in huts and burned to death. Their partially charred bodies were recognizable on the photograph....

With tired steps we prisoners dragged ourselves to the camp gates. Timidly we looked around and glanced at each other questioningly. Then we ventured a few steps out of camp. This time no orders were shouted at us, nor was there any need to duck quickly to avoid a blow or kick. Oh, no! This time the guards offered us cigarettes! We hardly recognized them at first; they had hurriedly changed into civilian clothes. We walked slowly along the road leading from the camp. Soon our legs hurt and threatened to buckle. But we limped on; we wanted to see the camp's surroundings for the first time with the eyes of free men. "Freedom"—we repeated to ourselves, and yet we could not grasp it. We had said this word so often during all the years we dreamed about it, that it had lost its meaning. Its reality did not penetrate into our consciousness; we could not grasp the fact that freedom was ours.

We came to meadows full of flowers. We saw and realized that they were there, but we had no feelings about them. The first spark of joy came when we saw a rooster with a tail of multicolored feathers. But it remained only a spark; we did not yet belong to this world.

In the evening when we all met again in our hut, one said secretly to the other, "Tell me, were you pleased today?"

And the other replied, feeling ashamed as he did not know that we felt similarly, "Truthfully, no!" We had literally lost the ability to feel pleased and had to relearn it slowly.[29]

Using Reading 12

When the Americans entered the concentration and extermination camps of Belsen, Buchenwald, and Dachau they took films of what they found. The British, French, and Russians also took films.

General Eisenhower, later to be President of the United States, viewed the camps. He sent a special American news team to Europe to "report the existence of atrocities in Germany...." "His purpose in giving us the assignment" wrote one newsman, "was to make the American people realize the incredible extent of the Nazi crimes so that the guilty would be justly punished—and here I repeat and emphasize, the words *justly punished*, not by Gestapo-like lynchings but by fair trials where a guilty man is found guilty and an innocent man has a fair opportunity to prove his innocence." The chapter on judgment will explore these trials more completely.[30]

Ronald Reagan was attached to a military branch in World War II whose job it was to edit the combat film taken by every branch of the service. He had access to and saw a film report for the general staff documenting the liberation of the camps entered by American troops. He too remembers seeing the townspeople of Weimar being marched to Buchenwald to see the horror.

*The day's quota of prisoners who had died in the camp were parked in a truck in the front yard. The furnace gates had not yet been cleared of unconsumed joints and skulls. The piles of bone ash had not been removed from the backyard.**

Reading 13

American Army Officials' Reports of Atrocities

One newsman reporting for *Army Talks* and a member of Eisenhower's special group asked a victim why he was in the camp. He replied: "Because I am a Jew. You understand that? Because I am a Jew."[31]

After the Allied films were made they were shown in nearly all theaters and Army posts in the country and individual atrocity photographs were displayed in many store windows. According to an Army reporter,

Newspapers have been inclined to omit the more gruesome shots, but photomagazines have withheld little if anything from their readers. Both have carried full eye-witness accounts of correspondents who visited Dachau, Buchenwald and other Fascist death factories. Radio, too, had done a good job of covering a story which should be convincing to the last doubter—if one exists—that our enemies in legalized Europe followed a policy of legalized barbarism.[32]

U.S. Army officers entered Buchenwald on April 12, 1945. On that day the Army forced the townspeople of Weimar to march to Buchenwald to see for themselves. This march was photographed. The following is a

---

*From a speech to the Holocaust Remembrance Committee.

story based on Army officers' reports of Army officers now stored in the U.S. National Archives.

"*Afterwards many of these citizens, although the camp had been in their midst nearly 13 years, had the gall to pretend that they had never heard of it, that they did not hold themselves responsible for such proceedings."*

As the Americans approached, the SS attempted to evacuate some of the "valuable" prisoners. Columns of 2,000 each were marched into the woods to be shot on April 8 and 10, but in the excitement and confusion almost 1,000 escaped. Inmates claimed that there were orders to kill all 20,000 but the on-rolling tanks stampeded the SS personnel.

They had little time to tidy up. The "strangling room" was freshly painted, the hooks removed, the holes plastered over. But Americans were able to examine and understand the cycle of operations: French P.O.W.'s gave them a guided tour.

Brigadier General General Eric F. Wood headed an official American party which inspected the camp on April 16, two days after the arrival of American personnel and supplies. He described the 20,000 survivors—all males—as "intelligentsia and leadership personnel from all of Europe; anyone and everyone of outstanding intellectual or moral qualifications, or of democratic or anti-Nazi inclination of their relatives"—parliamentarians, professors, generals, editors, professional men.

"A particular inclination for incarcerating prominent Jews was manifest," he wrote. There were 4,000 of them, and they were given "even worse treatment" than the others.[33]

Americans reacted strongly to Buchenwald, partly because they had eyewitness reports from the liberators.

Lieutenant Col. C.R. Codeman, a senior aide to General Patton, wrote an article for *Atlantic Monthly* "because I thought I ought to. . . . It probably won't be believed even with the dozens of photographs, but there it is. Take it or leave it. Leave it, and there will be another war in ten years."

Buchenwald was on the outskirts of Weimar. Codeman wrote: "If you didn't know what it was, you might take it for the entrance to a third-rate amusement park. In a sense it was like that to the SS."

The Nation reported that many soldiers advocated letting "the Poles, Czechs, Russians and Jews be turned loose on the German prisoners of war." But, *The Nation* reported, Army officers were trying to curb this kind of talk, for the "tremendous anti-German feeling could take on a definitely Nazi character if allowed to get out of hand." The article commended the Army officers in charge of Buchenwald for "their cool, unbiased and fair treatment of German civilians." Some individuals, mostly noncombatant observers, were beginning to talk of German bestiality as being something racial and genetically transmitted. "These people are obviously a little carried away by what they have seen."

Newsweek reported that many Americans were angered when they contrasted the Buchenwald story with the fair treatment given to German P.O.W.'s at Fort Dix, some of whom were said to be still pro-Nazi.

A colonel at Fort Dix admitted to being worried about these "healthy Nazis" in his prison, but he said that "a resurgence of Nazism is a problem for the peacemakers to handle"—not for him.

A congressional delegation came home from Buchenwald divided over the issue of whether to charge the entire German nation with responsibility. Some favored this. Others thought too little was known about whether the German people were really aware of what was going on.[34]

Reading 14   What Did Americans Believe?

A reporter from *Army Talks* wrote that the evidence of atrocity was so overwhelming that all those who covered the event were very careful to describe it accurately, fearing it would weaken the case to do otherwise.

Because during World War I many stories of atrocities were later exploded as Allied propaganda, many people who heard about Nazi concentration camps believed the stories were Allied propaganda to rouse citizens against Germany. Polls were taken in the United States after the war to find out the effect that the news accounts, films, and radio programs had on the American people.

The George Gallup Poll asked the following questions in May 1945:

Do you believe stories of German atrocities? Should movie houses show atrocity pictures? Should all German people in Germany be made to see atrocity films? Should all German prisoners in the United States be made to see atrocity films?[35]

The polls showed that the accounts of atrocities were accepted by an overwhelming majority of Americans as the "plain uncolored, if revolting truth. . . ."[36]

Using Reading 14

According to the Army correspondents, those who didn't want the films shown in the U.S. thought that the films were "too revolting for public consumption or that benefits of public viewings are questionable."[37]

Reading 15   Other Documentation of the Atrocities

Eyewitnesses, survivors, and the Nazi officials themselves have left us with an abundance of materials that document the Holocaust. Many victims risked the short time remaining in their lives to preserve the truth for the future. The pleas of this victim are indicative of the struggle under extreme conditions to preserve a record for future generations:

> . . . I regard it as a sacred task . . . for everyone, whether or not he has the ability, to write down everything that he has witnessed or has heard from those who have witnessed—the atrocities which the barbarians committed in every Jewish town. When the time will come—and indeed it will surely come—let the world read and know what the murderers perpetrated. This will be the richest material for the mourner when he writes the elegy for the present time. This will be the most powerful subject matter for the avenger. . . . We are obligated to assist them, to help them, even if we must pay with our own lives, which today are very cheap.

Many risked their lives and the lives of others by burying eyewitness records in the ground. One victim understood his obligation to history to be more valuable than life.

My work was primitive, consisting of packing and hiding the material... it was perhaps the riskiest, but it was worth doing. We used to say while working: we can die in peace. We have bequeathed and safeguarded our rich heritage. I don't want thanks. It will be enough for me if the coming generations will recall our times. We were aware of our obligation. We did not fear the risk. We reckoned that we were creating a chapter of history and that was more important than several lives. I can say with assurance that this was the basis, the dynamic of our existence then. What we could not cry out to the world, we buried in the ground. May this treasure be delivered into good hands, may it live to see better times, so that it can alert the world to what happened in the twentieth century.[38]

The most extraordinary archive ever created was buried at Auschwitz. It consisted of eyewitness testimonies written by members of the Sonderkommando ("special commando"), a work squad of Jewish prisoners whom the Germans had temporarily spared from the gas chambers. Their task was to remove the dead from the gas chambers and cremate them. In due time the members of the Sonderkommando were themselves gassed and replaced by new workers. In the full realization that they would not survive, some members of the Sonderkommando, under conditions of extreme peril, wrote accounts of the events they had witnessed. They buried their records in the ashes that covered the ground at Auschwitz. These were found after the war, in bad condition, some scarcely decipherable. One testimony began:

Dear finder, search everywhere, in every inch of ground. Dozens of documents are buried beneath it, mine and those of other persons, which will throw light on everything that has happened here. It was we, the commando workers, who deliberately strewed them all over the ground, as many as we could, so that the world should find material traces of the millions of murdered people. We ourselves have lost hope of being able to live to see the moment of liberation.[39]

Russian troops liberated Auschwitz in January 1945 and they left it standing. It has been preserved by the Polish government. The slogan over the gate—*Arbeit Macht Frei* (works make you free)—is still standing. A visitor can see the monument dedicated in 1967 to those who died in Auschwitz.

On the monument he may read a series of memorial plaques in 18 languages, but none of them are in Hebrew or Yiddish. And none will tell him what he already knows—that most of all of those who died at Auschwitz were Jews. He can only weep.[40]

Using Reading 15

Shortly before he was murdered at the Maidanek concentration camp in 1943, Dr. Ignacy Schipper warned that Western society would be reluctant to acknowledge the destruction of European Jewry.

Everything depends on who transmits our testament to future generations, on who writes the history of this period. History is usually written by the victor. What we know about murdered peoples is only what their murderers vaingloriously cared to say about them. Should our murderers be victorious, should they write the history of this war, our destruction will be presented as one of the most beautiful pages of world history, and future generations will pay tribute to them as dauntless crusaders. Their every word will be taken for gospel. Or they may wipe out our memory altogether, as if we had never existed, as if there had never been a Polish Jewry, a ghetto in Warsaw, a Maidanek. Not even a dog will howl for us.

But if we write the history of this period of blood and tears — and I firmly believe we will — who will believe us? Nobody will want to believe us, because our disaster is the disaster of the entire civilized world. . . . We'll have the thankless job of proving to a reluctant world that we are Abel, the murdered brother.[41]

Consider with students the motivation of those who deny the particular Jewish victim of the Holocaust or those who deny that the event occurred. See the overview and the introduction to Chapter 11 for further development of the notion of revisionism and denial.

Reading 16 Hope

The following is one survivor's reflection on the power of hope.

There are a great many of us who know the unspeakable bitterness aroused by everything reminding us of how millions of men and women like ourselves died in complete disarray and without any means of defending themselves, killed like cattle in a slaughterhouse. For my part, I have always firmly refused to accept any pathetic statements of a religious or a nationalistic sort, whether sincere or only apparently so, as explanations of what happened. For the contemporaries of this cataclysm, there is no consoling explanation, nor could there ever be, no comforting word that could put an end to the profound disquiet on the part of survivors who refuse to forget that, only yesterday, the fact of their birth condemned them without appeal to suffer an absolute degradation and to disappear from the world, a defenseless prey. Only a complacently deficient memory would allow us to forget that the earth refused our feet even as it remained firm under the steps of all the others — including our best friends, who had everything in common with us, everything but their origin.

Hope pushes them to fight anew each day for one day more, since the coming day could be the one that will bring freedom. . . . Never had hope provoked so ill as in this war, as in this camp. We were never taught how to rid ourselves of hope. And that is why we are dying in the gas-chambers.[42]

Using Reading 16

This reading reminds us again to consider the behavior of those who created these choiceless situations, the victimizers. Now is the time to help students define those questions that they are left with after reading this chapter.

Reading 17 I Do Not Know Why

Before education about the Holocaust began to find its way to the public, many learned about it from Elie Wiesel, author of *Night* and other works on the Holocaust. Wiesel is the Honorary Chairman of the President's Commission on the Holocaust. The following is an excerpt from his book, *Legends of Our Time*.

I attended the Eichmann trial, I heard the prosecutor try to get the witnesses to talk by forcing them to expose themselves and to probe the innermost recesses of their being: Why didn't you resist? Why didn't you attack your assassins when you still outnumbered them?

Pale, embarrassed, ill at ease, the survivors all responded in the same way: "You cannot understand. Anyone who was not there cannot imagine it."

Well, I was there. And I still do not understand. I do not understand that child in the Warsaw Ghetto who wrote in his diary: "I'm hungry, I'm cold; when I grow up I want to be a German, and then I won't be hungry anymore, and I won't be cold anymore."

I still do not understand why I did not throw myself on the Kapo who was beating my father before my very eyes. In Galicia, Jews dug their own graves and lined up, without a trace of panic, at the edge of the trench to await the machine-gun barrage. I do not understand their calm. And that woman, that mother, in the bunker somewhere in Poland, I do not understand her either; her companions smothered her child for fear its cries might betray their presence; that woman, that mother, having lived this scene of biblical intensity, did not go mad. I do not understand her: why, and by what right, and in the name of what, did she not go mad?

I do not know why, but I forbid us to ask her the question. The world kept silent while the Jews were being massacred, while they were being reduced to that state of objects good for the fire; let the world at least have the decency to keep silent now as well. Its questions come a bit late; they should have been addressed to the executioner. Do they trouble us? Do they keep us from sleeping in peace? So much the better. We want to know, to undersand, so we can turn the page: Is that not true? So we can say to ourselves: the matter is closed and everything is back in order. Do not wait for the dead to come to our rescue. Their silence will survive them.[43]

Using Reading 17

Consider why we seek and accept simple answers to complex questions. Discuss how a curriculum that raises more questions than it gives answers defies traditional notions of education.

Reading 18

Where Are the Camps Now?

Today at Dachau the materials are gone and the concentration camp itself has vanished. In its place are three memorials. One is a set of stone blocks, placed one upon the other, with a Menorah carved on the uppermost stone. Engraved in German, Hebrew, and English is the inscription, "Remember the Victims."

The second memorial to the victims of Dachau is a Carmelite convent known as the Convent of Atonement. Here live 21 nuns who have taken a vow never to leave. The prioress of the convent was a member of the group led by a Jesuit priest, Alfred Delp, one of those executed by the Nazis for his part in the attempt to assassinate Hitler on July 20, 1944.

Why did the Carmelites put a convent there? They gave this answer: The ground Dachau stood on can never be allowed to return to "normal" use. The convent is there to remind the visitor that when he leaves bright and busy Munich and arrives at Dachau, he is in another world.[44]

The memorials built by the Polish government on the site of the former Treblinka concentration camp are unique in Europe. In the center of what was formerly the large compound stands a single stone sculpture. Surrounding that central point and filling the former courtyard are 15,000 gravestones. The visitor will not immediately recognize them as gravestones until he reads the inscriptions carved into each of them. No two stones are alike. They are in fact 15,000 pieces of sculpture, each distinctive, each portraying one victim's anguish.[45]

Using Reading 18

In one class two students argued over whether the camps should be left standing. "Yes, if my mother had been there I would want to know what she went through." "No, not me," responded another student, "I don't want them left up for others to learn how easy it is to do such evil."

If the teacher did not view *Kitty Returns to Auschwitz* earlier in the chapter, it would be appropriate here. The section on memorials in the last chapter might be used here also.

A student responds:

I read the column on Auschwitz. Somehow this may seem crazy to you, but I would like to go there. I think it would be good for me. I just can't believe that millions of Jews died there, but if I see it for myself maybe somehow I will believe it. I would like to see how someone suffered because I have not really suffered much in my life, and I think I would be changed greatly if I went.

Today many classes of students from Germany and other parts of Europe visit Dachau and Auschwitz as part of their education.

Reading 19

The Art of the Victims

The art of the victims, produced by incarcerated professional artists between 1939 and 1945, survived from almost all the concentration camps, labor camps, ghettos, and hide-outs across Europe. It has become a subject of popular exploitation in the recent Gerald Green film for television, "Holocaust," which includes a distorted account of the "Painter's Affair" of 1944 in Theresienstadt. This unofficial or illegal art produced by numerous unconnected individuals was clearly art of "social conscience" and humane responsibility. . . .

The art was produced furtively, under conditions of extreme brutality, lack of artistic materials, and imminent threat of death. Although the work includes a heavy amount of portraiture and scenes of daily life, there are also abstractions completed by the victims (the works of Otto Freundlich, for instance). It is still far too early to theorize about schools and styles of art produced, since very basic information is still being accumulated about the nature of creativity under duress.

The victims were portrayed with honesty and dramatic reality in many localities such as Dachau, Dora Mittelbau, and others. The social responsibility to tell this history of the camps makes the surviving works of art an extremely important historical document about conditions and events from 1939 to 1945.

Most of the artists used pen and pencil, but a number of watercolor works have survived. The works of art produced by the victims of Nazi Germany are a testimony to the reality of a world of agony. They are historical evidence of a unique kind and transmit the camp experience to posterity; this experience is confirmed by written evidence. However, these artists differed from their predecessors (Goya, Gillray, Gericault, and Barlach, for example). Previous socially conscious artists rarely suffered as much as the people they portrayed in their works; this division was erased with the victim-creators of 1939 to 1945. An ethical person as well as an artist may lack the power to prevent or stop the horrors he or she witnesses; however, the inmate artists transcended the events in which they were unwilling participants. The visual record of the camp inmates differed from that of the emigrants. The latter's work is close to the genre of political protest art, while the former fits the more timeless humanistic tradition of Brueghel's *Massacre of the Innocents*.[46]

Citations

Chapter 8

[1] William Shirer, *The Rise and Fall of the Third Reich*, (Simon and Schuster, 1960) p. 969.

[2] Published by Transaction, Inc. from *Taking Lives: Genocide and State Power* by Irving Horowitz. Copyright © 1980 by Transaction Books. p. 25.

[3] William Styron, "Hell Reconsidered," (a review of Richard Rubenstein's *The Cunning of History*) *New York Review of Books*, June 29, 1978.

[4] This material in slightly altered form is taken from Professor Lawrence Langer's work in progress: *Versions of Survival: The Holocaust and the Human Spirit*, to be published in the spring of 1982.

[5] Adapted from *Man's Search for Meaning* by Viktor E. Frankl. copyright © 1962 by Viktor E. Frankl. Reprinted by permission of Beacon Press, p. 65.

[6] Langer, *Versions of Survival*.

[7] Judith Sternberg Newman, *In the Hell of Auschwitz* (N.Y. Exposition Press, 1963) pp. 42-43.

[8] Philip Hallie, "From Cruelty to Goodness," *The Hasting Center Report*, Vol II, No. 3 (June 1981).

[9] From *Legends of Our Time* by Elie Wiesel. Copyright © 1968 by Elie Wiesel. Reprinted by permission of Holt, Rinehart and Winston, Publishers, pp. 172-173.

[10] Hallie, "From Cruelty to Goodness."

[11] Lucy Dawidowicz, *A Holocaust Reader* Published by Behrman House, Inc., New York City, p. 119. Used with Permission.

[12] Information taken from Martin Gilbert, *Auschwitz*, p. 69.

[13] Rudolf Hoess, *Commandant of Auschwitz* (World Publishers, 1959) pp. 222-223.

[14] *Holocaust*, Israel Pocket Library (Keter Books, 1974) p. 98.

[15] Hoess, *Commandant of Auschwitz*, pp. 205-221.

[16] Henry Friedlander, *Toward a Methodology of Teaching About the Holocaust* (original paper), 1978.

[17] Frankl, *Man's Search for Meaning*, pp. 43-46.

[18] Reprinted from a pamphlet *In Everlasting Remembrance: A Guide to Memorials and Monuments Honoring the Six Million* (New York American Jewish Congress, 1969) p.21.

[19] *The Holocaust;* (Yad Vashem, Jerusalem, 1975) time line.

[20] Martin Gilbert, *The Holocaust* (Hill and Wang, 1978) p. 16.

[21] *Holocaust*, Israel Pocket Library, p. 1.

[22] Shirer, *Rise and Fall of the Third Reich*, p. 968.

[23] Styron, "Hell Reconsidered."

[24] Frankl, *Man's Search for Meaning*, pp. 9-11.

[25] Richard L. Rubenstein, *The Cunning of History* (Harper & Row, 1978).

[26] Styron, "Hell Reconsidered".

[27] Frankl, *Man's Search for Meaning*, pp. 6-8.

[28] Harriet Tarnor Wacks, "Looking Backwards to the Future," *The Journal*, March 1, 1979.

[29] Frankl, *Man's Search for Meaning*, pp. 61, 62, 87, 88.

[30] *Army Talks*, July 10, 1945, U.S. Army Document.

[31] Ibid.

[32] Ibid.

[33] I.L. Kenen, *Buchenwald: They Won't Believe It*.

[34] Ibid.

[35] *Army Talks*.

[36] Ibid.

[37] Ibid.

[38] Dawidowicz, *A Holocaust Reader*, pp. 6-7.

[39] Ibid., p. 8.

[40] *In Everlasting Remembrance*, p. 22.

[41] Alex Grobman, Los Angeles *Herald Examiner*, (July 12, 1981).

[42] Manes Sperber, *A Tear in the Sea* (New York: Bergen Belsen Memorial Press.

[43] Wiesel, *Legends of Our Time*, p. 184.

[44] *In Everlasting Remembrance*, pp. 20, 22, 32, 34-5.

[45] *In Everlasting Remembrance*, p. 21.

[46] Sybil Milton, "Artists Versus Hitler: The Social Responsibility of the Artist in Germany," paper presented at the International Conference on the Lessons of the Holocaust, Philadelphia, October 1978.

Many ex-Nazis that Hilberg interviewed claimed that, "I was ordered to do it." When Hilberg asked to see records of orders, he was often told that, "I was given the order orally." Even worse was the explanation that, "It was expected of me."

Dear Party Comrade Bormann:
We have cleaned up the Jewish question in the Netherlands.... The Jews have been eliminated from the body of the Dutch people and insofar as they have not been transported to the East for labor, they are enclosed in a camp . . . about 8-9,000 Jews have avoided transport by submerging (in hiding). By and by they are being seized and sent to the East; at the moment, the rate of seizures is 5-6,000 a week. The Jewish property has been confiscated and is undergoing liquidation.... The question of Jews in mixed marriages is still open. Here we went further than the Reich and obliged also these Jews to wear the star. I had also ordered that the Jewish partner in a children's mixed marriage should likewise be brought to the East for labor. . . ."[6]

The massive bureaucracy set up for the redistribution of all that belonged to Jewish citizens is indicated in the following summary:

All cash proceeds in German notes were to be deposited to the Reichsbank account of the SS . . . which managed the economic enterprises and administered the concentration camps. Foreign currency (specie or paper), precious metals, jewelry, precious or semiprecious stones, pearls, dental gold, and scrap gold were to be delivered to the WVHA for immediate transmittal to the Reichsbank. All timepieces, alarm clocks, fountain pens, mechanical pencils, hand- or electric-operated shavers, pocket knives, scissors, flashlights, wallets and purses were to be sent to a WVHA installation for cleaning and price estimation, and then forwarded, for sale, to the combat troops. Men's underwear, men's clothing, including footwear, were first to fill staff needs at the concentration camps and then to be sent, for sale, to the troops as an undertaking of the Ethnic German Welfare Office (VOMI). The proceeds were to go to the Reich. Women's clothing, underwear, and footwear and also children's clothing and underwear were to go to the VOMI for cash. Pure silk underwear was assigned to the Ministry of Economy. Eiderdowns, quilts, blankets, dress materials, scarves, umbrellas, canes, thermos bottles, ear mufflers, baby carriages, combs, handbags, leather belts, shopping bags, tobacco pipes . . . were to go to VOMI, with specific provisions for payment. Bed linens, sheets, pillowcases, handkerchiefs, washcloths, tablecloths were delivered to VOMI for cash. All kinds of eyeglasses and spectacles were assigned to the Public Health Office for sale. High class furs, dressed or undressed, were to be delivered to WVHA; cheaper fur goods (neckpieces, hare and rabbit furs) were to be delivered to the Clothing Works of the Waffen-SS at Ravensbruck.[7]

How could such a big operation, carried on in many localities and requiring substantial amounts of personnel and transportation, be concealed for so long? There was a war on and security was strict. It was not healthy for people to show too much interest in what "action groups" were up to, what was going on in "labor camps" or in who was being moved where on trains. . . .

Most important, nothing like this had ever happened before, and people were simply unable to imagine that it could happen. True, human beings had been killed en masse before, but never so cold-bloodedly

Victims were transported in cattle cars from all over Europe to concentration camps.

and systematically, by industrial mass production (or rather, mass destruction) methods. Everyone knew, of course, that Jews were constantly being deported to the East; but the public was led to believe that the deportees would be resettled or, at worst, used as slave labor.

Apart from its unprecedented horror, the mass murder program was hard to credit at first because of its utter irrationality. Even in the Nazis' own perspective, it made no sense. From the German military machine's viewpoint, it made no sense to divert to the killing operation manpower and railroad equipment that were badly needed for the front; from an economic viewpoint, it made no sense to kill people who could do urgent work, much of it skilled. How could anyone know that hatred, arising from quasi-religious fanaticism, would prove stronger than the most pressing practical considerations.

For over a year the secret held, and by the end of that period, late in 1942, most of the Jews were dead. Even in Poland; where the actual killing was done, the truth did not leak out until the summer of 1942. Only in August of that year did the people of the Warsaw ghetto learn about the death factory working overtime in nearby Treblinka. . . .

The outside world was even less able to grasp the truth than those directly concerned. For example, in May 1942 the Polish Government in Exile in London transmitted a report from the Bund, the Jewish Socialists, in Warsaw that 700,000 Jews had been killed as part of a mass murder plan. The report came to *Jewish Frontier,* a respected and responsible magazine published in the United States, but the editors there felt it could not be true. They finally printed parts of it tucked away in the back of the August and September issues, without mentioning that the

Bund said the events were part of an extermination program for the Jewish people as a whole.[8]

... When the terrible truth about the "final solution" became clear to some Jews, they urged the others to resist physically. Realists accepted the fact that Hitler meant to annihilate every Jew in Europe, but the majority of Jews could not believe this would happen. Partly because the Germans shrouded their evil work in utter secrecy. Partly because the Germans used many forms of deception to confuse and mislead their victims. And perhaps most importantly, because the very idea of mechanical and systematic mass murder struck most people—everywhere in the world—as utterly inconceivable. It seemed infinitely different from the earlier examples of what came to be known as genocide. It went far beyond the reach of the human imagination. As Dr. Louis de Jong, a Dutch historian of the Holocaust once said, "Our mind, once having grasped the facts, immediately spewed them out as something utterly alien and unnaturally loathsome." A group of Jehovah's Witnesses, who were put in the death camp at Birkenau, by the side of the gas chambers and crematoriums said later, "One day we would believe our own eyes; the next day we would simply refuse to do so." Another Hollander, Emile Franken, was one of a group in Birkenau which saw the crematorium chimneys smoking day in and day out. But the inmates, "the people themselves," he said, "pretended that the place was a brickyard or a soap factory. This mass delusion lasted for four weeks." He was the only one among them who could accept the unbearable truth.

The gas chambers spelled death not only for oneself but for husband, wife, children, grandparents, relatives, friends. How many among the millions who died in them could face that awesome truth? Professor de Jong concludes:

"We should be committing an immense historical error, were we to dismiss the many defense mechanisms employed by the victims—not constantly, mind you, but by way if intermittent distress signals—as mere symptoms of blindness or foolishness; rather did these defense mechanisms spring from deep and inherent qualities shared by all mankind; a love of life, a love of family; a fear of death, and an understandable inability to grasp the reality of the greatest crime in the history of mankind, a crime so monstrous ... that even its perpetrators (the sadists and other perverts among them excepted) were unable to dwell on their activities for too long."[9]

Using Reading 3

Walter Laqueur documents the response to the "knowing" about the mass exterminations by the majority of Germans, Jewish organizations, and Allied leadership in order to understand why it was kept a secret. He finds that the response was a continuation of denial and suppression. For Jew and non-Jew "the ability to absorb information but not believe it was the universal pattern."

Even when Jews did know they toned down their appeals to the Allies, fearing—correctly—that the full truth would be taken as exaggeration, as another bit of Jewish or Zionist propaganda to be filed and dismissed.

What is amazing is the amount of information available, how fast it came in, and how many different sources supplied it. It came by word of mouth, by personal letter, by coincidence and accident; it arrived by way of underground organizations, journalists, survivors who escaped, agencies in the neutral countries, official diplomatic channels and clandestine contacts, and finally through individuals with nothing at stake beyond private conscience. Until the Nazis caught them, for example, the Swiss colony in Warsaw conducted a covert courier service that delivered written reports (and even film footage) to London via Sweden. The Polish underground sent regular radio messages to the Polish government-in-exile in London, including carefully documented statements prepared by Emmanuel Ringelblum and his circle in the Warsaw Ghetto. Thus, in December 1941, when the first of the death camps, Chelmno, began to gas victims in moving vans, dumping them into mass graves, three grave-diggers escaped to Warsaw and told their story to Ringelblum, who wrote a detailed description of operations at Chelmno. It reached London in June and appeared in American newspapers in July 1942. . . .

The Jews denied reality out of fear and helplessness, the Germans denied it out of guilt, the Allies denied it out of shame, but also for reasons of expediency and a limited but steady strain of antisemitism.[10]

The United States rejected requests to bomb the gas chambers and crematoria at Auschwitz. Even though the attack would have killed many of the victims, those in favor of the bombing believe it would have saved others; one million Hungarian Jews might have been saved.

Beginning in April 1944, the Allies ordered aerial photographs of Auschwitz. These photos showed prisoners undergoing disinfection and standing in line to be tatooed, the gas chambers and crematoria, and in one photo, a line of 1,500 people from 85 railroad box cars being lead into the camp.

In the United States, besides those at high government positions who knew, there is evidence that there was an attempt to inform the readers of the leading American Protestant journals about the death camps.

Robert Ross in Religious Studies at the University of Minnesota found that American Protestants neither paid attention to the reports nor acted upon the knowledge. There was, he said, an absence of moral outrage.

By 1943 Protestant journals had fully reported the Nazi persecution of Europe's Jews: deportation and massacre, gas chambers, crematoria, and starvation, the transport trains and the death camps. Yet the reports were often couched in skepticism, reflecting the editors' fear that they might be fooled by propaganda—false atrocity stories during World War I had taught them to doubt. Even by July 1944, when the Russian army liberated the death camp Majdanek, editor Charles Clayton Morrison of the The Christian Century *was reluctant to part with his assumptions about wartime propaganda. Not till he saw pictures of a death camp in the spring of 1945 was Morrison convinced: "The thing is well-nigh incredible," he wrote. "But it happened."*[11]

"So It Was True!" This headline in *The Signs of the Times* is, for Ross, an apt summary of editorial reaction—mingled surprise, despair, and resignation—in the spring of 1945.

Reading 4 A Minister Looks at the Way Christians Acted in the Nazi Era

In this interview Reverend Dr. Carl Scovel talks with a journalist about his interest in Christian resistance in Nazi Germany. Dr. Scovel spent six months in a Japanese concentration camp with his missionary parent and three siblings. He considers himself a "child of World War II." One reason he became interested in Christian resistance was because of "those situations where a person is called by conscience to conflict with a culture in some way."

While in Germany in 1971 and 1973, he learned about the "conflicts between priest and pastors and the government and about the conflicts between the Christian laity and the government. Those conflicts... took place for many reasons, but they were also genuine religious conflicts. Nazism was a kind of religion, a pseudo-religion. [Those] churchmen who resisted Nazism were the ones who saw the conflict. There were many other churchmen who tried to see no conflict who did not see Nazism as a religion—I think very few ever did.

"There were some super-Nazis who sent their kids to Nazi schools, who had their kids baptized in Nazi baptisms, who had Nazi weddings. There was a very small group that was super-religious, but even Hitler himself made fun of them. Hitler was just the absolute pragmatist. He had not stuck with this thing.... I think for a few Nazis it was a cult, a religion, but there were an awful lot of others who were pretty skeptical about it, pretty dubious. And of course the Christians who resisted it understood that Hitler's real attempt was to wipe out the church.

"Very few churchmen understood that.... I don't think there can be any question that once the war was over, he intended either to wipe out the church or to reduce it to such a state of subservience that it would be meaningless—Jews first, Christians second."

"The churchmen—the priests and the pastors—knew a lot more than the laity did. For instance, by 1942, all the bishops, both Protestant and Catholic, knew about the extermination of the Jews—or by early 1943—but I think not a great many of the laity did. Of course, they knew their Jewish neighbors and friends had all left. The question was, did they believe the government propaganda that they were all in labor camps or something like that?

"But the laity didn't know as much as the church leaders did, and the church leaders didn't all know the same amount. So I think there was a significant difference. The laity by and large tended to react on local and emotional issues—I think that's a good point.

"There were certain lay individuals who were really outstanding leaders—a number of them who were in effect trying to set up a substitute government once Hitler was overthrown. There were individual resisters. There was a conscientious objector—there was a book written about him—who lost his life because he wouldn't fight in the war—truly an amazing man.

"And there was Kurt Goerstein, who appears in the play *The Deputy*—again a striking guy who did more than any person to spread the news about the death camps throughout Germany. He joined the SS in order to find out what was going on, and once he found out he went to anybody who'd listen to him and tell them what was happening—an amazing guy."

"The Catholic experience and the Protestant experience were totally different—two separate histories as far as Germany from 1932 to 1945 goes. The first thing you have to remember is that the Catholic Church signed a concordat with Hitler in July 1933, and that concordat in my opinion was a pair of handcuffs on the Church. Both Pius XI and Pius XII considered it a real protection of at least German Catholics.

"The Catholic bishops—yes, they did protest certain kinds of government measures, and they resisted the state's encroachment on the church.... There was one great protest made about Hitler's first experiment program—of the mentally retarded. In that case, the church and notably the Catholic Church really brought that program to a full halt. That was the most dramatic protest of the Church. On the other hand, they didn't do for the Jews what they were willing to do for the mentally retarded—and the differences between them is just a painful, painful indifference.

"I think the Pope was very tentative. I think he thought the concordat was much more of a protection than I personally think it was. Of course he knew a lot more than I did. . . .

"The frightening thing is that the present Pope was the head of the passport division of the Vatican, which handed out visas and permits right and left to known Nazis after the war, getting them to South America. It was just amazing—amazing because the Catholic Church knew that the Nazis were their enemies.

"What the Nazis did to the Polish priests—they shot them in droves. They literally jerked them off to concentration camps. They did this to Catholic priests and bishops in other countries as well. In other words, the German Catholics were relatively safe compared with Catholics in Hungary, Czechoslovakia, Poland and so forth—and the Pope knew all this but he was afraid that if he protested, it would be even worse."

"The Protestant church followed a different route. What Hitler tried to do was organize a national Protestant church, and most of the bishops and ministers joined that church. But about 10 percent of them refused to join and organized in Nazi Germany an independent church, the Confessing Church, and that church in one form or another stayed intact throughout the war.

"Now, they made a super amount of compromises, but they did do some good things. In the first place, they were the only semi-independent organization in Germany throughout the war. Secondly, they did protest twice the extermination of the Jews and in very mild language—so incidentally did a couple of Catholic bishops. At the end, the thing that was interesting to me was that a couple of these ministers in this little church, the Confessing Church—when I say church I mean an organization—hid Jews during the last two, two and a half years of the war. I had interviews with some of these people when I went over in 1973, very interesting people.

"But interestingly enough, I'm not sure I would say that Protestants resisted more than Catholics did. . . . You have to realize that the Catholic Church caught it much harder than the Protestant church. Far more priests died in the concentration camps than did Protestant ministers—relatively few Protestant ministers—hundreds of Catholic priests, maybe 4,000 from all over Europe. I don't know how many of these were Germans.

"The group that suffered the most were the Jehovah's Witnesses. . . . They were amazing. They were adamant. I think 97 percent of them were in concentration camps at one time or another during the war. Perhaps a third died during the war."[12]

Using Reading 4

Dr. Scovel's research on church resistance in Europe reinforces the notion that those individuals and groups who "believed in their freedom used their freedom." Dr. Scovel warns that the "interest in the Nazi era is often not for the right reasons." Too often its a "fascination with violence, the horror . . . a romanticization of Nazism that's totally inaccurate."

Reading 5

The Response of the Vatican

The role of Pope Pius XII and the Vatican response to the events of this history are the subject of serious analysis and interpretation. When accounts of the "final solution" were reported to Pope Pius, no strong statements were made, nor was Hitler excommunicated from the church. According to Abram Sachar:

The consistent rationale offered for the silence was that it was necessary first to corroborate the reports. Under pressure, there was an annoyed response that "in order to avoid the slightest appearance of partiality, His Holiness had imposed upon himself, in word and deed, the most delicate reserve." The "delicate reserve" was maintained even as Jews were being rounded up in Rome itself. Later, much later, a Papal spokesman indicated that the Pontiff had decided, after many tears and many prayers, that a denunciation of the Nazis from the Vatican might further rouse the ferocity of the Nazis and result in more, rather than fewer, deaths. There were, of course, not too many left to worry about after six million had been murdered. Monsignor Montini, later to become Pope Paul VI, added: "The time may come when, in spite of such a grievous prospect, the Holy Father will feel himself obliged to speak out." But that time never came. The duty to speak out was always counterbalanced by the fear of weakening Germany and opening the way to the triumph of atheist communism.[13]

Using Reading 5

When students ask about those institutions that had the power to make a difference, it is important to consider the responses of the Vatican and its leadership before and during the deportation of Jews from Rome.

No protest was heard from Pius XII when, in 1935, Germany promulgated its own infamous statutes of racial purity in the Nuremberg Laws.... The roundup of Jews by the Nazis began in Rome in the fall of 1943.

On October 18, over one thousand Roman Jews, more than two-thirds of them women and children, were deported from the Eternal City to Auschwitz. On October 28 the German ambassador, Ernst Heinrich von Weizsacker, reported to Berlin: "Although under pressure from all sides, the Pope (Pius XII) has not let himself be drawn into any demonstrative censure of the deportation of Jews from Rome...."[14]

Reading 6

The Bystanders

And what was said long ago is true: Nations are made not of oak and rock but of men, and, as the men are, so will the nations be.
—Milton Mayer

Using Reading 6

We have studied many of the responses of individuals and groups as they became aware of the victims of Nazi tyranny. Nations also responded in a variety of ways as revealed in the following two selections. The first is a brief summary of the debate in the United States over the Wagner-Rogers Bill to save 20,000 Jewish children. The second deals with the response of Denmark to the Nazi deportations of that country's Jewish people.

The response or nonresponse of nations was far more complex than we have presented here; yet these two selections offer some insight into the decisions of policy makers and citizens as they become aware of the plight of victims. One of the first questions students asked in class was, "Where was the United States?" In his book, *While Six Million Died*, Arthur Morse concentrates on the bystanders, and asks, "What did the rest of the world and, in particular, the United States and Great Britain know about Nazi plans for the annihilation of the Jews? What was their reaction to this knowledge?" *The Politics of Rescue* by Henry Feingold is appropriate reading on this topic. Students might also read the chapter in *While Six Million Died* on the voyage of the St. Louis that concludes with this question from a Nazi newspaper:

We are saying openly that we do not want the Jews while the democracies keep on claiming that they are willing to receive them — and then leave the guests out in the cold! Aren't we savages better men after all?

Why did the United States and other countries participate in the 1936 Olympic games in Berlin? In light of all that was known at the time about Nazi persecutions and discrimination toward Jews, why was there a lack of response to the refugee problem at the Evian Conference, an international conference in 1938 held specifically to deal with the refugee crisis. Why were so many conscientious leaders and "humanitarians" suspicious and unwilling to act upon the accounts of persecution in the news?

A large part of this curriculum has dealt with the responses of the victims and the victimizers, but if we are to understand fully why and how the Holocaust happened, we must also examine the response of the bystanders. In particular, what did the most powerful Ally, the United States, do to aid or rescue the victims of the Holocaust? For the sake of simplicity and clarity, this section will focus on some key political and social forces that influenced American decision-making during the thirties and forties. It will ask students to put themselves in the position of American policy-makers, in order to understand why certain decisions were made. At the same time, students should be encouraged to ask whether the decisions made were right and whether the United States should or could have acted differently.*

Reading 7

1933-1942: The Fallen Torch

The United States, prior to this period, had a long and proud tradition of offering a haven for the oppressed. The early settlers such as the Pilgrims fled religious oppression in England. The Irish sought refuge in the U.S. from persecution by the British. At the turn of the 20th century, Eastern European and Russian Jews, victims of bloody pogroms, poured into New York City. Yet, during the thirties, many Jews who were trying to escape Nazi persecution were unable to enter the United States.

One group of Jews stole a boat in Holland in 1938. There were 13 of them. None of them knew how to sail, but they managed to cross the Atlantic and land on a little cay very close to Tortola and Beef Islands in

---

*For further information read "Why Auschwitz Was Never Bombed" by David Wyman, *Commentary*, May 1978, pp. 37-46.

the British Virgin Islands where a young man and a young woman, Americans, were living an idyllic existence. The Jews wanted to go to Cuba so that they could then get to the United States. They were sick and physically and emotionally exhausted except for a baby who had been born aboard the boat. The young couple helped them plan their navigation but when they arrived in Miami they were turned away because they had no papers. And so they sailed to South America and were all lost at sea.

Immigration statistics dramatize the abrupt change in U.S. policy. From 1820 to 1933 when Hitler took power, over 37 million immigrants entered the United States. From 1933 to 1943, only 341,567 citizens from Germany or its allies were permitted to enter the United States.

Why couldn't the millions of Axis citizens find refuge here?

Why had the United States abandoned its historic role as a haven for the oppressed?

To answer the first question, one has to examine congressional legislation enacted earlier that severely limited the number of immigrants who would be admitted to the United States. Prior to and during World War I, many groups, such as the Immigration Restriction League, claimed that many immigrants were racially inferior and were corrupting American society. After the war, the Red Scare fanned distrust of foreigners and many workers feared that immigrants would compete for scarce jobs. The stereotypes about immigrants, bigotry, and economic concerns led to the passage of the Quota Act of 1921 and the Immigration Act of 1924, which cut immigration by almost 80 percent. Reflecting the bias against immigrants from Eastern Europe, the Congress imposed much more severe quota limits on those immigrants and provided large quotas for the British and Irish. Immigrants had to prove that they would not become a "public charge" by producing a police certificate attesting to good character. Obviously, it was difficult for many Jews to obtain that from the Nazi-dominated police.

In the early thirties, the United States and other Allied nations talked about the rescue of Jews, but they did not act. In 1938, the United States sponsored the Evian Conference in which thirty-two nations discussed ways of aiding refugees from the Axis countries. The United States, however, refused to change its immigration policies, so few of the other nations were willing to take dramatic steps on their own. The Conference did agree to form an Intergovernmental Committee on Refugees, but that committee had limited funding and it could not persuade the great powers to accept larger numbers of refugees. The League of Nation's High Commissioner for German Refugees was so disturbed by the pitifully insufficient efforts of the Allies that he resigned in 1935.

This inactivity was noticed by Hitler and the Nazi press. Hitler commented in the thirties: "Through its immigration law, America has inhibited the unwelcome influx of such races as it has been unable to tolerate in its midst. Nor is America now ready to open its doors to Jews fleeing from Germany." A Nazi newspaper exclaimed after the Evian Conference: " . . . no state is prepared to fight the cultural disgrace of central Europe by accepting a few thousand Jews. Thus the Conference serves to justify German's policy against Jewry." Several times, Hitler cynically offered to deliver the Jews to any nation that would have them; but he knew that there would be no takers.*

---

*Information collected by Kenneth Schwartz.

Using Reading 7

For centuries those escaping poverty and politics have looked to the U.S. as a haven. Recently the photographs of the Vietnamese "boat people" and the Haitians have raised similiar questions about the responsibilities of nations for others. Those issues are far too complex, however, for simple comparisons and quick judgments. Discuss with students what opportunities there were to use the Evian Conference to stop Hitler.

Reading 8

A Decision Not to Save 20,000 Jewish Children: The Failure of the Wagner-Rogers Bill

Perhaps the most poignant and revealing example of the American response is the Wagner-Rogers Bill. Prior to 1939, several nations had made modest efforts to rescue German-Jewish children; Holland admitted 1,700 young Jews, and Britain, 9,000 Jews. Inspired by those examples, a group of clergy persuaded Congressman Robert Wagner, author of the famous pro-labor Wagner Act, to co-sponsor legislation that would admit 20,000 Jewish children over two years. Under the act, which was introduced in February 1939, the number of children admitted would not be subtracted from the established quotas; otherwise, the bill would save Jewish children at the expense of other Jews. The children would be subsidized by Jewish agencies and they would not even be permanent citizens, but would return to their parents after the war.*

It is important to remember some of the events taking place at about the time the Wagner-Rogers Bill was introduced. A few months before, on November 9, the Nazis had conducted their "night of broken glass" in which riots left about one hundred Jewish people dead and many of their stores, homes, and synagogues destroyed. It also marked the beginning of deportations to the concentration camps. In January, Hitler publicly warned the impending annihilation of the Jewish race of Europe. It was becoming clear to Jewish people living in Germany and to many concerned Americans that the best hope for Jews, particularly the children, was to get them out of Germany.

The United States had been trying to survive a decade of severe depression and many desperate people searched for scapegoats. Millions of Americans listened to the antisemitic speeches of Father Charles Coughlin who called the "night of broken glass" a defense mechanism against the Jewish Communist conspiracy. A public opinion poll was taken in April of 1939—at the very same time that Congress was considering the Wagner-Rogers Bill. It revealed that 42.3 percent of the American people believed that antisemitism was the result of unfavorable Jewish traits. In another poll that same year, most people agreed that among all the immigrant groups, Jews and Italians were the worst citizens.

A number of religious and civic organizations spoke out in support of the bill. The prominent Quaker, Clarence Pickett, warned that if the United States did not respond, it would be forsaking its mission to the world; "The issue is whether the American people have lost their ability to respond to such tragic situations. If it turns out that we have lost that ability, it will mean that much of the soul has gone out of America." A bishop from Chicago said, "In providing [these children] a sanctuary

---
*Information collected by Kenneth Schwartz.

where they can grow up in the ways of peace and walk the paths of righteousness, we will help not only them but ourselves . . . we still demonstrate to the world our own devotion to the sanctity of human life."

Francis Kinicutt, president of the Allied Patriotic Societies, led a force of thirty organizations to oppose the bill. He claimed that the bill was for Jews and sponsored by Jews. "The bill," he suggested, "if passed, will be a precedent . . . in response to the pressure of foreign nationalistic or racial groups, rather than in accordance with the needs and desires of the American people." Other opponents stressed that the Jews were not the only victims of persecution. For example, "If this bill passes, there is no reason why we should not also bring in twenty thousand Chinese children. Certainly they are being persecuted too." Several congressmen picked up on this theme and asked supporters of the bill whether they would agree to admit Polish, Russian, or French children. When one supporter replied that the need was greatest for Jewish children, a congressman suggested that there was a Jewish conspiracy behind the bill. One opponent revealed to a friend one of his real fears which was that " . . . twenty thousand children would soon grow into twenty thousand ugly adults."

Because of pressure by numerous lobbying groups and because of their awareness of antisemitism in America, the congressional committee dealt a death blow to the bill. It was agreed that the 20,000 children would only be admitted as part of the regular immigration quota, not in addition to that quota. That meant that Jewish children would be admitted at the expense of Jewish adults.

The only chance for saving the bill rested with the President and the executive agencies, but as one official wrote, "There is a lot of sentiment about (these children) but the enthusiasm is liable to wane at the end of a long period." Even though Eleanor Roosevelt pushed the President to support the bill, he still responded with one note of appeal, "File—no action, FDR." The Secretary of State told the congressional committee that the bill would raise difficult administrative problems.

The bill was finally reported out to the full Congress on July 1, 1939, but the chief sponsor could no longer support his own bill because of all the changes. He said, "The proposed changes would in effect convert the measure from a humane proposal to help children who are in acute distress to a proposal with needlessly cruel consequences for adults in Germany. . . . " In July, the sponsor of the bill to rescue 20,000 Jewish children from persecution withdrew his bill.

It is interesting that several years later, the Congress passed a bill to evacuate British children who were endangered by the Nazi attack on England. These children who were admitted to America were not considered as refugees and none were Jewish.*

Using Reading 8

To understand this section, the student should be familiarized with the legislative process. The teacher should stress the importance of actions taken in congressional committees; because each congressman is concerned with so many issues, the full Congress must delegate much responsibility to the particular committee that is expert in a given area, such as immigration. In addition, the teacher should discuss the influence of lobbying groups on the legislative process; lobbying groups have the funds and organization to get congressmen elected and thus

*Information collected by Kenneth Schwartz.

congressmen listen. Finally, the teacher should point out that the President has a crucial role and his position on legislation and the positions of officials in the executive agencies can determine whether a bill succeeds or fails.

Reading 9

Two Decisions: One Saved Lives and One Would Not
Abram Sachar recounts two further incidents involving the possibility of saving Jewish lives.

In 1940, a refugee ship carrying Jews who had escaped from Vichy, France was turned away from Mexico and ordered back to Europe and certain doom. It stopped for coal at Norfolk, Virginia, and a Jewish delegation pleaded with Cordell Hull, the Secretary of State, to offer temporary asylum to the refugees. Hull pointed to the American flag and said that he had taken an oath to protect it and he would not break the law of his country. He was reminded by Dr. Nahum Goldmann that some anti-Nazi German sailors had leaped overboard from their ships, and that the Coast Guard had saved them and given them sanctuary at Ellis Island. Dr. Goldmann suggested that a message might be sent to the ship suggesting that the refugees jump overboard for they would surely be rescued by the Coast Guard. Hull sharply upbraided Goldmann as the most cynical man he had ever met. Dr. Goldmann replied, "I ask you, Mr. Secretary, who is the cynical one? I, who wish to save these people, or you, who are preparing to send them back to their death?" In the end, through the personal intercession of Eleanor Roosevelt, this small group of refugees was saved. . . .

In 1943, a possibility opened for the rescue of twenty thousand children when Sweden was prepared to request their release. They would be cared for in Sweden if Britain and the United States would share the cost of food and medicine, and place them, after the war, in Palestine or in some other haven. There was no problem of covering costs; private philanthropy was readily available, and Britain agreed. But the proposal was shunted from one office to another in the State Department for the whole of the year in which the crematoria operated. This was the period when thousands of Nazi prisoners of war were housed in comfortable American camps. It was suggested that similar camps might be opened for children, as enemy aliens, as a stopgap until the gas ovens stopped functioning. But the proposal roused no interest. One State Department official noted that any rescue concentrating on Jewish children might antagonize the Nazis, and prevent other possible cooperative acts. At the end of the year, when another million children had died in the crematoria, the proposal was dropped.[15]

Using Reading 9

The argument ascribed to the Pope and to the American State Department official are similar in content: Making a stand to rescue Jews might antagonize the Nazis and prevent other possible cooperation. It is said for the Pope his anticommunism was a consideration; for the United States it was decisions regarding the waging of the war.

Later, in the chapter on the genocide of the Armenian people during World War I, we learn about those western nations that refused to mediate, or take in escaping, starving people. The newspapers today are filled with similar stories. What principles are involved and do nations have an obligation to save lives whenever they can?

Reading 10 **Rescue in Denmark**

Harold Flender, author of *Rescue in Denmark*, was present at the trial of Adolf Eichmann in Israel where he was reminded of the "apathy and toleration—and sometimes approval—of the Nazi bestiality by many of the people of the occupied countries, including Austria, Poland, Czechoslovakia and Ukraine. The roll call of shame was long and embraced much of Europe.

During the trial Flender heard mention of Denmark. At that time he decided to research the reactions of Danes to the orders of their Nazi occupiers regarding the Jews in Denmark.

In October 1943, the Nazis decided to round up Denmark's eight thousand Jews for shipment to the death camps. The entire country acted as an underground movement to ferry the eight thousand to Sweden. It was one of the few times that Eichmann had been frustrated. He visited Copenhagen in a rage—but to no avail. The Jews were saved....

Before instituting anti-Jewish measures in the countries they occupied, the Germans tried to ascertain to what extent their actions would be supported by the non-Jewish populations of these countries. In Poland and Slovakia, for example, their research revealed that they could start Jewish persecution at any time with impunity. Not only would the Poles and Slovaks refrain from protests, they would help. The Ukrainians outdid the Nazis in slaughtering the local Jewry. The numerous Polish and Slovak atrocities against the Jews and the Ukrainian massacre of 100,000 Jews at Babi Yar are proof of the accuracy of the German predictions. In most of the countries under their domination, the Germans reached the conclusion that arrest and internment of the Jews would meet with little or no opposition.

Their research revealed only one outstanding exception: Denmark....

Many Danes spread stories that the king and members of his family had actually worn the yellow Star of David, and by doing so caused the Germans to rescind the order that all Danish Jews were to wear the armband.

Actually, none of these stories is true. King Christian X never made the statement attributed to him. He never wore the armband, never even said that he would wear it. Having been advised of the Danes' intense antipathy to antisemitism, the Germans never attempted or even threatened to introduce the yellow Star of David in Denmark....

The Danish Jews were aware of these open defiances by their fellow Danes of Nazi antisemitism. It bolstered their confidence and later inspired them to turn without hesitation to their friends, their neighbors, and even to total strangers, for aid. Their attitude was in sharp contrast to the attitude of so many Eastern European Jews, who, when asked years later at the Eichmann trial in Jerusalem why they had not attempted to escape, replied in effect: "To whom could we turn? We knew no one would help us...."

Jorgen Knudsen, a young, newly married ambulance driver, was leaving his apartment to report for work when he noticed some of his student friends rushing up and down the street stopping people. When he asked them what they were doing they informed him....

"Warn all your Jewish friends," said one of the students.

Knudsen had never thought in terms of Jewish or non-Jewish friends. Friends were friends. Names might be an indication, but for the moment he couldn't think of a single friend with a Jewish-sounding name.

He had to do something. On the street corner was a telephone booth. He entered it and ripped out the telephone directory. Hiding it under his coat, he walked rapidly to the garage where his ambulance was parked. Sitting behind the wheel of the ambulance, he opened the directory, and with a pencil circled what were obviously Jewish names. He did not report with his ambulance for hospital duty that day. Instead, he drove throughout Copenhagen calling on total strangers to give them the warning. When people he called upon became frantic because they had no one to turn to, he piled them into his ambulance and drove them to Bispebjerg Hospital, where he knew Dr. Karl Henry Koster would be willing to hide them.

Knudsen's spontaneous action was typical of the behavior of a large segment of the Danes. When questioned later as to why he acted the way he did, Knudsen matter-of-factly replied, "What else could I do?"—a statement of refreshing contrast to what was said by so many Germans and other nationals who, when asked why they never lifted a finger to aid the Jews, replied, "What could I do?". . .

Why did Dr. Koster work to save the Danish Jews? "It was the natural thing to do. I would have helped any group of Danes being persecuted. The Germans' picking on Jews made as much sense to me as picking on redheads."

Why did Ole Secher? "We just had to. We—that means some of my medical student friends and myself—just felt that we had to do something about this particular situation. There was nothing else we could do. . . ."

Why Nurse Jansen? "I was brought up to believe in democracy and to believe that you have to be willing to fight if you want to preserve that democracy. As for helping Jews, I didn't feel any particular responsibility for Jews. As a matter of fact, I never thought of them as Jews or anything else. They were merely my countrymen and they needed my help."

And Jorgen Knudsen? "It was never a question of Jew or non-Jew. It was a question of people in distress. I would have helped anyone to escape from the Gestapo.". . .

"Because the entire medical profession stood together as a single unit in opposition to antisemitism, our efforts in behalf of our countrymen of the Jewish faith were that much easier," said Dr. Koster. "We knew that the Germans couldn't arrest all of us."

Why did the Eges help the Jews? . . .

"We helped the Jews because it meant that for once in your life you were doing something worthwhile. There has been a lot of talk about how grateful the Jews should be to their fellow Danes for having saved their lives, but I think that the Danes should be equally grateful to the Jews for giving them an opportunity to do something decent and meaningful. It was a terrible time, but I must confess that it was also a wonderful time, a happy time. Yes, I don't think that we were ever happier. Our activities gave us a special feeling of oneness. We were together. Nowhere were we refused.". . .

"We've got to do something to fix those Germans," said Kaier.

Ronne passed on to Kaier the news he had learned about the raids to arrest the Jews. "How about helping the Jews to get across to Sweden?" asked Ronne. "That would be one way of getting back at the Germans."

Kaier was immediately enthusiastic over the idea. "Yes," he agreed, "that *would* be a hell of a way to get back at them!"

"We would also be doing a very humane thing in helping our fellow countrymen of the Jewish faith," said Ronne.

"Don't give me any of that!" snapped back Kaier. "I don't give a damn about the Jews one way or the other. I'm only interested in seeing what I can do to annoy the Germans. I think it'll be great sport to see how many times we can fool them."[16]

Using Reading 10

The Danish people were not alone in acting to save their Jewish population. There were individual acts of courage and humanity in Germany, in the camps, and in occupied countries. Henry Cargas and others have written about the *righteous gentiles*, and Philip Hallie has described the French village of Le Chambon, which acted to save Jews. But,

It was only in Denmark that almost everyone, from king to fisherman, took an active role in rescuing the Jews. It was only in Denmark that after World War II over 98.5 percent of the Jews were still alive.[17]

In a section of *Rescue in Denmark*, Harold Flender reflected on the question, why did the Danes act as they did?

There is no answer. There are many answers. And we will never know all of them. If we could, we should be able to solve the problem of man's inhumanity to man. More important, we should be able to establish a formula for humanity. But it is worth examining some of the answers.

One important factor is Denmark's geographical proximity to neutral Sweden and the fact that after 1943 Sweden was willing to accept all refugees who reached her shores. The Danes at least had a refuge to which they could send their Jews. The same could not be said for the peoples of most of the other German-occupied countries.

Luck too played its part. The Danes were fortunate in that the German head of shipping operations in Copenhagen, Duckwitz, was so opposed to the Nazi persecution of the Jews that he was willing to risk his life by revealing to the Danes secret information about the preparations for the raid. Had the Danes not received Duckwitz' advance warning, they would have had little if any opportunity to act. And Duckwitz was not the only German in Denmark opposed to Nazi racism. Many of the Wehrmacht troops sent to occupy Denmark were older men, often in their forties and fifties. Unlike the younger Germans, they had no great belief in the New Order. In several instances Wehrmacht officers were known to have been uncooperative in the Gestapo's drive to arrest the Danish Jews. On one occasion, a Wehrmacht officer in Amager, upon being told by a subordinate the Jews were boarding fishing vessels in the harbor, was said to have replied, "These people are the Gestapo's responsibility, not ours. Now let me finish my drink in peace."

For many Danes, the rescue of the Jews was primarily an act of protest against the German occupation. By the fall of 1943, the bestial character of Nazism was abundantly evident. The widely distributed publications of the Danish underground press had informed the people of German atrocities throughout the continent. In addition, large numbers of Danes were furious over the severe food rationing that had been imposed upon them by the Germans. They yearned for a chance to protest. That opportunity came with the persecution of the Jews. Getting the Jews safely to Sweden was tantamount to slapping the faces of the Germans.

For many of the younger Danes, love of adventure was often the initial motivation. Because Germany had treated Denmark with kid gloves during the early years of the occupation, these Danish youths had little notion of the brutality with which the Germans carried out their reprisals. There was no Danish Lidice.

Leadership was certainly an important factor. The king, church leaders, the heads of the medical profession, student groups and business organizations set examples which inspired others to emulate their stubborn resistance.

The large numbers of intermarriages between Jews and Christians in Denmark must also be taken into account. Many Christian Danes had close Jewish relatives, and rare was the Danish Jew without a Christian member of the family to whom he could turn in distress. And if there were no relatives, there were almost always close friends. The Danish Jews were never forced to keep to themselves, and never voluntarily kept to themselves.

All of these factors played their part, but they do not answer the key question of why the entire Danish population acted spontaneously to help.

That answer is to be found in the Danish tradition of democracy.

To understand the differences between peoples, we must examine their traditions. It is difficult to find traditions more extreme than those of Denmark and Germany.

In Germany, crimes against the Jews were not originated by the Nazis. History shows that the Germans began early with their persecution of the Jews. Easter was celebrated in Mainz in 1283 by the killing of ten Jews by a Christian mob. Two years later, at Munich, another group of German Christians set fire to a synagogue and burned to death 180 Jews. In 1286, at Oberwesel, a German mob killed forty Jews. The pattern continued well into the Middle Ages. The founder of Protestantism, Martin Luther, demanded that Germany rid itself of the Jews by seeing "that their synagogues or schools be set on fire, their houses be broken up and destroyed . . . and they be put under a roof or stable, like the gypsies. . . . "

Denmark, on the other hand, has no tradition of antisemitism. . . . The Danish Parliament in 1690 rejected the idea of establishing a ghetto in Copenhagen, calling its very concept an inhuman way of life. In 1814, all racial and religious discrimination was declared illegal in Denmark. The Danes who saved the Jews are products of a Danish tradition of democracy that has always found abhorrent any form of racism.

To understand why the Danes acted as they did, one must know that for centuries the Danish outlook in all areas of life has been oriented toward humanitarianism, decency, concern for all citizens. Denmark is one of the world's oldest democracies, economically as well as politically, with emphasis on equality as well as freedom. Education has long been of primary importance, illiteracy nonexistent, and all schools, from kindergarten through the university, are free. The University of Copenhagen was established before Columbus set sail for the Indies. The Danes' concern for all of the people is seen not only in free education, but in the field of social security, in which Denmark has long been a leader. Unemployment insurance, workmen's compensation, socialized medicine and old age pensions for every Danish citizen were a way of life in Denmark long before World War II. All of these things undoubtedly went into the shaping of the modern Dane, giving him confidence, belief in his own worth and a sense of responsibility toward his fellow countrymen.

What the Danes did was the natural response of a democratic people.[18]

Some people believe that if your country did something before you were born that you are guilty also and should feel bad. But it wasn't your fault. Really, all humanity should feel guilty and in the same way we have a right to feel good about what the Danes did because we're all members of the human race.
—*an 8th grade student*

The following message was sent to the Danish people by the Danish bishops of the Lutheran Church on October 3, 1943.

The Danish bishops have on September 29th, this year, forwarded the following communication to the leading German authorities through the heads of the government departments:

Wherever Jews are persecuted as such on racial or religious grounds, the Christian Church is in duty bound to protest against this action:

Because we can never forget that the Lord of the Christian Church, Jesus Christ, was born in Bethlehem of the Virgin Mary according to God's promise to His Chosen People, Israel. The history of the Jewish people before the birth of Jesus contains the preparation for the salvation God has prepared for all mankind in Christ. This is shown by the fact that the Old Testament is part of our Bible.

Persecution of the Jews conflicts with that recognition and love of man that are a consequence of the gospel which the church of Jesus Christ was founded to preach. Christ is no respecter of persons, and he had taught us to see that every human life is precious in the eyes of God (Galatians 3:28).

We understand by freedom of religion the right to exercise our faith in God in accordance with vocation and conscience, and in such a way that race and religion can never in themselves be a reason for depriving a man of his rights, freedom, or property.

Despite different religious views, we shall therefore struggle to ensure the continued guarantee to our Jewish brothers and sisters of the same freedom we ourselves treasure more than life itself.

The leaders of the Danish Church have a clear understanding of the duty to be law-abiding citizens and would never revolt needlessly against those who exercise the functions of authority over us—but our conscience obliges us at the same time to maintain the law and to protest against any violation of rights.

We will therefore unambiguously declare our allegiance to the doctrine that bids us obey God more than man.[19]

Activity 11

Film: *Denmark 43*

In this film a class of Danish students relives the story of a Danish coastal town that ferried Danish Jews to neutral Sweden during October 1943. Guided by their teacher, the students reenact the escape from the town of Gilleleje. They hide in church lofts; they meet to plan strategy; they set to sea in small boats.

Using Activity 11

The following questions are suggested in the film's study guide.

• Some scholars suggest that the Danes were motivated to act more from hatred of their occupiers than in response to the plight of the Jews. Should this statement be considered revisionism? How can we judge?[20]
• Were the facts of geographical proximity to Sweden and of Denmark's relative freedom under the occupation the main factors, or was something more intangible responsible for saving almost the entire Jewish population of Denmark? Why were other countries unable to save their Jews?

The following student responses represent opposite reactions to the film:

Today we saw a movie that was interesting but useless. There was no possible way for one to feel the pain, the horror, and the dread that the Jews felt. Anybody who thinks he can should think deeply.
— 8th grade student

The Danish people were real to me. They represented the ideals that I had always believed in. Realizing the danger to the Jews (who were their neighbors and part of their community) they did all they could to save them.
— high school student

Activity 12

Film: *Avenue of the Just*
This film documents actual stories of people who risked their lives in countries throughout Europe to save Jews. Had there been more people like those in the documentary, this history would have been quite different.

Using Activity 12

If the film is not available, the following brief descriptions also document others in Europe who saved Jews.

Dr. Adelaid Hautval

Dr. Adelaid Hautval, a French Protestant, was in a French prison for an infringement of the permit regulations in crossing the occupied zone of France. She had insisted on wearing the yellow star as a protest against the Gestapo's treatment of French Jews who were thrown into prison with her. She was branded a lover of the Jews and sent to Auschwitz in 1943. She was asked on at least five occasions to help with experiments on the Jews and each time she refused. On one occasion an SS asked her how it was that as a psychiatrist she could not see the Jews were different. She replied: "I can see several people who are different from me, beginning with you." Dr. Hautval knew that it was impossible that she would ever get out of the camp alive. "The Germans will not allow people who know what is going on here to get in touch with the outside world. So the only thing that is left is to behave for the rest of the short time that remains as human beings."

As a result of her refusal to take part in the Nazi experiments, she expected to be punished. A German political prisoner advised her to do as the SS had ordered because an execution squad instructed to deal with special offenders was to come to the camp the next day. That night, as she awaited the squad, the German colleague managed to smuggle her to another part of Auschwitz.

"What I did was nothing," stated Dr. Hautval. "And besides, if I had the luck to be able to refuse, it was certainly not due to myself, but simply because I had in me an instinct which told me that there were more important things than saving one's own skin."*

Dr. Gertrude Luckner

Dr. Gertrude Luckner, a German Roman Catholic social worker, editor, and writer, helped save hundreds of German Jews from the Nazis and, as a result, was tortured and imprisoned for two years in a concentration camp.

During World War II, Dr. Luckner worked with such German Jewish leaders as Rabbi Leo Baeck to esablish contacts throughout Germany to help Jews escape the Nazis. "I was a kind of courier," Dr. Luckner said. "I went from one Jewish family to another, from city to city. But there was little I could do. Help is always slower than the need is."

She was arrested by the Gestapo in 1943, and imprisoned in the Ravensbruck concentration camp for women, a camp that specialized in gynecological experimentation and torture.

The Gestapo interrogated her for nine weeks, to find out who her contacts were in the German Caritas Association (the Catholic welfare organization under whose auspices she worked). "But I didn't give them what they wanted," she said. When the Gestapo asked who her bosses were, she replied: "My Christian conscience."[21]

Fucia Burzminski

In Israel, those non-Jews who saved the lives of Jews plant a tree on the Avenue of the Just. Fucia Burzminski is one of the precious few to be officially recognized by the title, The Righteous Among the Nations. She was awarded the Yad Vashem certificate and medal this past fall 1980 in ceremonies at the Israeli Consulate in Boston.

Father Maxmillian Kolbe

Shortly after the outbreak of World War II in September 1939, Father Maxmillian Kolbe was arrested by the Nazi authorities. He was released on November 9, 1939, after spending some time in a prison in Germany and in a detention camp in Poland. On February 17, 1941, Father Kolbe was again arrested by the Germans. Although he was never formally charged with a crime, we can surmise that he was included among the members of the Polish civil, religious, and cultural elite who were fated to die because of their potential power to muster opposition to the German occupation forces.

After spending three months in the Pawiak Prison in Warsaw, Father Kolbe was transferred to Auschwitz. At Auschwitz, Father Kolbe was assigned to a Polish prisoners barracks in the main camp. Never very physically healthy, Father Kolbe slowly began to succumb to the harsh conditions of the concentration camp. Polish survivors who were imprisoned with him recall how Father Kolbe served as a source of spiritual strength for his imprisoned countrymen.

Sometime in the end of July 1941, the prison guards discovered that a prisoner from Block 14, Father Kolbe's barracks, had escaped. As punishment for the escape, 10 prisoners were randomly selected for execution. Among the prisoners selected was a Polish army sergeant, Francis Gajowniczek.

When Gajowniczek learned of his fate he screamed out, "My poor

*Based on an article "Who Shall Live? Who Shall Die?" by Haliam Tennyson.

wife, my poor children, what will happen to my family!" Dr. Nicetus Francis Wiodarski, a witness to the selection recounted, "After the selection of the 10 prisoners, Father Maxmillian slipped out of line, took off his cap, and place himself before the commandant. Astounded, Fritsch (Lager Fuehrer Captain Fritsch) asked him: "What does this Polish pig want?" Father Maxmillian pointed with his hand to the condemned Gajowniczek and replied: "I am a Catholic priest from Poland; I would like to take his place, because he has a wife and children." From astonishment, the commandant appeared unable to speak. After a moment he gave a sign with the hand. He spoke but one word: "Away!" Gajowniczek received the command to return to the row he had just left. In this manner Father Maxmillian took the place of the condemned man.

Father Kolbe and the nine other condemned men were taken to Block 11, or as it was commonly called by the inmates of Auschwitz, "the Block of Death." Their fate was to slowly die from starvation.

On August 14, after almost two weeks of starvation, Father Kolbe was injected with a lethal dose of poison. Death followed immediately.[22]

Raoul Wallenberg

Raoul Wallenberg was sent to Budapest, Hungary, on July 9, 1944, by the government of Sweden with the purpose of saving Jewish lives during the closing stages of the war. In the midst of the Nazi effort to eliminate Hungarian Jews, Wallenberg distributed over 20,000 Swedish passports to Budapest Jews and arranged shelter for 13,000 Jews in safe homes, rented by Wallenberg and designated by a Swedish flag.

At one point, Wallenberg stood on top of a deportation train and handed Swedish passports to all who could reach them. Through his insistence, the people holding Swedish papers were released.

On January 17, 1945 (three and a half weeks after the Russians entered Budapest), Wallenberg travelled 120 miles to the east to meet with Russian officers and arrange for Russian help in protecting citizens from local violent gangs. He never returned.

The Soviet Union claims that a prisoner named Wallenberg died in his cell on July 17, 1947, from a heart attack, but there have been many accounts since that time which indicate that Wallenberg may still be alive. Recently Raoul Wallenberg was made an official United States citizen.*

Le Chambon

The town of Le Chambon in southern France led by its Protestant minister, Andre Trocme, saved about 2,000 Jewish people during the Nazi occupation of France. The effort to save lives in Le Chambon was done in secrecy in people's homes. "Decisions that were turning points in that struggle took place in kitchens, and not with male leaders as the only decision makers, but often with women centrally involved." The story of this town was written by Philip Hallie in *Lest Innocent Blood Be Shed* (Harper and Row, 1979).

Many teachers would prefer to end the curriculum with stories of rescue. The reality is that such acts of courage, as comforting as they are, were rare. Had there been more such acts, this curriculum would be about saving lives, not taking lives.

---

*A more detailed account can be found in *The New York Times Magazine*, "The Lost Hero of the Holocaust: The Search for Raoul Wallenberg," March 30, 1980.

Reading 13 **The Road Not Taken**
Two roads diverged in a yellow wood,
And sorry I could not travel both
And be one traveler, long I stood
And looked down one as far as I could
To where it bent in the undergrowth;

Then took the other, as just as fair,
And having perhaps the better claim,
Because it was grassy and wanted wear;
Though as for that passing there
Had worn them really about the same,

And both that morning equally lay
In leaves no step had trodden black.
Oh, I kept the first for another day!
Yet knowing how way leads on to way,
I doubted if I should ever come back.

I shall be telling this with a sigh
Somewhere ages and ages hence:
Two roads diverged in a wood, and I
I took the one less traveled by,
And that has made all the difference.[23]
—Robert Frost

Citations **Chapter 9**

[1] *Study Guide: Joseph Schultz* (White Plains, New York: Wombat Productions Inc. Reprinted by permission of Wombat Productions.)

[2] Deborah Alper, 8th grade paper, Brookline, Mass.

[3] Robert Coles, "Belfast's Children", *The New Republic*, October 14, 1981.

[4] Much of this information is summarized from *Documents of Destruction* by Raul Hilberg.

[5] Raul Hilberg, *Documents of Destruction* (Quadrangle Books, 1971). Reprinted by permission of the New York Times Book Company, pp. 148-149.

[6] Ibid.

[7] From *The War Against the Jews* by Lucy S. Dawidowicz. Copyright © 1975 by Lucy S. Dawidowicz. Reprinted by permission of Holt, Rinehart and Winston, Publishers, pp. 197-198.

[8] Yehuda Bauer, *They Chose Life* (New York: The American Jewish Committee, 1973) pp. 30-31.

[9] From *Never to Forget: The Jews of the Holocaust* by Milton Meltzer. Copyright © 1976 by Milton Meltzer. Reprinted by permission of Harper & Row, Publishers, Inc., pp. 139, 140.

[10] Walter Laqueur, *The Terrible Secret* (Boston: Little, Brown, and Co., 1980).

[11] Robert Ross, "So It Was True: The American Protestant Press and the Nazi Persecution of the Jews," speech given at the National Conference of Christians and Jews, Spring 1978.

[12] "A Minister Looks at the Way Christians Acted in the Nazi Era," *The Boston Globe*, December 12, 1973. Reprinted courtesy of *The Boston Globe*.

[13] From *The Course of Our Times* by Abram L. Sachar. Copyright © 1972 by Abram L. Sachar. Reprinted by permission of Alfred A. Knopf, Inc.

[14] Eva Fleischner, ed., *Auschwitz: Beginning of a New Era?* (KTAV Publishing House, 1977) p. 104. Reprinted with permission of The Cathedral of St. John the Divine, New York City and KTAV Publishing Company, New York City.

[15] Sachar, *The Course of Our Times*, pp. 262-263.

[16] Harold Flender, *Rescue in Denmark* (New York: Manor Books, 1963) pp. 13, 25, 28, 29, 30, 47, 93, 94, 97, 110, 117.

[17] Ibid.

[18] Ibid., pp. 205-208.

[19] Source unknown.

[20] *Study Guide: Denmark '43* (Learning Corporation of America, New York).

[21] "Hebrew Union Cites a Catholic for Aiding Jews in Nazi Germany," *The New York Times*, June 6, 1977. © 1977 by The New York Times Company. Reprinted by permission.

[22] Warren Green "Anniversary of Death of Father Kolbe, Martyr of Auschwitz," *St. Louis Jewish Light*, August 12, 1981.

[23] From *The Poetry of Robert Frost* edited by Edward Connery Lathem. Copyright 1916, © 1969 by Holt, Rinehart and Winston. Copyright 1944 by Robert Frost. Reprinted by permission of Holt, Rinehart and Winston, Publishers.

10 Judgment

Crimes against international law (and this applies, of course, to the Holocaust) are committed by men, not by abstract entities (such as states).
—Professor John Fried

Overview

In this chapter students learn about the international war-crimes trials. As they read testimony of victimizers and victims, they think about consequences, punishment, revenge, retribution. They wonder, is it fair to condemn a man for what he has done under military order or a decree of a tyrannical dictatorship? Is the term *war criminal* appropriate for an Eichmann? Simon Wiesenthal says not; the atrocities of the extermination camps were not acts of war.

According to John Fried, Special Legal Consultant to the U.S. War Crimes Tribunals, Nuremberg, 1947-1949:

The Hague and Geneva agreements assert that there are limits in what men may do against their fellow men in war. Because of its magnitude and the incredible mass atrocities which accompanied it, the Second World War led to war-crimes trials on an unprecedented scale. Although some 10,000 people were tried between 1945 and 1950 and are still being tried before West German tribunals, the 13 Nuremberg trials of 199 individuals have become symbolic of the entire war-crimes process.[1]

The documentation from Nuremberg shows how antisemitism was used by the Nazis, and how many of the accused, their lawyers, and defense witnesses excused or justified anti-Jewish policies that, when combined with other policies, led to the Holocaust. This is important not only historically but also because such arguments are still heard today.

Reading 1

Dogma Makes Obedient Ghosts

There are those who say technology killed people at Auschwitz. However, Jacob Bronowski warns us that those who assert a dogma that closes the mind betray the human spirit, for it can turn a "nation, a civilization, into a regiment of ghosts—obedient ghosts, or tortured ghosts."

It is said that science will dehumanize people and turn them into numbers. That is false, tragically false. Look for yourself. This is the concentration camp and crematorium at Auschwitz. This is where people were turned into numbers. Into this pond were flushed the ashes of some four million people. And that was not done by gas. It was done by arrogance. It was done by dogma. It was done by ignorance. When people believe that they have absolute knowledge, with no test in reality, this is how they behave. This is what men do when they aspire to the knowledge of gods.

> *Science is a very human form of knowledge. We are always at the brink of the known, we always feel forward for what is to be hoped. Every judgment in science stands on the edge of error, and is personal. Science is a tribute to what we can know although we are fallible....*
>
> *I owe it as a scientist to my friend Leo Szilard, I owe it as a human being to the many members of my family who died at Auschwitz, to stand here by the pond as a survivor and a witness. We have to cure ourselves of the itch for absolute knowledge and power. We have to close the distance between the push-button order and the human act. We have to touch people.*[2]

Using Reading 1

Consider with students how this quotation anticipates the content of the chapter. Who or what, according to Bronowski, is responsible for the Holocaust?

Reading 2

Don't You See, We SS Men Were Not Supposed to Think...

Rudolf Hoess, the Commandant at Auschwitz, was asked if he had ever considered whether the Jews whom he had murdered were guilty or had in any way deserved such a fate. In this reading he explains,

> *Don't you see, we SS men were not supposed to think about these things; it never even occurred to us. — And besides, it was something already taken for granted that the Jews were to blame for everything.... We just never heard anything else. It was not just newspapers like the Stuermer but it was everything we ever heard. Even our military and ideological training took for granted that we had to protect Germany from the Jews.... It only started to occur to me after the collapse that maybe it was not quite right, after I had heard what everybody was saying.... We were all so trained to obey orders without even thinking that the thought of disobeying an order would simply never have occurred to anybody and somebody else would have done just as well if I hadn't.... You can be sure that it was not always a pleasure to see those mountains of corpses and smell the continual burning. — But Himmler had ordered it and had even explained the necessity and I really never gave much thought to whether it was wrong. It just seemed a necessity....*[3]

> *I must emphasize here that I have never been personally against the Jews. It is true that I looked upon them as the enemies of our people. But just because of this I saw no difference between them and the other prisoners, and I treated them all in the same way. I never drew any distinctions. In any event the emotion of hatred is foreign to my nature. But I know what hate is, and what it looks like. I have seen it and I have suffered it myself....*

> *When in the summer of 1941 Himmler gave me the order to prepare installations at Auschwitz where mass exterminations could take place, and personally to carry out these exterminations I did not have the slightest idea of their scale or consequences. It was certainly an extraordinary and monstrous order. Nevertheless the reasons behind the extermination program seemed to me right. I did not reflect on it at the time. I had been given an order, and I had to carry it out. Whether this mass extermination of the Jews was necessary or not was something on which I could not allow myself to form an opinion, for I lacked the necessary breadth of view.*[4]

Using Reading 2

Hannah Arendt's comments about Adolf Eichmann are relevant to this reading. She accuses Eichmann of thoughtlessness, the Socratic evil. How, she reasons, could a man who thought, who considered the meaning of his actions, have done Eichmann's work? Thinking, she said, is the urgent work of a species that bears responsibility for its own survival. She implores us to think with her, to philosophize by criticism or agreement, to carry on thinking, the authority by which we survive in human form. She asks in *Thinking:*

Could the activity of thinking as such, the habit of examining whatever happens to come to pass or to attract attention, regardless of results and specific content, could this activity be among the conditions that make men abstain from evil-doing or even actually condition them against it?

Ask students to go back to the reading and underline every time Hoess uses the words *think, thinking,* or *thought.* Then ask students to read Hoess' comments in light of Hannah Arendt's description of thoughtlessness. Do students find a relationship between evil doing and the activity of thinking?

In this passage Hoess explains that he cannot form an opinion on his actions because he lacks the necessary breadth of view. Can students explain this statement?

Consider who was most guilty? Individuals? Groups? What were people guilty of? What would the charges be?

What types of punishment are available? What is the goal of the punishment? Should there be a trial? Are there different forms of punishment for individuals and groups? The following are student questions:
- What should the sentence be?
- Can a whole nation be guilty?
- Who do you punish? When do you stop?
- How do you punish and not generate new hate?
- Is an eye for an eye an appropriate punishment?
- How can a punishment be used to prevent a similar happening?
- What does forgiveness have to do with punishment?

Teachers might choose to study one case such as Streichter or Hoess in order to think about choices, motivation, actions, and responsibility and the notion of only following orders.
- Are you guilty if you are obeying the law of the state?
- Is there a higher law to obey than a state law?
- What is international law?

Reading 3

What Was Nuremberg?*

Nazi conduct in World War II was so shocking that the countries on which the war had been forced made the punishment of the guilty a principal war aim. This was formally announced for the first time from

---

*Most of the information about the Nuremberg trials in Readings 3-17 was gathered and written by John Fried, formerly a special legal consultant to the U.S. War Crimes Tribunals, Nuremberg; expert, Judge Advocate General's Office, U.S. Department of Army; co-editor, as representative of U.S. Judges, *Trials of War Criminals Before the Nuremberg Military Tribunals,* Washington, D.C., Gov. Printing Office, Vols. 1-14, 14,000 pages.

London in January 1942, and afterward repeated several times, especially in a joint U.S.-British-Soviet Declaration in the summer of 1943.

The principal aims of the greatest trial in history that was held after the war, from November 14, 1945, to October 1, 1946, were:

a. to establish an overall record of what had happened.

b. to re-establish, in the most solemn form possible, the validity of the fundamental rules of international conduct that the Third Reich had so blatantly disregarded.

c. to bring leading personalities of the Nazi period to justice, and to punish them, if found guilty, for their *own individual* share in the catastrophe.

Using Reading 3

It should be noted that the establishment of *individual* guilt or innocence completely refutes the erroneous view, which is still being heard, that the trial was a revenge against the German people, or declared all Germans guilty, and the like. On the contrary, by undertaking the highly difficult task of establishing the *personal* guilt or innocence of specific individuals for events that covered many years and took place over almost an entire continent, the Tribunal did as little to judge all Germans as a trial of, say, twenty-two important New Yorkers would judge all New Yorkers.

On the other hand, the concrete planning of the trial had to wait until it was certain which of the top Nazi leaders would at the end be in the hands of the wartime Allies. If, in addition to Hitler and Goebbels, more of them had committed suicide at the last moment; or if in addition to the arch-criminals, Himmler (who probably killed himself) or Eichmann (who was discovered in Latin America years later), more of them had disappeared without trace; or if more of the leadership had fled to countries that would have refused to extradite them (just as Holland had refused to extradite the fugitive German Emperor William II for trial by the World War I Allies), the Nuremberg trial would have lost its impact. In particular, its unique aspect, namely, to give the protagonists the historic chance to present in open court their own explanations, defenses, and confessions, could not have been achieved.

Furthermore, every trial depends on the evidence produceable in it. The findings of the Nuremberg trials could not have been as revealing and incontrovertible as they are, except for two extraordinary circumstances: (a) the final collapse came so swiftly that masses of top-secret official documents of the Nazi period were (with some notable exceptions, especially of Hitler's personal files) not destroyed; and (b) although many of them had been carefully hidden, at least a large part of them were discovered by the invading Allies.

Only in this way was it possible for the Nuremberg prosecution to produce in court, after sifting through hundreds of thousands of papers and files, which were never meant to be divulged, several thousand official records, instructions, reports, minutes of conferences, letters, etc. that revealed the whole Nazi panorama. Primarily these documents, often addressed to, written by, or reporting to the individual Nuremberg defendants, condemned them. Only in this way do we now know, for example, the minutes of the Wannsee Conference where the groundwork for the "final solution" was laid; or SS-General Stroop's report about the last heroic battle in the German-erected Warsaw Ghetto; or the detailed statistical reports about the massacres by the Einsatzgruppen; or about the inner workings of Himmler's SS and police empire; and so on.

In the following readings about the Nuremberg Tribunals, the word *Judgment* will often be used to mean the commentaries from the trials, including the many decisions handed down by the judges.

Reading 4	**In What Way Was Nuremberg Unique?**

The international Nuremberg trial was structurally like other criminal trials: judges were judging defendants who had been charged by the prosecution in a written indictment, who were defended by counsel of their own choosing, who had the right to plead their own cases, to offer their own defense witnesses and other defense evidence, to cross-examine witnesses, etc.

The differences from ordinary trials were: (a) the trial's international character, with prosecutors and judges from four different nations: Britian, United States, France, and Russia. (This, incidentally, made the trial multilingual—English, French, German, and Russian.); and (b) that these four countries had drawn up a charter to make this unprecedented combined trial by four nations possible.

Using Reading 4

The famous charter was signed by the four countries in London on August 8, 1945. It is therefore sometimes called the London Charter, but since it formed the basis for the big Nuremberg trial, the Nuremberg Charter is more commonly used. (The city of Nuremberg was chosen for symbolic reasons. Nuremberg had been before World War II the city of the Nazi movement where the annual huge rallies, marches, and torch parades, regularly addressed by Hitler, were to demonstrate the power of Nazism and where, incidentally, the notorious anti-Jewish Nuremberg race laws were announced.) It was considered appropriate to try the major Nazi criminals in that city, which was now largely in rubble—a reminder that the regime had also brought enormous damage and losses to the Germans themselves.

There are some basic misconceptions about Nuremberg:

- that it was an innovation, an invention of Nuremberg, after World War II to *prohibit* certain wartime actions, such as the killing or torturing or maltreatment of civilians or of prisoners of war, or wantonly burning down houses or places of worship, etc.
- that it was an innovation or invention of Nuremberg to *punish* individuals, regardless of their position, for such atrocities.
- that at Nuremberg the German people as a whole were tried or found guilty.

Reading 5 **Obeying Orders**

Others at the International Tribunal at Nuremberg held views similar to those of Rudolf Hoess.

[Ohlendorf] was the leader of Special Task Unit D, which, under his direction, murdered about 90,000 Jews. He described in detail how he had the male Jews shot and had their wives and children liquidated in gas vans. "It was all directly ordered by Himmler on behalf of the Fuehrer, so he had to obey." The same view was voiced by Field Marshal Keitel: "I had absolutely no command function!"

Another instance of this attitude was that afforded by Joseph Kramer, who gassed about eighty Jewish prisoners for the "scientific" research of Professor Hirt. To the question what he would have done if the first attempt at gassing these people had failed, Kramer replied: "I would have tried once again to suffocate them with gas, throwing another dose of gas into the chamber. I had no feelings in carrying out these things, because I had received an order to kill the eighty inmates in the way I already told you. That, by the way, was the way I was trained. . . ."

The thought that he would ever be called to account for his outrages had never occurred to Hoess, for, as he said, everyone in Nazi Germany was convinced that the man who gave the orders was responsible. For this reason he felt himself betrayed by the suicide of Himmler, for the latter had not been loyal to the device of the SS: "My honor means loyalty."[5]

Using Reading 5

As Hannah Arendt traces her impulse to think about thinking from the time she sat and watched Eichmann* at his trial, so too do students feel compelled to think about judgment. Throughout the course, materials and methods stimulate the student to recognize the complex dilemmas inherent in this history, and as they recognize the conflict of issues and opinions, they reason carefully and then make judgments.

These readings and testimonies, excerpted from the Nuremberg trial records or from interviews of Nazi officials, were chosen to stimulate discussion about the motivation and reasoning of the victimizers. It is important to take time with these accounts since they raise again the basic questions of human behavior and morality. Students are asked to think and reflect about how others think.

John Fried explains the purpose of the war-crimes trials in this way:

The awesome, unprecedented nature of the Nazi war crimes demanded a response from the victorious Allies after World War II. That response, embodying the shock and outrage of mankind, was the Nuremberg Tribunals, in which the Nazi leadership was tried for its crimes.

The Allied judges sought . . . to decide . . . if the Nazi civilian and military leaders had instigated a war of aggression and then pursued that war by unacceptable means and in violation of normal standards [and] to determine an individual's responsibility for crimes which could not be disputed. No one, that is, could deny the reality of Dachau and the mass slaughter of civilians; the question to be answered was: who was responsible?

The defendants argued that they were bound by orders or by obedience to still higher leaders. Denying responsibility for Nazi atrocities, the Nuremberg defendants forced the judges (and in reality world public opinion) to come to grips with an ancient and difficult dilemma, i.e., how can an individual refuse orders from a superior, or from the State itself, even if the orders violate moral and legal codes? How could a German general, let alone a private, refuse to act when ordered? And should the individual be held responsible for those orders?[6]

---

*Long after the Nuremberg trials, Eichmann was discovered by Israeli agents at his hiding place in Latin America, brought by them to Jerusalem, and after trial by Israeli court, sentenced to death and hanged.

CIVILIZATION TRIES 20 TOP NAZI

BEHIND LAWYERS SIT EIGHT OF THE 20 DEFENDANTS: FIRST ROW, GÖRING, HESS, RIBBENTROP, KEITEL; SECOND ROW, DOENITZ, RAEDER, VON SCHIRACH, SAUC

As common criminals against mankind, 20 ex-masters of Germany, of Europe and, they had hoped, of the world, went on trial Nov. 20 in Nürnberg, Germany. Judges and prosecutors represented the U. S., France, Great Britain and the U. S. S. R.. but

The trial is an ambitious attempt to forward human justice, an imaginative but risky innovation in international law. It assumes that the League of Nations was not fooling in 1927 when it declared

Hindenburg last testament in his own favor. Sch: in 1935 had been made "plenipotentiary-genera war economy." Keitel had conspired to assassi:

NAZI LEADERS SING THEIR SWAN SONG

final pleas at Nürnberg trial they blame the war and concentration camps on everybody but themselv

weeks ago in Nürnberg, after U.S., British, and Russian prosecutors demanded death

The others on trial, led by Göring, whose weight has tumbled from 264 pounds to a mere 187, sang Nazism's swan song to the end. They were as blind-nationalistic as ever. Hess, former deputy to No. 3, put on another slyly

For four hours the former masters of Hitle deadly world protested ignorance and innocen But they could not dent the case built up agai them over nine laborious months. In 1,100 hour session, the longest trial in history, the prosecut had introduced most of the 200 witnesses, 300, from the Germans' secret fi

ÜRNBERG TRIAL ENDS WITH DEATH SENTENCE

three exceptions the verdict of Nürnberg at the end of the greatest trial tory was "Guilty!" Since Nov. 21, 1945 the lawyers of the four participations had built up a staggering mountain of evidence that 22 accused Ger-had, in varying degrees, committed crimes against peace, plotted aggressive d partaken in atrocities beyond comprehension

self-confident men into a gray-faced, dejected group, as these pictures sho For Göring, von Ribbentrop, Field Marshal Keitel and nine others, the se tence was death by hanging. Hess, Funk and

---

Activity 6 **Film: *Nuremberg Trials***
This film contains actual footage of some of the trials.

The story of Nuremberg tribunals offers a concrete instance in which an individual's responsibility for a terrible crime is examined before the world. Not an abstract debate, but a life and death matter for the defendants, those age-old questions converged in the city of Nuremberg, and the standards established in that trial have become part of the unwritten law of nations in the years since.[7]

Using Activity 6

The following questions help students to consider the major issues of this chapter.

- What is the difference between war crimes and international crimes against humanity, as stated by President Harry Truman?
- What should an individual do in a group society that has gone berserk?
- What should an individual do when ordered by the government to commit an act contrary to his or her beliefs and to the beliefs of civilization?
- Under what laws or what moral code may a defeated nation be tried?
- Can the leaders of victorious nations try leaders of defeated nations when the actions of the victor are also questionable?
- Is there a personal human morality that transcends obedience to the social, military, or political group?
- Can one fulfill one's patriotic allegiance to a country while still defying the tyranny of that country's present leader?
- Would you have wanted a family member to make the decision to give up his life instead of following an order?

- How do you feel about the saying, "You've got to go along to get along"?
- When is it cowardly not to go along with the group, and when is it courageous to stand alone?
- Can you recall any times when you yourself felt that you did not approve of the moral behavior of your group? What alternatives did you have?

Does anyone accept guilt for the Holocaust? Not Americans, not Roosevelt or a previous Congress or an apathetic public. Not Europe — the countries were too weak to oppose Germany and too caught up in their own recovery from W.W.I. Not the Germans — probably most would claim they knew nothing about it, or, if they did know, that they had nothing to do with it. Probably not even Hitler — doubtless he would feel no guilt, only remorse that his "final solution" didn't succeed.

Then who? Who is guilty? To say that we all are — although it may very well be true — is too easy. A Holocaust can happen only because no one feels directly responsible for it. It makes it all the easier to kill by saying: "You're just as responsible as I am." But that won't stop the killings. Who is guilty? The man who gives the orders or the man who carries them out? . . . I don't feel guilty for the Holocaust. The fact that I wasn't even alive at the time would seem to prove my innocence. But mustn't we all, as members of society, take responsibility for the past, the present and the future of the society we live in?

—a high school student

Reading 7 Judgment

Abram Sachar comments on some of the Nazis who escaped punishment.

Some of the Nazi criminals were tried and punished. Most of them, however, faded into the anonymity of the postwar climate of reconciliation, and these included men who had been an integral part of the extermination machine. For example, during the war, tens of thousands of slave laborers were used by the Krupp works, the huge armaments combine. After the war, the head of the firm was judged to be too ill to stand trial. The son, Alfred, was sentenced to twelve years in prison. In less than three years he was amnestied. The giant armaments corporation was returned to the family, as well as the personal fortune of ten million dollars. Albert Speer, Hitler's Minister of Armaments and War Production, who planned and supervised the slave labor battalions for the war machine, esaped hanging and was given a long prison sentence. When released he wrote a mea culpa which became a best-seller, in which he confessed that he had fallen victim to the technological obsession of our times. He was extremely sorry that he had not investigated what was happening to the Jews, although he was warned that there were camps where the practices were unfortunate.* But, as a special legal consultant at Nuremberg pointed out, Speer approved on September 15, 1942, 13.7 million marks for building materials to construct three hundred barracks for 132,000 Auschwitz inmates, and there

---

*Gunter Grass, "We had to create a new word after the war: Schreibtischtater, The Murderer at the Desk." *Intellectual Digest* (April 1972).

were other clear evidences of his continuous personal involvement in the agony of millions; yet these items were omitted from his volume.[8]

In a recent *New York Times* letters to the editor column, the following letter appeared after the death of Albert Speer in 1981.

To the Editor:
... A few years back, I spent 10 days with Albert Speer in Heidelberg, producing a series of television interviews. During one interview, held on Speer's lawn, I began a question, "You were the only person at Nuremberg to admit his guilt..." and he stopped me with, "I did not admit guilt—I said I was responsible."

For all these years, I have mulled over his answer, not sure where his legal and ethical culpability ended and his responsibility began. I have come to the conclusion that Speer was a clever survivor who knew exactly what he was doing when he was on trial at Nuremberg, and I also agree that he was never truly repentant about his role in the Third Reich....

He was a charming, though methodical man. He knew exactly what he was doing, and his answers had been well thought out during his 20 years in Spandau.
—Mel London[9]

Reading 8 The Trials at Nuremberg

According to the Tribunal at Nuremberg:

The persecution of the Jews at the hands of the Nazi Government has been proved in the greatest detail before the Tribunal. It is a record of consistent and systematic inhumanity on the greatest scale.

The judges of the International Tribunal made a connection between the antisemitic policies and the aggressive war in Germany.

Indeed, the Nuremberg documentation and trials showed that the planners were fully aware of the monstrously evil character of the program. And yet, many of them and many of the executioners maintained that it was not criminal, but was required as the "final solution" of the Jewish problem in the interest of German or Aryan race purity, or for the reordering of Europe, or for the Third Reich's future position in the world. Germany, as a sovereign nation—so the argument went—had established a regime based on the leadership (Fuehrer) principle; the Supreme Leader was the absolute lawgiver; he had ordered the Holocaust, and his loyal followers had to carry it out.

Why, then, is the argument so absurd? Is it not true that Nazi law ordered the Holocaust, just as it ordered other mass atrocities and, above all, enabled the regime to unleash history's worst war so far—of which the Holocaust was but one, although unique, horrendous aspect?

The argument is absurd because it overlooks a crucial fact: namely, that even after the Hitler regime's abolition of all democratic and parliamentary safeguards, Germany was still bound by the *international* rules that determine the permissibility of *any* country's behavior. According to those rules (in short, under international law) no dictatorship, and no democracy either, may, for example, attack another country and then establish there an Auschwitz camp (as Hitler did in Poland).

It was this that U.S. Supreme Court Justice Robert Jackson, in his famous Opening Speech as Chief U.S. Prosecutor at the Nuremberg 4-

power tribunal in 1945 called the purpose of the unprecedented trial: namely a desperate effort to show that the entire disaster was due to cynical disregard for the most basic rules of international behavior. The Tribunal completely shared this view. It castigated in its Judgment the nature of the Third Reich, "with all its methods of terror, and its cynical and open denial of the rule of law."

Using Reading 8

Students must be reminded that although international law is sometimes violated, just as domestic law is sometimes violated, the entire course of civilization has been directed toward erecting *dams* against anything like Hitler's war and the Holocaust; and that Nazi ideology was a deliberate, frontal attack on the fundamental values and rules that had been gradually built up for the international conduct of states.

Reading 9

Documenting the Gradual Process of Dehumanization and Brutalization That Resulted in the Holocaust

The Nuremberg International Military Tribunal (IMT) took great care in establishing the gradual evolution from the founding on January 5, 1919, of the tiny political party that grew into the mighty National-Socialist German Labor Party (Nazi Party) until Hitler became Germany's Reich Chancellor, or Prime Minister, on January 30, 1933, and how he consolidated his power quickly and ruthlessly so that within about one and a half years he became the omnipotent dictator. This process itself showed an increasing habituation to brutality and sheer violence. Thus, the first step Hitler took after becoming Chancellor, and when his Party still had only a minority of 288 deputies of the 647 in the Reichstag, was to take "into so-called *protective custody* a large number of Communist deputies and (Communist) Party officials." Thereupon, the rump-legislature passed, under Hitler's threat of "further forceful measures," an act granting to the Hitler-dominated Cabinet "full legislative powers, including the power to deviate from the Constitution" — namely, to abolish first of all, the extensive Bill of Rights of the very liberal Weimar Constitution of 1919. There followed by April 1933 the dismissal of all non-Aryan and Communist civil servants, the destruction of the trade unions, the undermining of the position of the Christian churches, in short, what the judges call the crushing of opposition. This even included the blood bath of the Old Guard of Hitler's own SA storm trooper formations without trial and without warning. The opportunity was taken to murder a large number of (other) people who at one time or another had opposed Hitler.

Yet by August 1934, in a "Nazi-dominated plebiscite . . . 38 million Germans expressed their 'approval' of Hitler's decision to become 'both Reich President and Chancellor,' and with the military forces taking the oath of allegiance to the Fuehrer, full power was now in Hitler's hands. Germany had accepted the dictatorship with all its methods of terror, and its cynical and open denial of the rule of law."

This included, as the Judgment underscores, the systematic persecution of Germany's Jews as offical state policy.

The Judgment says:

The persecution of the Jews at the hands of the Nazi Government has been proved in the greatest detail before the Tribunal. It is a record of consistent and systematic inhumanity on the greatest scale.

The implied question of how this was possible the Judgment answers by quoting two statements made during the trial. One statement was made by witness SS General Back-Zalewski, a former leader of one of the *Einsatzgruppen* (Special Assignment Units) that together caused the death of about two million victims:

... when for years, for decades, the doctrine is preached that the Slav race and Jews are not even human, then such an outcome is inevitable.

The other statement was part of the testimony of defendant Hans Frank, Hitler's Governor-General of the Occupied Polish Territory:

We have fought against Jewry; we have fought against it for years; and we have allowed ourselves to make utterances and my own diary has become a witness against me, utterances which are terrible . . . . A thousand years will pass and this guilt of Germany will still not be erased.

The Judgment traces the gradual evolution of the anti-Jewish policy since its formulation in the Nazi party program of 1919. This is significant for Holocaust studies because it documents that the Holocaust was not a sudden phenonmenon but the climax of an ideology that became ever more oppressive and finally ever more murderous.

Thus, the IMT Judgment shows that the party program preached racial discrimination against the Jews; describes as clearly evil the exclusion of all racial Jews, regardless of religious affiliation, from German citizenship, which was to be restricted to persons of German blood; and points out the systematic brutalization and dehumanization. "Hatred of the Jews" was preached and they "were held up to the public ridicule and contempt."

Then, after Hitler came to power in 1933,

... the persecution of the Jews was intensified. . . . By the autumn of 1938, the Nazi policy toward the Jews had reached the stage where it was directed toward the complete exclusion of Jews from German life. Pogroms were organized, which included the burning and demolishing of synagogues, the looting of Jewish businesses. . . . The seizure of Jewish assets was authorized, and the movement of Jews was restricted by regulations to certain specified districts and hours. The creation of Ghettos was carried out on an extensive scale and "Jews were compelled to wear a yellow star on the breast and back."

The territorial conquests of Austria and the Sudeten were to be connected with "the solution of the Jewish Question" because "the destructive Jewish spirit" hampered "the power and the will of the German people to rise again."

A section of the Judgment dealing with the World War II period states:

The Nazi persecution of Jews in Germany before the war, severe and repressive as it was, cannot compare, however, with the policy pursued during the war in the occupied territories. Originally the policy was similar to that which had been in force inside Germany. Jews were required to register, were forced to live in ghettos, to wear the yellow star, and were used as slave laborers.

In the summer of 1941, however, plans were made for the "final solution" of the Jewish question in Europe. This "final solution" meant the extermination of the Jews, which early in 1939 Hitler had threatened would be one of the consequences of an outbreak of war. . . .

The plan for exterminating the Jews was developed shortly after the attack on the Soviet Union (which started on June 22, 1941).

The Judgment refers to two methods of extermination. The first was to massacre Jews on the spot, that is, actually in, or very near to, occupied towns and villages, without transporting the victims to concentration camps. This was done mainly by the *Einsatzgruppen* "who obtained the cooperation of Army commanders" as well as by another policy organization, called Security Police and Security Service. Always quoting from top-secret contemporary documents, the Judgment cites at some length a report by SS-General Stroop, about the destruction of the Warsaw Ghetto, which lasted from April 19 to May 16, 1943, and caused the death of over 56,000 victims. The Judgment also relied on contemporary films of "mass murders of Jews" as evidence. (It notes that altogether millions of feet of captured moving films and over 1,800 still photographs were used as exhibits during the trial.)

The systematic extermination of Jews in concentration camps was the second method; Auschwitz and Treblinka are mentioned as illustrations.

After describing various horrible aspects of the Holocaust, the IMT Judgment concludes its section on the Persecution of the Jews by accepting the estimate of Eichmann, who had been put in charge of the program by Hitler, that

... the policy pursued resulted in the killing of six million Jews, of whom four million were killed in the extermination institutions.

Using Reading 9

Holocaust teaching, according to Professor Fried, must convey that the unspeakable did occur, and that since Auschwitz has become the symbol of the Holocaust, there must never be another Auschwitz.

But it must also be education for tolerance—tolerance for Jews and non-Jews—against intolerance toward racial or religious or political or national groups. It would teach a strange type of tolerance, if the yardstick, the criterion for intolerance, was the horror of the Holocaust—as if the aim was only to make impossible similar systematic mass killings.

It is suggested here that, logically and chronologically and to give true historic insight, the Holocaust be taught as the ultimate climax of a gradual process, and that much emphasis be given to that gradual process. The Jewish Holocaust could not have occurred without a gradual habituation of all too many non-Jews to an ever-increasing brutalization and dehumanization—a habituation to the proposition that certain types of people, such as Jews, but not only the Jews, were "beyond the pale."

Discuss what the term *gradual habituation* means in regard to making judgments about responsibility for the Holocaust.

Reading 10

Julius Streicher

For his twenty-five years of speaking, writing, and preaching hatred of Jews, Julius Streicher was widely known as "Jew-baiter Number One."... Week after week, month after month he infected German minds with the virus of antisemitism, and incited the German people to active persecution. Each issue of *Der Stuermer*, published by Streicher, reached a circulation of 600,000 in 1935 and was filled with such articles, often lewd and disgusting. But as early as 1938 he began to call for the annihilation of the Jewish race (also outside of Germany). A typical leading article in September 1938 termed the Jew a germ and a pest, not a human being, but "a parasite, an enemy, an evil-doer, a disseminator of diseases which must be destroyed in the interest of mankind." Among other statements, the Judgment quotes from a leading article in the May 1939 issue (still four months before the start of World War II and twenty-five months before the start on the attack on Russia):

A punitive expedition must come against the Jews in Russia... the Jews in Russia must be killed. They must be exterminated root and branch.

As the war in the early stages proved successful in acquiring more and more territory for the Reich (so that more and more non-German Jews fell into Nazi hands) Streicher intensified his efforts to incite the Germans against the Jews. . . . Twenty-six articles from *Der Stuermer* published between August 1941 and September 1944, twelve by Streicher's own hand, demanded annihilation and extermination in unequivocal terms. . . .

By 1943, the magazine publicly admitted the ongoing extermination policy, which is interesting in view of the assertion that it was a carefully kept secret.

The Judgment's section on Streicher concludes:

Streicher's incitement to murder and extermination at the time when Jews in the East were being killed under the most horrible conditions clearly constitutes persecution on political and racial grounds ... and (therefore) a Crime against Humanity.

Using Reading 10

Since the IMT Judgment emphasized anti-Jewish indoctrination as a contributing factor to Nazi anti-Jewish policies and eventually the Holocaust, it is instructive to know that one of the twelve defendants sentenced to death at the trial was Julius Streicher.

The implied message for the future is that incitement to hatred and persecution on political and racial grounds, whether directed against Jews or any others, is evil and must be prevented.

Fostering "pogrom mentality" in local populations: "inciting of the population to abuse, maltreat and slay their fellow citizens ... to stir up passion, hate, violence and destruction among the people themselves, aims at breaking the moral backbone even of those the invader chooses to spare."

Students are intrigued and often amazed to learn that a man was made responsible for his words. He was punished for breaking the moral backbone of a citizenry, turning citizen against citizen.

Reading 11

Determining the Facts and Deciding Personal Guilt

The documents were in essence admitted by the defendants. What most defendants often vehemently denied was their *own personal involvement* in the specific criminal policies that were unanswerably proven by the documents.

It must, however, be understood that, apart from deciding the personal guilt or innocence of specific defendants, a main purpose of the trial was to establish the facts of the Holocaust. And regardless of whether specific facts could be laid on the shoulders of individual defendants, the objective facts remain proven.

The major war criminals declared guilty and sentenced to death were:

Herman Goering, who the IMT Judgment says "was the moving force for aggressive war, second only to Hitler"; "the creator of the oppressive pogrom against the Jews and other races, at home and abroad." [He] "developed the Gestapo and created the first concentration camps." Apart from ordering other anti-Jewish measures, "by decree of July 31, 1941, he directed Himmler and Heydrich to 'bring about a complete solution of the Jewish question in the German sphere of influence in Europe.' '

Joachim von Ribbentrop, Hitler's foreign minister, whom the IMT found guilty of having "played an important part in Hitler's 'final solution' of the Jewish question," citing his pressure to have Jews from several occupied and satellite countries "deported to the East." Thus on April 17, 1943, he informed in Hitler's presence the head of state of Hungary, Horthy, that the Hungarian Jews "must either be exterminated or taken to concentration camps."

Alfred Rosenberg, the famous Party ideologist whose book, *Myth of the Twentieth Century* has, as the IMT Judgment notes, "a circulation of over a million copies" and who was the Reich Minister for the Occupied Eastern Territories since July 17, 1941. IMT Judgment: "His directives provided for the segregation of Jews, ultimately in ghettos. His subordinates engaged in mass killings of Jews . . . . In December 1941, he made the suggestion to Hitler that in a case of shooting 100 hostages, Jews only be used. . . ."

Arthur Seyss-Inquart who, the IMT Judgment says, as Reich Commissioner for the Netherlands, after various other measures against the Jews there, finally decreed "the mass deportation of almost 120,000 of Holland's 140,000 Jews to Auschwitz. . . ."

Using Reading 11

The various aspects of the Holocaust were laid bare at Nuremberg mainly by contemporary official documentation. This was a unique aspect of Nuremberg. Never before had it happened that masses of top-secret documents, showing events that covered an entire era of history, were available at all, and much less, immediately after their occurrence. Nor had it ever happened, as it did happen at Nuremberg, that top decision-makers who temporarily had ruled over hundreds of millions of people and whose decisions are mirrored in that never-to-be-disclosed evidence, themselves gave their own accounts and their own comments on such evidence.

Reading 12

Other American Trials Held at Nuremberg, 1946-1949

After the end of the 4-Power Nuremberg trial, twelve trials were held in the same Nuremberg courthouse by tribunals exclusively composed of American judges. Almost 200 persons, many of whom had also played important roles during the Hitler regime, were tried. The prosecutors, too, were all Americans. The trials lasted from December 1946 to spring 1949. The law applied was essentially identical to that applied by the IMT. Various aspects of the Holocaust again were a main subject.

- 22 high government officials, among them three of Hitler's former cabinet members, diplomats and ambassadors, and the vice president of the Reischbank.
- 26 military leaders, including five field marshals.
- 56 high-ranking SS and other police officers, including leaders of the *Einsatzgruppen*, the head and other officials of Himmler's central office which supervised and issued the instructions for the entire concentration camp and extermination program, and 14 officials of several other SS organizations* engaged in racial persecutions.
- 42 industrialists, in the cases against German officials of three of Germany's major corporations, the Krupp, I.G. Farben, and Flick concerns, for offenses including the utilization, procurement, and maltreatment of foreign slave laborers, largely Jewish; and looting of foreign, again often Jewish, enterprises.
- 23 physicians, including Hitler's personal physician, the president of the German Red Cross, and the chiefs of the Medical Services of the Air Force (Luftwaffe) and of the entire armed forces (Wehrmacht), respectively for various types of "medical experiments" on concentration camp inmates, largely Jewish, including sterilization experiments on men and women.
- 16 jurists, including an Acting Minister of Justice and other high officials of the Ministry who, the Judgment found, drafted the special laws and regulations that gradually deprived many people, especially Jews and Poles, of the basic rights of a fair trial, ordered their indefinite transfer to concentration camps, and the like; and prosecutors who charged and judges who condemned them to death for trivial or trumped-up reasons. The American Judgment says of those Nazi judges that they hid the murderer's knife beneath their judicial robes.

Altogether the American Nuremburg tribunals sentenced 24 to death, 20 to life imprisonment, 98 to other prison terms, and acquitted 35. Four committed suicide during the trial, and the cases of four others were severed because they were found unable to stand trial.

Reading 13 War-Crimes Trials Held at Places Other Than Nuremberg

Thousands of other war-crimes trials were held by countries that had been at war with Germany; by the Americans in their occupation zone at Dachau; by the British, French, and Russians in their respective occupation zones of Germany; and in Belgium, Denmark, France, Greece, Holland, Norway, Poland, the Soviet Union, and Yugoslavia; and in the Pacific areas against Japanese war criminals, especially by the Americans in the Philippines and the Dutch in Indonesia.

Some European countries also tried their own Nazi collaborators. The three most prominent, who were sentenced to death, were the Norwegian wartime prime minister, Quisling, whose name became synonymous with such traitors; the aged Field Marshal Petain, head of France's

---

*The case has become known as the "RUSHA" case, after the initials of the principle of those racist organizations *(Rasse-und Siedlungs-Haupt-Amt,* Main Office for Race and Settlement Matters). Their program included, as charged in the indictment, "the kidnapping of 'racially valuable' children from the occupied countries for 'Germanization'; forced 'Germanization' of other foreign nationals who were considered 'ethnic Germans'; and the persecution and extermination of Jews throughout Germany and German-occupied Europe."

wartime Vichy regime (his sentence was commuted by General de Gaulle to life imprisonment), and Petain's prime minster Laval who had been a willing instrument in the destruction of the French Jews.

In 1961, Eichmann was sentenced to death and executed after a trial before an Israeli court at which the Holocaust was discussed in great detail.

Trials for Nazi atrocities have also taken place in East Germany.

Following the model for the 4-Power Nuremberg trial, an 11-nation trial was held by the International Military Tribunal of the Far East in Tokyo, starting in 1946. Prosecution and judges were from Australia, Canada, China, France, Great Britain, India, the Netherlands, New Zealand, the Soviet Union, and the U.S.A. The 28 defendants were Japanese wartime leaders including two prime ministers (one of them, Tojo, had been involved in the attack on Pearl Harbor), cabinet members, generals, etc. Even more complicated, covering an even larger area of the world, and more multilingual than its Nuremberg model, it lasted longer than the latter, ending in 1948.*

Using Reading 13

What are war crimes? In the strict sense, war crimes are any acts forbidden by the international rules of war. These rules consist mainly of written treaties, such as the Hague Regulations of 1907 that have been in force before, during, and since World War II, and also of unwritten "customs of war" that have been generally recognized as binding on all states.

These rules forbid, for example, murder (as distinguished from killing in legitimate combat); ill-treatment, or deportation to slave labor or for any other purpose, of civilians of occupied territory; murder and ill-treatment of prisoners of war; mistreatment including torture, failure to give adequate medical attention to the injured and sick, inadequate food or housing; plunder of public or private property; wanton destruction of cities, towns, or villages; etc.

However, in a wider sense, the term, *war crimes,* also comprises two other categories of offenses, namely, *crimes against peace,* which the Nuremberg Charter defines as "planning, preparation, initiation, or waging a war of aggression . . ." and *crimes against humanity.* This term is a collective name for the same types of atrocities, long since forbidden, as those listed under war crimes, but with the following difference: whereas, as seen, atrocities such as murder, etc., against civilians constitute a war crime only *if committed in occupied territory,* they constitute crimes against humanity, as do, in general, "persecutions on political, racial or religious grounds," if committed against members of *a nation's own population.*

---

*The relocation of Japanese Americans in the early 1940s in the U.S. and their exclusion from the protection of the Constitution's Bill of Rights are receiving scrutiny in 1981 by the Presidential Commission on Wartime Relocation and Internment of Civilians. The Commission will hear testimony and consider "whether a wrong was committed" and possibly recommend some form of redress. The videotapes of the hearings and the final report of the Commission will be available from the Superintendent of Documents in 1982. The questions about whose role it is to defend civilians and their civil liberties in times of national crisis, propaganda, emotion, and war in the United States, are still being debated today.

Loyalty is a matter of mind, not race, creed, color, or sex; however, the Japanese exclusion cases are still legal precedent.

Reading 14	**The Supreme International Crime** The IMT Judgment concluded that war is essentially an evil thing. *To initiate a war of aggression is therefore not only an international crime; it is the supreme international crime, differing only from other war crimes in that it contains within itself the accumulated evil of the whole.* *Those who plan and wage such a war, with its inevitable and terrible consequences, are committing a crime in so doing.* It must be noted that obedience to these principles would have made World War II and the Holocaust impossible.
Using Reading 14	The defendants did not contest the documentation showing plans for attacks but rather argued that aggression did not constitute a crime. Since we concentrate here on the Holocaust, it is essential to understand that the Holocaust was only made possible by the preceding "supreme international crime," as the IMT calls it, namely, the starting of wars of aggression in the first place. Only through the subsequent conquest and occupation of such countries as France, Belgium, Holland, Poland, and large parts of the Soviet Union, where the overwhelming majority of Europe's Jews lived, did these millions fall into Nazi hands and thus become victims of the Holocaust. To avoid any possible misunderstanding, the Judgment does not mean that the war crimes, including the Holocaust crimes, which it calls of a "scale never before seen in the history of war" and "attended by every conceivable circumstance of cruelty and horror," were inevitable. The statement means that *any* war has "inevitable and terrible consequences." Hence, even if there had been no war crimes, and no Holocaust, if instead the aggressor had fully obeyed the rules of warfare, the war would still have enormous death, destruction, and suffering as inevitable and terrible consequences. Since the Holocaust was intrinsically intertwined with, and only made possible by Hitler's aggressive war, but since, on the other hand, that war was waged by his army, air force, and navy, the question arises whether the millions of Germans in those services committed the crime of aggressive war by fighting in it? The answer, according to Nuremberg, is "no." The IMT and the American Tribunals restricted the personal responsibility for crimes against peace to persons who actually participated in, or actually influenced, the deliberate preparation, planning, initiation, or waging of aggressive war. Of the twenty-two defendants in the IMT case, only twelve were convicted under the crimes against peace counts; and none of the almost two hundred defendants in the American cases were convicted, although the American prosecution had charged certain military leaders and war manufacturers for their part in the preparation and planning of aggressive war.
Reading 15	**Responsibility for War Crimes** The Judgment found that, "Any person who commits a war crime is responsible therefore and liable to punishment," and "The fact that internal law does not impose a penalty for (such act) does not relieve the

person who committed the act from responsibility under international law."

In other words: Nobody who committed a war crime can claim to have acted properly because the domestic ("internal") law of his own country permitted or even demanded the crime. This is the crux of the matter, according to Professor Fried, and was the crux at Nuremberg. The internal law of Nazi Germany did, in fact, demand, for example, the extermination of the Jews of occupied countries.

Reading 16 Any Person Can Be Responsible

The defense at Nuremberg argued that the worst excesses, including the Holocaust, had been ordered by a head of state who was beyond the reach of human justice (divine right of kings); and that while some policies were wrong, they were carried out as "acts of state," not by individuals.

The Judgment found, however, that "any person" who commits a war crime is responsible for it: "The fact that a person who committed a war crime acted as Head of State or responsible Government official does not relieve him from responsibility under international law."

Using Reading 16

To the claims of immunity for officers of the state, the IMT Judgment gave a realistic answer:

Crimes against international law [and this applies, of course, to the Holocaust] are committed by men, not by abstract entities [such as "States"]. . . . The authors of acts which are condemned as criminal by international law cannot shelter themselves behind their official positions [as, say, Foreign Minister, or Chief of Staff, etc.] in order to be freed from punishment in appropriate proceedings. . . .

Neither the head of state nor others in high positions may invoke their country's sovereignty, when actually they abuse that sovereignty for grave international wrongs.

Reading 17 Was There a Moral Choice to Act Differently?

According to the *superior order principle*, a person who commits a crime is not *automatically* excused by the fact that he obeyed a law, or decree or an order from a superior, when he did what he did. Instead, he is only excused if he did not have a *moral choice* to act differently.

The Nuremberg judges defined "moral choice." One is not expected to be a martyr. One is not expected to obey a criminal order at the cost of his life. Moral choice is the choice that morality can demand.

Using Reading 17

Students sometimes find the distinctions related to the superior order principle difficult to understand in the abstract. Some concrete illustrations may clarify it. If a one-star general has prisoners of war shot upon capture, or bombs an undefended city because a two-star general ordered him to do that; or if a concentration camp commander has inmates sterilized because of orders by higher-ups, he will nevertheless in principle be personally responsible. Regardless of the race or religion, or number of victims, he will not be excused by the mere fact that he acted under orders.

However, as seen, this principle contains a general exception that makes it fair and realistic: if one had no moral choice, one will not be considered responsible for what one does.

What, then, is "moral choice"? If A puts a revolver to B's back and orders him to machine gun innocent people, then B has no choice. He becomes A's extended arm and it would be altogether unfair to punish or even reproach him for having obeyed the criminal order against his will. The same is true if the risk for the recipient of the criminal order is much, much less extreme.

As the Nuremberg Judgments show, the higher the position of the recipient, the greater will be the choice, or choices, that are realistically open to him, and that morality demands from him. The ordinary soldier can regularly not begin to argue with his superior without risking grave consequences for insubordination. But the situation becomes increasingly different, the higher the position of the recipient of the criminal order.

There were numerous occasions for upright people in the top positions who were involved in the process, without risking any dangerous consequences, to make their opinions known, to plead against criminal decisions; to ask, if this was of no avail, for transfer to another position, or to resign. All this was done, but too rarely. Persons in prominent positions need not disobey or protest. They can, and quite a few did, extricate themselves from becoming criminally involved, without even stating the reason for extricating themselves.

On the other hand, as the Nuremberg Judgments show, the standard by which to measure the behavior of an individual, must also weigh the risks he might run for himself and his family, against the magnitude of the evil he might prevent.* Armament industrialists were unable to convince the American Nuremberg tribunals that they would have risked being sent to a concentration camp, had they refused to accept foreign slave laborers, including emaciated concentration camp prisoners, for their factories. They did risk the loss of some government contracts, which weighed little in comparison to what was imposed on those workers in their factories.

Sometimes people raise the objection that the principle tends to weaken military discipline and that absolute obedience to orders is the first duty of the military, especially in wartime. This objection requires careful consideration of the following:

• First of all, a decent regime will not issue criminal orders. The very dilemma of whether to obey them will not rise because they will not be issued. It was precisely the systematic, governmentally organized mass criminality that made the Holocaust possible. Otherwise, there would have occurred individual outrages, as occur in a bitter war, but never anything faintly approaching that genocide.

---

*Illustration: Immediately before the liberation of Paris, the German commander there countermanded Hitler's personal order to blow up Paris. The fuses had already been laid to the most important buildings, to bridges, etc. But the general did not activate them. Hitler's furious outburst, "Does Paris burn?" had to be answered to him in the negative. Paris was saved, although the general risked being court-martialed.

• It is not true that the military code, even in Nazi Germany — and this was carefully discussed at Nuremberg — demanded "blind" obedience.
• Military discipline is essential, especially in battle. But the worst Nazi excesses, and above all the Holocaust, had absolutely nothing to do with battle. Large parts of Europe were for years under German occupation, and the Holocaust actions were taken, sometimes only days, but very often years after any battle that brought the victims under German domination.
• The Nuremberg documents and testimonies proved a phenomenon that exists in bureaucratic and military decision-making processes in every country: realistically speaking, important order-recipients are virtually always also order-givers.
• By elementary fairness, only somebody who is truly opposed to the crime demanded from him — who is not animated by the same criminal intent as the giver of the order can plead coercion. If, as was unfortunately so often shown in the Nuremberg documents, his own behavior, own reports, statements, etc., show that he was a willing partner, he is, under general rules of law and morality, as guilty as is his partner, although the latter may have a higher rank or position.
• This leads to some explanation of the unexplicable Holocaust: The Nazi leaders were good psychologists. The greater were the crimes they demanded, the less did they choose for them individuals who were not themselves in favor of the crimes. The executioners were selected for their appropriate character traits. The higher-ups knew well that they had to exclude "weaklings."

The Nuremberg Judgments pointed out that the Nazi mentality had spread wide enough, even in "respectable" circles, to lead to the consequences the world may never overcome.

This, in turn, also points to two positive lessons: (1) what must be prevented within each nation and internationally is a mentality of brutality, of hatred, of racial or other superiority, a mentality that commits the sin of putting entire people beyond the pale; and (2) the spread of such mentality must be prevented long before it even faintly approaches the dimensions and acceptance that led to the dark age of Hitlerism.

Reading 18   Adolf Eichmann

Where would we have been if everyone had thought things out in those days?

Adolf Eichmann's trial opened in Jerusalem on April 11, 1961. Eichmann had been in charge of the office of the Nazi security service responsible for "Jewish affairs and the 'evacuation' of Jews to concentration camps."

Hannah Arendt's reflections on her coverage of the trial were published in *The New Yorker* magazine in 1963. Her description of Eichmann as neither monstrous nor demonic, but thoughtless and unreflective caused great furor and debate in the United States. She recognized that Eichmann had knowledge and may have been intelligent but these attributes did not stop him from evil deeds. Her belief that thoughtfulness would better insure against evil doing was shattering to many who held that those responsible were "different" from other humans.

In Nazi Germany, we heard from the Nazi participants, thinking was not encouraged. Doubting was out, obedience was in. There were no opportunities for the inner dialogue with the self that allows for conscience. Academic freedom, which had characterized the German universities, was to be squelched; it supported individual thinking—the state demanded conformity and obedience.

Arendt suggests that there may be a disturbing lesson to be drawn from the almost total collapse of respectable society during the Hitler period. Is it possible that, in extreme situations, those who will prove themselves most reliable are not those who proclaim values and adherence to moral norms but the skeptics and the doubters, those who are used to examining things, to probing, to thinking?[10]

Eichmann, writes Father James Bernauer, represented a new criminality—"the more profound failure of the modern age, of us, to understand the novelty of genocide and the changed human condition which makes it possible." The Holocaust, he writes, was more than the inevitable product of long centuries of Christian antisemitism, "about which individuals can do almost nothing." The event was exceptional.

[It represented] the operation of a bureaucratic form of governance which allow[ed] isolated individuals not to feel responsible for participation in programs whose success require[ed] the contribution of vast numbers.... Eichmann's participation in genocide was an attack upon human diversity itself. His crime assaulted the very nature of the political realm, which has for its purpose the achievement of freedom and the preservation of pluralism.[11]

Using Reading 18

Martin Heidegger expressed his views on academic freedom in May 1933 at the University of Freiburg.

The university was to encourage obedience not thinking.

The much-praised "academic freedom" is not genuine. It was simply negative. It signified primarily lack of concern. It fostered an individual's favorite intentions and inclinations, and admitted no ties, no obligations in one's doing and in one's letting be. The concept of the freedom of German students is now restored to its truth.[12]

Hannah Arendt suggests that "Eichmann's distance from the killing process and his bureaucratic connections with it left him a space in which he could conceivably consider his job apart from its moral implications."[13]

Insights can be drawn from the controversy around Arendt's description of Eichmann.

Gideon Hausner "asked the court to consider Eichmann as a 'monster,' as the grand master over the Holocaust of six million Jews, ruthlessly dedicated in his hatred to the elimination of Jews from the earth."

But for Hannah Arendt, Eichmann was an ordinary man caught up in an "extraordinary time." "Eichmann served his Fuehrer and Germany, not his own sadism or evil ideology."[14] He did not recognize evil.

When the "final solution" decision was made, Eichmann recalled, "I now lost everything, all joy in my work, all initiative, I was, so to speak, blown out."

The sparks that flew over Arendt's claims reflected the need to understand the very basic moral questions of good and evil that Eichmann's existence raises. The debate offers no scapegoat on whom to blame the Holocaust, but it challenges us to found our insights on an understanding of the complexities involved in its study.[15]

Citations

Chapter 10

[1] John Fried, *Trial at Nuremberg: Freedom and Responsibility* (National Project Center for Film and Humanities and the Research Foundation of the City University of New York,© 1973).

[2] From *The Ascent of Man* by J. Bronowski, © 1973 by J. Bronowski. Reprinted by permission of Little, Brown and Company, pp. 370, 374.

[3] Excerpt from *Nuremburg Diary* by G.M. Gilbert. Copyright 1947 by Gustav Mahler Gilbert, renewed copyright © 1974 by Gustav Mahler Gilbert. Reprinted by permission of Farrar, Strauss and Giroux, Inc., pp. 259, 260.

[4] Rudolf Hoess, *Commandant of Auschwitz*, (World Publishing Company, 1959).

[5] Selection is reprinted from *Human Behavior in Concentration Camps* by Dr. Elie Cohen, by the permission of W.W. Norton & Co., Inc. Copyright ©1953 by Norton & Co., Inc., pp. 258-259.

[6] Fried, *Trial at Nuremberg: Freedom and Responsibility*.

[7] Ibid.

[8] From *The Course of Our Times* by Abram L. Sachar. Copyright © 1972 by Abram L. Sachar. Reprinted by permission of Alfred A. Knopf, Inc. pp. 260-261.

[9] Mel London, "Letters to the Editor," *The New York Times,* Sept. 3, 1981. © 1981 by The New York Times Company. Reprinted by permission.

[10] Father James Bernauer, S.J. "Eichmann Twenty Years Later," (*Commonweal*, July 31, 1981) p. e437.

[11] Ibid., pp. 436-437.

[12] Michael D. Ryan, translator and editor, "In a Political University, Freiburg, 1933" (working paper).

[13] Bernauer, "Eichmann Twenty Years Later."

[14] Hannah Arendt, *Eichmann in Jerusalem: A Report on the Banality of Evil* (New York: Viking Press, 1963) p. 54.

[15] Karla Goldman, "On Eichmann" (paper prepared at Wellesley College, 1981.) Available at the Resource Center.

11

The Armenians
A Case Of A Forgotten Genocide
Do We Learn From Past Experiences?

Peoples' human rights have been violated. They have been robbed of their property. They have had their goods stolen. Their legitimate aspirations were crushed. They lost their lives.

Overview

In this chapter students explore the history of the first genocide of the 20th century, the Armenian Genocide, and examine the opportunities the world missed to prevent the Holocaust just twenty years later. Until recently the silence on the genocide of the Armenian people has been almost complete and so the label the "forgotten genocide" takes on new meaning as students consider the question, "Can we learn from the past?"

When our students study the Armenian Genocide, they indict those who have kept silent, denying this history its place in education for future generations. How, they ask, can they be expected to learn from a past partially taught or not remembered?

Students have a profound trust and commitment to the power of "knowing" and we, their teachers, have begun to listen to their message more carefully.

The following are typical student reponses to the question, why do you think the course is entitled *Facing History and Ourselves?*

We have to face ourselves and our history to prevent another [genocide] from happening.

If we could just recognize the small steps before it gets serious, then we have a better chance of preventing it.

It makes you think of what we might have done.

The hope really does lie with education.

Although each historical event is ultimately unique, with its own time, place, and setting, we look to identify, when appropriate, recognizable parallels, shapes, patterns, and symptoms of genocide, so that we can heed Jacob Timmerman's warning that "Modern tyranny repeats itself." This history helps students to think about the potential for all of us to be the victim, the victimizer, or the bystander.

We can learn about the steps a nation takes toward creating and implementing state policy of genocide. Students will recognize the abuses of citizenship and human dignity and be more sensitive to the signs of dehumanization and racism after facing the Armenian Genocide and the Holocaust. They will have models for risk taking and resistance during times of choice, before they become trapped in a choiceless choice situation in which the consequences of making a decision or taking a stand are too horrible.

After this study students understand Henry Miller's commentary about the SS women guards at Auschwitz, "We've learned something new about the human race, and the news is not good." But for our students the lessons go an important step further — "Tell us what the adult world knows and trust that with that knowledge we can do better."

As sensitivity to the dialogue about human rights increases, and students begin to identify actions they think their leadership should take, they are beginning to take a stand. They think about the power of language to protect minorities, the potential of statements to spread a language of morality or to set standards for protecting human rights, and the responsibilities of citizens to join actively in knowing and taking action in order to prevent "bad history" from happening again.

In this chapter, students ask questions about human rights and constitutional law. They continue to think about what the world could or should have done differently during and after World War I. Are there way individuals and groups can make a difference? Do words about human rights make a difference? What is the role of human-rights policy and policy makers in our country today? How does a group move from being a protected minority to becoming the victim of genocide? And finally, had American leaders taken a stand, would this history have been very different?

Senator Paul Tsongas argues for one type of responsibility that nations can and should take toward any violation of human rights.

As easily as foreign leaders can deny rights, Americans can deny reality. But turning our eyes away from human suffering doesn't diminish it one bit. To do so merely diminishes us. Two centuries ago, we declared independence with a ringing statement of human rights. Now is no time for a declaration of indifference.

Official attention to human rights has worked. It was saved lives, reduced suffering and bolstered our credibility abroad.[1]

In the following excerpt from a speech on the International Year of the Child, Professor Frank Stone, feels a special responsibility to communicate what happened to the Armenians in the Ottoman Empire between 1915 and 1923.

Most of us who are adults today [also]come to the Armenian Genocide as "children." By this I mean that we are the second generation who have heard what happened from our parents, or in some cases the third generation where the people who suffered and died were our grandparents and their generation. We, in other words, increasingly are not the groups who under this Holocaust ourselves. And our position is a sensitive one because we have the responsibility of communicating what happened to the Armenians in the Ottoman Empire between 1915 and 1923 to our children. We have to find a way to convey the reality of what took place together with an understanding of the causes that permitted it to happen. If we fail, our children will not know and the possibility of still another genocide occurring will be increased.[2]

Part 1 A Case of Forgotten Genocide

Reading 1

Quotation
Adolf Hitler made the following statement in a speech to his commanding officers before the invasion of Poland in 1939.

Our strength is in our quickness and brutality. Genghis Khan had millions of women and children killed by his own will and with a gay heart. History sees in him only a great state builder. What weak western European civilization thinks about me does not matter.... I have sent to the east only my "Death Head Units," with the order to kill without mercy all men, women, and children of Polish race or language. Only in such a way will we win the vital space that we need. Who still talks nowadays of the extermination of the Armenians?

Using Reading 1

What did Hitler assume he knew about human behavior? The fact is that the Armenian Genocide has been ignored, sometimes denied, and almost completely forgotten, in textbooks and in the public memory. Refer to the opening statement of the curriculum for a more complete discussion of the power of denial!

In the documentary film *The Forgotten Genocide*, Professor Avedis K. Sanjian suggests that if the world had responded more vigorously to the first genocide of the 20th century, the Holocaust might not have occurred. This chapter describes the genocide of the Ottoman Armenians during the First World War. The genocide was carried out between 1915 and 1916, although the destruction of Armenian people and communities continued through 1922.

There was no word yet invented in the 1920s to describe what the world learned when the eyewitness accounts of the Turkish horrors were written and told to the world. During World War II the French government originated the phrase "crimes against humanity" to describe Turkish acts against the Armenians, but this phrase didn't incorporate the complex dimensions in regard to calculated state policies of large scale murder of one particular people. Later, after the Holocaust, the international lawyers assigned to bring German leaders to Trials, found it difficult to find a legal concept adequate for the crimes committed against the minorities of Europe. It was at this time that Professor Raphael Lemkin coined the hybrid word *genocide*. It combines the Greek *genos* (race, nation, or tribe) with the Latin suffix *cide* (killing). The word was adopted in the Nuremberg Trial, notably by the British prosecutor, Sir Hartley Shawcross, but this crime was included under the broader category of "crimes against humanity."*

Professor Frank Stone reminds us that behind the facts, categories, and distinctions are human beings.

... [If] the aim of genocide is to exterminate a whole section of the population... to destroy the intellectuals of that group [then the lessons of the Armenian genocide are instructive.] ... to extinguish all of the

---

*Countries are still debating whether or not to sign the UN Convention on Genocide. On December 9, 1948, the General Assembly adopted a Convention on Genocide. The Convention received sufficient adhesions to enter into force on January 12, 1951, but the U.S. has not ratified it (1982) partly because of a fear that foreign powers might seek to intervene in American racial difficulties. This information is taken from the New Catholic Encyclopedia, "Genocide," by W.V. O'Brien (McGraw-Hill, 1967) pp. 336-337.

community institutions . . . to wipe out its economic basis by confiscating all of its property and to force into exile everyone in the target group [then the lessons of the Armenian genocide are instructive] . . . A genocide kills. It is not heroic. Men, women, and children are destroyed. They die along the roads and in the fields. Their blood stains the highways and colors the streams. People are made destitute. Children are left without fathers and mothers or any other living members of their extended family. The normal leadership of the victimized group is wiped out for at least the next fifty years. A generation remains unborn.[3]

Genocide, Irving Horowitz warns, is part of a 20th century phenomenon. He writes:

The umbilical cord between genocidal practice and state power has never been stronger.

This raises an important question: Are there certain preconditions which increase the possibility of a government committing genocide?

This chapter begins to identify some of these preconditions for genocide in order to help focus this study on prevention and not primarily on the retelling of very horrible events.

However, since genocide is so difficult to imagine, and because it is so easily forgotten, ignored, denied, and even deliberately censored, it is imperative to document the events in history before analyzing the historical background for warnings, comparisons, and parallels.

Students learned in the chapters on the Holocaust how difficult, how impossible, it is to imagine extermination. We have no language for atrocity, explains Larry Langer, and so new words had to be invented by those in the labor camps; new images have to be evoked by those who write about these events and experiences, and the learner has to be aware of the continuous struggle the human mind makes to confront the horror, not just to cope with the information.

In this context then, students should learn that politicians and lawyers too have had to invent new words for unprecedented 20th century events.

Reading 2 **The Pattern of the Genocide**

The following reading summarizes the genocide of 1915:

The pattern was this. Initially all the able-bodied Armenian men of a certain town or village would be ordered, either by a public crier or by an official proclamation nailed to the walls, to present themselves at the *konak* [government building]. The proclamation stated that the Armenian population would be deported, gave the official reasons for it, and assured them that the government was benevolent. Once at the *konak*, they would be jailed for a day or two. No reason was given. Then they would be led out of jail and marched out of town. At the first lonely halting place, they would be shot, or bayoneted to death. Some days later the old men, and the women and children, were summoned in the same way; they were often given a few days' grace, but then they had to leave. It was their misfortune not to be killed at the first desolate place....

Instead they were forced to walk, endlessly, along pre-arranged routes, until they died from thirst, hunger, exposure or exhaustion. Most were driven south to the burning Syrian desert; a few from Cilicia were initially sent in a north-westerly direction, towards the marshlands of

Konya and the gloomy, empty landscape around the great salt lake. All suffered atrociously, as convoy after convoy, accompanied by gendarmes, was moved on. Very soon, under those conditions, when given food and water very erratically, if at all, life became unendurable. If they stopped, exhausted, they were mercilessly whipped by the Turkish soldiers (some regular, some irregular) until they continued. The soldiers accompanied them, and the local populations who were encouraged to attack them *en route,* saw them as good for only two things: gold and rape. Once on the move, any money was liable to be stolen from them (the lucky ones were able to purchase water). Attractive girls were either raped, then beheaded on the spot, or snatched away into a Turk's household.

Gradually the ranks of Armenians thinned, although remarkable survivals are recorded, such as a native of Hadjin, who survived a forced march all the way to Mosul; most died in these terrible convoys; the dead and dying, their throats parched, their lips cracked, their bodies racked with misery and pain, were left by the road, to be devoured, by day by the vultures, by night by the jackals.

Simultaneously, the government had arranged for their empty homes to be taken over by *muhajirs,* the 750,000 Turkish refugees, mostly from western Thrace, who had either been driven out or left voluntarily from the lands conquered from the Ottoman empire during the Balkan wars. This policy was devised by Dr. Nazim. Government resettlement of Turks, Kurds or Circassians was from this time onwards a central feature of the process of killing Armenians. Resettlement of refugees is too complicated a process to be conjured out of the air; the frequency with which it occurs in 1915 highlights again the deliberateness of government policy.[4]

By the autumn of 1915 most Armenians in the heart of Turkey (Anatolia) had been killed, but the policy of genocide continued throughout 1916 and after. Talaat Pasha, the Minister of the Interior, dismissed government officials who were too lenient in carrying out orders to deport or eliminate Armenians.

Women and children who had been taken into Turkish homes or into the Turkish orphanages — that is, institutions in which Armenian children would grow up as good Turks — were turned out. Talaat Pasha ordered Armenian orphans to be taken from these orphanages and killed; and he gave orders that Armenian women who had been forced to become wives of Turks should be put on the road to the desert. Later he ordered the seizure of Armenian children who had been adopted (and indeed Turkified) by Turkish families; they too were to be killed; and to the few remaining Armenian labour battalions extermination was ordered.[5]

The city of Aleppo was designated as a major collection point for Armenians before they were deported on long marches or to extermination camps such as Maskinah (Meskene), Rakka, Deir ez-zor, and Ras ul-ain. By late 1915, there were so many Armenian refugees concentrated in Aleppo that Talaat ordered them to be killed in Aleppo.[6]

Using Reading 2

The magnitude of the genocide carried out between 1915 and 1916 is recorded in the following estimates:

- In 1914 there were about 2,500,000 Armenians living in Turkey.
- About 250,000 escaped to Russia.

- About 1,000,000 were killed (half of these were women and children).
- About 200,000 were forced to become "Islamized."
- About 400,000 (most of whom were starved and in rags) were found by the Allies at the end of the war.[7]

Reading 3 **Armenians are Made Defenseless**

The genocide of the Armenian people in what is now called Turkey was planned and executed by the government of the "Young Turks," a group of Turkish leaders who revolted against the Sultan-ruled government of Turkey (Ottoman Empire) in 1908.

The "Young Turks" were members of the Committee of Union and Progress, and as their name indicated, they promised progress, adopting a constitution, ending exploitation by other countries, and denouncing the corruption and brutality of the Sultan Abdul Hamid.

Henry Morgenthau, the United States ambassador to the Ottoman Empire at the time, documented the steps taken by the Young Turk Government to remove weapons from Armenian soldiers and make them powerless. According to Morgenthau, Armenian soldiers who had been trained and armed by the Ottoman government were present in every Turkish city. "Before [Armenians] could be slaughtered," wrote Morganthau, "[Armenians] must be made defenseless." The following excerpt illustrates the first step in the pattern of the Armenian Genocide.

In the early part of 1915, the Armenian soldiers in the Turkish army were reduced to a new status. Up to that time most of them had been [soldiers] but now they were all stripped of their arms and transformed into workmen. Instead of serving their country as artillerymen and cavalrymen, these former soldiers now discovered that they had been transformed into road [workers] and pack animals. Army supplies of all kinds were loaded on their backs, and stumbling under the burdens and driven by the whips and bayonets of the Turks, they were forced to drag their weary bodies into the mountains of the Caucasus. Sometimes, they would have to plough their way, burdened in this fashion, almost waist high through snow. They had to spend practically all their time in the open, sleeping on the bare ground. . . . They were given only scraps of food; if they felt sick they were left where they had dropped: [The Turkish soldiers often stopped] long enough to rob them of all their possessions—even of their clothes. If any stragglers succeeded in reaching their destinations, they were [often] massacred. In many instances Armenian soldiers were disposed of [by shooting them] in cold blood. In almost all cases the procedure was the same. Here and there squads of 50 or 100 men would be taken, bound together in groups of four, and then marched out to a secluded spot a short distance from the village. Suddenly the sound of rifle shots would fill the air, and the Turkish soldiers who had acted as the escort would sullenly return to camp. Those sent to bury the bodies would find them almost [always] stark naked, for as usual, the Turks had stolen all their clothes. In cases that came to my attention, the murderers had added a refinement to their victims' sufferings by compelling them to dig their graves before being shot.

Let me relate a single episode which is contained in one of the reports of our consuls and which now forms part of the records of the American State Department. Early in July, 2,000 Armenian [ex-soldiers] were sent from Harpoot to build roads. The Armenians in that town understood what this meant and pleaded with the Governor for mercy. But this official insisted that the men were not to be harmed, and he even called upon the German missionary, Mr. Eheman, to quiet the panic, giving that gentleman his word of honour that the ex-soldiers would be protected. Mr. Eheman believed the Governor and [calmed] the popular fear. Yet practically every man of those 2,000 was massacred, and his body thrown into a cave. A few escaped, and it was from these that news of the massacre reached the world. A few days afteward another 2,000 soldiers were sent to Diarbekir. The only purpose of sending these men out in the open country was that they might be massacred. In order that they might have no strength to resist or to escape they were systematically starved. Government agents went ahead on the road, notifying the Kurds that the caravan was approaching and ordering them to do their . . . duty. Not only did the Kurdish tribesmen pour down from the mountains upon this starved and wakened regiment, but the Kurdish women came with butcher knives. . . . These massacres were not isolated happenings; I could detail many more episodes just as horrible as the one related above; throughout the Turkish Empire a systematic attempt was made to kill all able-bodied men. . . .[8]

Using Reading 3

A more complete history of the Ottoman Empire, the Sultans, and the Young Turk revolution is included later in this chapter.

Students should begin to speculate on the opportunities the Young Turks had to build a following, consolidate their power, and to carry out their promises of constitutional protection for all.

The majority of people living throughout the Empire were very poor. What economic decisions could have been made to improve these poor conditions? What decisions could have been made to help the majority of people who were uneducated and who had almost no control over decisions that affected their lives?

According to Howard Sachar, Henry Morgenthau never stopped transmitting detailed accounts of the "torture and massacre, by drowning, axing, bayoneting, by bullet and fire." Others witnessed the "Turkish method of killing an entire people." The following account by Sachar indicates the magnitude of the slaughter. The next readings will further detail the stages of the genocide.

On June 10, for example, the German consul at Mosul telegraphed Ambassador von Wangenheim news of the slaughter of 614 Armenian men, women and children who had been floated down the Tigris by raft; . . . the river was clogged with human bodies and parts of bodies. On June 18, the German consul at Erzerum witnessed the massacre of no less than 25,000 women and children in [a] gorge near Erzinjan. On October 8, 1915, four members of the German Mission staff at Erzinjan reported the mass deaths of women and children by starvation and thirst; local Moslems were forbidden to [help] the dying. There were other reports of cannibalism, of mass torture, of sexual mutilation. A few of these descriptions were provided by Turks themselves. Others . . . came from American missionaries in the interior.[9]

Remnants of the once proud and powerful Assyrians, another minority living mostly in the eastern mountains near Persia, were likewise deported and killed by the government in 1915. According to Christopher Walker, incidents of dispersion and massacres were carried out by the government against this group well into the mid-1930s.[10]

Reading 4 **Armenian Leadership Is Eliminated and Deportations Begin**

Beginning on April 24, 1915, Turkish police in the capital of Constantinople arrested 235 Armenian leaders, politicians, writers, educators, and lawyers, who were held in custody for three days and later sent to towns in the remote interior of Turkey. The arrests continued until 600 leaders were exiled. Few were allowed to return home, and most were killed or died of starvation.

At the same time, the arrests spread to the 5000 Armenians, mostly from poorer classes in the capital, who were also "deported," and killed. This day, April 24, is regarded by Armenians as a day of mourning; it was the beginning of the genocide.[11]

Suren Hekimian, an Armenian, was born in Kharpert in 1905. His father used to warn the Armenian Archbishop and other leaders not to do certain things to irritate the Turks. He remembers the deportation this way:

The Turks believed the Armenians were like a horse. You have to reshoe them once in a while to give them a lesson so they remember where they belong. So by doing those things [protesting] it never helped the Armenian people anyway. Then against that we used to suffer very dearly. So my father used to say, that isn't the way we want our freedom. Because we were so far out and no one could give us a hand therefore, we should be very careful and try to advance ourselves and have patience. Of course, the patience takes a long time but we had no choice because you see how when the time comes no one gives us a hand and we were all massacred.

Suren Hekimian remembers the deportations from his home when the town crier, an Armenian speaking Turk, started walking through the streets in June 1915.

"Listen Turks. It's the order of our Sultan that every Armenian has to be deported and no Armenians are going to be left in this city. Any Turk that hides Armenians, he and that Armenian are going to be hanged in front of his house together...."

His father had been in prison in April for ten days and was then deported. His mother was left to survive with her two children. When they realized that the deportations were really massacres she went to her "prominent Turkish neighbor." He sent a letter to the German boys' orphanage where he and his brother survived the deportations.

In 1916 Armenians came out of hiding because they thought that was the end of the massacre, but instead of safety the Armenians who came out were taken. His mother had survived with Protestant papers.[12]

Using Reading 4

The Minister of the Interior, Talaat Pasha, did not deny ordering the arrest in April of the Armenian leaders in Constantinople or the subsequent mass killing of the Armenians. He justified to Morgenthau what he called "deportations" on the grounds that some Armenians were in communication with the Russians.

"Deportation" was just a euphemism for mass murder. No provision was made for their journey or exile, and unless they could bribe their guards, they were forbidden in almost all cases food and water. Those who survived the journey landed up in appalling concentration camps beside the Euphrates, between Jerablus and Deir el Zor. Descriptions by visitors in 1915 and 1916 will show what the Turkish government intended by deportation. Moreover, no distinction was made between

innocent, suspect or guilty—a point which prompted a query from a correspondent on the Berliner Tageblatt; *any such distinction, Talaat replied, was "utterly impossible," since "those who were innocent today might be guilty tomorrow."*[13]

Reading 5   **Deportation Through the Eyes of an Armenian Child, 1915**
In this reading Veron, a young Armenian girl, describes deportation.

It happened on a Sunday.

We were going to be deported—and now I understood what "deportation" meant. We were given three days to gather together our belongings and to leave. No one knew where we were being sent. People were giving things away, talking to each other in high-pitched voices, then breaking down and sobbing. I no longer remember the sermon at church that Sunday, only the sorrow in the priest's voice that he was unable to suppress.

At first I wanted to ask questions, but what was happening was just too terrible. I made myself believe that everything was going to be all right. I prayed to myself, and I tried to reason: Why should the Turks be doing this to us? Why should they drive us away from our home? But I couldn't find the answer, and so I prayed to Father God to deliver us from this evil and to deliver me from my own confusion. . . .

[Before leaving the town of Konya, my father gathered our family together to talk about our situation.] . . . "Thus far everything has gone in our favor, but it will not be so easy once we reach Adana, which is not as civilized a city as Konya. We all know of the massacres that occurred there just six years ago. Everything depends on the humanity of the police and the native population. Right now we have certain material means, but because we have no rights, no court of appeal, everything can be taken away at any moment. Therefore, we must be cautious, clever, suspicious and careful of our every move. All escape routes have been sealed. We will rest here another day or two before joining the other caravans. May the grace of God be with us. . . ."

In the morning we began to pass tiny villages in the foothills, where Papa said the people of Adana came in the summer to escape the heat. The homes were built along the sides of the hills, and as we passed below them, the people came out and stood in long lines and stared down at us. We felt like insects at the mercy of creatures whose minds we couldn't read. The first line of witnesses watched us in silence, and I was relieved when they disappeared at the first turn in the road, but before long we came to another line of people, this time on the other side of the road. As we passed below them, I heard one man shout, "Infidel dogs." This prompted two young boys to pick up stones and hurl them at our procession. . . .

"My God," one man asked, "Do they mean to exterminate us all?" Someone gasped.

My father waited a long time before answering. "They want us out of the way, so they can fight against our allies. . . ."

We were passing through many little towns on our way to the mountain. Some of the people stared at us, but most of them either looked away or ducked inside the homes or buildings.

"They are sick and ashamed of seeing us," Mama said.

One man ran up to our wagon and tried to offer us some bread, but one of the guards rode up and knocked it from his hand. The man sat down in the dust and would not move, though each of the guards rode up to him in turn prodding him to move, until, finally, one of the guards spat on him in disgust.

"He is as tired as we are," Papa said. "There are times when one man alone must bear the conscience of an entire village."

When they arrived in Syria the Turkish guards left and Bedouin Arabs appeared. Survival in the desert became nearly impossible. For some Armenians with money for bribes, some food was gotten, but others were defeated by starvation and heat.

At Gatman, a camp, Veron describes the existence:

I shuddered when I saw the people in the camp. Everyone was sick with an illness that had changed his color, and people were dragging themselves back and forth from the area they were using for a toilet; but they were so weak that many of them were unable to push their way through the mud, and they were sitting and falling down, weak, exhausted, dying.

"Cholera," I heard Papa say, and I felt our wagon come to a halt.

The days came and went. My life was empty, and I felt empty; but every day was a little less sad than the day before, and little by little my hope started to come back. All I remember hearing during this terrible time were the words "Deir el Zor." It was a town in Syria south of us where they were sending all the Armenians to die. That's what Papa said. He said that he learned that once you went to Deir el Zor, there could be no escape. People were being sent there by the thousands. They were saying that it was the end of the line; the final station; the Armenian graveyard. I knew what death was now, and I knew that the Turks meant to kill as many of us as they could. I don't know why, but I wasn't scared. I felt secure because I had my papa, and I was sure he was going to take care of me.[14]

Using Reading 5

As we learned in earlier chapters, a survivor's tale is just that, a surviving person's story and just one experience. This history is about genocide, not survival.

Later Veron was victim again. After the Treaty of Sevres was signed Greece was given Smyrna (Izmir), in western Turkey, and she was evacuated by Turkish soldiers so that "wealthy Turks" could use the Armenian homes, and the soldiers could hide in the church. She was injured in the Greek attack and finally brought to an Armenian hospital in Smyrna. She learned that Smyrna was labeled "Infidel Smyrna" because it was in the hands of the Christians—"Greeks, Armenians and Europeans."

The trouble between Greece and Turkey increased in Smyrna, and finally in 1922, with most of the Greeks evacuated and the Americans refusing to mediate, the Nationalists of Kemal returned. It was proclaimed that anyone harboring Armenians would be killed. The Armenians took refuge in the Church while their homes were burned.

Reading 6

Armenian Armed Resistance: Three Examples

• In the town of Zeitun, in March 1915, a Turkish army went to subdue and "deport" its Armenian people who had had a history of trying to resist government policies. Christopher Walker suggests that the purpose of this mission was evident by the fact that Turkish refugees, called Mahajirs, were waiting outside the town preparing to take over the vacated Armenian homes.

Although Armenians from Zeitun had chosen to pay a tax rather than enlist in the Ottoman army, an Ottoman general ordered all qualified Armenian men to enlist. The leaders of Zeitun agreed to this demand, but one group of Armenian men refused and escaped to the hills. The forty or fifty men who remained in the town were "deported," eventually to be killed or starved to death in the desert.[15]

Even though the Ottoman government was at war with Russia and was suffering defeats at the hands of the advancing Russian armies, the Ottoman policy of deportation and killing of Armenians continued.*
• In April 1915 a United States missionary in the city of Van recorded that the Turkish governor Djevdet Bey issued an order to officials throughout the province which read:

The Armenians must be exterminated. If any Muslim protects a Christian, first his house shall be burnt, then the Christian killed before his eyes, then his [the Muslim's] family and himself.[16]

At first the Armenians tried to cooperate with Ottoman officials, but at the same time they prepared to defend themselves.

As the extermination reports became public there were desperate attempts at resistance. One such resistance point was in the Van Province. Here the Turks, reinforced by the undisciplined Kurdish tribesmen, had swooped down on villages whose young men had already been conscripted. They murdered about ten thousand of those who remained. Those who could, fled for refuge to the city of Van, where more organized defense was possible. There, for anguished weeks, an ill-prepared civilian populace held out against strongly organized Turkish military units. The Armenians dragged out some antiquated artillery; they manufactured other crude weapons — guns and bullets and grenades; they melted down their silver, their lead, their cutlery, their samovars. But even the bravest resistance could not withstand the military pressure, and ultimately the casualties went beyond fifty thousand. Then, miraculously, a Russian relief force broke through briefly and evacuated a remnant of the survivors. But it was not possible to transport the wounded, the aged, the crippled, and when the Turks occupied Van, these were all brutally dispatched.[17]

• The mountain of Musa Dagh was the scene of a third effort by Armenians to use armed resistance against Ottoman forces. When the order for deportations in this region came in July 1915, sixty families decided to obey the orders. All were eventually killed. The remaining families collected all the possessions they could carry and retreated to the top of the mountain to defend themselves. For fifty-three days the men, women, and children of Musa Dagh held off the Ottoman army, which had surrounded the mountain. The entire group of about 4000 Armenians were finally rescued by five ships (four French and one English).[18]

---

*When the war started the Sultan and his government proclaimed, through the chief religious leader in Constantinople, a Holy War (Jihad) against the Allies — and this included the Armenians. (Martin Halabian)

Using Reading 6

It is important for students to know about these examples of Armenian armed resistance, because Turkish sources consider them as examples of rebellion which, they claim, justified the Ottoman response of "deportations." Deportations became a euphemism for mass murders, and self-defense was the reason the government leadership gave for them, even though these murders began before Armenians decided to defend their families.

Franz Werfel's novel *Forty Days of Musa Dagh*, written in 1934, describes the struggle of these Armenian villagers.

Professor Frank Stone believes it is important to dispel "romantic thinking" about the Armenian Genocide. For example, he writes:

Another type of romantic thinking is that which questions why the Armenians couldn't defend themselves, or that fails to recognize any places where resistance to the process of extermination occurred.[19]

Reading 7

Individuals Recorded the Genocide During the War

One of the best known primary sources on the Armenian Genocide was the collection of eyewitness accounts compiled by a member of the British Parliament, Lord Bryce, and published as an official Blue Book in 1916. The British historian Arnold Toynbee edited this Blue Book, and in 1917 he condemned the Ottoman government and warned historians about the revisionists:

Turks will say [after the war], "We were at war. We were fighting for our existence. The Armenians were traitors at large in a war zone." But such excuses are entirely contradicted by facts. These Armenians were not inhabitants of a war zone. None of the towns and villages from which they were systematically deported to their death were anywhere near the seat of the hostilities.[20]

After the war, Toynbee repeated that the Ottoman leadership, known as the Committee of Union and Progress, was clearly responsible for carrying out a genocide. In 1969 Toynbee wrote:

I am old enough to remember the horror at the massacre of Armenian Ottoman subjects in the Ottoman Empire in 1896 at the instigation of the infamous Sultan Abd-al-Hamid II. But this act of genocide was amateur and ineffective compared with the largely successful attempt to exterminate the Ottoman Armenians that was made during the First World War in 1915 by the post-Hamidian regime of "The Committee of Union and Progress," in which the principal criminals were Tala't and Enver.[21]

Another source of information regarding the Genocide was the German missionary Dr. Johannes Lepsius, who had been the head of the German Protestant Mission in Turkey. During the war he recorded eyewitness accounts of the killing of Armenian people. After the war, Dr. Lepsius was allowed to use files from the German foreign ministry to publish his work, *Deutschland und Armenien, 1914-1918* (1919). When Dr. Lepsius returned to Germany during the war, he made every effort to persuade Germany to protect the Armenians, but his campaign seemed to have no impact on protecting Armenian lives.[22] Historian Abram L. Sachar states that the activities of Dr. Lepsius were so embarrassing to Germany, because Turkey was an ally in the war, that he was transferred to the Netherlands.[23]

In September 1916, Turkey demanded that the German ambassador to Turkey, Wolf-Metternich, be dismissed from his position after his report to Berlin on June 30, 1916, which read:

No one any longer has the power to control the many-headed hydra of the Committee [of Union and Progress], to control the chauvinism and the fanaticism. The Committee demands . . . annihilation of the last remnants of the Armenians, and the government must bow to its demands. The Committee does not only mean the organization of the ruling party in the capital; it is spread all over the provinces. At the side of each provincial governor [vali], and on down to each kaimakam, a Committee member stands, with instructions either to support or supervise. The expulsion of Armenians has begun everywhere anew. But the hungry wolves of the Committee can no longer expect anything from these unhappy people except the satisfaction of their fanatic rage for persecution. Their goods have long since been confiscated, and their capital has been liquidated by a so-called commission, which means that if an Armenian owned a house valued at, say, £T100, a Turk—a friend or member of the Committee—could have it for around £T2.[24]

Reading 8   **Newspapers and Magazines Recorded the Genocide During the War**

Hundreds of articles concerning the destruction of the Armenian people appeared in American and European newspapers and magazines. The following headlines give us an indication of the coverage. Full copies of *The New York Times* article mentioned here are available at the Resource Center.*

A Sampling of Newspaper Headlines from *The New York Times*, 1915

August 20, 1915	Turks Lock Them in a Wooden Building and then Apply the torch
September 16, 1915	Answer Morgenthau by Hanging Armenians He Protests Against the War of Extermination in Progress
September 17, 1915	Mission Board Told of Turkish Horrors Correspondents Confirm the Reports of the Wiping Out of Armenians
September 21, 1915	Bryce Says that All the Christians in Trebizond, Number 10,000 Were Drowned Only Power That Can Stop the Massacre is Germany, and We Might Persuade Her to Act
September 24, 1915	500,000 Armenians Said to Have Perished Washington Asked to Stop Slaughter of Christians By Turks and Kurds
October 10, 1915	Plea to America for Aid Made in Form of Letter to Aneurin Williams, M.P.
October 12, 1915	Massacres Renewed, Morgenthau Reports Fresh Outrages Upon Armenians Follow Bulgaria's Stand Favoring Turkey

*Extensive coverage in newspaper articles has been compiled in *The Armenian Genocide—First 20th Century Holocaust: The Events in Turkish Armenia (1914-1916) As Reported in the New York Times and Various Periodicals of the Time with Selected Entries to 1922*, compiled and edited by Richard Diran Kloian (Walnut Creek, California: American Commemorative Committee, 1980).

October 19, 1915	Turkey Bars Red Cross
October 22, 1915	Only 200,000 Armenians Now Left in Turkey More than 1,000,000 Killed, Enslaved or Exiled, Says a Tiflis Paper
November 1, 1915	Aid for Armenians Blocked By Turkey Attempts to Send Food to Refugees Frustrated, Says the American Committee
November 3, 1915	Five Missionaries Succumb to Shock of Armenian Horrors, Says Report
November 27, 1915	Armenians' Heroic Stand in Mountains All Finally Exterminated
December 12, 1915	German Missionary Says Turks Proclaimed Extermination as Their Aim
December 15, 1915	Million Armenians Killed or in Exile American Committee on Relief Says Victims of Turks are Steadily Increasing

A Sampling of Articles From American Magazines, 1911-1918

"Armenian appeal to America for Help," *Survey* (April 1917): 486-94.

"Armenian Tragedy," E. Chandler, *Current History Magazine, New York Times* (August 1917): 332-4.

"Armenian Massacres," L. Einstein, *Contemporary* (April 1917): 486-94.

"Armenia Calls," H. Morgenthau, *Good Housekeeping* (November 1918): 21.

"Report on Turkish Atrocities in Armenia," Lord Bryce, *Current History Magazine, New York Times* (November 1916):321-34.

"Assassination of a Race," *Independence* (October 1915): 96.

"Armenia's Scattered Children," *Literary Digest* (December 1913):1166.

"Death of the Armenian People," *Literary Digest* (October 1915):716

"Exterminating the Armenians," *Literary Digest* (October 1915): 767.

"For Armenia," *Nation* (October 1915): 426-7.

"Germany and the Armenian Atrocities," H. Strummer, *Current History Magazine, New York Times* (November 1917): 336-9.

"Germany's Sins Indicated By a German," *Literary Digest* (October 1915): 31-2.

"Horrors of Armenian Encampments," *Current History Magazine, New York Times* (February 1917): 837-8.

"Lord Bryce on the Armenian Atrocities," *Outlook* (October 1916)L: 347.

"Massacre by Degree," *New Republic* (January 1917): 351-3.

"Massacred Armenians," *Review of Reviews* (December 1917):648.

"Murder of Armenia," C.F.G.Masterman, *Living Age* (February 1916): 370-3.

"Protest of German Teachers Against Massacre of Armenians," *Current History Magazine, New York Times* (November 1916):335-6.

"Armenia's Needs," *Literary Digest* (June 1917): 1782-3.

"Rescue of Armenia," *Missionary Review of the World* (July 1917):808-809.

"Songs of Exile; Hymns and Poems Through Which the Armenians Have Cried Out Against Their Persecution," A.S. Blackwell, *Survey* (December 1915):257-62.

"Tragedy of the Caucasus,' D. Heald, *Scribner's Magazine* (November 1918):561-8.

"Turkish Foreign Minister's Defense of Armenian Massacres," Halil Bey, *Current History Magazine, New York Times* (December 1916):544.

"Why the Armenians Were Killed," *Literary Digest* (November 1916):1256.

"Worst Sufferer of the War," M. Howard, *Asia* (August 1917):433-9.

Using Reading 8

Students can identify some of the common themes which are emphasized by the various headlines.

What questions do these headlines raise? What is happening? Who is involved? Where is this happening? What new information would be needed to learn more about this situation?

Reading 9

Documents and Telegrams Record the Genocide

The grim reality of genocide is almost too brutal for any of us to contemplate. It is a harsh, distasteful fact that we would rather ignore.... We encounter a disturbing demoniac element in official policies and national events. I am referring to the telegraphic messages from the imperial government in Istanbul sent by Talaat Pasha to provincial officials and military officers in the provinces. I mean the eyewitness accounts of the forced marches of the elderly, women and children. The shooting of the men, looting, starvation, and rape. These are not pretty pictures and they contradict our view of humanity as basically good and decent. It is not a matter of condemning the perpetrators in this instance as much as recognizing the capacity for inhumanity to other human beings that is part of many social structures.[25]

Naim Bey as head of the Ottoman General Deportations Committee of Aleppo in 1915 collected documents which he gave to an Armenian, Aram Andonian, who worked in the capital, Constantinople, as a military censor for the Ottoman government. Andonian later translated the memoirs into English.

In his introduction to the memoirs of Naim Bey, Andonian described this Ottoman official as the wrong man to be in charge of deportations, "because he was not a bad man." Andonian continued:

I had heard a good report of him [Naim Bey] how he had actually helped some Armenian families to escape, taking nothing in return, in spite of the fact that his finances were not in a very brilliant condition. He might have demanded anything he liked from those families who were rich, and for whom being sent back to the desert would have certainly meant being condemned to death.[26]

The following description of a deportation of Armenian women and children was written before Naim Bey became head of deportations in Aleppo:

They used to come to the village every morning to beg. Some of them carried water, and tried to live on the crust of bread which they earned in that way.

It was summer as yet. They could shelter themselves in the clefts of some rock or mound, but when the winter came, one could hear the moaning of those that were dying of cold and hunger all through the stillness of the long night. The Circassians of the vilage heard them, too, but those dying moans touched neither their hearts nor their consciences.[27]

But Naim Bey also remembered a group of soldiers and village people who set up a few tents to help the Armenians survive a raging storm one evening. But as the deportations to Mesopotamia continued, people living in the area began to die from diseases such as typhus, which was caused by proximity to the thousands of Armenian people left to die throughout the countryside. Naim Bey mentioned to two other Turkish officials that the deportations should be "relaxed" since they endangered all the people of the area. One of the other officials responded:

... In this way we rid ourselves of two dangerous elements at once. Is it not the Arabs who are dying with the Armenians? Is it a bad thing? The road for Turkey's future will be cleared.[28]

The following order was received by the Deportations Committee of Aleppo, and the new Governor General was responsible for carrying it out:

To the Government of Aleppo:
March 9, 1915—all rights of the Armenians to live and work on Turkish soil have been completely cancelled, and with regard to this the Government takes all responsibility on itself, and has commanded that even babes in the cradle are not to be spared. Because instead of the indirect measures of extermination used in other places—such as severity, haste [in carrying out the deportations], difficulties of travelling and misery—direct measures can safely be used there, so work heartily.[29]

When Talaat Pasha, the Minister of the Interior, sent the orders to Aleppo to massacre the Armenians, some officials refused to cooperate. Jelal Bey, the Governor General of Aleppo, wired a message to Constantinople stating: "I am the Governor of this province; I cannot be its executioner."[30] He was dismissed at once, and Beker Sami Bey, a man who was also opposed to the massacres, was sent to Aleppo in his place.

Fikri Bey, the Chief of Police, was replaced because he refused to carry out the orders. But finally officials were sent to Aleppo who were willing to organize the massacres, and some of these officials became very rich as a result of their new government positions.

Talaat continually emphasized that secrecy was important and that no officer should be brought to court for acts of brutality against Armenians. According to Talaat, public complaints should simply be disregarded:

To pay heed to the complaints lodged by "Certain People" on all sorts of

personal subjects will not only delay their dispatch to the desert but will also open the door to a series of actions which may entail political difficulties in the future. For this reason no notice should be taken of those applications, and orders must be given to this effect to the officials concerned.
Minister of the Interior,
   Talaat[31]

The following telegrams were sent by Talaat Pasha to officials at Aleppo:

November 18, 1915 — Be careful that events attracting attention shall not take place in connection with those [Armenians] who are near the cities, and other centers. From the point of view of present policy it is most important that foreigners who are in those parts shall be persuaded that the expulsion of the Armenians is in truth only deportation. For this reason it is important that, to save appearances, a show of gentle dealing shall be made for a time, and the usual measures be taken in suitable places.[32]

December 29, 1915 — We hear that there are [foreigners] on the roads who have seen the corpses of the Armenians and are photographing them. It is recommended as very important that those corpses should be buried at once and not left exposed.[33]

November 23, 1915 — Destroy by secret means the Armenians of the Eastern Provinces who pass into your hands there.[34]

The government official in charge of Res-ul-Ain, a collection center for Armenians, was Ali Souad Bey who decided to allow the Armenians to live in the town rather than massacre them. This irritated Nouri Bey, who as a deportation official sent the following telegram to Souad Bey:

It is contrary to the sacred purpose of the Government that thousands of Armenians should remain in Res-ul-Ain. Drive them into the desert.

Souad Bey replied:

There are no means of transport by which I can send the people away. If the purpose which you insist upon is slaughtering them, I can neither do it myself nor have it done.[35]

Zeki Bey was the governor of Der Zor, another collection center. He used others to slaughter 200,000 Armenians.

The colossal amount of labour needed had stupefied him. He had been obliged to call to this assistance all the Circassians who had executed the massacres of Res-ul-Ain. But still the butchers were not enough for the victims. Seeing that the Circassians would not be sufficient to complete the work, Zeki Bey had promised the Arab Ashirats of Der Zor the clothes of the victims, if they would come and help in the killing. And they accepted the offer. Most of the Armenians were slaughtered by them.[36]

In order to keep the enthusiasm of the Turks for massacre up to the mark, Zeki Bey would often bend down from his horse, [Kill an Armenian child and then say to his followers] . . . "Don't think that I have killed an innocent being. Even the new-born babes of this people are criminals, for they will carry the seeds of vengeance in themselves. If you wish to ensure tomorrow, kill even their children."[37]

Throughout 1915 and 1916 telegrams explaining deportation procedures were sent to local officials throughout the country. Some of these instructions and orders were signed by Talaat Pasha; others were guidelines supposedly sent by the Government Assembly in Constantinople, the Jemiet, or Committee of Union and Progress. The following excerpts are from some of these telegrams:

March 25, 1915 — *To the delegate at Adana... It will be forbidden to help or protect any Armenian.*

The Jemiet has decided to save the fatherland from the ambition of this cursed race, and to take on its own patriotic shoulders the stain which will blacken Ottoman history.

The Jemiet, unable to forget all old scores and past bitternesses, full of hope for the future, has decided to annihilate all Armenians living in Turkey, without leaving a single one alive, and it has given the Government a wide scope with regard to this.

Of course the Government will give the necessary injunctions about the necessary massacres to the Governors. All the delegates of the Ittihad and Terakke will do their utmost to push on this matter.

The property left will be temporarily confiscated by any means that the Government thinks fit, with the intention of its being sold afterwards and the money used [by the Government].[38]

September 16, 1915 — *To the Government of Aleppo from Talaat... It was first communicated to you that the Government, by order of the Jemiet... had decided to destroy completely all the Armenians living in Turkey. Those who oppose this order and decision cannot remain on the official staff of the Empire. An end must be put to their existence, however criminal the measures taken may be, and no regard must be paid to either age, sex nor conscientious scruples.*[39]

September 21, 1915 — *To the Government of Aleppo from Talaat... There is no need for an orphanage. It is not the time to give way to sentiment and feed the orphans, prolonging their lives. Send them away to the desert and inform us.*[40]

November 5, 1915 — *To the Government of Aleppo from Talaat... We are informed that Armenian children are adopted by certain Moslem families and received as servants when they are left alone through the death of their parents. We inform you that you are to collect all such children in your province and send them to the places of deportation...*[41]

November 18, 1915 — *To the Delegate at Adana... As announced in our dispatch dated February 8, the Jemiet has decided to uproot and annihilate the various forces which have for centuries been an obstacle in its way, and to this end it is obliged to resort to very bloody methods. Be assured that we ourselves were horrified at the contemplation of these methods, but the Jemiet sees no other way of ensuring the stability of its work.*

We are criticized and called upon to be merciful; such simplicity is nothing short of stupidity. For those who will not cooperate with us, we will find a place that will wring their delicate heart strings.[42]

In his memoirs, Naim Bey explained that the phrase "uproot and annihilate the various forces" meant the murder of other groups such as Greeks, Syrians, and Arabs, as well as Armenians.

December 17, 1915 — To the Government of Aleppo from Talaat . . . Communicate to those who wish to save themselves from the general deportations by becoming Moslems that they must become Moslems in their places of exile [the desert].[43]

January 15, 1916 — Collect and keep only those orphans who cannot remember the tortures to which their parents have been subjected. Send the rest away with the caravans.[44]

February 20, 1916 — To the Government of Aleppo from Talaat . . . The military authorities need Armenians that are of military age, for military service . . . we permit you to use them outside the town for road making or any other necessary work, on condition that their families shall be sent away with the rest of the deportees.[45]

At the end of his memoirs, Naim Bey commented on the response of many of the Turkish people to the government policy of eliminating the Armenian people:

Even Turkish elements like those who, in the time of Hamid II, had refused to take part in the massacres and had in some places protected their Armenian neighbors, enthusiastically welcomed the Government's project of exterminating the Armenians.[46]

He explained that there was so much hunger and misery throughout Turkey during the war years that

It was necessary to feed and deceive the people, and that could be done by means of the money and property that the Armenians would leave behind. The Turkish population . . . at the beginning made feeble assaults but, when they realized what the state policy was, they proceeded to wholesale slaughter and plunder.[47]

Using Reading 9

In April of 1915 Aram Andonian was accused by the Ottoman Government of giving information to the Armenian Patriarch (head religious leader) concerning the murder of an Armenian Bishop. Andonian was arrested and deported, but he later escaped. He then spent the next two and one half years being re-arrested, deported, escaping, and hiding, until finally he was rescued by some friends in Aleppo, where he remained until the British captured the city from the Ottomans.

Many Ottoman officials fled when the British arrived in Aleppo, but Naim Bey remained. It was then that Andonian arranged to meet with Naim Bey.

For several weeks Naim Bey gave Andonian information and original documents concerning deportations and massacres which passed through his office.

Naim Bey described in detail the attitude and policies of the Young Turk Government. Many scholars have considered these memoirs as an accurate account of this history, but the record is incomplete and many questions remain. For example:

• Naim Bey selected pieces of information from his files. What was contained in the documents which he did not reveal? Do these documents still exist today?

• Naim Bey was head of deportations. What decisions did he make? Why did he follow orders when he knew that the deportations would eventually lead to the murder of hundreds of thousands of Armenian people?

- These memoirs were translated by an Armenian who had survived this period of bloodshed. Did his experience affect his interpretations and translation of Naim Bey's writings?
- Suggested questions for dealing with documents in general: What type of document is it? Who wrote it? What information is contained in the document? Does the document give any clues as to what else was going on during the time it was written? What does the document emphasize?

Reading 10

Decree Issued Regarding the Armenians

Ottoman Government decrees of May 1915 regarding deportations appeared after the deportations from Cilicia and other massacres in the eastern provinces had begun. The following decree appeared in an Ottoman official journal, *Takvim-i Vekayi* on May 27, 1915:

If in time of war, the commanders of the armies, army corps, and divisions, or their replacements, as well as the commanders of independent military posts, who are subjected to an attack or to armed resistance from the populace, or who discover, under any form whatsoever, opposition to the orders of the Government or acts and measures for the defense of the state and the safeguarding of public order, are authorized and ordered to suppress them immediately and vigorously by armed force and to ruthlessly squelch the attack and resistance.

A. The commanders of the army, army corps, and divisions, can if military needs demand, remove and settle in other localities, individually or together, the populations of cities and villages who are suspected of being guilty of treason or espionage.

B. This law is in force from the moment of its publication.[48]

The decree was amended with provisions, but since the Armenians were never informed of the law and the rights granted to them, there were constant violations. On May 30, 1915, the decree added the following provisions:

1. to safeguard the person and possessions of the deportees until they had reached their destination and to forbid any form of persecution;
2. to compensate the deportees with new property, land, and goods necessary for a comfortable life;
3. to permit Moslem refugees to inhabit the abandoned villages only after having officially recorded the value of the homes and land and making clear that the property still belonged to the legal owners;
4. to sell or rent those fields, properties, and goods not settled by Moslem refugees and to keep in the treasury, in the owner's name, an account of the derived income, after first deducting adminstrative expenses;
5. to authorize the finance minister to create special committees to supervise these transactions and to publish circulars pertaining to the compensations for the properties and their protection;
6. to oblige all officials to comply with the law and report to the government during the course of its fulfillment.[49]

Using Reading 10

These documents raise again crucial questions about the use of law. Can laws hide illegal acts? How? Is "suspicion" sufficient reason to deport individuals, cities, villages? What justice is there behind this law?

A poster from the American Committee for Relief in the Near East.

If people are not informed about the law, how can it be enforced fairly? Should laws be made with input from all those to be affected? Were these documents sincere in view of the horrible events or just meant for world consumption?

Reading 11	**An Allied Response**

The Allied nations delivered an indictment to the Ottoman government on May 21, 1915 concerning the Armenian victims. They warned that responsibility for the crimes against "humanity and civilization" would be with Turkey:

Such massacres have taken place from mid-April at Erzerum, Terdjan, Eghine, Bitlis, Moush, Sasun, Zeitun and in all of Cilicia. The inhabitants of approximately a hundred villages in the vicinity of Van all have been killed and the Armenian quarter of Van beseiged by Kurds. At the same time, the Ottoman Government has acted ruthlessly against the defenseless Armenian population of Constantinople. In view of this new crime of Turkey against humanity and civilization, the Allied Governments make known publicly to the Sublime Porte that they will hold all the members of the Turkish government as well as those officials who have participated in these massacres, personally responsible.

The denial by Talaat Pasha:

Because some of the Armenians who are living near the war zones have obstructed the activities of the Imperial Ottoman Army, which has been entrusted with defending the frontiers against the country's enemies; because they impede the movements of provisions and troops; because they have made common cause with the enemy; and especially because they have attacked the military forces within the country, the innocent population, and the Ottoman cities and towns, killing and plundering; and because they have even dared to supply the enemy navy with provisions and to reveal the location of our fortified places to them; and because it is necessary that rebellious elements of this kind should be removed from the area of military activities and that the villages which are bases and shelter for these rebels should be vacated, certain measures are being adopted, among which is deportation of the Armenians.[50]

Using Reading 11

After World War I, many Americans contributed to Near East Relief, a semi-philanthropic agency that was only quasi-official.

A few thousand Armenian volunteers joined the Armenian Legion, set up by France.

According to Martin Halabian,* Russia helped as much as possible in battling Turkish forces in the eastern Armenian provinces of Turkey before the Bolshevik revolution.

The Ottomans defined the victims as the enemy and denied them the true protection of the law. Students might think again about the case of the Japanese-American citizens who were resettled to special American detention camps during World War II. What did these experiences have in common? What was different?

Recently the President's Commission investigating the removal of Japanese-Americans thought to be disloyal in America during World War II heard testimony about the need for a redress of the wrongs committed against these citizens in the name of the law.

Has Turkey today made any admission of guilt for lost lives or provided compensation for losses sustained by Armenians?

Reading 12

German Response to the Policy of Genocide

The only really effective and successful German action on behalf of the Armenians was a vigorous intervention by General Liman von Sanders towards the end of 1916, in favor of the Smyrna Armenian population. Von Sanders was then General Officer commanding Turkish and German forces in the Smyrna (Izmir) district, and his objections were based as much on military as on humanitarian grounds. The Smyrna Armenians were finally wiped out by the forces of Mustafa Kemal in 1922.[51]

According to Professor Frank Stone, although "many Germans were in the Ottoman Empire at this time and had great influence over their Turkish collaborators, they failed to intervene. The French hardly lifted a finger. The British accepted Armenian volunteers but did nothing to stop the genocide. And, as a matter of fact, at no point did the American

---

*Professor Halabian is Senior Lecturer in World History and Middle East History at Northeastern University.

government do anything substantial to halt the carnage in although Washington knew all about what was happening

The Germans, who had reorganized the Turkish Army and according to David Marshall Lang, had maneuvered the Ottomans into World War I, gave Enver and Talaat ideal conditions within which to carry out their plans. "... The Ottoman and German censorships prohibited all mention of these horrors in newspapers under their control, and reports of the massacres had to be smuggled abroad secretly."[52] The role of the German government in the complicity or active organization of the policies against the Armenians is controversial. Hovannisian suggests:

Certainly part of the German press bewailed the suffering of the Eastern Christians. The German General Staff and members of the Military Mission to Turkey condemned the radical measures of the [Young Turks] dictators, for the depopulation of vital farmland and the elimination of the most important professional and artisan classes caused immeasurable harm to the war effort of the Central Powers. Nevertheless, most official publications in Germany repeated Turkish charges against the Armenians and asserted that involvement in the internal affairs of an ally during time of war was imprudent. Ambassador Johann Bernstorff in Washington echoed these views and noted that the Armenians had brought the tragedy upon themselves. The Germans have been accused of direct complicity in the deportations, for the Berlin government had both the influence and the force to restrain its Turkish partner.[53]

According to David Lang:

Many German and Austrian diplomats, honorable men, were horrified at the monster which their masters had helped to conjure up. But, once the First World War had broken out, Kaiser Wilhelm could not risk losing the valuable ally — any more than Great Britain could have dispensed with the military might of Soviet Russia after 1941, however much British Conservatives disliked Stalin and all that he stood for. Nogales states: "The Ottoman Empire was without question the most important ally that Germany had during the World War. This is an incontestable fact which the Germans themselves are the first to recognize. While the Austrians openly pleaded for peace, and the Bulgarians kept up a continual complaint because of the constant decrease in rations, the Turkish soldier kept on bleeding and dying of starvation among the snows of the Caucacus and the sands of the desert without ever letting a complaint or a whisper of dismay cross his livid, fever-paled lips."

Locked in mortal combat on the battlefield of France, and in Poland to the east, the German General Staff had vital need of the invaluable support of Ottoman Turkey. The Young Turk ruling junta was well aware of its overwhelmingly strong bargaining position.

Thus it was that the Germans in Turkey had to acquiesce in the murder of Armenian employees of their own consulates and business concerns, and of Armenian pupils from their own German mission schools. In 1916, the German ambassador, Count von Wolff-Metternich, finally made himself so obnoxious to the Ottoman government through his humanitarian efforts that Enver and Talaat had him recalled to Berlin under a cloud of disfavor.

Thus it was also that the German socialist leader Karl Liebknecht, who courageously raised the Armenian issue in the German Reichstag, had to be put off by the Political Department of the German Foreign Ministry with unconvincing explanations.[54]

Using Reading 12

The German ambassador, Baron Hans von Wangenheim, brusquely turned aside every appeal for intercession with Germany's ally. He subscribed to the principle that the security of the state overrode all humane consideration. As he put it succinctly to the German naval attache, "The weaker nation must succumb."[55]

Professor Halabian states that, although Turkish soldiers continued to fight in the Causcasus, thousands deserted along the front in Palestine.

Reading 13 **An American Response: The Harbord Report**

After World War I, the countries involved met at the Paris Peace Conference. The Armenians were represented and tried to persuade the conference to support an independent Armenia, although by now the genocide had made them a minority in the land. Turkey denied the policies of genocide, and by the close of the conference, not one request by the Armenians for protection was endorsed by the Allies.

In July 1919, the United States sent Major General James Harbord to investigate the status of the Armenians living in the area between Russia and Turkey. The United States Congress was to consider whether the United States should accept a mandate over this area. If it were granted a mandate, it had the authority to reorganize the country by establishing a responsible government. The League of Nations planned mandates as a way to rebuild conquered countries torn by war.

The following excerpt from the Harbord Report lists reasons for and reasons against the United States accepting responsibility for these countries:

• *Reasons for:* As one of the chief contributors to the formation of the League of Nations, the United States is morally bound to accept the obligations and responsibilities of a mandatory power.
Reasons Against: The United States has prior and nearer foreign obligations, and ample responsibilities with domestic problems growing out of the war.

• *Reasons For:* The Near East presents the greatest humanitarian opportunity of the age — a duty for which the United States is better fitted than any other — as witness Cuba, Puerto Rico, Phillippines, Hawaii, Panama, and our altruistic policy of developing peoples rather than material resources alone.
Reasons Against: Humanitarianism should begin at home. There is a sufficient number of difficult situations which call for our action within the well-recognized spheres of American influence.

• *Reasons For:* America is practically the unanimous choice and fervent hope of all the peoples involved.
Reasons Against: The United States has in no way contributed to and is not responsible for the conditions, political, social, or economic, that prevail in this region. It [is] entirely consistent to decline the invitation.

• *Reasons For:* America is already spending billions to save starving people in Turkey and Transcaucasia and could do this with much more efficiency if in control. Whoever becomes mandatory for these regions we shall be still expected to finance their relief, and will probably eventually furnish the capital for material development.

Reasons Against: American philanthropy and charity are world wide. Such policy would commit us to a policy of meddling or draw upon our philanthropy to the point of exhaustion.

- *Reasons For:* America is the only hope of the Armenians. They consider but one other nation, Great Britain.

  For a mandatory [sic] America is not only the first choice of all the peoples of the Near East but of each of the great powers, after itself.

  American power is adequate; its record is clean; its motives above suspicion.

  Reasons Against: Other powers, particularly Great Britain, and Bolshevik Russia, have shown continued interest in the welfare of Armenia.

  The United States is not capable of sustaining a continuity of foreign policy. One Congress can not bind another. Even treaties can be nullified by cutting off appropriations.

- *Reasons For:* The mandatory [sic] would be self-supporting after an initial period of not to exceed five years. The building of railroads would offer opportunities to our capital. There would be great trade advantages.

  Reasons Against: Our country would be put to great expense, involving probably an increase of the Army and Navy. It is questionable if railroads could for many years pay interest on investments in their very difficult construction.

  The effort and money spent would get us more trade in nearer lands than we could hope for in Russia and Rumania.

- *Reasons For:* It would definitely stop further massacres of Armenians and other Christians, give justice to the Turks, Kurds, Greeks, and other peoples.

  Reasons Against: Peace and justice would be equally assured under any other of the great powers.

- *Reasons For:* America has strong sentimental interests in the region — our missions and colleges.

  Reasons Against: These institutions have been respected even by the Turks throughout the war and the massacres: and sympathy and respect would be shown by any other mandatory [sic].

- *Reasons For:* If the United States does not take responsibility in this region, it is likely that international jealousies will result in a continuance of the unspeakable misrule of the Turk.

  Reasons Against: The peace conference has definitely informed the Turkish government that it may expect to go under a mandate. It is not conceivable that the League of Nations would permit further uncontrolled rule by that thoroughly discredited government.

- *Reasons For:* "And the Lord said unto Cain, 'Where is Abel, thy brother?' And he said, 'I know not; am I my brother's keeper?'"

  Better millions for a mandate than billions for future wars.

  Reasons Against: The first duty of America is to its own people and its nearer neighbors.

Here is a man's job that the world says can be better done by America than by any other. America can afford the money; she has the men; no duty to her own people would suffer; her traditional policy of isolation did not keep her from successful participation in the Great War. Shall it be said that our country lacks the courage to take up new and difficult duties?

Without visiting the Near East it is not possible for an American to realize even faintly the respect, faith, and affection with which our country is regarded throughout that region. Whether it is the world-wide reputation which we enjoy for fair dealing, a tribute perhaps to the crusading spirit which carried us into the Great War, not untinged with hope that the same spirit may urge us into the solution of great problems growing out of that conflict, or whether due to unselfish and impartial missionary and educational influence exerted for a century, it is the one faith which is held alike by Christian and Moslem, by Jew and Gentile, by prince and peasant in the Near East. It is very gratifying to the pride of Americans far from home. But it brings with it the heavy responsiblity of deciding great questions with a seriousness worthy of such faith. Burdens that might be assumed on the appeal of such sentiment would have to be carried for not less than a generation under circumstances so trying that we might easily forfeit the faith of the world. If we refuse to assume it, for no matter what reasons satisfactory to ourselves, we shall be considered by many millions of people as having left unfinished the task for which we entered the war, and as having betrayed their hopes.

Respectfully submitted,
JAMES G. HARBORD
Major General, United States Army, Chief of Mission.[56]

Using Reading 13

This is an ideal reading to illustrate once again the complexities of decision-making for the government, the individual, and the group. As students clarify the reasons for and against, they will think about the consequences of taking a stand.

Have students categorize the arguments contained in the Harbord Report. For example, several of the arguments deal with the issue: Should the United States help the Armenians because our prestige as a world power is at stake, or will our involvement only tarnish our reputation and get us involved in more conflicts? What motivates a nation to care or not care for the needs of other people?

Armenians sacrificed their lives in the war effort based on promises by the Allies for protection after the war. Is the reputation of a government tarnished by breaking promises?

Certainly this exercise raises again all the major decision-making issues developed in the initial chapters of this curriculum. The thinking that students have done about individual, group, and national responsibility for one's neighbor is extended by this situation and specifically by this document. Have students decide on their stand and clarify their reasons either in discussion and or in writing. Give opportunity for reasoned debate, and encourage tolerance for opposing ideas. The complexities of this incident are echoed everyday in our newspapers. Ask students for analogies.

Reading 14

Surviving Armenians Declare A Republic

During World War I Russia and the Ottoman Empire (Turkey) had fought in the eastern provinces of Turkey, which were thickly settled by Armenians. In February/March 1917, the Russian Czar was overthrown and a provisional government was set up to function until a constitutional convention could meet to establish a parliamentary constitutional state. The Russian army in eastern Turkey, which included contingents of Armenian soldiers, continued fighting Turkish forces. In October/November of 1917 a second revolution, led by Lenin and the Bolsheviks, overthrew the Provisional Government and called for total withdrawal from the war.

When the Russian army in eastern Turkey and the Caucasus disbanded, the Armenian troops remained as a fighting unit and aligned themselves with forces that opposed the Bolsheviks and continued the war against Turkey. The region of Russian Armenia in the Caucasus and what little remained of the Russian-held territory in the eastern provinces of Turkey were now controlled by the Armenians. Armenian refugees in this region were now under the control of the Russian Armenian military and political regime. Although Lenin and the Bolsheviks made no claims to this region, the Armenians continued to hope that the Bolsheviks would be overthrown and a non-Bolshevik government established.

In May 1918 the Armenians declared their independence and established the Republic of Armenia in what was formerly Russian territory. Armenian refugees who had survived the genocide fled from their homeland in Turkish Armenia and settled in the impoverished Republic. Even though Turkey had recognized the existence of the Republic by signing the Treaty of Batum, Turkish forces continued to attack the Republic.

The Republic continued to fight for the Allied cause, especially in the protection of the city of Baku. The efforts of the Armenians delayed the capture of this important oil center for six months, thus depriving Germany of much needed oil for its war machine.*

Outside the newly created Republic of Armenia's borders the killing of Armenians continued. In Baku, 20,000 Armenians were slaughtered in September when the Turkish forces took control. In 1918 in the eastern provinces, according to Walker, between fifty and one hundred thousand Armenians were killed.[57]

Finally, on October 30, 1918, a defeated Turkey signed the Mudros armistice with the Allies, an armistice which, according to Arnold Toynbee, "made the military and naval situation of the Allies perfectly secure... but... no adequate provision was made for the security of the Armenians." No provisions were made for Armenian soldiers who had been fighting the German and Turkish forces.

In addition to the continued war with Turkey, the Republic was weakened in 1918 by two major events: involvement in a war with neighboring Georgia, which lasted through December of 1918 when the Allies arranged a cease-fire; and extreme winter weather.

The war was inconclusive for both sides. But the real damage was that, in the eyes of the world, here were two states, that had been amid the fire and ice of the last four years, which had suffered deprivation and fearful onslaught, but which were now, while the rest of the world was healing its wounds and longing for peace, laying into one another like two hostile cats.[58]

The severe winter conditions of 1918-1919 created extreme hardships for everyone in the region, and this, combined with the lack of shelter

---

*Martin Halabian

and food for the 300,000 Armenian refugees who had survived the genocide, made living conditions "catastrophic." Many European and American relief agencies sent large quantities of food and clothing in an attempt to ease the situation.

It is impossible to count the number of those who died in the terrible famine which affected Armenia from 1918 to 1920. The British High Commissioner in Transcaucasia saw dozens of emaciated victims collapsing and dying on the streets of Erevan. It is estimated that there were half a million homeless refugees from Turkish Armenia in and around Erevan in 1918.[59]

By the end of 1919, Turkey was in full control of its former Armenian eastern provinces, and Russia's Communist regime was again re-asserting its authority over Imperial Russia's Caucasian provinces. In December 1920 there was a Communist take-over of the Republic of Armenia, and it became part of the Soviet Union.

Turkey, under Kemal Ataturk*, signed a peace treaty with the Soviet Union in 1920, thus ensuring peace for the small Soviet Republic of Armenia. At this time, Armenian refugees from Turkish territory fled to Soviet Armenia for sanctuary.

During the establishment of Kemal Ataturk's Nationalist government, thousands of Armenian lives were lost. Walker estimates that about 250,000 Armenians were killed between 1919 and 1920 as they attempted to return to their homes from the deserts where they had been deported.[60]

Further heavy loss of Armenian lives occurred during the early years of the Kemalist regime in Turkey. In 1919, the victorious British and French occupied Cilicia and adjoining regions of southern Turkey, where there had been a large Armenian population [long pre-dating] the period of the Crusades. The ignominious rout of the French from the Marash region early in 1920 entailed a heavy death toll among those Armenians who had [returned] from exile in Syria.

Kemalist reprisals against Armenian civilians reached a climax at the Turkish recapture of Smyrna from the Greeks in September 1922. On this occasion, more than 100,000 Greek, Armenian, and other refugees perished in a terrible holocaust, when the Turks burnt down the Armenian, Greek, and European quarters, and machine-gunned families attempting to reach allied warships anchored close to the harbour.[61]

Using Reading 14

At this same time the Turkish government wanted to annex the whole of Transcaucasia, including Georgia, Armenia, and Azerbaijan, but the Georgians, fearing Turkey, declared their independence on May 26, 1918, and placed themselves under friendly German protection. Georgia was crucial to German strategic interests in the Caucasus. The decision by the Armenians to declare their independence in this region was forced upon them by the impending Turkish threat and the lack of protection from European powers.

---

*The history of the rise to power of Mustafa Kemal is complex and beyond the scope of this chapter.

Nearly 150,000 Armenians migrated from Turkey and settled in the Russian occupied areas. These migrations continued in spite of statements by Lenin and the Bolsheviks that Russian troops should withdraw from Turkish Armenia and allow for the right of all peoples to self-determination.

In January 1918 the Bolsheviks published a decree which stated the principle of self-determination and called for the return of Turkish Armenians who had recently migrated into the occupied area.

In March 1918, Soviet Russia agreed at the Treaty of Brest-Litovsk to end its war with Turkey and Germany by:

- giving up over a million square miles which was inhabited by nearly 60 million people.
- giving Turkey the right to rule over all Turkish Armenia.
- withdrawing Russian troops from Turkish Armenia within eight weeks.
- promising to use every means to disperse and destroy the Armenian bands operating in Russia and in the occupied provinces of Turkey.[62]

According to Hovannisian, the decree of self-determination and withdrawal of Russian troops was calculated to win the sympathy and support of the many thousands of war-weary soldiers and to undermine all opposing forces. Furthermore, Soviet leaders reasoned that the colonial peoples, once convinced of the good intent of the new Russia, would unite to struggle against the powerful imperialist and capitalist antagonists of the West.[63]

Irving Horowitz writes that between 1893 and 1923 roughly 1,800,000 Armenians were liquidated, while another 1,000,000 were exiled, without a single political or military elite within the state assuming responsibility for the termination of the slaughter, or for that matter, granting the Armenians national autonomy or territorial rights. [64]

And so the abomination of desolation had come to pass. A peaceful population of well over two million men, women, and children, the most skilled, industrious and educated element in Anatolia and Cilicia, had been murdered or dispersed. About a million and a half persons of both sexes perished by violence or hardships over the seven years from 1915 to 1922, and more than half a million were refugees in a score of foreign lands. Only about a hundred thousand Armenians remained, concentrated mostly in Istanbul and a few other urban centers."[65]

For further information on the history of the war, the Republic of Armenia, and the accounts of massacre in Smyrna and Marash, see the following:

- Richard Hovannisian, *Armenia on the Road to Independence* and *The Republic of Armenia, Volume I, 1918-1919* (Berkeley and Los Angeles, 1971)
- Firuz Kazemzadeh, *The Struggle for Transcaucasia, 1917-1921* (Oxford and New York, 1951)
- Marjorie Housepian, *Smyrna 1922: The Destruction of a City* (Faber, 1972)
- Stanley E. Kerr, *The Lions of Marash: Personal Experiences: American Near East Relief 1919-1922* (State University of New York Press, 1973).

Part 2 Do We Learn From Past Experiences?

Reading 15 **Conditions in Ottoman Turkey Before the Genocide**

Part I of this chapter documented the genocide of the Armenian people. In this second part information is presented about the political, social, economic, and cultural history of the region where Armenians lived before the genocide.

It is instructive to learn about the history of the Armenians and their ruling governments in order to further explore the critical question: How does a minority receive protection from the ruling majority? A study of the struggle of the Armenians for survival within the Ottoman Empire leads to a new understanding of the meaning of democracy.

As we read about the rule of the Ottoman Sultans and later the revolt of the "Young Turks," it is important to think about how each government used its leadership in regard to protecting human rights.

The history of the Armenian struggle for survival explores many of the opportunities the leadership of Turkey had to institute or enforce policies of protection toward its minorities. How then did the Armenian minority become victim to the policy of genocide?

As one looks back to the history before the genocide, there are certain preconditions which exist before policies of genocide are implemented.

One such precondition involves the defining of certain human beings as the "they" who because of certain characteristics are not as deserving or worthy as the "we." Within the strict social structure of the Islamic Ottoman world, the Christians and Jews and all other non-Muslims were the "they."

Perhaps, if we can identify those preconditions that come to exist in a society before genocide, then we can better appreciate the individual role in preventing such abuse. Although we recognize that no two events in history will share the same preconditions, we can recognize patterns of discrimination and hate which contribute to an atmosphere conducive to practices of dehumanization. If we learn who the Armenians were, where and how they lived, and then speculate about how their ultimate history might have been avoided, then truly the Armenians can serve as one case study and warning against genocide.

Using Reading 15

This chapter introduces students to a brief history of the Armenians and the Ottoman-Turkish Empire. Using the notion of identifying certain preconditions for genocide helps to focus this approach to a very complicated history. However, the danger is that students will draw simple lessons from this complex history. Preconditions may exist without a resulting genocide.

Does the actual writing of a constitution give the leadership of a country an opportunity to think and rethink the responsibilities of the individual citizen to the country and likewise the country to its citizens?

Since the Ottoman Empire was an Islamic theocracy in which religion played a critical role in the getting and keeping of power and in the decisions about the worth of human beings, then how could non-Muslim minorities expect to change the historical pattern? Similar dilemmas involving separations of church and state and the modern versus traditional worlds still cause great controversies today. (Modern Iran is a case in point.)

Could a Bill of Rights define and enforce protections for the individual, given the history and religion of the region? What opportunities were there for protection of Armenians?

Reading 16

A Child Is Taught the Difference Between an Armenian and a Turk

Veron, an Armenian child in the Ottoman Empire, remembers the disgrace she brought on her family when she cut her hair in bangs to look like the mayor's daughter, Lehman, who was Turkish:

"You should be ashamed of yourself," Auntie said. "Only Turkish girls wear their hair in bangs. You have brought a disgrace upon our family."

Later, the differences between Turkish and Armenian took on new and different meaning:

I had never thought about time or change. But slowly changes began to occur. Our lives went on as before, but now our days, which had always seemed to be lit by the sun, were being shadowed by a dark cloud.

For the first time I began to sense the seriousness of our problems with the Turks. I had always known that they were not our friends, even though there were some with whom we were friendly, but now it seemed, in truth, that they were our enemies. We were Christians, and they were Moslems, but it was not this alone that separated us; we were also different in language, race and custom. We did live on the same soil, but I was told that soil could be owned and that the present owner of this soil, which we had always called home, was Turkey.

Grandma had hinted in the past that there might be trouble between the Armenians and the Turks, but now it was being talked about more openly — not only by her, but by everyone in our quarter. I was told that the Turks had massacred several hundred thousand Armenians a few years before, in 1895, and then again in Adana, in 1909, when I was two years old. And now there were rumors that there would be more massacres. I wasn't sure what all this meant, but I could see that the elders were worried. This made me worried, too, and I began to talk about my fears with the other children. No one could understand what was happening, but I could see that they were uneasy, too. This made me aware for the first time that our fears were not imagined, not childish, but real and deep-rooted.

I began to hear whisperings — at home and at Grandma's, especially at night, when my parents thought we were asleep. But more than their whisperings, it was the way they looked, the way they talked and moved about, that made me know something was wrong. I began to hear words like "deportations," "massacres," "annihilation." I didn't like the sounds of the words, but mostly I didn't like the looks on their faces when they said these words.

It was around this time that the Turkish army drafted my uncles Apraham and Hagop. When I asked Grandma about this, she said something about the World War.[66]

Using Reading 16

We have learned that groups identify themselves by who and what they are not. In this case, the "we" are the Armenians and the "they" are the Turks. What good were these generalizations? Is it true that you have to be taught to hate, carefully taught, as the song goes?

Map 1 Ottoman Settlements, 1300

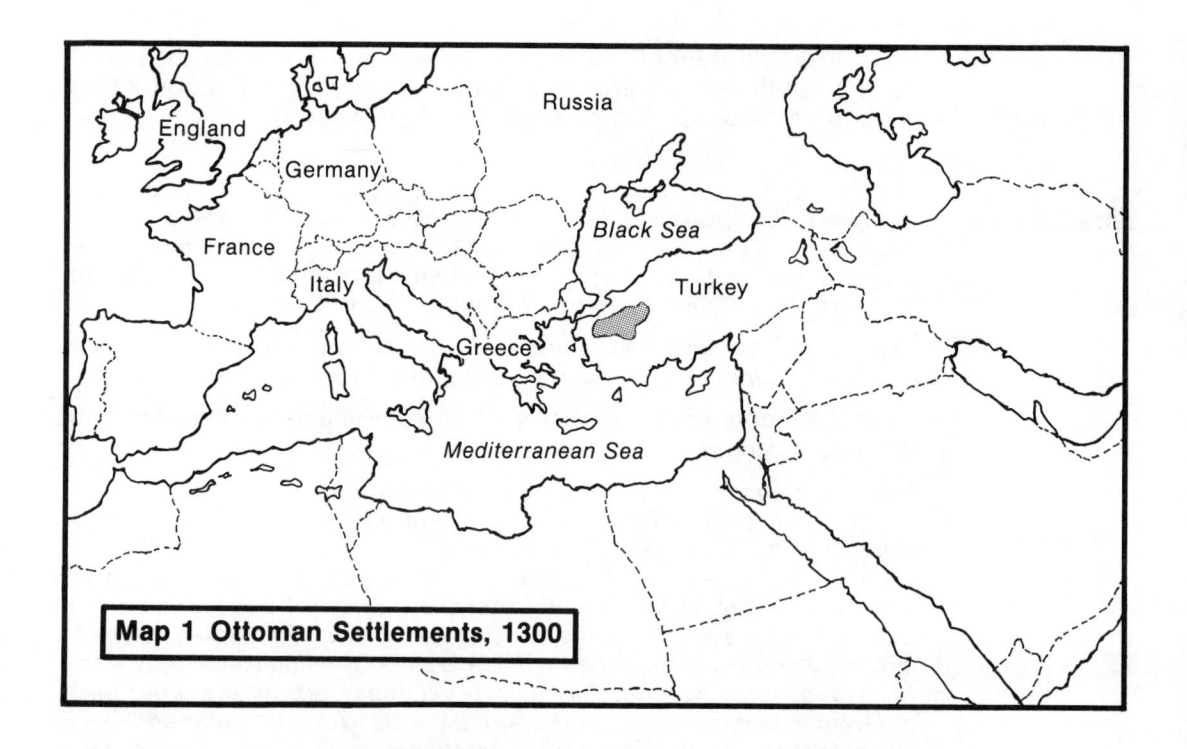

Reading 17 The Ottoman Empire Through the Use of Maps*

The Ottoman Empire existed for about 600 years (from 1453 to the end of World War I). Throughout this history, the Empire was ruled by a succession of Sultans who were descendants of the same family. The Sultan and his government agents ruled over a large area that included many nationalities.

The Sultan was descended from Turks, and Turks were Muslims, since they followed the religion of Islam. Up until the latter part of the 19th century, only Muslims were allowed to hold high government jobs or serve in the military. These positions could be held by a person from any nationality as long as they were converted to Islam. The Turks labeled non-Muslims living in the empire as *rayas*, which translated as "protected flocks or herds."[67]

The sequence of maps on these pages illustrates the growth of the Empire in territory and finally its decline in the 19th century.

MAP 1 The shaded area in Turkey shows where the Ottomans first settled around the year 1300. Ottoman expansion led to the fall of Constantinople in 1453, causing the fall of the Byzantine Empire and the establishment of the Ottoman Empire.

MAP 2 By 1800, the Ottoman Empire had reached its greatest expansion. Size, however, did not necessarily indicate strength. The Ottomans were often at war with various countries, and this drained the economic strength of the Empire.

MAP 3 By 1914, the Ottoman Empire had lost much territory as a result of revolts by peoples such as Serbs, Greeks, and Bulgarians who wanted their own independent countries.

---

*The maps were compiled from information in *The Times Atlas of World History*, Geoffrey Barraclough, ed. (Hammond, Inc., Time Books Ltd., 1970).

The Armenians 349

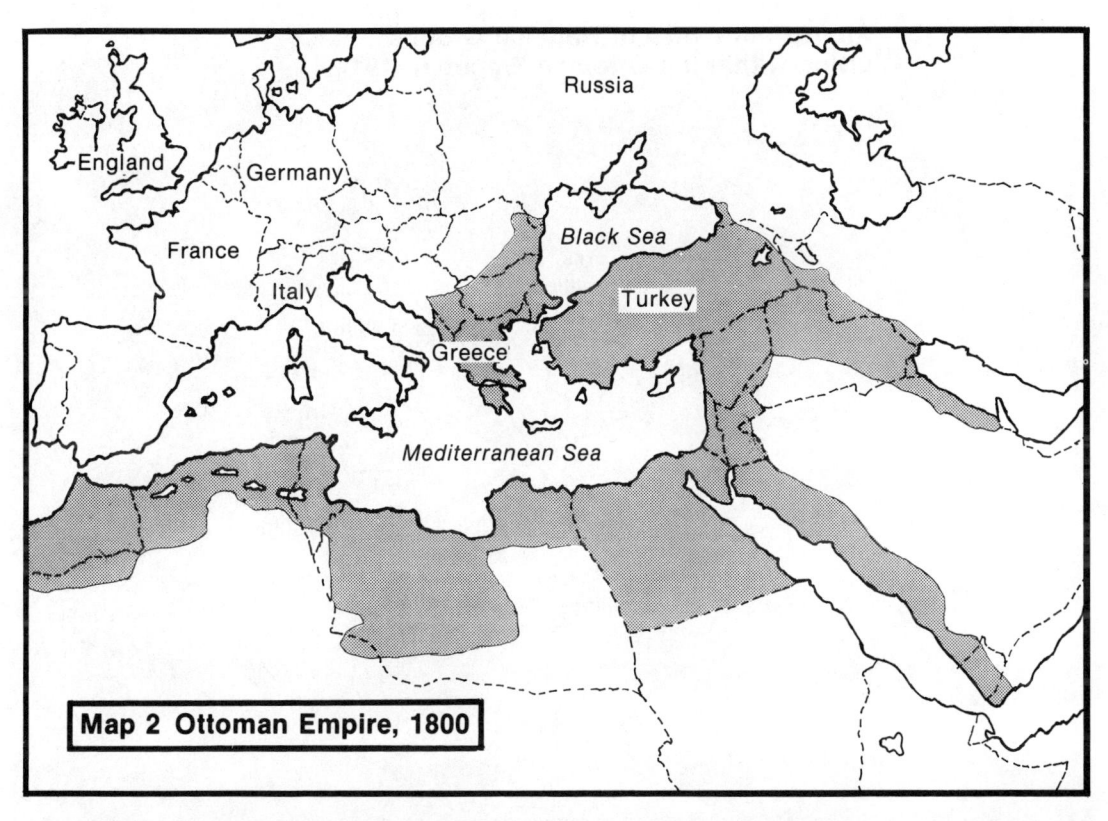

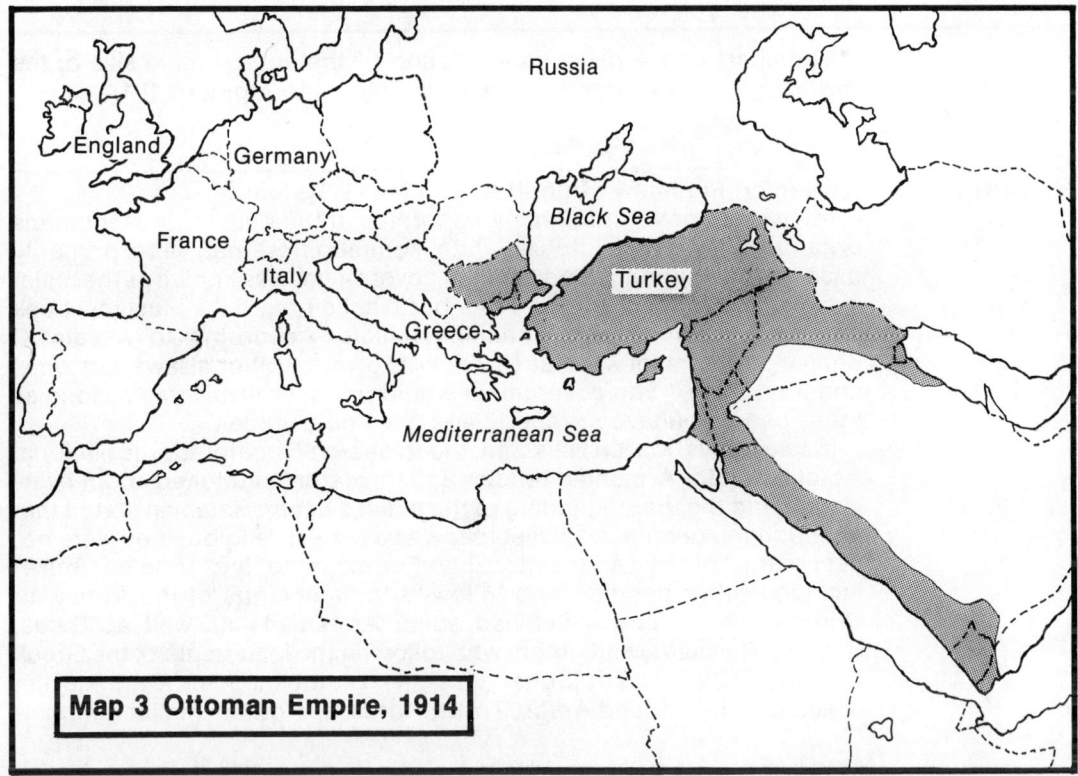

Map 2 Ottoman Empire, 1800

Map 3 Ottoman Empire, 1914

Approximate Size of National Groups Living within the Ottoman Empire in 1914.

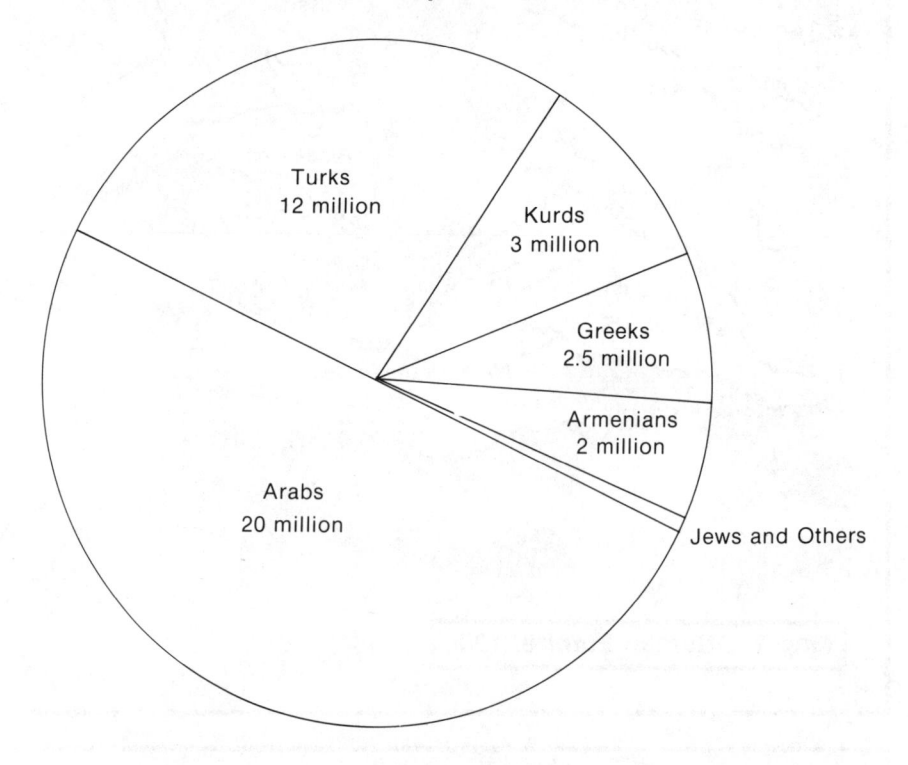

- Turks 12 million
- Kurds 3 million
- Greeks 2.5 million
- Armenians 2 million
- Jews and Others
- Arabs 20 million

The chart above gives an indication of the approximate size of the various groups of peoples within the Ottoman Empire in 1914.*

Reading 18	**Governing the Many Minorities: The Millet System**

In order to govern the many minorities in the empire, the Ottomans organized everyone into separate communities that were primarily based upon religion. This system of government was known as the millet system, and for centuries the four basic millets were the Muslim, Greek Orthodox, Jewish, and Armenian millets. According to Avedis K. Sanjian, each millet was free to follow its own "traditional laws, customs, and way of life." The government would protect the millets, "so long as these people behaved properly and gave no trouble."

In interviews, Martin Halabian, the Research Director for the National Association for Armenian Studies and Research, cautioned about oversimplifying the understanding of the millet system. Halabian stated that although the people in a millet followed a similar religion, they were not necessarily of the same nationality. For example, the Armenian millet included other peoples who followed the teachings of the Armenian Church. The Greek millet had some Armenians as well as Serbs, Bulgars, Russians, and others who followed the leadership of the Greek Orthodox Church. The Sultan was the religious leader of the Muslim millet, which included Arabs, Turks, Kurds, and other smaller national-

*Chart information from Martin Halabian.

ities. In the early years of the Empire Christian boys were taken from their families, brought up as Muslims, and trained for the bureaucracy of the Muslim millet. By the middle of the 19th century, Protestant missionaries from Europe and the United States began to attract individuals who had been expelled from the millets (mostly Armenians), often because they wanted certain religious, economic, or political reforms. The Ottoman government eventually recognized the creation of a Protestant Armenian Millet, which included many of these individuals. A Catholic Eastern Millet was also recognized by the Ottoman government in the 18th century and attracted a variety of groups, including Arabs, Greeks, and Armenians.

Each millet had leaders and councils who were responsible to the demands of the Sultan. The head of the Armenian millet was the Patriarch of the Armenian Church, while the Metropolitan of the Greek Church and the Chief Rabbi of the Jewish faith led their millets. For centuries the Armenian Patriarch had unlimited authority over all the other people within his millet, yet he in turn was subject to the wishes of the Sultan and the Ottomans. The Patriarch had the power to make political as well as religious and economic decisions for the Armenian millet. He organized the collection of taxes and had the authority to arrest people, bring them to court, or place them in jail. His authority was carried out by a small police force, and complaints of injustice were communicated to the Ottoman government through the Patriarch.

According to Halabian, people usually were born within a particular millet. Any person who didn't conform was ostracized and "drummed out," if not penalized or jailed. Since every non-Muslim millet had its own jails, such punishment could be carried out. However, in serious matters that required the death penalty, only the Sultan had the power to take a person's life.

There were reasons for an individual not leaving a millet. A person could not get married unless he or she received a certificate from the Patriarch. The names of all children had to be recorded with the police through the Patriarch, and likewise the Patriarch granted permission for a funeral. The consent of the Patriarch was required in order to receive a passport to travel anywhere in the country. Each year a millet had to pay a fixed tax to the government, and if people left, it meant a heavier burden was placed upon those who remained.[68] A person outside of a millet was like a person without a country and without rights.

Reading 19

Who Were the Armenian People of the Ancient Near East?

Armenians lived in the region of what is now Turkey for about 2500 years before the arrival of the Ottoman Turks. The following timeline indicates important dates in the long history of the Armenian people.

700 B.C. — The beginnings of an Armenian country.
100 B.C. — The greatest expansion of the Armenian country.
300 A.D. — Armenia begins to follow the Christian religion.
400 A.D. — Armenia conflicts with powerful neighbors such as the Roman Empire, and is reduced in size.
800 A.D. — Armenia divides into many small regions ruled by individual princes.
1000 A.D. — Seljuk Turks invade Armenia from the east and many Armenians emigrate west to organize a new country in Cilicia near the Mediterranean Sea.

1300 A.D. — The Ottoman Turks begin to expand throughout the region and Armenians are defeated and become a minority living in the Ottoman Empire.

The area where most Armenians lived has been referred to as the Armenian Plateau, a geographic area elevated like a table above the surrounding areas. The Armenian Plateau was of strategic importance to any army that wanted to control the region; many empires invaded the Plateau because it was

a land of rich natural resources, and an excellent base for military operations against enemies in the surrounding lowlands...The Plateau has served as the arena for countless rivalries and wars, its peoples have been subjected to many foreign lords, and its land has been repeatedly devastated.[69]

Richard Hovannisian writes:

By 1520, most of the Armenian Plateau had been included in the Ottoman realm. In the following decades, thousands of Armenians left the Plateau to settle in Constantinople and the western Anatolian Peninsula, particularly along the seacoasts. There, as interpreters, merchants, artisans, and traders, their importance exceeded their numerical strength. Some reached the higher levels of the administration and enjoyed the company of the reigning sultan. Most Ottoman Armenians, however, lived in the empire's eastern provinces where, from generation to generation, they tilled their fields. Although usually at peace with their Moslem neighbors and subservient to the Ottoman officials, the Armenians, as Christians, could not expect equality. Islamic law included special provisions concerning them, the dhimmi — the protected nonbelievers. In return for the privilege of professing their religion openly, they were required to pay special taxes and to submit to personal and collective limitations. Though some Christians surmounted this inferior status by converting to Islam, most Armenians held tenaciously to their native dialects and religion.[70]

Reading 20

Who Were the Armenians in the Ottoman Empire?

According to Christopher Walker, there are no reliable population statistics of the Ottoman empire. In 1854 a foreign traveler, M.A. Ubicini, estimated that the Armenian population was about 2,400,000. Although Walker agrees that there were some large areas where Armenians were in the majority, he considers Ubicini's estimate to be high. In 1882 the Armenian Patriarch gave a population of 2,660,000, of whom 1,630,000 were from the eastern region of Turkish Armenia. And in 1912 the Armenian Patriarch put the total Armenian population at 2,100,000. The reduction was due to the 1890s massacres and the migration of Armenians across the border into Russia.

... Armenians constituted about one-third of the total population of Turkish Armenia, and ... in an area where all the peoples were minorities, they were the largest...[71]

Walker continues:

Before... 1878, the Armenian population of the empire was made up, broadly speaking, of four fairly distinct groups.

Historic Armenia

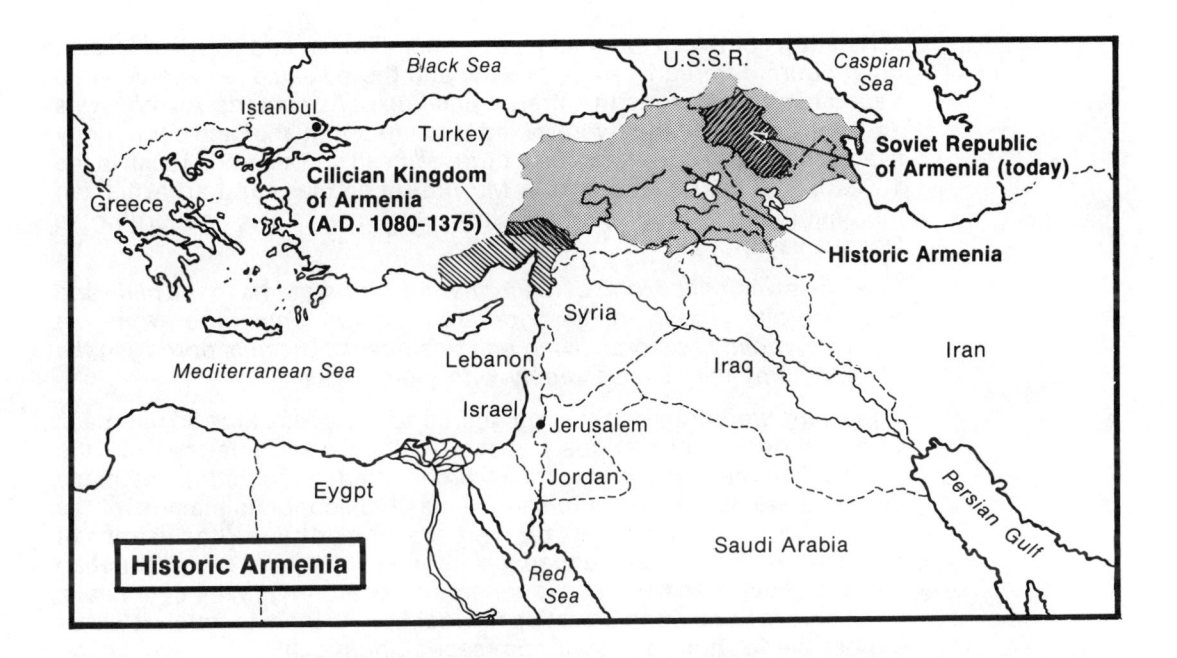

There were the rich men in Constantinople or Smyrna, who sometimes had close ties with the [Sultan]. This class was known as the *amiras*. At this stage they had little or no contact with their fellow nationals in Turkish Armenia, whom they described as *kavaragan*, or provincial.

Secondly, there were the traders and artisans in the towns in the interior of the empire. ...

Thirdly, there were the villagers—the peasantry who made a precarious living out of the soil and from their flocks (and who had done so for at least two millennia past); these men were frequently heavily in debt to local Turks or Kurdish beys. The peasantry are seldom discussed by travellers ... but of all classes they were much the largest. There were many entirely Armenian villages on the plains of Erzerum and Moush...

Finally, there were the mountaineers—men who led a bold, semi-independent existence, untouched by the Ottoman empire and its tax-collectors. These included the inhabitants of Zeitun in Cilicia, and the inhabitants of the Sasun *caza*, a confederation of about 40 Armenian villages. The mountaineers were a hardy breed, tough and independent of spirit. In Zeitun they were masters of their own affairs. ... In Sasun, though paying tribute to local Kurdish beys [lords], they were able to live without the insidious humiliations of the plainsmen. In both places they were armed, manufacturing the weapons themselves. They were un-Ottomanized, and virtually untouched by the central government and its functionaries.

By the nineteenth century, the Armenian population in Turkish Armenia had become heavily intermingled with Kurds and Turks. Taking Turkish Armenia as a whole, the Armenians were outnumbered by the combined populations of Kurds and Turks; but it is unwise to put the latter two peoples together, since their outlooks and aspirations were often very different. ... In some places, such as the province of Van, sources agree that the Armenians constituted a majority over the combined total of the other peoples.

Relations between Armenians and their Turkish and Kurdish Muslim neighbours differed in each locality, and there seems to have been no general pattern beyond the inferior position of Armenians. All the towns and many of the villages were mixed Muslim-Christian. Each community lived in its distinct quarter. The picture of life in and around Moush in the 1860s is, for example, one of a Muslim ruling class and an Armenian merchant and entrepreneurial class. Armenians also, according to Consul Taylor:

form the principal portion of the industrious inhabitants in the plain and near the city, supplying all agricultural labour and trade, while the Muslims, mostly pastoral, living on the slopes of the hills bordering the plain, occupy themselves simply with their flocks.

Muslims were found at the top and bottom places of the social scale, with Armenians precariously (because they were unarmed) in the middle. But merely because they were located in the middle, cautions Taylor, it would be wrong to see them as the economic masters of the land. In Van, for example, Kurds were the monied class, "the usurers of the country." They demanded an interest rate from their Christian debtors of between three and four percent per month. Taylor comments, "... There is hardly one Christian not indebted to them for sums it will be impossible for him to pay without sacrificing his all."

National feeling, in the sense of an awareness of a unity of interest, barely existed among Armenians throughout the empire until the third quarter of the nineteenth century. Thus, the Armenians of Constantinople were involved in struggles from 1830 to 1860 which were in no way related to the oppression of the villagers in the eastern provinces. The condition of the peasantry in the east was virtually forgotten in the capital until the election to the patriarchate in 1869 of Mekertich Khrimian, a leading educator and deep lover of his people. And when, in the 1890s, the Sultan was organizing massacres of Armenians in the east, and was being accused of doing so by the European ambassadors, he could plead his friendship with leading Constantinople Armenians.

Despite the fact that government in imperial Turkey worked against Armenians, whether from the central policies of the Sultan, the traditional oppressions of the pashas, or the bully-boy extortions of the tax-gatherer, the Armenian people themselves made notable contributions to the public life of the empire.

In the provinces, Armenians filled significant if lowly positions in the administration. Typical posts held by them were those of inspector of forestry, municipal engineer, provincial translator, and assistant to the deputy governor. When the telegraph was introduced one frequently found an Armenian managing it. With the spread of elementary health care, Armenians often appeared as doctors and pharmacists. They were present in almost any venture which brought progress and improvement [in the Ottoman Empire].

But it was in the imperial capital that Armenians of the *amira* class distinguished themselves in a wide variety of activities, some of considerable importance in the running of the empire. From 1757 to 1880, with the exception of a thirteen-year gap, the Armenian family of Duzian (or Duzoglu) held the position of superintendent of the Ottoman mint. They dominated the office so completely that the records were kept in Armenian. Most of their employees were Armenian, too. The few factories which were established in the Ottoman empire before the

Crimean war were almost all funded by Armenian capital: and in many cases the factory managers were Armenian. The leading family in this sector was that of Dadian. In 1795 Arakel Dadian was appointed manager of the gunpowder factory at San Stefano; his son Hovhannes became director of the imperial paper mill in 1820, and later established the imperial silk mill at Hereke and an iron smelting foundry at San Stefano. He was also an innovator in small-arms manufacture. Further enterprise was shown by him in establishing a tannery and two broadcloth factories, to mention but a few; a list of all his interests would be lengthy. Another Armenian family, that of Kavafian, built and managed a shipyard in Constantinople.

Armenians did not, however, only hold positions requiring capital and commercial enterprise. Many were organised into trade guilds. At this end of the scale, the stevedores, of whom there were scores in Constantinople, men who used to carry enormous quantities of goods on their backs, were until 1896 almost invariably Armenians.

In a quite different sphere, that of culture, Armenians were also prominent in the nineteenth-century Ottoman capital, and their activities showed the way Turko-Armenian relations might have developed had they not been strangled by despotism and ideology. Armenians shone in two fields, those of architecture and the theatre.... The Balian family dominated Ottoman architecture. The father of this dynasty, and the most distinguished member of it, was Krikor Balian (1764-1831), who was accorded the title "architect of the empire."

The Turkish theatre was founded by an Armenian, one Hagop Vartovian, known to the Turks as "Gullu Agop."[72]

Reading 21   Policies of Discrimination Toward the Armenians

The Ottoman government labeled all Jews and Christians as *dhimmis,* or "tolerated infidels." Dhimmis were required to follow certain laws which did not apply to their Muslim neighbors. The following is a list of some of these discriminatory laws. Many of these laws applied to all non-Muslims, yet because of the focus of this chapter, specific reference has been made to the Armenians:

- Until late in the 19th century, Armenians were not allowed to join the military or hold government jobs.
- Unlike their Muslim neighbors (especially, Kurds, Arabs, and Circassians), they were not allowed to own guns.
- They were not allowed to testify in courts involving Muslims.
- An Armenian would receive the death penalty if he or she murdered a Muslim, but the death penalty did not apply to a Muslim who murdered an Armenian.
- An Armenian man could not marry a Muslim woman, but a Muslim man could marry an Armenian woman. (She would convert to Islam).
- Armenians were often not allowed to ride horses.
- Unlike their Muslim neighbors, Armenians were forced to pay additional taxes. The following represents two examples of these special taxes:

The Kishlak Tax meant that Kurds were given the "right" to live in Armenian homes during the winter months. The Kurds received this "right" by paying Ottoman officials a certain amount of money. The

356 Facing History and Ourselves

Ottoman government did not interfere when Kurds destroyed Armenian homes, robbed them, or murdered members of their families.
The Hospitality Tax required Armenians to provide free food and lodging for government officials for three days a year.[73]

Using Reading 21

Although all Armenians were subject to the discriminatory laws, the hardships the laws caused varied according to the community to which an Armenian belonged or his or her economic status. Armenians living in the capital of Constantinople experienced far less mistreatment than the majority of Armenians who lived in eastern Turkey. Likewise, Armenian businessmen and bankers who dealt with Muslims as well as non-Muslims were often able to avoid the severe hardships that faced Armenian peasants.

Many historians refer to reform movements in the Ottoman government designed to make changes for the Ottoman minorities who suffered along with the Armenians. There were more than 500 appeals from 1856 to 1876 calling attention to the suffering of the Armenians, who, like the Turkish Muslim peasantry, were victims in the 19th century "anarchic conditions" of the Ottoman Empire. These appeals detailed:

...the extortion, robbery, murder, abduction, and rape that had become commonplace in the Armenian provinces. Unable to endure the harsh exploitation, thousands of peasants forsook their native homes, allowing once-fertile fields to revert to wastelands. The appeals called attention to the law-abiding nature of the Armenians and their role as loyal taxpayers and tillers of the soil in contrast with the disloyalty of the nomadic marauders who paid no taxes and devastated the land.[74]

Reading 22

Armenian Schools Influenced the Movement for Reform

Throughout the 19th century, the Ottomans allowed the Armenians to build a network of parochial schools and colleges. Many Armenian intellectuals who graduated from these schools became leaders of the Armenian community and spokesmen for their cause.

Many Armenians who lived outside of Turkey attended European institutions of higher education, and groups inside and outside of Turkey raised money for educating Armenians. For example, Russian Armenians not only contributed money to their own institutions, but to the schools in Turkey as well.

In the 1830's Protestant missionaries from America were setting up schools which attracted some Armenians who wanted to take advantage of the more secular educational opportunities offered by the Protestants both in Turkey and abroad. Prosperous Armenian families also sent their boys to study at universities in the United States, Europe and Russia. Eventually even Turks benefited from the missionary schools and studies in Europe.

Late in the 19th century the Ottoman government became very suspicious of Armenian schools and often closed them down.

Using Reading 22

What might have supported these suspicions? For example, many graduates became leaders in the movement to change Ottoman laws. Russia and the Empire had a long history of conflict, yet some contributions for Armenian schools in Turkey came from Russian Armenians.

Reading 23   The Influence of the Armenian Newspapers and Writers for Reform

Along with the schools, Armenian newspapers and writers helped to influence the community's struggle to gain control of their own lives. Traditionally, the Armenian newspapers and journals had concentrated on religious matters, but in the last half of the 19th century these publications began to publish articles on Armenian history and customs. Editorials began to appear which expressed the struggle for freedom and explored possibilities for autonomy or independence from the Ottoman government.

Khrimian Hairig, aware of the hardships and oppressive conditions of Armenians living in the eastern provinces, educated young men who wanted to participate in the nation's struggle for freedom. His articles not only described the miseries of the Armenians but gave encouragement and sometimes "advocated rebellion against oppression." The following passage is from Khrimian Hairig's journal:

Let us stop crying, let us be courageous, and let us fight ... we are not chickens, we are also men and children of men.... Let us wipe our tears not shed them.... Those that cried, cried and passed on. They were the old. We must follow the new....[75]

Grigor Ardzruni, another writer, published his newspaper in the Caucasian Russian capital of Tiflis near the Turkish border. The following excerpt was written by Ardzruni at the time of the Berlin Treaty in 1878:

If Turkey vanishes from the face of the earth as a nation, the Armenians of Turkey must try every means to join Russia. But, if subjugation is against Russian policies and ideals, the Armenians must try every means not to fall under the exploiting and oppressive hands of the insidious, selfish British.... Then the only thing left for the Armenians of Turkey to do is to strike out for independence and in this situation, too, our only hope is the help of Russia. And for Russia, too, it is better to have a small independent Armenia as a neighbor—always faithful and grateful to Russia—than an insidious, selfish oppressive, and always enemy neighbor like the British.[76]

The poet Rafael Patkanian (pen name—Kamar Katiba), "advocated that the Armenians forget the past and be born again to a new life." He wrote:

My hands, my feet, the chain of slavery ties,
Yet Europe says, "Why do you not arise?
Justice nor freedom shall your portion be;
Bear to the end the doom of slavery!"
Six centuries, drop by drop, the tyrant drains
The last remaining life blood from our veins;
Yet Europe says, "No strength, no power have they,"
And turns from us her scornful face away.[77]

And the novelist Raffi (Hakob Melik-Hakobian), who was born in Persia, was familiar with Armenians living in Russia, Turkey, and Persia: Louise Nalbandian describes Raffi and some of his ideas in the following excerpt:

Raffi believed that man is born free and has a right to remain so. If man is enslaved, he becomes morally weak and intellectually stagnant —and all the more so as his condition is more oppressed. Raffi argued that a free atmosphere was needed for the Armenians to develop to their utmost capacity, and education was essential for arousing the people to the realization of the need for freedom; and since only an educated and informed public could serve the national struggle, a new, enlightened generation must take up the task of spreading education. . . .

He also contended that the Armenians must rely on their own powers and that assistance from foreign countries could not be expected, since the latter had clearly proved that their actions were motivated solely by selfish interests. . . .

Raffi believed that "Patriotism and nationalism are holy duties for every individual and the war for freedom and protection of the fatherland is a holy war."[78]

Using Reading 23

• Notice some of the common themes expressed in the excerpts quoted above.

"We must follow the new"

"educate a generation of young"

"a new enlightened generation must take up the task of spreading education"

"education was essential for arousing the people to the realization of the need for freedom"

"independence"

"must rely on their own powers"

• Could such language have been threatening to any Armenians as well as to the Ottoman government? Why was it appealing to social activists who were determined to end oppression?

• Why was educating the young so important to these reformers?

• Students might think about their own education. What goals do teachers, principals, administrators, parents, and students have for education in our schools today? Is active participation in solving social injustices one of the goals of our schools? Should it be a goal? What kinds of student participation would be appropriate? Not appropriate? How can education be used to oppress people? How can it be used to liberate people?

Reading 24

Armenians Look to Europe to Support Reform and Protection

Russia defeated Turkey in the Russo-Turkish War of 1877-1878. By the terms of the Treaty of San Stefano (Article 16, Russia gained control of the eastern provinces of Turkey. This meant liberation of the Armenians from Turkey in these provinces, but not in the western area of Turkey. Russia also gained control of the water outlets to the Mediterranean Sea.

England, France, and Germany were concerned about the impact of the Treaty of San Stefano, so the powers met in Berlin. Under pressure, Russia signed the Treaty of Berlin, which replaced the Treaty of San Stefano and compelled Russia to return most of its huge territorial gains, especially in the eastern provinces (Article 16).

The Armenians of eastern Turkey were extremely unhappy about the Treaty of Berlin because most of the area in which they lived was once again under Ottoman authority.*

The Armenians had hoped that the European countries would put pressure on the Sultan to change the unfair laws which existed for all Christians living in the Empire. The final agreement at Berlin with regard to the Armenians and other Christian minorities was as follows:

- The Sultan would *promise to protect* the Armenians against attacks by Kurds and Circassians.
- The Sultan would *promise to reform* the discriminatory laws against Christians. Certain European governments would *supervise* the situation to make sure that the Sultan carried out his promises. The Sultan was also to *report his reform* measures to the European governments.

Using Reading 24

Armenians were concerned that without armed protection, they might be used as a scapegoat in a country that had just lost a war.

Christopher Walker concludes that one of the factors which supported the corrupt and economically decaying Ottoman Empire was the major European powers who wanted the Empire to exist. None of the powers was willing to let the Empire's remnants fall into the hands of another competing power. The European countries attempted on many occasions to pressure the Sultan into making reforms and guaranteeing the security of minority groups such as the Armenians. However, the living conditions of minorities within the Empire was relatively unchanged, and the European powers continued to reap economic advantages from their investments in Turkey.[79]

Reading 25

A Minority Is Not Protected from Massacres

Throughout the 19th century, various minorities across Europe and the Middle East rose up and demanded their independence in order to establish their own nation states. As shown by the maps in this chapter, the Ottomans in the 19th century lost considerable territory to peoples such as Serbs, Bulgars, Rumanians, and Greeks, who no longer wanted to remain under Ottoman authority. At times the Ottoman government responded with a policy to massacre an entire community when it felt threatened by rebellious activities.

For example, according to professor Avedis Sanjian, the Christian quarters of the city of Damascus were attacked by Muslims in 1860, resulting in the slaughter of 10,000 people. Many Kurds, Turks, and other Muslim peoples were also abused by Ottoman officials. Yet these minorities were unable to get support from each other. In fact, in certain instances the Sultan was able to make them jealous and suspicious of each other. To create hatred and fear between Armenians and Kurds, the Sultan created in 1891 a fighting force known as the Hamidiye; only Kurds were selected for the Hamidiye. They served to control Armenian

*Information from Martin Halabian.

areas, especially in eastern Turkey. The Hamidiye strove to prevent Kurds and Armenians from cooperating with one another.

As the Ottoman Empire struggled to stay alive, it reacted to real or imagined threats with terrible measures. In the following readings, we learn about the Armenian massacres that were preconditions for the policy of genocide carried out by the Young Turk government in 1915.

Using Reading 25

Discuss and diagram different ways in which a conflict between a minority and a ruling group could be resolved. For example:

ruling group >CONFLICT< minority group

- The ruling group could dominate and control the minority.
- The minority group could dominate and control the ruling group.
- One group could assimilate the other.
- One group could withdraw and migrate.
- Both groups could coexist as neighbors and maintain their own identities.
- One group could eliminate the other.

Students could apply these diagrams to contemporary relations between groups in their neighborhoods or school, or to historical examples such as the treatment of the Native-Americans and the black people in America.

Reading 26

A Question of Survival for the Armenians of the Ottoman Empire

Tracing the history of how the Armenians tried to find protection within the Ottoman Empire includes a careful look at how they used or were used by Turkey's enemy, Russia. Documents published by the Bolshevik government that replaced the Russian Czars revealed "that the Armenians were dupes and pawns in the game of international politics."[80]

Prior to World War I, Czarist Russia and Ottoman Turkey fought in eastern Turkey. Each time Russian troops withdrew from this border region (in 1828, 1877, and 1894) large numbers of Armenians fled from Turkish control. Although the Russian occupations often received "vigorous public enthusiasm," most Armenians in Turkish Armenia did not look to Russia for protection. In fact most Armenian leaders in the Ottoman Empire "considered self-administration within the framework of the Ottoman Empire as the most desirable improvement."[81] However, cooperation with either side often "brought instant reprisal from the other."

However circumspect and correct the Armenian national leadership tried to be, there were actions by individual groups and communities that could and did immediately set off the hostility of the opposing force.[82]

Using Reading 26

Some scholars argue that Armenians were seen as a threat to the Ottoman Empire because some advocated independence; yet other scholars document that the Armenian minority only desired to be autonomous. The impulse behind any activity of the Armenians in relation to the two major forces in eastern Turkey was for protection and survival. Increasingly, however, the Armenians became victimized by the drive for power inside and outside the Ottoman Empire. The late 19th century was a time of horrible massacres for minorities in the Ottoman Empire.

Students should also consider that there is a long history of division of the Armenian people among Czarist Russia, Persia, and Ottoman Turkey. For centuries the Armenians found themselves minorities in powerful imperial countries that were mutually antagonistic. Thus, to be loyal as the clients of one "fatherland" was to be regarded as a threat in the other two countries. Added to this condition was the fact of the "inner diaspora," the Armenians who had relocated in parts of these countries other than those originally their homeland, and the "outer diaspora," those relocated in Europe and elsewhere in the world. Unfortunately for the Armenians, most of their leaders and intellectuals were members of the "inner" or "outer diaspora," making concerted actions extremely difficult.[83]

Some scholars have speculated that critical opportunities for insuring the protection of minorities within the Ottoman Empire were missed. Perhaps the genocide of the Armenian people and the massacres of so many others might have been avoided.

Seventeen years after the Treaty of Berlin, the Sultan had 300,000 Armenians massacred. Thirty years later, in 1909, Armenians were massacred in Adana. Shortly afterwards the Sultan was deposed by the government of Talaat and Enver Pasha, and a new Sultan was enthroned. Under this new leadership between 200,000 and 400,000 Greeks were deported by the Ottoman government to the interior of Turkey, where at least one-quarter of this minority starved.[84] It was also during this period that hundreds of thousands of Armenians were massacred.

Reading 27 Background to the Massacres of the Armenians, 1894-1896

Early in the 19th century the Ottoman Empire had to confront movements from within its empire for independence, and the Empire lost some territory—Greece in 1829, for example. In the late 19th century losing territory to minorities who rebelled or demanded autonomy or independence was linked to a fear of encroaching European powers. Therefore the late 19th century uprisings to gain "liberation" or "protection" were seen as a direct threat to the Empire from within and without.

In the case of the Armenians, who for centuries had been called by the Ottomans the "Sadik Millet," or the "faithful community," the change to being labeled as the enemy and unworthy of protection was a critical precondition to their ultimate victimization in the genocide of 1915.

When Armenian leaders began to demand protection from discrimination, corruption, and violence in the last half of the 19th century, the Ottoman response was tragic.

Although there were activities sponsored and carried out by Armenian revolutionary groups, they had no organized mass support among the Armenians. When there were revolutionary activities, thousands of Armenian people who were nonparticipants were killed by the government and by government-instigated groups in retaliation.

The Armenian groups were not united in order to carry out a revolution. The older generation had developed school systems which produced many revolutionary leaders, yet many older Armenians did not approve of the violent tactics or ideas which were held by some of these young leaders. All Armenians wanted reforms, but most Armenians refused to join the revolutionary factions; in fact, many actively opposed the revolutionists. Most of the Armenian clergymen did not become involved and concerned themselves only with "religious matters."

The massacres of 300,000 Armenians in 1894-1896 were said to be in response to the activities of the Armenian revolutionary groups. But the slaughter of hundreds of thousands of innocent Armenians ordered by the Sultan to punish them for the political activities of minor political groups was a crime against humanity.

Using Reading 27

The following are some events that took place just prior to the widespread massacres of Armenians in 1895:

- *1881-1890:* Small Armenian political groups began to organize. The goals of these groups were varied — some demanded reforms; some encouraged Armenians to defend themselves with arms; others advocated revolution to establish a separate Armenian state within Turkey. The activities of these groups increased Abdul Hamid's mistrust of all Armenians.
- *1891-1892:* Abdul Hamid created a cavalry of Kurds (nomadic Muslims), known as the Hamidiye, for the purpose of terrorizing Christians and especially the Armenian communities of eastern Turkey.
- *1893:* Armenian revolutionaries posted placards in towns (central and western Turkey) encouraging Muslims to revolt against the Sultan.[85]
- *1894:* When the Armenian villagers of Sassun refused to pay an additional "protection tax" to local Kurds, the Kurds requested and received military support from the Ottoman government. After the Armenians were defeated, they were promised amnesty, but instead many were massacred. Diplomats, missionaries, and journalists from Europe and America criticized the Ottoman government. "A European commission of inquiry reported that the remains of Sassun had acted in self-defense, while the Ottoman officials maintained that they were rebels whom it was necessary to suppress."[86]
- *1894:* An Armenian demonstration in the capital of Constantinople demanded reforms and shouted, "Liberty or Death." Police killed many of the protesters, and this was followed by ten days of street violence in which Armenians were slaughtered by local Muslims. The police did not intervene.
- *1894:* The Armenian community of Trebizond was massacred by local tribesmen and Turkish armed forces.[87]

Reading 28

The Massacres of the Armenians, 1894-1896: A Precondition for Genocide

Armenians in the last half of the 19th century adopted a variety of measures to protect themselves from the discrimination and violence which was inflicted upon them. Despite attempts to secure reforms, and despite the promises for protection by Sultan Abdul Hamid II in particular, the situation did not change. The massacres of 1894-1896 were "part of a premeditated Ottoman policy . . ." by the government of Abdul Hamid and his agents:

The evidence of those on the spot suggests overwhelmingly that the government was responsible: the planning and forethought (first the killers went in, then the looters followed, and the whole operation was started and ended by a bugle call) and the participation of troops in the killings—these things show that the government itself was guilty....[88]

Some believe that Abdul Hamid wanted to eliminate the Armenians because he viewed them as a large Christian minority which was an obstacle to his "pan-Islamism," an effort by the Sultan to make Turkey a "rallying point" for all Muslims against the exploitation and domination of Europe and Russia.

In the eyes of the mass of his [Abdul Hamid's] subjects he had reestablished a strong, traditional Islamic regime, freed from foreign interference and influence, which they could understand and respect as their own. In their Sultan-Caliph his people recognized those personal qualities of austerity, sobriety, and piety which as Moslems, inspired by a Puritanical spirit, they were proud to respect....

In the isolation of his capital Abdul Hamid turned all eyes away from the West, as a remote and alien world. Its misguided political views and institutions and actions were sternly ignored by his censored press. His intelligentsia were indoctrinated with a belief in the superior culture of a medieval Islamic past."[89]

As illustrated by the maps of the Ottoman Empire in this chapter, the Ottomans lost considerable territory in the 19th century. Abdul Hamid was determined to make the Turkish peninsula (Anatolia) an Islamic stronghold against non-Islamic countries. He strengthened his contacts with Islamic communities both inside and outside of his borders. Although some government positions were held by Christians and most were given to Turks, Abdul Hamid made a special effort to appoint Muslims from other nationalities as well.[90]

The following excerpts from Lord Kinross indicate that the Ottoman government conducted an official military campaign in 1895 against the Armenians, especially in the region of eastern Turkey:

Their tactics were based on the Sultan's principle of kindling religious fanaticism among the Moslem population. Abdul Hamid briefed agents, whom he sent to Armenia with specific instructions as to how they should act. It became their normal routine first to assemble the Moslem population in the largest mosque in a town, then to declare, in the name of the Sultan, that the Armenians were in general revolt with the aim of striking at Islam. Their Sultan enjoined them as good Moslems to defend their faith against these infidel rebels. He propounded the precept that under the holy law the property of rebels might be looted by believers, encouraging Moslems to enrich themselves in the name of their faith at the expense of their Christian neighbours, and in the event of resistance, to kill them. Hence, throughout Armenia, "the attack of an ever increasing pack of wolves against sheep..."

Each operation, between the bugle calls, followed a similar pattern. First into a town there came the Turkish troops, for the purpose of massacre; then came the Kurdish irregulars and tribesmen for the purpose of plunder. Finally came the holocaust, by fire and destruction, which spread, with the pursuit of fugitives and mopping-up operations, throughout the lands and villages of the surrounding province. This murderous winter of 1895 thus saw the decimation of much of the Armenian population and the devastation of their property in some twenty districts of eastern Turkey. Often the massacres were timed for a Friday, when the Moslems were in their mosques and the myth was spread by the authorities that the Armenians conspired to slaughter them at prayer. Instead they were themselves slaughtered, when the Moslems emerged to forestall their design. The total number of victims was somewhere between fifty and a hundred thousand, allowing for those who died subsequently of wounds, disease, exposure, and starvation.[91]

Most historians suggest that about 300,000 Armenians lost their lives in the Ottoman Empire between 1894 and 1896.

Reading 29   Massacres of Armenians in Adana in 1909

In 1908 there was a revolt by many liberal Turkish leaders and members of the Sultan's army against the Sultan. These "Young Turks" of the Committee of Union and Progress (CUP) promised to bring back the Constitution of 1876 which guaranteed many freedoms and rights for all people living in the Ottoman Empire. They also denounced the corruption and brutality of the Sultan, and gave warning to other countries to stop exploiting their country. It was a time of hope and joy for the majority of people living in the Ottoman Empire.

Exhilarated by assurances of a new era of brotherhood and toleration, Turks, Greeks, Arabs, Jews, and Armenians embraced each other in the streets, in public meetings, in joint thanksgiving services.[92]

Another historian wrote:

There have probably not been many movements in recent history that have exhibited the unrestrained and touching joy that greeted the victory of the Young Turks.... There was literally dancing in the streets. Jew embraced Moslem, Armenian embraced Turk, and an era of good will appeared to be dawning.[93]

Even revolutionary groups such as the Dashnaks and Hunchaks supported the Young Turks. One of the reasons the Young Turks became involved in an overthrow of the Sultan was that they were frustrated by the way he allowed other countries to exploit the Ottoman Empire. They were angry at the control that other countries, especially France, had over the Empire because of large investments of money.

Another factor that contributed to the hostile attitude of the Young Turks toward other countries was the loss of more Ottoman territory between 1908 and 1914. Some areas were simply annexed (taken); other areas declared their independence from the Empire, and some countries went to war and won territory. This breakup of the empire resulted in greater mistrust of non-Turkish groups of people living within Turkey. These Young Turks believed that the Ottoman Empire would be strong and powerful if it operated as a constitutional monarchy with more modern concepts of government.

In 1909 supporters of Abdul Hamid staged a counterrevolt to try and regain control of the country. It was during this time that violence broke out in the city of Adana. According to David Lang,

It is not clear which faction was responsible for the outbreak—the Young Turks or partisans of Abdul Hamid. It is possible that it was simply a spontaneous outbreak of mob violence and Muslim fanaticism. About 30,000 Armenians perished.[94]

Christopher Walker suggests that "Without the local hatreds, the explosion of violence would not have occurred." Walker concludes that local antagonisms between Armenians and Muslims probably had more to do with causing the massacre than the influence of outside agitators.[95] The fact remains that the Young Turks did not take steps to protect the Armenians or to punish those responsible for the massacre.

In Adana, a city in Cilicia,* on March 31, 1909, Turkish armed mobs with the local authorities attacked the Armenian population. When the European ambassadors at Constantinople heard of the massacres they complained to the Sultan, and eight battleships from the governments of Britain, Russia, France, Germany, Italy, and the United States were sent to the area. The following is one description by Avedis Sanjian of the massacres of Adana:

On April 2, by [direct] orders of the Turkish government, the bloodshed at Adana stopped but the mobs spread their atrocities against the defenseless Armenians throughout the province. Moreover, a Turkish battalion of regular troops, brought to Adana [supposedly to restore order], joined hands with the [locally armed men] in completing the destruction and plundering of the town's Armenian population. This second and more violent massacre lasted from the arrival of the troops on April 12 until April 14. The *pogrom* [an organized massacre] in the province of Adana took a toll of about 30,000 Armenian lives, mostly male. Thirty-seven towns and villages, 50 churches and schools, and more than 5,000 houses and shops were destroyed. . . . At Antioch, contrary to the [promises] of the district governor that no harm would come to the Armenians of the city if they surrendered their arms, local Turkish mobs massacred approximately 500, comprising about half the number of the community. When survivors fled to the nearby mountains, their houses and shops were ransacked and burned.

The *atrocities* came to a halt at the end of April, 1909, leaving in their wake the massive task of rehabilitating survivors. In the gigantic effort of feeding, clothing, and housing the thousands of victims, reconstructing homes, [churches, schools, and businesses], the Armenian authorities were [helped by a variety of organizations from other countries] . . . [The Turkish government also provided money and] material assistance in the rehabilitation and economic recovery of the Armenian communities . . . which had suffered most at the hands of the Turks.

[The Young Turks sent a tribunal (military judges) to Adana to judge who was responsible for the massacres]. It soon became apparent, however, that these tribunals were instructed not to apprehend and punish the guilty, but to prove that a [serious] armed rebellion by the Armenians had provoked the violent retaliation of the Turks. In consequence, twelve innocent Armenians . . . received death sentences and 44 were imprisoned. Some 50 Turks received death sentences, but only 20 were actually executed [and the main leaders] were left unpunished.

[Many Turkish politicians criticized the judgment of the tribunal and two separate investigative commissions were sent to the area. Both commission reports agreed that the Armenians arrested were innocent. The names of the actual organizers of the massacres were given to the Turkish government. The government did make an official statement confirming the innocence of the Armenians, but the actual leaders of the massacres were never seriously punished].[96]

---

*Cilicia was heavily populated by Armenians; it was the region of the last Armenian kingdom that fell in 1375 after having given assistance to the Crusaders for decades.

Many people observed the violence at Adana, and their eye-witness accounts have been preserved as a challenge to those who claim the massacres were insignificant. Here are some excerpts from their testimony:

Dr. Herbert Adams Gibbons (author, scholar): I was in Adana (Cilicia) in April, 1909.... Their [Armenian's] blood was spilled before my eyes.... I was with them in different places after the fury of massacre had passed.

David Brewer Eddy (author): Men were hunted in the most horrible manner. Women were forced to watch the death of their husbands and little children while they themselves were reserved for an even worse fate. The murderers would make the most solemn promises of protection, tricking the villagers into giving their arms and then slaughter them in their defenseless condition.... Sailors from British and American warships... said they had never seen anything to compare with the destruction of life and property in this district. From three to five thousand people fell in Adana alone, while something like 20,000 perished in the outside districts. Whole villages were wiped out.

Dr. Fridjtof Nansen (Norwegian explorer and diplomat): Not only did Young Turkish officers and soldiers join in the looting, but the [punishments for these crimes] were a scandal. The known leaders of the massacres went scot-free, while a few murderers chosen at random were hanged—with some Armenians who had resorted to armed resistance in defense of themselves and their families.

Dr. Chambers (director of American Missionaries at Adana): The massacre began all over again furiously on the 12/25 of April, the soldiers and the [local armed men] began a terrible volley of firearms on the Armenian school where around 2,500 persons had taken refuge. When the building caught fire and when the refugees tried to save themselves by running outside they were fired upon; many perished in the flames.... The government [Turkish] help was absolutely insufficient and the measures taken to protect the goods and the persons are entirely ridiculous. A group of soldiers are engaged in plundering.[97]

Using Reading 29

These actions are seen as a precondition to the genocide of 1915. Notice how often the above accounts mention the participation of soldiers in the killings and the lack of government control of the situation in Adana. There is a translation by Haigaz K. Kazarian entitled "Minutes of Secret Meetings Organizing the Turkish Genocide of the Armenians" that does reveal that government leaders planned the massacres. However, an historian, Gwynne Dyer, has challenged the accuracy of this document by suggesting that it "is mostly based on the highly improbable anti-CUP tract written in exile by the opposition Turkish journalist Mevlanzade Rifat."

Reading 30 **A Philosophy of Discrimination: A Precondition for Genocide**

The Young Turks originally promised equality and first-class citizenship to unite all people of the Empire, regardless of religion and nationality. But they began to develop a unique philosophy, one that stressed special Turkish history and a special future. This new philosophy of "Pan-Turkism" was a Turkish racial ideology. Muslims were considered superior to Christians, and Turks deserved a "privileged position" in the Empire over all other nationalities, including the Arab Muslims.

David Lang writes:

The policies of the Young Turk junta were given a veneer of respectability by the adoption of a new ideology known as pan-Turkism or pan-Turanianism. The best-known exponent of this doctrine was Zia Gok Alp (1876-1924). Gok Alp was a devotee of the French sociologist Emile Durkheim (1858-1917) and his published works are notable for their reasonable tone and persuasive style. However, as a close friend of the Interior Minister Talaat Pasha, and a member of the Central Council of the Committee of Union and Progress, Gok Alp carries a heavy burden of responsibility for the Armenian genocide of 1915.

Gok Alp's philosophy was coloured by the Turkish military disasters of the late nineteenth and early twentieth centuries. The Turks had been set upon by Russian, British and Italian imperialists and driven from their ancient dominions in the Balkans, the Mediterranean and North Africa. Therefore the Turks must take refuge in their ancient national traditions, and be proud, instead of being ashamed, of their Turkic ancestry.

It was now the duty of the Turks to "know themselves," to rediscover the soul of the people, which could be done by research into the history and culture of the ancient Turks, and by examining those aspects of Turkish popular culture which faithfully retained their authentic character.

Gok Alp's essays glorified the warlike Turks of old, and described their political and cultural achievements, their extensive pre-Islamic Turkish kingdoms, and the feats of Attila, Jenghiz Khan, Timur, Babur and the early Ottoman sultans. For Gok Alp, the ancient Turks were distinguished by many excellent qualities: hospitality, modesty, courage, and so on. They did not oppress other nations, their god was one of peace, and they eschewed imperialistic ambitions. The great Turkish conquerors sought only to unite the scattered Turkic tribes. The Turks, both in ancient and in modern times, had a worthy mission, namely to realize the highest moral values and to prove that sacrifices and heroic deeds were not beyond human strength.

This fine-sounding programme looks very well on paper. But, in the hands of the Young Turks, who had seized power by terror and assassination, Gok Alp's theories were political dynamite. They could be and were exploited as the basis for a typical master-race ideology, jointly glorifying both ethnic Turkism and the Islamic faith, and consigning non-Turkish non-Muslims like the Greeks and Armenians to exile or extermination.[98]

The Young Turks began to develop a policy of Pan-Turkism which would force all people to become more Turkish. The Turkish language was required for conducting business. Non-Turkish newspapers and clubs were closed, and all groups of people could now be drafted into the army. Some of the Young Turks hoped for an even wider extension of the idea of Pan-Turkism that would eventually include all people of Turkish ancestry living throughout Asia.

Henry Morgenthau's memoirs describe this Pan-Turkish policy:

[*The Young Turks were determined to eliminate Christian schools in Turkey, or at least to change them into Turkish institutions*]. *Similarly, they attempted to make all foreign business houses employ only Turkish* labor, insisting that they should discharge their Greek, Armenian, and Jewish clerks, stenographers, workmen, and other employees. They ordered all foreign houses to keep their books in Turkish; they wanted to furnish employment for Turks, and enable them to acquire modern business methods. The Ottoman Government even refused to have any dealings with the representative of the largest Austrian munition maker unless he admitted a Turk as a partner. They developed a mania for suppressing all languages except Turkish. For decades French had been the accepted language of foreigners in Constantinople; most street signs were printed in both French and Turkish. One morning the astonished foreign residents discovered that all these French signs had been removed and that the names of streets, the directions on street cars, and other public notices, appeared only in those strange Turkish characters, which very few of them understood. Great confusion resulted from this change, but the ruling powers refused to restore the detested foreign language.[99]

As the policy of Pan-Turkism began to develop, stronger measures were taken not only to force people to become more Turkish but to make "Turkey exclusively the country of the Turks." Many non-Turkish people were suspected of being traitors and were arrested and deported (removed) from the country. Individuals who objected to government policies were often executed.[100] As Henry Morgenthau stated:

Indeed, the Greeks were the first victims of this nationalizing idea. I have already described how, in the few months preceding the European War, the Ottoman Government began deporting its Greek subjects along the coast of Asia Minor. These outrages aroused little interest in Europe or the United States, yet in the space of three or four months more than 100,000 Greeks were taken from their age-long homes in the Mediterranean [area] and removed to the Greek Islands and the interior. For the larger part these were [actual] deportations; that is, the Greek inhabitants were actually removed to new places and were not subjected to wholesale massacre. It was probably for the reason that the civilized world did not protest against these deportations that the Turks afterward decided to apply the same methods on a larger scale not only to the Greeks but to the Armenians, Syrians, Nestorians, and others of its subject peoples. In fact, Bedri Bey, the [Chief] of Police at Constantinople, himself, told one of my secretaries that the Turks had expelled the Greeks so successfully that they had decided to apply the same method to all the other races in the empire.[101]

Without the Christian-Armenians and other minorities, the Young Turks could Turkify elements of the empire under their form of nationalism. Enver, the Turkish military leader, dreamed of a Pan-Turanic empire free of all elements who were not pure Turkic. "As long as there were Armenians, foreign intervention, as experienced during the latest episode of the reform question, would pose a constant threat to the sovereignty of Turkey."[102]

Using Reading 30

David Lang comments on the Pan-Turkish movement.

The irony of all this is that the leaders of the Young Turk party were themselves of the most diverse ethnic origins: Talaat Pasha was a Muslim Bulgarian "pomac," while Enver Pasha's mother was Albanian, and he had a Circassian grandmother. The original centre of the movement was Salonika, a city of Greek Macedonia.

> It is also worth noting that the Anatolian Turks generally differ greatly from their distant kinsmen in Turkestan and other Turkic areas of Asia and eastern Europe. Ethnologically, the Anatolian Turk represents the most varied conglomerate imaginable. He is a mixture of decendants of the invading Seljuq Turks, combined with Greeks, Slavs, Kurds, Persians, Armenians, Georgians, Circassians and Arabs; many Turks may be described as barbarized Byzantines and Cappadocians. The pure "Turanian" type has become so effaced that traces of it are rarely seen among the settled population.
>
> Authentic Turkish and Turkmen tribes in Anatolia and Asia Minor tended until recently to live a separate, nomadic existence.... They have never had any interest in or indeed knowledge of theoretical pan-Turkism as a doctrine.[103]

According to Martin Halabian, the Young Turks attempted to persuade the chief religious leader of Islam in Mecca to declare a holy war on the Allies. However, the Islamic leader (who was an Arab) declared his support for the Allies against the Ottoman Empire, and the Arab revolt in the Empire began in 1915.

Reading 31 — The Armenians Are Defined as the Enemy: A Precondition for Genocide

The Armenians were almost a protected minority under the Young Turks, but they became defined as the enemy, a step which can be seen as another precondition for genocide.

By February of 1914, the Ottoman government and European nations had agreed to a plan for the establishment of two Armenian provinces to be supervised by the European nations. Many Armenian leaders supported the plan, which included many of the critical reforms they had requested. "But at this moment of triumph, when the strivings of the nineteenth-century Armenian political mind seemed in large part gratified, when national-cultural autonomy was in sight, all was obliterated with a single stroke." Turkey became involved in the First World War when Turkey attacked Russia in October of 1914. The agreement to create two Armenian provinces was canceled.

The outbreak of the war just as the Armenians were finally legitimizing their place in the world of nations was disastrous. The almost protected minority fell victim to the machinations and decisions of the war, which played a significant role in allowing for the definition of an internal enemy.

> With the Ottoman Empire committed to war, the Turkish Armenian leaders exhorted their people to fulfill every obligation of Ottoman citizenship. Their apprehensions were eased somewhat when Enver Pasha himself praised the valor of the Turkish Armenian soldiers. Such attestations, however, did not forestall the implementation of the [Young Turk's] plan for what was to be the first genocide in modern history.[104]

The case of the Armenians supports the notion that there is a relationship between a policy of genocide and the process by which a particular political party—the Young Turks, in this case—overcomes various kinds of opposition in its rise to power. As it consolidates all power under the one party, it becomes easier to decide and carry out policies of genocide. And during wartime, the deterrents against genocide are reduced because the events become obscured by the activity of war. In war, the act of taking the lives of a minority group—those defined as the alien or the traitor, are justified by the perpetrators (i.e. Nazis and Turks) because they are seen as a threat, the enemy.

The Armenians were considered a threat because the Turkish Empire regarded their demands for reform and autonomy to mean a demand for independence from the Empire. Turkey feared losing its territory at a time of increasing nationalism and European and Russian imperialism. Also, Armenian leaders often relied upon pressure from European countries to support their claims for reform within the Ottoman Empire.

The Ottomans therefore often regarded the Armenians as a foreign ward that could be ravished periodically when her European great-aunts and uncles were not looking."[105]

Although most Armenians maintained a correct attitude vis-a-vis the Ottoman government, it can be asserted with some substantiation that... the sympathy of most Armenians throughout the world was with the Entente, not with the Central Powers. By autumn, 1914, several prominent Ottoman Armenians, including a former member of parliament, had slipped away to the Caucasus to collaborate with Russian military officials. Such acts provided the [Young Turks] with the desired excuse to eradicate the Armenian problem and eliminate the major racial barrier between the... peoples of the Ottoman and Russian empires.[106]

Also during war the perpetrators calculate the cost of each next step against the victims. The awaited response of outrage or help from other nations sometimes comes in the form of censure, which has been no deterrent to acts of genocide. Most often the response of the outside world is silence.

Hovannisian writes that the special calamity of the Armenians was that their tragedy became "merged in the general tragedy of World War I."

The sad truth must be recorded that it was well nigh impossible in 1915 to get worked up about mass tragedy, any kind of mass tragedy, in remote forgotten corners of the earth. The world was at war. Millions were being killed and maimed everywhere.[107]

Using Reading 31

One way a nation rebuilds its natonal identity after a defeat in war is by identifying the new enemy and/or the internal traitor. One way a group can develop its identity is to distinguish itself from others, either by stating what the group represents and advocates or by defining those characteristics that distinguish it from other groups. In other words, if you like what you are, then what you are *not* can be construed as bad, a way of thinking which inevitably leads to prejudice and discrimination, whether adopted by an individual or a nation.

These stages of prejudice and discrimination during times of war can be seen as steps toward dehumanization of a people and a precondition for the taking of lives.

The history of the Holocaust and the Armenian Genocide shows the special relationship of genocide to war. Examine the meaning of the statement that the special calamity of the Armenians was that their tragedy became merged in the general tragedy of World War I.

Reading 32 **War and Genocide**

During a war there are certain conditions that make it easy for nations to ignore genocidal practices. In 1914 the Ottoman Empire became involved in the First World War on the side of Germany and Austria-Hungary. At this time Ambassador Morgenthau recorded the following statement by Talaat Pasha regarding Turkey and the war:

At this moment it is for our interest to side with Germany; if, a month from now, it is our interest to embrace France and England we shall do that just as readily. . . . Russia is our greatest enemy and we are afraid of her. If now, while Germany is attacking Russia, we can give her a good strong kick, and so make her powerless to injure us for some time, it is Turkey's duty to administer that kick!

According to Morgenthau, Talaat told him that

Turkey had decided to side with the Germans and to sink or swim with them. He went again over the familiar grounds, and added that if Germany won — and Talaat said that he was convinced that Germany would win — the Kaiser would get his revenge on Turkey if Turkey had not helped him to obtain this victory. Talaat frankly admitted that fear. . . was driving Turkey into a German alliance. He analyzed the whole situation. . . .[and] said that nations could not afford such emotions as gratitude, or hate, or affection; the only guide to action should be cold-blooded policy.[108]

German military officers often referred to Turkey as the "problem child"; nevertheless, the Germans attempted to build, train, and modernize the Turkish army and economy. German officers practically controlled the entire Turkish military. Many of the Turkish armies were commanded by German officers, yet Enver Pasha and his advisors decided the matters of highest policy. In fact, Enver seemed determined to prove to the Germans that Turkey could carry its weight in the war. Enver and the Germans viewed Turkey's role in the war as basically *defensive*. Its immediate job was to help isolate Russia from its allies.[109]

An important area for combat between Ottoman Turkey and Russia was the border region of the Caucasus Mountains and the eastern provinces of Turkey. This was also the homeland of a large number of Armenians who, if they wanted to remain neutral, would find it impossible in the war-zone area. Since Armenians were drafted into both Ottoman and Russian armies, their tragic dilemma over allegiance was particularly difficult. During the winter of 1914-1915 an entire army under the command of Enver Pasha was destroyed in this region, and Enver accused the Armenians of helping the Russian army to win.

The merchants of the large cities, primarily Christians, faced extreme hardships during these war years, and many of these hardships were inflicted by their own government. The following excerpt from Morgenthau's memoirs describes *requisitioning* (collecting of food and materials) which was ordered by the government in order to support the large Turkish army:

The requisitioning that accompanied the mobilization really amounted to a [complete] looting of the civilian population. The Turks took all the horses, mules, camels, sheep, cows, and other beasts that they could lay their hands on; Enver told me that they had gathered in 150,000 animals. . . . This system of requisitioning, as I shall describe, had the inevitable result of destroying the nation's agriculture, and ultimately led to the starvation of hundreds of thousands of people. But the Turks, like the Germans, thought that the war was [going] to be a very short one, and that they would quickly [recover from the hardships placed upon the peasants. The government also requisitioned materials from merchants and shopmen].

But practically none of these merchants were Moslems; most of them were Christians, though there were a few Jews.... They would enter a retail shop, take practically all the merchandise on the shelves, and give merely a piece of paper in acknowledgment. As the Government had never paid for the supplies which it had taken in the Italian and Balkan wars, the merchants hardly expected that they would ever receive anything for these latest requisitions. Afterward many who ... were politically influential, did recover to the extent of 70 per cent — what became of the remaining 30 percent is not a secret to those who have had experience with Turkish bureaucrats.

Thus for most of the population requisitioning simply meant financial ruin. That the process was merely pillaging is shown by many of the materials which the army took, [supposedly] for the use of the soldiers. Thus the officers seized all the mohair they could find; on occasion they even carried off women's silk stockings, corsets, and baby's slippers... caviar and other delicacies. They demanded blankets from one merchant who was a dealer in women's underwear; because he had no such stock, they seized what he had, and he afterward saw his... goods [in his competitor's shop]. The Turks did the same thing in many other cases. The... system was to take movable property wherever available and convert it into cash; where the money ultimately went I do not know, but that many private fortunes were made I have little doubt. I told Enver that this ruthless method of mobilizing and requisitioning was destroying his country. Misery and starvation soon began to afflict the land. Out of a 4,000,000 adult male population more than 1,500,000 were ultimately enlisted and so about a million families were left without breadwinners, all of them in a condition of extreme destitution. The Turkish Government paid its soldiers 25 cents a month, and gave the families a separation allowance of $1.20 a month. As a result, thousands were dying from lack of food and many more were enfeebled by malnutrition; I believe that the empire has lost a quarter of its Turkish population since the war started. I asked Enver why he permitted his people to be destroyed in this way. But sufferings like these did not distress him. He was much impressed by his success in raising a large army with practically no money — something, he boasted, which no other nation had ever done before. In order to accomplish this, Enver had issued orders which [made] the evasion of military service [the same] as desertion and therefore punishable with the death penalty. He also adopted a scheme by which any Ottoman could obtain exemption by the payment of about $190. Still Enver regarded his accomplishment as a notable one.[110]

Using Reading 32

Once Turkey decided to enter the war, requisitions were necessary to supply and feed a large army which would have to fight Russia, England, and France. In the above reading, Morgenthau described the system of collecting supplies as reckless and unfair. Consider these questions:
• What might have been done to make it a fairer process of requisitioning supplies?

- If we take some of the ideas of Pan-Turkism mentioned earlier, and we connect them with the methods used to requisition supplies—what dangers could this present for Armenians and other non-Muslim peoples living in Turkey at the time?

Reading 33

Armenian Relations with Russia—1914

When war broke out in 1914, Armenians in the Armenian region of the Russian Empire were optimistic that the Ottomans would be defeated and that the Czar would carry out his promise to free the Turkish Armenians. At first the Czar encouraged Armenians to join his war for the liberation of Turkish Armenia, but in 1916 this support was suddenly withdrawn. According to Richard Hovannisian,[111] documents now show that "... Russian postwar plans for Turkish Armenia did not, by any interpretation, include autonomy." Rather, the plan was to annex the region for resettlement by Russian people. Since Russian armies controlled the region by the summer of 1916, Hovannisian states, "there was no longer any need to expend niceties upon the Armenians."

Using Reading 33

The Russian Foreign Minister stated that one of Russia's chief objectives in the war was the "... complete liberation of Armenia from the Turkish yoke."[112] However, this history clearly demonstrates that although Czarist Russia wanted to pacify its various minority groups, it was also suspicious of efforts by minority groups to gain autonomy. A memorandum from the Russian Minister of Agriculture, Krivoshein, to the Russian Foreign Minister Sazonov in March 1915 documents Russian plans for Armenian lands:

The success of our military activities on the Turkish front gives reason to think that, more or less, in the near future, we will have the opportunity to rectify our Caucasian boundary and to round out our possession of Asia Minor and Armenia.

Martin Halabian points out that along with Czarist Russia, England and France made no provisions for Armenian self-rule or national independence. In fact, the three powers signed a secret treaty, the Sykes-Picot treaty, whereby the Ottoman Empire was to be partitioned among them. According to Halabian, that treaty was exclusively a big power "land-grab," without concern for the Armenians and other minorities. Later, provisions were made for the Arab states.

Reading 34

Taking Lives: The Deportations of 1915

In the description of the political, economic, social, and cultural status of Armenians in the Ottoman Empire before 1915, certain preconditions for the ultimate taking of Armenian lives have been identified. This reading describes the early stages of the mass genocide that is documented in Part I of this chapter.

In 1915 deportations of the Armenians began, initially in the name of national security but soon in the name of total annihilation. "People's human rights [were] violated. They [were] robbed of their property. They ... had their goods stolen. Their legitimate aspirations were crushed. They lost their lives." Within a setting of racism, certain people considered unworthy of life were massacred village by village and city by city.

Tens of thousands were sent, barefoot, almost without clothes, through defiles and pathless steppes, into the deserts and the mountains, most of them dying of fatigue, or starvation, or thirst, or from the cruelty of the accompanying guards. The survivors were shot or drowned or axed when they reached their wilderness of desolation. The staggering aspect of the whole inhuman process was its efficiency.[113]

Using Reading 34

Accounts of the Genocide were presented first in this chapter because a background study of the Ottoman Empire, the millet system, and the history of Ottoman Armenians is often so unfamiliar and complex for students and teachers that they avoid studying the Genocide of the Armenian people altogether. When the accounts of the Genocide are studied first, students are provoked to learn about preconditions to the Genocide.

Reading 35

Confronting This History

The history of the genocide of the Armenian people and the Holocaust are events of the 20th century which are ignored or avoided in textbooks and classrooms. Because these events tap very strong emotions in the survivors, and because the prejudices based on hate take a long time to die, these histories are controversial, emotional, and painful. Teachers have found it difficult to teach about racism and the misuse of power.

This curriculum is an attempt to give teachers and students access to difficult history which we believe we have an obligation to confront in order to better prepare for the realities of a very complicated world.

These events are particularly instructive because they yield contemporary lessons about the use and abuse of power and about the rights and responsibilities of human beings for the protection and survival of one another. These are 20th century events, unique and particular in many ways, yet universal in so many others. To face this history, we believe, we must also face ourselves. Pogo said, "We saw the enemy and he is us!"

Using Reading 35

At this point in the curriculum it might be useful to return to the Overview at the beginning of the book and think about why these events are not taught and their lessons are not learned.

In the Republic of Germany today students and teachers are learning about the Holocaust because "it was widely feared that youth would grow up ignorant of their history and vulnerable to Nazi prejudices and to dictatorial philosophies of government."[114]

We find similar sentiments expressed by Professor Frank Stone as he writes why it is important for Turkish youth to be allowed to investigate the history or the Armenian Genocide:

It is particularly important that Turkish youth be allowed to investigate the historic facts of the era that began late in the nineteenth century and led up to the genocide early in the twentieth. I don't suggest this as an attack on the national honor of Turkey, but rather as an investigation of what can result from misguided leadership and a rigid bureaucracy in many nations. Many Turkish youth must find out what socially dysfunc-

tional structures can cause, or risk creating new ones that could lead to another disaster. Frankly, I cannot understand why the present government of the Republic of Turkey perceives itself to have any stake in defending the policies that were implemented during the declining years of the Ottoman Empire or instituted by a new Republican regime that was struggling to establish itself.[115]

The media and press coverage of recent actions of the Armenian Secret Army for the Liberation of Armenia gives publicity to the group who claim to be avenging the massacres of Van in 1915. According to a recent article in *Newsweek,* the radicals want to avenge the massacre, reunite the scattered Armenians, and re-establish an independent Armenia in a lost homeland spreading across the borders of Turkey and the Soviet Union.[116]

Perhaps, if educators had remembered this history, contemporary events regarding some Armenian actions would be different.

Reading 36 **For Many Armenians the Anger and Hate Continues**

Many Armenians today believe that had there been international war crime trials similar to those held at Nuremberg after World War II, then much of the life-long hatred could have been dissipated.

*While the Jews had their Nuremberg and the Asiatic Nations had their Tokyo, where is the international tribunal that will hear, at long last, the Armenian complaint against Turkey for the mother genocide of 1915-1921?**

Charles Baboyan was born in Aintab in 1890. He describes his life-long hate this way:

In my time, more or less, the Armenians and Turks kind of looked at each other as enemies. The Turks started killing instead of protecting them. At the end, the Turks tried to kill all the Armenians. The Armenians even now . . . they demonstrate and I don't blame them. I can never forgive a Turk. All I've seen and all I've heard; all that my family suffered. Most of my family members are killed or drowned. My sister drowned herself not to be subject to the Turks. I feel the same way now. They might be angels but still I don't forgive them.[117]

Using Reading 36

Discuss and define retribution. What justice would have been appropriate to Armenian survivors of the genocide after the 1920s? What justice would be appropriate now?

What argument would students consider fair to give Mr. Baboyan if they didn't agree with his stand on forgiving?

Reading 37 **The Response of a Nation: Turkey**

Since the Genocide, officials, scholars, historians, and witnesses have debated the *intent* of the Ottoman government during the First World War. A full and open examination of Turkish documents and records has not been permitted by the Turkish government.

---

*J.H. Tashjian, *Genocide, the United Nations and the Armenians*, (Boston: The Armenian Committee For the Independence of Armenia, May 1967) p.11; Quoted in Sachar, *The Course of Our Times*, p. 256.

The following excerpts are included to indicate the content of the debates:

• In this excerpt from a paper presented by the Turkish-American Cultural Society of New England (Spring 1971), the Ottoman Empire is defended:

The repression of Armenian insurgency movements in Turkey can in no way be compared to Hitler's planned genocide of the Jews. Hitler's genocide was the result of a racial policy. The Turkish reaction to Armenians was the self-defense of an endangered people. The true historical fact is that the Ottoman Empire was perhaps the most tolerant government of its times of the religion and culture of the peoples under it. . . .

The Turks were faced not only with the loss of most of their homeland, but also with the annihilation of most of the Turkish population in these areas.

Remembering only the Turkish reprisals against the Armenian insurgents without recalling what motivated the Turks brings to my mind one very appropriate example from recent American history: the rest of the world still remembers Hiroshima, while Pearl Harbor is all but forgotten.

• In this excerpt from *The First Turkish Republic,* Richard Robinson views the Armenians as a threat to the Ottoman government:

The Armenian community let it be known that it would not support the Ottoman war effort, and encouraged by President Wilson's principle of self-determination, moved to create an independent Armenian state. To the Ottoman authorities, these activities constituted wartime treason and they reacted violently. Most of the Armenian population was forced to flee and large numbers perished at the hands of the Turks. These Turkish reprisals recharged the racial-religious animosity of the earlier period of Armenian troubles before 1900. Though the fact does not in the least excuse Turkish behavior on this occasion the Turks did consider the Armenian defection as treason, a stab in the back that was all the more painful because of Turkish military reverses. It is also quite clear that the Armenians reciprocated in kind, and many Turks lost their lives violently.[118]

• Marjorie Housepian rebuts Robinson's interpretation:

1. To begin with, there is no evidence, and Robinson's sources offer none, that "the Armenian community let it be known that it would not support the Ottoman war effort."

2. Nor has Robinson studied the deportation routes, which show that Armenians were being uprooted not only from the relatively small area by the Russian border, but also from such vastly dispersed towns and villages as Ismid, a few miles from Constantinople, and Musa Dagh, near the Mediterranean sea, not to mention all the scattered towns in between.

3. [In other writings, Robinson's claims] that "the Russian army drew recruits out of Turkish Anatolia" has not been established, but [he] may be referring to the fact that many male Armenians who escaped into Russia during the genocide subsequently enlisted in the Russian army. Obviously, this was a result, and not a cause, of the exterminations. . . .

4. Since President Wilson did not reveal his principle of self-determination until 1918, it could not have encouraged the Armenians to create anything in 1915. . . .
5. It is true that an independent, and short-lived Armenian state was created in 1920 by the Western powers who signed the Treaty of Sevres. Its creation, however, was again a result, and not a cause, of genocide. If the Armenians were ever guilty of reciprocating in kind, it was while they were defending this state several years after they had experienced genocide. Finally, that the "Armenian population was forced to flee," is merely Dr. Robinson's euphemism for a deliberate uprooting.[119]

Using Reading 37

It is important for students to recognize the tensions which these events still provoke for scholars. Comparing conflicting interpretations, analyzing data, identifying sources, and reading critically before making judgments are the task of the history student. However, to give credence to claims of denial, to reverse history beyond the recognition of its survivors, is not legitimate historical scholarship.

Although we dismiss the book written by Arthur Butz, *The Hoax of the Holocaust*, as inaccurate and ludicrous, and we dismiss those who deny that the genocide of the Armenian people ever happened, we are reminded that denial sometimes gets more publicity and is easier to accept than the tedious search for careful historical scholarship, which demands our active participation in thinking.

Recently a French court found guilty and fined a professor who denied the Holocaust ever happened. Is this an appropriate and effective stand for a court to make in regard to this history? Have students consider the reasons for taking such a stand.

Reading 38

When History Is Avoided—The Lessons Are Denied

It is a sad fact that when history is ignored, the lessons are denied future generations and prevention is not given a real chance.

Frank Stone writes:

Even within the Armenian American community, many people are under- or misinformed. Most other people obtain little information about the Armenian Genocide and much of what they do get is either garbled or very romantic. . . .

An entire way of life was destroyed forever in the seven short years between 1915 and 1922. Nothing that we can do will [restore] it, but places where our children can experience what that lost world was like can and should be created. In others words, lively teaching museums on the world of the pre-genocide Ottoman Armenians must be established. Youth must be able to see what Armenian life was like in a town like Bitlis, Dort Yol, or Harput (Kharpert). They should be able to get insights about Armenian village life, crafts, industries, social customs, and home life. They should be able to explore the Armenian life style in the Ottoman capital city of Istanbul (Constantinople) before the holocaust. This will have to be done either through regional centers or with travelling exhibits so that many people can have the experience.

Certainly, then, we owe it to Armenian children, youth and adults in the Armenian Soviet Socialist Republic and elsewhere in the inner and outer Armenian diaspora to provide accurate information so that they can understand what happened. But, equally, we owe the same type of learning opportunity to Americans of other ethnicities. American Jews, for instance, will be better able to comprehend the holocaust during the Second World War when they know about the Armenian Genocide that took place during World War One. And Americans of other cultural backgrounds should have the opportunity to study what their government did and did not do to intervene when the Armenians were being annihilated. Similarly, British, French, Germans, Greeks, Italians and Russians — to name a few — need Armenian Genocide Studies because their national policies were deeply intermingled with "The Armenian Question" and what was undertaken as its "final solution."[120]

Citations

Chapter 11

1. Paul Tsongas, "Human Rights: Helping the Foes" *Boston Herald American,* May 18, 1981. Reprinted by permission.

2. From a talk by Frank Andrews Stone, Professor of International Education at the Univ. of Conn., entitled, "Armenian Genocide Studies in the International Year of the Child," April 22, 1979.

3. Stone, "Armenian Genocide Studies."

4. From *Armenia: The Survival of a Nation* by Christopher J. Walker. Copyright © 1980 Christopher J. Walker. Reprinted by permission of St. Martin's Press, Inc. pp. 202-203.

7. Ibid., p. 226.

6. Ibid., p. 226.

7. Ibid., p. 230.

8. Henry Morgenthau, *Ambassador Morgenthau's Story* (New Age Publishers, copyright expired 1919) pp. 301-304.

9. From *The Emergence of the Middle East, 1914-1924* by Howard M. Sachar. Copyright © 1969 by Howard M. Sachar. Reprinted by permission of Alfred A. Knopf, Inc. pp. 102-103.

10. Walker, *Armenia: The Survival of a Nation,* p. 215.

11. Ibid., p. 209.

12. From oral history tapes by Bethel Charkoudian, Armenian Library and Museum of Belmont, Mass. (transcribed and edited by Barbara Perry).

13. Walker, *Armenia: The Survival of a Nation,* p. 210.

14. Abridged from pp. 29-31, 48, 60, 65, 72-73, 77, and 95-96 in *The Road From Home* by David Kherdian. Copyright © 1979 by David Kherdian. By permission Greenwillow Books (A Division of William Morrow & Company).

15. Walker, *Armenia: The Survival of a Nation,* information from pp. 203-205.

16. Ibid., p. 207.

[17] From *The Course of Our Times* by Abram L. Sachar. Copyright ©1972 by Abram L. Sachar. Reprinted by permission of Alfred A. Knopf, Inc. p. 253.

[18] Walker, *Armenia: The Survival of a Nation*, pp. 223-225.

[19] Stone, "Armenian Genocide Studies."

[20] Viscount Bryce, *The Treatment of the Armenians in the Ottoman Empire 1915-16*, 2nd ed. (report published in Beirut, 1972).

[21] Arnold Toynbee, *Experiences* (Oxford Archive Press, 1969), pp. 241-242.

[22] Walker, *Armenia: The Survival of a Nation*, pp. 230, 231, 234.

[23] Sachar, *The Course of Our Times*, p. 251.

[24] Walker, *Armenia: The Survival of a Nation*, p. 235.

[25] Stone, "Armenian Genocide Studies."

[26] Aram Andonian, *The Memoirs of Naim Bey* (Armenian Historical Research Association, 1965), pp. x-xi.

[27] Ibid., p. 2.

[28] Ibid., p. 6.

[29] Ibid., pp. 15-16.

[30] Ibid., p. 8.

[31] Ibid., p. 18.

[32] Ibid., p. 52.

[33] Ibid., p. 54.

[34] Ibid., p. 55.

[35] Ibid., pp. 22-23.

[36] Ibid., p. 29.

[37] Ibid., p. 46.

[38] Ibid., p. 49-50.

[39] Ibid., p. 64.

[40] Ibid., p. 60.

[41] Ibid., p. 59.

[42] Ibid., p. 51.

[43] Ibid., p. 64.

[44] Ibid., p. 61.

[45] Ibid., p. 57.

[46] Ibid., p. 67.

[47] Ibid., pp. 68-69.

[48] Richard G. Hovannisian, *Armenia on the Road to Independence, 1918* (University of California Press, 1967), p. 51.

49 Ibid., p. 50.
50 Ibid., p. 51.
51 David Marshall Lang, *The Armenians: A People in Exile*. (George Allen and Unwin, 1981), pp. 35-36.
52 Ibid., p. 34.
53 Hovannisian, *Armenia on the Road to Independence, 1918*, p. 54.
54 Lang, *The Armenians: A People in Exile*, pp. 35-36.
55 Sachar, *The Course of Our Times*, p. 254.
56 Dickran H. Boyajian, *Armenia: The Case for a Forgotten Genocide*, (Educational Book Crafters, 1972) pp. 197-204.
57 Walker, *Armenia: The Survival of a Nation*, p. 230.
58 Ibid., p. 268.
59 Lang, *The Armenians: A People in Exile*, p. 36.
60 Walker, *Armenia: The Survival of a Nation* p. 230.
61 Lang, *The Armenians: A People in Exile*, p. 37.
62 Richard G. Hovannisian, *The Republic of Armenia, Vol. I: 1918-1919* (University of California Press, 1971), pp. 20-21.
63 Ibid., p. 20.
64 Irving Horowitz, *Taking Lives: Genocide and State Power* (Transaction Books, 1980).
65 Lang, *The Armenians: A People in Exile*, p. 37.
66 Kherdian, *The Road From Home*, pp. 29-30.
67 Avedis K. Sanjian, *The Armenian Communities in Syria under Ottoman Dominion*, (Harvard University Press, 1965). Reprinted by permission of Harvard University Press.
68 Ibid.
69 Hovannisian, *Armenia on the Road to Independence, 1918*, p. 2.
70 Ibid., pp. 24-25.
71 Walker, *Armenia: The Survival of a Nation*, pp. 94-98.
72 Ibid.
73 List was compiled from:
Martyrdom and Rebirth (The Lydian Press, 1965), pp. 7-8.
Helen Fein, *Accounting for Genocide: Victims and Survivors of the Holocaust (Free Press, 1979)*, p. 56.
Avedis K. Sanjian, *The Armenian Communities in Syria Under Ottoman Dominion*, p. 274.
74 Richard G. Hovannisian, "Rewriting History," *Ararat*, (Armenian General Benevolent Union of America, Summer 1978).
75 Louise Nalbandian, *The Armenian Revolutionary Movement: The Development of Armenian Political Parties Through the Nineteenth Century* (University of California Press, 1963) p. 54.

76 Ibid., p. 55.
77 Ibid., p. 63.
78 Ibid., pp. 64-65.
79 Walker, *Armenia: The Survival of a Nation*, p. 173.
80 Hovannisian, *Armenia on The Road To Independence, 1918*, p. 58.
81 Hovannisian, *Armenia on The Road to Independence, 1918*, p. 16.
82 Sachar, *The Course of Our Times*.
83 Stone, "Armenian Genocide Studies."
84 Sachar, *The Emergence of the Middle East 1914-1924*, p. 309.
85 Lord Kinross, *The Ottoman Centuries: The Rise and Fall of the Turkish Empire*, (William Morrow & Co., Inc., 1977), pp. 556-557.
86 Hovannisian, *Armenia on the Road to Independence, 1918*, p. 27.
87 Kinross, *The Ottoman Centuries*, p. 558.
88 Walker, *Armenia: The Survival of a Nation*, p. 171.
89 Kinross, *The Ottoman Centuries*, pp. 552-553.
90 Ibid., p. 553.
91 Ibid., pp. 559-560
92 Sachar, *The Emergence of the Middle East*, p. 12.
93 Boyajian, *Armenia: The Case for a Forgotten Genocide*, p. 46.
94 Lang, *The Armenians: A People in Exile*, p. 14.
95 Walker, *Armenia: The Survival of a Nation*, p. 118.
96 Sanjian, *The Armenian Communities in Syria under Ottoman Dominion*, pp. 279-282.
97 Boyajian, *Armenia: The Case for a Forgotten Genocide*, pp. 48-50.
98 Lang, *The Armenians: A People In Exile*, pp. 17-18.
99 Morgenthau, *Ambassador Morgenthau's Story*, p. 285.
100 Sachar, *The Emergence of the Middle East*, pp. 12-13.
101 Morgenthau, *Ambassador Morgenthau's Story*, p. 323.
102 Hovannisian, *Armenia on the Road to Independence, 1918*, p. 54.
103 Lang, *The Armenians: A People In Exile*, pp. 18-19.
104 Hovannisian, *The Republic of Armenia, Vol I*, p. 12.
105 Fein, *Accounting For Genocide*, p. 12.
106 Hovannisian, *Armenia on the Road to Independence, 1918*, p. 42.
107 Ibid.
108 Morgenthau, *Ambassador Morgenthau's Story*, pp. 124-125.
109 Sachar, *The Emergence of the Middle East*, pp. 32-35.
110 Morgenthau, *Ambassador Morgenthau's Story*, pp. 64-66.

[111] Hovannisian, *The Republic of Armenia, Vol. I*, p. 15.

[112] Sachar, *The Course of Our Times*, p. 252.

[113] Source Unknown.

[114] Walter F. Penn, "The Great Evasion: Teaching the Third Reich in Postwar Germany" (Wheeling College Annual, 1980).

[115] Stone, "Armenian Genocide Studies."

[116] John Brecher and Timothy Nater, "France: The Hundred Years' War," *Newsweek,* Oct. 5, 1981.

[117] From oral history tapes, Armenian Library and Museum, Belmont, Mass.

[118] Marjorie Housepian, "The Unremembered Genocide," *A Commentary Report*, The American Jewish Committee, New York.

[119] Ibid.

[120] Stone, "Armenian Genocide Studies."

12 Facing Today and The Future

The unleashed power of the atom has changed everything except our way of thinking.
— Albert Einstein

Overview

Information about the Holocaust and the Armenian Genocide is difficult to learn and impossible to know. Yet students who struggle with this history describe profound changes in their thinking. One student wrote:

I feel as though something I have had all my life has been taken away from me, something that can never be totally restored. I almost feel so awful without it, perhaps it's a form of innocence, a removal of my protective blinders. We all in our struggling humanity have to clutch to our eyeballs to keep out the cold light of despair. Looking at things as they really are is a form of growing up.

But awareness is just the beginning! Now students search for appropriate connections from the past to the present as they think about how they can make a difference in the urgent problems facing the world. Information about food, energy, population, human rights, breakdown of community, and nuclear arms control confront them in some fashion every day. And what they have learned is that to do nothing is a choice not to participate in global survival. "With a little help from us," wrote Alvin Toffler, we could "turn out to be the first truly humane civilization in recorded history."

This curriculum must provide opportunities for students to explore the practical applications of freedom, which they have learned demand a constant struggle with difficult, controversial, and complex issues. The responsibility that citizens have for one another as neighbors and as nations cannot be left to others. This history has taught that there is no one else to confront terrorism, ease the yoke and pain of racism, attack apathy, create and enforce just laws, and wage peace but *us*. Information and experience in the political system can challenge the fear, the propaganda, the training in obedience and the lack of information that discourage active decision making about today and the future.

In this spirit educators can heed the warnings of those 20th century scientists who used their genius for creativity and invention but who left the decision making about the use of their ideas to others. Philip Morrison remembers the heavy weight of responsibility he felt for his part in creating the atomic bomb, which changed the world forever. He wrote, "We each did our own thing and hoped the leadership would know what to do. That was a mistake."

Education has a vital role to play in the shaping of the future. It can go beyond providing opportunities for practicing tolerance for differing views, for learning skills needed to confront complicated and controversial social, economic, and political issues, and for observing models of involved social action. It can help students recognize those pressing concerns of humanity that transcend individual stands, different political parties, and relative values, and that demand dialogue and concern in order to insure our survival.

"It is a lot to ask the human imagination to imagine massive death, collective death, holocaust with the possibility of total annihilation," wrote Robert Lifton. We too recognize that it is hard to accept the discomfort and anxiety that accompany a turning toward awareness; perhaps all we can ask for is a struggle against numbing.

Reading 1

Remembering History

Throughout history human beings have tried to memorialize important events, ideas, and people so that others might be witness to the lessons of the events and remember the participants. It is intriguing just to look around our own city for monuments that we often take for granted. For example, if we lived in Washington, D.C., we would visit the Senate Building and see George Washington dressed in a Roman toga, or Arlington Cemetary monuments built in memory of great leaders. In Rome, a city of monuments, the memorial to Victor Emmanuel stands out.

Often after wars, monuments are built to memorialize a general, a brigade, or a battle. For the Holocaust and Armenian Genocide, buildings, museums, and original art pieces have been constructed as memorials.

A monument is a reminder of a person, an idea, or an event. It can take many shapes: architectural, verbal, sculptural, musical, or combinations of many forms. The authors of this curriculum believe education about these events is an appropriate and powerful living memorial. What do you think?

Consider the following questions as you think about monuments:

• What kind of visual form will be appropriate to express 20th century genocide?
• What form might monuments to the Holocaust or Armenian Genocide take? Should there be separate memorials to each event?
• How can these events, so horrible and difficult to imagine, be expressed, memorialized, or commemorated?
• Can artists portray the hope that mankind will overcome this kind of evil?

Using Reading 1

For many students and teachers the close of this curriculum demands more than traditional classroom endings. As one student approached the last chapter he said, "This can't be the end; we can't just stop talking about this stuff!" For him, as for many others, the end becomes a beginning.

In some classes students use art projects, final journal presentations, slide tapes, and poetry to make personal statements in response to this history. For some these statements remain personal; for others it is important to make them public in some way.

A lesson on monuments can be done in conjunction with an art teacher or as part of classroom activities. In a complete unit on

A student monument, *To a Soldier Thinking About What He Should Do*

monuments, available at the Facing History and Ourselves Resource Center, Barbara Traietti Hearne describes lessons on integrating arts as final projects for students.

Students make monuments to personal and important ideas, persons, and events. Some deal directly with the Holocaust, others are more indirect, and some do not deal with it at all.

This activity allows students to make the connections to what they are studying in a form that allows for sharing on many different levels. Through working with materials—"real stuff"—they are able to clarify and redefine their thoughts and feelings, as they control and manipulate clay, wire, or plaster.

One student's monument was to education. This became important to her after studying the section in social studies about the education of the Nazi child. She said she valued her education much more after that. Another student said he started making a monument to a soldier doing his duty—obeying orders—fighting for his country. After trying many clay heads to fit his clay figure he said his monument changed. The figure looked more as though the soldier were thinking. The whole concept changed for this student through working out ideas in materials. Thinking became more important as he considered what duty meant.

Monuments can take many forms and use many symbols to express what is to be remembered. It is curious to think about those Holocaust survivors who returned to their homes to find them desecrated and destroyed. This "cultural genocide" leaves no trace of the historical roots of a people.

Reading 2

Ongoing Questions

A major theme of this curriculum is that there are no simple solutions to complex questions. It might be helpful to consider whether this study has left you with more questions than answers. List some of the questions you have now and think back to check if these questions were some of the same questions you had at the beginning of this study. Consider if one test of a good curriculum is whether the materials can answer your initial questions.

The following list of ongoing questions may help you to clarify your reasoning at this time.

- What should an individual do in a group society that has gone berserk?
- Does individual responsibility cease in wartime?
- What price must the individual be prepared to pay for his or her moral commitments?
- Is there a personal human morality that transcends obedience to the social, military, or political group?
- Is there such a phenomenon as a "just" war? If so, when does war become "unjust"?
- How does it feel to speak out against injustices when your words create a disturbance of the popular status quo?
- How do you make a decision when your individual moral commitment is in direct conflict with social demands?
- What is meant by the "crime of silence"? What is political apathy?

Using Reading 2

These questions can be used to provoke discussions or as a guide for final essays or papers. Writing projects give the students an opportunity to reflect and clarify relevant and important issues and concepts. In the following excerpt an 8th grade student remembers his encounter with the curriculum:

A long time ago, I sat in a 7th grade class. I was dumb then, or at least that's what I feel now.

Oh, I couldn't wait to see all those movies with these armies blowing up cities and shooting at each other. For some strange reason, I loved watching war movies. I didn't mind watching all those innocent people die in battle. I couldn't wait to see pictures, and learn about different planes, tanks, and battleships.

Yup, that's what I thought I was going to learn during 8th grade social studies. Well, I was wrong, but I won't regret it either, because what I did learn will probably change the way I think, and look out on life for the rest of my life.

Another student remembers the lessons he learned after interviewing his parents for his assignment on education:

I found out that some of my ideas were very different from my parents'. When I thought of why, it was because my thinking was shaped by your ideas, but when I thought harder, I realized that I was getting my ideas from both you, my parents and friends. They weren't ideas, actually it was just trying out other people's ideas, and when I get older, all those other people's ideas will have some way influenced (or the opposite) my own ideas, based on what I think.

Finally, this student makes his connections:

When I saw the first unit, I thought we were going to be taught just another ordinary social studies project, so my goals were to simply get through with passing grades, but after we got into the unit, I discovered that I was a very different person. My mind thought differently when I found out about Hitler's idea of what the perfect person was. It was called the white, blond-haired, blue-eyed Anglo-Saxon Protestant boy. My first thought was, Hey, that's what I am; by Hitler's terms, I must be perfect. Then it sunk in that I am not any different from the other kids in my class, except of course that I am a little smaller, but that by no means makes me perfect or even a little bit better than my Jewish friends. I am beginning to think even now, what they would have done with me, an Anglo-Saxon Protestant who didn't believe in Hitler. Boy, that's weird.

Reading 3 — Confronting Controversy

It is traditional in the United States to argue and debate as people decide which ideas, which political party, and which leader will govern them. The content of these debates usually focuses on the appropriate way to define and live the "good" life, make and enforce laws, and identify and confront problems. People express their ideas and attract support as they appeal to followers and voters in public and private speeches, in magazines and newspapers, and in political campaigns. Often the amount of information available is so great and the techniques and methods used to deliver the messages so sophisticated that the average person finds it difficult to make careful decisions on every issue.

Throughout this book we have recorded the testimony of those who said it was easier to avoid or ignore what was hard to think about. Simple solutions to complex problems were quicker and easier. "No one had time to think. And if we did who wanted to?" remembered one German citizen about the time before the Holocaust.

We need practice in confronting what is hard to think about. We believe that participating in decision-making about difficult and controversial issues gives practice in listening to different opinions, deciphering fact from opinion, confronting emotion and reason, negotiating, and problem-solving. In the political arena, where ideas compete with each other for support, choosing a side ensures against apathy and encourages political participation.

It is instructive to look at examples of controversies that have captured the attention of the American public. One such controversy is the American Civil Liberties Union case against the state of Arkansas. The state's "Balanced Treatment for Creation-Science and Evolution-Science Act" requires that the creation story from the Bible be given equal time whenever evolution is taught. The American Civil Liberties Union says the law violates the First Amendment prohibition against laws that establish religion and that it violates academic freedom. Although the Scopes trial in 1925 presented the American public with a chance to take a side on this same question, the issue has arisen again.

It is interesting to think about why this issue has returned. Certain popular issues re-emerge because they reflect the tensions over conflicting values in a society and appeal to already existing religious, racial, ethnic, and economic divisions. Besides involving arguments about faith and religion; this First Amendment case is made more controversial because a judgment depends on an understanding of sophisticated scientific information about the origins of humankind.

The following statements are indicative of the powerful feelings this debate touches in those who have reflected on the case in public:

• The current support for this law comes out of three forces, wrote Ellen Goodman, a syndicated columnist: "a skepticism about scientific certainty, a continuing unease with the human implications about evolution and a desire to smooth over controversy by allowing two views to be taught 'equally, fairly.' But the problem is that equal is not fair. A fine political solution can be a disastrous educational solution."[1]

• The state of Arkansas contends that creationism is supported by scientific evidence, and it argues that the American Civil Liberties Union is trying to shut out "ideas with which they disagree because they are incompatible with their personal religious or philosophical views."[2]

This is exactly the type of controversy that demands careful consideration, because the outcome of this debate will affect hundreds of school boards' decisions about how science will be taught by teachers and thought about by students.

Another issue that taps strong opinions and emotions and that also touches on ideas of freedom and coercion is debate about the role of the Moral Majority in the United States.

The Moral Majority has taken many public and controversial stands, some of which have been met with vigorous opposition. In many communities in the United States the mere mention of the Moral Majority brings debate. It is just such debate that we feel should be encouraged in public forums so that the meaning for individuals and groups can be openly considered. The name calling and labeling which proponents and opponents of this group have engaged in should indicate the importance of the issues and emotions that the debate touches.

A careful analysis of this popular topic will reveal some of the ideas debated when individuals and groups compete to influence the political process by gathering support for their notion of what is valuable for society.

The first reading is paraphrased from part of a speech to the freshman class at Yale by the President of the University. He discusses freedom and the threats to the values he believes in. In the second excerpt, Jerry Falwell, a Baptist minister who heads the Moral Majority, Inc., describes his beliefs for *Newsweek* magazine.

A. Bartlett Giamatti, President of Yale University

Dr. Giamatti believes that a liberal education is "an education in the root meaning of 'liberal'—'liber'—'free'—the liberty of the mind free to explore itself, to draw itself out, to connect with other minds and spirits in the quest for truth." The goal of such an education is to make a person both flexible and "intellectually discerning," and "to teach us to meet what is new and different with reasoned judgment and humanity."

Freedom must be based on a respect for an external order in the form of laws and the processes of laws, and also an "internalized order that grows with self-government, self-civilizing." There must be order before there can be human freedom. A goal of education should be to explore with students both the responsibilities and pleasures derived from an understanding of the connection between order and freedom.

Dr. Giamatti has specific reasons for discussing a liberal education. One reason is that the ideas provided by such an education are important in our daily lives. Another reason, he believes, is that in America today there are "powerful voices which attack and will continue to attack these very ideas."

A self-proclaimed Moral Majority, and its satellite or client groups, cunning in the use of a native blend of old intimidation and new technology, threaten the values I have named. Angry at change, rigid in the application of chauvinistic slogans, absolutistic in morality, they threaten through political pressure or public denunciation whoever dares to disagree with their authoritarian positions. Using television, direct mail and economic boycott, they would sweep before them anyone who holds a different opinion.[3]

Jerry Falwell, head of the Moral Majority

When liberals first began attacking the Moral Majority, they said we had no right to speak out. When it was pointed out that the liberal agenda was well represented in the 1960s and '70s in the government, in the streets and in liberal churches, the liberals conceded that while we had the right to speak, it was wrong for us to try to "impose" our moral viewpoint on everyone else.

Of course, there was nothing wrong, so far as liberals were concerned, with "imposing" their own views, whether those views had to do with civil rights, the Vietnam War, busing, the eradication of unborn babies through abortion. Liberals could impose their views because liberals were right! And they call us arrogant!

The Moral Majority was founded in June 1979 to address four basic issues. First, we are pro-life. . . . Second, we are pro-traditional family. . . . Third, we are pro-morality. . . . Fourth, we are pro-American, and that means we stand for a strong national defense, believing that freedom is the ultimate moral issue. . . .

To suggest that I am a modern-day Pavlov who, upon ringing my bell, causes millions of Americans to salivate to whatever political tune I am playing is as illogical as it is ludicrous.

The Moral Majority has touched a sensitive nerve in the American people. Many Americans are sick and tired of the way their government has been run. They are tired of being told that their values and beliefs don't matter and that only those values held by government bureaucrats and liberal preachers are worthy of adoption in the area of public policy. Our people are the preciously inactive, turned-off voters who believed that who wins an election doesn't matter. The 1980 election showed that people can make a difference. It is the liberals, not the religious conservatives, who politicized the Gospel.

The Moral Majority is not a Christian or a religious organization (however, as a fundamentalist, I personally object to categorizing fundamentalists as bellicose and anti-intellectual). We are made up of fundamentalists, evangelicals, Roman Catholics, conservative Jews,

Mormons and even persons of no religious belief who share our concerns about the issues we address.

We believe that people can disagree with us and not be relegated to an "immoral minority." We believe a person can be just as good a Catholic, a fundamentalist, a Jew, a Mormon or whatever, and disagree with us or all our issues.

We do not endorse political candidates, nor do we have a "hit list." We do not judge the quality of a person's relationship to God based on his or her voting record.

The Founding Fathers, contrary to what our liberal friends believe, wanted to preserve and encourage the church, not to restrict it or its influence. For them, the separation of church and state was a check on the *government*, not the church. The First Amendment prohibits the government from establishing a church (as had been done in England). It does not prohibit the churches from doing anything, except collecting taxes. Any person who suggests that separation of church and state requires more than this—that it requires churches to remain silent on "political issues" or preachers to be neutral on candidates or religious organizations to pursue only "spiritual goals"—is simply grinding his own ax rather than reading the law.

Let's remember that all law is the imposition of someone's morality to the exclusion of someone else's morality. We have laws against murder, rape, incest, cannibalism and stealing. No doubt, there are murderers, rapists, practitioners of incest, cannibals and thieves who are upset that their "rights" have been denied. But in order to provide for the common defense and promote the general welfare, it was deemed necessary to pass such laws. . . .

There is something worse than war, and worse even than speaking out. It is silence! The grossest immorality has been perpetuated not by those who carried it out, but by those who remained silent and did nothing. We may not always be right, but we will never stand accused of doing nothing.[4]

Using Reading 3

Help students to analyze the content of the issues, identify the major themes and claims, take the perspectives of the two speakers, and define the tools and processes by which ideas can be delivered. Consider also the intensity and dedication with which individuals and groups give their messages.

In these readings students can begin to identify the beliefs, attitudes, values, and skills of some of those who provide the ideas for public controversy. Hopefully, as students become familiar with the nature of controversy, they will become tolerant of differing ideas and willing to participate in the political system which expects debate. Understanding the concepts of political decision-makers, the process of political decision-making, the nature of political institutions, and the culture of a people is necessary for responsible, active, and effective citizenship.

Recently, the American Civil Liberties Union reported a growing attack on the Bill of Rights in America. Certainly this reading reflects on the vitality of First Amendment issues, since the protections they guarantee are continuously tested by those who take a stand for what they believe.

It might be useful to ask students to write down their own definition of *moral majority* before class discussion. Identifying the many responses that the label stimulates calls for class structure. Modeling a discussion that is certain to identify and produce controversy is a critical task for the teacher. Since the subject touches emotions so quickly, the class might be challenged to agree on an appropriate approach to discussing controversial issues. Remember, the history teaches us, it is easier to avoid and ignore what is hard to think about. This history tells us again and again how hard it was to think and how difficult it was to say what one believed for fear of ridicule, or later for fear of losing one's job, family, and life. Practicing debate *now* should be easy if one considers the consequences of waiting until it is too late.

Reading 4

Forming Consensus

Throughout history there are examples of times when an issue emerges that captures the allegiance of groups who traditionally are of opposing views. The rising issue overrides the parochial concerns of separate political parties, one-issue groups, individual lobby groups, and fringe groups, and what emerges is a movement, a consensus, around what has become a universal concern. The history of the end of the American involvement in the war in Vietnam is an example of such a movement.

A more recent example of a consensus growing around an issue has been concern over the role of arms control in avoiding a nuclear disaster.

Examining the arguments of those who want to avoid nuclear war reveals a variety of approaches to the use of nuclear weapons. For example, President Ronald Reagan, in a speech about nuclear weapons, said that nuclear war is evil in itself and that the goal is to limit the deploying, developing, and testing of nuclear weapons. He believes that it is a great achievement that the world has avoided using nuclear weapons in warfare for thirty-six years.

Eugene Rostow, former director of the Arms Control and Disarmament Agency in the United States, believes that all wars are potential nuclear wars and that unless the Soviet Union stops risking wars with each new expansion, no treaty will be meaningful. He argues that arms control is not effective. These arguments are capturing the attention of the world.

The debate about arms control agreements is complex and worthy of careful consideration.

Using Reading 4

As people debate the use of nuclear technology, they took many sides over the issues raised by the morality of military research, the test ban treaties, arms build-up, deterrence, and potential for total annihilation.

Consider the following statements indicative of the debate over the morality of working on military weapons today. Richard Ellis wrote in a letter to the editor of *The Boston Globe*:

I used to wonder how people in Germany under the Third Reich could have worked over drawing boards and in factories producing gas chambers and incinerators for the death camps.

Now I wonder, with what morality, this democracy, with congressional approval and public funding, proceeds to design and manufacture nuclear bombs capable of incinerating millions of civilians, their homes and their children, in one instantaneous flash.[5]

But Dr. John Browne of the nuclear weapon facility at Los Alamos wrote:

We need good people in weapons work because it is a national policy that nuclear weapons will be used as a deterrent. Most scientists... find the technological problems posed by nuclear weapons challenging... quite different from normal physics.

Questions about the use and abuse of nuclear technologies are subject for debate and decision-making for students and adults.

Reading 5

Making Connections About the Future

Students in this study have made connections from the Holocaust history to important issues in their lives by borrowing metaphors from the nuclear world. For example, one student describes those who encouraged Nazism in their children this way: "That's like dropping an atomic bomb; you may drop it now, but in 30 years the effects of the radiation are still lethal."

Curiously, the leadership of the movement against the nuclear arms race also borrows terms used to describe Holocaust events, in order to help pierce the wall of "psychic numbing" which they believe keeps people from confronting the potential dangers of nuclear disaster. The leap in the imagination, which some of the events of the Holocaust provoke, forces some recognition about the unprecedented nature of such impending horror.

After the Holocaust and with the dropping of the atomic bomb on Hiroshima, humanity learned that it could exterminate a species by its own technology. "After the Nazi death camps and Hiroshima, the imagery of mass extinction became the property of common man and woman but this imagery," according to Robert Lifton, "has not today been confronted because the anticipation of a still greater Holocaust is too painful!"*

---

*From "The Threat of Nuclear War: Biological, Psychological, and Social Dimensions," a talk delivered at Harvard Medical School, December 1981.

Using Reading 5

Although the history of the Holocaust does share certain basic principles with a study of potential nuclear holocaust, it should not be used to draw too strong parallels.

Yet one distinction developed for this curriculum, the distinction between coping with horrible information and the new thinking and vocabulary needed for confronting such horrible events, is useful as we attempt to understand the world of nuclear weapons today.

It is important to note that the explanations educators give for perpetuating the silence about nuclear issues are the same as those given for avoiding a confrontation with the Holocaust; the subject is too painful, too controversial, too emotional, and therefore too easily mistaught. Teachers used to having the right answers for students or simple explanations for complex questions find the methodology and content needed to teach this material challenging to their traditional teaching methods and authoritarian role, and therefore difficult to attempt. However, despite initial misgivings, most teachers have welcomed information and classroom-tested materials. They have attempted to struggle with the issues because *not* to confront them is a dangerous and impossible choice. The danger is to enlist students in the political campaigns of the teacher. The history teaches how easy it is to march in formation without thinking.

Reading 6

Should Children Be Educated About Nuclear War?

In October 1981, Ellen Goodman, a columnist for *The Boston Globe*, wrote that two out of three adults believe there will be another war in the next few years. She wrote:

This season, I know very few people who think Russians or Americans can win a nuclear war. But I know many who fear we could wage one. "We are living," said Eugene Rostow, "in a pre-war and not a post-war world...."

It's always hard to think about the unthinkable. It's hard even to give up the sense of fate and exchange it for struggle.

But if 68 percent of us expect the worst without fighting it, we will also be responsible for the worst.

We will end up helping to fulfill Einstein's worst prophecy: "The splitting of the atom has changed everything save man's mode of thinking.... Thus we drift toward unparalleled catastrophy....[6]

Using Reading 6

Some educators have begun to argue that continued adult denial of the information regarding potential nuclear annihilation is harmful to our students. Medical and psychiatric reports* document that students know a lot about their nuclear world but have few adults to turn to for more understanding and for models of direct action. The fear of "futurelessness," a lack of expectations for the future, the search for easy, simple sanctuaries are all notions reflected in students' thinking today, and these facts present an immediate and crucial challenge to their teachers. (Lifton suggests that we must revitalize our professions in order to confront and address the ultimate human threat, and he recognizes teaching and learning as a form of action.) Students who express a negative and hopeless quality about the nuclear world find it increasingly difficult to trust the adults who are supposed to be the protectors of the permanence of the world. Students can choose between turning to cynicism about the political process or following role models who are participating in the dialogue about universal priorities—but only if their teachers help them become aware of the nuclear threat of survival and teach them how to make a difference.

Consider Jacob Bronowski's plea for informed decision-makers:

And we are really here on a wonderful threshold of knowledge. Knowledge is not a looseleaf notebook of facts. Above all, it is a responsibility for the integrity of what we are, primarily what we are as ethical creatures. You cannot possibly maintain that informed integrity if you let other people run the world for you while you yourself continue to live out of a ragbag of morals that come from past beliefs. That is really crucial today.[7]

In this chapter students confront the complexities of the decision-making around nuclear issues and define the motivations and reasoning given by the various participants affecting the use and abuse of nuclear technology. At the same time, they learn about a variety of perspectives while practicing dialogue with conflicting ideas and motives. The curriculum emphasizes decision-making in times of peace and war and demands that students carefully evaluate evidence and recognize the dimensions of a particular decision. Every lesson is based on the belief that there are not simple solutions to complex problems.

Teachers report that students come to class with anxiety, misinformation, and a deeply personal and profound concern for understanding the information coming to them from the media and rumor. This project has been challenged to aid teachers and students to understand the complexities of national affairs so that they may participate knowledgeably and responsibly in world affairs. In order for a democracy to work, the citizenry must be informed and empowered. In order to practice prevention, it is important to let children know the truth about war, and the people behind it—not in propaganda or tricks but by straight forward truth.

Activity 7

Film: *Machine*

Since questions of taking a stand increasingly involve a judgment about facing today and the future in regard to technology and science, it is important to focus attention on who is responsible for what science creates.

The animated film *Machine* views the history of "man in relation to an idea which results in an invention which after time and with new adaptions comes to dominate and finally take over the inventor." The following quotations should help focus discussion on the issue of who is responsible for an idea and for the invention.

It is up to the scientist to create and invent. It is society's role not ours to monitor the use or judge its acceptability.
—Edward Teller

Is it true that the concepts of science and those of ethics and values belong to different worlds? I do not believe so.
— Jacob Bronowski

Using Activity 7

Machine, a film of powerful images and many messages, demands more than one viewing.

It is appropriate to remember that an introduction to the use and abuse of technology must be balanced, in order that students not retreat to a negative view of invention in which all science and scientists become suspect.

A discussion about the relationship of ethics and science might be appropriate here. Consider Jacques Ellul's statements about technology's effect on human behavior in his book *The Technological System*. He wrote that technology is independent of political, moral, and economic influences and that human beings in the technological system tend to behave more and more like the components of a system. "... The technician does not tolerate any insertion of morality in his work," wrote Ellul.

After viewing *Machine,* a student wrote:

I keep waiting for somebody to take control and be in charge of things. Like when something happens at school I hope a teacher will come out and break it up. Sometimes I think about a nuclear war and wish somebody with all the answers could take care of it and keep it from happening. It's depressing to think that we're the net in the movie. Am I supposed to do something? I think about the people who stood by and let the Holocaust happen and I wonder what we're all doing now .... Maybe if everyone would talk more like we do in this class we would get the energy and courage to do something.

Reading 8

A Scientists' Petition Before Hiroshima

Before the first atom bomb was finished, it was learned that Germany was not close to developing a bomb, as rumored, and that Japan was weakening. Several of the scientists working on the Manhattan Project considered alternatives for preventing what they described as their "monstrous brainchild from being unleashed upon the world."

The atomic scientists discussed the problem at all the project's installations, but the chief center of agitation was at the University of Chicago Laboratory. There, on June 11, 1945, seven scientists of the Committee of Social and Political Implications, headed by Nobel Prize winner James Franck, produced the following celebrated protest statement. Noteworthy among its signers was Leo Szilard, the man who, with Einstein, had fathered the whole project. Franck went to Washington to present the petition to the Secretary of War, Stimson, but Stimson was out of town and the petition was left with one of his assistants.

The scientists on this Project do not presume to speak authoritatively on problems of national and international policy. However, we found ourselves, by the force of events, during the last five years, in the position of a small group of citizens cognizant of a grave danger for the safety of this country as well as for the future of all the other nations, of which the rest of mankind is unaware. ... We believe that our acquaintance with the scientific elements of the situation and prolonged pre-occupation with its world-wide political implications, imposes on us the obligation to offer ... some suggestions. ...

> One possible way to introduce nuclear weapons to one [sic] world—which may particularly appeal to those who consider nuclear bombs primarily as a secret weapon developed to help win the present war—is to use them without warning on selected objects in Japan....
>
> Russia, and even allied countries which bear less mistrust of our ways and intentions, as well as neutral countries may be deeply shocked by this step. It may be very difficult to persuade the world that a nation which was capable of secretly preparing and suddenly releasing a new weapon, as indiscriminate as the rocket bomb and a thousand times more destructive, is to be trusted in its proclaimed desire of having such weapons abolished by international agreement. We have large accumulations of poison gas, but do not use them, and recent polls have shown that public opinion in the country would disapprove of such a use even if it would accelerate the winning of the Far Eastern War.... [It] is not at all certain that American public opinion, if it could be enlightened as to the effect of atomic explosives, would approve of our own country being the first to introduce such an indiscriminate method of wholesale destruction of civilian life.
>
> Thus . . . the military advantages and the saving of American lives achieved by the sudden use of atomic bombs against Japan may be outweighed by the ensuing loss of confidence and by a wave of horror and repulsion sweeping over the rest of the world and perhaps even dividing public opinion at home.
>
> From this point of view, a demonstration of the new weapon might best be made, before the eyes of representatives of all the United Nations, on the desert or a barren island. The best possible atmosphere for the achievement of an international agreement could be achieved if America could say to the world, "You see what sort of weapon we had but did not use. We are ready to renounce its use in the future if other nations join us in this renunciation and agree to the establishment of an efficient international control."
>
> After such a demonstration the weapon might perhaps be used against Japan if the sanction of the United Nations (and of public opinion at home) were obtained, perhaps after a preliminary ultimatum to Japan to surrender or at least to evacuate certain regions as an alternative to their total destruction. This may sound fantastic, but in nuclear weapons we have something entirely new in order of magnitude of destructive power....
>
> Nuclear bombs cannot possibly remain a "secret weapon" at the exclusive disposal of this country for more than a few years. The scientific facts on which their construction is based is well known to scientists of other countries. Unless an effective international control of nuclear explosives is instituted, a race for nuclear armaments is certain to ensue following the first revelation of our possession of nuclear weapons to the world. Within ten years other countries may have nuclear bombs, each of which weighing less than a ton, could destroy an urban area of more than ten square miles. In the war to which such an armaments race is likely to lead, the United States, with its agglomeration of population and industry in comparatively few metropolitan districts, will be at a disadvantage compared to nations whose population and industry are scattered over large areas.[8]

On June 16, 1945, Leo Szilard, fearful that the scientists were still not being heard, wrote a letter directly to President Truman and went to

Washington to urge personally that the use of the bomb be blocked. He circulated petitions requesting that the atomic bomb should not be used in World War II.

A petition addressed to the President carrying a majority of the scientists' signatures read:

We respectfully petition that the use of atomic bombs, particularly against cities, be sanctioned by you as Chief Executive only under the following conditions:

Opportunity has been given to the Japanese to surrender on terms assuring them the possibility of peaceful development in their homeland.

Convincing warnings have been given that refusal to surrender will be followed by the use of a new weapon.

Responsibility for the use of the atomic bombs is shared with our allies.[9]

Less than two months later the United States used the first atomic bomb on Hiroshima. Subtle and complex international relations played a part in the decision to use the atomic bomb. Using the second atomic bomb on the city of Nagasaki raised ethical dilemmas still being debated by scientists and the American public.

Using Reading 8

Since Leo Szilard was relatively unknown, he had used Einstein's name to promote the construction of a nuclear weapon:

Einstein agreed, although he confessed relative ignorance about nuclear chain reactions. Szilard wrote a draft and presented it to him for his signature on August 2. It spoke of the "vast amounts of power and large quantities of new radiumlike elements (that) would be generated" by a nuclear chain reaction set off in a large chunk of uranium.

The message finally went to Roosevelt. Later, Einstein did write and sign two follow-up messages which, together with the first, led to the 1942 formation of the Manhattan Project, which developed the bombs dropped on Japan in 1945. Szilard was one of the project's guiding forces; Einstein had nothing whatsoever to do with it. "I ... only acted as a mailbox," Einstein later wrote. "They brought me a finished letter, and I simply mailed it."[10]

A curriculum about decision-making in a nuclear age can give students a chance to make judgments about today and their future, within the context of recent 20th century history. And, perhaps with study about nuclear history, students will understand what Jacob Bronowski, the author of The Ascent of Man, felt when he first visited Nagasaki in 1945. There he met abruptly what he calls the "Universal Moment—the experience of mankind." He wrote:

On an evening like that evening—sometime in 1945—each of us in his own way learned that his imagination had been dwarfed. We looked up and saw the power of which we had been proud loom over us like the ruins of Nagasaki.

Reading 9 A Debate About Budget Priorities

In the United States, political decision-makers have been actively debating aspects of the nuclear weapons race in the Congress. These debates over the costs to society of increased military budgets have not centered only on the dangers of nuclear technologies.

Decisions concerning nuclear matters in Europe are traditionally discussed in a tight elite circle of scholars and officials, and not widely shared with parliamentarians or the public.[11]

Reading 10 What Can One Person Do To Affect Decision-Making?

If we listen attentively, we shall hear amid the roar of nations and empires, the faint fluttering of wing. The gentle stirring of life and hope. Some say this hope lies in a nation, others in a man. I believe rather, that it is awakened, revised, nourished by millions of solitary individuals whose deeds and words everyday negate frontiers and the crudest implications of history.
—Albert Camus

People in the United States, Europe, and the Soviet Union have coalesced around the theme that there is now a growing threat of nuclear war. The leadership of these groups have chosen a variety of ways to express their anxiety and to mobilize public opinion. Their hope for consensus depends greatly on their ability to help others understand that nuclear holocaust transcends politics. Individuals active and effective in the debate about nuclear arms control do not advocate the same approach to resolving the difficult problems.

Using Reading 10

As students consider how to make a difference, it is important to think about the effect of isolation, which we have learned can be a precondition of totalitarian terror. Feelings of loneliness and uprootedness come because people are seen as superfluous in the modern world. "Terror can rule absolutely only over men and women who are isolated against each other."

Hans Morganthau said:

I aspired to understand the riddle of human existence, and I expected academic philosophy to show me the way; but academic philosophy did not do what I expected it to do. We expect the oracle to give us a clear-cut answer. What we get is an enigma compounding the riddle. What remains is a searching mind, conscious of itself and of the world, seeing, hearing, feeling, thinking, and speaking—seeking ultimate reality beyond illusion.

The following are student responses to lessons about decision-making in a nuclear age.

I think I will make a difference. Thinking has made me be more human if you can get more human. By that I mean being able to do something in the world not just vegetate. I'm joining a group now to see if I can help. Isn't that what education is—putting your learning to use?
—a student

Many groups have emerged in response to the issues of the nuclear world of today. Some students might be interested in contacting these groups and exploring their potential for making a difference. A partial list of citizen participation groups is available from the Resource Center.

"We are counting on your generation," said Leonard Bernstein, "to make a difference."

Citations

Chapter 12

[1] Ellen Goodman, "Equal Time in the Classroom," *The Boston Globe*, December 10, 1981, © 1981, The Boston Globe Newspaper Company/Washington Post Writers Group, reprinted with permission. p. 39.

[2] "Creationists Misapply Theory Court Told," *The Boston Globe*, December 10, 1981, p. 28.

[3] A. Bartlett Giamatti, "It Poses a Threat to All Free Minds," *The Boston Globe*, September 2, 1981.

[4] Jerry Falwell, "The Maligned Moral Majority," *Newsweek*, September 21, 1981, p. 17.

[5] Richard Ellis, Letters to the Editor, *The Boston Globe*, June 24, 1981.

[6] Ellen Goodman, "Thinking the Unthinkable—The Numbers Are Growing," *The Boston Globe*, October 8, 1981. © 1981, The Boston Globe Newspaper Company/Washington Post Writers Group, reprinted with permission.

[7] Jacob Bronowski, *Science and Human Values* (Harper and Row, 1972).

[8] "Before Hiroshima, A Report to the Secretary of War," *Bulletin of Atomic Scientists*, May 1, 1946. Reprinted by permission of *The Bulletin of the Atomic Scientists*, a magazine of science and public affairs. Copyright © 1946 by the Educational Foundation for Nuclear Science, Chicago, IL 60637., pp. 2-4.

[9] Jonathan Harris, *Hiroshima* (Addison-Wesley, 1970), p. 36.

[10] *The Boston Globe*, September 27, 1981.

[11] *The New Republic*, December 9, 1981, p. 5.

[12] Bernstein, "War Is Not Inevitable."

Illustration Credits: Lisa Colt, *p. 26;* TR Gilmore, *p. 30;* Franciscan Communications, *p. 39;* Courtesy of the Krant family, *p. 57;* From *Adolf Hitler, Bilder Aus Dem Leben Des Fuehrer, pp. 82, 179;* Tony Auth, *p. 111;* Leo Baeck Institute, *p. 118;* U.S. Government, *pp. 133, 168;* Yad Vashem, *pp. 203, 246, 274;* Monument by Tim Donovan, *p. 385.*

Maps and graph by Donald Gotz.

NOTES

NOTES

NOTES

NOTES

NOTES

NOTES

NOTES

NOTES

NOTES

NOTES